Country	GNP per Capita (U.S. Dollars)	Adjusted GDP per Capita (U.S. Dollars)	PQLI	Population (millions)
Finland	10770	9060	98	4.9
France	9760	10420	98	54.9
Gabon	4100	7510	35	0.8
Gambia	260	1370	16	0.7
Ghana	350	1140	48	12.3
Greece	3770	6040	91	9.9
Grenada	860	na	92	0.1
Guatemala	1160	2190	60	7.7
Guinea	330	1130	25	5.9
Guinea-Bissau	190	na	27	0.9
Guyana	460(1983)	1710	88	0.8
Haiti	320	710	43	5.4
Honduras	700	1580	63	4.2
Hong Kong	6330	6920	95	5.4
Hungary	2100	3890	93	10.7
Iceland	11020	9560	100	0.2
India	260	820	46	749.2
Indonesia	540	1350	58	158.9
Iran	2160(1977)	2610	57	43.8
Iraq	2410(1981)	2850	51	15.1
Ireland	4970	5220	95	3.5
Israel	5060	6720	92	4.2
Italy	6420	7070	96	57.0
Ivory Coast	610	2160	40	9.9
Jamaica	1150	2190	91	2.2
Japan	10630	9100	99	120.0
Jordan	1570	1710	71	3.4
Kampuchea	100(1984)	na	33	33.0
Kenya	310	700	56	19.6
Kuwait	16720	na	78	1.7
Laos	na	na	39	3.5
Lebanon	1150(1983)	na	77	2.6
Lesotho	530	840	52	1.5
Liberia	470	1020	41	2.1
Libya	8520	na	57	3.5
Luxembourg	13160	9960	96	0.4
Madagascar	260	770	51	9.9
Malawi	180	540	29	6.8
Malaysia	1980	3600	73	15.3
Mali	140	400	27	7.3
Mauritania	450	1060	30	1.7

ECONOMIC
DEVELOPMENT

ECONOMIC DEVELOPMENT

Jan S. Hogendorn

Colby College

HARPER & ROW, PUBLISHERS, New York
Cambridge, Philadelphia, San Francisco, Washington,
London, Mexico City, São Paulo, Singapore, Sydney

1817

Sponsoring Editor: John Greenman
Project Editor: David Nickol
Cover Design: Miriam Recio
Text Art: Volt Information Sciences, Inc.
Production: Willie Lane
Compositor: ComCom Division of Haddon Craftsmen, Inc.
Printer and Binder: R. R. Donnelley & Sons Company

ECONOMIC DEVELOPMENT

Library of Congress Cataloging-in-Publication Data

Hogendorn, Jan S.
  Economic Development

  Includes bibliographies and index.
  1. Economic development.   I. Title.
HD75.H64   1987   338.9   86-27034
ISBN 0-06-042853-8

        89 90 9 8 7 6 5 4 3

To Dianne

CONTENTS

4 Domestic Saving and Investment   65

5 Foreign Flows to Fill the Gap Between Saving and Investment   111

6 Short-Term Borrowing: The Debt Crisis and the International Monetary Fund   146

7 Technology, Factor Proportions, and Dualism   174

12 Trade and Economic Development   329

13 Trade Policy and Economic Development   365

14 Trade in Manufactured Goods as an Engine of
   Growth   399

PREFACE

During my two decades of teaching development economics to undergraduates, I have often felt the urge to write a text that would better meet the needs of my diverse class enrollment. Many of my students have had only the first-year principles of economics course and are taking intermediate theory concurrently with my course. Some are not economics majors and will not be taking intermediate theory at all. At the same time, each class in development includes a large number of senior majors who have completed their theory courses and econometrics as well. The result of this mixture is that the students have generally been dissatisfied with the textbook—the sophomores and the nonmajors when a rigorous text assumes too much about their background, the seniors when a less advanced text fails to capture their interest. They have frequently told me so on the course evaluations at the end of term.

My response to these criticisms was to try my hand at writing chapter-length class handouts in subject areas where I thought improvements on available texts might be made. In preparing these, I resolved not to go beyond sophomore-level rigor of analysis, always keeping in mind Bohuslav Herman's apt comment that for this audience "what matters is the soundness of the economic principles used and not the elegance of the economic techniques employed."* I tried to achieve an up-to-date quality by always using the latest data possible from the most recent editions of the World Bank's *World Development Report* and the IMF's *World Economic Outlook.* Above all, I attempted to make the material interesting for the entire spectrum of my students.

My initial efforts were with what became Chapter 2 on measuring development, Chapter 5 on capital transfers, and Chapter 11 on planning. These areas had received dense, dry treatment in most available texts, at a level of rigor often beyond sophomores' abilities. In my approach to these topics, whenever a problem could be explored as a practical policy issue and could be illustrated with effective real-world examples, I attempted to do so.

Organization of the Text

The book is structured as a survey of the standard subject matter in the field of economic development but with some departures from the traditional sequence of most texts. I believe that the measurement of development (including national product and income, income distribution, and indicators of the "quality of life") should come early in the analysis, so this material appears in Chapter 2, immediately following the Introduction.

Chapter 3 presents a short survey of what is known about how countries develop, including the experience of today's developed countries during the periods when their advances yield the most useful lessons concerning the develop-

---

*Bohuslav Herman, "The Optimal International Division of Labour," in Gerald M. Meier, *Leading Issues in Economic Development,* 3rd ed., Oxford, 1976, p. 757.

ment process (Japan, 1880–1920; Russia and the Soviet Union, 1890–1940; and Germany 1870–1900). It also reviews the experience of three especially successful less developed countries—South Korea, Taiwan, and the Ivory Coast—in an effort to identify whether common factors figure in their development experience.

Chapters 4, 5, and 6 concern capital—saving, investment, the roles of international agencies and multinational companies, and an analysis of the debt crisis. I have placed these topics early in the text because, after a long period of reaction to the thesis that capital is a major factor in development, a reappraisal has come, and because the debt crisis has had such a profound impact. Additionally, students in recent years are more eager to study banking, credit, and investment than was true in the past, and I have found that early emphasis on these topics builds on their existing interests. These chapters also address monetary and fiscal policies (including taxation, fiscal deficits, and inflation) in the LDCs; I found it logically preferable to integrate these subjects with the problems of capital formation and capital flows rather than to put them into a separate chapter elsewhere in the text. A detailed treatment is given in these chapters to the distortions in capital markets, often introduced by government policies, that have received much recent attention in the development literature.

Chapter 7 is a conventional approach to factor proportions, technology, and dualism in industry that is unusual only in the degree to which it includes real-world examples.

Chapter 8 on population explores current national programs, both successful ones (Indonesia, Thailand, Singapore, and China), and the less successful (India and Pakistan). I find that the reasons why programs in general succeed or fail are nicely encapsulated in the experience of these six countries.

Chapter 9, on human capital, considers education, health, and nutrition both as factors in raising productivity and as "basic needs."

In Chapter 10 on rural development, the sections on the spread of the "high-yield" varieties and the consequences of their adoption, on rural credit problems, and on agricultural extension services are more comprehensive than in other texts of comparable scope. The length and coverage of this large chapter fully reflect the recent rise in importance of the rural sector in development economics.

Chapter 11, on planning and the market, compares the more questionable forms of comprehensive planning to "lighter" sectoral planning and reliance on market forces in the development process. I have tried to provide a more easily comprehensible treatment of cost-benefit analysis and shadow pricing than other development texts offer. Two appendixes cover technical aspects of the capital–output ratio in planning and examine the long-standing "balanced growth" controversy.

The greatest difference between this text and others in the field is embodied in Chapters 12, 13, 14, and 15, which consider the international economic aspects of development. The depth of coverage in these four chapters reflects my conviction that trade is now probably the single fastest path to development, but also represents a path that easily could be closed off by the developed world. Topics examined in detail include autarky and import substitution versus export promotion, prospects for the terms of trade, export cartels, depreciation of the exchange rate as a strategy, customs unions, and many additional issues. The increasingly crucial subject of developed-country protectionism, often touched only briefly in other texts, receives a thorough treatment.

Recommended Companion Volumes

I recommend that students using this text be encouraged to purchase the latest issue of the World Bank's *World Development Report,* available from Oxford University Press. This will provide convenient access to the latest available data. If additional readings are desired, the latest edition of Gerald M. Meier's *Leading Issues in Economic Development,* also from Oxford University Press, will serve as an excellent supplement.

Acknowledgments

Under the direction of John Greenman of Harper & Row, the typescript of this book went through an intensive review process. I did not always accept the reviewers' advice, and they thus cannot be responsible for any remaining flaws. But their suggestions resulted in a large number of improvements. The entire manuscript was examined first by Robert Christiansen, development specialist at the U.S. Department of Agriculture, and Wilson Brown of the University of Winnipeg in Canada. Then the revised versions of each chapter went to Patrick J. Gormely of Kansas State University, Whitney Hicks of the University of Missouri, and William E. Kuhn of the University of Nebraska. Their collective advice led to further improvements, as did comments received from Peter Kilby of Wesleyan University and Eugene R. Dykeman of Calvin College. My thanks to the Overseas Development Council of Washington, D.C., for allowing the use of the PQLI data shown on the endpapers, and to Professor Robert Summers of the University of Pennsylvania for making available the per capita product figures adjusted for purchasing power also shown on the endpapers.

Four individuals must have a special mention, for their influence on me has been of a personal nature as teachers or readers of my theses: William J. Barber and G. M. Meier at Wesleyan University and A. D. Knox and P. T. Bauer (now Lord Bauer) at the London School of Economics.

Student assistants at Colby College who helped me with data collection and location and verification of sources include Ban Chuan Cheah, V. C. Bushell, F. D. Delaney, C. Emond, J. Lord, and K. L. McPhail. The name and subject indexes were compiled at Colby by Jean Kroeck and Cindy Matrazzo. The Centre of West African Studies at the University of Birmingham furnished me with facilities and hospitality during the initial stages of this project, and its present director, Douglas Rimmer, influenced the text at several points.

My family bore the main burden of my long hours at the computer, at first with good-humored tolerance, later with stoic resignation, once even with a "wish to heaven you would finish." I appreciate their support and patience.

Jan S. Hogendorn

ECONOMIC DEVELOPMENT

chapter 1

Introduction: Studying Economic Development

Development economics is the study of how human economic circumstances change over time and how they can be made to change. This is a grand subject that spans continents and disciplines; the sheer scale and scope of its coverage make it the broadest subset of economics.

The subject matter of development is not divorced from the main body of economics nor are there any great differences in analytical methods. Completely new tools for analysis have not usually been necessary, and the standard ones are drawn from every branch of the discipline.[1] A textbook that explores development must touch on labor economics and industrial organization, money and banking and fiscal policy, international trade and international finance, transport and welfare and environmental economics, education and population and agriculture. To a large degree, the elementary insight that economics is the study of efficient choice among scarce resources, with a capacity to analyze the trade-offs (costs) of one policy versus another, is central to development studies, just as it is in so many other areas of the discipline.

DIFFERENCES IN THE VIEWPOINTS OF DEVELOPMENT AND OTHER BRANCHES OF ECONOMICS

Though much of the ground we cover is familiar to every economist, some major approaches of development economics will seem unusual to a student brought up in the neoclassical tradition of supply and demand and equilibrium. These different approaches attempt to deal with a number of situations quite unlike those of conventional economics.

One such approach is to view economies in terms of pervasive and persistent dualisms that, contrary to the neoclassical theories of markets and movements toward equilibrium, are not self-correcting. Urban dualism is the existence of an informal, small-scale, labor-intensive, low-wage sector of highly competitive family and individual enterprise alongside a modern, capital-intensive, high-wage industrial sector. The modern sector may employ world class technology, radically different from that in the informal sector, and often includes huge multinational firms as well as the large government firms (known as parastatals) that frequently do not follow the conventional rules of profit maximization.

Rural dualism takes the form of small family farms, sometimes heavily engaged in the subsistence production of food and other products for the family's own use, alongside large plantations, state farms, and mining enterprises using very different ratios of labor to capital and often paying much higher wages. This low-wage, agricultural subsistence sector holds huge numbers of people, with inadequate opportunities for employing them elsewhere.

Whole countries can be looked at as an aspect of dualism, for example, when public policy is characterized by an "urban bias" of favoritism toward the cities or when the relative stagnation of one country is compared to the dynamism of its neighbors. Even entire continents are broadly different in their economic performance, as we shall see.

Development economics also provides a different viewpoint in its treatment of international trade. The great debate between the trade optimists and trade pessimists endures. To the optimists trade is an engine of growth. To the pessimists trade risks "backwash effects," with exports growing slowly if at all, with inelastic demands that move prices against poor countries, and with those prices (and quantities and earnings) unstable, thus making development more difficult. These arguments have recently taken hard knocks, but there is enough realism in them, and repetition of them, to command attention. Worrisomely, protectionist policies in developed countries might radically change the rules of the game.

A further difference in development studies lies in the attention given to an apparent persistent tendency toward income inequality and the evaluation of frontal attack on the inequality by a basic needs strategy of direct action. Other differences are the attention given to the causes and effects of rapid population increase and the special concentration on how agriculture interacts with industry as a country grows.

A major field of study emphasized in development economics involves the perception that the system of market pricing may work less efficiently in conditions of poverty. There might be serious structural impediments to the smooth operation of a price system, including blockages, bottlenecks, rigidities, and lags, especially in supply. Enterprise may be deficient, responses slow or perverse. Lack of knowledge, inferior transport, and poor communication may hinder the path to equilibrium charted by supply and demand curves. One symptom of slow response by suppliers (or, low elasticities of supply) might be that inflation is quicker to break out and harder to control. Such structural arguments (all much debated) have for many years been used to justify government intervention in the economy via planning, the pros and cons of which are a staple of development theory and an element of high controversy as well. Often government itself may be part of the problem, with numerous prices kept unchanged by official decision, including foreign exchange rates, interest rates, prices charged by parastatals, or prices paid for agricultural products. This distorts the information carried by the price system and especially distorts the flows of investment.

Perhaps the greatest difference between development and traditional economics is not the models, but the mood. Development has a special immediateness because it grapples with human misery, poverty, disease, and the attempts to correct them. The closeness to these problems and the awareness of so much to be gained by their elimination gives enormous human interest to the subject; a first visit to a poor country brings quick understanding why such a country may view its struggle to develop as a war, or even a great crusade.

REQUIREMENT: A WIDE-RANGING MIND

Development is an area of economics where the lessons of other disciplines must be drawn on frequently. These lessons are not only useful, but can be critical for the work of the economist.

Law and order or the lack of it, the degree of democracy and personal trust, behavior based on a desire for power as opposed to economic gain, the struggle of ethnic groups within a country, the constraints of family and religion are all broadly important, but these institutional areas are often not defined or discussed very clearly by economists. In much of their research insufficient work is done on how these factors influence the "economic" factors. Researchers may ignore them or may acknowledge their existence and then, in effect, discount them by holding them constant, *ceteris paribus*.[2] But they cannot be ignored by a development specialist; sociology, anthropology, political science, and history are all important in our study. This is no doubt one reason why an economist narrowly trained in the standard tools of the profession may feel uncomfortable with this subject and may in an understandable reaction accuse it of being "soft." The experienced development economist cheerfully admits to this accusation, believing that wide application of the lessons of other disciplines adds to the intellectual vitality of such studies and is essential for progress in the field.

The development economist can profit also from some knowledge of personal psychology—how to deal with and understand people. If old policies are to be scrapped, new policies effectively implemented, or present policies defended and appreciated, then a convincing message must be conveyed to government administrators and politicians. These officials, with training and background different from the economist, are often distrustful of academic models and perhaps of academics themselves. Also, these officials must consider political as well as economic realities. They know that a policy change, however much it contributes to efficiency, will have its losers, and the losers may possess political influence and economic power.[3] Policies concerning taxes, subsidies, land, trade, foreign exchange, credit, and pricing of public goods have implications of penalty and reward for political enemies and supporters. Thus the advice of the development economist, however sensible, may be rejected. A desire to promote national unity, or heal ethnic divisions or project an image of "progress" can also spur politicians toward economic programs that might appear less than fully rational to economists. Politicians might thus give otherwise unexpected high priority to heavy industries such as steel, or a policy of import substitution to reduce "dependence," or defense of a "strong" foreign exchange rate, or modern tanks and planes for the military, or wide-bodied jets for the national airline and a superhighway in from the airport, or magnificent avenues and buildings in the capital city.[4]

In the face of all this, the economist who can present a model, expound it effectively, and explain the difficult points in an understandable and convincing way is an especially valuable person. There is abundant evidence that proper policy can promote development, while mistaken policy impedes it; this puts a grave responsibility on economists to communicate effectively. It also calls for perception that "first-best" solutions representing the most sensible economic response to problems may for political reasons be less desirable than "second-best" solutions. The advisor who can work effectively within these constraints, recommending policies that *can be adopted* and that will work almost as well as the first best, may be even more valuable.[5]

The student of this subject must be always on guard. The sheer vastness of development economics brings a pronounced tendency to generalize prematurely about what it is that causes development.[6] Capitalist catchwords and communist nostrums of all kinds abound in the literature on less-developed countries. Beware the hedgehog theories, to use Paul Streeten's words, theories of single causation that reflect little complexity in a subject that is assuredly complicated. A useful trait for a development economist is, as we shall see throughout, a healthy skepticism in the presence of "true believers" who profess to know exactly how development occurs and precisely what obstructs it. Perhaps even some humility is required—an appreciation of how little is sometimes known of the human and social constraints on progress.

To be sure, a development economist does not need all at the same time to be a sociologist, anthropologist, political scientist, historian, practicing psychologist, skeptic, and humble student—but it helps.

IS THERE A TYPICAL POOR COUNTRY?

There are some striking similarities among the more than 100 countries that make up our subject area. Almost always, the poorer the country, the smaller the percent of its population employed in modern industry. There will usually be a large pool of underemployed labor, and often much open unemployment as well in the cities, that have proven very difficult to absorb. The vast farming and service sectors will be very low in productivity. Exports usually consist only of primary products and labor-intensive manufactures, the proceeds from which pay for the imports of essential capital goods that cannot be produced at home. Whatever the goods produced, their production is often not as labor-intensive as might be presumed from their relative supplies of labor and capital (the reasons are ones of economic policy, as we shall see). Whether their exports are primary products or manufactured goods, their trade is still for the most part with developed countries and not with each other.

But there is also tremendous diversity, and the economist must avoid the bad habit of "lumping." Some countries have large populations, some have small; some are geographically big, some are little; some are rich in natural resources, some are resource-poor; most were once colonies, some were not; a few are honest in their public services, many are corrupt; some are democracies, some are authoritarian dictatorships, many lie somewhere in between. Adding to the diversity, there are examples of both very rapid and very slow growth in each of these groups.[7]

There are other contrasts as well. The poor countries with their very different types of government structure have very different attitudes toward government regulation of the economy. Some direct their development efforts toward increasing the conventional measures of per capita income and output; others emphasize the creation of an economy that will foster national self-reliance and self-respect; yet others focus on Marxian "modes of production" and movement toward a "socialist economy." They have dissimilar policies on international trade, from heavy protection to low barriers or even none at all (Hong Kong). Some are highly trade dependent (a high ratio of exports and imports to GNP), while some are not.

Finally, there are vast differences in income and welfare, no matter how they are measured. If gross national product is the measure, the 1986 *World Development Report* listed 40 "least-developed" low-income countries with per capita GNP of under $400, 75 more middle-income economies in the range from $400 to a little over $7,000, joining 7 high-income oil exporters, 19 developed "industrial market economies," and 8 "Eastern European nonmarket economies."[8] GNP data for most of these countries are shown on the endpapers.

Even continents are quite different in terms of income and population and hence of income per person. Table 1.1 shows the percentages accounted for by the less-developed countries (LDCs).

Possibly, the differences among countries and geographical areas will one

Table 1.1 POPULATION AND INCOME BY CONTINENT

	Percent of World Population	Percent of World Income
Caribbean, Central America, South America	9.2	6.4
Africa	12.4	3.3
Asia	59.7	9.2

World income is defined as gross domestic product (see Chapter 2 for details). The USSR, the Marxian socialist economies of Eastern Europe except Hungary and Yugoslavia, countries for which data on national income were not published in the 1985 report, and countries with populations numbering under 1 million are not included in the totals for either world population or world income.

Source: Calculated from World Bank, *World Development Report, 1985,* Tables 1 and 2. (References to the *World Development Report* are hereafter cited as *WDR.*)

day grow so pronounced that development economics as we know it will disappear, to be replaced by regional studies of particular areas.[9] In any case, the differences point to the difficulty in finding universal solutions. Policies that work well in Southeast Asia may not necessarily succeed in sub-Saharan Africa. An awareness of diversity and what it means is a valuable trait for an economist to have.

CAN THE GAP BE CLOSED? TWO VIEWS

With all the differences among the less-developed countries, there remains the common characteristic, the unifying theme so to speak, of poverty. Economic growth, if rapid enough, could presumably close any gap between poor and rich and eventually render our subject obsolete. The optimistic view of this possibility points to the fact that real growth for the third world as a whole has not been particularly slow in a comparative sense in recent years, as Table 1.2 shows. Note how the less-developed countries as a group have outperformed the developed countries for nearly two decades, except during the recession years of 1983 and 1984 and the tie projected for 1986, and how the non-oil LDCs on the whole did even somewhat better, exceeding the performance of the developed countries in every year shown.[10]

Even in terms of output per person, overall LDC performance has been relatively good in spite of problems with rapid population increase. From 1965 to 1984 average annual growth was 2.8 percent for the poorest 29 countries and 3.1 percent for 60 middle-income LDCs, compared to 2.4 percent for the developed countries.[11]

The broad averages do conceal some serious disappointments, however. Growth in the lowest-income countries looks far less favorable when China and India are excluded, with 14 of them registering a per capita increase in GNP of less than 1 percent from 1965 to 1984.[12] Asia has done much better than either

Table 1.2   ANNUAL PERCENTAGE CHANGES IN OUTPUT

	Average 1968–1977	1978	1979	1980	1981	1982	1983	1984	1985	1986
Developed countries	3.7	4.2	3.3	1.2	1.4	−0.4	2.6	4.7	2.8	3.0
All LDCs	6.2	5.1	4.3	3.5	2.2	1.6	1.3	4.1	3.2	3.0
Non-oil LDCs	5.4	6.1	4.6	4.6	2.7	2.5	3.0	5.5	4.8	4.6
Asia	5.4	9.1	4.4	5.5	5.5	5.0	7.4	7.9	6.1	5.5
Latin America	6.0	4.1	6.0	5.3	0.9	−0.9	−3.1	3.1	3.8	1.6
Africa	5.3	1.1	3.2	3.8	1.7	0.8	−1.5	1.6	1.6	2.8

Output is defined as real GDP. The 1986 figures are estimates.
Source: International Monetary Fund, *World Economic Outlook, 1986,* p. 179.

Latin America or Africa. (As usual there are large variances: Hong Kong, Singapore, South Korea, and Taiwan have exceptionally good records; Malaysia, Thailand, and Indonesia have done well; performance has been poor in Kampuchea, Laos, Nepal, and Vietnam.) Sub-Saharan Africa has the worst record, with an actual decline in output per person in nine countries during 1965 to 1984. The poorest countries in that region produced less per head in 1985 than they did a quarter-century ago in 1960.[13] (Again there are exceptions: Botswana, Cameroon, Ivory Coast, Kenya, Lesotho, and Malawi have registered good performance.)

Even given the disappointments, however, many areas compare quite favorably to Britain at the start of the Industrial Revolution (less than 1 percent per capita growth from 1700 to 1780) or in its heyday (about 1 percent, 1780 to 1880), or to the United States (less than 2 percent, 1840 to 1960).[14] Looking at all the geographical areas and income groups, only in sub-Saharan Africa was per capita growth notably worse over the last two decades than was true of these two industrial giants during their own period of development.

These are not the only statistics that contribute to a mood of optimism about the prospects for LDCs as a whole (always remembering the large variation in the performance of individual countries). During the decade of the 1970s manufactured exports of LDCs increased at a remarkable 15.9 percent a year. That doubled their share of the developed country manufactures market from 1.7 percent in 1970 to 3.4 percent in 1980. Such growth was impressive, because world trade increased only 0.9 percent per year during the period from 1913 to 1939 and less than 4 percent annually during 1873 to 1913. Even in the recent years of global recession, 1980 to 1984, the countries that mainly export manufactures grew 5¾ percent, aided in part by welcome growth in such trade among the poor countries themselves. (Primary product exporters grew only 1 percent in the same time period, due partly to the poor performance of their main exports and partly to the fact that these countries included some whose policies seemed most in need of reform.)

Gross investment reached 25 percent of GNP (compared to 19 percent in the United States) in 1984—a figure with few precedents in historical experience. Life expectancy has risen as much in the past 20 years (from an age somewhere in the 30s in many countries to an average age of 60 even in the poorest) as it did in developed countries during the whole nineteenth century. Adult literacy rose from a third in 1950 to over a half in 1980. Interdependence with developed countries increased broadly. Recently, 38 percent of all U.S. exports and 46 percent of Japan's went to LDCs. The United States sells over 40 percent of its agricultural exports, nearly 60 percent of its wheat, 60 percent of its cotton, over two-thirds of its rice, and half its machinery to LDCs, and now ships as many manufactured goods to these countries as to Europe, Japan, and the Communist countries combined.[15] At the same time about one quarter of U.S. imports came from LDCs, 45 percent if oil is included. Of American non-oil raw material imports, more than 30 percent came from the LDCs; of food imports, over 50 percent. Finally, a quarter of U.S. private foreign investment is in LDCs, and on average it must be more profitable than elsewhere, because 34 percent of our earnings on such investment is derived from these countries.

Even the oil shocks and the food shock of the 1970s did not altogether dispel the new optimism. The oil shocks raised the value of fertilizer, transport, and energy imports from only 10 percent of LDC merchandise exports in 1960 to 43 percent in 1980; the food shock tripled the cost of the LDC food import bill between 1972 and 1975. Both shocks represented a massive transfer from the poor to the rich. Yet the years of the oil shocks, 1974 to 1976 and 1979 to 1980, were relatively stable compared to the virtually complete collapse of the world financial system after 1929. It is true that the shocks created a crisis of large international debts; even so, there was no breakdown.

But there is pessimism, too, an old pessimism and a new one. The old pessimism stems from the figures for per capita income, which reveal a huge gap. To show this, let us add all developed countries and high-income oil exporters to Table 1.1. The resulting Table 1.3 shows 81.3 percent of the world's population earning 18.9 percent of world income. This income gap shows in many areas; consider some examples. Indian income per head in 1984 was $260; that is 1.69 percent of U.S. income, which was $15,390 in that year; Switzerland's was over $16,000. The LDCs consume energy at a level only 6 percent of the energy use of the developed countries; it has been estimated that for every car in a poor country there are over 50 in the rich world, for every telephone there are 16, for every horsepower of factory machinery there are about 60. The gap shows also in education; 99 percent of the population of the rich world is literate, only 50 percent of the poor. It shows in health. On average an individual can expect to live 76 years if born in a developed country, only 60 years if not (and only 48 years in sub-Saharan Africa).[16] Low-income countries suffer an infant mortality rate seven times higher than developed countries. The difference between birth and death rates is reflected in the rate of population growth; in the developed countries population is increasing at an annual rate of 0.7 percent, while in the poorer countries the average is 2.0 percent, 2.6 percent with China and India excluded. (These figures are, however, below the peak reached in the 1960s.)

Economic growth in the LDCs, if fast enough, could close these gaps, but for most catching up with the developed countries seems hardly possible, even

Table 1.3 POPULATION AND INCOME

	Percent of World Population	Percent of World Income
Caribbean, Central America, South America	9.2	6.4
Africa	12.4	3.3
Asia	59.7	9.2
All developed countries and high-income oil exporters	18.6	80.9
USA	5.8	33.7

Totals do not add to 100 percent because of rounding off. The high-income oil exporters are Saudi Arabia, Libya, Oman, Kuwait, and the United Arab Emirates.
Source: Calculated from *WDR 1985,* Tables 1 and 2.

in the long run. Mathematically, the absolute gap in income will increase whenever the ratio of per capita income, rich to poor, is greater than the inverse ratio of their growth rates.

$$\frac{Y_A}{Y_B} > \frac{\%\Delta Y_B}{\%\Delta Y_A}$$

where Y is per capita income, $\%\Delta Y$ is the growth rate of income, A is the developed country, and B is the LDC. For example, if the growth rate of income for South Korea (B) is 6 percent and that for the United States (A) is 3 percent, and U.S. income is $12,000, then South Korea will be falling behind at its current per capita income of $2,110. It would be closing the absolute gap only if its income exceeded $6,000; above that level the condition that Y_A/Y_B be less than $\%\Delta Y_B/\%\Delta Y_A$ for the gap to close is satisfied.

Here is another way to look at this. Switzerland and Burkina Faso (Upper Volta), in West Africa, both grew at 1.4 percent between 1965 and 1983. In 1983 Switzerland's per capita income was $16,290; thus the increment from 1.4 percent growth would have been $228.06 per person. Burkina Faso's income was $180; 1.4 percent of that is $2.52 per person. That means the absolute gap became far wider. Fewer than 10 LDCs would close the gap with the rich countries in a hundred years at present rates of growth; fewer than 20 would do so in a thousand years.[17]

These per capita income statistics represent the old pessimism. The new pessimism is based on some recent discouraging developments.[18] The world recession, which began in 1979 and hit all western industrial economies, had some very serious side effects for LDCs, effects that have not entirely dissipated.

Monetary policy was used by developed countries to fight inflation, while fiscal policy has been stimulative. The resulting runup in real interest rates, quickly passed on to the LDCs because of variable credit terms, posed a major burden for the countries that borrowed heavily in the 1970s. Debt service payments of interest and principal in the mid 1970s absorbed about 13 percent of non-oil LDCs' export earnings. That figure grew to some 20 percent during the debt crisis of the 1980s.

The world recession meant a reduction in the demand for poor-country exports and also declines in their price, that is, a shift in their terms of trade (which had already fallen from an index number of 111 in 1960 to 89 in 1980, with 1975 = 100). This spread the recession widely in the third world, and we have already seen (in Table 1.2) that growth in real output was cut approximately in half in the non-oil LDCs (1981 and 1982 compared to 1968 to 1978) and cut even more in the oil exporters. The result was that average GNP growth for two years in the 1980s was slower in the LDCs than in the industrial countries, the first time this had happened in many years. The slow growth of the 1980s, when combined with rapid increases in population, means that per capita output in the LDCs will be only slightly higher (current estimate an increase of 0.1 percent) at the end of 1986 than it was in 1980.

The recession brought a rise in protectionism in many developed countries, including the United States, much of Europe, and Australia. In Europe an especially high rate of unemployment (11.25 percent on average in 1985) was fertile ground for protectionist sentiment. In the United States a historically large federal budget deficit was a cause of abnormally high interest rates, which in turn stimulated inflows of foreign funds seeking to earn the high dollar interest returns. The resulting strong dollar made imports to the United States relatively cheap, caused a severe trade deficit, and further fueled the drift toward protectionism.

Though the recession did eventually ease, with recovery gathering momentum especially in 1984, the problem of slow growth in the developed countries still lingers on, adversely affecting future prospects for the LDCs.[19] The year 1985 was disappointing; developed-country growth fell sharply (to 2.8 percent from 4.7 percent a year before), cutting the growth in world trade from 9 percent in 1984 to only 3 percent in 1985. As a result, the LDC terms of trade fell even further, by another 2 percent. The most recent projections of the International Monetary Fund (IMF) in 1986 suggest that developed-country growth in 1986–1987 will be only 3 percent or a little more and will not be higher than that during the remainder of the 1980s. The volume of world trade during these years is expected to grow no more than 5 to 5.5 percent per year, significantly below the average of 7.7 percent reached during 1968 to 1977. If protection intensifies, it may do worse, and indeed the sharp decline in the volume of world trade in 1985 may partly reflect this. The combination of protection and stagnant developed-country GNP would make it far more difficult for LDCs to develop by means of an export strategy. The prognosis for trade-led growth is therefore both cloudy and worrisome. Should the sharp decline in oil prices early in 1986 prove to be permanent, the worries would be much eased. It would be risky to count on that permanence, however, as we shall see in Chapter 15.

WHAT'S IN A NAME?

Probably no branch of economics has had more difficulty in finding acceptable names for its subject matter. The very concept of a developed country is itself unclear, being wholly relative to time and place. How can we say that there is today any developed country, when another century or two may find (as, indeed, we all hope fervently) that the human condition is bettered beyond present expectation or belief. Egypt under the Pharaoh Ramses, China of the Ming and T'ang dynasties, India under the Mughals, Turkey under the Byzantines (Constantinople of the "gilded streets" wrote the scholar-monks of Europe during the Dark Ages), and Tunisia in Roman times (called "the breadbasket of Rome" by the ancient Latin authors) all were once regarded as among the richest in their world. They have all continued to grow, probably even in per capita terms, but they are now backward by comparison to others, so people call them poor. In this sense all countries are developing. Poor and rich, we must always remember, are relative terms applicable only to a particular time and place. Keep this context in mind when we use the term *developed country.* Misunderstanding might be avoided by the qualified term *more developed country* (MDC), which is now often used. But it has the disadvantage of introducing yet another set of initials into a subject where there are too many already, so we shall avoid it in this book.

Another aspect of appropriate naming is what to call a poor country.[20] The word *backward* was used in the nineteenth century, just as the phrase *rude and barbarous* had been employed in the eighteenth. These terms' demeaning reflection on race, religion, and social institutions now cause acute embarrassment. The word *poor* is fully appropriate, but it is a stark term, too stark for human nature, and it is often avoided. In fact, the unpleasantness of the condition means any label begins to wear badly with repetition, and the subject matter of this field has been renamed not once but several times.

Undeveloped and *underdeveloped* both had currency, and the latter term is still used. The new name became *developing country,* but for some nations this was patently not true, and it was followed soon after in the 1960s by *less-developed country,* or *LDC.* The poorest in this group are sometimes classed as *least-developed countries,* LLDCs, or as *low income countries,* LICs.

The *Third World* has a bit of a mysterious ring. I have heard it said that this was a mistranslation of the French *tiers monde,* used by a journalist to describe the poorest one-third of the world's countries. In this same vein, the First World is the developed lands, the Second World is the communist countries, and some use Fourth World to designate the least developed. The low ranking of the LDCs on this list causes resentment and many scholars in these countries avoid using the term.

A much higher number, the *Group of 77* is in use. The G-77 is the LDC club in the United Nations that actually now contains far more members than that; the number commemorates the 77 LDCs that attended the original meeting of the United Nations Conference on Trade and Development in 1964. A smaller *Group of 24* influential LDCs often serves as spokesman for the larger assembly, and the G-24 may be found bargaining with the developed countries' *Group of 10* in international negotiations.

A geographical designation is also employed, the North for the developed countries and the South for the LDCs, reflecting the fact—we must examine whether it is coincidence—that most poor countries are located in the tropics.

Your author prefers the name LDC because it accurately reflects the knowledge that today many countries are relatively "less developed" than others. (Conveniently, it is also the shortest of the names.)

GROWTH VERSUS DEVELOPMENT

An important additional aspect of the choice of names lies in the usage of two terms, *growth* and *development.* In the past the two were used synonymously, and many writers still do use them interchangeably.[21] But there is an important distinction that can be made, and it is a useful one. It is helpful to use the word *growth* broadly to refer to an increase in output or income and to reserve the term *development* for the underlying structural, institutional, and qualitative changes that expand a country's capabilities. A clear example of this usage can be found in a book by Robert Clower and his associates, *Growth Without Development,* which traces the growth of Liberia's economy through rising exports of rubber from plantations owned by foreign firms. Though GNP was rising, even in per capita terms, the benefits had little impact on most of the Liberian people.[22] By contrast, economic "development" suggests that growth in one sector (plantations) should have a substantial effect on other sectors as well and that the benefits, including more than income growth, should be shared by a large proportion of the population. The outcome is that development will most often mean growth as well, but growth unfortunately need not mean development.

Exactly what the term *development* conveys has been vehemently debated, a debate that is difficult to conclude because the term encompasses a large number of value judgments. There is no universally accepted standard for economic development, so perhaps a rough consensus is the best that can be expected. For our purposes, let us join the great majority of economists who have largely rejected the idea that some measure such as national product or national income is an adequate gauge of development. Product and income statistics are useful and important, to be sure, but development is a process of structural change in the way goods and services are produced and the way people live; understanding the process is central to the subject.

Let us then, noting the lack of consensus, begin with the following definition of development: the process through which over a long time period the real per capita income (output) of a country rises with the understanding that not just an elite few, but the general mass of population is the beneficiary of the increase. To this we add the further understanding that the rise in income (output), if it is to be termed development, must be accompanied by changes in basic conditions, including improved diets, better health, lower infant mortality rates, better clothing and housing, rising literacy, and an improved physical and cultural environment. In short, not just national product, but the *content* of the national product, is important. The composition of that content determines the "quality of life."[23] This quality goal is now considered to be of crucial significance by almost all development economists in determining whether progress has taken place. (The word *progress* could do more service in our subject, but it is now little used by economists.) Some attempts have recently been made to measure this broad concept, as in the "physical quality of life" index discussed in Chapter 2.

The dichotomy between growth and development has recently given rise to the so-called basic needs approach. Its advocates argue that the most fundamental requirements of *all* people should be met before the less essential needs of the few are met. This approach involves raising income-earning opportunities for the poor and public assistance in providing food, water, health services, sanitation, and education. All of these are intended to reach the lowest income groups and are expected to encourage their participation in the economy. The aim is to bring welfare improvements at lower levels of income and in a shorter time than would have been achieved by concentrating on income growth alone. Many supporters of a basic needs approach see traditional growth patterns as a flawed "trickle-down" process.

There is an element of controversy here, in that there may or may not be a significant trade-off between growth and basic needs. Some believe that only after productivity is raised—which economists consider the key to income growth —can a country be concerned with basic needs. Doing it the other way round means higher government taxes to finance the programs at the expense of saving and investment, thus in the long run lowering the welfare of all. Certainly, there is the suspicion that an overemphasis on basic needs *can* impede growth. Sri Lanka in the 1960s and 1970s, Jamaica in the 1970s, and Tanzania for long periods are cited as examples. Others believe that the basic needs approach *itself* raises productivity, because productivity depends in part on health, nutrition, and education. Raising the quality of labor will thus raise output; it will also have a negative feedback on population growth and, so it is argued, will thus reduce the population problem.

Though the controversy continues, there is at least some evidence to show that growth and development, income increases and basic needs, do not represent a trade-off, but are complementary goals. The likelihood of complementarity is suggested in the last paragraph. Basic needs programs require resources to implement (hence growth promotes basic needs). At the same time basic needs fulfillment can stimulate output (and thus growth) through higher labor productivity. World Bank economists, using multiple regression techniques on cross-country data for per capita income, investment, change in imports, literacy, and life expectancy, have shown the basic needs variables significantly correlated to the growth variables. Countries with life expectancy 10 years higher than would have been predicted by per capita income had a change in income 0.7 to 0.9 percent better than expected. Education, health, and nutrition are arguably thus central to *both* growth and development.[24] The concept of growth with equity, rather than the concept of a struggle between growth and equity, appears to be gaining ground.

ARE GROWTH AND DEVELOPMENT DESIRABLE?

An opinion is sometimes voiced, especially in the developed countries and perhaps more frequently in the late 1960s and early 1970s than today, that on balance economic growth and development are not desirable because their costs outweigh their benefits. The "no-growth" advocates base their position on the triple concerns of pollution, depletion of natural resources, and the psychic costs of a consumer society. These advocates argue that "progress" means pollution of the environment and the inevitable exhaustion of an already dwindling stock of natural resources (topics returned to in Chapter 16). Such "progress" means trading a poor life, but one that is calm and uncomplicated in a secure social structure, for impersonality, tension, unhappiness, and rootlessness; for the unworthy ends of acquisitiveness and materialism; for the monotonous and repetitive work that characterizes the assembly lines of the developed countries.[25]

The arguments are eminently debatable but we shall spend little time here on this debate because in any practical sense the decision is not in our hands. There will be a relentless drive toward higher material standards of living because, like it or not, there is overwhelming evidence that the people and their political leaders in the poor countries, democratic or dictatorial, have wanted it, now want it, and will continue to strive for it. Quite obviously, *they* consider the benefits far greater than the costs. It must be admitted at once that higher material standards of living do not necessarily make people "happier." Richard Easterlin has noted, in what is now known as the Easterlin paradox, that opinion surveys in high-income countries do not reveal greater happiness than do similar surveys in low-income LDCs.[26] But higher living standards do give people more control over their own lives by increasing the range of human choice. Sir Arthur Lewis, in one of his more memorable passages, put it this way: "What distinguishes men from pigs is that men have greater control over their environment, not that they are more happy."[27] Karl Marx made the same point when he spoke of "replacing the domination of circumstances and chance over individuals by the domination of individuals over chance and circumstance."[28]

This is indeed what development offers to the people of the LDCs; it offers choice, the possibility that life will be more humane and at a better standard. The standard we speak of is not necessarily just goods, though these are highly desired. People can afford to choose more leisure if they want it, instead of facing the constant necessity of working to survive. Activities can broaden to include art, music, reading, movies, sports; it is surely no coincidence that in America football, baseball, and basketball and in Europe soccer all became popular in the 50 years before the First World War, fruits of economic growth, so to speak.

Especial beneficiaries of development are the women of the third world, just as women benefited in the developed countries by being freed from their drudgery. In the poorest LDCs girls are often married at 13 or 14, have borne several children before 20, have aged rapidly by 25, and are perhaps toothless by 35. They sew the clothes by hand, carry the water, pound the grain, and tend the children. Their only opportunity to leave the house or fields may be to carry the goods the family wants to sell to market. Women working in the fields grow half the world's food, but own little land, receive little credit, and get little attention from mostly male agricultural and development advisors. It is hardly a surprise then that while the 1970s margin of life expectancy of females over males was 8 years in the United States, it was -2 in Bangladesh, -2.5 in India, -0.5 in Iran, only $+2$ in Indonesia, $+0.5$ in Iraq, $+1$ in Algeria, and $+3$ in Brazil. The scope for improvement in this margin as income grows is demonstrated by the much higher differential in the richer LDCs, for example, $+6$ in South Korea and Argentina. Writes Arthur Lewis in another striking passage, "it is open to men to debate whether economic progress is good for men or not, but for women to debate the desirability of economic growth is to debate whether women should have the chance to cease to be beasts of burden and to join the human race."[29]

Another well-known economist, Kenneth Boulding, advances the argument of choice in a different form. In a stagnant no-growth economy, says Boulding, "a gain by one person almost always has to be achieved at the cost of a loss by another. Under these circumstances, even personal betterment is viewed as a political struggle, for the person who moves to a better opportunity in effect pushes somebody else to a worse one."[30] Boulding suggests that as a response to the intense political tensions, authoritarian governments will arise to solve them. Economic development can ease the tension. With development when one person gets more, another person need not necessarily get less—the other person may get more, too. In short, without development an economy operates as a "zero-sum game" in which the gains to some are obtained by taking from others, while with development the problem is the much easier one of perhaps giving somewhat more to some than is given to others.

Henceforth, we will assume that development is desirable for the world's poor countries because that is their choice. The remainder of the book will not consider "whether to develop," but "how to develop."

NOTES

1. Compare Gerald M. Meier, *Emerging from Poverty: The Economics That Really Matters,* New York, 1984, p. 135. The methodology of development studies receives a lengthy review, sometimes quite critical, in a special issue of *World Development,* 14, no. 2 (1986), entitled "The Methodological Foundations of Development Economics."
2. In part this reflects a chart in William Loehr and John P. Powelson, *The Economics of Development and Distribution,* New York, 1981, p. 413.
3. See Paul Streeten, "A Problem to Every Solution," *Finance and Development,* 22, no. 2 (1985):16.
4. Some of the examples in the text are adapted from Ian M.D. Little, *Economic Development: Theory, Policy, and International Relations,* New York, 1982. Analyses of nationalist aims and their impact on economic performance are an important new departure in development economics. A useful work is Dudley Seers, *The Political Economy of Nationalism,* New York, 1983.
5. See Meier, *Emerging from Poverty,* pp. 228–230.
6. See Assar Lindbeck's comment in Sven Grassman and Erik Lundberg, eds., *The World Economic Order: Past and Prospects,* New York, 1981, pp. 556–557.
7. A recent study published by the Overseas Development Council presents disquieting evidence that authoritarian regimes performed significantly better in terms of economic growth, from 1970 to 1982, than did democratic countries. This gives some credence to the old view that more "discipline" is necessary for successful growth than democracies are usually able to muster. But the sample size of 10 countries was small, and during the period the democracies accumulated much less foreign debt and achieved more income equality. See Atul Kohli, "Democracy and Development," in John P. Lewis and Valeriana Kallab, eds., *Development Strategy Reconsidered,* Washington, D.C., 1986. Kohli argues that to maintain political stability during the oil crisis, authoritarian regimes were forced to borrow greater amounts abroad.
8. GNP and income figures here and henceforth are mostly the latest available at the time of publication, taken from Tables 1 and 2 of the World Bank's *World Development Report, 1986.* Current population figures are also in Table 1. Most statistical data in the remainder of this book, when not otherwise footnoted, is either taken directly from the annex to the 1986 report, "World Development Indicators," or is calculated from it by the author. References to the *World Development Report* are hereafter cited as *WDR.*
9. Compare Little, *Economic Development,* p. 16.
10. For a discussion of the figures and additional data, see International Monetary Fund (IMF), *World Economic Outlook, 1986,* pp. 1, 4, 179, 185. Also see *World Economic Outlook, 1985,* pp. 1, 15, 67, 70, and 205.
11. *WDR 1986,* pp. 180–181. China and India pull up the figures for the low income countries substantially, because their performance, particularly China's, was good and the figures are weighted by population.
12. The group average excluding China and India was 0.9 percent.

13. World Bank, *Financing Adjustment with Growth in Sub-Saharan Africa, 1986–90,* Washington, D.C., 1986. For an analysis of why Africa's record has been so poor, see this work and another World Bank study, *Toward Sustained Development in Sub-Saharan Africa,* Washington, D.C., 1984.

14. The historical growth rates in Britain and the United States have been studied by Simon S. Kuznets; the figures are from his *Modern Economic Growth: Rate, Structure, and Spread,* New Haven, 1966.

15. U.S. Department of State, "U.S. Prosperity and Developing Countries," *Gist,* January, 1985.

16. It should be pointed out that the life expectancy figures (from *WDR 1986,* Table 1) include the effects of high infant mortality. The average 18 year old in sub-Saharan Africa has a very much better chance of surviving to, say, age 70 than does an infant at birth.

17. This paragraph was suggested by David Morawetz, *Twenty-Five Years of Economic Development 1950 to 1975,* Baltimore, 1977, pp. 26–30. There is another mathematical rule, the "rule of 72," that is helpful in calculating the rapidity of growth. Take any growth rate and divide it into 72. The result is the number of years needed to double income at that growth rate. Example: growth is 10 percent a year; $72/10 = 7.2$. It will take 7.2 years for income to double. (If you were tempted to say it would take 10 years at 10 percent a year, you forgot about compounding.) The result is close to what would be obtained with a more sophisticated formula. The actual correct answer is 7.27 years. See Stanley Fisher and Rudiger Dornbusch, *Economics,* New York, 1983, p. 369.

18. The details are from IMF, *World Economic Outlook, 1984, 1985, and 1986;* and Arjun Sengupta, "Recovery, Interdependence, and the Developing Economies," *Finance and Development* 22, no. 3 (1985): 11–14.

19. The data are mostly from IMF, *World Economic Outlook, 1986,* pp. 3, 48, 179, 200.

20. See Albert O. Hirschman, "The Rise and Decline of Development Economics," in Mark Gersovitz et al., eds., *The Theory and Experience of Economic Development,* London, 1982, pp. 387–388.

21. Similar near-synonyms exist in other major languages. In French many authors use *croissance* and *développement* to mean the same thing; in German *Wachstum* and *Entwicklung* serve the same purpose, as do *crecimiento* and *desarrollo* in Spanish. See Fernand Braudel, *The Perspective of the World,* vol. 3 of *Civilization and Capitalism,* New York, 1984, p. 303.

22. Robert Clower, George Dalton, Mitchell Harwitz, and A. A. Walters, *Growth Without Development,* Evanston, Ill., 1966. This excellent example of the distinction was first called to my attention by Charles P. Kindleberger and Bruce Herrick, *Economic Development,* 3rd ed., New York, 1977, p. 3.

23. Compare Gerald M. Meier, *Leading Issues in Economic Development,* 4th ed., Oxford, 1984, pp. 6–8, whose lead I followed here.

24. For a survey of the basic needs approach, see Frances Stewart, *Basic Needs in Developing Countries,* Baltimore, 1985; and Paul Streeten with Shahid Javed Burki, Mahbub Ul Haq, Norman Hicks, and Frances Stewart, *First Things First: Meeting Basic Human Needs in Developing Countries,* New York, 1981. For the correlation between basic needs variables and economic growth variables, see Norman Hicks, "Growth vs. Basic Needs: Is There a Trade-Off?" *World Development* 7, nos. 11/12 (1979):985–994. Because of some loose definitions used by proponents of a basic needs approach, there has recently been something of a reaction against it, especially among the ranks

of the more highly quantitative economists. See Pierre Landell-Mills' review of the Stewart volume in *Finance and Development* 22, no. 4 (1985):58.

25. Compare E. Wayne Nafziger, *The Economics of Developing Countries,* Belmont, Calif., 1984, pp. 36–37.

26. See R. A. Easterlin, "Does Economic Growth Improve the Human Lot? Some Empirical Evidence," in Paul A. David and Melvin W. Reder, eds., *Nations and Households in Economic Growth: Essays in Honor of Moses Abramovitz,* New York, 1974.

27. W. Arthur Lewis, *The Theory of Economic Growth,* London, 1955, p. 421.

28. Karl Marx and Friedrich Engels, *The German Ideology,* 1846, quoted by Amartya K. Sen, "Development: Which Way Now?" *The Economic Journal* 93 (December 1983): 754. For perceptive comments on how increasing the range of choice can be painful in a traditional social setting, see Henry J. Burton, "The Search for a Development Economics," *World Development* 13, nos. 10/11 (1985):1099–1124.

29. Lewis, *Theory of Economic Growth,* p. 422. The differences between female and male life expectancies are from *WDR 1980,* p. 91. Portions of this paragraph were suggested by William J. Baumol and Alan S. Blinder, *Economics: Principles and Policies,* New York, 1979, pp. 753–754, and *The Economist,* July 13, 1985, p. 38. The literature on the role of women in development is rapidly growing, and "women's issues" have become a major area of study. Females have an especially important part to play in population control, human capital improvement, and rural development, as discussed in Chapters 8 to 10. A generous selection of sources can be found in Uma Lele, "Women and Structural Transformation," *Economic Development and Cultural Change* 34, no. 2 (1986):195–221. Also see Iftikhar Ahmed, *Technology and Rural Women,* London, 1985, and Sue Ellen M. Charlton, *Women in Third World Development,* Boulder, Colo., 1984. An important earlier source is Ester Boserup, *Woman's Role in Economic Development,* New York, 1970.

30. Kenneth E. Boulding, *Economics as a Science,* New York, 1970, p. 86.

chapter *2*

Measuring Economic Development

The debate on the meaning of economic progress—growth in income and output versus underlying change in a country's social and economic structure—is reflected in the methods used to *measure* movement in an economy. The standard measures of output and income are gross national product (GNP), gross domestic product (GDP), and national income. These tools are universally used. But there are problems with measuring output and income. Even greater difficulties beset the employment of these tools to measure well-being or satisfaction or the standard of living or to judge the "progress" of different countries or the same country over time. Uncritical use of output and income statistics can lead to poor policy, poor planning, and incorrect conclusions, so we shall examine carefully each of the potential problems.

PROBLEMS WITH MEASUREMENT

There are a number of difficulties, some more serious than suggested in the neat quantitative tables of the international organizations, that interfere with accurate measurement of GNP or national income in the LDCs. We discuss two of these.

First, Marxian economists tend to exclude many services from the nation's total output, concentrating on the production of goods. On the side of national income, the Marxian theory that all value stems from labor content colors their view of capital, land, and natural resources and leads to the exclusion of interest and rent. The result is called net material product (NMP). This is a compelling reason why national income and product figures for LDCs such as Albania, Angola, Cuba, Kampuchea, Laos, Mozambique, North Korea, and Vietnam are

18

often excluded from the statistical tables of books on development economics—
they are not comparable with the GNP measures of the market economies. The
World Bank states that published estimates of GNP per capita in the centrally
planned economies must be "treated as tentative."[1]

Second, and more importantly, it generally follows that the poorer a country, the poorer its ability to collect statistics. No doubt some marketed product
and the money income so generated get overlooked simply because a less-
developed country is likely to have a less-developed statistical bureau.[2] But the
problem is more fundamental: Nonmarket transactions with no money flows,
which are important in the LDCs, are exceedingly difficult to deal with. The
subsistence sector of an LDC's economy—goods and services produced for one's
own use, such as food, housing, do-it-yourself carpentry and construction, transportation, the water supply—is likely to be extremely large. The types of work
typically done by women, including porterage, marketing in village markets, food
preparation, and water provision, may be unpaid for. The phenomenon extends
to exchanges within kinship groups, in which relatives are helped not for pay, but
in return for some help tomorrow or to satisfy traditional obligations.

How are relevant statistics assembled? In a few cases the procedure of the
developed countries is followed and little or no attempt is made to value subsistence production. The omission is a serious one, startling even, and the accuracy
and hence usefulness of the national accounts are reduced accordingly.

Most LDCs do attempt to value subsistence production. Where the attempt
is made, however, the problem of what prices to use arises immediately. Take food
as an example. What price should be applied to a pound of home-grown yams
consumed in Ghana? The market price? But which market, because town markets
are divided from one another by a lack of transportation? And what should be
done about the wide seasonal price fluctuations? Worse, as Phyllis Deane has
pointed out, what if the goods, being mostly subsistence production, are traded
on the market only in small quantities? The demand curve for, say, bananas may
be highly inelastic because of the limited market, which will thus be thin and
volatile. A rise in banana output of 10 percent might have a substantial impact
on price, perhaps a fall of 50 percent. Measuring all banana output, including
subsistence output, in terms of market price would then paradoxically show the
area to be worse off than before!

Statistical departments generally react to these problems in one of two ways;
they use either a "high" estimate or a "low" estimate for income from the
subsistence sector. As it is commonly true that the poorer the country, the larger
the subsistence sector as a proportion of the whole, then the resulting inaccuracy
in GNP is relatively greater for the most poverty stricken. The motive to minimize subsistence income statistics stems from the connection between low income
and some World Bank financing, credit terms from rich countries, or tariff
preferences, all more liberal for the poorer LDCs. Arguing from a position of
poverty also has a certain moral value in North-South negotiations. A motive to
overstate is a government's desire to "showcase" its excellent performance for
domestic or international political reasons. On occasion one finds even the statistical departments themselves owning up to the seriousness of the data weakness.

There was once a sentence in the preface to the national accounts of Zambia, for instance, admitting that "the figures for subsistence output in the national accounts are purely token figures and it is important to remember that a revised scheme of evaluation would alter the results radically."[3]

The same type of problem affects the measurement of GNP when barter occurs, rather than monetary transaction in markets. Seldom is the attempt made to estimate for the national accounts the value of goods exchanged via barter. Finally, there is the output and income from unreported cash transactions and from illegal activities. The inclusion of the "underground economy" of barter transactions, unreported cash transactions, and illegal activities would raise U.S. GNP anywhere from 3 to 20 percent according to various estimates.[4] If, as appears to be so, these types of transactions constitute a larger proportion of an LDC's total output than of a developed country's, then including them would raise income even more.[5] In a few countries (Burma, Bolivia, Colombia, Jamaica, Peru) illegal drug exports may yield very large but uncounted revenues, sometimes thought to be greater than from any other single export item.

PROBLEMS WITH GNP AS A MEASURE OF WELFARE

If measurement is a problem, how much more difficult is the attempt to make any correlation between a country's total output or income (even if measured accurately) and that country's welfare or standard of living. A principles of economics textbook covers in detail the traps—population, distribution, "what goods," leisure, durables, and psychic considerations—set for the unwary one who tries this in a developed country. The problems are even greater for an LDC.

Income and Population

Obviously, if the same total amount of GNP or national income is earned by two different size populations (say, Japan with 100 million and Britain with 50 million), other things being equal, the individuals in the country with the smaller population will be better off. Aggregate measures are thus inappropriate, and it is customary to employ figures for per capita GNP and income.

The use of per capita figures introduces yet another chance for error, because census data must be used. The United Nations has worked diligently to improve population estimates (see the endpapers), but census data in LDCs can still contain serious inaccuracies. In some rare cases there has been no census at all, as in the Republic of Guinea, where population figures are based on a survey taken in 1954–1955. Sometimes the data are compiled when taxes are collected, so the tax evaders are not counted. Sometimes political power depends on census results, as when legislative seats are apportioned by population, so the counting is corrupted. (The national censuses of 1962 and 1973 in Nigeria, Black Africa's most populous and richest country, were voided for political reasons, and no further attempt has ever been made. In Uruguay, following a census in 1907, politics prevented another until 1964.[6]) Seasonal migrations interfere with accuracy. Nomads, who can move across borders as they choose, will do so when the census-cum-tax man pays a visit to collect the tax on cattle charged in some African countries.

Thus the use of questionable census data to compute GNP per capita can cause even greater error in that figure than in GNP alone. (Understating total GNP while also understating population could, ironically and accidentally, decrease the degree of inaccuracy in GNP per capita. This presumably does sometimes occur.) Note in addition that some parts of GNP are calculated using population figures; census errors thus feed back into the GNP itself.

Income Distribution

GNP and income per capita say nothing at all about the *distribution* of the output and income. The implications for welfare can be large, and income distribution issues have become central in the "growth versus development" debate.

Unequal distribution can affect welfare negatively in several fairly obvious ways. If it is the result of a small number of rich becoming more affluent at the expense of a mass of poor growing poorer, then increasing social and political tension would appear almost inevitable. There will be negative ramifications for standards of health and nutrition; birthrates might rise to make up for the higher infant mortality. This is not to mention the complete ethical unacceptability of further impoverishing the poor to benefit those already much better off than they.

If all incomes are increasing, but growing faster for the rich, then social and political tension may still result, but it may not if absolute incomes have more meaning for people than relative incomes or if there seems to be a significant chance for the poor eventually to move into upper-income groups.[7]

The large potential impact of inequality on welfare is disturbing because data appear to support the belief that income distribution will be persistently less equal in LDCs than in developed countries. The first generation of development economists was little aware how troublesome and long-lasting this condition could be.

There are seven main causes for greater income inequality in the LDCs. (1) Most important for some areas, land ownership and access to land are for historical and social reasons highly unequal. (2) Significant shortages of some professional and technical personnel—teachers, engineers, scientists, computer specialists, economists, physicians—drive up their relative remuneration compared to the rest of the population, thus ensuring unusual disparities in income. (3) Widespread existence of imperfect factor mobility, imperfect information, and monopoly power based on economic or political strength may make existing disparities difficult to close. (4) Inequalities can be perpetuated by a social structure that excludes people on the basis of caste, race, sex, or religion from jobs, landholding, and other means to produce incomes. (5) Even where governments wish to move toward more equity, taxes and transfer payments are less effective in changing the distribution of income than they are in the developed world, because the mechanisms themselves are less developed. (6) Government pricing policies, subsidies, taxes, credit, foreign exchange allocations, land policies, and the like may be used to reward supporters and penalize opponents and the powerless. (7) Population growth means an increase in the percent of young people in the population. Inequality rises even though the distribution of income stays the same within any given age group. Though this symptom is ultimately self-correcting, it is still real and appears in the statistics.

Unequal distribution is especially pronounced in parts of Central and South America (where land ownership is highly skewed) and in some of the oil-producing states, but it seems to affect all types of LDCs. Until recently, there was little available information on income distribution, and change was impossible to assess.[8] In the 1970s, however, much more attention was focused on the issue, methods of measurement were refined, and the data available became much more comprehensive. (Whether the data are uniformly *better* is open to question. Sometimes the figures for income distribution are calculated from very imperfect information, and less confidence may be placed in them than even in the figures for income and product.)

Economists measure the degree of income inequality with the Lorenz curve, a graphical representation of data named after the American statistician C. Lorenz, who developed it in 1905.[9] The diagram (Figure 2.1) shows the percentage of income earned on the vertical axis and the percentage of the population earning that income on the horizontal axis. If income is distributed equally throughout the whole population, then the poorest 30 percent of the population

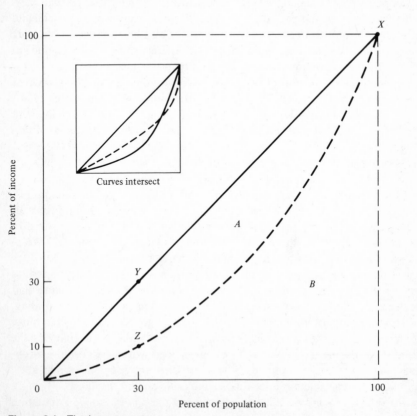

Figure 2.1 The Lorenz curve.

Table 2.1 PERCENTAGE SHARE OF TOTAL DISPOSABLE HOUSEHOLD INCOME IN INDIA BY PERCENTILE POPULATION GROUPS

Lowest 20%	Second 20%	Third 20%	Fourth 20%	Highest 20%
7.0	9.2	13.9	20.5	49.4

Source: WDR 1986, p. 226.

earns 30 percent of the income as at point *Y,* while at point *X* 100 percent of the population earns 100 percent of the income. If income is *not* distributed equally, then the poorest 30 percent of the population might earn only 10 percent of the income, as at point *Z.* If distribution is equal, then the Lorenz curve is a 45° line sloping up from the origin of the figure; if distribution is unequal, the curve is bowed away from the 45° line. The greater the bow, the larger the degree of inequality. A potential problem arises in the comparison of countries or time periods if two curves intersect (as in the diagram's inset). It is then hard to state which curve represents the greater inequality; a normative judgment must be made because some parts of society are more equal, and some are less equal.

A Lorenz curve is rather cumbersome, and it is possible to present the same underlying information on distribution in a numerical format. The method favored by the World Bank is to array the distribution by quintiles (20 percent of the population).[10] For example, India's income distribution is given by quintiles in Table 2.1. The poorest 20 percent of the population earns 7 percent of the

Table 2.2 PERCENTAGE SHARE OF TOTAL DISPOSABLE HOUSEHOLD INCOME BY PERCENTILE POPULATION GROUPS

	Lowest 20%	Second 20%	Third 20%	Fourth 20%	Highest 20%
Kenya	2.6	6.3	11.5	19.2	60.4
Peru	1.9	5.1	11.0	21.0	61.0
Zambia	3.4	7.4	11.2	16.9	61.1
Brazil	2.0	5.0	9.4	17.0	66.6
South Korea	5.7	11.2	15.4	22.4	45.3
Sri Lanka	7.5	11.7	15.7	21.7	43.4
Tanzania	5.8	10.2	13.9	19.7	50.4
Yugoslavia	6.6	12.1	18.7	23.9	38.7
United States	5.3	11.9	17.9	25.0	39.9
United Kingdom	7.0	11.5	17.0	24.8	39.7
West Germany	7.9	12.5	17.0	23.1	39.5
France	5.3	11.1	16.0	21.8	45.8

The figures in the table are for widely different years. Data, not all shown in the table, indicate that France's income distribution (with Australia's and New Zealand's) is currently least equal among the developed countries. *Source: WDR 1986,* pp. 226–227, and for Tanzania *WDR 1985,* Table 28, pp. 228–229.

income; the richest quintile earns 49.4 percent. Figures can be added across columns. For example, the lowest 40 percent of the population by income earned 16.2 percent of all income. Some examples of especially great inequality and relatively more equality are presented in Table 2.2, along with some developed country comparisons.

When comparing two countries, if one has a greater percentage share of income accruing in at least one quintile below the highest and is at least equal in the other three below the highest, that country is said to have "Lorenz dominance" or to "Lorenz dominate" the other country. Sri Lanka, with percentage shares of 7.5, 11.7, 15.7, and 21.7 for the quintiles below the highest clearly "Lorenz dominates" India's 7.0, 9.2, 13.9, and 20.5.

Often, though, the comparison is more ambiguous; one country might have a higher share in one of the quintiles and a lower share in another. In this situation Borda scores, named for their formulator, may be used. A country is given a ranking of 1 in each quintile where it has the highest percentage, a ranking of 2 where it has the second highest percentage, and so forth. The rankings are totaled to obtain the Borda score for each country. Referring back to Table 2.2, for the four countries in the middle of the table the Borda scores are as follows:

Country			Borda score
South Korea	$4 + 3 + 3 + 2$	$=$	12
Sri Lanka	$1 + 2 + 2 + 3$	$=$	8
Tanzania	$3 + 4 + 4 + 4$	$=$	15
Yugoslavia	$2 + 1 + 1 + 1$	$=$	5

In the first column of figures, Sri Lanka gets the "1" because the lowest 20 percent of its population receives the greatest percent of income among the four countries. South Korea gets the "4" because its poorest 20 percent receives the least income among the four. Low Borda scores indicate a more equal distribution of income in comparison to another country; in the example just shown, Yugoslavia has the most equal distribution of income, and Tanzania the least. The Borda method seems eminently sensible, but it has been little used in practice.[11]

Another method of comparison yields a number for each country derived from areas on the Lorenz curve diagram. Recall that the more unequal the distribution, the more bowed the Lorenz curve will be. The greater bow increases the area marked a on Figure 2.1 and decreases the area marked b. The calculation $a/(a + b)$ is called the Gini coefficient, after the Italian statistician who first formulated it in 1912. The more unequal the distribution, the larger the area a, and thus the higher the Gini coefficient.

Recent Gini calculations are given in Table 2.3.[12] Compare the high coefficients for many LDCs with the lower Ginis for developed countries and the low coefficients for a few LDCs. The main problem with Ginis is that countries with quite different income distributions can have similar coefficients. This would be true when two Lorenz curves intersect, as in the inset in Figure 2.1. Thus the

Table 2.3   GINI COEFFICIENTS FOR SELECTED COUNTRIES

Ecuador	0.66	Thailand	0.50
Zimbabwe	0.62	Tunisia	0.50
Brazil	0.61	Philippines	0.50
Iraq	0.61	Chile	0.49
Honduras	0.61	Zambia	0.49
Mexico	0.58	Tanzania	0.48
Jamaica	0.56	India	0.46
Venezuela	0.52		
Canada	0.32	United States	0.31
United Kingdom	0.32	Japan	0.31
Sri Lanka	0.37	South Korea	0.36
Pakistan	0.37	Taiwan	0.32
Malaysia	0.36		

Source: M. S. Ahluwalia, "Income Inequality: Some Dimensions of the Problem," in Hollis Chenery, M. S. Ahluwalia, C. L. G. Bell, J. H. Duloy, and R. Jolly, *Redistribution with Growth,* London, 1974.

distribution by quintiles favored by the World Bank, even though it requires dealing with more than one number for each country, has risen in favor.

Whatever technical measure is employed, any movement toward income equality in the LDCs has been limited. Typically, in an LDC the richest 10 percent of the population still receives 30 to 40 percent of the pretax income, whereas in a developed country the richest 10 percent receives only 20 to 30 percent. (This relative difference does not overcome the absolute difference, however. The rich in the developed countries are richer than the rich in the LDCs.)

Hollis Chenery, formerly vice president for research at the World Bank, has concluded that only a handful of countries—including Costa Rica, Israel, South Korea, Taiwan, and Yugoslavia—have managed to combine growth with a significant shift toward equality in income distribution. Chenery notes that rapid growth in underdeveloped countries has been of little or no benefit to perhaps a third of the population because of the unequal distribution of the gains.[13]

There are indications that trends in income distribution follow a pattern during the development process. Over time a curve plotting the Gini coefficient often assumes an inverted U-shape (see Figure 2.2); the U generally has gradually sloping, rather than steep sides, indicating that the observed tendency is relatively weak.[14] The thesis of the inverted U-shaped curve of Ginis is usually based on country comparisons (cross-section analysis) because data limitations make comparisons over time (time-series analysis) difficult. Only time-series data can indicate that a given *individual country* is behaving in the fashion shown by the U-shape; because of the scarcity of such data, the theory is controversial.[15]

There are, however, logical reasons to believe in an inverted U of Ginis. A compelling one is that in a poor, stagnant country the onset of growth will raise some peoples' income (entrepreneurs, the skilled, those in the locations where

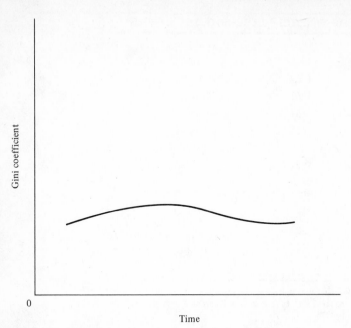

Figure 2.2   The inverted U-shaped curve of the Gini coefficient.

growth first occurs) before it touches others. Another reason involves the shift in a country's structure of production. A small structural change involving movement from a poor (rural) sector to a higher-income (urban) sector could lead to increased inequality. A commonsense way of seeing this is to picture a society wherein the whole population, with equal incomes, is in agriculture. Then shift one person into a new, higher-paid industrial sector. Immediately inequality increases and the Gini rises. This effect would be diluted as growth proceeds, but it would occur nonetheless. A further cause of the inverted U might be that a very poor country has little population growth; death rates are too high to allow it. With income growth population also grows, and this has an effect on the Gini. The percentage of younger people in the population increases; the weight of their low or nil incomes therefore rises; the Gini indicates increased inequality. Morton Paglin showed for the United States in the 1970s that a third of all U.S. inequality is due to changes in the age-income profile, and, of course, U.S. population growth is relatively low.[16] The existence of an inverted U-shaped curve might indicate that, to increase the equality of income distribution in the medium term, special programs targeted toward distribution might be needed, since growth in the same time period will predictably lessen equality.

Whether or not growth brings a more equal distribution can conveniently be illustrated via a so-called Kuznets curve (Figure 2.3), named for Harvard economist Simon Kuznets. The per capita income of the top 40 percent of the population is plotted on the vertical axis and the per capita income of the bottom 60 percent on the horizontal axis. A line through the origin (a Kuznets curve) shows unchanging income distribution as income grows. Thus at point *A* the top 40 percent of the population is receiving $800 in income per person, the bottom 60 percent $200. Further up the curve at point *B* economic growth has raised the

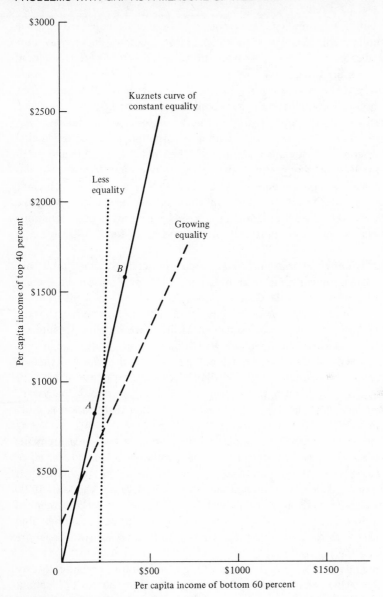

Figure 2.3 The Kuznets curve.

figure for the top 40 percent to $1,600 and the bottom 60 percent to $400. Note that points *A* and *B* show no change in distribution. If income growth is accompanied by a change in distribution, the curve will not intersect the origin. If distribution is less equal, that is, richer people's income is expanding faster than poorer people's, the line intersects the horizontal axis (the dotted line in the figure). A line intersecting the vertical axis (the dashed line) represents more equality with income growth, that is, the income of the poor is expanding faster than the income of the rich.

The Kuznets curve in Figure 2.4 plots the combined information for over

50 countries, with a weak tendency for incomes to become less equal with growth up to a per capita income level of about $800, and some slight tendency to more equality after that point. The smaller lines show the individual performances of six countries, with Sri Lanka and Taiwan moving toward more equality, Brazil and Mexico toward less, and South Korea and Yugoslavia about the same. Note, incidentally, how the Mexican experience contrasts with the general conclusion that beyond some turning point, rising income tends to lessen inequality.

If a government chose to focus attention on attempts to lessen inequality, the country's income statisticians could modify their national income and product figures to reflect the changes in income distribution. Such "poverty weighting" would typically assign a larger weight to a dollar's worth of increased income to the very poor, a lower weight to a dollar increase for the rich. Poverty-weighted income figures could be used for planning purposes by a country choosing among various projects and pursuing increased income and more equal distribution at the same time.

Another aspect of distribution that deserves notice is the wide difference that may exist geographically within an individual LDC. In England the average income in any given region of the country varies only about 10 percent from the national average. In the United States such regional differences are larger, but the variation is still at most only about 60 percent. LDCs face much more internal disparity. In Brazil the state that contains Rio de Janeiro has an average income 10 times that of the poor states in the northeast. Peru's coastal area has an income 12 times that of the Amazonian states. Similarly, compare Indonesia's rich Java to poor Sumatra or Turkey's wealthy Aegean coast and Istanbul to the backward east. These and many similar examples make it clear that distribution is more unequal in the LDCs.

A further aspect of inequality is called "absolute poverty." Measurements have been made to show what proportion of the population is below some absolute level of income that would purchase some minimal level of sustenance.[17] If absolute poverty is defined as an income of 200 U.S. dollars per capita in 1975, needed to buy a daily food ration containing 2,250 calories, then the percent of the population in this condition can be seen in Table 2.4 to be sometimes high even in countries with relatively high income. (None of the countries shown are classified among the poorest LDCs.)

In low-income LDCs, the percentage of the population in absolute poverty was estimated by Ahluwalia, Carter, and Chenery to be about half in 1975, about 13 percent in the higher-income countries, and 38 percent in the entire group.[18]

A final difficulty with distribution is the probability that some income earned within a country's borders will accrue to foreigners. The technical definition of gross national product (GNP) is the factor income earned in the production of goods and services by the citizens of a given country. It is the total domestic and foreign output claimed by residents. As such it is equal to all income earned from domestic output plus investment receipts and worker remittances coming to residents from abroad, minus these incomes earned domestically but accruing to foreigners. An alternative concept, gross domestic product (GDP) measures the factor income earned in the output of goods and services within the

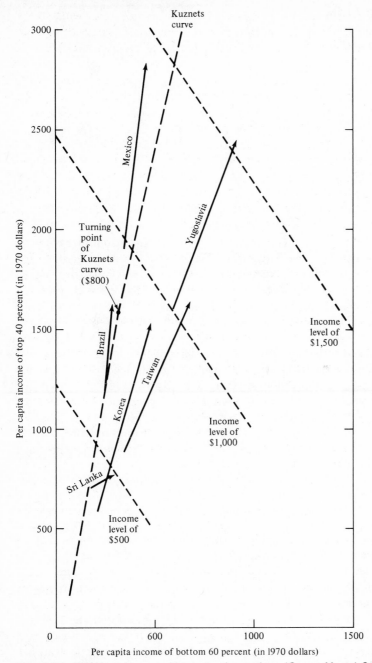

Figure 2.4 The Kuznets curve with country observations. (*Source:* Montek S. Ahluwalia, Nicholas G. Carter, and Hollis Chenery, "Growth and Poverty in Developing Countries," in Hollis Chenery, *Structural Change and Development Policy,* New York, 1979, p. 467.)

Table 2.4 PERCENTAGE OF POPULATION IN ABSOLUTE POVERTY (1975)

Senegal	29%
Colombia	14%
Turkey	11%
Peru	15%
Mexico	10%

Source: Ahluwalia, Carter, and Chenery, "Growth and Poverty in Developing Countries," in Hollis Chenery, *Structural Change and Development Policy,* New York, 1979, pp. 460–461.

borders of a country, no matter whether the income earned from that output is claimed by residents or by foreigners. The difference can be quite large. Venezuela's GNP was only 90.0 percent of its GDP in 1980, indicating that 10 percent of its factor income accrued to foreigners. The figure for Honduras in 1980 was 92.9 percent, for Nigeria 93.8 percent. In most LDCs the figure for GNP is smaller than for GDP. (In the United States GNP was 99.65 percent of GDP in 1984.)

The emphasis in the last few pages on methods for measuring inequality reflects the extent to which "growth with equity" has become a central position among economists. The inclusion of equity goals was a long time in coming, because development specialists were typically more concerned with efficiency goals involving a higher national product. As we saw in Chapter 1, though a conflict between economic growth and equity is possible and must be guarded against, there is evidence that the two goals are complementary rather than exclusive.

What Goods?

We have given substantial attention to unequal income distribution as a major obstacle in equating GNP or income with welfare. But there are others. An additional barrier, also large, is that the national accounts do not differentiate among *what goods* are being produced. War goods? (Real national product in Hitler's Nazi Germany more than doubled before the final collapse.) Capital goods, as in a country attempting to grow rapidly through heavy investment, but dire shortages of consumer goods? (China's investment is said to have reached 44 percent of output during the "Great Leap Forward" after 1958; the load was insupportably heavy, and the economy suffered severe damage.)[19] Manufactured goods fostered by government tariff protection, so that their recorded values are thereby inflated? Consumer goods, but with investment neglected, so that a future penalty of reduced output must eventually be paid? Do some of the products in the GNP reduce the quality of life, as when more cars cause massive traffic jams in the cities or more telephones overload the system so less than half the calls go through? Are the goods perhaps produced by unsafe methods, causing heavy pollution and even loss of life? (Nearly 500 people were killed in an explosion at a PEMEX refinery in Mexico City late in 1984; on December 3, 1984, a cloud of methyl isocyanate, accidentally released from an insecticide plant owned by a Union Carbide subsidiary, killed over 2,000 people and injured tens of thousands more in Bhopal, India.)

Does some expenditure lead to long-term environmental damage? The high dam at Aswan on the Nile caused downstream salinization in the Nile delta; salinization has also been extensive in Pakistan's irrigation dam and ditch program on the Indus River. Cutting trees for fuel and construction may lead to deforestation. Since forested land holds rainfall runoff very much better than denuded land, floods and landslides may result (Nepal) and hydroelectric dams may silt up (Philippines).[20] In the national accounts all of these goods are lumped together with those that do no damage or have no adverse long-run economic consequences. Nothing is reflected in the GNP beyond the market value of the good or service produced.

Notice also the problem facing the GNP accountant when some goods are simply not available. What will GNP have to say about the drying up of the gasoline supply because of congestion at the ports or some shortage of foreign exchange? Perhaps there is no bread because a license for wheat imports was mistakenly not issued last week. Perhaps the electricity goes off every evening between 5 P.M. and 8 P.M. because otherwise the generators would be overloaded by the peak demand, so some sections of the power grid are simply shut off. Perhaps the antique water system is closed down during certain daylight hours because population has outgrown its capacity. All these things can and often do happen, but their crucial importance for welfare is not reflected in the national accounts. The gasoline, bread, electricity, and water that are not sold are, of course, not included in the GNP, but periodic nonavailability of goods surely lessens welfare more than indicated by the reduced figure. *Permanent* nonavailability has an even greater impact. The health of citizens is unlikely to be much better even after a 20 percent improvement in their income if there is neither hospital nor doctor for 100 miles.[21] Countries A and B might therefore have equal per capita income, but A's citizens chase about frantically searching for needed goods whose supply has been interrupted, while B's inhabitants find full shelves in the marketplaces and public services working well. The implications for welfare can be large.

The question of what goods are in the GNP is also influenced by geography, with distinct implications for the standard of living. In temperate zones heated homes and warm clothing are necessary. A country in those latitudes will have to devote a fair portion of its GNP just to ward off the cold, and it will have to have a higher GNP than a warm country in order to achieve welfare equality. Peru and Turkey suffer from earthquakes and Bangladesh is hit by vicious cyclones (as hurricanes are called in the Bay of Bengal) almost every year, while other countries are not as subject to recurring natural disasters and not at all subject to cold. Income of $1,000 does not provide equal welfare in different areas when there is a different bill for heated homes, warm clothing, and disaster relief.

Product Quality, Leisure, Durable Goods, Psychic Concerns

Next is the problem of *product quality.* One thousand dollars' worth of Fiat made in Italy may appear at first glance to be exactly the same as $1,000 worth of the supposedly identical Spanish-made SEAT or the Romanian equivalent, but the quality of the product can and often does differ substantially. The gasoline may be the regular price, but the octane disconcertingly low, so that in many an LDC a high-performance car will not only knock, but will run two or three minutes after the ignition is turned off due to carbon buildup. There may be weevils baked into the bread and little pebbles in the rice; the first is hard on the appetite, the second on the teeth. A dollar's worth of Indian cloth may wear out sooner, or later, than a dollar's worth of Philippine cloth. The competition that would force prices to reflect quality differences is meanwhile not operating effectively because of high barriers to international trade.

Leisure is not included in the national accounts and GNP as a measure of welfare suffers accordingly. A country may secure higher output per head simply by reducing leisure, an aim of the Red Guards in China, the Stakhanovites in the USSR, and the factory committees in Cuba. Similarly, a rise in welfare because economic development allows an increase in leisure does not show up in the GNP. (Leisure time in the United States during the three and a half decades after 1929 increased 22 percent, but this is not reflected in the national accounts for the period.)[22] Between 1950 and 1973 leisure per adult male (a better measure than per person because women have joined the labor force in large numbers) grew 16 percent or more in Germany, Denmark, and Sweden, but only 6 percent in Britain and 4 percent in France.

More prosaic perhaps, but important, is the treatment of *durable goods.* These goods—the cars, the stoves, the refrigerators, etc.—are conventionally put into the GNP in the year they are produced and sold. Yet a durable good continues to perform an economic service long after its initial purchase. In theory one would want to measure not the purchase price of the durable, but instead the services that flow from it over the years. (Obviously, the car that lasts 15 years and 150,000 miles yields more services than the car junked after 4 years and 40,000 miles.)

From the standpoint of welfare, there are thus two sides to this issue. Developed countries have more durable goods, and thus their welfare is understated by their GNP. Also important, however, is the fact that LDCs keep durables in service much longer. Welding car bodies, soldering loose connections, wiring up carburetors, cannibalizing radios and cars and bicycles, all contribute to keeping durables in service much longer than they ever would be in a rich country. The welfare of an LDC is thus also understated by GNP, possibly in greater proportion than that of a developed country. The other side of this particular coin is that the tension of daily life rises appreciably, perhaps most apparent to the casual visitor when a wheel on his taxi drops off. (The poor condition of vehicles is certainly one reason why auto accidents kill far more people in the LDCs than in the developed countries, for example, 16 times more per vehicle-mile in Nigeria than in the United States.[23]

Finally, there is the problem of *psychic cost* and income, meaning that in the national accounts there is no place for working conditions and job satisfaction. Even if they had equal incomes, the farmer working in the enervating torrid heat and humidity of West Africa or Southeast Asia would certainly be in a different welfare position from the farmer in North America. One never gets completely acclimated—not even after a lifetime of adapting to the environment—to 100° heat, 90 percent humidity, and heavy labor with hand tools, all at the same time. For this reason alone, each dollar earned will come with more difficulty and psychic cost. Before World War II, much attention was given to this problem, but unfortunately often with a connotation of racial inferiority. Gunnar Myrdal surveyed this question aptly in his magnum opus, *Asian Drama.*

> It needs to be explained . . . why the climatic factor is almost entirely neglected in the literature on development problems . . . , why there is so little specialized research on the economic effects of climate and the possibilities for their amelioration, and why the development plans of these countries are almost entirely silent on this subject. This present-day lack of interest in climatic conditions is in sharp contrast to the thinking about underdevelopment in pre-independence times. Among the stereotyped opinions then elaborated to explain the poverty of the underdeveloped countries—more specifically, the lack of drive, enterprise, and efficiency of other peoples—were theories that all this was attributable to the unbearable climate and its effects on soils, crops, animals, and people, and on the pattern of civilization in general. . . . It was a doctrine consonant with the vague beliefs in the racial inferiority of the colonial peoples. In any case, this pessimism supported the common view badly needed as a rationalization of Western colonial policy, that little could be done to improve the productivity of the colonies and the life of the colonial peoples. That this interest in the climatic conditions, and especially the glib popular theories concerning their effects, served opportunistic ends should not, of course, be taken to mean that these conditions are unimportant or even that all the observations made in the pre-independence era were incorrect. Yet the reaction to this type of thinking has been so complete that, as we have pointed out, climate is no longer discussed as an important factor in economic development.[24]

It should not be ignored.[25] A hot, humid climate *does* interfere with work. An East African topsoil baked by the sun into an impenetrable hard pan surface can cause the rapid wearing out of iron and even steel plows; a tropical downpour can wash out a farm road or ruin an irrigation ditch in a few moments. Such frustrations have a psychic impact that does not appear directly in the national accounts, the ability of which to measure well-being is thus lessened.[26]

PROBLEMS IN USING GNP TO MAKE COMPARISONS OVER TIME

Perhaps the most confusing use of the national accounts is the attempt to make comparisons with them. "India's GNP is now 40 percent larger than it was in 1975" is an example of comparison over time. Such statements are subject to serious questions as to accuracy.

Any student of economics can explain that over time inflation will affect the figures for nominal income and product, making accurate comparison impossible without some adjustment for the price increases. This is accomplished by means of a weighted price index. But the poorer a country and the less developed its statistical services, the less frequently one might expect adjustment in its price indices. The commodities included and the weights used go out of date; it is not unknown for some indices to have reflected the same commodities and weights for 20 and even 30 years, and although such cases are exceptional, it is common to find that the price indices of LDCs are adjusted far less frequently than those of the developed world.

Development itself changes prices because of supply shifts, and this introduces an index number problem into any attempt to correct for inflation. A country that has undergone some development will often find that goods of little importance in consumer spending a few years ago, and which have thus received small weights in the country's price index, are now more important. Because of their growing abundance, these goods may be rising in price less rapidly than other goods. That will make a difference in calculating real GNP, depending on what type of price index we employ.

Most of the world utilizes base-weighted price indices, the base being the average price level in an earlier year, for example, "if 1980 = 100, then 1986 prices = 165." This index is called a Laspeyres price index, after its formulator, Etienne Laspeyres. One could also use a terminal-year price index, with, say, 1986 = 100 as a base. Prices in previous years would then show lower numbers, 1980 = 88, for example, if inflation has occurred. This is known after its developer as a Paasche index. Terminal-year pricing using current weights was once rarely encountered, since to keep it up to date an explicit index so constructed has to be on a new base that changes every year. However, the World Bank is in effect shifting toward this method because the implicit GNP deflator now emphasized in the Bank's statistical calculations uses current weights.[27]

Depending on which index is used, the measured amount of real growth over time will be significantly different.[28] A geometric average between the Laspeyres and the Paasche results, called a Fisher's Ideal Index, can correct for this index number problem, but it is more complex to operate and has found little use. Basically, this problem is just ignored by the vast majority of people who use GNP statistics. (The International Comparison Project discussed later in this chapter has made a point of showing what differences occur when Laspeyres, Paasche, and Fisher indices are used.)

PROBLEMS IN USING GNP TO MAKE COMPARISONS
BETWEEN COUNTRIES

"India's GNP per capita is triple that of Burma" is an example of a comparison between countries. An immediate problem is encountered. To make any statement of this kind, one has to put the respective GNPs into the same currency. Conventionally, the U.S. dollar is used as the measuring rod. Thus India's GNP in rupees is converted into dollars at the prevailing exchange rate, and Burma's GNP in kyats is also converted into dollars at its exchange rate. The two can then be compared to each other, to any other country whose GNP is converted into dollars, or directly to the GNP of the United States. The publications of the United Nations, the International Monetary Fund, and the World Bank do just this, converting local currencies into dollars so that a comparison can be made. It is the most common form for showing differences in income.

There is a serious flaw in the method, however. A country's exchange rate, whether it be rupees or any of a hundred other currencies to the dollar, may not reflect closely the actual purchasing power of the money. Numerous currencies in the LDCs are fixed at some artificial level by the government, a level that may have little relation to supply and demand for that currency in international trade and on foreign exchange markets. Buying and selling such a currency may even be prohibited except through the central bank. Little useful information may thus be conveyed by the official exchange rate, of which there may even be more than one if a multiple rate system with preferences for exports and penalties for imports is in use. The official rate may be so far from what would obtain on a free market that the statisticians will try to find a more reasonable proxy, such as the rate for illegal foreign exchange transactions on a black market. Even the black market rate, while an improvement, may not approximate what a free-market equilibrium price would have been because of the risks involved in buying or selling on that market.

Yet more discouraging for accurate comparison is that the problem persists even if the exchange rate is demonstrably a free-market equilibrium price that does yield useful information. Take a reasonably free-market rate such as 900 South Korean won equal 1 U.S. dollar. This rate reflects the purchasing power of the dollar in Korea, or the won in the United States, over goods and services traded internationally. But the rate reflects *only* that, and the relative purchasing power over goods and services not in international trade is not shown by the foreign exchange rate. This shortcoming is sure to be important when comparing an LDC to any developed country, because a large volume of goods and services never enters international trade at all. Included may be goods whose transport cost is high (fresh foods) or nearly impossible (house construction) and services (haircuts, domestic service, taxi rides) where transport of the service is quite impossible.

If the prices of the nontraded goods and services were proportional to the prices for goods in international trade, this would make no difference, and the foreign exchange rate would give an adequate comparison of the purchasing power of the two currencies. But the prices of nontraded goods are (unfortunately for the statistician) likely to differ substantially. In most LDCs capital ordinarily is scarce and labor is cheap. Goods embodying plentiful labor will thus be cheaper than in a developed country. Services usually embody more labor than capital, and so do many labor-intensive unstandardized products that do not enter international trade. Thus we can assume that these nontraded goods and services are relatively cheaper in LDCs than are the traded goods. It comes down to the probability that a dollar when converted into a foreign currency will buy more in the foreign country than it will in the United States. In India, for example, the price for goods not entering international trade has been estimated at about 13 percent of the price in the United States. Similarly, a study by Lloyd Reynolds involving retail price information collected at Shanghai noted a large discrepancy in purchasing power. The same cereal diet, two-room apartment, and use of public transportation that cost $900 in Shanghai at the official dollar/yuan exchange rate would have cost $4,800 in Ann Arbor, Michigan. Chinese per capita GNP of $310 per year (1984) looks much better in this light.[29]

This phenomenon was once often called the Gilbert and Kravis effect, because Milton Gilbert and Irving Kravis first estimated how much the real income of a country might be understated through the use of foreign exchange rates. The original Gilbert and Kravis study showed per capita GNP in eight western European countries and the United States during the 1950s, when labor was clearly much cheaper all over Europe than it was in the United States. Gilbert and Kravis found that converting the GNPs into dollars at prevailing exchange rates undervalued 1955 output in a range of 18 to 70 percent for the European countries studied. More recent studies of LDCs have estimated that use of the exchange rate for comparative purposes understates per capita GNP some 200 percent for countries with per capita output of about $600 and understates it by an even greater 300 percent when per capita output is about $200. (The same effect is true historically; economic historians estimate that U.S. real per capita income in 1860 was probably nearly double the calculated figure when purchasing power adjustments are taken into account.)[30]

Recently, the problem of using foreign exchange rates to make the conversion has grown much worse, since swings in the dollar of 10 or 20 or even 30 percent a year have occurred against some foreign currencies. When exchange rates vary, GNP will shift, and the change can be large! For example, Japan's per capita GNP was 47 percent above Great Britain's in 1978, but 5 percent lower in 1980. The reason was not that Japan's growth suddenly slowed and Britain's spurted; quite the opposite, Japan's growth rate was faster during the whole period. The entire explanation is that the pound sterling appreciated against the dollar and the yen depreciated.[31]

Such examples have spurred new work by the World Bank to compute the purchasing power of income, in an attempt to correct for the Gilbert and Kravis effect. The new work is called the International Comparison Project, or ICP, and is headed by Kravis himself, Alan Heston, and Robert Summers at the University of Pennsylvania.[32] The ICP involves 151 expenditure categories within the GDP version of national product. A weighted average world price is determined for each commodity. (Kravis has said that this weighted price structure bears a rough resemblance to the price structure of Italy.)[33] A purchasing power parity foreign exchange rate is calculated on this basis, the idea being to get an "international dollar" with the same purchasing power over total foreign country GDP. In essence, the output of every country is valued by a single set of prices—a common measuring rod. Using 1975 prices, purchasing power parity foreign exchange rates were calculated originally for 16 and later 34 countries (15 of them in Europe).[34] The most recent data, now based on 1981 prices, are shown on the endpapers.

The best methodology presently available, the ICP comparisons yield an outcome that is dramatically different from the orthodox method, as Table 2.5 shows. The difference in some sample per capita GDPs calculated by the purchasing power method as a percentage of the same GDPs calculated by using official foreign exchange rates is in Table 2.6.

The whole exercise leads the prudent economist or statesman to tread cautiously when comparisons of national income or product are made, recalling always that they are only rough approximations of reality. The implication is not that national product comparisons should be abandoned, but that they should be

Table 2.5 GNP CALCULATED BY FOREIGN EXCHANGE CONVERSION AND BY PURCHASING POWER CONVERSION, 1977

	Per Capita GDP (in Dollars)	
	Foreign Exchange Conversion	Purchasing Power Conversion
Low-income LDCs	$170	$484
Middle-income LDCs	$1,140	$1,863
Developed countries	$6,980	$6,187

Source: Column 1 is from *WDR 1979,* pp. 126–127. Column 2 is from Irving B. Kravis, Alan W. Heston, and Robert Summers, *World Product and Income: International Comparisons of Real Gross Product,* Baltimore, 1982, p. 343.

Table 2.6 GDP CALCULATED BY PURCHASING POWER METHOD AS PERCENT OF GDP CALCULATED BY FOREIGN EXCHANGE RATE METHOD, 1975

Sri Lanka	365	France	91
India	323	Netherlands	89
Pakistan	312	West Germany	88
Colombia	283	Denmark	79
Philippines	251		
Kenya	195		
Mexico	170		

Source: Irving B. Kravis, Alan W. Heston, and Robert Summers, *World Product and Income: International Comparisons of Real Gross Product,* Baltimore, 1982, p. 12.

made in a more thoughtful manner. "As things are," says Kravis, "the enormous authority of our leading international institutions is placed behind numbers that are poorer measures of real comparative GDP than others that are available. The result is a constant stream of citations of erroneous international comparisons of national real products in newspapers, journals, and even in scholarly papers."[35] Perhaps not surprisingly, given the political implications of this research (LDCs are not quite so poor as the usual statistics show), some LDCs have opposed continuation of the project, and UN funding has been considerably reduced. But the purchasing power adjustments should not in any way lessen our concern with poverty; they simply make our knowledge of it more accurate.

OTHER INDICATORS OF ECONOMIC PROGRESS

Such cautions concerning product and income calculations in recent years have led to a search for various alternatives and supplements. These supplements employ nonmonetary real indicators as a measure of "social development" and standard of living.[36] The indicators include the percentage of the labor force in agriculture, literacy rates, school enrollment as a percentage of the relevant age group, life expectancy, infant mortality, and all the following measured per capita: calorie supply, energy consumption, number of vehicles, consumption of iron, steel, and cement, purchases of consumer durables, number of radios and telephones, consumption of meat, and quantity of letters sent. Weights for leisure and income distribution are sometimes included. Indeed, some of these social development indicators can be fully as flawed as GNP where income distribution is concerned, if the poor are left out from any advance.[37] Whatever the indicators chosen, there is the obvious difficulty that combining them must involve weighting based on some system of values, and it will be very difficult ever to reach a consensus. Young people, for example, may prefer a good score in education to a good score in health, while old people might favor the reverse. "Meat consumption" in the list above may be of far less interest in India than in Argentina. The problem of inability to agree on a generally accepted list would seem serious.[38]

    The best-known of these attempts is simpler and less subject to debate over values, the physical quality of life index, or PQLI, pioneered by the Overseas Development Council in Washington. The PQLI is an index number based on the percentage of literacy, infant mortality, and life expectancy (after age 1, so as not to double count infant deaths). PQLIs have now been calculated for the entire world (see the endpapers). They range from a present low of 16 to 17 in Afghanistan, Gambia, and Somalia to a high of 100 in Iceland and 99 in Norway, Sweden, and Japan. The world average is 69, the LDC average is 61, and the developed country average is 96 (97 in the United States).

    Comparisons based on the PQLI may differ substantially from comparisons based on GNP, as shown from the following data published in 1985. Kuwait with its huge per capita GNP of $17,880 had a PQLI of only 78, actually beaten by "poor" Sri Lanka, whose low per capita GNP of $330 concealed a high PQLI of 85. A more dramatic view of PQLI's corrective value can be found if we comb the statistics a bit further. Gambia, on Africa's west coast, had a somewhat higher

GNP per capita ($360) than did Sri Lanka. But Gambia's PQLI was only 16, compared to Sri Lanka's 85. Infant mortality was 196 per 1,000 live births in Gambia compared to only 43 in Sri Lanka; life expectancy was 36 years as opposed to 69; 20 percent of the population was literate compared to 86 percent, but Gambia's GNP was the higher of the two![39]

The PQLI concept has its own controversies. It is strongly correlated with per capita GNP, and the definition is very narrow, leading some to call it more a "quantity" of life index than one of quality. There is debate on the subject. But the availability of PQLI data has clearly added another useful dimension to the comparison of countries, and the concept is now well established.

So to summarize: The difficulties of measuring development are so significant that no one statistic will serve. We know that some countries are rich, some are poor, and some are very poor. We know that some countries are growing and that some are not. We know that PQLIs have been increasing during the last three decades and that the percentage in absolute poverty as measured by income has been declining, so that whatever the inherent weaknesses in the data, these major measures are at least not diverging. But we should be exceedingly wary of any statement of precision in this area. For those seeking exactitude, a combination of real per capita GNP alongside a table of ICP adjustments and nonmonetary real indicators plus a physical quality of life index will greatly lessen the degree of error.

The end result is really a value judgment. Perhaps a reasonable one is as follows. However inadequate GNP is as a measuring rod, it is hard to imagine significant long-term development without a rise in per capita GNP—and this statement as much as anything explains the concentration on that much-maligned measure.[40] But it is also important to study what has happened to unemployment, inequality, and the qualitative dimensions of poverty; and if these are worsening, then even a fast growth in GNP is not development.

NOTES

1. *1981 World Bank Atlas,* Washington, D.C., 1982, p. 24. When such figures are included in tables of GNP, they are frequently only for the Eastern European countries. The data have usually been obtained by a rather rough method involving the measurement of NMP equivalent for 12 Western European countries in 1970. Then a ratio of NMP to GNP in these countries is calculated to obtain GNP for the Marxist countries. Finally, the ratio $\Delta NMP/\Delta GNP$ is calculated for the Western European countries and extrapolated forward to obtain the current GNP figure for the Eastern European countries. The results of a new World Bank research project on the subject have just been published by Paul Marer, *Dollar GNPs of the USSR and Eastern Europe,* Baltimore, 1986.
2. In a few instances the absence of data is so formidable that GNP is not calculated at all or, if calculated, is so doubtful that the World Bank does not publish the information in its annual *World Development Report.* Included in this category in 1986 were Bhutan, Brunei, Chad, Comoros, Djibouti, Equatorial Guinea, Lebanon, Maldives, Seychelles, Solomon Islands, Tonga, Vanuatu, and Western Samoa.
3. From a lecture by A. D. Knox at the London School of Economics.

4. There is a thorough survey of U.S. transactions of this nature in Carol S. Carson, "The Underground Economy: An Introduction," in *Survey of Current Business,* May 1984, pp. 21–37.

5. Revision of the Nigerian national accounts in 1979 raised national product since 1973 by over a third in some years. See Douglas Rimmer, *The Economies of West Africa,* New York, 1984, p. 268.

6. See R. K. Udo, "Population and Politics in Nigeria," in J. C. Caldwell and C. Okonjo, *The Population of Tropical Africa,* London, 1968, for details of the withdrawal of the 1962 census. The long hiatus in Uruguay's census is noted by Bruce Herrick and Charles P. Kindleberger, *Economic Development,* 4th ed., New York, 1983, p. 124.

7. See Albert O. Hirschman, "The Changing Tolerance for Income Inequality in the Course of Economic Development," *Quarterly Journal of Economics,* 87, no. 4 (1973): 544–566; to which I was led by Rimmer, *Economies of West Africa,* pp. 42–51.

8. Gerald K. Helleiner, "The Refnes Seminar: Economic Theory and North-South Negotiations," *World Development* 9, no. 6 (1981):542.

9. The methods for measuring income distribution receive a detailed study in Jacques Lecaillon et al., *Income Distribution and Economic Development: An Analytical Survey,* Geneva, 1984. The dates of the Lorenz curve and Gini coefficient (see below) are from Subrata Ghatak, *Development Economics,* London, 1978, p. 15. There is an overview of the subject, with many citations, by William R. Cline, "Distribution and Development: A Survey of Literature," *Journal of Development Economics* 1 (1975):359–400; and a thorough study by Gary S. Fields, *Poverty, Inequality, and Development,* Cambridge, 1980.

10. The data can be by household or individuals. For a critical analysis, see Lecaillon et al., *Income Distribution.*

11. For a discussion of Lorenz dominance and Borda scores (named for Jean-Charles Borda, an eighteenth-century French mathematician), see the work of A. K. Sen reprinted in Gerald M. Meier, *Leading Issues in Economic Development,* 4th ed., New York, 1984, pp. 79–80.

12. See M. S. Ahluwalia, "Income Inequality: Some Dimensions of the Problem," in Hollis Chenery, M. S. Ahluwalia, C. L. G. Bell, J. H. Duloy, and R. Jolly, *Redistribution with Growth,* London, 1974. Other calculated Gini coefficients differing somewhat from those shown in the text are given in Lecaillon et al., *Income Distribution,* chap. 2. A recently calculated world average Gini is a high 0.67. See Margaret E. Grosh and E. Wayne Nafziger, "The Computation of World Income Distribution," *Economic Development and Cultural Change* 34, no. 2 (1986):347–359. In addition to the Gini coefficient, there is another method for measuring income distribution called a Theil index, named for Henri Theil. More advanced treatises in income distribution can be consulted for details.

13. Among many works on the subject by Chenery, see Montek S. Ahluwalia, Nicholas G. Carter, and Hollis B. Chenery, "Growth and Poverty in Developing Countries," in Hollis Chenery, *Structural Change and Development Policy,* New York, 1979, chap. 11; Chenery et al., *Redistribution with Growth* (the statement in the text is from p. xiii, to which I was led by Meier, *Leading Issues,* 4th ed., p. 9); and the accessible article "Poverty and Progress—Choices for the Developing World," *Finance and Development,* 17, no. 2 (1980):12–16.

14. The inverted-U hypothesis was first advanced by Simon Kuznets in 1954. By now there have been many tests, discussed in Lecaillon et al. *Income Distribution,* pp. 10–14.

15. Compare the comments by William Loehr and John P. Powelson, *The Economics of Development and Distribution,* New York, 1981, pp. 129–130, in connection with the

studies of Kuznets, Kravis, Oshima, Paukert, Adelman and Morris, Chenery, and Roberti.

16. See Morton Paglin, "The Measurement and Trend of Inequality: A Basic Revision," *American Economic Review* 65, no. 4 (1975):598–609, to which my attention was called by Loehr and Powelson, *Economics of Development and Distribution,* p. 115.

17. The tying of the absolute level to fulfillment of some minimum level of caloric needs appears reasonable, but has also sparked controversy. Different climates and work environments would lead to different caloric needs even for the same person; other requirements such as vitamins, protein, etc., are not considered, and there has been debate on the appropriateness of the 2,250-calorie benchmark. See Peter Cutler, "The Measurement of Poverty: A Review of Attempts to Quantify the Poor with Special Reference to India," *World Development* 12, nos. 11/12 (1984): 1119–1130; and E. Wayne Nafziger, *The Economics of Developing Countries,* Belmont, Calif., 1984, p. 111.

18. The figures given in Table 2.4 have been adjusted in several ways to account for inflation and difficulties in comparing incomes through exchange rate conversions. (Both topics are taken up later in this chapter.)

19. Ding Chen, "The Economic Development of China," *Scientific American* 243, no. 3 (1980):159.

20. *WDR 1984,* p. 95. In addition there is the obvious increase in the price of the wood itself, by 10 times in Ethiopia during the 1970s, for example. In that country wood now claims as much as 20 percent of household income.

21. From Amartya K. Sen, "Development: Which Way Now?," *The Economic Journal* 93 (December 1983):756.

22. From Theodore Morgan, *Economic Development: Concept and Strategy,* New York, 1975, p. 83, quoting W. Nordhaus and J. Tobin.

23. *WDR 1980,* p. 54.

24. Gunnar Myrdal, *Asian Drama: An Inquiry into the Poverty of Nations,* New York, 1968, pp. 678–679.

25. The subject has been treated by Andrew M. Kamarck, *The Tropics and Economic Development: A Provocative Inquiry into the Poverty of Nations,* Baltimore, 1976; and by B. F. Hodder, *Economic Development in the Tropics,* London, 1980.

26. Our discussion of GNP's imperfect ability to reflect welfare could go further afield into many aspects of social organization not closely associated with standard economics. Two such aspects are the possible presence of *prejudice* or *authoritarian government.* Though practically no country is free from some aspect of one or the other, some countries clearly suffer more than the average. Examples of prejudice in LDCs would include anti-Jewish in the Arab states, anti-Palestinian in Israel, anti-black among South Africa's whites, anti-Indian in East Africa, anti-"untouchable" and anti-Sikh in India, anti-Chinese in parts of Southeast Asia. The litany appears, depressingly, very long. Where tension due to prejudice is at a high level, welfare is correspondingly reduced, though this does not appear in the GNP. The same is true for an authoritarian government. Life in Hitler's Nazi Germany seems to have had its parallels in the very recent history of some LDCs, Uganda, for example, or Kampuchea, in which a dollar's worth of national income presumably brought far less satisfaction to the recipient than it did in some more fortunate neighbor. See W. Arthur Lewis, *Racial Conflict and Economic Development,* Cambridge, Mass., 1985.

27. Technically, the Bank values current production at base-year prices, rather than using an explicitly calculated price index. This method yields the so-called implicit GNP

deflator. The GNP deflator is obtained by dividing nominal GNP by real GNP. Since the calculation in effect uses present-year weights for output, it is thus an example of the Paasche method.

28. A numerical example may be helpful in tracing through this index number problem, which is rather difficult to grasp in the abstract. It will demonstrate a case where real growth differs depending on the choice of price index. Say Brazil produces two products, cars and rice. The figures below are invented for easy calculation; prices are in Brazilian currency (C). Car output in 1980 totaled a small 100 units, at a relatively high price of C1,000 per car. Rice output was much greater, 900,000 bushels at C1 per bushel. Total current GNP in 1980 was thus C100,000 in car output plus C900,000 in rice output, or C1 million in all.

From 1980 to 1986, there was substantial inflation. But at the same time car output expanded a great deal, to 1,000 cars, while rice production went up only a little, to 1 million bushels. The relatively greater abundance of cars restrained the price increase for them to 100 percent, the price becoming C2,000 per car; while the rice price went up by a considerably greater 200 percent, to C3 per bushel. Thus current GNP in 1986 is:

1,000 cars × C2,000 per car	= C2 million
1 million bushels rice × C3 per bushel	= C3 million
Total current GNP at 1986 prices	= C5 million

Obviously, part of the 1986 GNP, which has grown 5 times since 1980, is due to inflation. But how much growth has occurred in real terms? It depends on the form of price index we employ. Let us first use a conventional explicitly calculated Laspeyres price index that weights according to the importance of goods in some base year, such as the consumer price index or producer price index. In that case the weights in the base year are 10 for cars and 90 for rice, since 10 percent of spending was on the former, and 90 percent on the latter, in 1980. We must now find the weighted price index for 1986. Following the standard method taught in a principles of economics course, we multiply the weight (W) times the percentage increase in each price expressed on a base of 100 (R). R is therefore 200 for cars and 300 for rice. We then sum the results.

R		W		R×W
200	×	10 =		2,000
300	×	90 =		27,000
sum of		R×W =		29,000

This sum, when divided by 100 is the weighted price index. Thus 29,000 ÷ 100 = 290 (indicating that in weighted terms, prices rose 2.9 times between 1980 and 1986). The final step is to calculate the real GNP for 1986 in 1980 prices, following the conventional formula that current GNP ÷ the weighted price index = real GNP. Thus,

$$\frac{C5 \text{ million}}{290} = C1.72 \text{ million}$$

Real GNP in 1980 prices was thus C1.72 million in 1986, meaning that real GNP was 1.72 times its figure in 1980.

But we also could have used another procedure, valuing 1986 output at the prices obtaining in 1980 rather than using an explicit price index. Doing so in effect weights according to the current importance of goods, and is thus an example of the Paasche method. Look at the different result:

1986 output	×	1980 price =	Value of 1986 output in 1980 prices
1,000 cars	×	C1,000 =	C1 million
1 million bushels	×	C1 =	C1 million
Real 1986 GNP at 1980 prices			= C2 million

Using this procedure, we find that real GNP has increased 2 times since 1980, over 16 percent more than in our earlier example. For an explanation of this knotty problem, see Edwin Mansfield, *Microeconomics,* 3rd ed., New York, 1979, pp. 99 ff.; and Robert J. Barro, *Macroeconomics,* New York, 1984, pp. 16–23.

29. Lloyd Reynolds, "China as a Less Developed Economy," *American Economic Review* 65, no. 3 (1975):418–428; and the comments by Benjamin Higgins and Jean Downing Higgins, *Economic Development of a Small Planet,* New York, 1979, p. 283.
30. See Simon Kuznets, *Economic Growth of Nations: Total Output and Production Structure,* Cambridge, Mass., 1971; and Nafziger, *Economics of Developing Countries,* p. 24.
31. Irving W. Kravis, "Comparative Studies of National Incomes and Prices," *Journal of Economic Literature* 22 (March 1984):2.
32. The sophisticated work of the International Comparison Project is discussed in detail in Irving B. Kravis, Alan W. Heston, and Robert Summers, *International Comparisons of Real Product and Purchasing Power,* Baltimore, 1978; Irving B. Kravis, Alan W. Heston, and Robert Summers, *World Product and Income: International Comparisons of Real Gross Product,* Baltimore, 1982; Robert Summers, Irving B. Kravis, and Alan W. Heston, "International Comparisons of Real Product and Its Composition: 1950–77," *Review of Income and Wealth* 26, no. 1 (March 1980): 19–66; Irving B. Kravis, "Comparative Studies of National Incomes and Prices," *Journal of Economic Literature, 22 (March 1984):1–39;* Robin Marris, "Comparing the Incomes of Nations: A Critique of the International Comparison Project," *Journal of Economic Literature* 22 (March 1984):40–57; and Irving B. Kravis, "The Three Faces of the International Comparison Project," *The World Bank Research Observer* 1, no. 1 (1986):3–26.
33. Kravis, "Comparative Studies," p. 33.
34. A short-cut involving multiple regression analysis uses a few variables taken from trade and inflation data that closely duplicate ($R^2 = .99$) the results for the original 16. It has been applied to all remaining LDCs.
35. Kravis, "Comparative Studies," p. 37. There is an area of academic debate as to whether the importance of developed countries in the weighted world average price level skews the results (only slightly, argues Kravis), and whether the prices of services are treated correctly. See Kravis, "Three Faces," pp. 21–22.
36. Familiar attempts include Wilfred Beckerman, *International Comparisons of Real Incomes,* Paris, 1966, p. 29, and Wilfred Beckerman and Robert Bacon, "The International Distribution of Incomes," in Paul Streeten, ed., *Unfashionable Economics,* London, 1970. Also see Gerald M. Meier, *Leading Issues in Economic Development,* New York, 1976, 3rd ed., p. 12; Morgan, *Economic Development,* p. 81; and Ghatak, *Development Economics,* p. 13.

37. Ian M. D. Little, *Economic Development: Theory, Policy, and International Relations,*
    New York, 1982, p. 14.
38. See Muriel Nissel, "Indicators of Human Betterment," in Kenneth E. Boulding, ed.,
    The Economics of Human Betterment, Albany, N.Y., 1984, pp. 15–35, especially pp.
    28–29. Another and altogether different approach might be to measure well-being with
    reference to what use is made of available time: paid work, including breaks and travel;
    unpaid work on preparing food, obtaining water, child care, shopping and marketing,
    etc.; sleep; and free time including education, leisure, and recreation. This approach
    is examined by F. Thomas Juster, Paul N. Courant, and Greg K. Dow, "A Theoretical
    Framework for the Measurement of Well-Being," *Review of Income and Wealth* 27,
    no. 1 (1981); and see Nissel, "Indicators of Human Betterment," pp. 18–21.
39. The GNP figures for Kuwait and Sri Lanka are from *WDR 1985,* pp. 174–175. The
    GNP for Gambia and the PQLI statistics are from John W. Sewell, Richard E.
    Feinberg, and Valeriana Kallab, eds., *U.S. Foreign Trade Policy and the Third World:
    Agenda 1985–86,* Washington, D.C., 1985, pp. 214–215, 218–219. Figures differ some-
    what in *WDR 1986,* and indicate a lower GNP for Gambia. But the point remains
    the same.
40. Compare Ghatak, *Development Economics,* p. 14.

chapter 3

What Causes Development? The Lessons of Experience and a Forward View

This chapter is an overview of what are thought to be the main causes of economic development. This view is based on the experience of today's low-income countries during the last quarter century and today's rich countries during their period of early development.[1] The discussion serves an important purpose for the book as a whole in that it provides a broad framework for subsequent chapters that examine these causes in detail. We will find no single "engine" of causation, but instead a group of five important factors that propel the process, their significance varying from country to country: (1) increased saving and investment and acquisition of appropriate technology, (2) agricultural improvement, (3) a growing foreign trade with close attention to comparative advantage, (4) an economic system that allows for efficient allocation, and (5) human resource development.[2] It should be understood that the process is not mechanical, automatic, and fully predictable. Progress in each of these areas appears valuable, but experience shows it may not always be a necessary condition for growth. Neither will it always be a sufficient condition; following the recommended policies does not carry a guarantee of success. But proper policy certainly appears to improve the odds.

CRITICAL FACTORS FOR DEVELOPMENT

The first factor propelling the process of economic development is increased productivity through *saving* and *investing* a larger proportion of national income and product. Investment is the process by which capital is formed—the tools, machines, structures, inventories, and other man-made improvements of the

45

economy. Capital, whether directly productive or for social improvement, is lacking in the underdeveloped world. There is less equipment per worker, often a shortage of housing and transport, low stocks of inventory, and frequently an inappropriate level of technology embodied in the capital. The lack of capital is caused by a low level of saving and investment. Saving is more difficult when incomes are low; borrowing abroad is expensive, and foreign aid is difficult to obtain in sufficient quantity. From whatever the source, it is imperative that enough be saved and invested to increase the capital stock at a satisfactory rate. Only thus can the productivity of the labor force be raised, and productivity improvement is the key to higher incomes per person.

There is now, however, far less confidence than formerly among development economists that this capital formation should be accomplished by active state intervention through planning and by protection of the domestic market. (Deliberate government efforts to form capital in areas with widespread externalities, such as transport, communications, and education, have not suffered from this loss of faith.) Nor is there now much confidence that rural underemployment, often called "disguised unemployment," is the key to industrialization. These beliefs were a prominent feature of development economics 25 years ago. There are also serious concerns about the appropriate level of technology for the LDCs. Capital formation and technology are the subjects of Chapters 4 to 7.

The second condition for development is that performance of the agricultural sector improve. In the typical low-income LDC most people are small farmers, working manually with traditional techniques and with low output per farmer. (At the start of the 1970s an American agricultural laborer produced an average output per day 34 times larger than his or her African and Asian counterpart.[3]) This is surely understandable. Poverty itself means low capital per farmer. A tropical climate, rainfall cycles that are damagingly erratic, or land that is too swampy or too dry may all be enemies requiring far more capital to rectify than is available.

Unless both agricultural productivity and total farm production are increased, development will be difficult. The country that neglects agriculture will neglect the sector where (self-evidently for some of the least developed) it presently has the largest comparative advantage. If incomes do not grow in agriculture, the growth of domestic markets for a country's new output of manufactured goods will be limited.

Concentration on industry to the exclusion of agriculture will also lead to a problem of balance. A growing national income from new industries leads to a growing demand for agricultural commodities. Population growth leads in the same direction. If farm output does not increase to meet the new demand, how then will an industrial labor force be fed? Through imports, perhaps, but LDCs already spend some 25 to 33 percent of the revenue generated from their exports on imported food. Balance of payments problems are likely to arise unless agriculture receives attention, and this will be the more serious when foreign trade promotion is not a central feature in government economic policy. The results can be seen in the statistics, which show that on the average the lower the overall growth of an LDC, the poorer has been its performance in the farm sector.

High-growth LDCs have increased their agricultural output at a rate more than four times the level of the low-growth LDCs. The lesson seems clear enough that a stagnant agricultural sector is an inhibiting factor for development. The subject is treated in Chapter 10.

The third consideration is a country's foreign trade. Exports typically must move ahead rapidly, for only with the "push" of comparative advantage, doing what one does best, can a country reach income growth rates higher than achieved from purely local activities. Without exports, the imports needed for development cannot be acquired. (The only other possible means to pay for imports, an inflow of private foreign capital plus official loans and grants from the developed countries, seem very unlikely to alleviate this problem in the foreseeable future.)

The role of imports in the process is more crucial than often realized. The chance to acquire highly desirable new goods not available locally has worldwide been a fundamental stimulant to productive human effort. Complex capital goods may be very expensive if purchased locally, or may not be available at all. The technology embodied in the capital may be procurable only through imports.

Although the exports of LDCs are certainly rising, over time they have not risen as fast as those of the developed countries. The LDC share of the world's total exports, about one-quarter in 1955, had dropped to one-fifth 10 years later, where it remains. How are the LDCs to achieve acceptable export (and hence import) growth? They often find demand for the traditional plantation crops growing relatively slowly. Minerals may be better, but they are depletable, and in any case many LDCs are poorly endowed with natural resources. Manufactured goods, especially of a labor-intensive type, can be exported to the developed world, but there is significant danger that success in exporting makes an LDC subject to developed-country barriers to trade. Export promotion schemes make sense if they are tailored to present or predicted future comparative advantage. But neither general export promotion (with subsidies) nor general import substitution (with quotas and licensing) is sensible if it neglects the underlying comparative advantage of the country concerned. These issues are explored more fully in Chapters 12 to 15.

The fourth area that has recently come to be regarded as critical to growth is the ability to allocate resources efficiently. If government-administered prices fail to reflect opportunity costs, growth is hindered. The use of market prices more proportional to social marginal costs than controlled government prices is seen to be a "cheap" mechanism for allocation. The mechanism includes low administrative costs, high transmission of incentives, rapid signaling of scarcity and glut, and little in the way of corruption costs, since so much corruption is based on the ability to exploit the difference between an artificial price established by government and a free-market price based on marginal costs.

True, monopoly influence and small markets make the market system less than perfect. But the evidence grows that even an imperfect market is better than the controlled price structure so long used by so many governments. The LDCs have passed through a lengthy era of high tariffs and restrictive quotas on their imports, low (government-set) producer prices for agricultural commodities, widespread price controls on foodstuffs and transport, artificially low interest rates, and measures that raise labor costs. Often the foreign exchange rate has been sharply overvalued by government action, one unit of local currency then buying more dollars or other foreign exchange than would be true in a free market.

Each of these policies has its justifications. Protection against imports was and is popular among export pessimists—those who fear exports are subject to low growth in demand, high fluctuations in price, and lead to economic "dependency." Low producer prices in agriculture are justified on the grounds that supply is not very responsive to price, that larger farmers benefit from high prices more than the smaller, that these same high prices hurt low-income consumers, and that industrialization requires a transfer of income from agriculture to manufacturing. Price controls are rationalized as protection for the poor. Low interest rates are said to encourage investment and keep down the burden of the public debt. Minimum wage laws and pro-union legislation are advocated as a means to bring adequate income to the workers. Overvalued exchange rates are said to ease the burden of importing costly capital goods; with an overvalued rate the foreign exchange to purchase such imports appears cheaper.

There was always a large element of doubt in each one of these propositions, doubts that are carefully examined in the chapters to come. But nowadays there is *less* doubt that the country with large distortions (divergence from market prices) in its price system pays a penalty in reduced growth, whatever the reason the distortions were adopted in the first place. The World Bank has constructed index numbers indicating the extent of distortions in a country's price system. When it compared this measure to the rate of economic growth, it found a strong correlation between high distortion and slow growth in the sample of 31 countries studied.[4] The development economics of the 1980s has turned strongly to these micro issues of improving the efficiency with which resources are used. The subject is treated in Chapters 4 and 11.

The final area critical for development centers on the realization that progress will be difficult unless the quality of "human resources" is improved directly. Depending solely on growth of income to bring about educational improvement or reduce population pressure or alter inhibiting cultural and social institutions runs the risk that the growth in income will be slowed and the distribution of its benefits skewed. The need to concentrate directly on qualitative changes is more strongly felt now than it was 20 or even 10 years ago. There are many considerations concerning this area of human resources. Basic needs approaches may raise productivity directly because a healthier, better nourished, better educated labor force works with more efficiency. Rapid population growth may on the contrary make it more difficult to raise per capita national income and thus make necessary direct action. In some (though not all) LDCs the population is large and growing relative to the available land and natural resources; the overpopulation contributes to low investment, low labor productivity, and unemployment. Population grows faster because birthrates are high and death rates have been rapidly reduced due to advances in public health.

In addition to rapid population growth another negative factor on the human side is that the social and cultural value systems, including attitudes toward thrift, profits, risks, education, and even the view of work, may present obstacles.[5] The influence of the middle class of managers, technicians, and professional people may be slight and their numbers small. Education may be backward, with low levels of literacy. The legal and religious systems, the one often directly related to the other, may have a substantial impact on land tenure, credit and interest rates, taxes, and inheritance.

Property ownership or personal safety itself may be in doubt, as many an LDC faces problems of mismanagement, corruption, an uncontrolled army, a dictatorial government. Gunnar Myrdal has said that one great difficulty in the process of development is to get the profit motive out of government. Corruption makes daily life and business transactions more cumbersome, whether we speak of a major bribe or just a minor rip-off. Corruption frequently motivates public servants to slow down or obstruct in the hope of a fee. The widespread use of credit controls, tariffs, foreign exchange controls, and the like makes the corruption profitable and leads to illicit gains which, modest or vast, are ruinous to the morale of the remaining honest public servants. It delays all forms of economic intercourse, thus boosting costs, and diverts energies to concealment of private gain. Nigeria's most discouraging statistic, perhaps, is that a majority of new university graduates applying for federal civil service positions wanted to join the customs and excise department, where the bribes are fattest.[6]

Clifton Barton's research in South Vietnam showed how the propensity for power and the potential profitability for those government officials who set the prices, allocate the permits, and supply the licenses led to tremendous harassment of medium-scale businesses.[7] The smallest firms largely escaped the harassment; they were insufficiently visible. The largest firms employed specialists for expediting transactions, often with bribes, and had both political connections and clout. In between there was a middle ground of firms too visible to escape the attention of corrupt officials, but with few skills in dealing with them and few good strings to pull. Small firms may thus deliberately choose to remain small. The resulting scarcity of the vulnerable, middle-size firms has been termed a "Barton gap." Generally, corruption and its effects are too little studied by development economists, perhaps because those with the deepest interest and commitment feel the most embarrassed by the situation.[8] Population and human resource development are the central subjects of Chapters 8 and 9.

To say these five requirements of development are "known" does not mean that they are a certainty, but only that there is advance toward a consensus position among specialists that they are broadly necessary even if not always sufficient. Nor does it mean that these "knowns" are easily quantified. Even in discussing the causes of a growing GNP and national income, it is fascinating and challenging to discover how the most careful studies show that much of growth cannot be attributed to changes in physical inputs such as capital, labor, and natural resources. The attitudes, motivation, and social framework of a people loom much larger in development economics today than they did two decades ago. They are hard to measure, hard to change, not even easy for economists to discuss. But the attention devoted to them later in the book is an indication of their rising importance for the subject.

SECTORAL CHANGE IN DEVELOPMENT

Another "known" about development, this time less debatable, is that there is a typical pattern of changes that affects the various sectors of an economy in a predictable way. These sectoral changes were first analyzed in detail by the British economist Colin Clark and are thought to apply widely among diverse LDCs. The changes are certainly not linear and uniform, but to a greater or lesser degree, they do occur in all countries. Every economy can be divided into three sectors: a *primary* sector producing the so-called primary products—agricultural commodities, minerals, and the like; a *secondary* sector producing manufactures; and a *tertiary* sector producing services. There is impressive evidence that with economic development a movement occurs in the relative importance of these sectors.

Take a typical very poor LDC. Agriculture will make up the largest share of GNP, nearly 60 percent sometimes, about 40 percent on average. Services (the tertiary sector) will also be large, perhaps 40 percent on average, with many people engaged in petty trade, marketing, carrying goods from place to place, hauling water, and the like. When some development occurs, one expects growth in the secondary (manufacturing) sector and a drop in the primary and perhaps the tertiary sectors. Thus between 1960 and 1984 the share of agriculture in the national product of low-income LDCs sank from about 50 to 36 percent, while the share of manufacturing rose from 11 to 15 percent.

With further growth, as a country rises in the ranks of the LDCs, there is usually a considerable fall in the size of the agricultural sector (the average output share for middle-income LDCs was 24 percent in 1960 and 14 percent in 1984). Manufacturing rises (22 percent in 1984) to about the same share of production as in the developed countries. Numerous LDCs, among them Argentina, Brazil, Korea, Mexico, Peru, Philippines, Singapore, Taiwan, and Turkey now exceed the U.S. share.[9] Services remain largely unchanged.

As a country enters the ranks of the developed, one expects a further decline in primary production (agriculture's share of national product averages only 3 percent in the developed countries, 2 percent in the United States) and a rise in the tertiary sector (54 percent of national product in 1960, 62 percent in 1984, for the developed countries).

When expressed as a percentage of the *labor force,* these sectoral changes appear even more dramatic, although the incomplete specialization of many individuals means the statistics are far less trustworthy and must be treated with care.[10] In low-income LDCs the average percentage of the labor force in agriculture in 1981 (the latest year for which statistics are published in the *WDR*) was 72 percent (down from 82 percent in 1960) with some countries still over 90 percent; 11 percent was in industry, 16 percent in services. By comparison, only 2 percent of the U.S. labor force was in agriculture, while 32 percent was in industry and 66 percent in services. One main reason for the movement to services is consumer demand, which shifts toward travel, entertainment, restaurant meals, health care, banking, stockbrokering, insurance, and so forth, as income rises. The labor finding employment in the growing service sector becomes available when rising productivity, especially in agriculture, means less labor is required in that sector. The fastest growth rates, incidentally, are usually found in the countries that are increasing the size of the secondary (manufacturing) sector, for it is here that productivity can grow most swiftly, hence leading to the fastest increase in output.

The sectoral changes that accompany development are not uniform. Different countries move at different rates. But the changes occur in virtually all settings. It is thus rather a pity that they are much more certainly an effect of economic advance rather than its cause. If the sectoral movements were mainly causal, then government planners could conceivably "jump the gun," deliberately attempting to speed up the process. Unfortunately, as we shall see in Chapters 4 and 11, premature alteration of a country's economic structure in the absence of a solid foundation of successful growth is likely to be a high-cost method for accomplishing little.

IS GROWTH MORE DIFFICULT NOW THAN IT WAS?

Though there are many differences, today's developed countries had to overcome some of the same problems as today's LDCs. They were poor, they were agricultural, their growth was slow, many were historically feudalistic. But significant changes have taken place in the nature of the hurdles; they are not the same now as they were in the eighteenth and nineteenth centuries. In certain respects today's rich countries appear to have had some advantages at the start of their growth process not available to today's LDCs. In other ways the prospects for growth are more favorable now. What are these main points of difference?

We focus first on the disadvantages from the perspective of today's LDCs.[11]

1. The output levels measured by GNP of most LDCs are lower at the present time than the output levels that modern industrial countries possessed even *before* their industrial revolutions. The average per capita income of the poorest LDCs in 1976 (approximately $170) was in real terms probably about half that of the United States in 1776 or of Britain at the start of its industrialization in the eighteenth century.[12]

2. In a number of LDCs, especially parts of Asia, Central America, and Egypt, there is less land per capita and often less valuable natural resources than there were in the developed countries a hundred or two hundred years ago. There is usually no open frontier and thus no frontier spirit (Brazil is a notable exception). Population growth is often more rapid, due especially to the sharp decline in death rates. Numerous LDCs are registering population increases of about 3 percent. Europe and North America *never* had a natural rate of population change (excluding immigration) greater than 2 percent; and vast, underpopulated North America with immigration included did not exceed 3 percent even in the years of maximum influx from abroad.[13] Emigration is no longer much of a safety valve for population growth. Only those with training or skills find it legally

possible to enter a developed country, and few enough of these; only a few LDCs welcome unskilled workers.

3. Even though rural development has been a bright chapter in the recent experience of the LDCs, many poor countries face some greater barriers to raising agricultural productivity than the rich countries did a century or two ago. Numerous social factors, including land ownership, tenure patterns, and perhaps the extended family system, can retard rural progress. The climate and the soil can be enemies. The combination of low government procurement prices and (sometimes) narrow and undeveloped markets on which surplus produce can be sold constrains growth and inhibits change. Levels of capital, education, nutrition, and health may be low. Finally, general underdevelopment may mean less general effectiveness in mobilizing agricultural resources.

4. Nineteenth-century entrepreneurs were for the most part free to save and invest within a system of market prices, low taxation, and little direct production by government or government-controlled firms. In many of today's LDCs private entrepreneurs face a more hostile climate. In India, for example, three-quarters of all industrial assets are owned by nationalized firms. The management of such state firms there and elsewhere is usually marked by conservative practices; in most cases the public enterprises are simply not allowed to fail. Private competition may not be permitted or may operate under severe restraint. Prices, including exchange rates, may be much influenced by government action and in a way that reduces their value as indicators of scarcity, to a far greater degree than in the nineteenth century. Taxes, including foreign trade restraints and the costs of other government intrusions in the economy, can be high, and the greatest financial rewards may go to the corrupt or those who can wield influence in the public sector. Entrepreneurs find little opportunity to borrow in world capital markets; the sale of bonds and shares by firms in poor countries to tap the capital of rich countries is proportionately far less important now than it was before World War I. (The recent debt crisis, discussed in Chapter 6, involved overwhelmingly loans from banks to *governments,* not private entrepreneurs.) There are certainly some countries where the supply of private entrepreneurship is low, and some sectors where free markets are limited. Government programs under such conditions may be welcomed even when they fail. But where government impedes entrepreneurs and itself restricts the market, the climate is significantly different than it was in the nineteenth century.

5. It is probably fair to say that the stability of government institutions and legal systems was greater a hundred years ago in what became today's developed countries than it is today in many LDCs. In the former enforceable contracts involving land, labor, and business affairs have permeated economic relationships and have been standard for a long time. In today's LDCs, this is too often not the case. The benefits of stability and consistency are difficult to measure, but are surely large.

6. Finally, very rich and very poor countries must now coexist, where two hundred or one hundred years ago the gap between the richest and the poorest countries was not nearly so great as it is today. On a broad reckoning, in 1850

per capita income in the developed countries of the day was no more than 70% above that of the less developed. Today the gap is more like 1000%. For one carefully-studied example, Dahomey (now called the Republic of Bénin) in West Africa, had a national income estimated to be about ⅓ Great Britain's during the period of the Atlantic slave trade. This figure has sunk to only ⅟₃₀ now.[14] Modern communications make the great disparity very obvious; the poor feel their plight all the more. The resulting sense of confrontation has embittered relations between the LDCs and developed countries. (Other arguments based on the existence of rich and poor together are far more controversial. These "dependency" arguments hold the developed countries responsible to some degree for the poverty of the LDCs, either through the adverse effects of international trade or the exploitative investment strategies of multinational firms and lending institutions. Unlike the six disadvantages discussed above, these charges are much more debatable. They are treated in Chapters 5 to 7 and 12 to 15.)

There are, fortunately, substantial offsetting advantages for a country undertaking its growth now. For many though not for all, these advantages probably outweigh the difficulties, as demonstrated by the unexpectedly strong growth of numerous LDCs over the past 25 years. (Recalling the "new pessimism," however, there are no guarantees for the future.)

1. Late developers have access to new technology in quantity far greater and in quality immensely superior to that of past centuries. In spite of debates on the appropriateness of much of this to conditions in the LDCs, the consequences are highly positive.

2. There are specialized international institutions for financing development; foreign aid to stimulate economic growth was unheard of a hundred years ago. The dollar amounts are indeed limited, but can be of strategic importance.

3. Orthodox colonialism is largely a thing of the past. Many LDCs are for the most part free to consider their own economic interests, and usually even to put them uppermost, in their policy making and diplomacy.

4. World trade is certainly more open than it was in the eighteenth century. Even the nineteenth century, especially after the 1870s, was an age of high protection except in Britain. An LDC without a large home market can today take advantage of specialization through trade, and this appears a strong and largely uniform element in the recent growth of the most successful LDCs. Continuation of this favorable prospect for foreign trade is by no means assured. As exporting by LDCs increases, interest groups in the developed world arise with a strong desire to protect their high wages and profits. Through their lobbying free trade is attacked with tariffs, quotas, "voluntary" restraints, and the like. Thus far, though, the damage has been relatively limited, and opportunities for trade remain a major path to growth.

Whatever the obstacles today and in spite of the sometimes angry rhetoric emanating both from the LDCs and from the developed countries, on balance the barriers to economic advance are probably no greater than they were in the past and for some they have surely been lower. This is reassuring, though the absence of a guarantee that conditions will remain so adds a disquieting element of risk.

THE STAGES OF GROWTH

In any science progress is measured not only by the success of new models, but also by mounting evidence that some models lack credibility and should be modified or withdrawn. Nowhere is this more the case than in development economics, which has seen its share of discredited theory in the recent past. A few years ago it was widely believed that several important *stages* of growth could be identified and that a familiarity with these stages could make development planning more effective. By far the most popular of the stage theories, and the one that became perhaps the most familiar of all development models, was Walt W. Rostow's stages of economic growth. In his well-known 1960 book of that title, Rostow argued that any country proceeds through five stages of growth: (1) traditional society, (2) preconditions for take-off, (3) take-off, (4) drive to maturity, and (5) era of high consumption.[15]

Almost all attention to this model has focused on the preconditions and the take-off, which ingenious aeronautical analogy (says Gunnar Myrdal) is heard in every LDC. Rostow sees development as being caused by "leading sectors" in an economy, examples of which might be textiles in Great Britain late in the eighteenth century, railways in the United States during the nineteenth century, electronic goods and ships in Japan in the twentieth century. The take-off comes, according to Rostow, when the leading modern sectors break down the traditional resistance to growth, occupy a commanding position within the economy, stimulating changes in the political, social, and institutional framework, and thus replace stagnation with "self-sustaining growth." The major feature of the take-off is raising the level of net investment as a percentage of national income from 5 percent to 10 percent or more. Rostow points to the take-off as occurring in Great Britain between 1783 and 1802, in France between 1830 and 1860, in the United States between 1843 and 1860, in Japan between 1878 and 1900, and in Canada between 1896 and 1914.

Rostow's stage theory has generated enormous controversy, especially concerning the take-off. Much criticism has centered on the importance of the take-off. Rostow says that *sustained* economic growth requires a repetition of the changes occurring during the take-off process. But if this is so, then perhaps the take-off has a spurious significance. Growth may well falter after a take-off; there may be an emergency crash landing. Argentina is often cited as a country that apparently met the criteria for take-off around the turn of this century but then did not fly.

There are also problems of dating. Britain took a long time after take-off to reach the era of high consumption, as did Germany and even Japan. Canada took only a short time. The "stages" may not explain much of this.

It has also been argued, especially by Simon Kuznets, that far too much emphasis is placed on investment during the take-off. In Britain substantial investment was needed to improve agriculture and to build the "infrastructure" of transport and communication systems, but for both purposes the investment preceded the take-off, in what Rostow would call the precondition period. Kuznets thus argues that the model is too fuzzy.

Scholars during the past decade have focused on evidence of the gradualness and long continuity of growth rather than its sharp steps. Close investigations of British growth reveal the importance of the pump and steam power in the early eighteenth century, leading to a metallurgical revolution involving coal and metals, in turn accompanying (and promoting) an agricultural revolution, and all preceding the more famous Industrial Revolution later in the eighteenth century. Critics have also demonstrated the gradualness of growth in other industrialized countries. Special comment has been directed at the take-off requirement for investment to rise from 5 percent of national income to 10 percent or more. Recent studies indicate that any sudden shift of this sort is difficult to identify in most of the developed countries. The rise in investment was also a gradual one.

To sum up the criticism, economic growth usually does not "take off." The phrase catches attention, but it raises false hopes that there exists a master key always able to open the development door. Alas, there is no such key.

THE EXPERIENCE OF THE LATE STARTERS

If stage theories are out of fashion, there is still much to be learned from the experience of the "late starters"—the now developed countries that entered their period of growth *after* the Industrial Revolution in Britain.[16]

The experience of three countries stands out. The countries are Germany, the Soviet Union, and Japan. In all three there was a national push for development, with a pronounced emphasis on education, heavy capital investment, imported technology (often improved upon), and intensive effort by labor and management. But the individual details and emphases were different, and their respective development drives, especially in the case of the Soviet Union, did not always emphasize all five of the major factors discussed at the start of this chapter.

Germany   The key to German development, which achieved startling success in the last half of the nineteenth century, was the combination of science and education with new investment. Universal primary education was achieved early; science was emphasized in the curriculum; technical schools sprouted. The government subsidized research in the universities, leading most importantly to great advances in the chemical and electrical industries. Germany started as a borrower of technology, the borrowing encouraged by government policy, improved upon it, and put it in the hands of an educated work force. Simultaneously, the government encouraged scientific education and liaison between university professors and industry. In short, Germany was the country that did the most with "human capital" during its development.

The Soviet Union   Soviet economic development was marked by a number of important features. It successfully borrowed technology, with careful investigation of technical change abroad, and combined this with large-scale training of scientists and engineers (including many women). High levels of saving and investment were achieved quite early, with saving often 25 to 33 percent of GNP as compared to the 16 to 20 percent of the United States. The investment was

concentrated in capital-goods industries rather than on consumer goods, sometimes called the Fel'dman model after G. A. Fel'dman who developed it for the
Soviet Planning Commission in 1928.[17] There was high availability of labor from
the agricultural sector and high investment in education (often double that of the
United States as a percent of GNP). Finally, large-scale operations were achieved
with accompanying economies of scale (but collectivization of farming very probably retarded long-term growth in the agricultural sector). Foreign trade was *not*
emphasized, though of course trade is less necessary for countries that are extremely large and are well endowed with natural resources.

Japan   Among today's developed countries Japan was a hundred years ago the
most underdeveloped and most akin to a modern LDC. It was backward and
isolated, with a large population compared to its meager land area and a small
stock of natural resources. Japan began by lifting many of the restrictions on free
movement of people and goods that had marked the rule of the feudal shoguns.
There was an awareness that agriculture was the foundation of economic
strength. Land was turned over to the peasants, and even though the land tax,
used to finance substantial government participation in investment, was high, it
was paid at fixed rates on assessed valuation rather than (as had been the case)
on the size of the harvest. Thus farmers could keep the profits from any incre-
ments to production. Japan encouraged agriculture and labor-intensive manufactures for export, in the beginning particularly silk and low-cost dishware and
trinkets, thus thoroughly grounding its foreign trade on a comparative advantage
determined by factor proportions. As late as 1890, 68 percent of investment was
still in agriculture and labor-intensive light industry. The figure remained as high
as 32 percent in 1917. The major shift to capital-intensive heavy industry did not
take place until after World War II.[18]

Japan studied and imported foreign technology, welcomed but carefully
policed foreign private investment, and searched for lines of production that
might become more capital-intensive over time. The Japanese government was
development-minded. It successfully encouraged saving and investment, engaged
in public entrepreneurship but also encouraged private entrepreneurs, and funneled the relatively high tax collections into development expenditures. Japan's
government, institutions, and social framework all combined to generate high
levels of saving and investment. Saving, for example, came to be promoted by the
light taxation of interest income, by the poorly developed market for consumer
credit, and by the not-very-generous social security system, all reinforcing the
tradition of very high saving by entrepreneurs.

At first wages were quite low, unions were suppressed, and labor conditions
were poor. Few would recommend emulation. But the 1911 Factory Act, regulat-
ing hours and working conditions, surprised antagonistic employers by leading
to higher productivity. Eventually, income became quite equally distributed,
according to the latest figures somewhat more so than in the United States. The
Japanese were fortunate that so much went right in the process. Even the loss of
a disastrous war—in 1952, seven years after the war's end, per capita income was
still below that of Chile, Brazil, and Malaysia—proved only a temporary setback,

with Japan's figures now four times higher than Chile's, the richest of those three countries. Though per capita income is still somewhat below that of the United States, Japan's PQLI rose to equality in the early 1970s and is now 99 compared to 97 in the U.S.

These successes teach several lessons. We have already noted that all the countries were heavy savers and investors, technology importers, and education-minded. But the Soviet experience shows that development can occur even when policies are followed that most (Western) development economists would not recommend. Agriculture was not encouraged, the price system was little used as an allocation mechanism, "distortions" from market-clearing levels were high, and foreign trade was a minor factor. True, many economists would claim that these are the outstanding reasons for the USSR's stagnant performance in the 1970s and 1980s. But in spite of that, the country did develop, showing conclusively that there is more than one path to that goal.

THE EXPERIENCE OF THREE SUCCESSFUL LDCS

Twenty years ago Germany, the Soviet Union, and especially Japan were the main examples of development by late starters. Today the list can be expanded, and with the new names new insights have been gained into a range of potentially successful development strategies. There are a number of high-performance economies that could have been chosen for examination. Of the three selected, the first two are newly industrializing countries (NICs) illustrating a strategy of industrialization through trade and the third exemplifies a strategy of promoting primary product exports.[19]

South Korea and Taiwan These outstanding cases of poor countries transforming themselves are similar in many ways. The most obvious similarity, that they are Asian, has led some to conclude that there may be a "racial" component to development. Whether or not there is anything to such arguments, it is undeniable that as recently as just 35 years ago both countries were extremely poor, and being "Asian" did not seem to have helped.[20] Both had some advantages from Japanese colonization in the first part of this century; there was a manufacturing sector in Korea even before World War I (although it was mostly in the north, which became a separate country after World War II). There was also some industry in Taiwan from the 1930s. Though the nascent industries were ruined by World War II, much industrial experience and acquired skill survived.[21]

South Korea was not only poor, but was wrecked once again by the Korean War. About the time that war ended (1953), the country had fewer resources and a higher population density than the overcrowded Netherlands. Manufactured goods made up less than 10 percent of all output. Exports were still only a minuscule 3.5 percent of national product at the start of the 1960s, and per capita income in 1961 was only $80.

Aid from the United States was intelligently used, especially to assist with the establishment of an infrastructure of roads, railways, ports, communications, electricity generation, and a power grid. Korea emphasized education on its own;

a literacy rate of 30 percent in the mid 1950s had reached 93 percent by 1980. Repressive labor laws did not prevent wages from rapidly reflecting the increased demand for labor. Land reform and rural manufacturing enterprise contributed to keeping income distribution more equal than in most LDCs.

Export-led development was a key. The foreign exchange rate was kept from becoming overvalued (Chapter 13 discusses the adverse effects of overvaluation and its frequent occurrence in the LDCs). The price system was freed, so that prices reflected real costs and guided entrepreneurs toward labor-intensive manufacturing activities that had a comparative advantage. According to one recent study, "the allocation of factors has not been very different, at least since 1965, than it would have been under a free-trade regime."[22] To overcome infant industry problems, government promoted exports with subsidies and tax reductions, and actively though selectively intervened in investment decisions. It also utilized protective quotas against imports to develop the home market, especially in the 1950s and 1960s, and even in 1970 quota restrictions still applied to about 40 percent of basic imports. From about 1960, however, export promotion was increasingly emphasized, and by 1985 protection by quotas had largely been superseded by sweeping import liberalization. Tariffs are still high (averaging about 20 percent in 1986) but are coming down. Foreign investment, initially very difficult, was eventually made much easier.[23]

The result was real per capita growth of 6.6 percent per year in the period 1965 to 1984, reaching over 10 percent in some years. Saving was about 30 percent of national product in 1984, investment was 29 percent, and 1984 per capita GNP was $2,110. Exports, mostly manufactured goods, at $29 billion were over a third of GNP, making Korea the world's fourteenth largest trading nation. About a quarter of these exports are now heavy manufactured goods, including steel, ships, and cars; the economy resembles Japan's in the mid 1960s.

Korea's current dependence on the U.S. market, which took about 37 percent of its exports in 1985, is dangerous because of rising U.S. protectionism. There is also overconcentration in shipbuilding, textiles, and shoes, the government's support of industry has recently had some mixed results and there have been policy mistakes in agriculture. But Korea's growth still has been a remarkable feat, shocking no doubt to development pessimists.

Taiwan has been even more successful. In the 1950s this island refuge for the Chinese Nationalists was even more densely populated than South Korea; its density ranks second in the world (excepting the city-states Hong Kong and Singapore) just behind Bangladesh. Taiwan encouraged saving with high real interest rates. Plowing its relatively high taxes into development spending, the government sponsored export promotion in labor-intensive manufacturing and later in heavy industry. Most of the largest heavy industrial projects were undertaken by government because of the shortage of established firms capable of managing endeavors of such size. By and large Taiwan made fewer mistakes even than South Korea. Imports were largely freed from quotas in the 1960s, and the average rate of tariff is now about 9 percent although the duties on a fair number of imported goods remain high.[24] Local content and export requirements for foreign firms were originally common, but are now much relaxed. The exchange rate was not overvalued. Per capita income was about $3,000 by 1984. Manufactured goods exports rose at just under 30 percent a year from 1965 to 1981 and 21 percent even in the "slow" year 1984. The ratio of total exports to GNP, at about 55 percent, is the highest figure in the world among LDCs of any size. Of these, about 40 percent are now heavy industrial goods. Though it did not pass its first labor law until 1984, Taiwan has probably the most equal income distribution of any capitalist country. Like Korea, however, it is overly dependent on the U.S. market, which in 1985 took 48 percent of its exports.

Both Korea and Taiwan suffered from the oil and debt crises (Korea more so), with heavy industry overexpanded and inflation setting in. Both recovered rapidly.[25]

These two countries and the two city-states Hong Kong ($6,330 per capita income in 1984) and Singapore ($7,260) are the outstanding examples of newly industralizing countries.[26] Popular nicknames for them are the Gang of Four and the Four Tigers.

There are other NICs—Brazil, Mexico, the Philippines, Thailand, and Israel among them. Vigorous debate now centers on whether these NICs and other, yet poorer, aspiring ones can emulate the spectacular East Asian successes with export-led growth.[27] A great hope of poorer LDCs is that as the NICs grow richer, labor-intensive manufacturing in them will become increasingly more costly. Thus it is expected that comparative advantage in goods so produced will shift to the poorer economies, with the NICs providing new markets for the very goods they once produced before moving on to more capital-intensive items.

The debate concerns the degree to which exports of manufactures by NICs would impinge on developed-country markets and the extent to which protection would be stimulated by the impact. As a value judgment, it is probably correct to think (and the protagonists in the debate seem generally to share the opinion) that the 30 percent annual real growth in exports achieved over long time periods by South Korea and Taiwan will be difficult to generalize. If this figure were achieved by many countries in the long run, under modern political conditions it probably would stimulate industrial-country protectionism. But William Cline, a major skeptic on the possibility of generalizing a 30 percent growth rate in exports, nonetheless believes a "brisk" 10 to 15 percent growth rate should be possible for the LDCs over a long time period. The crucial point will presumably be the extent to which the political influence of industrial-country exporters will grow as their exports to LDCs grow, offsetting the protectionist lobbying of the affected industries. Another possibility that would reduce the pressure would be rapid expansion in trade among the LDCs themselves. We return to this important subject in Chapter 14.

Ivory Coast   This West African country has utilized an altogether different path, concentrating on primary product exports. To some observers, export-led development means concentration on manufactured goods, but if comparative advantage is likely to be in agriculture, minerals, or fuels for some time to come, then staying with these commodities would arguably be appropriate. There is a school of thought (see Chapter 12) that primary products are *not* appropriate for long-run export-led development because of unfavorable demand conditions, declining supply of natural resources, and low impact on the rest of the economy. The experience of the Ivory Coast contradicts significantly this view of export pessimism.

When independence was achieved in 1960, the Ivory Coast was very poor, with income per capita of only about $70. In 25 years (1950 to 1975), it raised its exports of cocoa by four times to become the world's third largest exporter; by 1985 it was number one. Meanwhile, its export of coffee went up five times, to third place in the world. There were numerous years during that time when earnings from exports were growing 10 percent annually. GNP growth has been slower, about 6 percent annually from 1970 to 1982, and in per capita terms much less than that, about 2 percent per year, 1960 to 1982, well below the performance of the Asian Gang of Four. But the Ivory Coast's natural population increase is high, at over 3 percent per year. For a country that has extremely high population growth, is an exporter of agricultural commodities, and is located in sub-Saharan Africa, where economic performance has generally been poor, GNP growth has been very good indeed.

The essential ingredients were a policy of remunerative prices for farmers, along with reasonable taxation of the export commodities to finance heavy investment in infrastructure, diversification of crops, improvements in agricultural credit, and establishment of an excellent agricultural extension service. The foreign exchange rate did not discourage exports. The positive response by farmers, as indicated by the growth in their production, surprised even the experts on the Ivory Coast economy.

The early 1980s were not kind to the Ivory Coast. The debt crisis hit hard and necessitated dramatic economic readjustments. The failure in the rains that affected so much of Africa in these years ruined the coffee crop and dried up the rivers that powered the new hydroelectric facilities, thus dislocating the electricity supply and industrial production. Even so, the Ivory Coast was still much more successful than its neighbors, and immigrants poured across the relatively open borders. The influx has probably added almost another 2 percent to annual population growth, resulting in the world's fastest increase in that figure excluding only the Middle Eastern oil states. All of this has caused per capita growth to slip. But it resumed its advance in 1985 and 1986, evidence that the Ivory Coast economy is not only successful but resilient.[28]

Does a common thread link the experience of the successful LDCs discussed above? To some degree, yes. Government intervention in the economy was carried out judiciously and effectively. None neglected agriculture. The foreign trade strategy of all actively promoted exports, usually paying close attention to existing or potential comparative advantage, and rarely promoting anything obviously *dis*advantageous. Government policies involved fairly uniform incentives and did not discriminate to any great degree against any existing sector. General import substitution was not encouraged. (Singapore, incidentally, has an even more liberal policy of letting the market separate winners and losers, while Hong

Kong is the only NIC to pursue a strategy of virtually complete free trade.) All the countries successfully managed to keep their price structures, including the foreign exchange rate, free from serious distortions. These are, presumably, useful lessons.

THE ROAD AHEAD

At this point in the text we turn to specific topics concerning growth and development. The broad framework has been sketched in this chapter: Growth is not the result of any *one* factor, but instead of a whole constellation of economic and social determinants. These include the availability of capital; labor (including human resource considerations such as education, health, and nutrition and the influence of income distribution); land and natural resource endowment; entrepreneurship and management ability; technical improvement in all its forms; and the psychological, cultural, and social differences (including government and attitudes toward foreign trade) that inhibit or promote growth.

This rather long accounting is worlds apart from models that seek to identify some paramount cause of growth, and even at the introductory level it requires a book-length study to consider the individual components. It clearly gives no easy description or prediction of growth, and since some of its components are inherently difficult to measure with precision, constructing a mathematical model of the growth process defined in this way is not very practical. But the experience of the last two decades shows that this is exactly the problem—the causes of growth are indeed complex, more so than was believed by the earlier generation of development economists who searched for single explanations with a notable lack of success.

And so to work.

NOTES

1. The mid 1980s have been years of stock-taking and critical assessment of what gains have been made in knowing how to develop. Several excellent articles and books in this vein can be recommended, including W. A. Lewis, "The State of Development Theory," *The American Economic Review* 74, no. 1 (1984):1–10; A. K. Sen, "Development: Which Way Now"; Gerald M. Meier, *Emerging from Poverty: The Economics That Really Matters,* New York, 1984; Ian M. D. Little, *Economic Development: Theory, Policy, and International Relations,* New York, 1982; and Henry J. Bruton, "The Search for a Development Economics," *World Development* 13, nos. 10/11 (1985). The rising dissatisfaction with development studies in the 1970s was nicely captured in David Lehmann, ed., *Development Theory: Four Critical Studies,* London, 1979.
2. In selecting the factors, I followed in part Meier's analysis in *Leading Issues in Economic Development,* 4th ed., Oxford, 1984, pp. 85–87.
3. Calculated from information in Subrata Ghatak, *Development Economics,* London, 1978, p. 7.

4. *WDR 1983,* pp. 57–63. See this volume's Chapter 11 for details.

5. Theodore Morgan, *Economic Development: Concept and Strategy,* New York, 1975, p. 30, and Everett E. Hagen, *The Economics of Development,* rev. ed., Homewood, Ill., 1975, p. 81.

6. Myrdal's views are in "Need for Reforms in Underdeveloped Countries," in Sven Grassman and Erik Lundberg, *The World Economic Order: Past and Prospects,* New York, 1981, especially pp. 518–525. For the information on Nigeria, see *The Economist,* May 7, 1983, p. 59.

7. Clifton Barton, *Problems and Prospects of Small Industries in the Republic of Vietnam,* Saigon, 1974. This work was brought to my attention by William Loehr and John P. Powelson, *The Economics of Development and Distribution,* New York, 1981, pp. 27–28.

8. Myrdal, "Need for Reforms," p. 523.

9. *WDR 1986,* Table 3, pp. 184–185.

10. See P. T. Bauer, *Reality and Rhetoric,* Cambridge, Mass., 1984, pp. 10–11. The figures here are from *WDR 1985,* Table 21, pp. 214–215, and not from *WDR 1986* which gives data for 1980.

11. This section utilizes in part the insights of Meier, *Leading Issues,* 4th ed., pp. 89–110, and the contributions of Simon Kuznets and Alexander Gerschenkron reprinted there. A recent insightful discussion of why the presently developed countries had historical advantages over the LDCs that promoted their growth is Nathan Rosenberg and L. E. Birdzell, Jr., *How the West Grew Rich,* New York, 1985.

12. John W. Sewell et al., *The United States and World Development Agenda 1980,* New York, 1980, p. 99.

13. Compare Michael P. Todaro, *Economic Development in the Third World,* 2nd ed., New York, 1981, p. 101.

14. The broad estimate is cited by Hans W. Singer and Javed A. Ansari, *Rich and Poor Countries,* Baltimore, 1977; and see William W. Murdoch, *The Poverty of Nations,* Baltimore, 1980, p. 246. For the Dahomean data, see Patrick Manning, *Slavery, Colonialism and Economic Growth in Dahomey, 1640–1960,* Cambridge, 1982, pp. 224–225.

15. W. W. Rostow, *The Stages of Economic Growth: A Non-Communist Manifesto,* Cambridge, 1960. For the critique of Rostow's stage theory, I have relied especially on the discussion in Benjamin Higgins, *Economic Development,* New York, 1968, pp. 174–187, and the various editions of Meier, *Leading Issues.* Also see E. Wayne Nafziger, *The Economics of Developing Countries,* Belmont, Calif., 1984, pp. 152–155; Hagen, *Economics of Development,* revised ed., pp. 99–100; and Morgan, *Economic Development,* pp. 105–107.

16. I utilized especially the work of Benjamin Higgins and Jean Downing Higgins, *Economic Development of a Small Planet,* New York, 1979, pp. 74–82, for the discussion of the USSR and Japan, and also some material on Japan from Loehr and Powelson, *Economics of Development and Distribution,* pp. 382–384. My general background on these three countries has been informed over the years by Gustav Stolper, Karl Häuser, and Knut Borchardt, *The German Economy, 1870 to the Present,* New York, 1967; Alec Nove, *An Economic History of the U.S.S.R.,* London, 1969; Maurice Dobb, *Soviet Economic Development Since 1917,* New York, 1948; Yoshihara Kunio, *Japanese Economic Development,* New York, 1979; Kazushi Ohkawa and Miyohei Shinohara, eds., *Patterns of Japanese Economic Development,* New Haven, 1979; Lawrence Klein and Kazushi Ohkawa, eds., *Economic Growth: The Japanese Experience Since the Meiji Era,* Homewood, Ill., 1968; William W. Lockwood, *The Economic Development of*

Japan: Growth and Structural Change, Princeton, N.J., 1968; and Angus Madisson, *Economic Growth in Japan and the U.S.S.R.,* New York, 1969.

17. From Nafziger, *Economics of Developing Countries,* pp. 294–295.

18. Loraine Donaldson, *Economic Development,* St. Paul, Minn., 1984, p. 110.

19. This section stems from Meier, *Emerging from Poverty,* pp. 57–65. For details on Korea, I used Edward S. Mason et al., *The Economic and Social Modernization of the Republic of Korea,* Cambridge, Mass., 1980; Yung Whee Rhee, Bruce Ross-Larson, and Gary Pursell, *Korea's Competitive Edge: Managing the Entry into World Markets,* Baltimore, 1984; and *The Economist,* October 5, 1985, p. 69. Harry T. Oshima, "The Transition from an Agricultural to an Industrial Economy in East Asia," *Economic Development and Cultural Change* 34, no. 6 (1986):783–809, gives details of Korea's policy mistakes in agriculture. For Taiwan, see Shirley W. Y. Kuo, *The Taiwan Economy in Transition,* Boulder, Colo., 1983. Also see the *Wall Street Journal,* January 8 and 27, 1986.

20. Compare Helen Hughes, *Policy Lessons of the Development Experience,* Group of 30 Occasional Paper No. 16, 1985, p. 14.

21. It should be noted that many among an already existing class of Korean managers and entrepreneurs fled to the south after World War II. Taiwan also received an influx of entrepreneurs and technically talented people during the exodus from the mainland in 1949. See David Evans and Parvin Alizadeh, "Trade, Industrialisation, and the Visible Hand," *Journal of Development Studies* 21, no. 1 (1984):33.

22. Mason et al., *Republic of Korea,* p. 6.

23. See U.S. International Trade Commission (ITC), *Operation of the Trade Agreements Program, 36th Report,* Washington, D.C., 1985, pp. 171–179, and *37th Report,* 1986, pp. 199–209.

24. *The Economist,* June 22, 1985, p. 69. Also see U.S. ITC, *Operation of the Trade Agreements Program, 36th Report,* pp. 164–171.

25. See Bijan B. Aghevli and Jorge Marquez-Ruarte, *A Case of Successful Adjustment: Korea's Experience During 1980–84,* IMF Occasional Paper No. 39, 1985; *The Economist,* June 22, August 24, October 5, and October 19, 1985; and U.S. ITC, *Operation of the Trade Agreements Program, 37th Report,* pp. 189, 199. There was a downturn in both countries' real growth in 1985, caused by the decline of world trade in that year. But compared to the developed countries (and many LDCs) growth remains high.

26. Average annual real per capita growth in GNP was 7.8 percent for Singapore, 1965 to 1984 and 6.2 percent for Hong Kong during the same period. These are world-class results. Singapore has recently encountered serious difficulties, however. Its government policy of promoting higher wages was designed to drive out low-wage, labor-intensive manufacturing in favor of higher-tech industries. The policy succeeded in giving that little city-state the highest wages of any Asian developing country. But the policy appears to have been premature. Growth fell sharply, to a negative figure in 1985, and unemployment mounted. In 1986 the government changed course, announcing a new policy of longer hours and little or no increase in wages during the next few years. See *Christian Science Monitor,* March 24, 1986.

27. The debate is nicely captured in William R. Cline, "Can the East Asian Model of Development be Generalized?" *World Development* 10, no. 2 (1982): 81–90; Gustav Ranis, "Can the East Asian Model be Generalized? A Comment," *World Development* 13, no. 4 (1985):543–545; and William R. Cline, "Reply," *World Development* 13, no. 4 (1985): 547–548. See also Evans and Alizadeh, "Trade, Industrialisation, and the Visible Hand," pp. 33–36. There is a comparison of various authors' lists of which

countries deserve the label NIC in Helen O'Neill, "HICs, NICs, and LICs: Some
Elements in the Political Economy of Gradation and Differentiation," *World Development* 12, no. 7 (1984): 711–712.

28. This paragraph was the outcome of discussions with officials of the World Bank's West
African Programs Section. Note should be taken that Ivory Coast per capita GNP
expressed in U.S. dollars tumbled during 1981 to 1985 because of the steep rise of the
dollar during that period. In 1981, $1 = 271.7 CFA francs (the currency used in the
Ivory Coast), while in 1984 $1 = 436.9 francs, so that a given GNP in francs declined
steadily in dollar terms. This is a good example of the exchange rate problem studied
in Chapter 2.

chapter *4*

Domestic Saving and Investment

This chapter begins our consideration of the first key element in the development process: capital formation through saving and investment. The early generation of development economists thought capital was the single critical factor in the development process, and the legacy of this belief has lasted to this day. Though the evidence has not confirmed their view that capital is the only key, it is certainly important. Additions to capital have the capacity to raise the productivity of labor and hence the demand for labor. In the long run the higher demand can raise the real wage and cause yet more investment in a "virtuous circle." A balanced perspective is much needed after a long period of overly great attention to capital in development, followed by what now appears an overly great reaction against it.

In the early days of the specialty, just after World War II and in the 1950s, Sir Arthur Lewis, Walt Rostow, and others established the position that a stagnant economy normally saves and invests about 5¢ out of every dollar of national income, or a savings ratio of 5 percent, while a growing economy manages to save and invest 12 to 15 percent of its income. They saw in that difference the essential strategy for any country desiring to develop.[1]

The theoretical linchpin connecting capital formation to economic growth was the capital-output ratio. This appealing concept of a relatively stable ratio between capital as an input and a growing output (GNP) as a result became a fixture in economic planning, as we shall see in Chapter 11.

In any discussion of capital formation in the context of underdevelopment, especially if attempts are made to correlate additions to capital with growth, there immediately arises a problem of definition. What *is* capital? Ordinarily, of course, we mean the accumulated stock of material resources that contributes through time to a larger flow of goods and services. But items fitting this definition in one country may not fit it in another. Put differently, a reasonable observer could agree that expenditures classed as consumption in North America or Europe may well form capital in Asia or Africa. Take, for example, the hand tools of the household or the farm—the hammers, hoes, sickles, and so forth. These are treated as consumption goods in the national accounts of a developed country, but they very arguably serve as capital in many an LDC. The bicycle, considered a consumption good in developed countries, is an important contributor to production in many LDCs. Bicycles are used to transport goods to market or as taxis. They are like a very small truck, except that they are able to go where the truck cannot. They can carry an enormous load, easily over 500 pounds, if they are wheeled along. Bicycles carry cocoa and peanuts in bags, cotton in bales, rubber in sheets, palm oil in drums, imported commodities in boxes, and disassembled artillery pieces and rocket launchers, as was common during the Vietnam War, when the North Vietnamese employed many thousands of cargo-carrying bicycles.[2]

Improved agricultural land provides a similar definitional problem. By conventional practice the clearing and improving of land and the planting of tree crops that take a long time to bear are not counted as capital formation. But what if much time and effort is devoted to clearing and planting as opposed to other types of capital formation? What if the agricultural sector is very large? A serious omission in the measurement of capital can result if these are overlooked, as ordinarily they are.

It is frequently recognized that output of some consumption goods has a capital aspect. Examples include education and health measures, which are commonly called "human capital" and increases in spending on them "human investment." In agriculture inputs with capital characteristics such as pesticides, fertilizers, and improved seeds have had an extremely important role in the "Green Revolution." Often their cumulative effect on yields has far outweighed the impact of capital as conventionally defined.

One can go a long step further, as with Gunnar Myrdal, and claim that the distinction between investment and consumption is not justified in an LDC even when speaking of consumer goods with no obvious capital characteristics whatever. Myrdal argues that higher consumption of goods in a poor LDC ordinarily raises production as a direct result. Thus consumption acts as investment, even though for definitional purposes it remains consumption. The clearest example is food. Observers of the LDCs can hardly doubt that in many of them larger supplies and better quality would, by improving nutrition, cause an increase in worker productivity and hence output. Or, to turn the example around, cutting the consumption of food would surely reduce output, perhaps substantially. Clothing shares this property to a lesser extent. (Housing does, too, but this is everywhere classified as capital.) Empirical evidence on the subject is presented in Chapters 7 and 9. Even more broadly, any new consumer goods (including imports), if made available, may have a capital aspect if they act on consumers as an inducement to better economic performance.

All these difficulties of definition must be kept in mind in the discussion to come. As Andrew Kamarck has argued convincingly,

> It is now time for economists working on problems of developing countries to accept fully the Fisherian definition of investment [from Irving Fisher's 1927 book, *The Nature of Capital and Investment*]: . . . any outlay made today for the purpose of increasing future income—whatever the asset (tangible or intangible, a piece of machinery or a piece of productive knowledge, a passable road or a functioning family planning organization) that is purchased with the outlay. . . . The whole apparatus of investment decision can be applied to this as it is applied now to the purchase of durable goods. The figures and calculations will be less precise, but the analysis and conclusions will be more correct.[3]

ASSESSING THE CONTRIBUTION OF CAPITAL

For a long period the crucial role of capital formation in the development process was more or less taken for granted, osmosis, so it seems, from the idea that poor countries are capital-short, while rich countries are capital-abundant.

The pioneering attempts at "growth accounting," rough and ready econometrics at the start but becoming increasingly more sophisticated, gave surprising results. Respected investigators writing in the 1950s and 1960s, including Alec Cairncross, Robert Solow, Moses Abramovitz, John Kendrick, Benton Massell, and others, all focusing on the United States, were united in their conclusion that the *physical quantity* of capital itself was less important than the *productivity* of that capital. The vivid implication of these studies was that there is much in the development process that capital cannot explain. Development economists rapidly became aware of these calculations. Although they applied only to a developed country, they certainly introduced a note of skepticism that grew into a great reaction against the belief that the sheer quantity of capital is central to development.

Prominent among the economists who continued these studies is Edward Denison.[4] Denison's 1962 study, utilizing Cobb-Douglas production functions and econometric methods to break down the contribution of separate productive factors to U.S. economic growth, showed for 1929 until 1957 that 91 percent of the increase in real income per worker during the period was due to causes other than capital, and only 9 percent was due to the physical increase in the size of the capital stock.

One might certainly argue—many did on becoming acquainted with Denison's work—that the United States from 1929 to 1957 was at an advanced state of development and that similar data for a prior period in American economic history would lead to different conclusions. But extension of the Denison methods to the earlier period of 1909 to 1929, though it raised substantially the significance of the quantity of capital, still left it far behind other factors in explanatory power. During this period Denison's results showed a much higher 29 percent of the growth in real income per worker was due to the increase in the volume of capital.

Though the quantity of capital was seen to be far more important than in the period 1929 to 1957, the findings still did not support the view of the pioneering development theorists that the role of capital was pivotal.

What then did Denison identify as the crucial causes of growing real income per worker in the United States, if, indeed, the volume of capital was not the primary determinant? He pointed instead to education, to an increase in the quality of each hour worked due to a reduction in number of hours worked, to technical progress (better knowledge about production), and to economies of scale. These explained the bulk of the increases in real income and were large enough to offset some reduction in hours worked per person as the work week was reduced in both time periods. Table 4.1 shows Denison's calculations in summary form, also including the years 1948 to 1973.

The Denison results for the United States, and several studies that have largely replicated those results for other developed countries, employ numerous restrictive assumptions, but there is no strong evidence that the use of the assumptions alters the results very much.[5] For a time these models made explanations of growth based on capital distinctly passé. Very probably this reaction against capital was pushed too far. One must guard against any quick assumption that the findings from U.S. and European historical experience can be transferred unaltered to today's LDCs. The United States was always, even in the early nineteenth century, relatively capital-intensive. In more labor-intensive countries, capital would be predictably more effective per unit because it is scarce.

Indeed, recent, though largely tentative, studies in the LDCs do revive the conclusion that capital per se is very important. There is, for example, a weak but noticeable correlation between today's LDCs with the highest output growth and the highest rate of capital accumulation.[6] Similarly, low growth and a low rate of capital formation are also correlated. This in itself is not proof of cause and effect, but some country studies of the Denison type have now been made that show capital formation contributing more to output per worker, and sometimes far more, than such studies show for developed nations. Modeling of this sort has suggested a contribution of capital of about half or a little more in Israel

Table 4.1 CONTRIBUTION TO GROWTH IN REAL INCOME PER WORKER, 1909–1973 (IN PERCENT)

	1909–1929	1929–1957	1948–1973
Volume of capital	29	9	15
Reduction in hours worked	−19	−33	−8
Education	29	42	19
Effect of fewer hours worked on labor quality	19	21	
Change in age and sex composition of labor force			−8
Technical progress (knowledge)	20	36	54
Economies of scale	23	21	15
Improved allocation of resources			15

Column totals do not add up exactly due to rounding off and omission of several minor items.

and even higher in some other LDCs (which, however, must be subject to a considerable discount in confidence because of weaknesses in the data).[7]

The rehabilitation of the idea that expansion in the volume of capital is important for economic change now is in full sway. The World Bank in 1985 introduced a new study with this sentence:

> This paper reaffirms certain notions that might have seemed self-evident in previous years but have now increasingly begun to appear contentious that growth in such pacesetters as the Republic of Korea, Japan, and Brazil has arisen principally from capital accumulation. . . .[8]

What, then, are we left with? We see that capital is one factor in the growth process, a factor that in the past received overwhelmingly the most attention, then fell in esteem, but is again returning to prominence. The controversy has been convincing in one respect. Almost all economists would now agree that changes in the quality of capital—its productivity—and not simply the quantity of it are a vital feature. Unfortunately, this has a disturbing aspect, because economists know considerably less about productivity than they do about quantitative applications of capital. This is due to the great variety of elements that lead to productivity change—education, technical progress, internal and external economies of scale, improved management and others.

It is these aspects, along with the hospitality or hostility of the social and institutional setting, that cause the wide divergences in effectiveness of capital investment among LDCs that at first glance seem astounding. If we define such effectiveness as a ratio between growth in GNP and the proportion of GNP invested, we find some LDCs investing a given proportion of their output obtain a rise in output *four times* higher than some other countries investing the same amount.

THE DISTRIBUTION OF INVESTMENT

One aspect of capital formation is highly visible in many LDCs, namely, the problems that arise when insufficient attention is given to the distribution of investment. In the popular mind investment is often equated with the establishment of industry and mechanized agriculture, especially the machinery associated with these activities. Rather surprisingly, perhaps, experience shows that the country devoting most of its investment funds to the machinery of industry and agriculture, as compared to other types of investment, is certain to pay a serious penalty of popular discontent and lopsided, inefficient development. In a working free market scarcity of capital in any given sector will be reflected by a high rate of return (marginal efficiency of investment) in that sector, and investment will flow to it. But if markets are working poorly or governments override their signals, then serious problems of misallocation may result. Both the LDC that plans its investment through the government and the LDC that channels private investment through government influence, advice, controls, and subsidized credit must be aware of this penalty.

Table 4.2 PERCENTAGE OF POPULATION LIVING IN SLUMS

Bogota, Colombia	60	Mexico City, Mexico	46
Calcutta, India	67	Nairobi, Kenya	70
Colombo, Sri Lanka	44	Recife, Brazil	50
Dakar, Senegal	60	Tunis, Tunisia	43
Dar es Salaam, Tanzania	50		

Source: UNESCO, *New Book of World Rankings.*

What are the sectors that are sometimes neglected? Why do the usual figures for capital formation over long time periods in the developed Western countries show only about 30 percent of all investment going to manufacturing and agriculture? The answer is found in four areas.[9]

Housing   The country that does not channel 20 to 25 percent of its investment into housing, perhaps even more for an LDC suffering from rapid population growth and a shift in population from rural to urban living, is in for some serious social consequences. Failure in this regard is familiar everywhere, and shanty-town slums have become a standard feature of urban life. New words find their way into many languages to describe these slum conditions: the *bustees* of Calcutta, the *gece kondu* of Istanbul, the *colonias proletarias* of Mexico City, the *poblaciones calampas* of Santiago de Chile, the *favelas* of Rio de Janeiro, and the *barriadas* of Lima. (The literal meaning of the first five of these names is, respectively, "registered slum," "put up in the night," "poor people's colonies," "population mushrooms," and a type of prolific flowering fruit tree). In many cities of the LDCs over half the population lives in slums or settlements of squatters.[10] Table 4.2 shows the most recently available figures.

Public Works and Utilities   The transport systems, power plants, water works, schools, and hospitals that make up the infrastructure or "social overhead capital" of an economy take up about 35 percent of total capital formation in the developed world. There is no reason to expect that LDCs can avoid spending at least this amount without suffering severely from inadequate capacity.

The results of deficiencies in these areas are both predictable and highly visible. Run-down electric power plants gasp and die at peak power load (usually when the lights are turned on at dusk). Sometimes the lights come on again after a few minutes; sometimes the wait can be for hours. A blown fuse in a transformer may mean days before overworked maintenance crews fix the problem. A fractured bearing somewhere in a hydroelectric installation may mean no electricity for weeks or months. The following item, from the weekly *West Africa,* concerns Sierra Leone, but could serve for dozens of other countries as well.

After several weeks of serious disruption in the supply of electricity in the western area, resulting in "utter public disgust," the National Power Authority has come out with the following release:

"The public is hereby informed that the exhaust gas turbocharger on one of the major engines at Kingtom Power Station failed during the early hours of Friday, May 11. Prior to this failure, the authority was unable to meet full demand in the western area due to lack of spare parts and standby generating capacity. As a result of the failure of the exhaust gas turbocharger, the authority is now able to provide less than half of the electricity demand in the western area. . . . Although every effort will be made to provide electricity to consumers, increased load shedding is inevitable.

The National Power Authority regrets the inconvenience to all consumers and assures them that immediate measures are being taken to rectify the situation. . . ."

Meanwhile, sources close to the authority disclose that unless the required spares are obtained swiftly, the western area stands the risk of getting engulfed in total blackout. Of the five generators at Kingtom, only one is said to be in satisfactory working condition. The others have been cannibalised to keep it going. Hardest hit are consumers in Greater Freetown area [the capital], where most of the industries are located.

An official of the Ministry of Energy and Power told *West Africa* that the machinery has been set in motion for the acquisition of new generators from Japan, but that this will take at least two years to materialise.[11]

The effects on an economy can be severe. The Indian government estimates that power cuts between 1975 and 1980 reduced the rise in real GDP in that country by 2 percentage points a year.[12]

Similar problems abound. Water-supply shortages are especially common in drier areas, with water often limited to only a few hours a day. One-fourth to one-third of urban dwellers in LDCs have no regular supply (and thus no sewage system either). Of all Tunisian dwellings, 76 percent have no plumbing; the figure is 70 percent in Nepal, 67 percent in Bolivia, 42 percent in Colombia, 41 percent in Mexico, and 0.1 percent in West Germany.[13]

Ill-kept highway surfaces can develop enormous potholes. Your author saw one in Algeria that could have swallowed a car with ease, but topped that one day in Cameroun where he came across a pothole that *had* swallowed a *truck*. Unpaved surfaces develop corrugations, hard ridges that build up laterally across the road. This washboard effect is caused by heavy traffic moving at high speeds over roads that are given little or no maintenance. Its results can be devastating to motor vehicles. (After a one-day trip on corrugation in West Africa, the author's VW bus was found to have shaken loose several nuts in the transmission, oil streaming from the apertures, and to have shaken a headlight out of its bracket, leaving it dangling from its wires at bumper level.)

Railway lines are often single-track, with so much congestion that crops for export rot in storage. The Ghana western railway "has stopped operating because of severe deterioration of the wooden sleepers [ties] that hold rails in place."[14] Bridges wash out and are not replaced for months or years. Ships anchor for days at overcrowded ports, waiting for berthing space and charging the "demurrage" (waiting time in port) that runs up shipping bills to sometimes spectacular levels in the LDCs.

These costs are obviously high in inconvenience, in shutdowns or slow-downs, in time lost, and in damage to equipment. Their costs, however, are sometimes little considered by the country concentrating its efforts on "directly productive" manufacturing or agriculture rather than on the neglected, underfinanced public works and utilities of the economy. The imbalance is clear, the penalty large.

Inventories A third area of potential neglect in planning investment is inventories. In a developed country inventories comprise 10 percent or more of net investment (12 percent is the usual benchmark), and short-changing here either through planning or through policies to protect the balance of payments can lead to extensive difficulties. The main symptom will be breakdowns in the supply of raw materials, spare parts, and final goods, as wholesalers and retailers find that their backlogs are easily exhausted.

In the underdeveloped world it is common to see a motorcycle or car temporarily off the road because some minor part cannot be obtained. For an egregious example, note the World Bank's estimate that in early 1983 70 percent of Ghana's busses and trucks were idle, due mainly to a shortage of tires and batteries, and about 80 percent of the country's railway locomotives were out of service, due to a lack of spares.[15] The little things of life taken for granted in a developed country—the tiny starter for a fluorescent lamp, for example, without which the lamp won't turn on—may be next to impossible to obtain. In Zambia recently the copper mines could not get spare parts, soft drinks were not being bottled because there were no caps, and no flour was being shipped from local mills, not because of a flour shortage, but because there were no sacks.[16]

Construction It is a common misconception that investment in manufacturing industry involves mostly machinery and equipment. On the contrary, in both developed countries and LDCs from one-half to two-thirds of gross fixed capital formation in manufacturing is in construction. The very fact that the magnitude of building activity comes as something of a surprise indicates that a shortage of construction capacity can be an unexpected bottleneck in the development process and that the human instruments of such activity—architects, builders, and trained construction workers, for example—are likely also to be scarce.

Under such circumstances the profits of contractors are likely to be larger than otherwise, and the shortage of trained supervisors too often results in bad designs and poor workmanship.[17] The most visible aspect of construction shortages is without doubt the unfinished project, just started or perhaps half completed, standing there in what amounts to a state of suspended animation for months or years waiting for the next stage of construction to begin.

FINANCING CAPITAL FORMATION

Where can an LDC obtain the capital it needs for development? How does it finance its capital formation? The answers to these important questions always involve either domestic saving or flows from abroad. A little simple algebra from the principles of economics course shows why.[18]

Take the fundamental proposition of national accounting that

$$Y = C + I + (X - M)$$

where Y = gross national product (total spending), C = consumption, I = investment, X = exports of goods and services plus income received from abroad, and M = imports of goods and services plus income paid abroad. Both government and private consumption and investment are included in $C + I$.

All this spending generates an identical flow of income (Y); this total income equals total spending. Of all income, some is consumed and some is saved (S). Thus

$$Y = C + S$$

(Again, government consumption and saving is included in $C + S$.) Then, since total spending equals total income, by substitution

$$C + I + (X - M) = C + S$$

From this equation, we can by simple manipulation easily discover the essential constraints on capital formation. Move $(X - M)$ to the right-hand side, reversing its sign; cancel C on both sides. The result is

$$I = S + (M - X)$$

The algebra is clear. A country's investment opportunities are determined by its potential for domestic saving (S) plus any net capital inflows from abroad $(M > X)$. (The only way for imports to exceed exports is for the country to borrow abroad; $M > X$ is thus equivalent to a capital inflow.)

The domestic saving can be (1) private and voluntary, which can then be loaned to businesses or the government by banks or other financial intermediaries, or (2) government saving, when taxes exceed current expenditures, thus making funds available for investment. This latter case includes the "forced saving" of inflation, whereby central bank creation of new money allows the government to bid resources away from the rest of the economy. The flows from abroad can be (1) long-term international loans, as from the World Bank, (2) official development assistance ("foreign aid") from governments abroad, (3) foreign private investment, called *direct* when it involves a controlling interest in a factory or mine (and hence usually involving the activities of multinational firms) or *portfolio* when, as with the purchase of a bond, it does not, (4) medium- or short-term loans from commercial banks, or (5) medium- and short-term loans from the International Monetary Fund (IMF). The domestic alternatives will be discussed in the remainder of this chapter, the longer-term capital flows in Chapter 5, and the shorter-term borrowing (which came to involve the debt crisis of the 1980s) in Chapter 6.

PRIVATE DOMESTIC SAVING (HOUSEHOLDS AND FIRMS)[19]

The level of saving within a country is, in modern economic theory, closely correlated with the level of disposable income. Thus a poor country will ordinarily mobilize less savings than a middle-income or rich one, both in total amount and percent of income saved. Indeed, low-income LDCs save on average only 7 percent of their GDP, while lower middle-income LDCs save 16 percent and upper middle-income countries 26 percent. Obviously, growth itself helps to alleviate the shortage of savings, since the ability to save rises with income. Econometric studies from some Asian countries show nearly 83 percent of the total variation in saving per head is explained by the value of income per head.[20] On the grounds of income alone, therefore, the LDC starts at a disadvantage; the poorer the country, the greater the difficulty.

Household saving, including the saving of small family businesses, usually predominates, often making up 60 to 70 percent of domestic saving.[21] Even in the poorest LDCs some household saving can be important for development in spite of the low income levels. Peasant farmers usually contribute to saving by giving up leisure, by clearing land, by retaining seed for output growth, and by putting in commercially valuable trees such as cocoa and rubber that take a long time to mature. (These activities represent real saving and real investment, combined in the same act.) Small, family-owned businesses in both urban and rural areas save and reinvest a substantial amount in low-technology pursuits such as making cement blocks, thatching roofs, constructing irrigation facilities, tool making, rice milling, food processing, and the like. As a country grows richer, the savings of this sector are likely to rise significantly and, in fact, have done so in the last two decades.[22]

An important debate on saving behavior concerns the question whether greater income inequality increases saving. If the wealthy save more, then allowing a more unequal income distribution (via abolition of the progressive income tax, for example) would by increasing saving promote investment. Generally, however, the statistics do not support the contention, there being no noticeable correlation between high income inequality and high saving. Some of the biggest savers (Algeria, China, Congo Republic, Singapore, South Korea, Taiwan, Yugoslavia), all saving over 30 percent of GDP and in the LDC "top 10," are among the countries with the greatest income equality.

Some factors affecting household saving are socioeconomic in nature. One such is the well-known "extended family" system, wherein parents, children, grandparents, aunts, uncles, and cousins are closely tied and perhaps live together in the same family compound. Each member is under an obligation to help the others. The impact on saving can be substantial. In some cases the result is negative. With the extended family acting as a social security system, relatives caring for the elderly, saving for retirement is less necessary. In addition, should a member of the family succeed in accumulating a significant increase in income, the relatives are there to claim their share. In response to the transfers, the successful family member would most likely reduce the amount saved. In some ways the extended family may instead encourage saving, working virtually as an internal capital market by pooling funds to promote a business venture or the education of a talented family member. Cases in point are the overseas Chinese, many Indian and Philippine families, and the Igbo (Ibo) of Nigeria. Family members may be a better risk as borrowers because knowledge about them is more complete, and pressure for repayment can be applied more directly. With the social security aspect noted above, the extended family may be rather more workable than usually appreciated by economists; the criticism of this institution as an obstacle to development has probably been overdone.

One inhibiting factor that may reduce the level of domestic household saving, again socioeconomic in nature, can be detected in many LDCs. If society is highly stratified, so that accumulated savings are of little help in advancing socially (India is a pertinent example), then an important incentive to save is destroyed. For this reason, large chunks of income may be expended on fancy clothing, extravagant ceremonial expenditures, and other conspicuous consumption, rather than for saving. Even without a stratified society, one may find conspicuous consumption permeates social relationships. The extravagance is sometimes competitive, as in the size and value of gifts exchanged on ceremonial occasions.

Religion is similarly a mixed case. Scholars such as R. J. Tawney and Max Weber have advanced famous theses on the contribution of Protestant Christianity to the rise of capitalism through a "saving ethic." A similar argument emphasizing religion has been made for Japan. But there are also religious factors that retard saving. Religious scruples against receiving a rate of interest are especially strong (and growing) in Islamic countries.[23] Banks stopped paying interest in Sudan in 1984 and in Pakistan in 1985. The prohibition has been strictly enforced in Iran since the fall of the shah; other Muslim countries have followed suit. True, Islamic law does allow for administrative charges and repayment for risk, and Prince Faisal of Saudi Arabia took part in 1977 in establishing national bank profit-sharing with borrowers and lenders, so that at least some "interest" could be charged and paid there and in the countries where this scheme has been emulated. Returns to saving are notably lower nonetheless. Even without the religious scruples, countries may still have stiff anti-usury laws that reduce interest receipts and stiff bank reserve requirements that have the same effect.

Saving may also be inhibited by inflation. Inflation is often a more serious problem in the LDCs than it is in the developed world. A normal response is to avoid its effects by buying and hoarding tangible goods, by purchasing land and buildings, or by any other purchase that will act as a hedge against rising prices. Similarly, governments may inhibit saving because the interest on accounts is easy to tax, and so are the accounts themselves via a "wealth tax." Households might then shun saving in this form as overly risky.

In spite of these inhibiting factors, household saving can still be enhanced by well-designed government policies. Governments have the power to attack inflation, to restore incentives to save, and to undertake pro-saving campaigns. Stimulation to saving can come from new institutions such as credit cooperatives, government combined plans for insurance and saving (as in Egypt), new pension funds, and post office savings accounts. In many countries banks have an urban bias; to counter this, governments can encourage branch banking outside major urban centers. The response is not likely to be overwhelming, but every little bit helps.

Corporate saving in the form of retained earnings is of importance in the excellent saving performance of the middle-income LDCs. Such saving often involves foreign firms (the multinationals) as well as domestic ones, a topic discussed in Chapter 5. In poorer LDCs less is to be expected. With capital markets thin, symptomatic of underdevelopment, firms realize that their own savings in the form of reinvested earnings are critical to their own expansion. Internal funds, derived from undistributed profits, must be relied upon because the costs for funds obtained externally are often high indeed.

Why is this so? It is often found that raising equity capital through share issues is not very practical because there is no easy way to sell the shares. The indigenous stock market is likely to be small, with little turnover, even if one exists. According to the *Wall Street Journal* (October 31, 1985), only 36 of Turkey's 496 listed stocks had any sales in a recent 8-month period, while Kenya's stock market in all of 1984 had a sales volume of only $10 million. Indonesia's exchange listed the stock of just 24 companies.

Even if shares can be sold, it is quite characteristic in most LDCs for the shares of a firm to be closely held by a founding family or group of families, with no real desire to dilute the ownership. Thus even where there is an active market, as in Hong Kong and Singapore, prices are volatile because only a smallish proportion of a company's shares are ever traded. Minority shareholders under such circumstances can be "taken for a ride," as the majority shareholders pay each other high salaries or otherwise divert the profits to themselves. The sale of shares is further inhibited.

Some international help is in the offing, however. An agency of the World Bank, the International Finance Corporation, in 1986 announced a small but innovative Emerging Markets Growth Fund (EMGF). This mutual fund will invest $50 million in the stock markets of nine LDCs, while selling its own EMGF shares in developed-country securities markets. If the plan succeeds—and LDC securities are frequently undervalued in relation to earnings—the International Finance Corporation would expand the idea. Should western investors find the EMGF shares attractive, the concept certainly has a potential to promote capital inflows. The amount of investment in the securities markets of the developed countries is extremely large, now about $3 trillion. Even a tiny trend toward the purchase of LDC stocks, less than 1 percent of which are currently owned by foreigners, might have a substantial impact.[24]

The alternative to sale of stock is to borrow from the commercial banking system, but firms following this route will typically find high interest rates. The high level of such rates is readily explicable. Loanable funds are usually in short supply. Governments, rather than supplying funds to the credit market, are often found in that same market trying to borrow for their own purposes. Banks and insurance companies, normally large suppliers of loanable funds, are often under the requirement of lending to the government so as to finance the government's own programs. Household saving will not be sufficient, as seen in the last section. Business corporations, themselves often subject to compulsory government bond-buying schemes, will usually either do their own investing or pay dividends.

Without credit bureaus (like Moody's), without national business publications and industrial newsletters, risks are harder to assess. The ability to enforce contracts by seizing assets or garnisheeing wages may be limited by the institutional setting. Small borrowers may vanish without a trace; large ones protected by friends in high places may thumb their noses and refuse to repay. The general lack of information is a major impediment to lending, thus raising the cost of credit (and explaining why membership in an extended family or ethnic group often serves as a proxy for credit worthiness).

The result is a supply curve for loanable funds positioned inward to the left, as in Figure 4.1. Meanwhile, the underdeveloped economy is typically short of capital; there are many profitable opportunities for its employment. Thus the demand curve for loanable funds is located out to the right. The combination of low supply and high demand results in a relatively high market rate of interest, shown at the equilibrium *r*. (Various barriers, including imperfect knowledge, risk, expectations of a currency devaluation, and pervasive government controls on capital movements, keep international flows of capital from equalizing interest rates across countries.) Not only will the rates be high, but highly variable as well. Advantageous ones will be granted to trusted borrowers, while strangers face much higher charges, so that over a wide range of credit markets there is no single rate of interest.

In some countries this description of conditions in LDCs must be modified

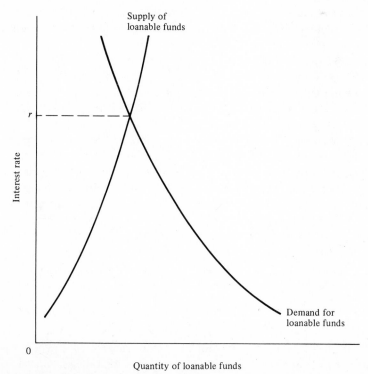

Figure 4.1 Low supply and high demand for loanable funds lead to a high market rate of interest.

to take account of a strange fact. In the organized, relatively developed sectors of the economy, businesses often have access to local capital, both short term and long term, at interest rates not much higher than have to be paid in capital-abundant developed countries or sometimes even lower, as in Ghana, the Ivory Coast, Nigeria, Tunisia, and Zambia, in all of which interest rates averaged less than 6 percent in the period 1971 to 1980 (see the nominal rates listed in Table 4.2 below). In three of these countries, average rates were below 4 percent!

How can it ever occur that interest rates in capital-short countries would be lower than in the developed world, conflicting as that does with the clear-cut prediction of Figure 4.1? The answer lies in government interference with capital markets, on the side of both saving and investment, through the use of controls. Especially important are the so-called selective credit controls used to allocate funds into specific types of capital formation and also to direct them toward specific firms. This is often combined with prohibitions on certain types of investment. The result can be very advantageous to established large-scale enterprises, usually the ones to benefit from the controls on interest rates. (Transactions costs are commonly lower when borrowing is large, so banks would generally choose to lend to established firms when interest rates are kept at below-market levels.) Such enterprises are frequently found leading the defense against any suggestion that capital be priced competitively. The main manifestation of the controls is ordinarily a tendency toward investment in projects where the marginal return to capital is low, toward overly high capital intensity, overcapacity, and slow completion of projects (since a delayed project costs its investors little). All of these practices contribute to a low efficiency of capital. All would be uneconomic at market rates of interest.

Another possible cause of low or even negative real rates of interest is that unanticipated inflation takes place. If borrowers' and lenders' expectations of inflation lag behind the actual rate of price increase, then the "inflation premium" built into the interest rate will not (at least temporarily) be sufficiently large, thus reducing real rates below nominal rates.

Whatever the reason, when real rates are very low or negative for long periods, they have an inhibiting effect on saving. Some recent examples of low or negative real rates are shown in Table 4.3. Understandably, the low real rates cause the public to hold its savings outside the domestic financial system, in turn encouraging credit rationing and slowing the development of financial institutions. Recent empirical work shows that a rise of 1 percentage point in interest rates would cause the amount saved to rise between 0.15 and 0.25 percent.[25] High priority in restoring positive rates of return to saving would seem clearly called for.

GOVERNMENT SAVING AND INVESTMENT

The discussion to this point amounts to saying that private saving and the capital formation generated from it are likely to be deficient in poor LDCs, with the deficiency correctable as growth takes place. This deficiency leads us to consider

Table 4.3 SELECTED NOMINAL AND REAL INTEREST RATES, 1971–1980

	Nominal rate	Real rate
Colombia	20.98	1.23
Malaysia	7.61	1.20
Thailand	9.66	0.16
Pakistan	8.39	−0.47
India	6.79	−2.24
Morocco	6.00	−2.55
South Korea	15.46	−2.67
Zambia	4.76	−2.95
Philippines	9.45	−3.27
Mexico	15.40	−3.65
Tunisia	4.00	−4.11
Kenya	5.37	−4.97
Bangladesh	8.14	−5.38
Tanzania	3.79	−7.31
Indonesia	11.06	−7.86
Nigeria	5.54	−10.80
Yugoslavia	9.91	−11.73
Ivory Coast	3.97	−12.90
Brazil	31.07	−13.25
Peru	22.96	−15.14
Uruguay	44.10	−18.58
Bolivia	13.66	−21.01
Ghana	5.29	−41.70
Argentina	58.95	−71.34
Chile	60.31	−118.42

The price index used in calculating the real interest rates is the GNP deflator. Note some of the low nominal interest rates in the middle column, confirming a point made earlier in the text.

Source: Deena R. Khatkhate, "Estimating Real Interest Rates in LDCs," *Finance and Development* 23, no. 2 (1986): 48.

the government as saver and investor. In the developing world government saving and investing can equal half or more of such activity in the economy. Almost the whole of it is carried on by government in the centrally planned economies.

The only way for a government to save is, of course, by taxing more than it spends (including the possible surpluses of public-sector enterprises). This surplus in the current budget could be used to finance private investment by placing the funds in private capital markets. Economists see much to recommend in such a policy. It could potentially increase the level of saving, encourage the efficient allocation of investment, and build the capacity of the private sector which is otherwise inhibited by lack of credit.[26] Only rarely, however, have LDCs used a budget surplus on any scale to mobilize funds for lending to the private sector on a competitive and neutral basis.[27] Much more commonly the government does the investing itself. Government investment can also be accomplished by borrowing from the private sector or by running a budget deficit, as we shall see.

Financing Government Investment Through Borrowing from the Private Sector

Government domestic borrowing potential, exercised through the sale of government bonds to its own public and business firms, is usually strictly limited in the poor LDCs. Most LDCs nowadays have one or more "development banks" which attract interest-bearing deposits from the public and lend the funds for development projects. They are substitutes for raising capital through the sale of bonds. Such banks often have the additional task of improving project appraisal methods, undertaking some equity investment themselves, and perhaps pushing funding toward the neglected agricultural sector. In the low-income LDCs they may receive foreign aid. Well-known institutions of this sort are the Industrial Credit and Investment Corporation of India and the Korean Development Finance Corporation.[28]

We have already noted the shortage of investable funds that afflicts most LDCs, and even payment of a high rate of interest on government bonds may be ineffectual in attracting funds because of alternatives elsewhere in the economy. Commercial banks may consider government bonds a poor place to hold funds, and in the early days of independence for the LDCs, when such banks were largely foreign-owned, this was especially a problem. At times some governments have lessened the attractiveness of their own bonds by arbitrarily altering their terms of issue or calling them back. Furthermore, an increase in government bond sales at any given time and given level of national income must imply either a matching reduction in funds available to the private sector, so that the total does not increase, or a voluntary reduction in private consumption. But reductions in consumption are clearly the more difficult to achieve the poorer the country is. Development, then, means that domestic borrowing will become easier as income rises, but little is to be expected from it in the earlier stages of the process.

A number of countries have at times required the *compulsory* purchase of government bonds out of wage and salary payments, an idea initiated by the Soviet Union. This practice has always been much more akin to taxation, however, as shown by the Soviet Union itself where interest on the bonds was first reduced and then eliminated and where repayments of principal were not made on numerous categories of the compulsorily purchased bonds. That such bonds have never been popular is an understatement. There were riots in Ghana and Guyana when similar schemes were introduced, and the author's own Turkish bonds, purchased with part of his salary in the 1970s in compliance with Turkish law when he was teaching in that country, have now lost most of their value due to inflation.

Financing Government Investment Through Taxation

If borrowing is largely ineffective at low levels of development, financing government investment then becomes a problem in taxation.[29] Direct transfers of goods
and physical controls on the movements of productive factors could be used
instead, but these are less efficient mechanisms and often generate more public
resentment.

At once a typical LDC runs into policy problems in its tax decisions. Any
kind of tax is almost certain to apply inequitably, affecting some of the population
more than others, for the simple reason that most forms of modern taxation will
not cover a very wide range of economic activity in the average LDC.

Another concern is that growth may be a tender shoot, easily discouraged
by high taxation. A recent 20-country study by the World Bank comparing low
tax and high tax nations at approximately the same level of development concludes that there is some correlation between low taxes and rapid growth.[30] Low
taxes might be expected to increase private investment, both domestically and by
foreigners, and to raise returns both to work and to innovation, augmenting the
supply of all of these. The study warns, however, against any simplistic notion
that cutting taxes is an automatic path to faster growth. Low taxes might still be
very complex or poorly administered. World recession, high interest rates caused
by heavy government borrowing made necessary by the slimness of tax revenues,
and causing a crowding-out of private investment, or overvalued foreign exchange
rates all might swamp the positive effect of the lower taxes. In any case, the
positive effects are unlikely to occur in the short run. It will take some considerable time before the low taxes might bring about the change in attitudes leading
to more work effort, more innovation, and more investment.

Effective collection of taxes is typically an arduous task for an LDC, usually
more difficult than in a developed country. The problem of how a government
is successfully going to collect the revenue it needs tends to submerge the question
of whether the means of collection is fair. There is thus often far less public
discussion and debate concerning tax incidence (progressivity versus regressivity)
than in the rich countries. In some LDCs, Mexico for example, the result is a quite
regressive tax system.[31]

Collection, then, is the crux of the matter. Income, output, and sales are
by definition all low in a poor LDC. It follows that any form of tax tied to these
will collect little. Thus it is not surprising that total central government tax
proceeds as a percent of GNP were much lower in LDCs than in developed
countries. In 1983 the figures averaged 27 percent for the developed countries,
ranging from 20 to 38 percent for the United States, Great Britain, and West
Germany, with the Netherlands higher at 53 percent and Japan lower. The
proportion was only 5 to 18 percent (14.2 percent average) for most low-income
LDCs and even below 1 percent in 1981 for troubled Uganda.[32] The figures reflect
the proposition that, with advances in income, proportionally more public services are demanded by the public. There are exceptions. Tanzania for a time
raised its figure to 30 percent, but at the cost of serious disincentive effects on its
entrepreneurs and farmers, and a retreat ensued. Large exporters of minerals can

also raise their tax take, as with Zimbabwe at 33 percent, Zambia at 25 percent, and Zaire at 20 percent. Even so, note that these figures, high for LDCs, are mostly well below the developed-country average.

Understandably, all LDCs search for types of taxes that collect more as national income rises. Technically, the responsiveness of the tax take to income increases is called the income elasticity of tax revenue. This figure can be derived from the so-called tax ratios: T/Y is defined as the average tax ratio; $\Delta T/\Delta Y$ is the marginal tax ratio; Expressed as a percentage, the amount by which tax revenues increase, $\Delta T/T,$ divided by the increase in income, $\Delta Y/Y,$ is the elasticity of tax revenue. Typically, this tends to be highest for excise and sales taxes, *not* as one might expect for income taxes, as we shall see. Taxes on foreign trade tend to be the lowest, ranking behind income taxes.[33]

Income, Property, and Inheritance Taxes   The personal income tax, heart of the revenue system in the developed world (representing 50 percent of U.S. government revenue in 1983), is particularly hard to collect and is of relatively minor importance in LDCs. In some countries this low importance is due to the realization that income taxes may discourage the profit-making entrepreneur from saving and investing.[34] In light of this realization Nicholas Kaldor proposed a tax reform for India that would reduce the disincentive effects on saving and investment brought by an income tax. He suggested an expenditure levy, that is, a tax applied only on expenditure, or the difference between income and saving $(Y - S = E)$. Such a tax on spending would tend to restrict consumption and increase saving. The idea has its attractions and it does have strong advocates in the United States and Western Europe, but to date only India and Sri Lanka have actually employed it.[35] It proved difficult to administer for the two LDCs that tried it. A major complication is that it requires the taxpayer to calculate changes in his total net worth, since drawing down past saving in any form can contribute to expenditure. India adopted it, repealed it because of these problems, readopted it, and finally re-repealed it. Sri Lanka repealed its expenditure tax as well.

The more significant reason why the income tax is of limited importance in most developing countries, however, is the fact that such a tax is distinctly difficult to operate under conditions of underdevelopment. The difficulties arise for the following reasons.[36]

1. There must be measurable income to tax. Where subsistence output is common or where barter is carried on, there are serious problems in determining how much income is subject to tax.

2. An extremely low rate of literacy, for example, around 30 percent of the population in India, Pakistan, Nigeria, and the Sudan, means limited ability to understand and to fill out income tax forms.

3. A shortage of suitable clerical skills means record keeping will be lax.

4. Where the notion becomes popular that the government is there to be cheated and that such cheating is socially acceptable, the income tax will yield a low return. Even in developed Italy, for example, large numbers of people do not file a tax return for this reason, and the size of the underground economy is estimated to be about a third of GNP. In Lebanon, before the civil war, only about

a quarter of the estimated amount that should have accrued through the income tax was actually finding its way to the treasury, with the government virtually powerless to increase its revenues from this source.

5. Many LDCs have undemocratic political structures run by wealthy merchants or landowners who themselves would be most affected by a progressive income tax, and their opposition is often adamant. It makes itself felt in low budgets and corresponding low levels of personnel for the taxing authority. Gunnar Myrdal says the question of the income tax is "drenched in hypocrisy."[37] Proposals for an income tax in Guatemala have more than once officially been termed a communist plot inspired by agents of Cuba's Castro.[38] The end result is that the aristocracy often escapes income taxation even when it is otherwise feasible.

6. An income tax requires an able and honest group of administrators. In many parts of the underdeveloped world there are deficiencies in accounting skills and many opportunities for bribery and corruption (both usually due to the low salaries noted above). The lack of skills and more-than-occasional dishonesty can breed a reaction in the form of massive red tape and formal procedures to ensure that taxes are paid, making the tax collection system even more difficult to administer. Many an airplane flight out of a country has been delayed when some traveller finds a required tax form is missing.

7. "Withholding" from wages and salaries is central to income tax collection in the United States and Great Britain. It was introduced in 1943 in the U.S.; with surprising candor the British call it Pay as You Earn, PAYE. But in the poorest LDCs withholding often will affect only government employees and a small group of workers and managers in private industries. The chances for tax avoidance are increased.

All these reasons mean that the income tax in LDCs is likely to bring in less per dollar spent on administering the tax system than will the same dollar used to support other types of tax collection. To be sure, such criticisms have not stopped poor countries from trying to obtain some income tax revenue from the well-to-do, especially when the wealthy are foreigners or some immigrant group lacking in political power. Even if the amount in money terms is not very significant, collection from the well-to-do gives an appearance of equity and has good propaganda value. But, on the whole, the poorer the country, the less success to be expected from an income tax. Thus only about 20 percent of all central government tax revenue is from income taxes in the LDCs, though the figure is higher in some countries where corporate profits from natural resource exports are large.

Another possibility is taxes based on property, which would seem relatively simple and efficient. It is difficult to conceal land, and it cannot be moved around like other assets. A land tax encourages cultivation and a move into the cash economy. It has the potential to broaden widely the tax base in the poorest countries. It promotes the sale of property by large landowners and may thus encourage productivity.[39]

In spite of these arguments, which for the most part are sound, the land tax has traditionally had even less success than the income tax. The difficulty in some

LDCs is that land tenure is not as we know it in the Western world. Rather than private ownership of land, ownership may be vested in an ethnic community or village or extended family. The land in such cases is held in common with no identifiable single owner. Individuals and families possess use rights, with the farm land reallocated from time to time so that no one has permanent control over the best land. This situation is not conducive to the usual form of property tax. Although it is theoretically possible for collection to be made by village elders on the basis of the entire community's holding, with each individual's share determined by the elders, it is rarely carried out in practice. (Uganda and Burma are countries with such a system.)

Even where land is held individually, parcels may be fragmented or ownership records may be badly outdated, so that administration is difficult. Assessment is also ticklish: Will the land's value be judged by its actual output or its potential output? (Nicaragua now relates its land tax to soil fertility, while in neighboring Honduras and Guatemala taxes rise when land is kept unused.[40]

Most commonly, the property tax presents problems when politically influential landowners of large estates (or *latifundia* in the literature) have the power to resist the tax completely or adapt it to their advantage. This occurs most often in Latin America and Asia. The political power of large landholders is the major explanation why on average property taxes collect only some 5 percent of all tax revenue, a figure that has been roughly constant for 20 years.

Another tax, that on inheritances, is even rarer and more limited in scope in almost all LDCs. Here again, the low occurrence of such taxes seems to reflect the balance of political power, with wealthy merchants and landowners allied in resisting such levies.

Consumption Taxes   For want of more effective taxes, many LDCs are forced to fall back on the taxation of local consumption, foreign trade, individuals on a "per head" basis, and on such eccentricities as a national lottery. These together often account for the lion's share of government revenue in the LDCs. Domestic excise (sales) taxes plus taxes on imports and exports frequently comprise 65 percent or more of that revenue. In the poorer LDCs taxes on foreign trade alone may make up over 40 percent of government revenue (the average for all low-income LDCs is about 33 percent) as against only 1.3 percent in the United States. The justification in every case is not that these taxes are fair, but that they work. Where ease of collection is significant, all of them will be found in operation.

Local consumption taxes of the excise and sales sort are collected at the wholesale point of production or at the retail level. Their importance in different LDCs varies, ranging from under 20 percent of government revenue in Cameroun, Ecuador, Egypt, Haiti, Indonesia, Jordan, Malaysia, and Turkey, to 40 percent or so in Chile, Ghana, India, Peru, Philippines, and Thailand, and up to nearly 70 percent in Yugoslavia. Their collection must be at individual factories or stores and hence is often spotty by comparison to import duties, which are collected at more easily policed ports of entry. Excise and sales taxes are most effective when applied to goods produced by a small number of firms and sold through a limited number of outlets which can be supervised by the tax authorities. They are almost impossible to collect, often the attempt is not even made, when production is widespread and sale is in local markets. They can be adjusted for progressivity by charging a higher rate on luxuries. Progressive excise taxes may be part of a scheme for achieving greater income equality, as they are in Tanzania, but progressivity adjustments introduce complexity and make administration more difficult.

A value-added tax (VAT) is a type of sales tax collected on each stage of production; it is central to the tax systems of Europe. VAT is too complex for many of the poorest LDCs because of its dependence on good record keeping, and only 17 LDCs were using this method in 1983.[41] But it is easier to administer than an income tax, and it has the splendid advantage over most other taxes of being in part self-policing. Those who pay the tax at each stage of production pay only on the value they add. For example, the firm that manufactures the paper on which a magazine is printed pays the tax on the value it added when the paper is sold to a magazine publisher. Hence the firm that publishes the magazine will want to ensure that the proper VAT receipt is sent along with every paper delivery from a supplier, so that it does not get stuck with the payment itself. Along with this remarkable element of self-policing is the further advantage that value-added taxes are collected only on spending, and not on saving. All in all, there seems a bright future for the VAT method in the LDCs.

Taxes on Foreign Trade   Import duties are the most important example of taxes on foreign trade. Such duties are ordinarily easier to collect than either a sales or income tax. It is much easier to police a country's ports of entry and even its borders, than it is to collect taxes in all local markets or implement an income tax. Import duties are at least a partial substitute for a corporate income tax on multinational firms whenever the full burden of the tax cannot be passed on to consumers.

It has been said in criticism that import duties are not progressive, weighing on rich and poor alike. But this is not necessarily so, as luxury consumer imports can easily be taxed at higher rates than are necessities, as is notably the case in Tanzania.[42] Alas, the tactic may backfire—there will then be a stronger incentive to produce the luxuries at home in the LDC. In a wide range of countries, import duties have been applied extensively in support of an import substitution policy designed to promote the domestic economy. When generalized import substitution is encountered, our topic turns from revenue collection to the nationwide effects on economic efficiency caused by the protection. This broad issue is central to Chapter 13.

Export taxes are also common and are certainly much in the news because of the long success of the OPEC oil cartel, essentially involving export taxation. Export taxes are simply money duties on goods shipped abroad, including agricultural and mineral products but hardly ever extending to manufactures because the average LDC wants to encourage their sales. Americans tend to find these taxes a bit unfamiliar, for the simple reason that they are explicitly barred in the United States by Article I of the Constitution. Export taxes are most effective revenue collectors when a country or group of countries has some monopoly power over the production of an essential item, oil, for example, or possibly copper, tin, uranium, and the like.

From the point of view of the LDC, the tax collects most when the foreign demand curve for the export being taxed is highly inelastic, as in Figure 4.2. Placing a per unit (ton, barrel, etc.) tax on the product is tantamount to shifting its supply curve upward, from S to S_t. This is because domestic producers willing to supply a given quantity at some given price will, after a tax, not be willing to do so unless they receive the previous amount plus the tax. The vertical distance AB in the figure is the dollar amount of the tax and is also the distance by which the supply curve is shifted upward. Note that the tax will in this case lower the quantity sold only slightly from OQ to OQ_1, will raise substantially the price the producer can charge from OP to OP_1, and result in a large increase in total revenue earned from the sale of the product from $OPEQ$ to $OP_1E_1Q_1$. As will be seen in later chapters, OPEC is the outstanding example of success for countries employing export taxation as a method of generating government revenue.

There are, however, a host of difficulties in using an export tax. Even when one country or small group of countries can exert quasi-monopoly control over the market due to limited supply and inelasticity of demand, thus passing export taxes on to consumers abroad (Brazilian coffee before World War II, Ghanaian cocoa and Pakistani jute to some degree in the 1950s, Chilean nitrates in the early part of this century), there is still a substantial risk.

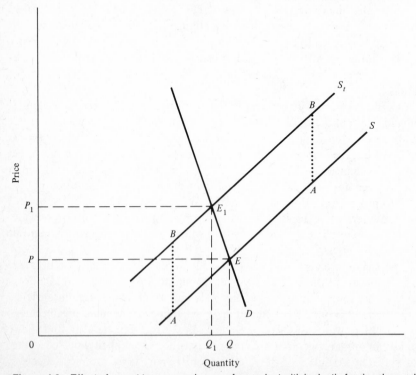

Figure 4.2   Effect of export tax on supply curve for product with inelastic foreign demand curve.

The most notorious example, from the point of view of the producer squandering a monopoly position, is that of Chilean nitrates. These rich deposits in the Atacama desert were, in the first decade of this century, essential both for fertilizer and in the manufacture of explosives. The latter attribute meant that the war machines of Europe and the United States were to a significant extent dependent on imports of the Chilean natural resource, with 65 percent of the nitrate market under its control just before the outbreak of World War I, and even more when neighboring Peru (and its bird guano islands) is included. But Chile's high export taxes encouraged technical research into synthetics, and at the Oppau plant of the German firm Badische Anilin und Sodafabrik a technical break-through led to the availability of synthetic nitrates drawn from nitrogen in the air. Chile was left with untold stocks of now much-depreciated nitrates, its share of the market down to only 25 percent in 1928 and even that retained only by severe price cutting. By better tax management all this might have been avoided. (The episode was perhaps even more upsetting to Allied war strategy. With German artillery firing more shells at the Battle of the Marne in September 1914 than in the whole of the Franco-Prussian War of 1870–1871, it was expected that the *Wehrmacht* would run out of ammunition by the start of 1915, since the naval blockade had cut off the supply of Chilean nitrates.[43] This was a case of the demand curve collapsing inward, even though supply was sharply restricted first by the tax and second by the blockade.)

Similarly, if less dramatic, high tax-induced prices for Ghanaian cocoa have stimulated the production of that product in the Ivory Coast, Cameroun, and South America; the production of coffee has spread in Africa, becoming an important crop in Kenya and Ethiopia, undoubtedly encouraged by the tax policies of Brazil and other Central and South American coffee producers. Pakistan's jute taxes encouraged a shift to other packaging materials. Steep increases in the Jamaican export tax on bauxite in the 1970s stimulated the production of that raw material for aluminum in Australia, Brazil, and Guinea. As a result, Jamaica lost much of its market share, its sales declining from 15 million tons a year in 1974 to somewhat less than 6 million in the mid 1980s. In technical terms, in these cases the price elasticity of demand facing a single country's export commodity was rising over time.

The greatest problem facing export taxation for most products is likely to be that any single LDC does not after all have monopoly power and therefore has far less than complete control over the world market price (that is, an individual nation faces a relatively elastic demand for its export). This being the case, for export crops or minerals the market price minus the tax represents the proceeds to the producer, whether that producer be peasant farmer or mining firm or plantation. Where this is so, the worry is that making exports artificially less attractive will cause producers to cut output sharply. The returns from marketing food domestically, or even subsistence production, will increase relatively; exports may decline, and *very* high taxation may even lead producers to withdraw effort from the money economy. Steep taxes on rubber output in colonial days had this effect in Indonesia, Sabah, and Sarawak, resulting in substantial cuts in production for export and increased effort in the subsistence sector.

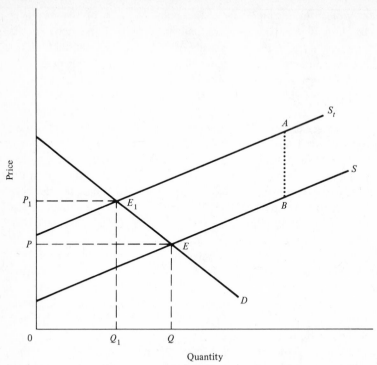

Figure 4.3 Effect of export tax on quantity produced for product with elastic supply curve.

Analytically, this involves an elastic supply curve, as in Figure 4.3. With supply elastic, a 10¢ tax per pound of rubber exports cuts production seriously. Before the tax price is OP and the quantity produced is OQ. A tax equal to AB raises the supply curve to S_t. For any given elasticity of demand, an elastic supply curve means a large cutback in output (here to OQ_1) and a smaller total revenue earned from the production of the commodity (here from $OPEQ$ to $OP_1E_1Q_1$).

On the other hand, there are some agricultural commodities very inelastic in supply, for example, the copra exports of the South Sea islands and West African palm oil. Many of the palm trees are long-lived, so that production from existing groves takes the form of gathering, but need not require planting for many years. Whatever the price, the fruit is there for the taking. A tax per unit of output on these crops is much safer and will not be expected to lower quantity significantly, as seen in Figure, 4.4, where OQ_1 is only slightly lower than OQ. Similarly, supply elasticity will be low for any crop where opportunities for substitution in production are limited.

With minerals there is the danger that costs of production including the tax will be forced too high for profitable operation. A first symptom is that low-grade ore will cease to be mined, as has happened from time to time with Bolivian tin.

A general problem with the taxation of commodity exports is that they do not ordinarily grow as fast as national product (manufactured exports often do grow as fast or faster than GNP). Too much dependence on taxing exports may

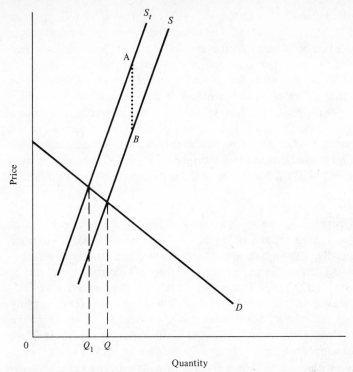

Figure 4.4   Effect of export tax on quantity produced for product with inelastic supply curve.

mean that the government captures only a declining share of national product. Further, such taxes make a country fiscally dependent on changeable foreign demand in the developed world, subject as it is to the recurring ups and downs of the business cycle.

In short, it seems reasonable to suppose that each individual export will require careful study to determine whether it should be taxed, with duties on some clearly causing more difficulties than duties on others. Lumping them together, though common, is unwise. But such levies are popular in any case, because they are easy to collect, hard to evade, and often fall on well-off, foreign-owned enterprises, such as plantations, mining firms, and oil companies. There is a darker side, however. The duties are often heaviest on the politically powerless and poor peasant producers of agricultural exports. Even though in theory the duties could be graduated to take account of the wealth and income of those taxed, this is seldom done.

Taxation of imports and exports need not be direct. Much the same effect can be achieved by a system of multiple exchange rates, with such rates used as a revenue-earning device equivalent to taxation. (More often, they are used as a substitute for devaluing the currency.) For example, take a mythical country Penuristan and its dual rate. All exporters who earn foreign exchange (say, dollars) must sell these to the government at a cheap price, say, $1 = 20 penuris. Meanwhile, the only legal way to obtain foreign exchange for imports, tourism, investment abroad, and the like is to buy the exchange from the government at an expensive rate, say, $1 = 30$ penuris. The Penuristan government thus obtains a revenue, akin to a tax, of 10 penuris on every dollar bought and sold. The real effect is a combined tax on exporters, who have to sell their dollar earnings at a penuri price that is overvalued, and a tax on importers, who have to buy their dollars at a price that undervalues the penuri. The economic effects are similar to direct taxation. Peru's long-overvalued sol caused a dramatic reduction in that country's exports of copper, lead, zinc, and silver, all of which boomed when the controls were removed. After a decline in the use of multiple exchange rates during the 1970s, there has been a recent resurgence. Twenty-five countries were using them at the end of 1984; Mexico at that time was operating five different rates.[44]

The Poll Tax   Historically, one of the most common and effective forms of taxation was the poll tax, sometimes called the head or capitation tax. It was once used almost universally, although its importance is now dramatically lower. It is levied on some basis such as "$5 per person per year." Of course, such a tax is extremely regressive, but it takes little paper work and administrative skill. A policeman does not even need to be literate to check whether a suspect is carrying his official stamped tax receipt. Some economists, such as P. T. Bauer of the London School of Economics, support the poll tax for another reason. It is not likely to reduce the supply of effort to the money sector or to agricultural exports, as may well happen with a tax on money income or a tax on exported commodities. The poll tax is in fact likely to cause an *increase* in the supply of effort to the money economy. Why? Because as a "lump-sum" tax it raises the marginal utility of income by reducing that income, but does not alter the reward for marginal effort. The result will ordinarily be more work to pay the tax, with leisure being sacrificed.

Unfortunately, in the hands of an authoritarian government an overly high poll tax may have the effect of lowering nutritional levels to the point where effort is reduced. Further, it has been used as a device to compel labor to enter the money economy, sometimes harshly as in the former Belgian Congo, Northern and Southern Rhodesia, and in South Africa. Among its side effects may be a disruption of local community life and the forcing of large-scale migration to the cities. These are reasons for the great decline in its use.[45]

The National Lottery   A last and much-used method of revenue collection in LDCs is the national lottery, whose ubiquitous ticket sellers throng the streets and marketplaces. Though they are popular with the government, which likes the revenue, and the public, who hope for a chance to get rich quick, the author has an especial antipathy for lotteries in poor countries. Cash is extracted from people far less able to pay than is true in rich countries. This might be harmless enough if the voluntary purchase reduced the consumption of no one but the ticket buyer, no matter how horrible the odds, but a large and dependent family may have no voice in the matter. A penny spent on the lottery by a poor man is all too conceivably a penny's less food for the children. True, people will gamble anyway, but government is uniquely able to lend legitimacy to the activity and advertise it widely. Such reasoning has, however, not been at all persuasive to LDC governments.

Taxation of Agriculture   Because of the difficulties in revenue collection, any alternative taxes with any promise of easy collection are sure to be welcomed. One such alternative, little emphasized in the rich countries, is taxing agriculture.

Since poverty and a dominance of agriculture are virtually synonymous, LDC governments early in the game turned their attention to agricultural taxation. This would have been true even if revenue collection were the only aim. Many countries have in addition attempted to transfer food output to the cities at below-market prices in (often ill-advised) attempts to promote the growth of manufacturing or to placate the politically more powerful and potentially troublesome urban populations.

There are many examples of agricultural taxation to finance growth outside of agriculture, either in cash (thus forcing the farmer to sell food or some crop for export in order to pay his tax) or in kind (collection of food that is taken to the cities). Probably the best-known example of deliberately depressing agriculture has been the Soviet Union, where explicit taxes plus forced deliveries at low compulsory purchase prices for farm produce have been the major tools. The taxation was accompanied by the mechanization of farming and large shifts of labor to the cities. Less harsh but equally effective in encouraging a shift were the high exactions on Japanese farmers after the Meiji Restoration of 1867–1868. It is said that farm productivity doubled in the 30 years before World War I, but that little increase in farmers' net real income occurred. Taxes on farming accounted for about 80 percent of total Japanese tax revenue in the period 1893 to 1897 and were still about 50 percent in 1913 to 1917.[46]

A familiar, more recent device for taxation in the agricultural sector is the agricultural (or produce) marketing board set up during and after World War II in countries that were formerly British colonies.[47] Various government organizations with similar titles serve the same function in the French sphere of influence and in parts of Latin America. Among the best-known of the marketing boards in the developing world are those of Ghana, Nigeria, Sierra Leone, Kenya, Uganda, Argentina, and the rather notorious one in Burma (and in the developed world those of Great Britain, New Zealand, the Canadian provinces, etc.).

These boards generally follow the same line of action. They are established with the seemingly sensible claim that they will buy the entire output of some particular export crop and pay a fixed price for it all season long. Such policy ensures against cheating by middlemen, as the marketing board price can always be received just by carrying produce to the nearest official buying station, of which there will be many. A second publicized advantage is the elimination of price variation during a season and the security provided thereby. There is none of the old uncertainty as to whether today's price will collapse tomorrow or be higher.

In almost every instance, however, these marketing boards became devices for heavy taxation. Their technique is simple. If cocoa is selling on the world market for $10,000 a ton, the Ghana cocoa marketing board might announce an official price of $8,000 a ton for the following year. It intends not to change that price even if the bottom drops out of the world market, and indeed the cash reserves of the various boards have been called upon to support above-market prices a fair number of times. (Boards in this circumstance have been known to stop buying, however, as recently happened in Kenya.) In normal circumstances the gap between the marketing board producer price and the world market price can be skimmed off and used for government development expenditure. Large sums have been acquired in this manner. (The export marketing boards must be distinguished from domestic food marketing boards, common in Africa, which by "selling cheap" act as a means for subsidizing consumers. Food boards that act in this way are a drain on public revenue rather than an addition to it.[48])

Political objections on the part of the peasant producers can be intense on the grounds that one of the poorer sectors of the economy is being singled out for heavy taxation. The objections can be forestalled by keeping all the revenues thus acquired in a reserve fund earmarked for "price stabilization." Then the cash can be used as interest-free or low-interest long-term loans for development projects or for subsidizing inputs (fertilizer, machinery), especially for the large farmers whose political protests might be effective. In Nigeria, for example, during the first decade of marketing board operations 36 percent of the accumulated stabilization reserve was distributed as development grants and 21 percent as development loans. In some countries the whole concept of a reserve was eventually lost, and taxation became the only function. The Ghana marketing board, for example, was not permitted to keep reserves after 1965.

Analytically, marketing boards can be viewed as in Figure 4.5, where S and

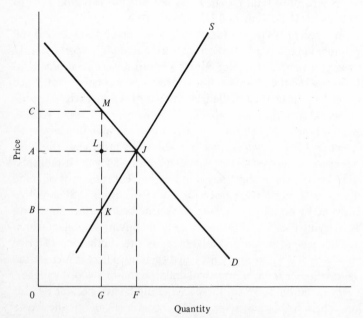

Figure 4.5 Analysis of agricultural marketing boards.

D are the supply and demand curves for a commodity in a free market, and proceeds to the producer at the equilibrium price are $OAJF$. If the marketing board sets a below-equilibrium price OB, quantity supplied will fall to OG. Producers earn $OBKG$; their loss is $BALK$ from taxation plus the loss because their output is reduced by GF. At first glance this appears to be $GLJF$, but the resources freed from not producing the quantity GF will be available for other, presumably less useful, purposes. In the diagram these alternative uses would yield producers $GKJF$, leaving a net loss of KLJ. The marketing board surplus is $BCMK$, of which $ACML$ came from supply reduction which raised the sale price of the commodity to OC, while $BALK$ is a transfer from producers.

The greater the elasticity of supply, the greater the shift by farmers to other products. The more elastic is demand the smaller the gain to the marketing board. Thus, the longer the period of marketing board operations (allowing time for farmers to substitute untaxed crops) and the less the importance of the covered crop on world markets (so that no price increase can be passed on to foreign consumers), the less effective the marketing board will be as an instrument of taxation.

Marketing boards certainly can mobilize financing for development purposes, but the adverse economic repercussions can be substantial. In Ghana, for example, implicit taxation via a marketing board reduced the real cocoa price by 44 percent between 1967–1968 and 1977–1978. The government had been taking 3 percent of sales revenue in 1947–1948, nearly 30 percent in 1953–1954, and 60 percent in 1978–1979. Across the borders in neighboring Ivory Coast and Togo, prices were much higher. There were three fully predictable effects: less work expended on cocoa, more on other crops, and extensive smuggling. Official marketing board exports fell from an average 430,000 metric tonnes per year in 1964 to 1966 to an average 202,000 tonnes in 1979 to 1981. During the same time period the Ivory Coast's cocoa exports rose from 84,000 to 298,000 tonnes per year. Rice and maize prices were not controlled by a marketing board. There was much shifting to these untaxed crops, which gave a net return about double that of cocoa. The estimate of cocoa smuggling in the late 1970s was a minimum of 10,000 tonnes; the actual amount may well have been about 45,000 tonnes. That amount would represent 15 percent of the value of Ghana's total exports of all products. The Ghanaian cocoa industry was thus left in an economic shambles, contributing to that once-fortunate country's political turmoil.[49]

Other marketing boards have also become highly politicized. A rice price unchanged for a decade by the Burma State Marketing Board was said to be instrumental in the downfall of a Burmese government. Of all the domestic measures to raise investment, the marketing boards are high on the list of those with unfavorable side effects.

Tax Reform   What can be said to summarize this section on taxation? In general what is needed is a system that will yield more as income grows, that is not too complex, that does not penalize saving, and that avoids massive distortions in production such as can happen in taxing agriculture and foreign trade. This is no doubt tantamount to saying that designing appropriate taxes for LDCs is a tough job! The author would recommend phasing in value-added taxes as soon as possible, eventually putting major emphasis on them, and perhaps exempting small firms and traders to reduce the administrative burden. Withholding could be introduced into the income tax system whenever feasible. In the long term it is crucially important to lower dependence on taxes directed at agriculture and international trade. But progress in reforming taxes is unlikely to be either easy or rapid.[50]

Cutting Current Spending

Are there items in the government budget that represent waste, extravagance, inefficient use of public funds? Undoubtedly, in many LDCs. Could such expenditure be reduced and the resources made available for investment purposes? Or could government investment that competes with and perhaps "crowds out" private investment be given over to the private sector? Conceivably, but with great difficulty because "wasteful extravagance" in an LDC is often the outcome of a political process wherein a government utilizes public resources to reward its loyal supporters, to "buy off" its potential opposition, and to purchase protection via the defense budget.

This politicization of economics is often highly visible, taking the form of (1) overstaffing of government and state-owned enterprises (parastatals), (2) subsidies that affect certain favored groups, (3) government projects selected for political effect rather than economic returns, and (4) surprisingly high spending on defense.

A well-managed development strategy will require substantial participation by government, but "participation" can translate into gross overstaffing in the government sector. Such overstaffing is rampant in many LDCs, a well-developed "spoils system" in otherwise less-developed lands, so to speak. In a study conducted 1982 the share of central government salaried jobs as a percentage of all salaried jobs was only 9 percent in the industrialized countries, but was 23 percent in the LDCs.[51] In some areas the figure was far higher: India 54 percent, Liberia 53 percent, Bénin 50 percent, Tanzania 46 percent. The *rate* of growth in LDC government employment in recent years (1976 to 1980) has often far exceeded the highest rates recorded in the developed countries: over 10 percent per year for Ecuador, Nigeria, Burundi, Mexico, and Zaire (15 percent), compared to 5 percent or less in Europe, Japan, and the United States (1 percent). In Brazil rampant overstaffing in state enterprises has been reported, with four times as many employees as necessary on the government railways and five times as many on government-operated shipping and in the Coffee Institute's warehousing.[52] The opportunity to use employment as a perquisite for supporters of a particular government has in many countries proved irresistible.

Subsidies for food, manufacturing, credit, seed, fertilizer, farm machinery, rural water supplies, electrification, and the like also have a strong political side to them. The subsidies can be substantial: bread priced at 1¢ per (small) loaf in Egypt, gasoline at 12¢ per gallon in Bolivia until August 1985. Politically well-organized urban workers benefit from the food subsidies; allied industrialists and merchants can be granted production subsidies and cheap credit; large and thus influential farmers can be made recipients of the subsidies in rural areas.

Another form of politicization of economics is the selection of government projects to reward loyal supporters. The authority to decide where to locate a project and who is to staff it gives politicians another instrument of political power. The presence in a country of many not very efficient projects underway, each with a large staff sporting the ruling party's colors on a sleeve, cap, or collar, becomes more understandable when viewed in terms of their political implications.

High defense budgets can be seen in the same way. A well-equipped military can reinforce the police in suppressing political opposition. Military adventures may provide a distraction from a government's problems and, in turn, make necessary defensive measures by neighbors. Modern arms may deliver prestige to the government of the day.

Whatever the reason, defense spending is surprisingly high (and rising) in many LDCs. It is growing faster (6 percent a year) than the incomes of the LDCs, and even more discouraging it is rising at 7.5 percent a year in the low-income countries and at 9 percent a year for "major weapons."[53] Having more than doubled in real terms during the past 25 years, it represents more than their governments spend on either health or education and almost as much as is spent on both combined: Table 4.4 shows the percentage of GNP devoted to defense and also defense as a percentage of all central government expenditure for selected

Table 4.4 DEFENSE SPENDING, 1983

	Percent of GNP	Percent of central government revenue
Canada	2.0	8.0
France	3.3	7.3
West Germany	2.9	9.3
United States	6.0	23.7
Burma (1982)	3.3	19.0
Israel	14.2	29.0
Morocco	4.6	14.6
North Yemen	15.9	36.7
Oman	27.9	51.3
Pakistan	6.2	34.8
Syria (1982)	14.3	37.7
Uganda	0.7	17.0 (34.5, 1981)
Uruguay	3.3	12.7
Zimbabwe	6.6	18.3

Total world armaments expenditures are presently running worldwide at over $900 billion per year, some 30 times more than all foreign aid and more than the total combined gross national product of the world's 34 poorest countries including China, India, and all of sub-Saharan Africa.

Source: Calculated from *WDR 1986*, pp. 222–223.

countries. On average in 1983, 19.5 percent of central government revenue in the low-income LDCs went for defense compared to only 14.3 percent in the developed countries. (The respective percentages of GNP were 3.2 and 4.3.)

Of course, Middle Eastern countries would say they have an excuse, and true, foreign aid pays for many of the weapons, but the table does give some idea of the potential for raising development expenditures if defense costs could be cut.[54]

The same logic applies to the other forms of government spending discussed above. Each, if cut, represents an opportunity to increase productive investment spending. Whether the opportunity will soon be seized is a difficult matter of politics and social psychology. It must be emphasized that the seeming irrationality of these types of spending is in the eye of the beholder. From the point of view of the ruling party, they are rational and perhaps even necessary if the government is to stay in office. The dilemma of a politicized economy looms ever more important as an obstacle to development, and the dilemma is not easily escaped.

This being said, it is necessary to caution the beginner in development economics that these criticisms can be overdone. In the developed countries the tide in the 1980s has been running strongly against government involvement in the economy, especially in the United States and Great Britain. This view has had a substantial influence on aid-giving institutions and on economists generally. But it must be remembered that in LDCs the infrastructure of transport, communications, and credit plus public goods such as education and health must to some significant degree involve government participation and investment. Any recommendation to cut bloated government spending, to reduce the crowding out of private investment, and to decrease the politicization of economics, presumably reflects a desire to increase the efficiency of an economy and further its development prospects. If a dedicated commitment to a free market ideology carries beyond this, so that desirable government investment in infrastructure is not undertaken and public goods are not provided in sufficient quantity and quality, then an economy will be less efficient, not more so. These choices are critically important, and the methods for making informed judgments are explored in Chapter 11.

Forced Saving: Inflation as a Tool of Development[55]

A government wishing to promote development has the alternative of turning to forced saving through inflation, whereby government spending is achieved by running an inflationary budget deficit financed by the creation of new money. There was once some enthusiasm for this tool as a growth strategy, as economists saw a difference between inflationary government spending that leads to no further flow of output and inflationary spending that raises the stock of capital goods and hence *does* lead to further output. Consider money creation to finance a budget deficit when that money is used to finance a war, or to pay the government's wage bill, or to construct public monuments or government buildings. In wartime the money supply will increase steadily just as the stock of consumer goods grows even smaller. Violent inflation can be the result. In the case of government payrolls or buildings at best there is no increase in the supply of consumer goods on the market; at worst there may be a decrease, when resources are diverted from the private sector. But economists long ago noted the *possibility* of engaging in deficit financing with a lessened inflationary impact by comparison with the examples of war or government payrolls and buildings just mentioned.

The diminished inflationary impact was thought to be most likely when deficit spending is used for financing capital formation that directly increases productive capacity. Recall that $S = I + (M - X)$. Say government, by running an inflationary budget deficit at a time of full employment, succeeds in investing more. If in addition no capital inflows occur, then the higher government spending diverts output from private consumption to the government by simply bidding away goods from the private sector, which in real terms must consume less and thus endures "forced saving."

This can be looked at in monetary terms as well. If government printing of money causes inflation, then the value of the already existing money stock held as transactions balances will decline. To restore the value of the money stock, holders will have to reduce their consumption to acquire the larger balances—"forced saving" in other words. A final possibility is that government tax revenue will rise more than proportionately because the tax system is progressive. The rise in government tax collection is the forced saving. (Usually it is the other way round. Government tax collection is unable to keep pace with the inflation, so that even more deficit spending will have to be engaged in than otherwise.)

One might think that such forced saving would be "purely" inflationary. But there is a possibility that the inflation so generated could be a limited one. What if the government budget deficit is used to finance productive capital formation? If the resulting capital successfully pours forth a stream of output, and this new output is then sold on domestic markets, the effect is to increase supply and restrain the rate of inflationary price increases. Thus in the long run inflation can tend to be "self-destructive."

How self-destructive it is depends on how quickly the new output is forthcoming and how large it is. The self-destruction of inflation is furthered if the profits from the new output are saved by the government, should production be under government auspices, or taxed away by government, should the profits be earned by private enterprise. If, however, the tax system depends heavily on excise and sales taxes, and if price controls are used against the inflation, then taxes may *fall* as a percent of GNP and this element of self-destruction will be lost. A serious obstacle to intelligent use of the self-destructive aspect is that the information needed to determine exactly the degree of permissible stimulus is difficult to ascertain. Worse, government willpower to avoid further non–self-destructive inflation may be lacking.

There might be other situations, usually more debatable, when a favorable case might be made for inflation. In countries where prices have been relatively stable (and there *are* still some), there may be significant "money illusion" for labor, landlords, and capitalists. All may decide to work harder (or allow the factors they own to work more intensely) in order to obtain a higher money income, even if real income does not increase. Because goods prices may rise

faster than costs, inflation could also redistribute income to profit-earning entrepreneurs, thus possibly promoting the prospects for development as the entrepreneurs increase their saving and investment. Simultaneously, inflation may
raise the rate of return on investment relative to general interest rates. This would
be true whenever the inflation premium in interest rates underestimates the degree
of actual price increases. Investment is thus stimulated. Unfortunately, all of these
possibilities run up against counter-arguments: Inflation may generate sufficient
social unrest so as to hinder development; the inflationary expectations of entrepreneurs may rapidly become entrenched, so that they switch away from long-
term investment and move toward the search for hedges and speculation. (Behavior changes in the face of persistent inflation will be discussed presently.)

A last possibility for deficit financing without *apparent* inflation is to institute a so-called disequilibrium system. Such a system involves the use of various
tools to suppress the inflation: price fixing, rationing, licensing of investment,
exchange control, government propaganda, and dozens of other measures. The
widespread use of these tools in wartime has led to an alternative name, the "war
finance approach." In essence this approach worked reasonably well in most
major countries during World War II. It certainly *can* work, when there is
sufficient popular enthusiasm for some cause so that the public accepts the
inflation-suppressing medicine.

More commonly, however, insoluble problems erupt. Lack of public support leads to the growth of large black markets, controllable only with an extensive police-state apparatus. LDCs employing a disequilibrium system often lack
the able and honest administrators needed to make the mechanism work. In fact,
of the countries that *could* use a disequilibrium system, it would appear that
LDCs as a group would be least able to do so for this reason. Finally, economic
theory tells us convincingly that the supporting price controls, rationing, and
other tools had better be very short-term in nature or else serious economic
distortions will arise as the price system fails to give adequate signals.

Advocates of inflation as a tool of development must consider a number of
detrimental consequences. Against any possible advantages, there will be the
likelihood of the following economic distortions, all of which could occur at the
same time and each potentially serious.

1. The impact on saving and investment may be adverse. Productive saving
will be reduced if people put their income into assets considered hedges. The belief
that land, buildings, gold, silver, jewelry, or stocks of goods will advance in value
with the inflation will cut into one source of productive investment.

2. Groups with political or economic power will attempt to defend themselves. Those with political influence push for government subsidies, supplements,
and price floors. Those with economic power use the strike. Groups with this sort
of leverage may well keep up with the inflation; their success may even fuel it.
In the LDCs this leaves only a few groups within society where consumption can
be squeezed by the inflation. Professional people, government employees, unor-
ganized industrial workers, and landless laborers are the most vulnerable, and it
is difficult to justify treading on these classes, some of which are small and
important for development and one of which (landless laborers) is very large and
very poor.

3. Inflation may *not* make investment more lucrative relative to interest rates if such rates rise fully to take account of the inflationary expectations of bondholders and other lenders.

4. Inflation may have serious effects on income distribution. It may frighten people who have just entered or are on the margin of the cash economy and drive them back to subsistence production due to their growing distrust of money. Large firms with access to government supported low-interest loans prosper in comparison with small firms.

5. There is a justified fear that inflation may be less easy to control in the LDCs for built-in fiscal reasons. The demand for modern, up-to-date social welfare programs in education, social security, health care, and elsewhere, may lead a country to inflationary spending. Public provision of food and transport may swell budgets, and subsidies in these sectors may go far beyond the ability of the public to pay for them in prices, rates, fares, and fees. Almost all LDCs with high rates of inflation have large public-sector deficits as a percent of their GNP. Commonly, public enterprises are run at a loss and suffer from swollen employment figures because of overhiring and the difficulty of firing or laying off employees. Meanwhile, tax yields may not rise in proportion to the inflation if income and corporate taxes are unimportant or are not progressive. With tax revenues not keeping pace, inflation is further fueled. Populist governments may raise wages and other spending without a tax increase, financing their programs by borrowing from a pliable central bank, which is seldom independent of the executive branch in the LDCs. The resulting inflation is often countered by freezing the prices of basic goods, with resulting shortages and inefficiencies.

6. If inflation is faster than in a country's trading partners, imported goods become relatively cheaper, while exports become more expensive. There is a rise in the value of the former, a fall in the latter. As a result, the foreign exchange rate will depreciate (if the rate is floating) or the balance of trade will move adversely (if the rate is fixed). Currency depreciation, by boosting the price of imports, feeds back on the rate of inflation when domestic substitutes are unavailable or high in price. Governments may impose protection to halt the slide of the foreign exchange rate (under floating rates) or the increasing balance of trade deficit (under fixed rates).

7. Foreign capital is repelled, while domestic savers attempt to invest abroad. The balance of payments is weakened.

The knowledge that inflation brings economic penalties has a further disturbing aspect. The economic structure of LDCs may be especially conducive to the transmission of the disease. Bottlenecks caused by shortages of skilled labor and certain indispensable types of capital equipment may always be close to the surface. Such bottlenecks arise long before full employment is reached in any LDC attempting to utilize deficit financing. In addition, resource immobility, itself a symptom of underdevelopment, means that transfers of resources into bottleneck areas are slow even at best. Lack of information and good economic data, high risk, and long-established traditional patterns of production, all contribute to the immobility. These factors lead to the conclusion that the basic structure of many LDCs may be more conducive to inflation than the more flexible structure of the developed countries.

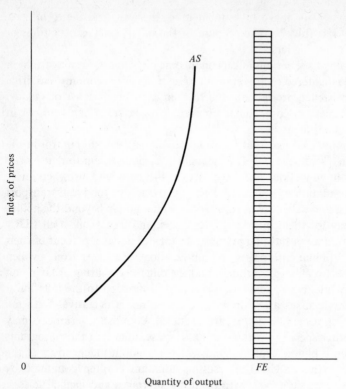

Figure 4.6   Susceptibility of LDCs to structural inflation.

This "structuralist" view of inflation was pioneered in South American, and particularly Chilean, academic circles. It suggests that the pure inflationary effect of money supply increases will, all things equal, set in *earlier* in an LDC because of the structural and institutional blockages. This conclusion is presented diagrammatically in Figure 4.6; note how aggregate supply in LDCs may turn nearly vertical at a point considerably below the output level that would bring full employment. When structural considerations are present, inflation might then be generated even without serious budget deficits and monetary overheating; "supply-side" reforms to lend greater flexibility to the economy would clearly be called for.

In reaction to what it saw as structural problems difficult to solve with conventional tools, Brazil in the mid 1960s pioneered *indexing,* a system wherein the effects of inflation are assimilated without attacking the causes. With Brazilian inflation running at over 90 percent in 1964, economists there, led by the influential planning minister Roberto Campos, felt that standard monetary and fiscal solutions would reduce growth too drastically. Their solution was to incorporate escalator clauses (known in the United States as COLA or cost of living adjustments) into almost all phases of economic activity. From small beginnings, by 1967 these clauses covered cost of living adjustments for wages, interest rates on bank deposits and bonds, taxes, and rents. The principle was later extended to the adjustment of asset values. In the full flower of indexing corporate stocks and bonds, government bonds and securities, savings accounts, and even legal judgments were written up according to the latest price index, the increases in value not subject to taxation. Brazilians argued that they could live comfortably with a much higher degree of inflation than could, say, the United States, where much less is indexed. There was some evidence on their side. The Brazilian average real growth rate in the years 1970 to 1977, 9.8 percent a year, ranked with a few other world leaders, despite the country's annual average inflation of 29 percent during this period.

But today the enthusiasm for indexing in Brazil and the numerous other countries that adopted some version of the scheme is much diminished.[56] Outside supply shocks, such as the OPEC oil crisis, in an unindexed country have only a temporary inflationary impact before their effect dies away. Indeed, even the structuralist argument as a whole explains only the original cause of inflation and not why it would spiral upward. Where indexing is widespread, however, a price rise triggers a wage rise and then another price rise in a vicious circle. The resulting rapid inflation is seen to carry costs even if adverse effects on income distribution do not occur (and the Brazilian experience gives reason to believe that the indexing has been somewhat more effective for holders of capital than for wage earners). One major cost appears to be the rapid obsolescence of knowledge concerning prices. In fully indexed Israel, for example, inflation in mid 1985 was running at around 400 percent a year; in equally indexed Argentina inflation in the year to May 1985 was 1,010 percent. This discourages people from shopping around; with such rapid change consumers lose track of how prices compare at different stores. In a recent survey, Israelis asked to state a price for the same type and brand of shoes gave answers varying by as much as 20 times. In Argentina supermarket managers in one chain were getting new price lists from headquarters on average once every 1.3 days.[57] Understandably, the term "menu cost" is used to describe this situation of outdated information. There are also so-called shoe-leather costs, the expenditure of time and money to move out of cash balances and low interest deposits into higher yields. With real rates of return of, say, 3 or 4 percent completely submerged by the wave of inflation, people search for assets where indexing works more quickly and avoid investing in physical capital where the return is in the future. A vivid example of shoe-leather costs in countries suffering from heavy inflation is the rush to sell the local currency for dollars or other foreign exchange as soon as any balances are obtained.[58]

Indexing is now seen too often to mean abandonment of the fight against inflation. In a reaction against this psychological surrender numerous governments have pulled back from the idea. In the developed countries Iceland in 1983 suspended its almost total index system as a major contributor to inflation, and Belgium, Finland, and Italy have retreated as well. Even in Brazil, the pioneer, the government lost its enthusiasm. It attempted, unsuccessfully for several years because of strong resistance from organized labor and firms desirous of protecting their flow of cheap credit, to reduce the degree of indexation. At long last in early 1986 wages were strictly controlled and prices and rents were frozen as part of the "Cruzado Plan" (see below). In effect, indexing had been abandoned.

**Table 4.5   ANNUAL AVERAGE RATE OF INFLATION
AND GROWTH, 1960–1981**

	Inflation (Percent)	Growth (Percent)
High inflation, high growth		
Saudi Arabia	19.2 (1968–81)	7.8
South Korea	18.3	6.9
Brazil	41.1 (1963–81)	5.1
Yugoslavia	16.0	5.0
Indonesia	31.1 (1966–81)	4.1
Turkey	20.0	3.5
High inflation, low growth		
Ghana	21.3	−1.1
Uganda	24.8 (1967–78)	−0.6
Zaire	28.5	−0.1
Peru	21.7	1.0
Uruguay	52.5 (1964–81)	1.6
Bolivia	13.1	1.9
Low inflation, high growth		
Singapore	3.6	7.4
Lesotho	10.3 (1971–81)	7.0
Tunisia	5.6	4.8
Thailand	5.8	4.6
Malaysia	5.9 (1970–81)	4.3
Low inflation, low growth		
Chad	6.0	−2.2
Zambia	6.1	0.0
Guinea	3.1	0.2
Ethiopia	3.3	1.4
India	7.6	1.4

Inflation is measured by average annual rates of change in the GDP deflator; growth is real GNP per capita. When the dates for inflation begin after 1960 or end before 1981, it is because the data for the entire period are not available in the *International Financial Statistics Yearbook.* The inflation figures for Chad and Guinea are approximate; their GDP deflators do not appear in the *Yearbook* and were obtained by averaging two series in the *WDR.*

Source: Calculated by the author from IMF, *International Financial Statistics Yearbook, 1985,* and *WDR 1983* pp. 148–149.

When we turn to the actual statistics of inflation in the LDCs, the evidence of its pros and cons is mixed. Inflation as a disease is somewhat more prevalent in the less-developed world than in the developed countries, with a median rate of a little over 12% from 1970 to 1981 in the former compared to a little under 10 percent in the latter. (Using median instead of mean prevents the hyperinflations in several countries from utterly skewing the results. The mean for the LDCs in 1985 was 39.3 percent.[59] But there is no persuasive evidence that slightly higher rates of inflation, or even rather rapid ones, do anything significant to discourage moderate growth in real terms. There are examples of both high inflation accompanied by high growth and high inflation accompanied by low growth in the period 1960 to 1981; similarly, one can find examples of both low inflation and high growth and low inflation and low growth, as seen in Table 4.5.

A statistical study of data from 77 countries over intervals of one to three decades since World War II concluded that "there is no significant relation between the average rate of inflation and the average growth rate of real GNP."[60] Thus one cannot predict on the basis of inflation alone, even when it is moderately high, as to whether development prospects are hindered or improved. One *can*, however, state flatly that hyperinflations *are* inimical to growth. There have not been too many of these, but even though the sample is small it does appear to convey a lesson (Table 4.6).

The serious hyperinflations of 1984 and 1985 in Israel, Argentina, and especially Bolivia, further confirmed that growth is very difficult under these conditions. Bolivia's was by far the world's worst in 1984, 2,700 percent, up from 329 percent in 1982. Nicely printed banknotes were the country's third largest import, after wheat and mining equipment. (They soon became torn and tattered since coins have disappeared, their value having vanished, and banknotes serve as the fractional currency. These wear out even faster than they would otherwise because of the tendency for the velocity of circulation to increase during a hyperinflation.) In February 1985 the most common banknote of 1,000 would buy one bag of tea; 68 pounds of the notes were needed to buy a television set, but the set and the tea would soon be yet more expensive, because in early 1985 inflation was running at an annual rate of about 12,000 percent, in some months reaching 50,000 percent. Real growth was negative, − 5.8 percent annually 1980 to 1984.[61]

Let us spend a moment considering what might be done if a country does find itself in a growth-inhibiting hyperinflation and attempts to bring it to an end with a stabilization program. What policy recommendations might be made?[62] A typical first step will be to withdraw the old currency and replace it with a new one that lops off a certain percent of the nominal value. Argentina in June 1985 issued a new currency, the austral, 1 of which equalled 1,000 of the old pesos.

Table 4.6   ANNUAL AVERAGE RATE OF INFLATION AND GROWTH IN COUNTRIES SUBJECT TO HYPERINFLATION

	Inflation (Percent)	Growth (Percent)
Bolivia (1945–1959)	1,257	−0.8
Argentina (1977–1983)	167.0	−0.7
Chile (1945–1959)	340	0.6
Chile (1960–1981)	140.6 (1973–81)	0.7
Brazil (1979–1983)	107.7	0.8
Paraguay (1945–1959)	381	0.9

Source: IMF, *International Financial Statistics* and *WDR*, various issues

The convenient 1,000 : 1 ratio seems to have set a pattern: Israel's new shekel, introduced in the summer of 1985, is worth 1,000 old shekels; Brazil in early 1986 opened its campaign against inflation of over 200 percent by replacing 1,000 cruzeiros with 1 cruzado.

A new currency will, however, be mere window dressing unless the rate of growth of the money supply is drastically reduced. This reduction will attack the main underlying cause of the hyperinflation, there being a rather strong correlation between money supply growth and rates of change in prices.[63] The public-sector deficit, doubtlessly huge and financed by money creation, will be sharply cut at the same time, perhaps by freezing wages and requiring the parastatals to balance their budgets. The subsidies will be cut back. (Bolivia's 12¢ gas was raised 10-fold in August 1985.)[64] Further to control price increases, tariffs will be reduced (generally to 10 percent in Bolivia) and quotas enlarged, providing more competition in the private sector. Sharp reductions in export taxation will have the same effect. Many restrictions on financial flows will be relaxed; the exchange rate may be floated. (In Bolivia in August 1985 the peso fell from 75,000 to 1.5 million to the dollar because of such relaxation and floating.) There may well be a break in the very efficient system of indexing, as in Argentina's wage freeze, Brazil's "Cruzado Plan" wage controls, and Israel's 1985 July/September austerity package. A temporary price freeze is likely to accompany these steps, as in Argentina starting June 1985, Israel from November 1984 and renewed in July 1985, and Brazil beginning in early 1986.

Such stabilization programs even if well designed are likely to carry a significant adverse side effect.[65] They may cause a recession, perhaps a sharp one with a steep decline in output and rise in unemployment, before the stabilizing is finally accomplished. The reason for this is that during the hyperinflation investment is disrupted and inefficiencies proliferate; it takes time as well as proper policy to turn this around. Chile, for example, defeated an inflation running at 500 percent in 1975 (down to 9 percent in 1981), but part of the cost of this victory was a crash that hit bottom in 1982 with an unemployment rate for a time as high as 20 percent and a temporary decline in output that was also about 20 percent.[66] (To a lesser degree, the United States encountered the same costs when in 1980 to 1983 it employed tight money to control its inflation.) Chile's "Chicago Boys," so named for their monetarist views imbibed in the University of Chicago economics department, showed a zealot's adherence to free markets, tight money (the money supply was reduced 5 percent between 1980 and 1981), and low tariffs (lowered from an average 100 percent to 10 percent). They managed a valuable repeal of many of the old restrictive union rules, instituted marginal cost pricing in energy and several other parastatals, scaled back the overextended social security system, encouraged saving with something like an expenditure tax, and lifted controls on many private firms (though this included banks, with the result that tight money took longer to accomplish). They did not, however, free the exchange rate, a major failure because the overvalued peso, worth perhaps 45 percent more than it would have been on a free market, discouraged exports and was heavily deflationary just as the world entered the recession of the early 1980s. A large devaluation in 1982 was not nearly enough to stem the deflation, and growth did not resume until 1984. There is still much catching up to do.

Even in the long run, there is no guarantee that a stabilization program will succeed, since such programs run the great risk of lacking credibility.[67] Very commonly, stabilization is implemented too little and too late, with the inflationary fires not adequately damped at the point where the government loses its will to continue the battle.[68] Next time around control measures will be viewed even more skeptically than before. All in all, the pain of hyperinflation and the difficulties of stabilizing an economy in its grip have made this a disease to be dreaded. The risk that governments attempting to use moderate inflation as a tool of growth will be unwilling or unable to keep this genie under control has much diminished any enthusiasm still felt for it.

NOTES

1. W. Arthur Lewis, *The Theory of Economic Growth,* London, 1955 chap. 5, pp. 201–303.
2. In their first major military victory of modern history, in 1954, it was this humble item of capital equipment that carried the parts of 105 mm howitzers over the mountains to secretly prepared positions from which they pulverized the great French base at Dien Bien Phu. Years later, they were the workhorse, so to speak, of the transport system on the Ho Chi Minh Trail during the Vietnam War.
3. Andrew M. Kamarck, *Economics and the Real World,* Philadelphia, 1983, p. 113. The chapter in which the quotation is contained, " 'Capital' and 'Investment' in LDCs," pp. 106–115, makes numerous valuable points.
4. See E. F. Denison, *The Sources of Economic Growth in the United States and the Alternatives Before Us,* New York, 1962; *Accounting for United States Economic Growth, 1929–1969,* Washington, D.C., 1974; and *Trends in American Economic Growth, 1929–1982,* Washington, D.C., 1985. Everett Hagen's texts influenced me in choosing to use the Denison figures.
5. E. F. Denison, *Why Growth Rates Differ,* Washington, D.C., 1967.
6. See Amartya K. Sen, "Development: Which Way Now?" *The Economic Journal* 93 (December 1983): 750–751.
7. E. Wayne Nafziger summarizes the studies in his *The Economics of Developing Countries,* Belmont, Calif., 1984, Table 12–1, pp. 277–278. See especially Sherman Robinson, "Sources of Growth in Less Developed Countries: A Cross Section Study," *Quarterly Journal of Economics* 85 (August 1971): 391–408.
8. See World Bank, *New Publications,* Spring 1985, p. 5. The study is Shahid Yusuf and Kyle Peters, *Capital Accumulation and Economic Growth: The Korean Paradigm,* Working Paper No. 712, 1985.
9. This method of approach follows Lewis, *Theory of Economic Growth,* pp. 209–213, and see Everett E. Hagen, *The Economics of Development,* Homewood Ill. 1975 rev. ed., p. 420.
10. For a study of the topic, see Peter Lloyd, *Slums of Hope: Shanty Towns of the Third World,* New York, 1979. Large-scale public housing has been a solution only in a few cases such as Singapore and Hong Kong, where relatively high incomes, good adminis-

trative skills, and social acceptability are the rule. Otherwise, public housing on a national scale has simply been too expensive for most LDCs to manage. See *WDR 1979,* p. 83.

11. Entitled, "Blackout, Blackout, Go Away" in the issue of June 4, 1984.

12. *The Economist,* January 12, 1985, p. 13.

13. There is much scope for capital saving in these public services. Standpipes cost only ⅛ as much as house connections to piped water; water-borne sewage systems are five to eight times more expensive than well-maintained community pit latrines. See *WDR 1979,* p. 82. The percentages in the text are from UNESCO's *New Book of World Rankings.*

14. *IMF Survey* 13, no. 21 (November 12, 1984): 340.

15. *Ibid.*

16. *Christian Science Monitor,* October 1, 1982.

17. See W. Arthur Lewis in Gerald M. Meier, *Leading Issues in Economic Development,* 3rd ed., Oxford, 1976, p. 825.

18. This section, and others elsewhere in the book showing the algebra of capital financing, draw on Eprime Eshag, *Fiscal and Monetary Policies and Problems in Developing Countries,* Cambridge, 1983, especially chaps. 3 and 4.

19. I found Hagen, *Economics of Development,* revised ed., chap. 13, helpful. The figures in the paragraph below are from *WDR 1986,* pp. 188–189.

20. Subrata Ghatak, *Development Economics,* London, 1978, p. 77, reporting work by Jeffrey Williamson.

21. V. V. Bhatt, "Improving the Financial Structure in Developing Countries," *Finance and Development* 23, no. 2 (1986): 20.

22. *Ibid.*

23. For a discussion (and a favorable view of the profit-sharing aspect noted below) see Moshin S. Khan, "Islamic Interest-Free Banking: A Theoretical Analysis," *IMF Staff Papers* 33, no. 1 (1986): 1–27. A longer review is Ziauddin Ahmad, Munawar Iqbal, and M. Fahin Khan, eds., *Money and Banking in Islam,* Islamabad, 1983.

24. See "Foreign Portfolio Investment for Development: An IFC Initiative," *Finance and Development* 23, no. 2 (1986): 23, and *South,* no. 66 April (1986): 87. Leading candidates for the first round of new purchases are the stock markets of Argentina, Brazil, Chile, India, Indonesia, Korea, Malaysia, Mexico, and Thailand. Other countries under consideration are Jordan, Nepal, and Turkey. The EMGF will not put more than 20 percent of its assets into any one country or over 5 percent in any one company.

25. For real interest rates, see also Anthony Lanyi and Rüsdü Saracoglu, "The Importance of Interest Rates in Developing Economies," *Finance and Development* 20, no. 2 (1983): 21. For the connection between low real interest rates and low saving, see M. J. Fry, "Savings, Investment, Growth, and the Cost of Financial Repression," *World Development* 8, no. 4 (1980): 317–327; and IMF, *World Economic Outlook, 1985,* p. 184. The contention that higher interest rates for savers will lead to higher levels of saving and investment is sometimes called the McKinnon-Shaw hypothesis after its formulators, Ronald McKinnon and Edward Shaw. Among their seminal works are McKinnon, *Money and Capital in Economic Development,* Washington, D.C., 1973, and Shaw, *Financial Deepening in Economic Development,* New York, 1973. For a generally sympathetic view of their work, see Lazaros E. Molho, "Interest Rates, Saving, and Investment in Developing Countries: A Re-examination of the McKinnon-Shaw Hypothesis," *IMF Staff Papers* 33, no. 1 (1986): 90–116.

26. Mario I. Blejer and Adrienne Cheasty, "Using Fiscal Measures to Stimulate Savings in Developing Countries," *Finance and Development* 23, no. 2 (1986): 19.

27. Bhatt, "Improving the Financial Structure," p. 20; Blejer and Cheasty, "Using Fiscal Measures," p. 19.

28. See Joslin Landell-Mills, "The Role of Development Finance Corporations," *Finance and Development* 22, no. 1 (1985): 43–45.

29. For thorough treatments, see Stephen R. Lewis, Jr., *Taxation for Development,* Oxford, 1984; and Richard Goode, *Government Finance in Developing Countries,* Washington, D.C., 1984. I also utilized Michael P. Todaro, *Economic Development in the Third World,* 2nd ed., New York, 1981, chap. 16; and Nafziger, *Economics of Developing Countries,* pp. 357–363.

30. See Keith Marsden, *Links Between Taxes and Growth: Some Empirical Evidence,* World Bank Staff Working Paper No. 605, 1983.

31. In Mexico, the average percent of income paid in tax by highest income taxpayers was 14.9; for the lowest it was 40.2. See A. J. Mann, "The Mexican Tax Burden by Family Income Class," *Public Finance Quarterly* 10, no. 3 (1982): 305–331.

32. Figures calculated by the author from *WDR 1986,* pp. 224–225. The other figures for tax collections later in the chapter are from the same source. See also Alan A. Tait, Wilfrid L. M. Grätz, and Barry J. Eichengreen, "International Comparisons of Taxation for Selected Developing Countries, 1972–76," *IMF Staff Papers* 26 (March 1979): 130.

33. See Michael Roemer and Joseph J. Stern, *Cases in Economic Development: Projects, Policies, and Strategies,* London, 1981, p. 218, citing work of R. J. Chelliah.

34. Perhaps the realization has come after a glance at India's tax system, which until 1985 was a good example. Business people earning 8 percent on assets of 250,000 rupees (= $20,000), if they paid the income tax, wealth tax, and "compulsory deposit," would have paid almost the whole of the $20,000 in tax. Higher returns to someone of greater wealth soon resulted in a negative return on investment. The average corporate tax rate in India was 60 percent. There was thus in that country much concealing of income, use of tax shelters, and bribery; much hidden wealth called "black money"; much cash for hoarding, property speculation, moneylending, smuggling, the financing of crime—but little for investment, with corporate saving abysmally low at around $400 million. The government then felt it must provide large loans to businesses, with long delays and extraordinary red tape. See "India's Private Sector: Red Tape, Black Money, White Hope," *The Economist,* October 11, 1980, pp. 79–80. Many of these problems still exist, but in March 1985 Rajiv Gandhi slashed tax rates, with apparently very favorable effects within a matter of months. *The Economist,* March 8, 1986, p. 37, reported that the collections from India's income tax had risen by 40 percent in fiscal 1985.

35. There is a readable review of the expenditure tax in Robert Tannewald, "Should We Adopt an Expenditure Tax?" *New England Economic Review,* March/April 1984, pp. 29–39. The comment on Kaldor and the vicissitudes in India and Sri Lanka are from Ghatak, *Development Economics,* p. 91.

36. Drawing on the work of Richard Goode and Walter Heller reprinted in Gerald M. Meier, *Leading Issues in Development Economics,* 1st ed., New York, 1964, pp. 115–127.

37. Gunnar Myrdal, "Need for Reforms in Underdeveloped Countries," in Sven Grassman and Erik Lundberg, eds., *The World Economic Order: Past and Prospects,* New York, 1981, p. 521.

38. Compare Hagen, *Economics of Development,* rev. ed., p. 357.

39. See the analysis in Lewis, *Taxation for Development,* chap. 7; and Ghatak, *Development Economics,* pp. 92–93.

40. Ghatak, *Development Economics,* pp. 92–93.
41. Malcolm Gillis, "Micro and Macroeconomics of Tax Reform: Indonesia," *Journal of Development Economics* 19, no. 3 (1986): 241.
42. See Reginald H. Green in Meier, *Leading Issues,* 3rd ed., pp. 836, 840.
43. For details, see Gerd Hardach, *The First World War 1914–1918,* Berkeley, Calif., 1977, pp. 31, 59, 266, 268–271.
44. *IMF Survey,* June 24, 1985, p. 197; José Saul Lizondo, "Unifying Multiple Exchange Rates," *Finance and Development* 22, no. 4 (1985): 23–24.
45. The much more sophisticated "lump sum" taxes adjusted for income and/or wealth, often supported by economists as promoting both effort and equity, have had virtually no trial in the LDCs (nor in the developed countries for that matter). These lump sum taxes would bring some difficulties of their own if they were utilized. For an understandable explanation, see Edmund S. Phelps, *Political Economy,* New York, 1985, pp. 316–323, 340.
46. Ghatak, *Development Economics,* p. 98, citing B. F. Johnston and J. Mellor.
47. This section draws heavily on Douglas Rimmer's analysis of marketing boards in "The Economic Legacy of Colonialism in British Tropical Africa," paper presented at a UNESCO conference, Lake Naivasha, Kenya, June 1981 (which contains the diagram used in the text), and in his *Economies of West Africa,* New York, 1984, pp. 164–173. The boards are surveyed in Kwame Arhin, Paul Hesp, and Laurens van der Laan, eds., *Marketing Boards in Tropical Africa,* London, 1985. Another good treatment of the boards (and of export taxation as well) is George S. Tolley et al., *Agricultural Price Policies and the Developing Countries,* Baltimore, 1982.
48. The food boards in Africa have been much criticized for their sometimes extraordinary inefficiencies. In some countries they "buy dear" to subsidize farm output in addition to "selling cheap," thus increasing their dependence on public tax revenues. See Arhin, Hesp, and van der Laan, *Marketing Boards in Tropical Africa,* and William O. Jones, "Economic Tasks for Food Marketing Boards in Tropical Africa," *Food Research Institute Studies* 19, no. 2 (1984): 113–138.
49. See especially *WDR 1983,* p. 77. Some reform finally came in the 1983–1984 crop year; the fixed cocoa price was raised from 12,000 cedis ($4,560) to 30,000 cedis ($11,400), but this did no more than offset the real decline since about 1975. See "Ghana Undertakes Major Adjustment Program . . . , " *IMF Survey,* November 12, 1984, p. 339; and David K. Willis, "Prescription for Change," *Christian Science Monitor,* November 29, 1984, p. 24.
50. See Gillis, "Micro and Macroeconomics of Tax Reform," pp. 221–254, for a review of Indonesia's new and sensible-sounding policies.
51. The figures here and below are from Peter S. Heller and Alan A. Tait, "Government Employment and Pay: Some International Comparisons," IMF, quoted in *WDR 1983,* p. 102. A comprehensive account of parastatals is Leroy P. Jones, *Public Enterprise in Less Developed Countries,* Cambridge, 1982.
52. Benjamin Higgins and Jean Downing Higgins, *Economic Development of a Small Planet,* New York, 1979, p. 241; *Wall Street Journal,* December 5, 1985.
53. See Joan Robinson, *Aspects of Development and Underdevelopment,* Cambridge, 1979, p. 124, with updating from Lester R. Brown, "Redefining National Security," *Challenge* 29, no. 3 (1986): 25–32; *WDR,* especially *1984,* p. 150; Olaf Palme et al., "Military Spending: the Economic and Social Consequences," *Challenge* 25, no. 4 (1982): 4–21; and Inga Thorsson, "The Arms Race and Development: A Competitive Relationship," in Charles Wilber, ed., *The Political Economy of Development and Underdevelopment,* 3rd ed., New York, 1984, pp. 500–501. There is a survey article

by Mary Kaldor, "The Military in Development," in Paul Streeten and Richard Jolly, eds., *Recent Issues in World Development,* Oxford, 1981, pp. 241–264.

54. That cuts can occur and can be significant is shown by the steady long-term reduction of defense spending in China, down by nearly half as a percent of GNP since 1972, and the even greater decline in Argentina between 1980 and 1984. See Brown, "Redefining National Security," pp. 30–31. Two articles concluding that a higher proportion of defense spending is correlated with lower economic growth are David Lim, "Another Look at Growth and Defense in Less Developed Countries," *Economic Development and Cultural Change* 31, no. 2 (1983): 377–384; and Saadet Deger and Somnath Sen, "Military Expenditure, Spin-Off, and Economic Development," *Journal of Development Economics* 13, no. 1 (1983): 67–83. An earlier contrary view can be found in Emile Benoit, *Defense and Economic Growth in Developing Countries,* Lexington, Mass., 1973.

55. This section draws on material in Hagen, *Economics of Development,* 1st ed. and rev. ed., chapter 14; Benjamin Higgins, *Economic Development,* 1st ed., New York, 1968, chap. 19, and rev. ed., New York, 1968, chap. 22; Charles P. Kindleberger, *Economic Development,* 2nd ed., New York, 1965, chap. 13 and Bruce Herrick and Charles Kindleberger, *Economic Development,* 4th ed.; and Meier, *Leading Issues,* 1st ed., New York, 1983, chap. 17; pt. IV; and 4th ed., pt. IV.D.

56. See John Williamson, ed., *Inflation and Indexation: Argentina, Brazil, and Israel,* Cambridge, Mass., 1985, for a collection of papers on the subject given at a conference sponsored by the Institute of International Economics in Washington.

57. *The Economist,* May 28, 1983, pp. 76–77; and *The Manchester Guardian Weekly,* September 16, 1984, p. 17.

58. The recent tendency to hold and use dollars instead of local currency has become pronounced in Bolivia and Israel. See C. L. Ramirez-Rojas, "Monetary Substitution in Developing Countries," *Finance and Development* 23, no. 2 (1986): 35–38.

59. The figures are from IMF, *World Economic Outlook, 1986,* p. 6; *WDR 1985;* and *Wall Street Journal,* December 26, 1985, p. 4.

60. Robert Barro, *Macroeconomics,* New York, 1984, pp. 447–449.

61. Sonia L. Nazario, "When Inflation Rate Is 116,000%, Prices Change by the Hour," *Wall Street Journal,* February 7, 1985. By June 1985 it appeared inflation for that year was running not at 116,000 percent, but "only" at about 50,000 percent. *The Economist,* June 15, 1985, p. 40. The real growth rate is calculated from IMF, *International Financial Statistics Yearbook, 1985,* p. 195.

62. A thorough review of anti-inflation policy in LDCs is William R. Cline and Sidney Weintraub, eds., *Economic Stabilization in Developing Countries,* Washington, D.C., 1981.

63. Very generally over a large sample of LDCs, a one percentage point increase per year in the rate of growth of the money supply is associated with roughly a one percentage point per year increase in the rate of inflation. The relationship is strongest when money supply growth is high (over 15 percent per year) or low (under 5 percent per year). The relationship is even stronger when changing demand for money as reflected by growth rates of output, interest rates, and financial innovation is allowed for. See Barro, *Macroeconomics,* pp. 152–158. Some countries are so distrustful of their ability to control their money supply that they actually issue no currency of their own and use foreign banknotes as their circulating medium. These must be acquired by the export of goods and services, thus representing a high-cost money. Inflation will, however, be unlikely to exceed the rate in the issuing country. Panama and Liberia use the U.S. dollar; several Pacific island nations use the Australian dollar; much of

former French West Africa uses a CFA franc (CFA standing for French African Community) tied tightly to the French franc. No country in modern times went so far, however, as did Cambodia ("Democratic Kampuchea") under the Pol Pot regime. It abolished money. The Cambodian economy was already in ruins, so less harm ensued than might have been expected. Money was officially restored when Pol Pot was overthrown in 1979.

64. *Wall Street Journal,* August 30, 1985.

65. A summary of the costs of stabilizing a serious inflation, citing numerous sources, is in Liaquat Ahamed, "Stabilization Policies in Developing Countries," *The World Bank Research Observer* 1, no. 1 (1986): 99–105. A special issue of *World Development* 13, no. 8 (1985) is entitled "Liberalization with Stabilization in the Southern Cone of Latin America." A special issue of *Economic Development and Cultural Change* 34, no. 3 (1986) is entitled "Growth, Reform, and Adjustment: Latin America's Trade and Macroeconomic Policies in the 1970s and 1980s." Also see Leland B. Yeager and associates, *Experiences with Stopping Inflation,* Washington, D.C., 1981.

66. Among interesting recent articles on the Chilean experience are Arnold C. Harberger, "Observations on the Chilean Economy, 1973–1983," *Economic Development and Cultural Change* 33, no. 3 (1985): 451–462; Sebastian Edwards, "Stabilization with Liberalization: An Evaluation of Ten Years of Chile's Experiment with Free-Market Policies, 1973–1983," *Economic Development and Cultural Change* 33, no. 2 (1985): 223–254; Sebastian Edwards, "Monetarism in Chile, 1973–1983: Some Economic Puzzles," *Economic Development and Cultural Change* 34, no. 3 (1986): 535–559; Ricardo French-Davis, "The Monetarist Experiment in Chile: A Critical Survey," *World Development* 11, no. 11 (1983): 905–926; and *The Economist,* August 10, 1985, pp. 60–62.

67. See Vincent Corbo, Jaime de Melo, and James Tybout, "What Went Wrong with the Recent Reforms in the Southern Cone," *Economic Development and Cultural Change* 34, no. 3 (1986): 607–640.

68. One reason why there will be skepticism about the government's intentions is that the inflationary creation of money may have come to provide much of the government's revenue through seigniorage. The term describes the "profit" from creating money very cheaply and then putting it into circulation at its face value. Such seigniorage made up almost half of Argentina's government revenue during the period 1960–75. Observers may doubt whether politicians will be willing to give up this lucrative seigniorage yield, whatever the deleterious effects of the resulting inflation. See Stanley Fisher, "Seigniorage and the Case for a National Money," *Journal of Political Economy* 90, no. 2 (1982): Table A2; and the discussion in Barro, *Macroeconomics,* pp. 195–196.

chapter 5

Foreign Flows to Fill the Gap Between Saving and Investment

The last chapter discussed domestic policies for saving and investment within the LDCs. This chapter goes on to consider the foreign alternatives for a country that wishes to invest more than it is willing or able to save domestically.[1]

Almost all LDCs do indeed invest more than they save at home. This is true especially of the least-developed countries, which in 1984, on average, invested about 16 percent of GDP, while saving only 7 percent. (The figures exclude high-saving India and China.) For the lower middle-income LDCs 1984 investment was 19 percent of GDP, while domestic saving was 16 percent. (By contrast, developed countries usually save more than they invest. Japan for example saved 31 percent of GDP in 1984, while investing 28 percent.)

Flows from abroad may take the form of borrowing or transfers from international institutions such as the World Bank, foreign aid from national governments, or private investment (portfolio or direct) by foreigners. In effect the rich world is not absorbing all its own output and is using some either for gifts to or as "claims" (in the form of loans or equity) on poor countries. This makes good economic sense. Rich countries are able to produce a surplus, while poor countries cannot. Financial capital is abundant in the developed world, and scarce in the LDCs; there are many favorable opportunities for profitable investment in the latter.

As capital flows from abroad, an LDC could finance investment for development purposes. In essence, the LDC incurs debt to the developed world and repays out of the higher national product made possible by the new investment. As long as the investments are profitable enough to pay the interest on the loans and yield a further net return, the process is a sensible one, filling a "savings gap"

111

between what can be saved at home and profitable investment opportunities. Most of today's LDCs do just this; and, indeed, so did many now-developed countries, especially the United States, which for most of the first 125 years after its founding ran a current account deficit, importing foreign capital (much from London) to finance its expansion.

Current account deficits *(M > X)* involving capital inflows from abroad are quite normal and desirable in the development process. But it is possible for things to go wrong, as we shall see in Chapter 6's discussion of the debt crisis.

BORROWING FROM THE WORLD BANK

Capital flows from international institutions are generally associated with the International Bank for Reconstruction and Development (IBRD), more commonly known as the World Bank. A product of the 1944 Bretton Woods Conference in New Hampshire, the World Bank is actually a family of three related institutions that administer three different sorts of lending to the LDCs. The parent World Bank itself, located in Washington, D.C., by tradition has an American president (Barber Conable since 1986). A European heads another product of Bretton Woods, the International Monetary Fund (discussed in Chapter 6). This clubby arrangement has not thrilled the LDCs.

The Bank's influence extends far beyond its capacity to make loans, since the publications of its research departments are read avidly by development economists everywhere. This book's footnotes fairly reflect the influence this research has on scholarship. Financial capital for development loans is raised in some small part through contributions from all member governments, currently numbering 150, but primarily by the Bank's sale of bonds on the world's capital markets, where the Bank is the world's largest nongovernmental borrower.

The parent World Bank, the first of the three related institutions, lends on regular commercial terms, with nearly $90 billion available (the Bank's capital was doubled in 1979 and raised again by $8 billion in 1984). It lends only to less-developed countries, and even among these it "graduates" its borrowers when per capita income reaches $2,650 1980 dollars. Almost all the authorized amount is usually loaned out at a given time; in the fiscal year ending June 30, 1986, lending was $13.2 billion. Until 1981 a fixed rate of interest was levied, and a variable rate since that date. The rate, set for six months at a time and 8.23 percent in the last half of 1986, is determined by adding a spread of ½ of 1 percent atop the "pool rate" of outstanding borrowing of the Bank. There have been times when this arrangement was a bargain, with private rates for dollar loans far above the Bank's figure; in 1985 they were comparable, which in part explains why lending was below the expected figure in that year. The Bank seeks to raise its lending to the $15.0 to 16.6 billion range in 1986 to 1988.

In lending for development projects in LDCs, the Bank estimates a likely rate of return; this must be above a minimum 10 percent for the project to go forward. Recently its average rate of return on all projects has been around 18 percent.[2] In 1985, 26 percent of World Bank loans were in agriculture, 25 percent were in the field of energy, 15 percent were in transport and communications, and just under that in industry. The remainder went largely for programs in population, education, health, and nutrition.

In recent years the Bank has moved into "co-financing," with governments and private banks as co-financers of projects. By 1982 about two-fifths of all Bank endeavors were so funded. In some recent years 40 to 50 percent of the money has come from these outside sources; the 1984 figure was about 25 percent. Since the debt crisis, co-financing has become less popular with commercial banks, but governments have made much use of the Bank's expertise by putting a part of their foreign aid into its projects.[3]

The second of the Bank's agencies, dating from the late 1950s, is the International Development Association (IDA). It is a major source of scarce concessionary or "soft" finance for the poorest LDCs. Its much smaller budget, recently between $3 and $4 billion per year, is obtained wholly from grants "replenished" every three years by developed-country governments, and not from capital markets. It is used for very much softer 50-year loans, interest-free except for a ¾ of 1 percent service fee, with a grace period of 10 years before repayment starts. About 120 LDCs, those with per capita income below $790, are eligible.

Nearly 90 percent of IDA credits have gone to the 40 poorest countries in this group, those with incomes below about $400 per capita. Twenty-seven other LDCs have been "graduated" because their incomes are above the allowed figure. The same standards for expected performance of projects are used for IDA credits as for parent World Bank loans, but far more of the loans (46 percent) are in agriculture. Recent rates of return, though more variable than the World Bank's are on average the same or slightly better, 18 to 22 percent, reflecting the great capital shortages in the poorest LDCs. In spite of this good performance, there have been some monumental failures of a few IDA projects, and nearly 9 percent of them have had a negative rate of return.

The biggest recipients by far of IDA loans are India and China; since funds are limited, it has proved necessary to put a ceiling on loans to them, and their share is dropping. Africa is gaining a proportionate share. The agency brings significant amounts of investment to the poorest countries (13 percent of the total in Bangladesh, for example) on much easier terms than would otherwise be obtainable. Importantly, it also serves to separate out the worst risks, protecting the World Bank's treasured AAA bond rating and thus allowing it to borrow on world credit markets at the most favorable terms.[4]

The third agency, dating from 1956, is the International Finance Corporation (IFC). It now has a British director. The IFC is even smaller than the IDA, authorized to loan a total of $1.3 billion since its capital was doubled in 1985. In the fiscal years 1985 and 1986, its actual disbursements were in the range of $600 to $700 million. It lends only for projects in the private sector of its 128 member countries, borrowing for this purpose from the World Bank and also (since December 1984) floating its own bonds on world capital markets. Because much syndication of loans takes place with private investors, about five times more than the stated value of IFC loans is actually invested in LDCs through that agency's activities. In addition, the IFC's new Emerging Markets Growth Fund, discussed in the last chapter, will aid LDC stock markets.

Due to the fact that the IFC lends only in the private sector and advises on ways to improve local capital markets, it has been much preferred to both IDA and the World Bank by the Reagan administration in the United States; this once little-known agency fits in well with the private enterprise proclivities of that administration. Many mainstream development economists, reflecting on the mixed record of public enterprise in the LDCs, also see some advantage in the IFC's approach. These same economists are, however, less comfortable with any assumption that the private sector *alone* is necessarily a better milieu for development than an appropriate public-private mix. Private entrepreneurs, however talented and hard-working, face great barriers in the poor LDCs that loans, even generous ones, are unlikely to overcome fully. They must cope with an inadequate infrastructure of transport and communication, limited education, overly rapid population growth, plus poorly developed institutions for money and credit management and marketing. All are areas that may not respond rapidly to individual entrepreneurial effort in the private sector and have the potential to block that effort. It seems fair to suggest that only in a country already approaching developed status are these problems likely to be inconsequential.

The new prominence of the IFC and the debates concerning it fully reflect the politicization of other Bank activities. Some wish to impose a human rights test on lending, in particular to punish South Africa's racist policies. Conservatives, especially in the United States, have criticized the parent Bank and IDA for lending to communist governments (Vietnam is a member, for example) and to "socialist" governments such as India and Tanzania; under the World Bank group's various charters no discrimination in lending is permitted. They attack loans for projects such as textile mills, the output from which, when exported, would compete with U.S. producers. They criticize what they see as an overemphasis on government projects generally, rather than on private enterprise, hence their preference for the IFC. By way of rebuttal, a recent U.S. Treasury study states that 43 percent of World Bank and IDA lending was to the private sector and only 8.2 percent was deemed "directly competitive" with that sector. In addition, the IFC itself has started to lend to communist countries, a Yugoslav natural gas firm receiving the first loan of that sort in 1984, followed by a big one to the Guangzhou Peugeot Automobile Company for a French-Chinese pickup truck.

Even so, the result has been serious difficulty in raising the agreed upon share of U.S. government funding, especially for IDA where all moneys come from official sources and not the capital markets. Congress has several times delayed and stretched out the U.S. contribution (now $500 million, or 59 percent of the cost of an Ohio-class Trident submarine), leaving that agency on the point of a temporary shut-down and reducing its present funding by one-quarter to about $3 billion a year. Thirty-one out of the 32 IDA donors wanted to continue funding at the old $4 billion figure, but the United States, still contributing 27 percent of IDA funds (down from 42 percent when the agency was new) got its way.[5] As with the World Bank itself and the IFC, one response to IDA funding difficulties has been the syndication of loans with private lenders and governments. Some change in the U.S. views came at the Bank's conference in Seoul, Korea, during October 1985, when an idea to make available new funds for a lending pool to aid sub-Saharan Africa was advanced by the United States. Part of this "Baker Plan" initiative, named for Treasury Secretary James Baker, also involves the International Monetary Fund. This special fund lent $782 million in fiscal 1986.

The LDCs also have their own criticisms of the World Bank family, the chief being that the majority of the Bank, IDA, and IFC loans have been for specific projects only—a factory, a railway, a port facility. Due to the gestation period for any project, this means that the Bank's annual disbursements are usually below half the sums approved for lending. LDC governments, and many economists as well, often contend in addition that capital needs cannot easily be identified on a specific project-by-project basis. LDCs would prefer more latitude to use Bank funding generally to support current spending programs connected with capital projects. The teachers' pay will be every bit as much a drain on a government budget as the capital cost of a school building. Further, it is difficult to support positive policy changes and economic reforms with project loans alone and a project will not be very attractive if the economic environment surrounding it is unsound.

Project lending does have some advantages from the Bank's point of view: loans not specifically allocated to a project might end up being used for arms purchases, wasted, or misused. Of course, if the LDC would have used its own funds for the project had the Bank not financed it, then the loan is "fungible"— the resources freed by the loan could in any case have been used to buy arms, been wasted, or been misused. But the Bank has recognized that the arguments against loans for projects only have merit and that good projects are not enough where the underlying economic policies are flawed. In 1980 it made its first "structural adjustment" loans to Turkey, Kenya, and Bolivia.[6] So far 16 countries have received 29 such policy-reform, rather than project, loans, most for adjusting to the debt crisis, the energy crisis, and for export promotion. They generally include some Bank involvement in economic policy and often aim to dismantle the structure of controls and increase the influence of free market pricing. The structural adjustment loans are released in installments and so can be dispensed far more rapidly than project assistance. By fiscal 1986, they had risen to some 23 percent of total loans, up from 17 percent the year before. Such lending clearly has similarities to the International Monetary Fund activities discussed in the next chapter and may suggest, as some have argued for years, that a union of the two organizations, both founded at Bretton Woods, might be pursued as a long-term goal.

The 1980 Brandt Commission, an international body chaired by former West German Chancellor Willy Brandt, posed some further criticisms of World Bank project lending.[7] Small projects are less favored than large, since monitoring the small ones is administratively expensive for the Bank. New investment gets priority over improvement in the efficiency of old investment, because working capital balances covering labor costs and raw materials procurement are not generally eligible for financing. There is also a suspicion that capital-intensive projects are preferred to those that are labor-intensive, because the capital-intensive type of technology is more readily available in the developed world.

Another Brandt Commission objection concerned the "gearing" of the Bank's operations. Currently, the Bank operates under conservative rules that permit it to lend only up to the amount of its capitalization—the total committed, but not actually paid in, by the Bank's member governments. Remember that most Bank lending is actually financed by the sale of its own bonds on world capital markets. The record of loan repayments is excellent, the Bank's prestige is high, and there would presumably be little difficulty in expanding bond sales to a significant degree, "attracting deposits" so to speak, just as does every domestic bank. Thus, argued the Brandt Commission, it would make sense to change the ratio of loans-to-capital from its present conservative 1 : 1 to a higher figure, possibly 2 : 1. Note that commercial banks are typically geared at 16 : 1. The objection that the new lending would be inflationary could be met by the reply that "new money" is not created; buyers of World Bank bonds do not acquire demand deposits, but instead long-term obligations.

Another option would be for the Bank to reduce the amount of capital its members are required actually to pay in. That figure is currently 7.5 percent; if reduced to 5 or 3 percent, capitalization could then be raised and more funds obtained on the bond markets. Interestingly, alone of World Bank members, the U.S. Congress has to approve the whole of any increase in capital as new spending in the budget, even though a call has never been made beyond the 7.5 percent that has to be paid in. Nor is it really likely that any call will be made in the foreseeable future, since the Bank carries virtually no bad debts, even after the debt crisis—its policy is not to reschedule. Alternatively, much the same effect could be achieved if the Bank acted more directly as the guarantor of private-sector loans to LDCs. A charter for a Multilateral Investment Guarantee Agency with a rather small capital of $1 billion was approved by the Bank's executive directors in 1985, with governments paying in 10 percent, giving promissory notes for another 10 percent, and the remaining 80 percent being "callable capital." Lastly and more conventionally, the Bank's capitalization could simply be raised; if the increase were $40 billion, then lending could be expanded by about half. Many economists find attractive these ideas to raise the Bank's lending potential.

In addition to the World Bank family, there are three other international lending agencies, smaller, operating only in specific geographical areas, but run on lines similar to the World Bank. These are the Inter-American Development Bank, founded in 1959, which lent $3 billion in 1983; the Asian Development Bank, founded in 1964, which lent $2 billion; and the African Development Bank, founded in 1966 and much the smallest, which lent $0.93 billion. Each borrows on world capital markets and lends mostly on near commercial terms. Each has a soft-loan affiliate, a "fund" resembling the IDA, established with rich-country contributions, and the Inter-American Development Bank set up an IFC-like agency lending to private enterprise in 1986. Rates of return have been similar to those of the World Bank.

The lending of the World Bank family and the regional development banks is important; it amounted to about $21 billion in 1984, compared to $35 billion for foreign aid and under $10 billion for direct investment. Its capital flows, together with the co-financing it manages and the research expertise it brings to development issues, give the Bank family a unique place in promoting economic change in the LDCs.

FOREIGN AID (OFFICIAL DEVELOPMENT ASSISTANCE)

For the poorest of the LDCs, those least able to borrow on commercial terms from private capital sources or to qualify for World Bank loans, foreign aid from the developed countries and oil states (often called ODA for official development assistance) is an important source of funds. The poorest, who manage as a group to cover only 5 percent of their collective balance of payments deficit by bank loans and have dim prospects of receiving more, in fact have little alternative to seeking foreign aid (which, incidentally, at least allowed them to escape the worst rigors of the debt crisis). In the early 1980s aid was financing one-fourth of the imports of the poorest countries and one-seventh of their investment.[8]

Without such finance infrastructure development may be difficult and so delay foreign investment. Aid may give a chance to "buy off" with better designed alternative programs those who gain from policies such as protectionism and cheap urban food. In the sense that it can finance policy improvements, aid may be a catalyst rather than a competitor for development via private enterprise. It can also finance health and education programs, agricultural research, roads, ports, and power stations that may not pay off for 30 or 40 years; even if the return is high, delays this long make such programs unsuitable for financing in the current private market for lending.[9] Since aid is usually either in the form of grants or "concessional" loans with an interest rate below the market rate, any problems of servicing a large debt are much muted when such assistance is the vehicle for the transfer. Finally, aid is often packaged with good technical advice, help with management, and institution building, all less feasible with private lending.

The position of foreign aid in the present political climate is much more a pragmatic than an idealistic one. Though some countries, mostly small (all of Scandinavia, Belgium, the Netherlands, Canada) appear to act from principles of ethics, accepting that the present world distribution of income ought to be rectified, and perhaps even accepting that there is a "right" or "entitlement" for poor countries to receive aid, most do not. Such moral arguments as debated by scholars who work on the ethics of economics—Amartya Sen, John Rawls, and Robert Nozick among others—appear to have little impact on many major aid givers.[10] In these including the United States, foreign policy goals have a decided edge on moral arguments.

In 1985 the net flow of official development assistance, both grants and low-interest loans, amounted to just over $35 billion, of which some 83 percent came from the western developed industrial countries, 8 percent from OPEC oil exporters, and an additional 8 percent from communist countries. Although the $35 billion total represents a quintupling of aid flows between 1970 and 1985, much of the increase was in fact not used for capital formation, but to finance balance of payments deficits run up after the huge rise in oil prices. (However, aid for this purpose has an indirect impact on capital spending, which otherwise might have been sharply reduced had the aid not been available.) The quintupling is less impressive in real terms. Corrected for inflation, aid grew only a little less than one-third in the two decades since 1965. In that year the developed nations had been giving 0.49 percent of their combined GNP to the LDCs, but by 1985 the figure had fallen back to 0.35 percent.

Following the 1970s surge in oil prices, aid patterns shifted as grants from OPEC oil exporters increased remarkably. Some of these (mostly Muslim) countries have taken their Koranic charitable obligations, or perhaps their urge to play realpolitik, very seriously. OPEC disbursed only $0.4 billion in aid as recently as 1970, but that figure had soared to over $8 billion in 1981. By 1985 it had fallen back by more than half to $3 billion (still nearly 0.9 percent of national product). With the sharp decline in oil prices in early 1986, OPEC aid will fall further yet. The most generous donor has been Saudi Arabia, giving away about 5 percent of its national product, over half of OPEC's total aid. The lion's share of this, 80 percent or more from 1977 to 1981, went to Arab countries, Syria and Jordan in the lead. Less than 10 percent went to the least-developed LDCs. OPEC members frequently engaged in co-financed projects in which they added funds to those already raised by an international lending agency such as the World Bank or one of the regional development banks.[11]

Aid from the USSR and the communist countries of Eastern Europe, at about 8 percent of all foreign assistance, was 0.21 percent of national product in 1984. The figure is low because the interest and repayment terms are fairly tough; three-quarters goes to Cuba, Mongolia, and Vietnam.[12]

There is even a little aid from the LDCs themselves, though far less than a billion dollars in total. India and China have been significant contributors, mostly in the form of technical assistance; recently, China was giving 0.07 percent of its GNP. Others giving some aid include Argentina, Brazil, Colombia, Greece, Israel, Korea, Mexico, Portugal, Spain, and Venezuela. It does seem entirely reasonable that countries receiving aid in the past should, as they develop, give aid themselves. In time this would mean a sizable augmentation of the amount of aid available.

The greatest hope for increased aid lies, of course, with the richest economies, and the United Nations Conference on Trade and Development (UNCTAD) has for some years applied pressure for a new aid target, originally that 0.7 percent of rich-country GNP would be devoted to aid programs by 1980. Many developed countries accepted the challenge, and five (the Netherlands, Norway, Denmark, Sweden, and France) have reached the goal. But the 1980 target date was not met because West Germany and Japan did not accept the timing, and the United States (0.24 percent in 1985, 0.20 percent in 1981) did not even accept the target itself. Currently, the United States is the most parsimonious in terms of percent of GNP, though it is still giving twice as much in absolute terms as the next largest donor. Britain and Japan are not particularly generous either.

The Future for Foreign Aid Programs

Recent years have seen both favorable and unfavorable developments in the foreign aid picture. On the plus side for aid proponents, during the 1970s there was a movement toward channeling aid to the most needy countries.[13] The important decision was taken by the developed countries that all aid to the poorest LDCs (34 at the time) would be grants, not loans; this was followed in March 1978 by a decision to write off the loans made earlier to this group, $6 billion in all, on which $500 million of repayment and interest was being made annually, a burdensome flow from the poorest to the rich. Even for the better off LDCs, there has been a similar tendency to replace loans with grants; about two-thirds of all aid is now in the form of grants. Repayment of principal and interest on foreign aid debt is thus steadily shrinking, and already by 1977 was well below 5 percent of the other foreign debt owed by the LDCs.

A grant element is often present in loans to LDCs when, most importantly, the interest rate is below that available on the open market, with longer repayment periods allowed (the average maturity is now a long 30 years), or when there is a grace period with no repayment required (7 years is average). If this grant element is at least 25 percent of the value of a loan, the aid is considered "concessional." Technically, the concessional element in loan aid is the difference between the amount of the loan and the present discounted value of the stream of repayments. This concessional element also grows if aid is disbursed quickly, as opposed to a lengthy gestation period of disbursements. Outpayments which take a long time can easily cut the concessionary element in half. There is often some trade-off between the total volume of aid a donor provides and how concessional that aid is. Concessional aid is particularly apt when a long-term activity generates little immediate revenue with which to repay loans and where charging for a loan-financed service would cut its use by the poor, for example, immunization, or clean water supplies.[14]

More aid is being channeled through international agencies such as the World Bank, so reducing charges of political meddling, often bringing good advice, delivering more assistance to the very poor, and cutting the duplication of effort that sometimes occurs among many individual donors.[15] Multilateral aid, as this is called, more than doubled in the 1970s, reaching 34 percent of the total in 1980 before falling back to 30 percent in 1985. Of the grants and loans made country to country, called bilateral aid, about a third has been free for use as the recipient LDC chooses, while the rest has been for specific projects. The most important project areas have been electricity, water, and sewage schemes; education, including some 100,000 students from LDCs attending universities and technical schools in developed countries; and agriculture.

The less favorable view of the subject involves some controversial features of foreign aid programs that have been criticized both by recipients and by many in donor countries as well. One serious problem is that bilateral aid is so often "tied," that is, the recipient is required to spend the funds received on goods produced in the donor country.[16] More and more aid is given with such strings attached. Tied aid was only 25 percent of all bilateral assistance in 1972, but the figure was 54 percent in 1982–1983; the United States was tying about 70 percent of its bilateral aid in 1982, and Britain about 75 percent. Donors like tying because every dollar of aid means automatically a dollar of exports, important if balance of payments problems are present or if exporters have a strong lobby. Recipients do not like the practice because the donor may not be the world's cheapest producer, sheltering its high-priced production behind protectionist walls. Business people facing a certain sale will raise their prices in any case. Tying may also mean accepting lower quality goods. Current estimates are that 15 to 20 percent of the money value of aid is lost to the LDCs because of tying; in some individual cases the loss is much higher. Clearly, tying also means aid is limited to covering foreign exchange costs and not local costs of projects, and as with World Bank loans, the tied aid is much more concentrated on capital outlays than on day-to-day recurrent spending. In fact, only some 8 percent of all aid, tied or untied, is used for this latter purpose. The concentration on capital may contribute to overly high capital intensity in aid-financed projects.

Closely akin to tying is the recent practice of awarding "mixed credits"— credit for the purchase of developed-country exports at below market rates of interest and so involving a subsidy.[17] Almost unknown until the late 1970s, except to their inventor the French, they reached about $3.5 billion per year in 1981 to 1983. France (with 45 percent of the total) and Britain (with 23 percent) have led in this practice. Mixed credits have resulted in sharp competition in the promotion of developed-country exports and have brought a clear bias toward capital intensity and import intensity. The credits have also mostly gone to the more well-to-do LDCs, where the competition for sales is the greatest and the possibilities for gain most lucrative. The United States once made little use of mixed credits and complained that it was an unfair trade practice, but by late 1985 it was retaliating with cheap credits of its own in at least five LDCs.

Another problem with aid is that the former colonial powers still have a few colonies that in some cases received huge amounts of money that is counted in the ODA totals. The French, for example, were recently giving $660 per capita to their island of Réunion in the Indian Ocean and $1,500 per head (tops in the world) to their South American colony of French Guiana.[18] Compare India's aid from all sources $2.10 per head in 1984 and Indonesia's $4.20 in the same year. Excluding this aid to overseas possessions drops France well below the UNCTAD target of 0.7 percent of GNP. Of all foreign aid given by the European Community, over 50 percent goes to the African-Caribbean-Pacific (ACP) states which, though they have only about a tenth of the third world's population, are almost all ex-colonies of the EC members. Aid under such circumstances can be used as a lever: France drastically cut its aid to the Republic of Guinea (old French Guinea) when that country would not accede to French policy, and the Netherlands did the same thing in 1983 to its old colony of Suriname.

In a similar but much more widespread way, foreign aid has increasingly become a tool of domestic and foreign politics, to be doled out to friends and clients or cut off with dramatic suddenness when differences arise. Political exigencies and economic need are far from the same thing, explaining why over half the world's bilateral foreign aid goes to middle-income LDCs that contain only some 20 percent of the world's "absolute poor."

The politics of the situation are obvious. The largest recipient of Soviet aid is Cuba. Much Scandinavian aid goes to "socialist" Tanzania and Vietnam. Israel and Egypt together get about 48 percent of U.S. bilateral aid, the former receiving about $300 per head of population.[19] By contrast, all the 40-odd remaining countries of black Africa get only 12 percent, and even among this remainder, for years Sudan got by far the most, presumably not because it is the neediest (it is close on this score), but because of its strategic position between Libya and Ethiopia and its long-standing support of U.S. policy. El Salvador gets more U.S. aid than any country except Israel, Egypt, Turkey, and Pakistan.[20] In recent years U.S. foreign aid has shifted heavily toward helping private enterprise (there is now a Bureau for Private Enterprise in the U.S. Agency for International Development) and to Economic Support Fund (ESF) assistance, designed to promote economic and political stability in regions where the United States has a special interest in security. ESF money is generally a nationwide subsidy and is seldom targeted specifically toward the poor. Less than 15 percent of U.S. bilateral aid was ESF money in 1980; in the 1985 budget the figure was 50 percent and even higher in the 1987 budget proposal. (This is a major reason why an LDC's military can be supported even without loans and grants. Aid is fungible; if a dollar is received for butter, the LDC can transfer a dollar to guns.)[21]

The shift away from economic aid for the poor seems to accord with the public mood. Opinion polls that ask what budget item should be cut first if cutting is to be done, find the public giving the spot of honor overwhelmingly (typically some 80 percent) to "foreign aid."

There is an unusual meeting of the minds between many radical and conservative economists, who carry the criticisms of aid a long step further. They argue that over time aid is certain to involve adverse effects on the recipient country. Such effects might include the politicization of domestic economic policy, as effort and trained personnel are thrown into the search for grants rather than into the battle for development,[22] and a damaging loss of self-reliance as aid strengthens the government sector at the expense of the private sector. It is argued that the aid may have little impact on growth. The proceeds may go not for additional capital formation, but to finance further consumption; they may also substitute for domestic saving. The programs may largely benefit the politician, the educated elite, the civil service, the military, and, more generally, urban areas as opposed to rural. When aid givers prefer "monuments" to their own generosity to projects with a high rate of economic return, the effect on growth will be smaller yet.[23]

Some of these problems have indeed been present in numerous recipient countries. The point can even be made that aid could conceivably be regressive for donors. Arguably, the tax systems that finance the foreign aid of many donors are somewhat regressive, with many loopholes for the rich and a heavier relative burden on the middle classes. Meanwhile, the benefits of aid transferred via these tax systems may go to a favored elite, as just noted. If foreign aid is to improve the world distribution of income, as Robert Lekachman of the City University of New York has pointed out, then taxing low- or middle-income American workers to support and enrich the entourage of some third world leader does not seem the appropriate way to go about it. Such complaints point to the need for reform in both donor and recipient.

Food aid is the focus of particular controversy. One-twelfth of LDC food imports come as a gift; the rest is purchased at market terms.[24] Such aid seems the essence of humane dealing with the third world. In cases of famine (discussed in Chapter 9), it can represent the difference between life and death and is thus the most immediately vital form of all aid. A little surprisingly, given these obvious merits, even this type of aid is controversial, with serious issues of long-term strategy. Usually food aid has involved the disposal of surplus agricultural commodities put into stock because of price support programs. Surplus disposal may lead to the incongruity of averting famine with U.S. shipments to poor countries of surplus tobacco (until 1980) and free cotton! Critics deplore the way large quantities of food aid can depress the free-market price and ruin the incentive to produce. For example, thousands of Indian farmers were bankrupted by U.S. wheat giveaways in the 1950s and 1960s. Food aid after the 1976 earthquake in Guatemala came on the heels of one of that country's largest wheat harvests; prices plummeted and made it harder for farming villages to recover.[25]

Much has been learned about "what not to do." About a third of U.S. food aid and almost two-thirds of the EC's is now sold on markets, with the local government using the revenue for seed and fertilizer (or sometimes perhaps for higher salaries and more armaments). The valuable but little-known UN World Food Program now handles some 20 percent of emergency food distributions (2.5 million tons out of 10.5 million in 1985), bringing a degree of planning and coordination to a sometimes haphazard effort. But when food aid is given it is still not easy to encourage local production and to keep in repair age-old famine defenses such as sale of substitute foods produced by farmers in other, less affected, parts of the country or migration of pastoralists to better pastures. It is difficult to prevent inappropriate consumption habits (say, a shift from local millet to imported wheat) from spreading. It is also hard to guard against corrupt practices, political manipulation by both donors and recipients, and the solidifying of government agricultural policies that depress farm prices. High taxation of farmers is obviously more feasible if large-scale food aid is being received.

The future of foreign aid is currently both cloudy and controversial. It is still common to make startling comparisons—U.S. aid was 2 percent of GNP during the Marshall Plan, but only ⅛ of that now; total aid from all sources is equal to less than 18 days' worth of military expenditure or two months' worth of rich-country alcohol and tobacco consumption—but invidious comparisons of this sort obviously have little effect on the general public of most donors and the spirit of sacrifice is in short supply. The Brandt Commission tried to rekindle interest in economic aid with a plea for the target of 0.7 percent of GNP by 1985 (and 1 percent by 2000), plus a special effort to quadruple aid for the poorest LDCs. But the 1985 target represented a five-year delay from the old date (during which time aid actually fell even in nominal terms in 1981, 1982, and 1983). It was missed by an embarrassingly wide margin just as the old one was.

Aid once seemed the central topic in development. Not so now. In the third world attention is, understandably given the record, swinging away from it except in the very poorest who have little other choice or in the favored few (such as Israel, Egypt, and Cuba) whose strategic positions ensure a continued or increased flow. The old slogan "Trade not aid" is obviously winning out. At the start of the 1980s the LDCs were earning nearly $320 billion in foreign exchange from their combined merchandise exports (not including the high-income Arab oil states), almost 10 times the $35 billion in aid; the trade-aid ratio had been only 4 in the early 1960s. Whatever the value of aid, and it remains crucial for the poorest, "Trade not aid" appears to be both slogan and prophecy.

One last, perhaps unexpected footnote: As aid has become more politicized, there has been a rather quiet surge in effort from private voluntary organizations. Some of the names are familiar everywhere, while some are less well-known: the Red Cross and Red Crescent, Oxfam, CARE, Caritas, Catholic Relief Services, Save the Children, Interaction, World Vision, Misereor in Germany, Mani Tese in Italy, Maisons Familiales Rurales in France, the Aga Khan Foundation, and many others. They are philanthropic, often more trusted than governments, often free from political entanglements, and usually interested in helping those who need the help the most, especially through the development of local self-reliance. Though their transfers amount to only some 9 percent of government-to-government foreign aid ($3.1 billion in 1985), they are morally influential and (if a normative statement may be permitted) altogether laudable.[26] The momentarily famous Band Aid–Live Aid movement organized by Bob Geldof in the summer of 1985 raised a staggering $70 million for African famine relief. Is such voluntarism the shape of things to come? Will governments see merit in transferring some of their aid money to private voluntary organizations to capitalize on the latter's growing reputation? Perhaps.

AUTOMATIC TAXES AS A FORM OF AID[27]

"Automatic" taxes could provide new sources of finance for development, and a flurry of interest surrounded the subject after the Brandt Commission called for such taxes in its report. Most of the ideas are innovative; some are radical in concept. "Are not the world's oceans the heritage of all mankind?" asks the commission. As a common resource, could they not generate revenue for the common good?

One proposal is for a tax on fishing in international waters. Such a tax would raise revenue that could be devoted to development in the LDCs; it could also discourage the overfishing that is predictable when the resource involved is free for all to take as they can. There are estimates of $2.4 billion possibly generated by such a tax, not counting its desirable consequence of protecting the life of the world's fisheries.

There is also the prospect of mining the potato-size manganese nodules that litter large areas of the deep ocean floor. There are said to be some 1.5 trillion tons of these nodules, the bulk of them in the Pacific, recoverable by "water-beetle" minisubs, vacuuming, or bucket systems. Estimates on three exploration sites out of about a hundred feasible ones project over 60 million tons at each site, with a content of approximately 1 percent of nickel, copper, and cobalt, actually worth more than the manganese (29 percent) for which the nodules are named. The estimated value of production from the three sites, on the order of $16 billion, could be taxed on recovery, generating perhaps half a billion dollars annually at 1970s prices. But mining will be very expensive, and the mineral markets are currently depressed. A number of U.S.-based consortia have cut back their activities, and estimates that production would probably begin in the 1990s have now been pushed back to 2000 and after.

Offshore oil could be taxed in a similar fashion. Taxing oil from wells drilled beyond ocean depths of 200 meters would be lucrative, $1.5 to $3 billion annually if the UN's suggested rate of 7 percent is applied and oil is selling at $15 a barrel.

As an alternative to taxation, licenses to fish, mine, or extract oil could be auctioned.

In September 1980 a Law of the Sea Treaty was agreed to after 7 years of negotiations that began in Caracas in 1974 and eventually involved 150 countries. Under this treaty a United Nations Commission on the Law of the Sea (UNCLOS) would put into effect one of the ideas above, namely, the collection and distribution of funds obtained from seabed mining. An International Seabed Authority would oversee the activity on behalf of all countries, not just those doing the mining. It would grant permits to private mining firms. Its rules would be determined by voting in which majorities would have to include the mining countries. The Authority would collect royalties on private production for the nonmining developing countries and also undertake some production itself.

The United States originally supported the proposal, but changed position in 1981 and in 1982 announced it would not sign the treaty. U.S. objections centered on the Seabed Authority's rules. (1) Private enterprise would be burdened by the cost of having to prospect on two sites, but then could go forward on only one, the other being reserved for the Authority's own production. Costs would also be substantial because the planned fees are high, $1 million a year until production starts, and because taxes would be as high as 50 percent. (2) Even then, there would be no "right" to production. A private firm would have to reapply to start output, with an agreement to "sell" technology to the Authority. (3) The rate of extraction set by the Authority would be explicitly calculated to protect present producers. The benefits of such limitation on production would be reaped largely by the USSR and Gabon (the largest exporters of manganese), Zaire and Zambia (cobalt), Chile (copper), and Canada (nickel). There is no doubt that compensation payments to present producers are an economically more efficient method for dealing with the potential rise in production than are output limits, which encourage cartelization. (4) After 15 years new regulations, in which the mining countries lost their say, could be passed by a two-thirds vote. (5) There is no guarantee of a U.S. seat on the 36-member Seabed Authority. A last and unstated objection is surely that the current U.S. administration objects strenuously to any precedent declaring presently unowned natural resources a "common heritage" of mankind.

The treaty was signed anyway, by 144 states but not including the United States and Britain. Sixty ratifications will bring it into force without the participation of these countries. (By the start of 1985, there had been only 13.) Meanwhile, the United States and Britain have adopted legislation authorizing unilateral private seabed mining. Whether bankers would loan to private deep-sea miners in nonsigning countries is not clear.

There is a more radical school that proposes a tax on the production of *all* nonrenewable resources, even on land. Proponents of this descendant of the single-tax idea of Henry George state their conviction that the existence of mineral resources, as opposed to their discovery and extraction, is not in any way due to the genius or hard work of their owners. That the resources happen to lie in one country rather than another is sheer accident. A tax on this gift of nature can be justified both for equity and as a measure of conservation, claim its supporters. A 1 percent tax on output would be lucrative, collecting $5 billion or more. But the political obstacles to such a tax are obviously immense, and the prospects for passage virtually nil at present.

Similar long odds face other suggestions for automatic taxes made by the Brandt Commission: a levy on international trade, a tax on employment by multinational companies, a tax on military spending or arms exports. None of these has received much serious economic analysis. Taxes on international trade and employment would carry distortions that would have to be thoroughly investigated; a tax on armaments runs up against a move in the 1980s for far more expensive government commitments to improved weaponry.

FOREIGN PRIVATE INVESTMENT

Investment from private sources abroad is an important alternative for LDCs that wish to invest more domestically than they are able to save. Some $13 billion annually came in this form from 1979 to 1982, though the amount has now declined because of the debt crisis. To regain its 1975 peak in real terms, such investment would have to be nearly double the figure expected for 1986.[28]

Such private investment may be portfolio, that is, the purchase by foreigners of stocks or bonds, but not involving a controlling ownership. It may also be direct, meaning the creation or acquisition of capital assets which are owned fully or in amounts large enough to imply control. The dividing line between the two is not always very clear. Australia has a 25 percent minimum figure of equity ownership for the term direct investment to apply. France uses 20 percent; the United States, Germany, and Sweden use 10 percent. Great Britain and Japan make a value judgment and do not employ a fixed dividing line.

Portfolio Investment[29]

At the turn of the century private, nonbank portfolio investment was important, with investors in developed countries actively buying the shares and bonds of firms in the United States, Canada, Australia, New Zealand, Argentina, Chile, and others. Britain was the chief source of the flows, investing 5 percent of its GNP abroad in the period 1870 to 1913. The funds, over one-quarter of all British saving, were used especially for railways and utilities (nearly two-thirds of the total) and for many types of heavy industry. There was also a vigorous government bond market involving the securities of national and regional governments. Both for private and government borrowing the interest rates on the bonds were generally fixed and the maturities very long (99-year bonds were not uncommon). After World War I the United States emerged as the major source of capital, still long-term, although the balance swung to borrowing by governments.

There had been some troubles in this market for a long time, with repudiations in Peru and Turkey in the 1870s and in Argentina and Brazil in the 1880s and 1890s. These did little harm. But the financial disasters of the 1930s were much more general. After Germany's default in 1932, many LDCs followed suit. In all of Latin America only Argentina continued to service its debt during the Great Depression. The result was severe restriction of this market, and for many years after World War II private investors understandably considered portfolio investment in the LDCs a highly risky proposition. There are few recourses for a private holder of an LDC government bond if default occurs, since the principle of "sovereign risk" permits governments to disallow suits against itself within its own borders. Neither were the LDCs very receptive to portfolio investment, which was discouraged with high taxation, foreign exchange restriction, and limits on the types of shares that could be held by foreigners.

As a result, such flows were only half a billion dollars or less annually in the 1960s and up to 1975, often as much as 10 times below the figure for direct investment. There was a revival in the years 1977 to 1979, mostly via bond issues in the Eurobond market and in the national markets of Switzerland and Japan. In 1978 bonds floated by a small number of high-reputation LDCs reached nearly 15 percent of the value of all international bond issues, involving a useful $5 billion. But with the debt crisis of the early 1980s, this portfolio revival went into retreat, to some 3.5 percent of all international bond issues in 1983 and 1984. (It should be remembered that the LDCs have *indirect* access to the bond markets via the bond-financed lending of the World Bank and the regional development banks.)

Direct Investment: The Multinationals[30]

Private direct investment has in most years been much larger than portfolio investment, as well as much more controversial, since it involves the activities of the so-called multinationals (abbreviated MNE for multinational enterprise, or MNF for multinational firm, or MNC for multinational corporation.) Such enterprises usually have a home base with operations abroad. The UN and many scholars argue that the word *multinational* is thus not fully appropriate and prefer the term *transnational.*

There are about 10,000 such firms holding assets in more than one nation; about 50 percent have their home in Europe and 25 percent in the United States. Most (61 percent) have only one or two branches abroad, and about 380 MNEs do much the greater part of all foreign investment. The top ten in 1985 were GM, Royal Dutch Shell, Exxon, Mobil, British Petroleum, Ford, IBM, Texaco, Chevron, and GE. In terms of total assets abroad, U.S.-based firms own nearly half, with the British in second place. Their operations are imposingly large in scale.

The foreign sales of affiliates of U.S. firms in 1977 were over five times larger than total U.S. exports in that year; foreign sales of manufactured goods by U.S. MNEs were as much as 20 percent of the domestic sales of these same firms; for every four workers employed in U.S. manufacturing, one was employed abroad by an affiliate of a U.S. firm.[31]

Though three-quarters of this accumulated private direct investment has been in the developed world and only one-quarter in the LDCs, its significance for development is large and in the 1970s the LDC share was growing. New multinational investment in these countries reached $14.8 billion in 1981, up from an average of $2.8 billion annually in the early 1970s. The biggest portion of the shift was due to changes in direction in the United States, which accounts for nearly half the direct investment in the third world, largely in Latin America. Japan also raised its investment, mostly in Asian LDCs, to two-thirds of its total flows abroad. This trend came to a halt with the debt crisis. New investment sagged to only $10.9 billion in 1983, with U.S. MNE investment in Latin America halved, and the Japanese figure for all LDCs down to just 46 percent of its total in 1981–82.

There is, interestingly, some multinational investment flowing from one LDC to another. Examples of moderately large investors are Brazil (active in the Middle East and West Africa), India (active in Indonesia and Malaysia), Hong Kong, Singapore, and South Korea. LDC multinationals are said sometimes to provide more labor-intensive technologies and to be politically more acceptable than their developed-country brethren.[32]

The investment of MNEs in developing countries has most often followed the growth of new markets in these countries for goods where the firms' superior technology and popular brand names lend advantages over domestic firms. Rather commonly, they seek to establish operations inside the protectionist barriers of an LDC pursuing an import substitution strategy. Generally, they prefer investing where markets are relatively similar to those at home, or where the combination of factor inputs is comparable to those the firm is already skilled at handling. MNEs have no special advantage in designing products or marketing goods in environments far different from those they face at home nor in organizing and managing factors of production when the mix and qualities are far different from what they are used to. That is one important reason such firms either avoid very poor countries or address themselves only to the middle- and upper-class markets familiar to them from their home operation.

Less frequently, though more in the news, MNEs have sought new sources of inputs. Examples include minerals and oil to offset declining reserves at home and to capture part of the rents on especially valuable deposits. Labor also can be an attraction, as when a multinational moves an operation overseas in search of cheaper wages, thereafter exporting the product back to the home market and elsewhere. As a company's multinational operations have proliferated, the knowledge available to it about other markets increases, as does its confidence in that knowledge, which now comes at low cost. This is a reason why MNE reactions to changing economic conditions are both more rapid and tuned more finely than they were two decades ago.[33]

About a third of MNE investment has been in manufacturing, another third in oil, a tenth in mining, while the remainder, just under a quarter, is in the service sector, the most rapidly growing of them all. Taking the LDCs as a whole, it is commonly found that about 30 percent of their manufacturing output is produced by the multinationals. Sometimes it is much higher, for example, nearly 60 percent in Singapore.

In general, the poorer the country, the smaller its domestic market, the lower its stock of skilled labor, the less committed it is to private enterprise, and the less stable its political-economic environment, the less private investment it receives. About 50 percent of all such investments went to Latin America and the Caribbean in the period 1970 to 1983; Brazil leads the LDCs as a recipient. Some 30 to 40 percent went to Asia, mostly East Asia, with Singapore hosting nearly half the total. The least goes to sub-Saharan Africa, and the figure is falling (to 11 percent in 1980 to 1983). Investment is heavily concentrated in countries that have promoted export-led growth; though the information is fragmentary and the range of data is wide, the share of exports accounted for by foreign majority–owned affiliates includes Hong Kong 10 percent, Taiwan over 20 percent, South Korea over 15 to 31 percent, Mexico 25 to 34 percent, Brazil 43 to 51 percent, and Singapore 70 to 84 percent.[34]

The amounts involved were once the largest form of private flow until the surge of bank lending discussed in Chapter 6. As bank lending subsided after 1982 because of the debt crisis, direct investment was again gaining proportional ground.

Contrary to the early work on the subject, the most important benefits brought to the LDCs by the multinationals are not directly associated with the capital transfer itself. These benefits are wide in scope. The investment may make available, in larger quantity and better quality, goods and services formerly high in price, so that consumers gain. The government may garner extra tax revenue from the expanded operations of foreign firms. Additional domestic investment may be stimulated because the new foreign operations open up profitable opportunities for supplying them with components or raw materials. The multinational may reduce production costs through its coordination of marketing and its ability in planning. The MNE may bring nonmarket, cost-reducing externalities to its hosts, including the technical knowledge that flows to the branches of an MNE; managerial ability, organizational competence, and the capacity to avoid the waste and inefficiency that might be present if the project were forced to depend on indigenous talent alone. These nonmarket advantages, especially the transfer of knowledge in all its forms, are now emphasized by most scholars as the key explanation why multinationals prefer to operate in an LDC themselves rather than licensing production to local firms. Some of these advantages will, of course, accrue as profit repatriated abroad by the MNE, but some will be reinvested or will be paid to local factors of production. Finally, the MNE can be an influential lobbyists for world free trade if it wishes to export some of its production from the LDC, because tariffs and quotas in developed-country markets will interfere with these plans. A country with little clout in the U.S. Congress or parliaments of the EC when it pushes for free trade may find it has puissant allies in its corps of multinationals.[35]

Even the role of the multinationals in investment itself does not primarily involve the direct transfer of capital into an LDC. A large amount of capital is transferred by means of commercial bank loans to LDC subsidiaries of MNEs. To a significant degree, often more so than the direct and indirect capital transfers, MNEs also add to saving by building retained earnings, which may be reinvested in the operation. Much of this saving is still foreign, done by the corporate shareholders in the parent country who receive lower dividends than they would have otherwise. (In the figures for foreign direct investment, these reinvested earnings are included. They presently make up about half the total.) To the degree that multinationals serve to raise local income, they also play a part in stimulating *domestic* saving, as already noted in Chapter 4.

Benefits and Costs of Multinational Operations

Ownership by foreign firms is much more visible both physically and politically than are bond holdings and bank loans. This makes the operations of multinationals a highly controversial topic, involving a wide variety of issues some of which are only vaguely related to saving, investment, management and technology. But a country cannot have these inflows without facing the other issues as well, so it is convenient to take them up here. LDCs have indeed gone through a long stage of learning how to deal with multinationals. The early "acceptance" school of thought gave way to "rejection" in many countries. Nowadays an "assertive pragmatism" marks policy in most countries, though acceptance and rejection can still be found.[36]

What positive and negative arguments can be made for the operations of these firms? Concerning their transfer of capital into a recipient LDC, the "normal" microeconomic argument in its favor is that foreign investment benefits both parties to the transaction. For the LDCs in particular the rise in real income is in amount greater than the profits earned by the investor and repatriated to the foreign country. The argument is presented in simple diagrammatic form in Figure 5.1.[37] A rich and capital-abundant country's marginal product of capital (*MP* of *K*) is shown by the downward-sloping line relating to origin *O* (on the left side of the diagram); a poor and capital-short country's *MP* is drawn relating to origin *O'* (on the right). Assume a large stock of capital *(OK)* in the rich country. If profits per unit (*OA*) are equal to the marginal product of capital (KB = OA) total returns to domestic capital are *OABK*. Assume a small quantity of capital *(O'K)* in the poor country. Total returns to domestic capital in the poor country are thus *O'KCD*. Since the area under an *MP* curve is the return to all factors, then *O'KCJ* is the total income earned, and this minus the return to capital is the return to other factors, *(O'KCJ − O'KCD = CJD);* This return will be wages if our model is limited to just the two factors capital and labor.

Now consider what happens if rich-country owners of capital seek out the higher per unit returns in the LDC by making a transfer *KK'* of that factor to the poor country, either by lending or direct investment (including reinvested earnings). Transferring that amount will equalize the return on capital in the two countries, since the two *MP* curves cross there (at point *E*).

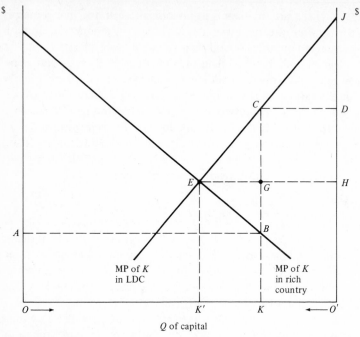

Figure 5.1 Advantages of MNE Investment.

First, note the advantage to the rich country. Total incomes earned at home fall by $K'EBK$ because of the capital transfer, but returns from the new investment in the LDC are $K'EGK$. There is a clear gain of BEG, thus providing the motive for the transfer from the investor's point of view. (Indeed, the yield on U.S. investment in manufacturing in the LDCs has recently averaged about 19 percent, more than double the average yield in developed countries. The average risk on an individual investment in an LDC is higher, of course, but then the geographical diversification of the investments serves to spread it.[38])

Now the advantage to the poor country. It loses $K'EGK$ either as interest on borrowing or profit repatriation on direct investment, but it gains $K'ECK$ in greater total income, thus increasing total income ECG. The "world" is ahead by $BEG + ECG = ECB$.

Note the interesting effects on income distribution. In the poor country domestic capitalists find their returns reduced to $KGHO'$, but the real income of labor has risen to EJH, an increase of $ECDH$. Much of this rise is a transfer away from domestic capitalists to labor in the amount $GCDH$, but the rest is a net addition to the incomes earned in the country receiving the capital.

The model portrayed here is within a framework of competition and full employment and ignores the possible monopolistic or oligopolistic behavior of MNEs discussed below. But it does make a salient point that on occasion is forgotten: Adding to capital where capital is scarce is likely to bring benefits.

Against these benefits must be weighed the costs, both economic and political. There is an active mythology concerning the multinationals much of which, both pro and con, is politically motivated and has a strong emotional content that must be recognized. Hard-line defenders of free enterprise may see nary a negative, pointing to the overwhelming advantages of competition in free markets. The opposition, sometimes xenophobes with a "blame the foreigner" attitude, deplores foreign control over a country's resources and may see nefarious exploiters wherever it looks (indeed, foreign firms can often make convenient scapegoats). Other opposition can come from local firms who fear the competition and from trade unions in the home country who claim that jobs are exported. Here we shall attempt to confine the discussion to economic analysis and forgo the rhetoric.

The major economic complaints are (1) excessive repatriation of profits with associated balance of payments problems and crowding out in local capital markets, (2) the high cost of enticing the MNEs through tax reduction or other means, (3) their monopolistic behavior, with overpricing, political meddling, and stultifying effects on domestic entrepreneurship and management, (4) their overcharges for patents and technical knowledge through the use of an internal price system for transfers between branches of the same firm, (5) their marketing of inappropriate goods, and (6) their use of inappropriate technology. Below we expand on these accusations, weigh them, and allow the multinationals an opportunity for rebuttal.

Repatriation of Profits   Repatriation of profits has been criticized as leading to lower levels of reinvestment in the country concerned, with attendant greater dependence on local capital markets and the crowding out of local borrowers. The repatriation involves foreign exchange, which has to be generated somehow. In an efficient economy with floating exchange rates and following the dictates of comparative advantage, this may not be a serious problem. But protectionism in the developed world plus artificial exchange rates in the LDCs defended by controls on currency movements may mean that obtaining the necessary foreign exchange is not so easy.

A defender of the MNEs would argue that the fault lies with the controls and the protectionism rather than with the multinationals; if the MNE's investment is otherwise beneficial, it makes much more sense to attack these problems directly. The defender would also point out that the sheer size of repatriated profits is not necessarily evidence of wrongdoing. All things equal, one would expect profits to be higher where capital is in short supply (and, indeed, predicted high returns should actually increase an LDC's leverage during the bargaining over entry by an MNE). A common measure of high profits, comparing repatriated earnings to new investment by a single MNE or by the multinationals as a group in a given year, is illegitimate, or so the defender would argue. Though this information is easily obtained from the balance of payments data, the comparison should instead be between repatriated earnings and the stock of capital accumulated from *previous* investment and on which the returns have been earned.[39]

Another consideration is that the reinvested earnings of the multinational provides low-cost improvement for the balance of payments, if the funds would otherwise have had to be borrowed abroad. In any case these flows are not the only influence on the balance of payments; the positive increase in exports and decrease in imports caused by the MNE would also have to be considered.

As to the argument that crowding out of local investment will occur, MNEs and their supporters maintain that if the investment is otherwise beneficial, it should be pursued. Any crowding out would be of investment with lower rates of return.

Cost of Attracting Multinationals   There is a cost to be considered whenever tax reductions, rebates, concessions, large investment allowances and low interest rates, cheap locations for factories, tariff protection, and public subsidies are granted to attract multinational companies to a particular LDC. A recent survey by the U.S. Commerce Department of U.S. branches of MNEs abroad showed 26 percent of them had been granted at least one incentive to invest. Of this group, 20 percent received tax breaks and 9 percent even got direct subsidies.[40] Given the intense competition among LDCs for MNE investment, it is conceivable that in the short run these costs could be larger than the economic benefits provided by the firms' operations, with resources shifted from more to less efficient uses. Consumers and taxpayers from a poor country would thus subsidize a firm from a rich one. Even though LDCs would learn from the experience, the dimension and longevity of the losses might be great. (A code to harmonize these incentives among countries has been suggested but not adopted.)

Monopolistic Behavior   If there is price competition in world markets, we can define overpricing as

$$P_o = \frac{P_m - P_w}{P_w}$$

where P_m = the price charged by the MNE, P_w = the world price, and P_o = the percentage of overpricing.[41]

There is no doubt that price discrimination of this sort is frequently found. It is usually based on protection, however, as otherwise the differential could not be maintained. The defender of the MNEs would note that purely domestic firms, as opposed to multinationals, would also overprice if given the chance. In this sense, the LDC's own policies of protection lead to the exercise of market power. The multinational might, of course, lobby to this end, especially when negotiating its initial entry to a country.

Worldwide monopoly overpricing is much rarer, because an aspiring monopolist must face the potential competition from all countries, not just one. Some MNEs do appear to operate in a worldwide oligopolistic structure, where they are able to utilize price discrimination based on product differentiation, proprietary technology, or some other secure asset. Different prices can be charged in different countries simply by ordering branch managers not to engage in unauthorized international trade. Even so, it is clear that the oligopolistic behavior of numerous industries in a national market (steel, autos, aircraft, ships, electronic goods) is very much less so when the firms face competition from other countries in LDC markets.

Still, the lessons of the past warn that LDC governments had better be vigilant and that, where it exists, uncontrolled behavior by a large and monopolistic MNE can be far from benevolent. Multinationals might attempt to bribe public officials for their benefit (Lockheed being a well-known example) or even conspire to overthrow governments, as with ITT's moves against Chilean president Allende in the 1970s. But the ITT case of 1973–74 sparked worldwide protests and tightening up by both developed-country and LDC governments alike. A decade has brought greater experience and less naiveté; the ITT example now looks to be a low point rather than the trend.[42]

There have been points lower than that, however. It is salutary to trace the extraordinary life of the United Fruit Company to see why a country's public servants had best be on guard.[43] Central America was the fabled preserve of Unifruit, or *El Pulpo,* "the Octopus," as it was called. Close to a monopoly in the United States, its Norteamericano managers achieved virtually a monopsony in Central America from Panama to Guatemala, where at its maximum it captured 92 percent of the business. Unifruit owned port facilities, the railways, and even the electric utilities in some capital cities. Its Great White Fleet of steamers, made economic by their lucrative mail contract, controlled the shipping trade of several countries. Unifruit often operated the communications system. It made unsecured personal "loans" to dictators, including among the known ones $1 million to Guatemala's Ubico, whereupon the company's taxes were sharply reduced, and $1.25 million to Lopez in Honduras. It held large tracts unplanted (at one point 95 percent of its total holdings of 3 million acres in Guatemala, 42 percent of the country's arable land), apparently to reduce the potential for competition. Typically, it paid tiny taxes and was almost exempt from import duties. It massaged its Washington connections to advantage. In the 1950s Sullivan and Crowell, the law firm of Secretary of State John Foster Dulles, represented the company, and CIA director Allen Dulles was on the board of trustees. A propaganda film, *Why the Kremlin Hates Bananas,* showed El Pulpo fighting in the front lines of the Cold War.

Some would say this is what happens when MNEs are allowed to operate in a free market, but the point is different: A free market was *not* allowed to operate. Economic and political power were used by the company to eliminate competition, to keep taxes low, and to keep politicians pliable. In doing so Unifruit found willing allies in the military or in the wealthy oligarchic hierarchy. And the behavior was certainly not permanent, changing as its allies in government lost power. Consider that as early as the 1950s, Unifruit was being compelled by governments to share profits via taxation and abide by minimum wage laws, and it now pays wages far above the country averages, with admittedly superior housing and education for its workers.

Its reputation for invincibility was lost with the great and successful 1954 strike of its workers in Honduras, the original banana republic. By the mid 1950s its land holdings in Guatemala were only $\frac{1}{12}$ the old figure and a 30-percent profits tax had been levied by that country. Unifruit lost an antitrust suit in the

United States in 1958, had to sell part of its operations to Del Monte, and found it the better part of valor to replace direct land ownership and direct management with local arrangements among producers. Competition developed; the now poorly managed company, renamed United Brands, was near bankruptcy in the early 1970s. Its chief executive jumped to his death from his 44th-floor New York office in 1975. By 1981 the "dollar tax" on each bunch that had been a rallying cry for years in Costa Rica was actually being collected. The task of policing multinational behavior is far from hopeless, as the case of the now-detentacled octopus shows.

Further extensions to the argument that monopsonistic MNEs underpay for hastily extracted natural resources and usually process them not in the LDCs but in the developed countries are considered later in Chapters 12 and 15.

Overcharging for Patents and Technical Knowledge   The world trade in "know-how" is large—only $2.7 billion in 1965, over $11 billion 10 years later. Though most of this trade is within the developed world, the 10 percent or so between the developed countries and the LDCs can be a substantial percentage of the latter's export earnings and is more as a proportion of income than was spent by Europe, the United States, and Japan for imported technology during their periods of development. Over 11 percent of Mexico's export revenues, to take an example from a recent year, was paid out in royalties and fees for patents and technologies. Since the amounts involved are large, any potential for manipulation can be magnified in its effect.

Manipulation can arise because the payments often represent a transaction between a branch of a multinational firm in an LDC and another branch of the same firm somewhere abroad. Since the transaction is not on an open market, the "real" value is not easy to establish. The payment of whatever "transfer price" is chosen obviously boosts this year's profits for the branch doing the selling and reduces it in the branch doing the buying.[44] Often enough the transfer price will be an "honest" one, since it is in the MNE's interests to have an accurate profit yardstick to measure the success of its branches. But a canny corporate treasurer can try to achieve higher profits in countries with less stringent tax laws and lower profits where taxes are high through careful juggling of the transfer price. Many LDCs actually tax corporations at a lower rate than do developed countries, but the motive is still there if the shift avoids legal limits on profit repatriation, or refutes charges by politicians and trade unions that high profits are being earned, or conceals these profits so as not to encourage competitors. Perhaps holdings of a weak currency can be minimized. Finally, if the government bases price controls on costs of production, then the transfer price can be used to raise costs and hence permitted prices. (The transfer price issue also arises in the shipment of *goods* between branches of a multinational firm or for that matter between *any* indigenous firm and a foreign one. The price can be set with an eye on tariffs and other taxes. But overcharges for goods are usually more visible to the tax authorities by comparison with the question of a proper value for patents and technology.)

Since about 1981 national tax inspectors have tried to cope with the MNE transfer price problem using four main methods.[45] They try to apply a "comparable uncontrolled price," at which technology has been transferred after an arm's-length bargain. This is often hard to find. They attempt to calculate a "resale price," finding a price at which some technology left the group and applying that price when possible. They use "cost-plus," attempting to establish costs and then applying a markup. Finally, they fall back on negotiations with the MNE to see if the firm will accept a compromise solution. Large-scale simultaneous audits by two or more national tax authorities would help to cope with the problem and are in the offing.

In part due to the distrust of the multinationals' own accounting, a movement to tax them in a different way has sprung up, ironically in the United States itself.[46] This "unitary tax" idea was pioneered by the state of California and by 1984 had been adopted by 11 other states including Colorado, Florida, Indiana, Massachusetts, and New Hampshire. These states do not accept the declared profit figures of the MNEs. They instead estimate what percentage of a firm's activity is carried on in their jurisdiction, using a simple average of the firm's sales, assets, and employment in their state as a percent of the whole. This seems at least as reasonable as accepting the firm's own (sometimes mysterious) accounting. But the MNEs claim that there is a significant probability of double taxation, a big administrative burden, and a large temptation for LDCs to follow suit. They also dislike it because it forces disclosure of much more information than they would choose to give, and lowers the chances for allocating profits away from high-tax jurisdictions. (As so often in relations with multinationals, the prospect of losing investment proved too much for some of the unitary tax states. In 1984 and 1985 Indiana, Oregon, and Florida repealed the method, and the Massachusetts supreme court struck it down. In July 1985 the U.S. government announced it would prepare draft legislation to ban the unitary tax altogether.)

Inappropriate Goods   There has been recent intense criticism of some multinationals, with charges that they market inappropriate products in the LDCs. They cater to the demands of local elites, it is said, rather than to the needs of the common people. They transmit an undesirable home country ("Coca-Cola") culture, with their advertising leading demand.[47] They move the invisible hand rather than responding to it, according to their critics, whose evidence is thought provoking. These critics note the trend to bottled soft drinks instead of fruit drinks, detergents instead of soap. They stress a survey showing Samoans (in American Samoa) to be tremendously high per capita consumers of much-advertised Pepto-Bismol, in a society where no incidence of intestinal or digestive ailments had previously been visible.[48] They point to the rapidly rising consumption of cigarettes, freely advertised (with no health warnings) and frequently with higher levels of nicotine and tar content than in those marketed in the developed countries. They note sales of inflammable pajamas, and pesticides questionable from the point of view of safe use and environmental damage.

For those who believe consumers are better off when free to choose, some of these points will not be persuasive (and it must be remembered that no charge of inappropriateness is made against a wide range of MNE production). Unsafe products would seem, however, to be another thing altogether. The Carter administration took the step of restricting the export of goods banned or limited in the United States, but the Reagan administration lifted the ban and exports of these items are now running at over a billion dollars a year.[49] In December 1982 the UN General Assembly voted 146 to 1 with no abstentions to urge strict controls on the export of products the sale of which is banned in the exporting country. The negative vote was cast by the United States.

Much attention has been focused on Nestlé, the Swiss company that markets baby food on a worldwide basis, and other producers of infant formula. Many mothers switched to formula from breast-feeding, their switch encouraged by billboard advertising promoting the bottle as the "modern way" and by wide distribution of free samples in hospitals. These, together with the high birthrates in the LDCs, brought greatly increased sales. The critics noted the inability of the formula to transmit natural immunity to disease, the malnutrition resulting from improper administration of the product, and the incidence of diarrhea caused by inadequate boiling of the water used. Nestlé replied that undernourished mothers may produce milk deficient in nutritive value and that the labels now stated that breast-feeding is the superior method. But the criticism, including an international boycott begun in 1977, caused Nestlé to abandon consumer advertising and other promotional efforts. A World Health Organization code of conduct on infant formula, voted in May 1981, involved agreements with several producing multinationals to curtail or halt their direct advertising. The code passed in the WHO by an initial vote of 93–3 and a final vote of 118–1, with the United States always voting against. Nestlé not only accepted the code, but set up an independent audit board chaired by former Secretary of State Ed Muskie of Maine to conduct an ongoing review of company practices, and in October 1984 the consumer groups that had organized the boycott officially dropped it with the statement that the company had made "substantial progress" toward reform.

Other charges are aimed by the critics against the pharmaceutical multinationals, sometimes for the high prices of brand-name drugs that could be purchased much more cheaply under the generic label, sometimes for allowing the unrestricted sale of drugs that require prescriptions in the United States or Europe. Drugs are big business in the LDCs, which spend 50 to 60 percent of their health care budgets on them as opposed to only 15 to 20 percent in developed countries. Doctors in LDCs often own their own pharmacies. Lack of competition sometimes leads to big markups above the world price. Streptomycin recently was selling in Guinea at a price 12 times higher than in Egypt. In retaliation Bangladesh has banned 1,700 drugs, India uses unpopular price controls, and Sri Lanka has a state marketing agency that buys at world prices. The UN has singled out Parke Davis' Chloramphenicol, severely restricted in the United States because it can cause blood disease problems, but sold over the counter without prescription in many LDCs. Dipyrone, a pain killer that can cause fatal blood disease (the AMA says its "only justified use is as a last resort to reduce fever when safer measures have failed"), is severely limited in the United States, but is sold over the counter in some LDCs. In response to the problems of appropriateness and high cost, the World Health Organization has compiled a list of 220 drugs it considers most essential. For the LDCs, the WHO now undertakes large-scale buying in bulk of many of these, at prices often only about half what the drugs had been costing.[50]

The United States bans the export of drugs not approved by the Food and Drug Administration (FDA), but U.S. firms want the ban repealed. It may seem reasonable to ban such exports, but there is another side to the issue. The World Health Organization has noted that the export ban may keep efficacious medicines from being used to fight diseases that do not occur in North America and may discourage the use of some cheap (although possibly more toxic) drugs because they have not been approved in the United States. The drug companies say regulation should be the responsibility of the importing nation; critics point to the expense and technical barriers of having the LDCs do the testing. An economic office in the FDA to speed the obvious cases may seem sensible, but there is no such thing.

Inappropriate Technology   It is said that multinationals tend to favor capital-intensive production rather than the labor-intense production that is often more in line with LDC factor proportions. There are thus unfavorable repercussions for employment. Economists as opposed to politicians have tended to think that this last charge is especially important, and it will be considered at length in Chapter 7.

Controlling the Multinationals

Controlling the conduct of foreign firms was much emphasized by LDCs in the 1960s and most of the 1970s. As countries weighed the costs and benefits discussed above, they frequently decided against allowing unfettered operation by the multinationals. Many steps certainly *can* be taken. Whole industries can be declared off limits to the MNEs and reserved for local (often parastatal) enterprise. Controls can take the form of maximum allowable ownership and profit repatriation. Both 100 percent foreign ownership and uncontrolled profit repatriation are considerably rarer than they used to be. Of the affiliates of U.S. multinationals, only 44 percent of those established in the mid 1970s were wholly owned.[51] *Minority* participation became commonplace among European MNEs, 42 percent in the mid 1970s, and typical of Japanese operations, 74 percent in that time period.

There are often strict rules on local participation in the investment and management of the firm. Countries now commonly require that any expansion of an enterprise be accomplished through domestic participation, and a steady rise in the proportion of local stockholding may be mandated by law. In some instances joint ventures may be required from the time a firm is first established, and foreign shareholders may be under a legal obligation to sell out within a certain time period. Several South American countries (Bolivia, Colombia, Ecuador, Peru, Venezuela) are now operating under a 15- to 20-year provision that outside ownership be reduced to a 49 percent maximum. This has, however, had a depressing effect on foreign capital inflows, especially inhibiting transfers of confidential technology, so that these countries are considering a complete relaxation of the requirement. They may also be reacting to several other perverse developments: local stockholders sometimes prefer higher dividends to the reinvestment of retained earnings; and there is an increased incentive to engage in transfer pricing as a means to shift profits out of the LDC. The mandated local ownership may not even be a sensible use of resources whenever the rate of return is below those in the scores of substitute uses for the local financial capital. Just because the MNE is there is no guarantee whatever that its returns will be the highest available. Some countries have gone even further and have prohibited foreign ownership (equity holdings) altogether, which, however, obviously discourages MNEs from revealing technology and management methods over which they wish to retain complete control.

To counter the problem of inadequate training, quota targets (akin to equal opportunity guidelines in the United States) are now widespread, with countries mandating a certain percentage of local managers at junior and senior levels, the target number growing larger as time passes. (MNEs view these requirements with reluctance if employees once trained are likely to jump to a competing firm.) "Local content" requirements, mandating the use of domestically produced inputs and similar in their economic effects to import quotas, are now common, as are export requirements for some of the MNEs' final output.[52] The permitted amount of local borrowing may be limited by law. In an attempt to meet the problem of the transfer price, many governments now restrict royalties and fees to some fixed percentage of total sales in the country, though this has not been a full solution.

At the United Nations a debate has been underway on the adoption of a code of conduct to establish behavioral rules for multinationals operating in LDCs. The proposed code was at one time bitterly opposed by the developed countries, but now they are willing to give it some support since it is voluntary and does not require ratification. The present form of the code will lead to some release of previously classified MNE information in exchange for "reasonable safeguards" of confidentiality. Major areas of the voluntary code include consumer and environmental protection, guidelines on transfer pricing, and government agreement not to discriminate against MNEs in return for a right to limit MNE entry into some specific areas. Still open are discussions on how much diplomatic protection a home country can provide an MNE and whether to allow "slate-cleaning" contract adjustments, that is, adjustments that can wipe out provisions too advantageous to an MNE as opposed to the permanent "sanctity" of contracts.[53] The United States has announced it will not support any code provisions that are compulsory, discriminate against foreign enterprise, and apply just to MNEs rather than to all firms, including government ones. The U.N. is currently considering whether to convene another conference on the subject.[54]

Running parallel to the decision to place restrictions on multinational operations has been the realization that attracting direct investment is a competitive proposition. Numerous countries, particularly in Africa and the Caribbean, have failed to attract funds, controls or no, because their domestic markets are small and local natural resources are few. Unstable governments and changeable economic policies have proved even more discouraging to investors than have fixed rules on operations. Recognition spread that the restrictions could result in cuts in investment, even sharp ones, and so could prove counterproductive. Some governments, including Egypt, Jamaica, Korea, Mexico, Pakistan, the Philippines, and Turkey, once hostile to foreign investment, have now adopted much more flexible and accommodative policies. In this group are countries that for years were among the most bitter foes of the MNEs.

The upshot for today's multinationals with branches in the LDCs is a curious combination of sometimes very strict regulations and performance requirements with sometimes very liberal investment incentives. As a result of these mixed signals, there has recently been a steady shift in the character of multinational operations. Some LDCs are rapidly reducing equity-holding by foreigners. (The game must be carefully played: Coca-Cola and IBM left India in the 1970s when the order was received to reduce their equity to 40 percent.) Direct control by expatriate managers is being replaced by participation in management, contract arrangements, and technology deals. The trend is to what can be called the "Japanese model," since Japan in its development preferred to contract for capital and technology and provide Japanese managers rather than admitting the multinationals. The Germans used much the same tactics at an earlier time.

For an LDC without the entrepreneurial and managerial talent that the Japanese showed they possessed, controlling the multinationals is a contest that must be closely calculated. The aim, obviously, is to retain the benefits they bring while reducing their costs. Like a general, a gambler, or an oligopolist, an LDC government must weigh every decision concerning the MNEs in the light of what its "rival" will do. Will further regulation cut capital inflows substantially? Will access to the latest research and technological developments be curtailed? In short, will the economic penalties be worse than the benefits from any given regulation? The calculation is not an easy one where multinationals are free to move and where one of their chief complaints has always been the instability of the economic rules under which they must operate. If a prediction might be hazarded, MNEs will continue to threaten immediate withdrawal, they will constantly lecture the LDCs about overregulation and the large potential losses of valuable investment, and they will charge a risk premium; but in spite of their many threats to leave they will continue to bring capital and know-how to the LDCs because even with the regulations it is profitable to do so.[55]

Confiscation

Nationalization of MNE assets without adequate compensation, called confiscation or expropriation, is a side issue to this debate. From the point of view of a capital-hungry LDC, there is always the alternative of seizing assets. But doing so is likely to be devastating for future private capital inflows, not only by the affected firm but by other firms as well. U.S. aid must stop by law. Where wrangles over ownership and compensation are likely, commercial bank and World Bank loans will be less forthcoming. Foreign managers and technicians may depart. In technical terms, the present discounted value of the expropriated property would have to be balanced against the present discounted value of the reduced inflows and then weighted for political impact.

The tactic always has a high degree of political and emotional content. The fear of nationalization may be an important matter even in a country with no history of such events, especially when politicians put their rhetoric into high gear. Fear, even when largely groundless, can quickly result in big cuts in private foreign investment. Hence the importance for maintaining business confidence of the relatively recent but small government insurance plans, the Overseas Private Investment Corporation (OPIC) in the United States, similar European and Japanese agencies, and the Multilateral Investment Guarantee Agency being set up by the World Bank. OPIC issued $4.3 billion in insurance in 1984, a rise of three times in three years. Criticism of this otherwise sensible sounding idea has centered on the favoritism shown to relatively well-off LDCs and to large projects (83 percent of OPIC's newly insured commitments were to just 13 large projects valued at over $10 million each). Congress originally required OPIC to insure commitments only in low-income LDCs, but lifted that requirement in 1981.[56]

Expropriation was at one time particularly pronounced among plantations, mines, oil companies, banks, utilities, and transportation facilities. Some compensation was frequently made, but the amount of the payment (in the 1960s) averaged only about 40 percent of book value. Since that time, however, there has been a massive retreat by the LDCs from outright expropriation, caused, so it appears, by self-interest. Some countries have passed laws prohibiting the tactic, a number have even put the prohibition into their constitutions, and there are currently about 200 treaties involving the protection of investment, some of them part of the U.S. Bilateral Investment Treaty (BIT) Program. In the 1960s nearly three-quarters of the disputes involving U.S. firms abroad had to do with formal nationalization or expropriation. In the 1970s this figure fell to less than a quarter, and the bulk of the controversies came to be over contract or management issues.[57] Many of the cases are now negotiated in the World Bank's International Center for the Settlement of Investment Disputes (ICSID), which presently has 82 member countries. In recent years only a few LDCs have used expropriation as a major tool. In the period 1960 to 1977, nearly three-quarters (72.5 percent) of all reported seizures were concentrated in just seven nations—Algeria, Chile, Cuba, Ethiopia, Sri Lanka, Uganda, and Venezuela; Cuba and Uganda together were responsible for fully half of them.[58]

We have seen in this chapter that LDCs seek capital from abroad because they want to invest more than they are able to save at home. Generally, this makes good economic sense. But two of the most important ways in which capital can flow are foreign aid and investment by multinational firms; few areas of development economics are as politically "loaded" and involve such disputes and acrimony as do these two topics. For LDCs, what strategy to employ toward foreign capital is one of the most difficult questions to be faced; too often, the economic optimum and the political optimum will be far apart or even mutually exclusive. "Uneasy lies the head that wears a crown," said Shakespeare; life is not much easier for those who have to design public policy on foreign capital flows.

NOTES

1. The World Bank's *World Development Report 1985* focused on the contribution of foreign capital to economic development and is an excellent introduction to the subject.

2. The rates of return calculated here and below are from a recent U.S. Treasury study of 236 Bank-financed projects. An account of the Bank's record, published by the Bank itself, is Warren C. Baum and Stokes M. Tolbert, *Investing in Development: Lessons of World Bank Experience,* Washington, D.C., 1985. Rates of return were 10 percent or more in 79 percent of the projects studied; the returns were highest (20 percent average) in agriculture and lowest (13 percent average) in manufacturing. Only 14 percent of projects were judged to have had an unsatisfactory outcome. See *WDR 1985,* p. 103. Other data in this section are from Richard Feinberg, ed., *Between Two Worlds: The World Bank's Next Decade,* Washington, D.C., 1986; the survey in *The Economist,* September 27, 1986; and the World Bank's *Annual Reports.*

3. *The Economist,* August 27, 1983, p. 53; October 5, 1985, p. S25.

4. For the last two paragraphs, see Shahid Javed Burki and Norman Hicks, "International Development Association in Retrospect," *Finance and Development,* 19, no. 4 (1982): 22–25; *WDR 1984,* p. 49; and *The Economist,* September 14, 1985, p. 73.

5. The next replenishment, for 1988 to 1990, was being discussed at the time of writing. The negotiating range was $11.5 to 12 billion; this would represent a substantial real decrease from 1981 to 1983. See *The Economist,* April 5, 1986, pp. 16, 91, and September 27, 1986, p. S45.

6. Early in the Bank's history, just after World War II when the "Reconstruction" in its official title, IBRD, had some meaning, program loans accounted for nearly three-quarters of all lending. But by the 1960s and 70s, they had dropped virtually out of sight.

7. See *North-South: A Programme for Survival,* London, 1980, especially chap. 15.

8. *The Economist,* September 24, 1983, p. S46. The figure for investment financed by foreign aid reaches a hardly credible 98 percent in very poor Burkina Faso (Upper Volta). A new and definitive study is Robert Cassen et al., *Does Aid Work?* Oxford, 1986.

9. See Anne O. Krueger, "Aid in the Development Process," *The World Bank Research Observer,* 1, no. 1 (1986): 57–58, for a survey of the positive economic effects. Also see Gerald M. Meier, *Emerging from Poverty: The Economics That Really Matters,* New York, 1984, pp. 230–231; and *WDR 1985,* pp. 99–100.

10. See A. K. Sen, *On Economic Inequality,* Oxford, 1973, and "Ethical Issues in Income Distribution," in Sven Grassman and Erik Lundberg, eds., *The World Economic Order: Past and Prospects,* New York, 1981, pp. 464–494; Ian M. D. Little, "Distributive Justice and the New International Order," in Peter Oppenheimer, ed., *Issues in International Economics,* London, 1980, pp. 37–53; John Rawls, *A Theory of Justice,* Cambridge, Mass., 1971; and Robert Nozick, *Anarchy, State, and Utopia,* Oxford, 1974.

11. See Shireen Hunter, *OPEC and the Third World: The Politics of Aid,* Bloomington, Ind., 1984; Ibraihim F. I. Shihata and Naiem A. Sherbiny, "A Review of OPEC Aid Efforts," *Finance and Development* 23, no. 1. (1986): 17–20; and Zubair Iqbal, "Arab Concessional Assistance, 1975–81," *Finance and Development* 20, no. 2 (1983): 31–33.

12. The Soviets claim to donate 1.3 percent of their GNP, which would make them the world's leading donor in total amount, but independent analysts state that this figure is bogus. See *The Economist,* August 27, 1983, p. 28, and July 5, 1986, p. 32.

13. See J. M. Dowling and Ulrich Hiemenz, "Biases in the Allocation of Foreign Aid: Some New Evidence," *World Development* 13, no. 4 (1985): 535–541.

14. See Bruce Herrick and Charles Kindleberger, *Economic Development,* 4th ed., New York, 1983, pp. 445–446, and Danny P. Leipziger, "The Concessionality of Foreign Assistance," *Finance and Development* 21, no. 1 (1984): 44–46.

15. *WDR 1985,* p. 107, notes that in the early 1980s 60 donors were trying to administer 600 separate projects in Kenya. At the same time there were 188 projects from 50 donors in Malawi, 321 from 61 in Lesotho, and 614 from 69 in Zambia. "In such numbers, the effectiveness of aid can be severely reduced," says the *Report.* Some coordination has been achieved under World Bank and UN auspices, however, by aid groups ("consortia") and "round tables." In these groups donors consult on joint approaches; there are currently about 20 active consortia.

16. The data in this paragraph are largely from *WDR 1985,* p. 101.

17. See David M. Cheney, "The OECD Export Credits Agreement," *Finance and Development* 22, no. 3 (1985): 35–38.

18. *The Economist,* April 28, 1979, p. 45. The other figures in the paragraph are from *WDR 1986,* pp. 220–221.

19. *The Economist,* May 24, 1986, p. 26.

20. See *WDR 1985,* p. 101. With Sudan less friendly to the United States (and vice versa) in 1986, that country suddenly dropped out of the "top 10" recipients. Alfred Maizels and Machiko Nissanke, "Motivations for Aid to Developing Countries," *World Development* 12, no. 9 (September 1984): 879–900, show with multiple regression analysis that bilateral aid is often granted largely in support of donors' perceived interests rather than based on need. A trend toward giving aid based on need set in between 1969 and 1980, but has been reversed since that time in the United States and Britain. Recent data on aid flows may be found in Shahid Javed Burki and Robert L. Ayres, "A Fresh Look at Development Aid," *Finance and Development* 23, no. 1 (1986): 7–9. In this section I also utilized Richard Newfarmer, "A Look at Reagan's Revolution in Development Policy," *Challenge* 26, no. 4 (1983): 34–43.

21. The 1985 U.S. budget contained $5.8 billion in ESF money, $2.3 billion for development assistance, $1.5 billion for Public Law 480 (PL480 authorized U.S. food aid), $1.5 billion for the international institutions, plus some miscellaneous (Peace Corps, refugees), all totaling $11.7 billion. Military aid for equipment was $2.6 billion in grants, $0.7 billion in concessional loans, and $1.7 billion for loans at a market rate, which together with miscellaneous items totaled $5.9 billion. The 1986 request would cut economic aid 20 percent and raise military aid 11 percent. See U.S. Department of State, "Foreign Assistance Program: FY 1986 Budget and 1985 Supplemental Request," Special Report No. 128, May, 1985. In the 1987 proposal President Reagan asked for a further increase in aid of the security sort. See *The Economist,* February 22, 1986. Between 1981 and 1986 development assistance grew only 11 percent, while economic support fund assistance grew 66 percent and military assistance increased 81 percent. See *Wall Street Journal,* May 22, 1986, p. 64.

22. Paul Streeten has humorously but vividly pointed out that the personal characteristics of the aid-seeker must be carefully tailored to the national traits of the donor country. Thus, the grantsperson soliciting for British aid should have common sense, be able to laugh at English jokes, not have oily hair, and if a male dealing with males, not be too successful with women. "A Primer for Aid Recipients," in Streeten, *The Frontiers of Development Studies,* New York, 1972, p. 309. In the same essay (p. 307) he notes that aid is like making love to an elephant: there is no pleasure in it, you run the risk of being crushed, and it takes a long time to view the results.

23. See Keith Griffin and John Gurley, "Radical Analyses of Imperialism, The Third

World, and the Transition to Socialism: A Survey Article," *Journal of Economic Literature* 23 (September 1985): 1116–1117; and the various articles on aid by Lord Bauer of the London School of Economics, for evidence of some convergence of the critiques by radicals and conservatives. But a recent study of the problem by Anne O. Krueger and Vernon W. Ruttan, *The Development Impact of Economic Assistance to LDCs,* Washington, D.C., 1983, concludes that in general aid with all its problems has been beneficial to growth.

24. *The Economist,* May 26, 1984, p. 73.
25. For a discussion of adverse effects, see Cassen et al., *Does Aid Work?* and S. J. Maxwell and H. W. Singer, "Food Aid to Developing Countries: A Survey," in Paul Streeten and Richard Jolly, eds., *Recent Issues in World Development,* Oxford, 1981, pp. 219–240. Some details in this paragraph are from the *Wall Street Journal,* July 2, 1984.
26. See Robert F. Gorman, ed., *Private Voluntary Organizations as Agents of Development,* Boulder, Colo., 1984; and Vittorio Masoni, "Nongovernmental Organizations and Development," *Finance and Development* 22, no. 3 (1985): 38–41.
27. For this section I relied on the Brandt Commission Report, *North-South: A Programme for Survival,* London, 1980, chap. 15; Peter B. Kenen, "Debt Relief as Development Assistance," in Jagdish D. Bhagwati, ed., *The New International Economic Order: The North-South Debate,* Cambridge, Mass., 1977, pp. 68–69; Richard N. Cooper, "The Oceans as a Source of Revenue," in Bhagwati, *New International Economic Order,* pp 105–120; and Nural Islam's comment in Bhagwati, *New International Economic Order,* pp. 121–124; Permagnus Wijkman, "UNCLOS and the Redistribution of Ocean Wealth," *Journal of World Trade Law* 16, no. 1 (1982): 27–48; an article by Stephen Chapman on UNCLOS in *The New Republic,* April 21, 1982, pp. 17–20; and Scott Armstrong, "Seabed Mining," *Christian Science Monitor,* April 10, 1984.
28. See David Goldsbrough, *Foreign Private Investment in Developing Countries,* IMF Occasional Paper No. 33, 1985; and *The Economist,* March 15, 1986, p. 67.
29. For this section, I utilized *WDR 1985,* especially pp. 12–14.
30. For the pros and cons of multinationals, I benefited from Theodore H. Moran, ed., *Multinational Corporations: The Political Economy of Foreign Direct Investment,* Lexington, Mass., 1985; Thomas N. Gladwin and Ingo Walter, *Multinationals Under Fire,* New York, 1980; Jean-François Hennart, *A Theory of Multinational Enterprise,* Ann Arbor, Mich., 1982; Ian M. D. Little, *Economic Development: Theory, Policy, and International Relations,* New York, 1982, pp. 182–189; V. N. Balasubramanyam, *Multinational Enterprises in the Third World,* Thames Essay No. 26, London, 1980; C. F. Bergsten, T. Horst, and T. H. Moran, eds., *American Multinationals and American Interests,* Washington, D.C., 1978; Seymour E. Rubin and Gary C. Hufbauer, eds., *Emerging Standards of International Trade and Investment,* Totowa, N.J., 1984; and especially from the penetrating comments on this chapter by Wilson B. Brown of the University of Winnipeg. Two modern classics by Raymond Vernon are *Sovereignty at Bay,* New York, 1971; and *Storm Over the Multinationals,* Cambridge, Mass., 1974. *The Economist* publishes many articles on the activities of MNEs. For this section I utilized the issues of April 21, 1979; June 20 and December 12, 1981; February 19 and July 23, 1983; April 28 and May 5, 1984; February 9, July 13, and September 21, 1985; and March 15 and 22, 1986. Among the textbooks, I was guided by Michael P. Todaro, *Economic Development in the Third World,* 2nd ed., New York, 1981, chap. 14; and Gerald M. Meier, *Leading Issues in Economic Development,* 4th ed., Oxford, 1984, pts. V.D and V.E.
31. Peter B. Kenen, *The International Economy,* Englewood Cliffs, N.J., 1985, pp. 157–158.

32. See Louis T. Wells, Jr., *Third World Multinationals: The Rise of Foreign Investment from Developing Countries,* Cambridge, Mass., 1983. A skeptical view of the supposed advantages is Sanjaya Lall et al., *The New Multinationals: The Spread of Third World Enterprises,* Chichester, 1984. Singapore has even invested in the United States, in electronics, and South Korea in semiconductors.

33. See Raymond Vernon, "Multinationals Are Mushrooming," *Challenge* 29, no. 2 (1986): 41–47.

34. The figures are for various years, from studies by D. Nayyan and S. Lall. See Hubert Schmitz, "Industrialization Strategies in Less Developed Countries: Some Lessons of Historical Experience," *Journal of Development Studies* 21, no. 1 (1984): 10–11. The exports have been much stimulated by the relatively new system of value-added tariffs now in use in both Europe and the United States and discussed in chapter 14.

35. Economists sometimes speak of multinationals as "filling gaps" in economic development. Their gap models usually emphasize the role of foreign companies in (1) bringing saving from abroad so that domestic investment can be larger than domestic saving; (2) generating foreign exchange receipts and so filling a gap between the desired earnings of foreign exchange and what a country could otherwise acquire through exports, aid, etc., in the absence of the multinationals; (3) alleviating the shortage of managerial and technical skills; and (4) mobilizing new government revenue through taxation of the multinationals, thus filling a gap between the revenues a government wants to expend and what it can acquire through local taxation. See Todaro, *Economic Development in the Third World,* 2nd ed., pp. 403–404.

36. The terms are used by S. P. Schatz, "Assertive Pragmatism and the Multinational Enterprise," *World Development* 9, no. 1 (1981): 93–105.

37. Illustrating the MacDougall-Kemp model, from G. D. A. MacDougall, "The Benefits and Costs of Private Investment from Abroad: A Theoretical Approach," *Economic Record* 36 (1960): 13–35; and M. C. Kemp, *The Pure Theory of International Trade,* Englewood Cliffs, N.J., 1964. The diagram is adapted from R. J. Ruffin, "International Factor Movements," in Ronald W. Jones and Peter B. Kenen, *Handbook of International Economics,* vol. 1, Amsterdam, 1984, pp. 255–256. See also Meier, *Leading Issues,* 4th ed., pp. 323–324.

38. See *The Economist,* March 15, 1986, p. 67.

39. Loehr and Powelson, *Economics of Development and Distribution,* p. 304.

40. Reported in *The Economist,* December 12, 1981, p. 81.

41. The formula is from Subrata Ghatak, *Development Economics,* London, 1978, p. 198.

42. Often enough the political pressures are the other way round, as in the attempts by Arab states to persuade the MNEs they host to embargo trade with Israel or in moves by the United States to alter its firms' behavior in South Africa.

43. See Walter Le Feber, *Inevitable Revolutions,* New York, 1983, for a discussion of the company. Unifruit is also discussed in Jan S. Hogendorn and Wilson B. Brown, *The New International Economics,* Reading, Mass., 1979, pt. V.

44. For transfer pricing see Hogendorn and Brown, *New International Economics,* pp. 374–375; David Colman and Frederick Nixson, *Economics of Change in Less Developed Countries,* Deddington, 1978, p. 227, citing S. Lall; *The Economist,* June 20, 1981. The same principle can apply to the allocation of overhead expenditures within the firm.

45. See *The Economist,* June 20, 1981, pp. 108–109.

46. See Vernon, "Multinationals Are Mushrooming," pp. 46–47; U.S. Department of State, "Examining the Unitary Tax," *Current Policy No. 564,* 1984, and articles in *The Economist,* May 5, 1984, and July 13 and September 21, 1985.

47. See William Loehr and John P. Powelson, *The Economics of Development and Distribution,* New York, 1981, p. 301. John Kenneth Galbraith has been a leading exponent of this view, especially in *The New Industrial State,* Boston, 1967; and *The Affluent Society,* Boston, 1958.

48. See *The Economist,* June 6, 1981, p. 102.

49. See Charles O. Agege, "Dumping of Dangerous American Products Overseas: Should Congress Sit and Watch," *Journal of World Trade Law* 19, no. 4 (1985): 403–410. Foreign governments do, however, have to be notified under U.S. law that a banned product is being exported.

50. All of these cases have been reported in *The Economist* in recent years. See note 30, and the issues of October 2, 1982, and May 31, 1986.

51. Previous experience was, however, very different, so that 83 percent of U.S. multinationals are still majority owned and 71 percent are wholly owned. See B. L. Barker, "A Profile of U.S. Multinational Companies in 1977," *Survey of Current Business* 61, no. 10 (1981): 38–57.

52. Export requirements can have a "beggar-thy-neighbor" impact if a multinational reduces exports from country B in order to meet the new target imposed by country A. See Vernon, "Multinationals Are Mushrooming," p. 44.

53. Discussed in *The Economist,* September 12, 1981.

54. U.S. ITC, *Operation of the Trade Agreements Program, 37th Report,* 1986, p. 119.

55. This section, and other analyses of MNEs in this chapter, have been informed by Gerald K. Helleiner, *International Economic Disorder: Essays in North-South Relations,* Toronto, 1981. Some data are from his "Intrafirm Trade and the Developing Countries: An Assessment of the Data," *Journal of Development Economics* 6 (1979): 391–406. Also see Meier, *Leading Issues,* 4th ed., pp. 322–331, 339–343; and Herrick and Kindleberger, *Economic Development,* chap. 22. The final sentence is adapted from Carlos Diaz-Alejandro, "The Less Developed Countries and Transnational Enterprises," in Sven Grassman and Erik Lundberg, eds., *The World Economic Order: Past and Prospects,* New York, 1981, p. 251.

56. Such plans usually insure less than 10 percent of total direct investment, however, far lower than the total amount of insurance written since more than one policy can be taken out to cover various types of risk. OPIC's policies are usually for 20 years, far longer than presently available private insurance, and they also usually cover "civil strife." Even so, private insurance for political risk (pioneered by Lloyd's of London) has grown, and now covers an estimated $8 billion in foreign investment. See *WDR 1985,* p. 131.

57. Helleiner, *International Economic Disorder,* p. 169. The U.S. Bilateral Investment Treaty (BIT) program dates from 1981. It seeks to obtain agreements with LDCs guaranteeing certain rights and safeguards. A "model treaty" revised in 1984 is the basis for the negotiations. Seven treaties are expected to be ratified in 1986 and 14 more are being negotiated. See U.S. ITC, *Operation of the Trade Agreements Program, 37th Report,* 1986, pp. 110–111.

58. F. N. Burton and Hisashi Inoue, "Expropriations of Foreign-Owned Firms in Developing Countries," *Journal of World Trade Law* 18, no. 5 (1984): 396–414; M. L. Williams, "The Extent and Significance of Nationalization of Foreign-Owned Assets in Developing Countries, 1956–1972," *Oxford Economic Papers,* July 1975, Table V–1; and see Herrick and Kindleberger, *Economic Development,* pp. 473–474.

chapter 6

Short-Term Borrowing: The Debt Crisis and the International Monetary Fund

The capital flows from abroad discussed in the last chapter were long term, either grants or loans with long maturities, or direct investment. But the transfer of foreign resources need not be confined to these long-term flows. Commercial bank loans with short maturities will also serve, though with greater risk for the LDCs as the debt crisis of the 1980s plainly demonstrates. The basic proposition is once again that a country can consume and invest no more than it can produce at home plus any deficit in the current account balance $(M - X)$.

All *can* go well. An LDC can borrow from private banks and then use the foreign exchange made available to finance crucial imports of capital goods and materials necessary to build a new road or port facility or factory. If the interest payments on the loans are moderate and do not change much, and if the income generated by the new projects is rapidly realized, then the greater economic strength allows the debt to be financed in timely fashion, and the strategy is successful.

But there can be serious trouble. What if the interest charged on the loans is variable and rises? Perhaps banks refuse to renew old loans so no new flows come in to help fund the repayment of the old. Instead of using the foreign exchange to finance productive investments providing the future means to repay, a country might choose to consume beyond its means while it can, or might invest inefficiently, or might use the funds for political purposes or for its military. In that case the economy may grow too slowly to service the required transfers of interest and repayments of principal.[1]

If all these eventualities were to happen at the same time, there might be a crisis. They *did* happen at the same time, and there was a crisis, a dangerous one, in the early 1980s. Though the word *crisis* is widely used, it is not completely correct because it signifies something temporary, as in the turning point of a disease. We cannot be sure this is true of the debt problem, which seems to be more like an ongoing malaise.

THE ERUPTION OF THE DEBT CRISIS[2]

The crisis of 1982 to 1984 grew slowly from innocent roots put down in the mid and late 1970s. When commercial banks in developed countries and the LDCs began the rapid expansion in their relationship, it was initially widely applauded by most observers.[3] It brought profit to the banks, or so they believed. It brought no tying or politically difficult conditions, as did foreign aid. Plenty of funds were available, because of the early 1970s increase in world oil prices. OPEC deposited its continuing windfalls largely with developed-country commercial banks (about 50 percent in the 1974 oil shock and 65 percent in 1979), causing substantial excess liquidity in the banking system. OPEC approved of the lending because the recycling of funds kept the system healthy, but without risk to OPEC since the loans were the responsibility of the banks. Supporters of aid approved because the expanded relationship of banks and LDCs transferred resources on a scale beyond what was politically possible otherwise. Western governments in general were enthusiastic; it cut the need for foreign aid and was a stopgap that avoided emergency responses to OPEC.

The banks, lacking perfect foresight, had little reason to question the developments. For many years their losses on international loans had been proportionately less than on domestic loans, and many LDCs boasted better records of economic growth than did the industrial countries over a space of several years leading up to the lending boom. Lending reached vast proportions, until by the end of 1982 total non-oil LDC debt to commercial banks was just over $354 billion, 53 percent of a total debt of slightly more than $669 billion. LDC debt had grown about seven times since 1971, at which time bank loans were only 23 percent of the total. In some years annual growth in net bank lending was in the range of 25 to 30 percent, and the proportion of bank loans to all lending reached 70 percent. These loans were about 6 percent of the total assets of the lending banks. Debt, only 14 percent of developing country GNP in 1970, was nearly 34 percent in 1984.

Very poor LDCs were never able to borrow much from commercial banks because of their unfavorable economic prospects; 87 percent of their debt in 1980 was to governments and international agencies. Most of the commercial bank loans (about two-thirds) were to 13 relatively well-off LDCs. There was high concentration (slightly over 50 percent) in Argentina, Brazil, Mexico, and South Korea. (Korea's adjustment to the economic conditions that brought near catastrophe to so many others is a remarkable success story.) Nearly a third of the commercial bank lending was by U.S. banks; their loans of over $98 billion were 8 percent of their total assets and 186 percent of shareholders' capital at the end of 1982. The loans to Latin America alone were 120 percent of capital for all U.S. banks. The nine largest U.S. banks were much more exposed: the equivalent of

288 percent of their capital in loans to LDCs; 177 percent to the Latin American borrowers.

The crisis erupted forcefully and suddenly with Mexico's announcement in August 1982 that it was in difficulty. The announcement brought an obvious high risk of default, a risk of insolvency for major banks unable to collect principal and interest payments, even perhaps the risk of another Creditanstalt. (The collapse of that Vienna bank and the resulting world banking panic was one cause of the Great Depression of the 1930s.) Paul Volcker, chairman of the U.S. Federal Reserve System, called the potential threat to the international financial system essentially unparalleled in postwar history.[4]

THE CAUSES OF THE CRISIS

It is important to understand the causes of the crisis and what might be done to avoid a repetition. Analysts with the full benefit of hindsight point to three major factors: (1) the world recession of the early 1980s, (2) the sharp increase in interest rates starting in 1978, and (3) the strength of the dollar.

The world recession of the early 1980s cut developed-country imports and thus reduced the exports of the LDCs. The usual estimates of the relation (elasticity) between developed-country growth and their imports is that a 1 percent change in the rate of growth causes a change in imports ranging from about 1.2 to 2.2 percent. Imports from the LDCs are even more sensitive since the demand for many industrial raw materials produced by these countries shifts rapidly with the business cycle. Not only was the world recession deep, but it was severely underestimated by most reputable forecasters. The International Monetary Fund, whose forecasts are regularly published and widely respected, had to cut its best estimate of LDC growth in half for 1981, and the Organization for Economic Cooperation and Development (OECD) projection for industrial country growth for 1982 of +1.5 percent had to be revised downward to −0.5 percent at the end of the year. There was thus a sharp decline in LDC export performance, with a rise in volume of only about 1 percent in 1982.[5]

At the same time the major OPEC oil price increase of 1979 meant a further drain on foreign exchange earnings, just as those earnings were falling because of the decrease in LDC exports. The petroleum necessary for industry, transportation, and the manufacture of artificial fertilizer was now much higher in price. IMF studies indicate that a $1 per barrel rise in the price of OPEC oil meant $2 billion more in annual spending on oil by the LDCs.

This stagnant demand for their exports together with the OPEC oil price shock affected earnings not only by reducing volume, but also by worsening the LDCs' terms of trade (the ratio between the prices paid for exports and the prices paid for imports, P_x/P_m; a fall means that a dollar's worth of exports buys less imports than before). This ratio declined 6 percent in 1980, nearly 4 percent in 1981, and nearly 3 percent in 1982. (The terms of trade of the industrial countries were also falling in this period, as they, too, are net oil importers.) The recession helped to generate intensified protectionist pressures in the industrial countries and in the LDCs as well.

Thus the "triple whammy" of reduced export volume, worsening prices, and increased protection made it far more difficult for LDCs to earn the hard currency needed to make debt payments. The IMF's *World Economic Outlook* for 1983 estimated that the recession could be blamed for about a third of the cumulative payments deterioration from 1978 to 1981, while over a quarter could be blamed on the adverse turn in the balance on oil trade.

The second cause of the debt crisis, responsible for perhaps another third of the deterioration, was the sharp increase in interest rates starting in 1978. Interest payments on LDC debt had been only 0.5 percent of their GNP in 1970, but had reached 2.8 percent in 1984. Why interest rates rose requires some explanation.

The commercial bank loans had come in large part from the Eurocurrency markets, still largely (70 percent) a dollar market at the start of the 1980s. Eurodollars are dollars held in bank accounts outside the territory of the United States, with London the most important center. OPEC governments and other holders of dollars deposited their surpluses in the Eurodollar market. By doing so, they earned interest; their deposits were liquid; and since they were not in the territory of the United States, there was some extra security that politics would not result in the seizure of the deposits.

The Eurodollar loans to LDCs came usually in the form of fairly short- and intermediate-term bank credits (seven years was the average in 1981). Often they were syndicated by a group of banks, at some spread over a variable interest rate, the so-called LIBOR or London interbank offered rate. The variability of this interest rate, extending over the entire life of the loans to which it applied, was a particularly important contributor to the crisis. The banks were not really to blame for floating the rates, by the way. Earlier in the 1970s, when serious inflation had occurred in the developed countries, they had frequently been locked into fixed low or negative real rates of return at great expense to them. Learning from that experience, they had protected themselves by insisting on variable rates that would reflect any future inflation.

The variable rates were typically adjusted every six months, with a spread intended to reflect risk. For example, before the debt crisis began Britain and France were paying a +0.875 percent spread over LIBOR for their Eurodollar borrowing at the same time Mexico was paying +1.625 percent, Brazil +2.25 percent, and Burma +2.5 percent.[6] The situation was harmless as long as it was stable, but from 1979 world interest rates rose sharply, carrying upward with them the variable rates paid by LDCs on their existing bank loans. The U.S. prime rate, much used for loans to Latin America, eventually peaked in 1981 at 20.50 percent; LIBOR reached 16.625 percent in the same year. (LIBOR had been only 9.25 percent in 1978.) Even that did not measure the whole burden, since in addition to the risk premium over LIBOR, LDCs were paying a management fee "up front" of 0.375 to 0.75 percent, and a facility fee on undrawn credit of 0.25 to 0.75 percent.[7] Added up these averaged 18 percent in 1981, compared to the average rate on official development loans of 2.5 percent. When adjusted for inflation, the resulting real rates on dollar loans were about 11 percent, the highest peacetime figure for centuries.

The rise in interest rates was generally due to tight monetary policy, particularly in the United States and Britain, designed to reduce the rapid inflation of the late 1970s and to resist the further inflationary impact of the oil price shock of 1979. Temporarily high interest rates would have been bad enough, but after the oil shock worked its way through the Western economies and monetary policy loosened, real interest rates *stayed* high, at 6 to 8 percent on short-term dollar loans (and slightly lower at 5 to 6 percent in other major currencies) in 1981 to 1983, compared to about ½ of 1 percent in 1974 to 1978. In 1977 and 1978, most real short-term rates had been negative—no wonder the LDCs had rushed to borrow! Since so much LDC debt was at floating interest rates, over 40 percent at the end of 1982 (and 62 percent for Latin America) compared to 23 percent in 1978 and 10 percent in 1970, the rise had a stunning impact. Interest costs rapidly doubled from what they had been in the mid1970s, following the rough rule of thumb that a rise of 1 percent in market interest rates raises the flow of interest payments from the LDCs after about a year by about $2 billion. (Of that sum, $1.35 billion would come from the three major borrowers, Argentina, Brazil, and Mexico.)

Most observers believe the persistent high real rates were due to a combination of temporary factors and more permanent structural changes in economic and financial circumstances. In particular they emphasize expectations and budget deficits.[8] Expectations of inflation were high and came down only slowly. Lenders thus demanded an inflation premium as well as a risk premium for uncertainty. Growing government budget deficits, especially in the United States, brought new demands for loanable funds and put an upward pressure on interest rates.

The high rates had an even greater impact on LDCs than might have been anticipated, because their effect was levered up by so-called front loading. Front loading means that the biggest burden comes early in the loan. At a 6 percent interest rate, a 10-year loan of $100 requires payment in the first year of $10 principal plus $6 interest for a total of $16. But if inflation of 10 percent causes interest rates to rise to 16 percent, the payment becomes $10 + $16 = $26. Because of front loading, with a 10 percent inflation the burden of the debt rises about two-thirds.[9]

The combination of high real rates on the variable-rate loans and front loading need not in themselves have caused a crisis, if export earnings were also strengthening and providing the means to repay. But, as we have seen, both prices and volumes were instead weakening. The outcome was that the debt service ratio (payments of interest and amortization as a percent of export revenue) rose for LDCs from 15 percent or less in 1973 to 1977 to 24.6 percent in 1982, the rise almost entirely due to the higher interest payments. Debt service had cost the LDCs $9 billion in 1970; the figure was $100 billion in 1984.

A third cause of the crisis was the very strong dollar, its exchange rate against other currencies about two-thirds higher by 1984 than it had been in 1979. Bank loans to LDCs were mostly denominated in dollars; in 1979 to 1983 loans in other currencies were only 30 percent of the total and only just over 10 percent in Latin America. The dollar then appreciated and also carried interest rates generally higher than other currencies. The Federal Reserve Bank of New York estimates that non-oil LDCs incurred extra expenses of about 12 percent from 1979 to 1982, which could have been avoided by a more diversified program of borrowing.[10]

Why *was* the dollar so strong for so long?[11] There appears to be no single explanation. Relative rates of inflation, historically the most popular theory to explain currency strengths, does not apply because German and Japanese rates of inflation, and more specifically unit labor cost increases, advanced less rapidly during the period of the strong dollar than did those of the United States. An excess of exports over imports would also account for the dollar's strength, but this is an implausible explanation since the United States went from a trade surplus in 1979 to 1981 to large trade deficits of over $35 billion in 1983, $102 billion in 1984, and about $150 billion in 1985, at the same time that Germany and Japan were running substantial surpluses of $13 billion for the former and $36 billion for the latter in 1984.

The more persuasive explanation appears to involve capital transfers, caused by high U.S. real interest rates that for some time were significantly above those of Japan, West Germany, France, and Britain. This differential sucked in financial capital from abroad and kept U.S. capital at home. Added to that, there were flows into the dollar due to unsettled conditions abroad, as from France, Mexico, and elsewhere in Latin America. It is believed there was a $50 billion capital flight from these areas between 1978 and 1982 due to politics, low or negative real interest rates, and overvalued foreign exchange rates that make the dollar artificially cheap.[12] The U.S. government did nothing to stem this flow when in 1984 it abolished the 30 percent withholding tax on interest payments to foreigners owning dollars securities in that country. At the same time Japan liberalized its financial markets and that savings-rich nation rapidly became the major supplier of funds to the United States. Together, these factors appear to explain the dollar's strength.

The reason U.S. interest rates were so high for so long, though controversial, seems predominantly to involve the great budget deficit question. The structural (or high-employment) deficit, predicted in the $200+ billion range in the late 1980s even as the economy recovers, served to push up interest rates because it represented a heavy demand for loanable funds by government. To the degree that the large U.S. tax cuts of 1981 and the deductibility of interest payments stimulated borrowing, this too contributed to the pressure on demand. The deficit also affected interest rates through the expectations of borrowers and lenders concerning the possible reignition of inflation.[13]

The expansionary stimulus of large deficits was surely needed in the United States under the economic conditions of the recent recession. But when historically high budget deficits, equivalent to 6 percent of GNP through 1988, were run as the economy recovered toward full employment, a serious dilemma was encountered. Large public-sector borrowing posed a choice between a substantial absorption of private saving with accompanying increases in interest that would serve eventually to choke economic growth or an accommodating monetary policy that would reignite inflation. A recognition of this dilemma is a reasonable explanation why long-term real rates exceeded short-term rates in the United States by a margin surpassing that of the other major developed countries, and why both U.S. short- and long-term real rates exceeded the rates in these same countries.[14] It is true that both nominal and real interest rates were falling during the period 1982 to 1985, but the differentials in favor of the United States stayed significant, peaking in mid 1984. The differentials narrowed after that, but the dollar still kept rising—somewhat puzzling, and perhaps suggesting that investors were impressed by the pro-business climate in the United States and the good prospects for keeping inflation under control. Perhaps there was even something of a "speculative bubble."

TO WHAT EXTENT DID POLICY MISTAKES CONTRIBUTE TO THE CRISIS?

The impact of the crisis can be briefly summarized. The number of nations in arrears on their international loans was 32 at the end of 1981, and the total amount of the arrears was over $6 billion. In quantitative terms Mexico, Brazil, and Argentina presented by far the greatest difficulties. Rescheduling (delayed repayment) negotiations mounted rapidly: 6 cases in 1980, 13 in 1981, 12 in 1982.[15]

Did the commercial banks and the LDCs contribute to their own difficulties by reckless mistakes of policy? To some degree, yes. By hindsight, of course, the banks lent too much and lent without sufficient care. They had too little experience assessing risks in circumstances very different from their usual business and relied on overly simple tests that were not good "leading indicators" of trouble ahead.

Judged by the information available at the time, however, the conclusion that the banks were reckless is less firm. The officially published statistics for "credit worthiness" did not show cause for alarm until 1981 at the earliest and not clearly until 1982. The private bond markets showed little concern; interest rates on Mexican bonds did not rise until a matter of weeks before the dramatic Mexican announcement of August 1982 that it could not meet its obligations.[16] Even after that the higher spreads over LIBOR to reflect risk proved to be a poor predictor of difficulty. By the time the banks recognized that there was a crisis, cutting off lending would have been too late to stave it off and by virtually ensuring default would have been counterproductive.

One major criticism of bank behavior can be called the "small bank" problem.[17] Small banks, which joined LDC lending late in the game, soon reduced that lending the most and gave the greatest difficulty in renegotiating the obligations. The large number of banks involved (560 lent to Mexico) and the inexperience of the small ones with such transactions initially made the negotiations cumbersome. Some of the small banks, as well as some of the big ones, had a lesser share of the loans, and thus with less to lose, apparently felt they could hold out for stiffer terms. Since in a syndicated loan each participant has to approve if the terms are changed, the negotiations were usually difficult. Advisory committees were eventually pieced together; these, with some arm twisting by governments, reduced but did not eliminate the problem. In 1986 proposals were being made for a "supercommittee" or "superbank" that could speed agreement and eliminate the small bank veto power.

The banks were also too quick in reducing the maturity of new loans, and this applies especially to U.S. banks who led in this move.[18] They may thus have hoped to increase their influence on economic policies, or they were using shorter maturities as a substitute for reducing loans outright. They certainly wanted to lower their own long-term exposure. But they did not see the extent to which the shortened maturities could cause a liquidity crisis if unexpected shocks had to be faced, just when the shorter terms of the loans were increasing the debt service payments coming due.

To what extent did LDC policies contribute to the crisis? There seems little doubt that in an understandable attempt to ward off the effects of the deepening recession, prolonged heavy borrowing was continued past the point of prudence, and some LDCs deliberately chose the troublesome short-term loans to avoid the higher spreads on the already costly medium- and long-term loans. Domestic fiscal deficits in the LDCs were allowed to expand, partly financed by the borrowing but in large part by domestic money creation that was inflationary. The non-oil LDCs ran average budget deficits of 3 percent of GDP in 1977 to 1979, rising to 4.5 percent on a weighted average basis, 6 percent median, and over 10 percent in a fair number of countries in 1982. Between 1979 and 1982 the public-sector deficit of Argentina rose from 7 to 14 percent, Brazil's from 8 to 16 percent (and a whopping 24 percent in 1984), and Mexico's from 7 to 18 percent.

Such large deficits were often permitted because of the politics of budgeting in the LDCs, already discussed in Chapter 4. The leadership in many countries was unwilling to cut the flows to the urban workers benefiting from cheap food and subsidized public services, to the business sector via cheap credit and subsidies, to the military, to their supporters in the form of government jobs and large projects, and (sometimes) to themselves. The difficulties of restraining this spending, as long as foreign bank loans were still available, proved insurmountable. The shortened maturity of the loans did not stop the borrowing, as a number of LDC governments demonstrated they had a short time horizon. "Keep up the spending now; let a future generation deal with the problem" seemed to be the motto for some. Even after the flow of loans was stemmed, the deficits continued, with governments often turning to inflationary money creation for financing them. The median money supply change in non-oil LDCs in 1982 was $+18$ percent.

The resulting inflation would have caused the real exchange rate to depreciate, but often countries resisted the depreciation and maintained an overvalued rate that squeezed exports and introduced other damaging efficiency distortions. Recent econometric calculations by the IMF confirm how direct this relationship is.[19] A 1 percent increase in the ratio of fiscal deficit to GDP in a non-oil LDC causes an average deterioration in the current account by about 0.5 percent. By contrast, a 1 percent fall in industrial-country growth rates or a 1 percent rise in the real foreign interest rate produces a deterioration of *less* than 0.5 percent in the current account.

The recognized importance of public-sector deficits in the debt issue is the reason why the IMF, in lending to help countries cope with the debt crisis, has insisted on sharp reductions in these deficits, even at the expense of high political costs in the countries concerned. The targeted adjustments in deficits as a percent of GNP have been large: a reduction by almost half (14 to 8 percent) for Argentina and by more than half for Brazil and Mexico between 1982 and 1985.

The real exchange rate has also been an important issue. The IMF calculations reported above indicate that on average a 1 percent appreciation of the real exchange rate causes a deterioration in the current account of about 0.5 percent.[20] The IMF presents evidence that countries that avoided an overvalued real exchange rate, allowing it to fall when their rate of inflation exceeded that of trading partners, have registered better records in both export performance and in overall growth. Relative depreciation is by no means a panacea, however. To obtain a favorable result, it may have to be bolstered by allowing more freedom in exchange transactions. Adjustments in the price system to reflect the market more adequately may be called for. Other useful policy changes might include withdrawal from a generalized system of import substitution through protection, perhaps moving to more realistic market interest rates to avoid a flight of capital, or perhaps the adoption of an "incomes policy" to limit wage and price increases. But it remains true that the deliberate maintenance of an overvalued rate on balance invites trouble. The conclusion from IMF studies of an 82-country sample is that countries willing to adjust both their fiscal deficits and relative overvaluation of their currency were significantly more successful in maintaining GNP growth rates and shares in export markets.

MEETING THE CRISIS

The crisis was contained during 1983 and 1984, but not without cliff-hanging negotiations constantly in the news. The banks and the LDCs had clear reasons to avoid a default, and they were eventually able to bargain a series of country-by-country rescheduling agreements, almost always involving a postponement of principal repayments but not of interest payments. (It bears mentioning that about 100 countries have continued to make both principal and interest payments, without rescheduling.[21])

There were 31 rescheduling agreements, with 21 countries, in 1983, 21 agreements in 1984, and 31 in 1985. In that year the total involved was $93 billion, 13 percent of LDC debt.[22] The biggest ones, with Mexico and Brazil, came in 1984, and the toughest one, with Argentina, was completed (?) at the start of 1985. The agreements with the smaller borrowers are generally on a year-by-year basis. The largest borrowers have obtained more favorable multiyear agreements, typically postponing the payment of 80 to 100 percent of principal over six to nine years (Mexico's until 1990), with a grace period of two to four years. The loans are repackaged with a new schedule of interest rates and fees, in the earlier agreements sometimes higher than the original ones, but now usually lower, with longer maturities, and with "humps" of repayment smoothed over. However, the results of all reschedulings thus far will eventually mean higher repayments in total, with less now and more later.

Long-term rescheduling makes much more sense than the year-to-year agreements, because the process of arriving at several short-term agreements is repetitious and time-consuming, and the time span involved is not long enough to allow a focus on needed policy reforms. But, as noted, the banks have agreed to a multiyear format only when the borrowers have been large, thus lending credibility to the old saw, "If you owe me a thousand dollars, you have a problem; if you owe me a million dollars, I have a problem."

During the rescheduling developed-country government funds were often utilized to prevent immediate defaults and give time to work out an acceptable agreement. Frequently, policy changes in the debtor were required and supervised by the IMF ("conditionality," discussed later in this chapter). "Bridging loans" were advanced, especially by the IMF, the Bank for International Settlements in Geneva, and the U.S. Treasury. On one occasion the bridging loans even included LDC lenders that were themselves debtors, as when Brazil, Colombia, Mexico, and Venezuela pledged $100 million in 1984 to keep Argentina from a default that could have caused a chain reaction.

A predictable repercussion among the private banks, caused by the unwelcome rescheduling, was a drastic cut in their willingness to lend outside the agreements to countries perceived as high risks or, indeed, to any LDC borrower at all; the flow of such borrowed funds fell 72 percent between 1981 and 1983. Some of the reduction was in the very short-term loans called export credits that finance the international shipment and billing of goods in international trade, much the same way a consumer is temporarily financed by a credit card. The decline in this funding was immediately damaging for foreign trade, and the banks had to take special measures to restore the funds.

Whether the temporary easing of the crisis will prove permanent remains to be seen. Major factors will be the strength and steadiness of economic recovery in the developed nations, the height of real interest rates, and the size of budget deficits, especially in the United States. The degree to which protection against LDC imports becomes the rule will be a crucial element. The tightening of textile barriers in 1984–1985, and the U.S. and EC decisions to restrain steel exports from countries such as Brazil and Mexico do not bode well.

The fall in oil prices is especially helpful to non-oil LDCs, because it contributes to a restoration of more favorable terms of trade. It also directly reduces inflation 0.5 to 1.0 percent for every 10 percent drop in oil prices and improves the current account balances of the nations concerned. The gain is shared both by developed and underdeveloped countries. The decline in oil prices will also relatively appreciate the currencies of countries without oil vis-à-vis the dollar, because the United States produces much of its own consumption.

Another advantage will accrue to the LDCs that used their borrowed money primarily for investment purposes rather than to prop domestic consumption or for defense spending. Until the crisis struck, most borrowing countries were in fact raising their investment levels. Such countries will experience favorable long-run repercussions when the results of that investment generate future export growth. Of course, the productivity of this investment, indeed *any* investment, is not guaranteed. Economic conditions can change and play havoc with the relationship between investment and GNP, as seen during the 1980s recession, and any new capital might be used inefficiently. But the situation is certainly to be preferred over one in which most of the borrowed money disappeared into consumption or helped finance a war (Argentina and the Falklands/Malvinas) or flowed abroad as capital flight, with no long-run improving effects on the economy.[23]

FACING THE FUTURE

By 1985 many signs were more favorable than most informed observers had thought imaginable just two years before. The exports, imports, and GNP of the debtor LDCs had all risen since 1983. Real interest rates had declined sharply, from nearly 8 percent in 1984 to an average of only about 4 percent in mid 1985, and by the end of 1985 the interest rate differential favoring the United States had disappeared. In March 1986 real rates in the U.S. at 3 percent were now *below* real rates in Japan, Germany, and France (all 4 percent) and Great Britain (6 percent). Short-term debt also fell rapidly, from 30 percent of LDC exports in 1982 to under 20 percent in 1984. The combined current account deficit of the LDCs, $103 billion in 1982, was only $38 billion in 1984 as economic recovery sucked in LDC exports to the developed world and as import-reducing adjustments took place.[24] (The reduction in LDC imports had sharp repercussions for the developed countries, too. For example, imports from the United States to the five biggest Latin American borrowers fell 48 percent in 1981 to 1983, contributing importantly to the worsening U.S. trade balance.) Debt service (principal and interest as a percentage of exports) fell from nearly 25 percent in 1982 to 22.5 percent in 1984, and as conditions improved, capital flight declined sharply.[25] Bank exposure has fallen significantly, from 186 percent of capital at the end of 1982 to 141 percent in July 1985, reducing the risk of a major bank collapse.[26] Information on the size and terms of bank debt was now much better, due to efforts by the IMF and by the LDCs themselves, which scrambled to centralize and computerize their statistics. (Information on short-term export credits is still weak, however.) The surprises of the past, when inadequate information among the borrowers and lenders led to severe underestimation of the amount of debt, are now less likely to be repeated. More LDCs have implemented formal ceilings on the amount that the public sector will be permitted to borrow, especially useful when uncoordinated borrowing by state corporations and the military had run up the size of debt.[27]

Some other events in the developed countries were also favorable. Though the dollar continued to strengthen in the first quarter of 1985, thereafter it weakened as U.S. interest rates eased, falling on average 15 percent against other major currencies between March and September. In September, there was an accord to bring down the dollar yet further, agreed upon by the U.S., Britain, West Germany, France, and Japan. Together these countries sold some $10 billion on currency markets to further the fall. By March 1986 the decline from a year before had reached 25 percent, bringing the dollar to only a little over 10 percent above its 1975–84 average.[28] The accord did not of itself change underlying economic conditions, but it did show a new sense of purpose. The new determination was underscored by passage in the United States of the Gramm-Rudman-Hollings deficit reduction bill; the bill mandates elimination of the deficit over a six-year period through spending cuts. In Europe there seemed new impetus for improving economic growth by increasing flexibility in labor markets; Germany and Japan were easing their very restrictive budgets to promote expansion through fiscal means.

On the other side of the coin, however, the flow of bank loans to the LDCs has fallen sharply, and one must go back all the way to 1973 to find the flow of bank finance to poor countries as low as it was in 1985.[29] Net borrowing from private creditors, which peaked at $76 billion in 1981, was only $4.5 billion in 1985. Most of what remained was "involuntary," part of the rescheduling agreements. The oil states stopped supplying liquid funds to the banking system; as oil price increases slowed and then reversed, their huge trade surpluses turned to deficits. At the same time the record government budget deficit in the United States was absorbing large quantities of loanable funds, with that country now borrowing far more savings abroad than all the LDCs put together. Essentially, via interest rates the U.S. government was competing with the LDCs for borrowed funds and was winning. New laws on bank lending in the U.S. and elsewhere reinforced the bankers' sudden caution.[30] One regulation adopted by the U.S. Federal Reserve System requires banks to write off from 10 to 75 percent of their "value impaired loans," interpreted to mean countries which are in de facto default. (But this small group of countries, including Bolivia, Nicaragua, Peru, Sudan, and Zaire, is not very important for the debt issue as a whole because the total size of its indebtedness is minimal.) All these events have worked to constrict lending. The bankers are clearly now very skeptical, and their confidence will take time to rebuild.

A more serious development had surfaced during 1985. The worldwide economic recovery of 1984 slowed sharply in the latter part of the year, and growth prospects appeared increasingly stagnant. IMF projections for developed-country GNP growth were scaled back in October 1985 to 2.8 percent from April's projected 3.1 percent. U.S. unemployment was stuck at about 7 percent, with Europe's unemployment much worse at over 10 percent. In this fertile breeding ground for protectionism, several stringent quota measures seemed likely to pass in Europe and the United States. The low developed-country growth meant that LDC export volume would also grow much more slowly; the IMF's original 1985 growth estimate of 7.6 percent was reduced to 4.1 percent, and when the year was over actually turned out to be a very disappointing 0.4 percent.[31] As a result commodity prices continued to decline, and both trends would worsen if indeed protectionism did pick up.

There was increasing concern that this slow growth would bring a new recurrence of the debt crisis. With LDC export surpluses again dwindling, and debt service rates still very high in some countries (Argentina 80 percent, Mexico

59 percent), there seemed to be a more hostile mood. President Alan Garcia of Peru announced that his country would simply stop paying more than 10 percent of its export revenue in debt service and that if pushed, Peru would withdraw from the IMF. Later, in February 1986, Peru unilaterally lowered the interest rate it was paying. (U.S. banking regulators immediately slapped a special reserve requirement on loans to Peru.)[32] Nigeria followed, limiting its payments to 30 percent of export revenue. Mexico, with a far larger debt, gave the biggest problems. The IMF in 1985 was poised to discipline that country for failing to meet some of the rescheduling conditions; this was averted at the last minute when Mexico City was hit by a devastating earthquake. Again the problem arose in early 1986, made worse by the sudden fall in oil revenues as OPEC lost control. President de la Madrid implied that Mexico would not be paying its current interest bill or, if it did, the payments would not be on time and perhaps would be linked to the price of its oil.[33] The rich countries were clearly more concerned about a sharp decline in their exports if the debtors turned inward, and the Latin American debtors were showing some signs of adopting a common front.

In 1986, with its "Baker Plan" named for Treasury Secretary James Baker, the U.S. government was attempting to persuade the commercial banks to expand their lending by $20 billion to the 15 LDCs in greatest difficulty. It was also supporting increased World Bank and regional development bank lending ($9 billion), plus more IMF assistance, in return for a greater commitment by the LDCs to economic reform.[34]

In July 1986, the first results of the new plan looked promising, with the acrimonious Mexican discussions suddenly leading to an outcome much better than anticipated. A package of new credit was announced by the World Bank, the IMF, and the Inter-American Development Bank, with the commercial banks being pressed to extend $6 billion in additional loans. Including funding from the U.S. government, the whole amount was a remarkable $12 billion. In a major innovation, the agreement was tied to the price of Mexico's main export, oil. Thus if oil falls below $9 a barrel, more loans will automatically be made available, but if it rises above $14, the loans will be repaid early. A substantial effort toward economic restructuring is provided for in the agreement, with much of the World Bank's portion of the loan devoted to financing it.[35] This first result of the Baker Plan was an encouraging recognition that recycling of funds had to play a part, and that meeting the crisis by simply contracting the economies of the debtor LDCs was neither good economics nor pragmatic foreign policy. The Mexican agreement may well presage more liberal treatment for other countries harmed by sharp declines in the prices paid for their major exports.

REFORM PROPOSALS

Has the debt bomb been defused or is it still ticking? Much would seem to depend on whether LDCs see an advantage in defaulting. When the time comes that principal repayments are required under the rescheduling agreements, what if real interest rates are very high and little new lending is forthcoming? What if the world economy is sluggish and racked by protectionism, so that the principal and interest on the old debt must be obtained not from increased exporting but from further compression of imports? Then the net transfer of resources will be strongly away from LDCs and to the developed world, and some countries may see default as a viable option.

This continuing specter has led to a variety of reform proposals designed to ward off a recurrence of the crisis.[36] None of the proposals is close to implementation at present, but each would attract much more interest if and when the crisis again intensifies.

1. Longer-term, fixed-rate lending would clearly be an advantage to LDCs. But the bond market is conservative, and prospects for LDC bonds are limited. Of the $20 billion raised over the last decade, some two-thirds was obtained by just three countries, Mexico, Brazil, and Israel. There was a spurt in that market starting in 1976 that peaked in 1978, but for now borrowing is limited to the more well-to-do countries with a sound reputation that takes time to acquire or restore. Thus proposals have been advanced that developed-country governments might aid banks in converting high-interest, short-term debt into long-term debt at fixed and lower rates of interest. The government, a new agency perhaps, might buy the debt from banks at, say, a 10 percent discount. The banks would absorb the loss. Such a solution would be difficult; the banks would like neither the government intervention nor the losses.

2. More equity financing and less contractual lending would be a help. Direct or portfolio investment, paying dividends from profits rather than interest, would, of course, pay *no* dividends in a slump, which would prove highly advantageous if crisis conditions were to recur. The investor, and not the LDC, would bear the risk when exchange rates change. Equity-like features might possibly be built into securities, so that some portion of the total yield to the holder might be calculated on changes in the borrower's GNP, or change in export earnings, or the prices of major export commodities, or the like. All no doubt true, but equity financing raised only $15.6 billion for the LDCs in 1981, much more than the bond market, but way below what came from bank financing. The World Bank's IFC is attempting to assist by encouraging a mutual fund whose managers will trade shares on LDC stock markets while representing about 10 institutional investors in the developed countries. Such trading may lead other investors into LDC stocks. As we have already seen, however, some LDCs that have borrowed do not welcome equity investment.

3. Letting banks simply absorb all the losses themselves is a populist suggestion sometimes heard, but this seems a high road to bank failures and financial disruption. Senator Bill Bradley's plan to cut interest rates on the debt and write off 9 percent of its value over 3 years is an example of this approach used in moderation.

4. A taxpayer bail-out of the banks in case of default is at the opposite extreme. Schemes to involve industrial-country governments in picking up the risks from the commercial banks have been aired, but would surely encounter serious resistance from the taxpaying public. In any case, the necessary funding would no doubt come in major part from aid budgets, so that the very poor LDCs would suffer to help the middle-income who have borrowed the most. Such a solution would also send signals to countries with a debt problem that they could

expect continued government intervention whenever they refused to pay, thus leading to future difficulties.

5. A shift by commercial banks toward originating loans and then selling them off into a secondary market could, as prices fluctuate, give useful early warning to borrowers and lenders alike. Such "transferable loan instruments" have up to now been used only in the developed countries.

6. There are "lender of last resort" ideas in which the IMF and World Bank could play an expanded role. The IMF might involve itself directly in the establishment of credit terms both for new loans and renewals, adopt a longer time frame than now possible, and stand ready to assist banks in jeopardy because of their loans to LDCs. The World Bank might pay more attention to structural rehabilitation through co-financing with the banks.[37] Both proposals would, if adopted widely, require substantial additional funding, and a new "Marshall Plan" of long-term loans to debtors seems politically out of the question at present. (It must be said that if the alternative ever becomes universal default and financial collapse among the banks, then a new Marshall Plan might suddenly appear very cheap!)

7. There is a Brazilian suggestion for indexing the principal of a loan, but not the interest, so avoiding the front-loading problem. Thus a $100 loan at 5 percent interest would after a year of 10 percent inflation be written up to $110, requiring repayment of $5.50 interest + $11 principal = $16.50 instead of the $25 in the example given earlier. But this reasonable-sounding proposal would put great pressures on banks to do so domestically as well as internationally and to index their deposits so as to match assets and liabilities; banking would undergo fundamental changes, and fundamental changes are hard to implement.

8. A "capping" proposal would put a maximum on the interest rate that had to be paid, either by extending the maturity of the loan whenever market rates were above the cap or by requiring a "balloon payment" at the end of the loan's life to make up for any shortfall. Alternatively, inpayments could be required at the higher cap rate should market rates fall below it, with the surplus thus obtained compensating for any earlier deficit. The major worry about the capping schemes is what would happen if rates climbed above the cap and stayed there long enough to create a much enlarged future burden. If the plan were simply a disguise for a developed-country takeover of the debt, again strong taxpayer resistance would be encountered.

9. Finally, an insurance program might be implemented, with losses after some "deductible" limit covered up to the resources in the insurance fund.[38] Costs might be met by a premium on bank loans or by tapping the rescheduling fees that banks have been charging, possibly supplemented by government money. This proposal raises many questions. Would an insurance plan be voluntary or compulsory? Who would set it up and be responsible? Would it be joint with borrowers? If government money were used, would it be an unwarranted bail-out for banks? Any such insurance plan appears a long way from implementation.

All these proposals will be judged by the criterion "who gains, who loses." The ones that do not lower the long-term burden on the LDCs will leave intact a risk of eventual default and a banking crisis. Those that do reduce the debt burden will be expensive either for the banks or for developed-country taxpayers. Unless the situation deteriorates substantially, the most likely outcome is probably some additional lending in return for some further restructuring of policy by the LDCs.

Up to now the debt crisis has been kept within bounds, and the efforts to do so even reveal some encouraging signs of cooperation among nations. But another bout of recession with high interest rates, if it occurred, could cause an immediate threat of serious financial disruption. Even after years of coping with the crisis, it is not clear how quickly help could be made available during some future emergency. With luck, perhaps we shall not learn.

THE ROLE OF THE INTERNATIONAL MONETARY FUND

The debt crisis brought to prominence as never before the International Monetary Fund (IMF). A product, with the World Bank, of the Bretton Woods Conference of 1944, its headquarters also in Washington, D.C., the IMF has via its strict conditions on lending become the chief "policeman" of the debt issue. It is also important to the poorest of the developing countries; until the crisis hit, some two-thirds of total IMF commitments were going to nations that received only about 7 percent of commercial bank loans. The Fund, headed since 1978 by Jacques de Larosière of France, is a fascinating institution. The vigorous debates over its role are the more comprehensible when one understands something of its mechanics, which is where we shall commence.

From the very beginning countries have "joined" the IMF by initially paying in a subscription fee, or quota, made up of 75 percent of their own national currency and 25 percent in hard currencies, mainly the dollar or nowadays the special drawing rights (SDRs) of the IMF (considered below). To join the Fund, Portugal, for example, paid in $18.8 million worth of hard currency and $56.2 million worth of its own escudos as its membership fee. It is these quota inpayments from its 151 members that furnish the cash that the IMF then lends to those in need, along the lines of a neighborhood credit union on a giant scale.

The IMF's eighth review of quotas in 1983 raised the quotas 47.5 percent from a little over $60 billion to about $90 billion. More is available from a group of developed countries united in the so-called General Arrangements to Borrow (GAB).[39] Formerly a small program of $6.5 billion, the funds from which were lent only among the members of the group, during the debt crisis the GAB was nearly tripled in size to $17 billion and its resources were made available as supplementary loans to the IMF's general lending.[40] Some economists believe that the new reliance on borrowed GAB money, in lieu of a larger quota increase, marks a conservative turn, since the major developed countries and not the IMF retain ultimate control over these funds.

Of the whole of the IMF's quotas, only about half (perhaps $45 billion) is really "usable," since many countries, especially LDCs, have inconvertible currencies so surrounded by exchange controls that no one would want to borrow them. The billions of "soft" Ghanaian cedis or Nicaraguan cordobas or Burmese kyats and the like held on the books of the Fund are for any practical purpose virtually useless. Even a relatively hard currency such as the Paraguayan guarani might be traded only in thin markets with high exchange costs and would thus be lent infrequently and only to a neighboring trading partner such as Argentina, Brazil, or Uruguay. Thus in 1985 only some 39 percent of the IMF's quotas were actually lent out.

When the quotas were last increased in 1983, two-fifths of the increase were distributed according to the existing distribution, initially and somewhat obscurely determined within the IMF on such criteria as the size of a country's national economy and its "economic importance." About three-fifths of the increase came as selective adjustments to reflect changes in the world economy, for example, higher shares for Japan and Saudi Arabia, lower for Great Britain.

Quotas range from very large (United States, about $18 billion) to tiny (Republic of the Maldives, $2 million). The quota size also determines the number of "votes" a country has in the Fund's decision-making process. The United States, with 20.08 percent of the voting power, is still well above the 15 percent needed under the IMF's bylaws to veto any key issue.

An LDC can borrow from the Fund with varying degrees of ease, which is an element of great importance in the debt crisis. A first borrowing, or drawing, is virtually automatic and without strings. A country simply calls for the return of its original 25 percent share (called the "reserve tranche," *tranche* being French for "slice") paid in hard currency. After that, it may borrow the "first credit tranche," another 25 percent, with virtually no strings. Three further credit tranches may be borrowed in each of three subsequent years, and each amounting to 25 percent of the original quota. Since 1981, if the IMF approves a member's plans for economic reform (say, in an attempt to cope with the debt crisis), the member can borrow more: currently (1986) a further 90 percent of quota annually for three years under the "enlarged access" policy. Some of this money the Fund has borrowed to lend again.

An exception to the percentage limits is made when the IMF executive board declares that balance of payments needs and the strength of a country's adjustment effort justify an advance to 110 percent of quota per year for three years.[41] This decision-making power, which could make terms easier or harder for a given member, is a departure from past practice wherein each country received the same treatment. With the enlarged access policy, further loans from 270 to 330 percent of quota can be obtained in a three-year period, in addition to the normal lending. But all is subject to a cumulative upper limit of 400 to 440 percent of quota. Beginning in 1981, the "no-strings" tranches do not have to be borrowed before the credit tranches and can be kept for a rainy day.

The usual terms are that the loan must be paid back in three to five years, with the repayment in hard currency, at a 1986 interest rate of 6.50 percent on the credit tranches, a zero rate on the reserve tranche, and whatever the Fund has paid plus 0.2 percent when money borrowed by the Fund is involved. (Since borrowing by the IMF is recent, and since market interest rates have been high, the average rate charged rose sharply during the debt crisis.) All loans until 1985 were repaid, but in 1985 and 1986 several countries, including Guyana, Liberia, Peru, Sudan, and Vietnam, were far behind in their repayments.[42] The IMF cannot by its rules reschedule. In case of nonpayment it can either declare a country ineligible for future loans, as was done with these five, or as a last resort boot the country out.

Obtaining the second, third, and fourth credit tranches and money from the extended access policy involves an ever-greater degree of IMF supervision, including substantial consultation with the officials of the Fund and a visit by an IMF financial team. Typically the IMF will require as prerequisites for borrowing cutbacks in budget deficits including subsidies to various sectors of the economy (included in 91 percent of all IMF programs from 1981 to 1984), reduction in the rate of monetary expansion (in 98 percent), measures to restrain wages and prices (in 88 percent), devaluation of an overvalued exchange rate, and some dismantling of protectionist trade barriers. It will also often require government action to make the price system reflect true costs more accurately and some turn toward the encouragement of exports. This conditionality of lending—34 such programs were in effect at the start of 1985, compared to an average of only 8 in 1971 to 1973—has proven by far the most controversial aspect of IMF operations in recent years. In the 1980s over three-quarters of the Fund's loans were on conditional terms from the higher tranches, the situation usually reassessed every three months by the governing board.[43]

During the debt crisis the LDCs raised a chorus of complaint against IMF conditionality, urging that it be scrapped. Their arguments are usually that the conditionality has become tougher, with stiffer terms toward borrower domestic policies and that low-income groups within a country bear the brunt of the adjustment. They say the deflationary policies required by the IMF are one-sided, the painful contraction of employment and consumption being borne by the LDCs alone, and not by the countries whose oil price policies (for example, OPEC) or interest rate policies (for example, the United States) certainly contributed to the underlying problem. The deflation spreads, so claim the critics, since the deflating countries import less; thus exports are reduced everywhere, even in countries not previously in difficulty.

The IMF replies that the terms are not tougher, but that the underlying economic conditions have become much worse. As compared to the 1970s, the IMF now has to do much more to ensure that credit is advanced from private sources (the banks) as well, and without conditionality there would be far less of it. The Fund also argues that painful adjustment is inescapable anyway. Countries cannot continue spending policies that exceed resources. Also, without the IMF the adjustment would be far more disorderly, perhaps with high inflation and severe import restrictions causing reduced growth and more unemployment, which in turn would make foreign funds impossible to obtain. The proper question is not whether adjustment is painful, says the Fund, but what the situation *would* have been *without* that organization's lending.

It adds that harm to lower-income groups is a result of a country's own political choice.[44] The choice might be made to cut defense expenditures or capital outlays, rather than programs that affect the poor. Thus the Fund does not accept responsibility for choosing where the social impact of its policies will be. In any case, it claims, some of the requirements should actually increase income equality.

Restraints on subsidies (gasoline or food, for example) will harm the middle class to be sure, but not the rural poor who do not receive them. In addition, the structural changes to promote agricultural exports and rural development might have the same effect of increasing equality.

The IMF also argues vigorously that the supposed deflationary consequences are not nearly so severe as the critics imply. This view received support in an important 1985 study by Khan and Knight, which reviews the results of IMF conditionality and presents simulations of their long-term effects.[45] The authors of the study agree that a deflationary bias is certainly imparted by the more restrictive monetary and fiscal policies. But they present evidence that this consequence is largely offset by the supply-side reforms that reduce the distortions in the economy. The time path, they suggest, is usually a rather brief deflation followed by a beneficial impact on growth as the supply-side reforms take hold. A study by Morris Goldstein claims that any induced macroeconomic effects on other countries are small; simulations indicate a fall in the imports of countries with IMF programs (almost 8 percent) led to a fall in industrial-country GNP of only 0.1 to 0.2 percent.[46]

Be that as it may, following the imposition of IMF conditions the recession, even if temporary, can be severe, and the political situation deteriorated in some countries to the point where street fighting occurred. Often the condition causing the most political turmoil is the scaling back or elimination of food subsidies in urban areas. A dozen people were killed in Peru in 1978 when General Francisco Morales Bermudez doubled food, fuel, and transport prices to meet a condition for an IMF loan. Rioting over IMF terms took place in Brazil, the Dominican Republic, Ecuador, and Egypt in the 1980s. Governments have even been overturned; resistance to the IMF played a role in coups in both Ghana and Nigeria, also in the 1980s.

Economists are often of mixed minds on the issue of conditionality. Sometimes it is agreed that the Fund's teams of experts have been insensitive to the demands of domestic politics, and the public requirement of an immediate devaluation and severe cuts in consumer subsidies before new IMF loans are made can be bitter medicine for the government in power. More circumspection and attention to "face saving" could presumably be employed. When a country suffers a large drop in export revenues, as did Mexico in 1986 because of the decline in oil prices, spending cuts may have to extend to capital improvements and even maintenance. Deteriorating roads, a decaying railway system, and power stations wearing out have all suddenly become part of the Mexican economic scene, as that country strains to pay its debts. On the other hand, the Fund's economic prescriptions for budgeting, money creation, and foreign trade appear generally sensible; its insistence that ill-advised government policy is as important an obstacle to development as inadequate resources is a valuable contribution. The conditions can be remarkably useful to a government that wants to take painful economic action, but finds it difficult to do so unaided because the political repercussions would be intense. The blame for taking the action can in this view be transferred abroad; useful policies can after all be implemented; the protests from the government's standpoint are more smoke than fire. Another argument is that the Fund's conditions can take a collective view, discouraging beggar-thy-neighbor policies that promote recovery in one member at the expense of others. A final consideration is that if the IMF were to become more lenient in its conditions, it would no longer serve as a de facto guarantee to commercial banks that reasonable economic policies were being implemented by a debtor LDC. Without that guarantee, commercial bank financing might be far harder to obtain.

The IMF also has two additional programs that have recently become important, reaching 20 percent of all IMF transactions in 1985. The Compensatory Financing Facility (CFF) was introduced in 1963. It is designed to allow borrowing above the normal access (specifically, another 83 percent of quota) when total earnings from primary product exports fall short of their average over a recent period of years. Borrowing from the CFF was not subject to conditionality before 1983, but it was made so in that year, marking yet more IMF emphasis on its stabilization plans.[47]

The CFF is now integrated with a new Cereal Imports Financial Facility, dating from 1981, which allows borrowing to finance grain imports during periods of abnormal price rises. Another 83 percent of quota can be borrowed to cover the margin by which cereal grain costs exceed a five-year average.[48] (The compensatory financing and cereal imports schemes are linked by the limitation that total borrowing under the two programs together cannot exceed 105 percent of quota.)

The LDCs have called for the ending of conditionality on CFF loans, payment according to need instead of quota size, and extension to cover changes in interest costs on debt, but no move in these directions is currently visible, primarily because of the increased costs involved. We shall return to the topic of compensatory finance in Chapter 15.

REPORT CARD: THE IMF AND THE DEBT CRISIS

The IMF has been central in the effort to contain the debt crisis. Could it have done better? Perhaps, in several respects. First, the developed nations have been unwilling to vote quota increases sufficient to keep pace with the growth of the world economy. Even with large dollar increases, IMF quotas as a percentage of world exports or world GNP are now less than half what they were 30 years ago. In any case, the poorest countries and those deepest in debt would have difficulty in making the repayments; critics say all along there should have been a way to subsidize interest payments from the poorest borrowers.[49]

Second, the IMF's terms of lending are short term, with the associated conditionality covering a space of only two or three years, while the problems of the debt crisis would seem to require a longer strategy of adjustment. IMF conditions are thus forced to focus overly on demand restraint rather than on the valuable supply-side adjustments. Another result is that after a period of heavy lending, as in the debt crisis, the flow of finance is reversed as the loans are repaid. In 1985, for example, repayments were almost as large as new loans, and the net addition to resources by the Fund was, disappointingly, a little less than half a billion dollars.

These objections have been met with an extended fund facility that does make some loans available on a longer-term basis (up to 10 years) to aid in structural adjustments in production, trade, and prices. In addition, a new program was announced in 1986. This $3 billion structural adjustment facility is for the 60 poorest member countries. China and India have announced they will not use it; sub-Saharan Africa is expected to receive almost 80 percent of the money. An eligible country will be able to borrow an additional 47 percent of quota in three installments, at a low interest rate of 0.5 percent. Repayment will not start for 5 years and will end in 10. The new plan will be developed in concert with the World Bank and will focus on supply-side reforms. A borrowing country failing to meet targets for restructuring its economy will not be given the next installment of the loan.[50] But the amounts for both the extended fund facility and the new structural adjustment facility are far smaller than for normal lending. (In 1986 another new idea being circulated was for a fund to succor low-income oil exporters, such as Mexico, Indonesia, and Nigeria, in distress because of the major fall in oil prices early in that year.[51]

The Fund also has to cope with increasing criticism, not just from LDCs concerned with conditionality, but from the developed countries themselves. There are those who oppose funding for the IMF. On the right the criticism focuses on budgetary demands, on the agency's internationalism, on the fact that communist countries (Afghanistan, Hungary, Nicaragua, Romania, Vietnam) are among its members, and on what they believe is lack of support for a completely free market. On the left the complaint is that the IMF favors stability over growth, with policies that raise unemployment and lower standards of living, leading to the rise of authoritarian regimes which, without the loans, would collapse.

Whatever kernel of truth such arguments may have, IMF loans have been important in adjusting to the debt crisis. On balance it is hard to see how the massive debt reschedulings would ever have been accomplished without that organization. How else could fiscal, monetary, trade, and price reforms have been negotiated so as to encourage lenders to keep the flow of loans coming, even at their current reduced rate?[52] The complaints of the "free marketers" seem especially wide of the mark, since during the debt crisis IMF conditionality very generally encouraged market-oriented policies and the elimination of distortions to trade. The great weakness revealed by the debt emergency was another one entirely, namely, the Fund's inability to influence the countries that contributed to the crisis because of their policies, but did not need to borrow. Thus there was no conditionality for the OPEC countries that administered the oil shock, nor for the U.S. deficit imbroglio that ran up interest costs, nor for the swings of European and American monetary policy that led first to inflation and then to sharp recession, nor for the protectionists with their trade barriers. By its rules the IMF can require adjustments only among its borrowers, the unfortunate LDCs who, not blameless themselves, are also victims of these policies. Ideally, perhaps, the IMF should have more ability to influence the actions of its members when these actions cause global damage among its other members.

SPECIAL DRAWING RIGHTS

A last activity of the IMF, interesting and controversial, has the potential to increase long-term capital formation in the LDCs. This activity is the issuance of special drawing rights (SDRs), new international reserves created by the IMF and distributed to its members in accordance with the size of their quotas. The last new allocation of SDRs (12 billion) was in 1979 to 1981, bringing the total in existence to 21.4 billion. (This was about 60 percent of outstanding IMF loans in mid 1985.) Each SDR was worth a little less than 1 U.S. dollar in early 1985, while in September 1986, the figure was $1.21. Its value is determined by a weighted average of five major currencies, the weights established by the share of the currencies in world trade and in reserves held by central banks. Currently, the SDR's value is calculated from a basket consisting of the U.S. dollar (42 percent), German mark (19 percent), Japanese yen (15 percent), French franc (12 percent), and British pound (12 percent). The basket is adjusted every five years, with the next alteration scheduled for 1991. It is unlikely that the currencies presently employed will change, since there is such a large gap between these currencies and the sixth most important. SDRs may be transferred between governments in settlement of balance of payments deficits. Countries holding more than their allocation receive a rate of interest from the IMF; countries that have "spent" their SDRs pay a rate of interest plus a small charge. These rates (5.85 percent and 6.00 percent, respectively, on August 11, 1986) are fixed weekly and are made up of the weighted average short-term interest rates in the money markets of the five countries whose currencies determine the value of the SDR.

Up to now, the LDCs have benefited little from SDR creation because collectively their quotas are small. There are, however, innovative ideas to combine SDR creation with more financing for the LDCs in what has come to be called the SDR link.[53] The link is an old idea, dating back to an earlier scheme called the Stamp Plan, devised by the British economist Sir Maxwell Stamp. The Stamp Plan was to introduce something like the SDR as a way of distributing new purchasing power to the needy. Instead of distribution according to quota, the plan envisaged the new credits as aid to LDCs, countries being able to make purchases internationally with the credits and repaying the IMF for these credits many years hence on easy terms.

With the coming of the SDR, the idea surfaced again and received support in the 1980 report of the Brandt Commission.[54] Some proponents favor an "organic link" in which the IMF articles would be amended to raise the quotas of the LDCs; they would thus receive a greater proportion of newly created SDRs. The realization that this would be time-consuming and involve much in-fighting over quota sizes gave rise to the "inorganic link" proposal of voluntary contributions of developed-country SDRs to the LDCs, with no change in quotas. Such a plan could be more rapidly adopted, but, obviously, there would be doubts as to whether all developed countries could always be relied upon to make their voluntary contributions. (Only the French gave any support to the "reverse link," which would have excluded LDCs altogether from receiving any of the newly created SDRs.) In Peter Kenen's version, countries borrowing from the IMF might receive newly-created SDRs instead of dollars, etc., in exchange for their own currency. Those in greatest need would thus be the recipients of the assistance.

The SDR link proposals have the advantage of avoiding any repugnant political strings attached to "normal" foreign aid. If the decision were taken to transfer resources via SDRs, a new problem would arise, however. The recent era of high market rates of interest meant that under present rules LDCs would have had to pay these high rates if they used their new and larger allocations. To counter this flow, either the interest paid on the use of SDRs would have had to be lowered below that paid on accumulations, or preferential rates for LDCs would have had to be negotiated. If neither is possible, then when interest rates are high new SDRs might have to be made available to the World Bank or UN agencies or national governments as a basis for development grants.

The major objection to the SDR link, as to the original Stamp Plan, has always been its inflationary potential. The need for development funds, so it is said, will be much higher than the optimal need for international reserves. As world trade grows (and presuming a need for reserves even under floating rates as major nations manage their floating and smaller countries continue to fix their rates), the need for reserves grows also. The result of an SDR link would be inflationary only if the newly created reserves outran the growing liquidity demand for them. To be sure, if the LDCs *themselves* determined the amount to be created, the charge of inflationary potential would undoubtedly carry great weight. In the 1970s the LDCs did not abate their calls for new SDR issues even when world inflation hit its peaks in this period. But since it now takes an 85 percent vote of the IMF to create new SDRs, and LDCs have only 31 percent of the votes, the volume of SDRs would remain under developed-country supervision unless arrangements were drastically changed. There is thus little likelihood of the money creation running out of control.

Even if through some unknown means the LDCs should seize the decision-making process, the goods furnished in exchange for the SDRs would still come from the developed countries, which would always have an option simply to pull out of the scheme. It is, however, doubtless true that an SDR link would have greater first-round multiplier effects than the present system of SDR creation, because all the new SDRs would surely be spent. (Under today's system many countries hold their SDRs without spending them.) SDR creation under a link plan would have to be correspondingly less than otherwise to avoid inflationary repercussions.

Other objections to a link are that the SDR would become politicized, the poorest would not get the most aid, and the valuable economic restructuring required under IMF loans would not accompany the new SDRs.[55]

The question is currently in abeyance. The governing committee of the Fund did not recommend a new distribution of SDRs in either 1984 or 1985. From 6 percent of world reserves in 1972, the SDR had slipped to only half that in 1983. It cannot at present be said whether this provocative method of providing a capital transfer to the LDCs will ever be utilized.

ENVOI

The debt crisis and the role of the IMF in assisting the LDCs to survive it were topics little imagined 10 years ago. For a time in the early 1980s they became the most threatening and portentous issues in all of development economics. The whole episode has already been damaging, with day-to-day turns of events and a certain breathless quality not usual in the study of economics. Should the crisis recur to the point of international financial panic or collapse, the prospects for LDC development would be set back severely, perhaps for many years. Should it be brought under control, however, the outlook for increased flows of private capital to needy countries would become much brighter.

NOTES

1. Compare Peter B. Kenen, *The International Economy,* Englewood Cliffs, N.J., 1985, pp. 279–280.
2. There is a large recent literature. *WDR 1985* addressed the issue, and there is an excellent and readable overview by Norman S. Fieleke of the Federal Reserve Bank of Boston, "International Lending on Trial," *New England Economic Review,* May/June 1983, pp. 5–13. Both are much depended upon here, and the Fieleke article provided the framework for the debt section. I also utilized IMF, *World Economic Outlook, 1984,* pts. 1, 3, 4; *1985,* chaps. I, II, and supplement no. 2; *1986,* chap. 5; "LDC Debt Crisis" with articles by Rudiger Dornbusch, William R. Cline, Gustav Ranis, and Martin Feldstein, *Challenge,* 27, no. 3 (1984); Henry S. Terrell, "Bank Lending to Developing Countries," *Federal Reserve Bulletin,* October 1984, pp. 755–763; Eduardo Wiesner, "Domestic and External Causes of the Latin American Debt Crisis," *Finance and Development* 22, no. 1 (1985): 24–26. Kristin Hallberg, "International Indebtedness in 1984: Origins of the Problem and Issues for the Future," in Michael K. Claudon, ed., *The World Debt Crisis: International Lending on Trial,* Cambridge, Mass., 1986, is thorough and authoritative. Other sources include IMF, *Foreign Private Investment in Developing Countries,* IMF Occasional Paper No. 33, 1985; Donald R. Lessard and John Williamson, *Financial Intermediation Beyond the Debt Crisis,* Washington, D.C., 1985; Rudiger Dornbusch, *Dollars, Debts, and Deficits,* Cambridge, Mass., 1986; Jeffrey Sachs, "LDC Debt in the 1980s: Risk and Reforms," in Paul Wachtel, ed., *Crises in the Economic and Financial Structure,* Lexington, Mass., 1982; and the World Bank's voluminous *World Debt Tables,* annual, which contain the raw material for any study. I also made use of material in the *Wall Street Journal,* June 22, 1984; *The Economist,* February 19, 1983; September 24, 1983, pp. S30–S45; April 14, 1984, p. 77; June 2, 1984, pp. 87–88; September 1 and 8, 1984, pp. 59–60, 86; October 5, 1985, special section; October 12, 1985, pp. 75–76; January 11, 1986, pp. 71–72; March 15, 1986, pp. 67, 82, 101; and almost every recent issue of the *IMF Survey.*
3. *The Economist,* July 9, 1983, pp. 14–15.
4. Statement before the House Banking Committee, February 2, 1983, cited by Fieleke, "International Lending on Trial," p. 6.
5. The figure is for LDCs that do not export fuels. The volume of exports by the indebted LDCs actually fell by 0.7 percent in 1982; exports of the "major borrowers" went down by 3.3 percent.
6. Edmar Lisboa Bacha and Carlos F. Diaz-Alejandro, *Financial Markets: A View from*

the Semi-Periphery, Yale Economic Growth Center Discussion Paper No. 367, 1981, p. 32.

7. *Ibid.,* pp. 32, 34.

8. See the explanation in the IMF's *World Economic Outlook, 1985,* pp. 123–129. See also Sylvia Ann Hewlett, Henry Kaufman, and Peter B. Kenen, eds., *The Global Repercussions of U.S. Monetary and Fiscal Policy,* Cambridge, Mass., 1984.

9. The example is adapted from *The Economist,* September 24, 1983, pp. S32–S37.

10. "Currency Diversification and LDC Debt," *Federal Reserve Bank of New York Quarterly Review* 8, no. 3 (1983): 19–20.

11. In addition to sources cited in note 2, I used Otto Emminger, *The Dollar's Borrowed Strength,* Group of 30 Occasional Paper No. 19, 1985.

12. The World Bank estimates that capital flight from 1979 to 1982 was actually greater than capital inflows (137 percent) in Venezuela, and high as a proportion of inflows in Argentina (65 percent) and Mexico (48 percent). There is a discussion in *WDR 1985,* p. 64. More recent estimates for 1983 to 1985 by Morgan Guaranty suggest that, for the 10 biggest Latin American debtors, capital flight was 70 percent of all net borrowing, with the figure 178 percent for Mexico. See *The Economist,* March 8, 1986, p. 106. For an unorthodox view of capital flight that in part blames developed-country banks for the phenomenon, see James S. Henry, "Where the Money Went," *The New Republic,* April 14, 1986, pp. 20–23.

13. I utilized "The Persistence of High Real Interest Rates," in IMF, *World Economic Outlook, 1985,* pp. 123–129. A new study by Vito Tanzi, "Fiscal Deficits and Interest Rates in the United States: An Empirical Analysis, 1960–84," *IMF Staff Papers,* 32, no. 4 (1985): 551–576, suggests that the U.S. fiscal deficit has contributed somewhat less to high interest rates (perhaps one-third of the rise in real terms) than have changes in tax laws, financial deregulation, continuing tightness in monetary policy, shrinking OPEC surpluses, greater merger activity, and other influences. Econometric modeling by Jeffrey Sachs and Warwick McKibben, *Coordination of Monetary and Fiscal Policies in the OECD,* NBER Working Paper No. 1800, 1986, suggests that an increase in the U.S. fiscal deficit of 1 percent causes nominal interest rates to rise by 2 percentage points after five years, and the exchange rate to appreciate by 3.3 percent.

14. This case is modeled by Paul R. Masson, "The Sustainability of Fiscal Deficits," *IMF Staff Papers,* 32, no. 4 (1985): 577–605.

15. For this section, I followed especially Fieleke, "International Lending on Trial," pp. 8–10. Even in the years when there was no "crisis," some countries had problems in making their payments. In the fifteen years from 1955 to 1970, Argentina, Brazil, Chile, Ghana, Indonesia, Peru, and Turkey rescheduled a total of 17 times. A few became veterans. Zaire, for example, rescheduled six times between 1975 and 1983.

16. See Sebastian Edwards, *The Pricing of Bonds and Bank Loans in International Markets,* NBER Working Paper No. 1689, 1985.

17. See Willene A. Johnson, "Bank Size and U.S. Bank Lending to Latin America," *Federal Reserve Bank of New York Quarterly Review* 8, no. 3 (1983): 20–21.

18. See Jane Sneddon Little, "Eurobank Maturity Transformation and LDC Debts," *New England Economic Review,* September/October 1983, pp. 15–19.

19. Moshin S. Khan and Malcolm D. Knight, "Sources of Payments Problems in LDCs," *Finance and Development* 20, no. 4 (September 1983): 2–5.

20. *Ibid.*

21. *WDR 1985,* p. 6.

22. When the debt is owed to or guaranteed by governments, the rescheduling is done

within the so-called Paris Club, staffed by French Treasury officials and dating from 1956. Here creditor nations negotiate the rescheduling with debtors. When the debt is owed to commercial banks, the rescheduling is done by teams put together for the purpose. This began only in the late 1970s. Since the teams often meet in London, the name "London Club" is sometimes used. See *WDR 1985,* p. 27. A thorough survey of the reschedulings, with details of the individual agreements, is K. Burke Dillon et al., *Recent Developments in External Debt Restructuring,* IMF Occasional Paper No. 40, 1985. Also see M. S. Mendelsohn, "Commercial Banks and the Restructuring of Cross-Border Debt," Group of 30, New York, 1983. The 1985 figures, involving 12 agreements with commercial banks and 19 in the Paris Club, are from *The Economist,* July 12, 1986, p. 98.

23. Two recent studies conclude that, until the onset of the crisis, the great preponderance of debt *was* used to finance capital formation and not consumption in the debtor LDCs for which the statistics are good enough to analyze. After 1979 more debt financing was used to meet balance of payments difficulties, so that the contribution of debt to growth was diminished. See Iqbal Mehdi Zaidi, "Saving, Investment, Fiscal Deficits, and the External Indebtedness of Developing Countries," *World Development* 13, no. 5 (1985): 573–588; and *WDR 1985,* pp. 46–51.

24. Much larger adjustment was undertaken by the seven biggest borrowers, whose combined current account deficit fell from $40 billion in 1982 to $1.5 billion in 1984. For an analysis of the particular severity of the problem in Latin America, see Stephany Griffith-Jones, *International Finance and Latin America,* New York, 1984.

25. IMF, *World Economic Outlook, 1986,* p. 67. The 1985 figure for capital flight was thought to be only 25 percent of the 1982 figure. The data are weak, however.

26. Morgan Guaranty calculation reported in *Christian Science Monitor,* August 1, 1985.

27. *WDR 1985,* pp. 71–76, surveys the types of controls that various LDCs have put into place on external borrowing.

28. IMF, *World Economic Outlook, 1986,* pp. 35–36.

29. See Jack M. Guttentag and Richard J. Herring, "Commercial Bank Lending to Less Developed Countries: From Overlending to Underlending to Structural Reform," *Brookings Papers in International Economics* 16 (June 1984): 1–52; and IMF, *World Economic Outlook, 1986,* pp. 8, 68.

30. The U.S. International Lending Supervision Act of 1983 now requires among other things (1) the holding of reserves against some international assets; (2) tightened disclosure requirements on loans; and (3) increased frequency of reporting. See Henry S. Terrell, "Bank Lending to Developing Countries: Recent Developments and Some Considerations for the Future," *Federal Reserve Bulletin* 70, no. 10 (October 1984): 758.

31. IMF, *World Economic Outlook, 1986,* p. 200.

32. Peru's strategy is discussed in *The Economist,* July 19, 1986, p. 33.

33. *The Economist,* June 14, 1986, pp. 19–20, 73–74; *Wall Street Journal,* June 23, 1986.

34. At the same time, the U.S. was proposing a special World Bank/IMF program for Africa, mobilizing $3 billion in a jointly administered, highly conditional operation discussed later in the chapter.

35. *The Economist,* July 26, 1986, p. 73; *Wall Street Journal,* July 15, 1986.

36. See C. Fred Bergsten, William R. Cline, and John Williamson, *Bank Lending to Developing Countries: The Policy Alternatives,* Washington, D.C., 1985; Frances Stewart, "The International Debt Situation and North-South Relations," *World Development* 13, no. 2 (1985): 197–200; David Felix, "Latin America's Debt, *Challenge* 28,

no. 5 (1985):44–51; *The Economist,* February 19, 1983, p. 85; *IMF Survey,* December 5, 1983, pp. 374–375; May 21, 1984, pp. 154–155; October 19, 1985, p. 90; and March 18, 1986, p. 69.

37. The agreement with Mexico in July, 1986, incorporates some aspects of this proposal.

38. See Henry C. Wallich, *Insurance of Bank Lending to Developing Countries,* Group of 30 Occasional Paper No. 15, 1984.

39. It should be noted that the dollar amounts here and in the remainder of the chapter are actually not in dollars, but are in the IMF's special drawing rights, or SDRs, which are explained later. One SDR originally equaled 1 U.S. dollar, but the SDR now floats and its value in dollars can vary. The dollar figures in the text are calculated on the assumption that SDR 1 = $1. In early 1985, when SDR 1 = $0.96, these dollar figures would have been slightly lower; in September, 1986, when SDR 1 = $1.21, they would have been 21 percent higher. To obtain exact dollar amounts for a given date, the dollar figures in the text must be adjusted by the value of the SDR in dollars on that date. The GAB was established in 1962, and originally included 10 countries (hence the much-used name, "Group of 10"): United States, West Germany, Japan, Britain, France, Italy, Canada, Netherlands, Belgium, and Sweden. Switzerland was formally added in 1983 after many years of association.

40. Saudi Arabia in a separate arrangement similar to the GAB added another $1.5 billion to the total at the same time the latter was reformed in 1983. Small amounts have also been borrowed from the Bank for International Settlements.

41. The levels quoted are for 1986 only. Since 1984 the figures have been renegotiated every year. The 1984 figures were 102 percent or 125 percent annually; in 1985 they were 95 percent and 115 percent. Note that the 1986 figures thus represented a significant reduction from 1984. Some part of the lending (140 percent of quota) can be obtained in the "extended fund facility" with a longer repayment period of 4 1/2 to 10 years.

42. *Wall Street Journal,* April 10, 1985, and March 28, 1986; *The Economist,* August 23, 1986, p. 68.

43. There is a survey of the subject by John Williamson, ed., *IMF Conditionality,* Washington, D.C., 1983. A trenchant critique of the conditions for Brazil that focuses on the deflationary aspects is Celso Furtado, *No to Recession and Unemployment: An Examination of the Brazilian Economic Crisis,* London, 1984. For figures on the number of programs, see Morris Goldstein, *Global Effects of Fund-Supported Programs,* IMF Occasional Paper No. 42, 1985. Goldstein also provides the information from which the percentages used in this paragraph were calculated; see p. 9 for the data.

44. See Charles A. Sisson, "Fund-Supported Programs and Income Distribution in LDCs," *Finance and Development* 23, no. 1 (1986): 33–36, and Jacques de Larosière, "Does the Fund Impose Austerity?" IMF, Washington, D.C., 1984. It is true that LDCs approaching the IMF for loans cannot be certain at that moment what the conditionality will eventually involve. The lack of knowledge may delay the country's own adjustment efforts. Thus Peter Kenen's recent proposal for "shadow conditionality," wherein the IMF would make it known what the general conditions would be should a country seek loans, makes sense. This would save valuable time, eliminate surprises, and encourage sensible adjustment before a loan is granted. See Peter B. Kenen, *Financing Adjustment and the International Monetary Fund,* Washington, D.C., 1986.

45. See Moshin S. Khan and Malcolm D. Knight, *Fund-Supported Adjustment Programs and Economic Growth,* IMF Occasional Paper No. 41, 1985.

46. Goldstein, *Global Effects of Fund-Supported Programs.*
47. See Sidney Dell, "The Fifth Credit Tranche," *World Development* 13, no. 2 (1985): 245–249.
48. A recent discussion of food financing is Barbara Huddleston et al., *International Finance for Food Security,* Baltimore, 1984.
49. See the Brookings study by Richard Goode, *Economic Assistance to Developing Countries Through the IMF,* Washington, D.C., 1985.
50. See *The Economist,* April 5, 1986, p. 91. This new program resembles the World Bank's IDA. It is a descendant of the old "Trust Fund" which has now expired. Under earlier rules the IMF required in-payment of gold to cover the first 25 percent of a country's quota. This was called the "gold tranche." (Nowadays this has become the "reserve tranche," payable in hard currency, as we saw above.) In 1976 the IMF decided to return ⅙ of its gold to its members and to sell another ⅙ of its total holding of 25 million ounces to finance loans to developing countries. In a series of some 30 auctions lasting until March 31, 1981, the IMF sold what amounted to about 60 percent of one year's production of new gold, worth over $3 billion at prices on the open market always several hundred dollars an ounce above the outdated official price of about $40 an ounce which the IMF had been using to value its gold. The proceeds (the Trust Fund) were used to finance loans to poor LDCs at concessional rates. The IMF in doing so was clearly reacting to the common complaint in the LDCs that its quota structure was highly discriminatory toward poor countries. The repayment of these Trust Fund loans is the major source of funding for the new structural adjustment facility.
51. Goode, *Economic Assistance to Developing Countries Through the IMF.*
52. Some of the major rescheduling agreements actually *increased* the flow of lending, at least temporarily, with a significant amount of IMF pressure applied to this end.
53. See Graham Bird, "The Benefits of Special Drawing Rights for Less Developed Countries," *World Development* 7, no. 3 (1979):281–290; Geoffrey Maynard, "Special Drawing Rights and Development Aid," *Journal of Development Studies,* 9, no. 4 (1973):518–543; Geoffrey Maynard and Graham Bird, "International Monetary Issues and the Developing Countries: A Survey," and "Postscript," in Paul Streeten and Richard Jolly, eds., *Recent Issues in World Development,* Oxford, 1981, pp. 343–373; Gerald K. Helleiner, "The Less Developed Countries and the International Monetary System," in Helleiner, *International Economic Disorder: Essays in North-South Relations,* Toronto, 1981, pp. 130–165, especially pp. 153–161; Y. S. Park, *The Link Between Special Drawing Rights and Development Finance,* Princeton Essays in International Finance No. 100, 1973; and John Williamson, "SDRs: The Link," in Jagdish N. Bhagwati, ed., *The New International Economic Order: The North-South Debate,* Cambridge, Mass., 1977. I relied heavily on the last of these.
54. For a recent review of the question see John Williamson, *A New SDR Allocation,* Washington, D.C., 1984. The Kenen idea is from his *Financing Adjustment and the International Monetary Fund.*
55. Noted by Goode, *Economic Assistance to Developing Countries Through the IMF.*

chapter 7

Technology, Factor Proportions, and Dualism

We turn now to the question of appropriate technologies for the LDCs.[1] *Techno* in Greek means "art," "craft," or "skill." Technology is the application of art, craft, or skill to a product or a process. Improvements in technique are a key factor in productivity increase. Technical change applies to far more than the improvements in physical capital usually associated with the word. It can occur in the seeds and methods of agriculture, in the organization of markets and of economic planning, in the control of population, in virtually any economic endeavor, large or small.

We are perhaps used to thinking of grand leaps in technology—industrial revolutions, agricultural revolutions, major transformations in transport (sail to steam, prop to jet), communication (pencil and paper to typewriter and adding machine to computer), or energy (wood to coal to oil). Any item of physical capital, however, no matter how simple it is, always embodies a technology. A humble screw in a machine can be made of iron, steel, steel alloy, aluminum, or other material; it can be manufactured by numerous different methods; it can be inserted by hand or by robot; it can have a metric pitch or one in inches, a slotted or Phillips or Robinson or Allen head, a flat or round top. At some point in the development of the screw each of these characteristics represented, on a small scale, a "technological change" with large implications for the usefulness of that little artifact.

Small or large, whenever we speak of an economic activity, we also speak of the technology bound up with it and hence of productivity. The topic actually applies so widely that it is convenient to divide it. The remainder of this chapter concentrates largely on technological change in industry. Technology in agriculture, in forming "human capital," in planning and markets, and in relation to economies of scale is considered in the following four chapters.

The rapid worldwide spread of technical knowledge has been an obvious outstanding feature of development in the last half of the twentieth century, and it seems certain that it will increase. Remember Edward Denison's claim (which has its critics) that economic growth may be more fully explained by differences in technologies than by unequal accumulation of physical capital. Technical research may be the most productive of all investment activities. Applied widely in many areas of output, with one innovation often leading to another, technology is a major defense against diminishing returns to capital accumulation.[2]

ALTERNATIVE TECHNOLOGIES

How does a country decide what factor proportions to employ as its economy grows, and how are such decisions made? Does it aim for capital-intensive methods embodying the most "modern" techniques found in the developed countries? Or does it strive to acquire labor-intensive technologies that conserve scarce capital and utilize the country's large labor force, at the expense of appearing less "up-to-date"? Perhaps some activities of an economy are highly capital-intensive, while at the same time others are highly labor-intensive. Such a situation is commonly called a "dual economy."

The question for this chapter is whether a country undergoing economic development should use a capital-labor ratio tailored to its factor proportions, or whether it should adopt "modern" technologies fitted to the capital-labor ratios of developed countries. In coping with the question, it is always necessary to ask another: What is the intended outcome of the choice? Maximizing output per head is the most familiar goal, no doubt, but a country's leaders may choose to maximize future as opposed to current output. They may also believe that the choice of technologies can play a part in social reform or in promoting social cohesion or in lowering class barriers, and so forth.[3] The effects of technology on saving and investment (hence on future income) and on income distribution are not considered in this chapter. We will return to these topics in Chapter 11.

Assume for now that the intent is to maximize present output. What then does economics have to say about the choice of technologies? The traditional argument of neoclassical microeconomic theory is clear and relatively simple. Standard theory suggests that the factors of production should be so allocated that the marginal physical product (MPP) per dollar spent on some given factor is equal to the MPP per dollar spent on any other factor. In the symbols of a first-year economics textbook, this is written:

$$\frac{MPP_L}{P_L} = \frac{MPP_K}{P_K}$$

This formula's ordinary meaning is that if the price of labor *(L)*, is extremely low relative to capital *(K)*, then output per dollar spent is maximized when the MPP of labor is very low and the MPP of capital is very high. For some actual enterprise, in a typical LDC heavily endowed with labor, this means in turn the employment of a great deal of labor and a relatively small amount of capital. For any given dollar outlay on labor and capital, output is the highest that can be achieved; said another way, for any given output the dollar outlay on labor and capital is minimized.

A set of production isoquants based on this logic shows diagrammatically the sacrifice of output when a capital-intensive technique is chosen in an economy with abundant labor and scarce capital (see Figure 7.1).[4] The quantity of capital is shown on the vertical axis, and the quantity of labor is on the horizontal. CI_1, CI_2, CI_3, and CI_4 are four isoquants showing production levels using a capital-intensive process, with the level of output increasing from CI_1 to CI_4. These isoquants show high capital intensity (a high capital-labor ratio) relative to the isoquants labeled LI. Note how along CI_4 factor proportions can be altered to include a little more capital and a little less labor, as at *OA* and *OB*, or a little less capital and a little more labor, as at *OC* and *OD*, while still producing the same quantity of output, as shown by the height of CI_4. But the technique itself is capital-intensive. Any combination along the CI isoquants requires more capital than labor relative to a labor-intensive technique such as shown by isoquants LI_1, LI_2, LI_3, and LI_4. Along the LI isoquants, the capital-labor ratio is always lower.

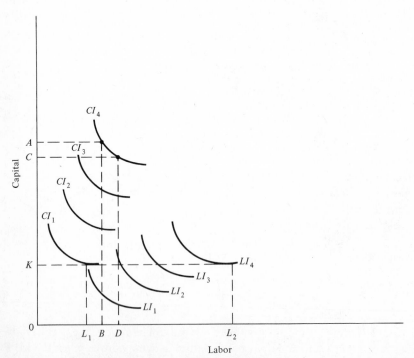

Figure 7.1 Production isoquants for capital-intensive and labor-intensive techniques.

If an economy possesses limited capital *(OK),* but a large quantity of labor *(OL$_2$)* then if maximum output is the goal, it is clearly a mistake to use the capital-intensive technology. That method would allow an output level equal only to CI$_1$; a shortage of capital precludes reaching a higher isoquant using this technique. A further disadvantage is that much available labor cannot be used in this sector: $L_1 L_2$ labor will not find employment there. Consider, however, adoption of a labor-intensive technique. Then *OK* capital, in combination with *OL$_2$* labor, is sufficient to allow a much higher output level, as at isoquant LI$_4$. (The "wrong" factor proportions will also cause a further sacrifice than this: Exports with the greatest potential comparative advantage will be penalized, with resulting reduction in the ability to acquire imports.)

In short, standard neoclassical theory suggests that the availability of factors will determine the appropriate technology. And, indeed, much economic behavior reflects just this, with studies usually indicating rather wide scope for substituting labor-intensive techniques when desired.[5] Certainly, the difference in employment can be large, depending on the technique used. A survey of plants in Indonesia showed labor-intensive techniques resulted in 13 times more employment than capital-intensive techniques for an equal output of cigarettes, 12 times more for flashlight batteries; 6 times more for tires, and 23 times more for soft drinks. Evidence from Colombia indicates that investment of over $100 million in the capital-intensive petrochemical industry up to 1965 caused a *decrease* in employment of 290 people and a gain of less than 1,000 jobs from the multiplier process in other industries. Analysis showed the same amount of investment in labor-intensive industries, such as shoes, furniture, and clothing, could have expanded employment by 47,500 jobs, over 20 percent of all industrial employment at the time, which would have led to 207,000 more jobs from the multiplier effect.[6]

Employment generation through labor intensity may be favored for another reason as well. If a value judgment is made that government is not up to coping with the possible unemployment and income redistribution aspects of capital intensity, then that, too, might point to the adoption of labor-intensive methods. This argument is controversial, however, because of the possibility of an adverse trade-off. The economist must be on guard when government promotes labor intensity as a tactic to increase employment, when that is not the most efficient combination of factors and so sacrifices output. A severe trade-off between more employment and less GNP would have to receive intense scrutiny. *Perhaps* markets are poorly developed, so that the absorption of the unemployed is long delayed and painful. *Perhaps* the government is incapable of capturing any part of the increased output, so unemployment compensation and training schemes are not feasible and the social consequences of the unemployment are too great to be borne. But *perhaps* proper policy would be to work on the inadequacies of markets, taxes, and transfer systems, rather than sacrifice the output. Chapter 9 returns to this issue.

In the past, often it seems without much debate and contrary to all the above, LDCs have tended to deal with this important issue by adopting the latest available technology—a sort of "international demonstration effect" at work, whereby satisfaction comes from obtaining the most modern Western or Soviet techniques. Frequently, such choices have been promoted by foreign consultants whose "culture-bound" experience is mainly with this type of technology. For other reasons as well there may be a bureaucratic bias toward capital-intensive techniques in the LDC. Foreign contractors may be thought more dependable and likely to produce on schedule. The bureaucrats in charge may view their local poor and uneducated labor force with mistrust and contempt. Managers may find it more comfortable to cope with fewer workers and deal primarily with trained engineers, so avoiding many problems in human relations. And a government may be locked into an initial choice of capital intensity by fear of appearing wasteful and indecisive if the choice is changed.[7]

Indeed, the latest available technology is usually capital-intensive, tailored to the labor-scarce factor proportions of the developed world where most of the research has been done. The LDCs currently hold only about a 3 percent share in the world's annual spending on science and technology.[8]

There are several arguments justifying the use of capital-intensive techniques even when labor is the most abundant factor. The arguments must be studied with care, because often they are used to rubber-stamp a decision already taken to opt for the most modern technique, based not on economic reasons but on demonstration effects. Five economic arguments used to justify high capital intensity are considered below.

Low Labor Productivity The marginal physical product of labor (MPP_L) may be so low on some particular project that the labor price cannot fall far enough to offset the low productivity. Wages for full-time labor are limited on the down side by the expenses of subsistence, and since a firm cannot pay less than that, it might find capital a preferable substitute because of its high productivity.

A major reason for such low labor productivity is malnutrition and illness in the work force, leading to tiredness, sickness, and general inability to stand up to the required working conditions. Calorie deficiencies have been reported from many parts of the third world. Disease brings absenteeism and low productivity even when on the job. A World Bank study in Indonesia in 1975 found that 85 percent of the workers in the construction and rubber industries were infected with hookworm, and 45 percent of these had the associated iron-deficiency anemia. The anemia, usually caused by inadequate absorbable iron in the diet, saps strength and leaves workers weak and listless. It is thought to affect between one-third and two-thirds of the population in many tropical LDCs, with the figure reaching 80 percent and more in India. In Africa mining companies often make a regular practice of feeding new recruits a nutritious diet for several weeks before putting the men into the mines; they reap a substantial reward in increased output per man hour from this "investment." Firms building the Pan-American Highway found it possible to raise labor productivity 200 percent by providing three balanced meals a day to the work force.[9] (Further empirical evidence on the role of health and nutrition in productivity is reviewed in Chapter 9.)

Workers might also not be used to factory methods, might be illiterate and uneducated, and might have only a passing attachment to their jobs, with high turnover and many missed days. All these are symptoms of what Harvey Leibenstein has called X-inefficiency, the inefficiency displayed when a firm has average costs higher than need be for a given quantity and quality of output, or, put another way, produces less than could be produced given its inputs. (Leibenstein has also argued that X-inefficiency may prevent the adoption of technologies requiring more intensive effort, higher literacy, etc. Here a country may be forced to continue to use an inferior technology by the underlying inefficiencies.) This amounts to saying that low wages may not after all be a good bargain for an employer if they do not compensate for even lower efficiency.

Artificially High Prices for Labor or Low Prices for Capital   A complication intrudes if the price of labor is kept artificially high, so that wages do not reflect labor's true abundance. Urban wages are often two or three times higher than the income level that can be earned in the farm sector and much higher than would occur in any competitive structure, even if there are large costs of job search and moving. What are the reasons for the large differential? First, government salaries may still be paid according to wage scales set in the colonial period or just after independence, when skills and education were more scarce. Second, the legal minimum wage may be high and sternly enforced. This is especially true in urban areas. (In Tanzania, for example, the legal minimum is three times that of India, even though Tanzania has the lower per capita income.)[10] Such laws may originally have been aimed at relatively vulnerable foreign firms, but political forces sometimes then spread their effects more widely. Third, strong trade unions, often operating first on foreign firms especially in mining, may lead to a dualistic wage structure in the rest of the modern economy (Chile, Venezuela, Zambia). Fourth, large foreign firms may pay higher-than-market wages to protect and promote their corporate image, as insurance against public hostility, as a matter of social conscience, or to guard against high turnover. If training costs are relatively large, the modern-sector employer may be able to minimize unit costs by cutting turnover, and above-market wages are one way to do so. Fifth, expensive social programs, such as pensions, compulsory health and safety measures in plants, family allowances, and fringe benefits, may raise labor costs by as much as 30 to 40 percent of the nominal wage bill.[11]

All this means dualism in the labor market, with wages artificially boosted in the modern sector and still low in the traditional sector. The high wages of the urban centers, which have often grown 4 or 5 percent a year in real terms, as fast as or faster than in the developed world, sometimes three or four times faster than the growth of real per capita national income, have been a great attraction to labor.[12] This wage differential is the main cause of the recent heavy migration from rural to urban areas. Over 30 percent of the addition to urban population in the LDCs in the past few years has been people from the farms. The figure was over 60 percent in Ghana, South Korea, and Tanzania and over 70 percent in the Ivory Coast and Uganda.[13] Urban population was only about a fifth of the whole for the LDCs of 1950, but it was nearly a third by 1975, with growth of some 4 percent a year, as opposed to only 1.2 percent in the urban centers of the developed world.

The dual wage structure also promotes the spread of urban unemployment.

High wages greatly enhance the supply of labor relative to the demand; thus many migrants are destined to remain jobless. Urban unemployment rates are especially severe in the age group 15 to 24, with figures over 20 percent commonly reported, in Colombia, Kenya, the Philippines, and Sri Lanka among many others.[14] We return to the subject of urban unemployment in Chapter 9.

The dualism can also be promoted from the capital side, if there are special stimuli for the use of capital. Examples have already been discussed in earlier chapters and include the subsidization of interest rates for large firms and the tying of aid from developed countries. Imports of capital may be encouraged by overvalued exchange rates or forgiveness of tariffs. In particular, *state* corporations may be called upon to pay only a small return on capital, or perhaps nothing at all. This is almost certain to ensure that they will end up highly capital-intensive and use too much capital in total in an organizational structure that is often overly expanded. Again, labor will appear expensive relative to capital, even though it is the abundant factor; there will be far less incentive to search out new technologies that are labor-using. Whatever the reason, be it artificially high prices for labor or artificially low ones for capital, the result is the same. The demand for labor is reduced and that for capital increased in any sector where policy alters prices. Technological dualism sets in.

Actual data showing the degree to which labor and capital costs are distorted are somewhat scarce. Even where data exist, there is a strong suspicion that the worst cases are not included. Table 7.1, taken from the work of Anne Krueger, shows the estimated percentage distortion in labor and capital costs for a selected group of countries at various time periods. Economists are not certain how large these distortions have to be before they become significant. Krueger's simulations suggest that for a given unit of capital, removing the price distortions would have increased labor use by 10 percent in Argentina, 15 percent in Brazil, and 271 percent in Pakistan.

The expected effect of a combined artificially high price for labor and artificially low price for capital can be seen diagrammatically in Figure 7.2a,

Table 7.1   DISTORTION IN LABOR AND CAPITAL COSTS

Country	Year	Change in Labor Cost (Percent)	Change in Capital Cost (Percent)
Argentina	1973	15	17
Brazil	1968	27	4
Chile	1966–1968	na	37
Hong Kong	1973	0	0
Ivory Coast	1971	23	15
Pakistan	1961–1964	0	76
South Korea	1969	0	10
Tunisia	1972	20	36

Source: Adapted from Anne O. Krueger, *Trade Strategies and Employment,* vol. 3, *Synthesis and Conclusions,* Chicago, 1983, Table 7.1.

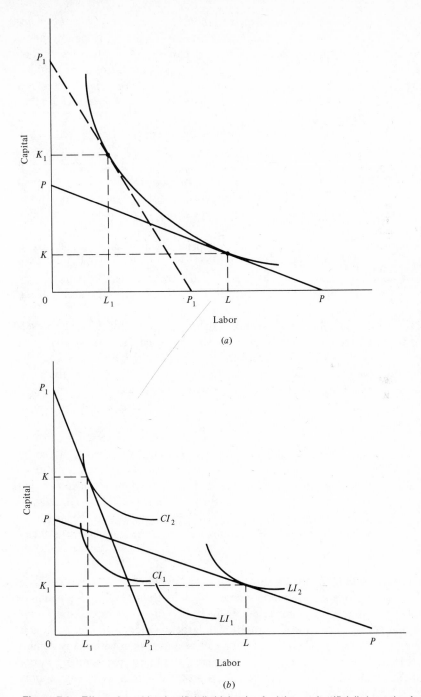

Figure 7.2 Effect of combined artificially high price for labor and artificially low price for capital.

which uses a production isoquant similar to those in Figure 7.1. *Given any choice* between labor intensity and capital intensity, along the single isoquant shown here, artificially altering the prices of labor and capital will alter the technology adopted. The line *PP* is a price line showing a small amount of scarce capital exchanging for a larger amount of abundant labor. Production is labor-intensive, with *OL* labor and *OK* capital being employed. If, however, the price of labor is boosted and the price of capital subsidized, as shown by price line P_1P_1, then managers choose different factor proportions. More capital is employed (OK_1) and less labor (OL_1). The type of technology in use and the resulting employment of capital and labor are here closely related to the price of these factors, even if artificial. Diminished employment possibilities for labor follow directly. Note in Figure 7.2a how only OL_1 labor finds employment on this project because of the choice of a capital-intensive technique, whereas with a labor-intensive technique *OL* labor was at work.

Alternatively, one could show relative prices, if artificially established at P_1P_1, causing a shift to a different (capital-intensive) type of technology as with the CI isoquants on Figure 7.2b. This is completely rational from the point of view of the firm making the decision, but it does not reflect the actual scarcity of the factors of production.

Numerous LDCs have recently come to recognize the difficulties for development when technological dualism becomes pronounced. In response, planners have frequently used a device called a "shadow price," which estimates what the price would have been in the absence of the distortion. Low shadow prices for abundant labor and high shadow prices for scarce capital can be used to guide decision makers in their choice of factor proportions. The topic is discussed in Chapter 11.

Another fairly common reaction has been the attempt to lessen the urban-rural wage gap.[15] Singapore, South Korea, and Taiwan have tried to do so by curtailing the strength of the urban-based trade union movement. A number of other nations, including Ghana, Indonesia, Sudan, and Thailand, have reduced their emphasis on minimum wage laws.[16] Others who have such laws (Brazil and Mexico) have set the legal minimum so close to the going wage that the laws have little effect.[17] There has also been a slowdown in the spread of expensive social security programs.

Factor Substitution Difficult   A third reason why capital intensity may occur in the modern sector of a labor-abundant country—why technological dualism may be found—is a matter of engineering. Here the argument is made that factor substitution is easy enough in the traditional, largely agricultural sector. This is illustrated in Figure 7.3, where production can be undertaken with many combinations of capital and labor, as shown by the smooth slope of the isoquant. Labor is cheap, shown by the flat price line *PP,* and production is labor-intensive, only *OK* capital being used alongside the large quantity *OL* of labor.

The situation will be very different if, in the modern sector of the economy, the opportunities for substituting between labor and capital are limited. Arguably, some modern industries present a capital-labor ratio that is largely fixed and

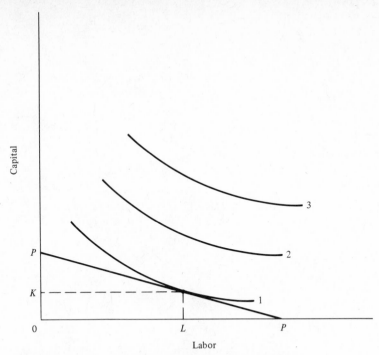

Figure 7.3 Factor substitution in labor-intensive production.

unalterable. For example, it is hard to imagine a labor-intensive nuclear power plant or labor-intensive gasoline production.[18]

If factor proportions are fixed for technical reasons, then output can be increased only by raising the inputs of capital and labor in the same proportion.[19] Figure 7.4a shows a capital-intensive situation in which the factor proportions are fixed. There is no possibility of substituting between capital and labor, shown by the L-shape of the isoquants, and the proportion between these two factors will thus remain constant at any level of output, as shown by the slope of the line OZ. Note that large quantities of available labor (OL_2) will not alter the outcome; at output level 1, L_1L_2 will simply remain unemployed in this sector. Only the availability of additional capital, OK_2 for example, would allow more labor to be employed. Alternatively, factor proportions might not be as fixed as this, but, as shown in Figure 7.4b, a large change in prices (from PP to P_2P_2) may be necessary for any shift to occur; a small change (to P_1P_1) leads to no factor substitution. The outcome is, in the modern sector, limited employment of labor for technical reasons. The excess labor can, however, find employment in the traditional sector (Figure 7.3), where factor proportions are variable. The large quantities available put a downward pressure on wages in that sector. With labor cheaper even than it would otherwise be in the traditional sector, there is little impetus to adopt higher-productivity methods.

The issue is an important one. If only a few products were involved, all might be innocent enough. But what if LDC elites are drawn to sophisticated

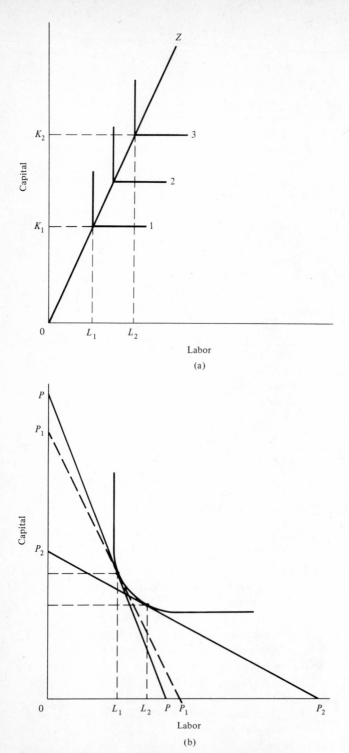

Figure 7.4 Fixed factor proportions in capital-intensive production.

consumer goods that must be produced by capital-intensive methods? Then the structure of consumer demand itself might push industry toward capital intensity. This particular technological bind would thus be due to a choice of products, and not to a choice of technology. The government of India has thought the problem sufficiently serious so that it has used the law to require entrepreneurs to search out more labor-intensive methods, with, apparently, some success.[20]

Technically, the question of whether labor and capital are substitutable for one another is one of elasticity, the elasticity of substitution of labor for capital. If a 1 percent rise in the price of capital relative to labor leads to a rise in labor use so that the labor-capital ratio grows 2 percent, then the elasticity of substitution in that industry is 2. Empirical studies show such elasticities in manufacturing most commonly lie between about 0.5 to 1.0, and that they are lower in manufacturing than in agriculture.[21] A high elasticity is shown in Figure 7.3, a low one in 7.4b, and zero elasticity in 7.4a.

The entire argument must be qualified to a degree. Within limits even great apparent fixity of factor proportions may be indirectly flexible. Equipment can sometimes be run faster or longer, with new shifts of workers. Transfers of input and output to and from the equipment may perhaps be accomplished in a labor-intensive manner. Some aspects of production, for example, packaging and labeling a product, may be more labor intensive than some central activity within the operation, thus making the whole operation less capital-intensive than it would otherwise be.[22]

There is a further problem with factor proportions when technical improvements take place. Such changes are more likely to occur in modern capital-intensive industry than they are in traditional farming or small business. In the traditional sector there is less emphasis on research, there are fewer inputs of complementary capital, and often production is on a very small scale. Technical improvements may therefore have considerably less effect in the traditional sector than they do in the modern one, thus perpetuating the technological dualism and the low wages and low productivity growth in much of the economy.

The model of fixed capital-labor ratios leads to some pessimistic predictions in countries with rapid population growth. In these countries, fixed capital-labor ratios in the advanced sector (or equally a belief by entrepreneurs that the ratios are fixed even if they are not) will mean that employment in the modern sector will not be encouraged by the tendency toward lower wages as population grows. Unless new investment is occurring at a rate fast enough to absorb the large numbers, the growing work force then has to find employment in the traditional sector. There is an ever-lower capital-labor ratio in that sector and even less land per unit of labor. The resulting fall in the marginal product of labor lessens any tendency to adopt labor-saving innovation in agriculture. Why bother if the labor is so cheap? Hence there may be a cut in the incentive to invest in agriculture. Labor-*using* innovation can, of course, be profitable under these circumstances and can still drive up rural wages.

Designing and Servicing Labor-Intensive Equipment   A fourth reason why capital intensity may be favored in the modern sector even in the face of high labor availability has to do with the design and servicing of machinery and equipment. Even the initial design of more labor-intensive alternative machinery calls for entrepreneurial ability, for fresh insights, and for research that costs money—all scarce in the LDCs. Typically, even multinational firms clever enough to manipulate transfer prices to maximize profits do not appear to do much research into the development of new labor-intensive processes.[23] They usually prefer to shift older equipment, which is ordinarily less capital-intensive, to their branches in the LDCs. Perhaps this is because they have the ability to seek out and find equipment of this sort all over the world, perhaps because they can obtain it at good prices due to their good bargaining position, or perhaps because they already own their own surplus stocks which might be easily shifted. Even when labor-intensive designs are available, it is frequently found that machines and equipment from the industrial countries can be more quickly serviced by trained personnel and are better provided with spare parts than equipment manufactured in the LDCs. The industrial countries tend to produce machines of greater capital intensity because of their relative labor scarcity; hence the bias. Say, a firm purchases labor-intensive machinery (from India or Brazil or from a local manufacturer). It runs the risk that a repair crew, perhaps only days away if the machine were made in West Germany or the United States, will take weeks or months to arrive from a manufacturer that produces on a much smaller scale and is far less experienced in such matters. It amounts to a question of risk. This problem has received less attention than it deserves.

Technology as a Competitive Device   Finally, capital intensity may be favored by firms that believe they will capture and keep higher returns when they employ sophisticated, hard-to-copy technology.[24] Competition can be kept at bay longer and more profitably when technology provides a barrier to entry, especially if the barrier survives the expiry of patent protection. Predictably, this behavior will be more likely among multinational firms, with their easier access to advanced technology. It should be noted, however, that MNEs are not generally more capital-intensive than are domestic competitors in the same industry. Their reputation for emphasizing capital is due instead to their tendency to concentrate in industries that are themselves capital-intensive and where their experience has given them advantages.

   In summary, it is a basic neoclassical presumption that relatively labor-intensive technologies are appropriate for countries where labor is abundant, but there are a number of significant impediments, from the point of view of a private decision maker, to adopting labor-intensive methods. The result is that no general rule is likely to be safe for any given private firm. A specific investigation will be necessary to ascertain whether, in any particular industry, the impediments will overcome the basic presumption. There is little reason to expect any great similarity in the decisions between countries or between industries in the same country because of the diversity involved. Short-run decisions for capital intensity, appropriate on a private basis where alternatives are not available or where servicing is poor, may be quite inappropriate in the long run when these problems have been overcome. From a social point of view ensuring that a country's factors are combined in an efficient way will involve attention to basic needs when labor productivity is so low that it offsets low wages, to government policy on wages and interest rates when these are the cause of the dualism, to the development of alternative technologies when appropriate substitutes are unobtainable, and to the provision of better servicing for these technologies when they do become available.

There seems no question that in the years to come, research on alternative technologies will be an exciting part of development economics. Even if progress is slow, however, there is no need to despair. The fastest growers of recent years have been countries with (initially) very cheap labor, including South Korea, Taiwan, Hong Kong, Singapore, and Japan for that matter. These have been successful, far beyond expectation, without much development of new labor-intensive methods beyond what could be achieved through management and organization.[25]

RECENT RESPONSES TO TECHNOLOGICAL DUALISM[26]

In the LDCs there has recently been an upsurge in concern for the problems of dualism just outlined. A number of countries have established institutes for research and for the spread of information on research with the expectation that the institutes will advertise, and perhaps develop, alternative labor-intensive technologies. Noteworthy examples include Ghana, India, Indonesia, and Mexico. (The other side of this coin is that the research may be pushed most avidly in protected industries, which could not compete without the protection. Where this is so, the resources may be "wasted" from a social point of view.)

On a small scale there is now some export of technology from one LDC to another, the major producers being Argentina (plants for fruit processing, meat refrigeration), Brazil (steel), Mexico (steel), India (textiles, sugar processing, solar-powered irrigation pumps, cement), and South Korea and Taiwan (electronics, light manufacturing). Except for India, these are all relatively high-wage LDCs, however, with their contributions of limited significance where labor is even cheaper. A little developing-country technology has even flowed to the North, particularly in energy. Brazil is a gasohol pioneer; India and China are leaders in the development of biodigesters that convert garbage to power. A story reported in the press shows how difficult things can be sometimes. India's sale to Tanzania of a "technically appropriate" system for turning waste into combustible gas backfired when it was found that Tanzania's wages (the legal minimum three times higher than India's) were too high to justify the Indian labor-intensive technology![27]

The LDCs are rapidly becoming more discriminating in their purchases of foreign technology. Sometimes in the past several local firms have each contracted to buy exactly the same imported technology from some foreign firm, the negotiations kept secret, of course, for commercial reasons. To economize on these costs, national registers of imported technology have been established by, among other countries, Argentina, Colombia, India, South Korea, and Mexico. The agencies in charge of the registers work to ensure that expensive duplication of technology imports is avoided. The World Bank has singled out the programs of Colombia and Mexico for favorable mention, noting their "significant success in reducing costs and acquainting domestic entrepreneurs with cheaper alternative technologies."[28] In Colombia the government's examination and appraisal of contracts involving technology led to a reduction in royalties paid of some 40 percent and also to a cutback on the restrictions for exporting goods produced with the new technologies. In the first year after Mexico's new technology law, 36 percent of all contracts registered with the government were rejected and thereafter renegotiated. Of these, 81 percent were objected to on the basis of excessive cost. Other reasons included limits on the volume of production and restrictions on export of the finished product.[29]

Ever since a United Nations conference on science and technology in 1979, there has been discussion of a "technology code" to control restrictive practices, but such practices have proved difficult to define. There is also an ongoing debate as to whether the code should be legally binding and backed by national law or simply take the form of guidelines. Agreement was expected in 1985, but negotiations broke down, and the draft code has been transferred to the UN General Assembly for further work.[30] At about the same time as the initial UN conference, President Carter was announcing his support for an innovative proposal: a new $90 million U.S. Institute for Scientific and Technological Cooperation. Long an idea of Mr. Carter's, the institute would have sought to develop alternative technologies adapted to third world conditions. But support was withheld in Congress, and no funds were appropriated.

PATENTS AND THE LDCS

Recently there has been concern in the LDCs with the present framework of patent legislation.[31] Patents clearly serve the very useful purpose of increasing the flow of new products and new technologies by rewarding their developers. Encouraging research by granting a temporary exclusive right to the inventor seems at first consideration fully as beneficial to a poor country as to a rich one. Yet there is some doubt.

International patent law stems from the Paris Convention of 1883, to which many LDCs adhere. The crux of the convention is its provision for equality of treatment between nationals of a country and nonnationals. Once a patent is filed for in a member country, there is a 12-month right of priority to file for the same patent in any other member. The patent holder is permitted to import the product embodying the patent from a country where he holds the grant to another where he also does; imports are usually forbidden to nonholders of the patent. Often, contracts involving patented products or processes involve controls on export as well. Of 247 contracts in four Latin American countries studied by UNCTAD in the early 1970s, 200 contained export-prohibition clauses and 12 more permitted export only to certain markets.[32]

LDC objections to the Paris Convention center on the manner in which the monopoly aspects of patents can be manipulated to their disadvantage. It is claimed that the benefits accrue mainly to firms in the developed nations, which typically hold 80 to over 90 percent of the patents taken out in the LDCs. By far the greatest share of patents issued to foreigners is held by holders in the United States, West Germany, Great Britain, France, and Switzerland (most by corporations, often as few as 2 percent by private foreign individuals, only 2/3 of 1 percent by holders in other LDCs). Even the residual of patents held domestically may include citizens acting as a front for foreigners, and a good portion of the remaining patents have little importance.

The chief criticism is that often the patents are taken out as a competitive tool to prevent the use of an invention and thus to allow the trouble-free importation of a product. Gerald Helleiner of the University of Toronto states that they are used "more to preclude the employment of technologies" in the LDCs than to increase their use.[33] The statistics seem to bear him out. In the early 1970s only 5 percent of patents issued in LDCs were actually being used, 95 percent were not. Certainly, at least a suspicion arises that the Paris Convention does not tend to encourage the spread of new technologies to industries in the developing countries. (The possible effects of such a situation, even if it does exist on a large scale, can be exaggerated because unpatented know-how and confidential processes are often more important than the patents.)[34]

One suggestion for reform is to encourage the compulsory licensing of patents to prospective users in an LDC. Such licensing is legal under the Paris Convention; so is complete revocation if the licensing arrangements do not work out. But the international rules are very stringent. Compulsory licensing is rare and revocation even rarer; the process is long and costly and usually seems not worth the trouble.

Another suggestion is to require the publication of the technical specifications of a patent when issued in an LDC under the convention, but these are often complex with a wealth of experimental detail that can be undecipherable.

Yet another idea for reform is shorter terms for patents in LDCs. In the United States the term is 17 years, but this is arguably a long period for protecting a monopoly position. Already numerous LDCs have shorter terms (the average for 45 third world countries is now 11 years), and there are calls to limit protection to as little as 3 to 6 years along the lines of the so-called utility model patents now used with great success in Germany and Japan.

More radically, some suggest replacing patents altogether in favor of a system of government prizes for new technology followed by free public use of the knowledge. Others argue that patents should apply more favorably to, or perhaps only to, locally developed technologies, and not to imports.

A new conference to revise the Paris Convention met first in Geneva in 1980, continued in Nairobi in 1981, and met in Geneva again during 1982 to 1985. Called WIPO, World Intellectual Property Organization, its main point of discord was over the granting of involuntary licenses of patents following non-use. After many compromises, a proposal did pass for compulsory licensing after 30 months of no working use, unless the patent holder could show due cause for the non-use. An exclusive license good for 4½ years would follow, to revert to the holder after that time. Also an LDC could revoke a patent after 5 years of non-use. It was agreed that revocation could occur only if a licensee did not come forward or did not use its license. Major barriers in the way of agreement were the opposition of Australia, New Zealand, and Canada, which were not extended the privileges just discussed, and of the United States, implacably opposed to nonvoluntary licensing as a confiscation of intellectual property. The United States has announced that it might stop attending WIPO conferences in the future.

The issue resolves into several pragmatic questions. Will changes in the Paris Convention lessen the flow of technology to the LDCs? If so, will the costs of this loss exceed the benefits of patent reform? "At issue," says Helleiner, "is the true shape of the supply schedule for the technology that is of greatest interest to the developing countries." Perhaps that supply schedule is inelastic in the present price range. This would even be probable if, as many believe, the present prices for technology far exceed the marginal cost of supplying it, and if the patents are seldom worked for competitive reasons. There is "no *a priori* reason to take the gloomy forecasts of businessmen . . . too seriously, since they are so obviously interested parties," says the Canadian economist.[35]

These are major issues for the 1980s.

NOTES

1. Standard works include A. K. Sen, *Choice of Techniques: An Aspect of the Theory of Planned Economic Development,* Oxford, 1960, and Sen's *Employment, Technology, and Development,* Oxford, 1975; Edwin Mansfield, *The Economics of Technological Change,* New York, 1968; Frances Stewart, *Technology and Underdevelopment,* London, 1977; and Stewart's "International Technology Transfer: Issues and Policy Options," in Paul Streeten and Richard Jolly, eds., *Recent Issues in World Development,* Oxford, 1981, pp. 67–110. A recent volume with an extensive review of the literature is Hubert Schmitz, *Technology and Employment Practices in Developing Countries,* London, 1985. A good introduction to the economic history of technology is Charles Singer et al., eds., *A History of Technology,* London, 1958. Informative essays from a symposium on technological change and industrial development were published in the *Journal of Development Economics* 16, nos. 1–2 (September/October 1984). There is an up-to-date study by Martin Fransman, "Conceptualising Technical Change in the Third World in the 1980s: An Interpretive Survey," *Journal of Development Studies* 21, no. 4 (1985):572–652. I also benefited from Ian M. D. Little's unorthodox critique in *Economic Development: Theory, Policy, and International Relations,* New York, 1982, pp. 176–181.

2. Denison has suggested that the country not spending something on the order of 1½ to 2 percent of its national product (some 10 percent of total investment) on research and development expenditure, not counting education, will be unlikely to maintain its productivity. The point about diminishing returns was made originally by Alfred Marshall. See Simon James, *A Dictionary of Economic Quotations,* London, 1984, p. 34.

3. Thus for long periods of time the Soviet Union favored factor proportions in industry partly aimed at long-term rather than short-term development, while the production decisions in countries around the globe from Cuba to Angola to Vietnam have been made in part because of their social effects, rather than aiming at a maximum of present output.

4. Most of the diagrams in this chapter either appear in or were suggested to me by the Herrick-Kindleberger text. See Bruce Herrick and Charles Kindleberger, *Economic Development,* 4th ed., New York, 1983, chap. 11. Also see Gerald M. Meier, *Leading Issues in Economic Development,* 4th ed., Oxford, 1984, pts. III and V.E, for analysis to which I frequently referred.

5. See the discussion by Fransman, "Conceptualising Technical Change," pp. 583–584.

6. For the Indonesian evidence, see Theodore Morgan, *Economic Development: Concept and Strategy,* New York, 1975, citing work of L. T. Wells, Jr. For the Colombian examples, see William Loehr and John P. Powelson, *The Economics of Development and Distribution,* New York, 1981, pp. 162–163, quoting a study by D. Morawetz.

7. For a discussion of locking in to a particular technology, see Harvey Leibenstein, *General X-Efficiency and Economic Development,* London, 1978, pp. 113–122. In this section I also utilized Loehr and Powelson, *Economics of Development and Distribution,* pp. 179–183, and Michael Roemer and Joseph J. Stern, *Cases in Economic Development: Projects, Policies, and Strategies,* London, 1981, p. 13.

8. Research in the LDCs is becoming increasingly important, however. See Fransman, "Conceptualising Technical Change," pp. 584–589.

9. Henry M. Levin, "A Benefit-Cost Analysis of Nutritional Programs for Anemia Reduction," *The World Bank Research Observer* 1, no. 2 (1986): 219–245; Loehr and Powelson, *Economics of Development and Distribution,* p. 225; Andrew M. Kamarck, *Economics and the Real World,* Philadelphia, 1983, p. 75.

10. *The Economist,* April 30, 1983, p. 100.

11. See Meier, *Leading Issues,* 4th ed., pp. 191–195. In much of Latin America, social programs are financed by a payroll tax. The employer's contribution (10 percent of the wage bill is not unusual) represents a direct increase in labor costs. Sri Lanka and Malaysia are notable examples of countries outside Latin America with these programs.

12. See H. A. Turner in Meier, *Leading Issues,* 3rd ed., p. 174.

13. See *WDR 1979,* p. 55.

14. From Michael P. Todaro, *Economic Development in the Third World,* 2nd ed., New York, 1981, p. 41, citing Edgar O. Edwards.

15. *Ibid.,* pp. 54–55.

16. *WDR 1979,* p. 54. Thailand's laws of 1974 and 1975 were carefully designed to cope with the obvious discrimination against low-paid female textile workers without imparting an upward bias to wages in the labor market as a whole. Monopsony power was counteracted without a change in the general wage structure. *WDR 1979,* p. 55. A contrary recent example is the 1980 minimum wage law in Zimbabwe, where press reports spoke of large-scale layoffs of labor the week the law was passed.

17. *Ibid.,* p. 54. India has used the more direct tool of labor courts, tribunals, and boards to enforce more moderate wage claims.

18. But then much of the *construction* of the nuclear plant or petroleum cracking tower could utilize labor-intensive methods, and Biafra produced gasoline (inefficiently) from crude oil in backyard stills during the Nigerian Civil War.

19. This assumes that the capital is being operated at full capacity. If the capital is idle part of the time (at night, say), then, of course, multi-shift working *could* change the capital-labor ratio.

20. Indian employment strategies are innovative, and are surveyed at length in Austin Robinson, P. R. Bhramananda, and L. K. Deshpande, eds., *Employment Policy in a Developing Country,* 2 vols., London, 1983.

21. See Todaro, *Economic Development in the Third World,* 2nd ed., p. 222, citing David

Morawetz; Pan A. Yotopoulos and Jeffrey B. Nugent, *Economics of Development: Empirical Investigations,* New York, 1976, pp. 151, 162. If the elasticity of substitution is in fact lower in manufacturing, that means problems of flexibility in labor absorption could potentially worsen as development proceeds.

22. See Little, *Economic Development,* pp. 178–179.
23. The statement is made by Howard Pack in Meier, *Leading Issues,* 4th ed., p. 355. This section reflects Pack's work.
24. See Stephen P. Magee, "Information and the Multinational Corporation: An Appropriability Theory of Direct Foreign Investment," in Jagdish N. Bhagwati, ed., *The New International Economic Order: The North-South Debate,* Cambridge, Mass., 1977, pp. 327–328. A general view of the multinationals and technology is J. Davidson Frame, *International Business and Global Technology,* Lexington, Mass., 1983.
25. Compare Little, *Economic Development,* p. 181. Little has examined the technological choices of these countries in "The Experience and Causes of Rapid Labour-Intensive Development in Korea, Taiwan Province, Hong Kong, and Singapore, and the Possibilities of Emulation," in Eddy Lee, ed., *Export-Led Industrialisation and Development,* International Labour Office, 1981.
26. *WDR 1979,* especially p. 66, is informative concerning these responses.
27. *The Economist,* March 24, 1979, p. 122.
28. *WDR 1979,* p. 66.
29. Gerald K. Helleiner, *International Economic Disorder: Essays in North-South Relations,* Toronto, 1981, p. 52. This work, p. 173, also contributed to the next paragraph.
30. U.S. ITC, *Operation of the Trade Agreements Program, 37th Report,* 1986, p. 119.
31. In this section I drew heavily on Peter O'Brien, "Developing Countries and the Patent System: An Economic Appraisal," *World Development* 2, no. 9 (1974):27–36; and on Gerald K. Helleiner, "International Technology Issues: Southern Needs and Northern Responses," S. P. Magee, "Information and the Multinational Corporation," and Charles P. Kindleberger, "Response," all in Bhagwati, *New International Economic Order,* pp. 295–343. I also utilized Constantine V. Vaitsos, "The Revision of the International Patent System: Legal Considerations for a Third World Position," *World Development* 4, no. 2 (1976):85–102; and Pedro Roffe, "Abuses of Patent Monopoly: A Legal Appraisal," *World Development* 2, no. 9 (1974):15–26. Another major article is Edith Penrose, "International Patenting and the Less Developed Countries," *Economic Journal* 83, no. 331 (1973):768–786.
32. Loehr and Powelson, *Economics of Development and Distribution,* p. 186.
33. Helleiner, *International Economic Disorder,* p. 171.
34. Following Little, *Economic Development,* p. 245.
35. Helleiner, *International Economic Disorder,* pp. 175–176.

chapter 8

The Population Problem

This chapter considers the population problem in economic development.[1] A large and rapidly growing population influences economic development in several ways and arguably accounts to a significant extent for the low per capita incomes and slow growth of poor countries. In no other area of development economics has there been a more dramatic change in attitudes and prospects. Whereas about 1975 abject pessimism was the rule—and justified pessimism at that, given the then available information—today, more rapidly than was once thought possible, there is progress to report. It now appears that the world's population growth rate peaked around the year 1970.

THE PRO-NATALIST POSITION

But is there really a population problem at all? This is a fair question to ask, as do Julian Simon and other "revisionists" in their defense of rapid population growth.[2] Why the fuss, say these "pro-natalists." Why should not more people be considered an *augmentation* of resources, rather than a problem?

There are indeed arguments for population growth in certain circumstances. Demonstrably, population size can be so small in relation to land area that there are severe diseconomies of scale in transport, utilities, other public services, and the production of goods. North America in the nineteenth century and Australia early in the twentieth were both areas where a large and growing population allowed more efficient use of natural resource endowments plus the development of larger markets with the attendant realization of scale economies. Technological change was thereby enhanced, and the risks associated with investment were reduced.[3] But these areas had abundant resources and high income, reflected in a well-developed infrastructure of transport, communications, storage, and power; and they also had stable governments able to cope administratively with a rapid increase in population. Education and public health were well developed and improving, meaning that the growing population brought a flexible, qualitatively better labor force.

It is much more difficult to make this argument for most of today's LDCs. With their low levels of capital and their masses of unskilled, uneducated labor, it is doubtful what obvious economic gains would flow from rapid population growth even in areas of low density such as Brazil or parts of West Africa. It is doubly difficult to see any advantage in countries (Egypt, Bangladesh, China probably) where population per acre of cropland is already considerably higher than that of the Netherlands, the developed country with the densest population.[4] And even where more people might eventually be advantageous, as they were in the North America of the frontier era, the immediate costs of rapid population increase may for years submerge the eventual benefits, long delaying any positive effects.

There are also noneconomic arguments for rapid population increase, with some observers in the LDCs taking the position that despite population pressures, the goal of greater numbers should nevertheless be sought for religious, social, and political reasons.[5]

The religious beliefs of several groups lead them to the position of opposing population control. The Roman Catholic church, some conservative Muslim mallams (Saudi Arabia banned all contraception in 1975), many Hindu priests, and lately some fundamentalist Christians are opposed on moral grounds to birth control by artificial means.[6] This is not necessarily a pro-natalist position, since one can certainly oppose rapid population growth, but at the same time find artificial means for slowing the growth unacceptable. Even so, it would seem that rejection of the major means for controlling population increase would inevitably have the result of larger numbers.

It is perhaps somewhat surprising, therefore, that there is little correlation between national religions and the birth rate, with the lack of correlation pronounced for some Catholic countries. Birth rates in the United States, for example, are above those of Catholic Belgium,[7] France, and even Italy, a relatively low-income developed country. Catholic France was historically the pioneer in fertility decline, showing how difficult it is to achieve a fully satisfactory explanation for the desire to limit population growth. France had a devout, predominately peasant population and a rather slow pace of development, but the fertility decline among the French far outpaced that of richer, Protestant, modernizing, urbanizing England until late in the nineteenth century.[8] In Canada the image of Catholic Quebec as extremely conservative is shaken by the statistic that birthrates are lower there than in any other Canadian province. Over a decade ago (1973) there was already government-supported family planning, often the preferred euphemism for birth control programs, in Catholic Peru, Honduras, Bolivia, and Colombia. Conservative, Catholic, overpopulated El Salvador officially adopted family planning in 1974; even more conservative Guatemala in

1975. There have been large decreases in birthrates recently in Catholic Chile, Panama, and Venezuela. Religion, it seems, has less influence on this vital matter than was once supposed.

Some Marxists and other radicals, particularly in Latin America, are often found in opposition to birth control programs on the grounds that such programs, by alleviating some of the misery of overpopulation, will only delay the needed thoroughgoing economic revolution of society. Control of population is thus seen as counterrevolutionary. Much Marxist writing contends that birth control will not be needed after the revolution either, because in a reformed society population growth will not impede development.[9]

Right-wing nationalists and conservatives often take the same position against birth control for a different reason, namely, that military as well as economic power depend on population size. There is sometimes an anticolonial aspect to their argument. The "mother country" had a period of rapid population growth, and so should the now-independent nation. The implication is that population control entails an attempt to maintain an inferior status quo. The pro-natalist position emphasizes not only economies of scale and an augmentation of labor supply, but also protection of currently underpopulated areas from covetous neighbors. It sees military power, political power, and the "vitality" of a younger age structure all stemming from population growth. These arguments are commonly heard in Latin America (especially Argentina and Chile) and in Israel, but nowhere more so than in the former French colonies, especially in West Africa. Of the 22 non-oil LDCs without any public support of family planning, 11 were formerly French. One, Cameroun, recently banned contraception altogether.[10]

The argument that military power is enhanced by the availability of conscript soldiers is certainly persistent and might be persuasive, if true. It seems seriously flawed, however. One would have thought that the history of war from Alexander the Great to nuclear weapons shows conclusively that it is technology, good management, and national product, not sheer manpower (especially when undereducated and malnourished) that strengthens military capacity. How else to explain Alexander's victories over the masses of Asia, or British power in the nineteenth century, or the well-oiled Israeli military machine in a country with a small population (in spite of that country's pro-natalist policies), or, conversely, why Bangladesh is not a great power or India a juggernaut.

THE COSTS OF RAPID POPULATION GROWTH

By what reasoning might one conclude that rapid population growth is detrimental to development? Perhaps the simplest argument is a statistical one, extrapolating from recent growth rates to estimate what will happen in the future. This statistical evidence points to the appropriateness of the term "population explosion." On rough estimate, it took perhaps 4 million years until the earth reached its first billion of population about the year 1800, 130 years to reach the second billion in 1930, 30 years to the third billion in 1960, 15 years to the fourth billion in 1975, and news reports announced that the the fifth billion had been reached just 11 years later, in 1986. Population experts now estimate stability will eventually arrive, but not until the start of the second decade of the twenty-second century when there will be about 10.5 billion people. Growth *rates* of population exhibit similar increasing trends. From almost no growth, 0.03 percent, between A.D. 1000 and 1750, the rate went to approximately 0.5 percent in 1900, 1 percent in 1930, just over 2 percent in the 1970s, before a predicted retreat to about 1.4 percent around the year 2000.[11]

Startlingly gloomy predictions, though tongue-in-cheek because of their bizarre implausibility, are sometimes used to dramatize the problem. They extrapolate forward from the growth rate reached in about 1970. At that rate, 6½ centuries in the future there would be only 1 square meter of land per human being. Or, if population grew at the same rate for 12 centuries, the weight of the people would exceed the weight of the earth. Or, in 60 centuries—not very long in terms of our planet's history—the earth would be at the center of a sphere of humans expanding at the speed of light![12]

Arguing from compound growth rates and their effects centuries hence, even if it is obvious that something must eventually be done, will not be taken very seriously by LDCs concerned with their prospects in the more immediate future. In this shorter time frame economists and demographers do not as a rule speak of apocalypse and catastrophe from rapid population increase, but instead of lower quality of life and less opportunity for improvement. They emphasize how, if neglected, the problem will be ever harder to solve because a bigger population base today provides the potential for an even greater increase tomorrow.

The Burden of Dependency

The first serious effect of rapid population growth on development flows from the resulting adverse changes in the age composition of the population. In a country where population is growing slowly, no particular age group predominates, and there are far more people of working age (15 to 65) than there are children or the elderly. The effect of rapid population growth is to increase sharply the percentage of children in the population, an effect intensified by the LDCs' concentration on infant and child mortality reduction. Typically, 40 percent of the population in the LDCs is less than 15 years old, or 65 and over, a figure that increased by 5 to 15 percentage points between the 1940s and the 1960s. The normal figure in rich countries is a little over 30 percent.

These dependents, contributing relatively little in labor power, but making heavy demands on food, shelter, clothing, and education, are an extra burden on an LDC's resources. The term "burden of dependency" has been coined to describe the situation. The percentage of dependents in LDCs is not as high as would be true if the over-65 age group were as large as it is in the developed world, but the problem is serious nonetheless. Table 8.1 shows the percentage of dependent population of selected countries in 1984. It points to a sharp contrast between the poor and the rich. Note that a poor-country figure of 50 percent

Table 8.1   THE BURDEN OF DEPENDENCY: PERCENT OF POPULATION IN AGE GROUPS 0–14 AND 65+, 1984

Canada	32	Egypt	43
France	34	India	44
Italy	33	Kenya	55
Japan	32	Mexico	47
United Kingdom	35	Nigeria	51
United States	34	Pakistan	47
West Germany	31	Sudan	48
		Syria	51
		Tanzania	50
All developed countries	33	All LDCs	
		Low income	47
		Middle income	44

An alternative method of expressing the burden is the dependency ratio, the number of people under 15 and 65 and over for every 100 people between 15 and 64. That ratio was over 80 for the LDCs, compared to a little over 50 for the developed countries at the start of the 1980s.
Source: WDR 1986. pp. 238–239.

translates into about one dependent for each worker, while the rich-country average of 33 means one dependent for every two workers.[13]

The result is that even if economic conditions were exactly the same in every way between the countries on the left and right of Table 8.1 except for the burden, then the burdened nations would suffer lower growth of per capita income because of having to divert a substantial amount of their resources to meet the needs (food, housing, education, etc.) of their young. In the countries with really rapid population growth, in the 3 to 4 percent range (Kenya and Malawi among others), it is estimated that education costs could be cut sharply, by as much as 50 to 60 percent over 30 years, if the increase could be slowed to a more moderate rate.[14] The funds would be freed for other uses, for example, improving the *quality* of education, or other investment, or consumption. The dependency argument alone is therefore a powerful incentive to control population growth. The problem is ultimately self-correcting after population increase is brought under control (Taiwan's dependency burden fell from 45.1 percent in 1960 to 35.7 percent in 1975), but this is little consolation in the short run.

Capital Widening Versus Capital Deepening

With rapid growth of the labor force a given stock of capital has to be expanded (capital widening) or the productivity of labor will fall, causing wage incomes to decrease as well. A country thus must use some of its material resources simply to keep pace. If, however, population growth is limited, the same resources allow a greater quantity of capital per worker (capital deepening) with resulting higher productivity and growing wage income. The infrastructure of an economy—its railways, highways, ports, electric power grid, telecommunications, etc.—will be harder to provide and harder to improve if substantial saving must be devoted to capital-widening.

Consequences for the Young

Several adverse consequences for children can result from rapid population growth. On a national level the greater the drain of keeping pace with the burden of dependency and the need to widen capital, the less the potential for spending on improved health care, better schools, and higher nutritional standards.

On the family level saving is likely to decrease, since more of current income must go for consumption, so worsening educational prospects and security itself. The dilution of family resources as income is spread among larger numbers can contribute to malnutrition of the children. There was a 16 percent greater probability of malnourishment in Colombian families with five or more children compared to four or fewer; 38 percent in Thailand when comparing four or more to three or fewer.[15] The result is more sickness and hence a much higher risk of infant mortality.

A large number of closely spaced young children contributes to a weakened mother, premature weaning, and hence a much higher risk of infant mortality. Demographers estimate that an average decline in infant mortality of 10 percent (or up to 30 percent in some countries, Pakistan, for example) would be registered if the time interval between births were increased beyond 3 years.[16]

The children of large families are likely to have lower birth weights and to be physically smaller, with a higher incidence of infectious disease (more than twice as high for family size eight than family size three in one study[17]). There is possibly even an adverse effect on intelligence, according to some reports. The children of large families tend to perpetuate the cycle by having more children themselves.

The surfeit of young, inexperienced, low-productivity workers, with relatively poor prospects for modern-sector jobs may have to be absorbed in the rural labor force or in "informal sector" city jobs such as porterage, shining shoes, hawking small quantities of merchandise, or producing cheap handicrafts. The less equal distribution of income so generated can mean bitter people and disappointed hopes, with a severe increase in political tension.

These young people may also face a bleak environment of deteriorating soils and fuel and fresh water shortages if the pressure on land (for farming) and forests (firewood for cooking) leads to erosion, silted rivers and dams, encroachment by deserts, and the like.

Even if these problems are avoided, there will be adverse esthetic and psychological effects from the overcrowding: the high costs ("social scarcity" it is sometimes called) of obtaining quiet and privacy, of escaping congestion, of access to wilderness and unspoiled streams, meadows, and woodland, and of uncrowded housing. It is common to ignore these concerns and to say they do not matter, but to do so is to dismiss the importance of the quality of life, which you and I in the developed world would certainly not abide if it were our lives thus blighted.[18]

Malthusian "Trap" Models

Another approach to population increase as a detriment to economic development is the longstanding legacy of the "gloomy parson," T. R. Malthus, in the
early part of the nineteenth century. Malthus argued that unrestrained population
growth would keep per capita incomes limited to a subsistence level. Whenever
income rises above subsistence, procreation would expand, and the greater numbers would push income per capita down again. Income is thus "trapped," unable
to expand because of population pressure.

Though once the centerpiece of population economics, and with some
validity when applied to eighteenth century England, the Malthusian trap models
have been found to apply poorly to the underdeveloped countries in the twentieth
century.[19] Their focus was on per capita income as the only determinant of
population growth, whereas we shall see that income growth, income distribution,
and determinants within the family are all more important. Cross-section analysis
among countries actually reveals quite poor correlation between per capita incomes and birth rates. There is a better fit (though still weak) between *growth* of
per capita income and a decline in birth rates, and a still better one between
income inequality and high birth rates.[20] Whatever their faults, however, the
Malthusian models did serve to convince economists that a population battle is
easier fought on more than one front. As we shall see, progress is much more
likely when direct measures to control population are undertaken simultaneously
with measures to raise growth rates of income and to ensure that the very poor
share in the gains. Doing all together means that no single policy must be pushed
to heroic extremes. The most favorable legacy of the Malthusian models, then,
is the wide acceptance of a strategy that combines a population program with a
program that focuses on income and income distribution.

THE POPULATION EXPLOSION

Why Birth Rates Are High

So much for the consequences of rapid population growth. Let us now turn to
the demographic details that underlie the so-called population explosion. This
and the following section discuss the substantial changes in both birth rates and
mortality that have occurred historically in the LDCs, especially over the past
three decades.

Central to demographic detail is the fact that human beings have the ability
to achieve very high birth rates, usually fully adequate to offset high death rates
even under primitive conditions. Table 8.2 shows some current birth rates, calculated as the number of live births per thousand of population and called the
"crude birth rate." Though the statistics are subject to a wide margin for error,
they do show dramatically that some countries have birth rates at just about the
natural maximum—a rate of 50 per 1,000 is extremely high and is seldom exceeded. (The highest birth rates ever recorded are among the Hutterite religious
sect, many followers of which live in Canada. A religious duty to bear children
has led the Hutterites to an average of 11 children per woman, 500 births per

**Table 8.2 CRUDE BIRTH
RATE (LIVE
BIRTHS PER
THOUSAND OF
POPULATION),
1984**

Bolivia	43
Ethiopia	41
Iraq	45
Kenya	53
Mexico	33
Nigeria	50
Pakistan	42
Tanzania	50
Singapore	17
South Korea	20
Taiwan (1983)	21
Great Britain	13
Japan	13
United States	16
West Germany	10

Source: WDR 1986, pp. 230–231.

1,000 women per year in the age group 25 to 29, and a crude birth rate on the order of 85 per 1,000.)[21] The highest national birth rates in 1984 were 54 in Malawi and 53 in Kenya. That the typical high rates for LDCs can be changed is shown by the rates for Singapore, South Korea, and Taiwan, where rates have been reduced (via somewhat Spartan methods, to be sure) almost to the low levels found in the developed countries. In these countries, rates of 13–16 such as those of Japan and the U.S. are typical.[22] The average for all low-income LDCs (excluding China and India) has slowly come down from 47 in 1960 to 42 in 1984.

Birth rates in most LDCs are high nonetheless. We have already seen several macro reasons that influence government policy and attitudes toward family planning. There are also micro reasons that encourage the production of children, based on what is perceived as biological and economic necessity at the family level.

The social milieu may be an incentive for large families. The concept of "machismo" or manliness in Latin America leads to a high personal value put on family size as evidence of virility. In pre-revolutionary China, traditions of ancestor worship meant more benefits to the departed when the descendants were large in number. There may be a bias in favor of sons (especially strong in China and Korea), which encourages "trying again." With child mortality high, parents might decide to have as many as five offspring simply to ensure that one boy would survive.[23]

Large numbers of children may be thought to guarantee an adequate labor supply for farming. Some useful work can be obtained from about the age of 7, and with wages low, any lost income to the mother may be minimal compared to the later economic returns from the children. Perhaps half the costs of a child (goods and services, mothers' lost wages) may be offset by these early earnings, based on a study in the rural Philippines.[24] Numerous children also serve to ensure that this labor supply will be available in spite of the high child mortality characteristic of less-developed, rural areas. Many families still appear to act on these premises, and birth rates often are a quarter more in rural regions than in urban surroundings.

Similarly, numerous children act as insurance for the parents' old age or in case of disability. The offspring serve as a social security system for their mother and father. In Indonesia, Korea, the Philippines, Thailand, Turkey, and other countries surveys find 80 to 90 percent of parents intend to rely on this form of old age insurance.[25] The children in turn count on the grandchildren for the same service a generation hence. The greater the numbers, the less the burden on each individual. In numerous cultures boys are looked upon as likely to produce higher incomes than girls, so adding to the preference noted on the last page.

Considerable evidence has been collected on the influence of these factors on procreative decision making. Surveys from widely separated points showed a *desire* for large families, as well as the obvious existence of such families. Such surveys in the 1960s asking "What number of children do you desire?" commonly received replies above 4: in Tunisia and in eastern Java 4.3, near New Delhi in India 4.0, in India's Mysore state 4.2.[26] In short, the availability of cheap, effective means of contraception will by no means solve a population problem if families are large because parents desire them to be large.

Why Death Rates Have Declined

At the same time birth rates have stayed high, for understandable economic and social reasons, death rates have fallen sharply. Representative crude death rates (deaths per thousand of population), shown in Table 8.3, reveal spectacular declines from the 30 or so that was typical prior to World War II. The world's highest death rate in 1960 was 35 in Guinea. The highest in 1984 were Guinea and Sierra Leone at 26. For the LDCs as a whole, death rates averaged 24 per 1,000 in 1960 and 16 per 1,000 in 1984 in low-income countries and 17 and 10, respectively, for middle-income countries. Both are now approaching the 9 per 1,000 that is the average for the developed countries.

In Table 8.3 there are some figures that are noticeably low if 9 or 10 is considered "normal." How can the citizens of Singapore and Taiwan die at only half this rate? Have they outdone Ponce de Leon and found an elixir of life? No, more prosaically it has to do with the age distribution of the population. There are simply so many young people (in one recent year, over 55 percent of

**Table 8.3 CRUDE DEATH
RATE (DEATHS
PER THOUSAND
OF POPULATION),
1984**

Bolivia	15
Ethiopia	24
Iraq	10
Kenya	13
Mexico	7
Nigeria	16
Pakistan	15
Tanzania	16
Singapore	6
South Korea	6
Taiwan (1983)	5
Great Britain	12
Japan	7
United States	9
West Germany	11

Source: *WDR 1986,* pp. 230–231.

Singapore's population was under 21) due to earlier rapid growth that fewer deaths occur in the population as a whole.

In all the LDCs death rates have dropped dramatically in a process of change with three identifiable stages. In the first stage, usually occurring earlier in this century, the imposition of law and order (often by colonial rulers) plus the provision of better transport meant that food production and distribution improved markedly. As a result the periodic famines of an earlier period became much rarer. In India, for example, the construction of a railway system made it possible to ship food from areas of relative plenty to those of scarcity, and famines in that country thus became considerably less severe than those of earlier centuries. Areas where long-distance commerce in bulky items was once difficult (Mali, Ethiopia, Cambodia) have had serious food shortages in recent years, but these shortages have not caused anywhere near the number of deaths that would have resulted in the days before the paved highway, the airstrip, and the modern port.[27]

The second stage begins with the arrival of public health programs. These involve water supplies and sanitation in many towns and vaccines against the great killer diseases—typhus, typhoid, cholera, and yellow fever. Smallpox has been eliminated and plague virtually so (more than 10 million people in the LDCs are thought to have died of plague from 1900 to 1920).[28] Most important of all was DDT to kill the anopheles mosquito and hence to halt the transmission of malaria. Malaria is not particularly fatal per se, but a body weakened by it is often easy prey to some normally mild ailment. It was thus really the biggest killer. When DDT was introduced, its effect was immediate and stunning. Thirty-nine countries wiped out the disease, for the time being at any rate; 19.6 million cases were reported in 1955, only 50,000 in 1961. In Ceylon (now Sri Lanka) the first big anti-malaria campaign in 1946 brought the crude death rate down from 20 in that year to 14 in 1947. (A revisionist literature notes that mortality also declined in areas not affected by malaria, and that some important share of the decline was due to higher income and more equal distribution of it.)[29] The chemical also gets the major credit for raising Mexican life expectancy from 36 to 60 years between 1930 and 1964, from 38 to 58 in Mauritius between 1940 to 1960, and from 45 to 65 in Taiwan in the same years.[30]

The third stage, achieved by all the developed countries and by a few LDCs, involves the provision of widely available intensive medical care through hospitals and clinics. This last step is the factor that pushes the death rate down to the 10 or so of the United States, Britain, France, and Italy. In the underdeveloped world reasonable care along such lines can usually be found only in some South and Central American countries (Argentina, Chile, Costa Rica, Panama, Trinidad, and Venezuela for example) and occasionally in Asia (Hong Kong, Malaysia, Sri Lanka, Singapore, South Korea, and Taiwan). Most other countries are just embarking on the third stage, and their death rates still show the effects of high child mortality, largely due to diarrheal disease and gastroenteritis, flu, and pneumonia, which at present are not easy to combat outside the confines of a modern clinic or hospital.[31] Many LDCs have age-specific death rates (that is, rates within age categories) rather similar to those of the developed countries for the adult years, but their crude death rate is "spoiled" by high infant mortality.[32] In some countries over 50 percent of all deaths are among children under 5; over 30 percent among children less than 1. Even so, life expectancy at birth has shown remarkable improvement, as shown in Table 8.4.

Population Growth Rates

The slow decline in birth rates in combination with the rapid decline in mortality is the main reason for the population explosion. On occasion, a high rate of immigration also contributes. The rate of growth of population is calculated by subtracting the crude death rate (CDR) from the crude birth rate (CBR), and then moving the decimal point one place to the left to express the rate of growth as a percentage (number per hundred, instead of per thousand). For example,

Table 8.4 LIFE EXPECTANCY AT BIRTH (IN YEARS)

	1950	1984	Percent Increase
Developed countries	68	76	12
Low-income LDCs	41	60	46
Middle-income LDCs	46	61	33

Source: Calculated from WDR, various issues.

using the data from Tables 8.2 and 8.3, for Bolivia CBR — CDR = 43 — 15 = 28, an increase of 28 per 1,000 per year or 2.8 percent. Selected rates of growth are given in Table 8.5.

The figures in Table 8.5 can be illuminated by looking back at the birth and death rates of Tables 8.2 and 8.3. There are several considerations: (1) The countries with the largest population increase are those where birth rates have fallen little or not at all, while death rates are sharply down (Kenya, Iraq) or those where birth rates have fallen, but previous population growth has left the country with numerous young people and an especially low death rate (Mexico). (2) Smaller increases are recorded when the first or second stage is not yet complete, so that death rates have not fallen very far (Ethiopia). (3) *Some* LDCs have registered remarkable success in controlling the population explosion (Singapore, South Korea, Taiwan, and a few others). (4) The developed countries have in recent years reduced their birthrates so substantially that population growth is often zero or even negative.[33]

The population gap between rich and poor is amply demonstrated by the average figures for 1984. In that year the annual growth rate was 2.6 percent for the poorest 34 of the world's countries (excluding China and India), 2.3 percent

Table 8.5 ANNUAL GROWTH RATE OF POPULATION (CRUDE BIRTH RATE — CRUDE DEATH RATE, EXPRESSED AS PERCENT), 1984

Bolivia	2.8
Ethiopia	1.7
Iraq	3.5
Kenya	4.0
Mexico	2.6
Nigeria	3.4
Pakistan	2.7
Tanzania	3.4
Singapore	1.1
South Korea	1.4
Taiwan (1983)	1.6
Great Britain	0.1
Japan	0.6
United States	0.7
West Germany	−0.1

Calculated from data in Tables 8.2 and 8.3.

for 60 middle-income LDCs, and only 0.5 percent for the developed countries. (Historically, as noted in Chapter 3, natural population increase did not exceed 2 percent in any presently developed European or North American country.)

WHY BIRTH RATES DECLINE—A CHANGING DESIRE TO BEAR CHILDREN

With this background, we must ask *why* birth rates decline, as inexorably, sooner or later, they seem to do in countries undergoing development. On the level of the family, a number of important reasons can be detected, all of which work in the same direction—fewer children.

Many observers would no doubt point to the availability of cheap, effective techniques of birth control. It seems well established, however, that the techniques are less important than the incentive and desire to use them. France, for example, realized a substantial decline in its birth rate in the nineteenth century, long before the arrival of safe, effective methods. For that matter, the primitive contraceptive methods of the later Roman empire, involving a number of anti-sperm chemicals, were reasonably effective more than a millenium before. There is, of course, no doubt that the pill, IUDs, and safe sterilization all help, but it remains to be explained why people *want* to use the techniques.

The more persuasive answer lies in the phrase costs and benefits. The monetary and nonmonetary costs of having many children rise with economic progress. At the same time a number of economic benefits tend to decline.

1. Many children bring nervous strain in modern housing, where the units are often small. The modern family in a developed country is much more mobile, moving from place to place and job to job more than was true in the past. The resulting mental stress is higher as a result. Modern societies thus have much in common with the hunter-gatherer peoples of prehistoric times in terms of children's costs, whereas sedentary agriculturalists in their extended family structure have less of such costs and more benefits (as noted, children can help in production and, with parents living longer, give support in old age).

Hunter-gatherers had to space births because the mother could not easily carry more than one child. Births were typically spaced three to four years apart instead of the two years common among sedentary agriculturalists. This trait can be seen today among the Dobe !Kung of Botswana, who average 4,200 kilometers a year with all their baggage.[34] A Dobe !Kung woman who spaced her children two years apart would in a ten-year span spend eight years carrying two children and move a baby-weight of 17 kilograms. With children spaced four years apart, however, the woman in the ten-year period would spend no time at all transporting two children and move a much lighter baby-weight of just 9.2 kilograms. The motive for family size limitation is thus obvious.

Such limitation among the hunter-gatherers, likely as true of the Pleistocene as of today, is achieved by three main means. First, sexual abstinence may be practiced for a year or as much as two after the birth of a child. Second, since breastfeeding suppresses ovulation somewhat, extended nursing, for $2\frac{1}{2}$ to $3\frac{1}{2}$ years, delays the conception of the next child an average of 2 to 10 months.[35]

Third, infanticide is another method. It is said to occur in possibly 15 to 50 percent of all births among Australian aborigines; 1 percent is admitted among the Dobe !Kung, though the figure is thought to be greater. Infanticide played a major part in the early decline of population growth in Japan; the practice, once applied especially to female babies, is now universally illegal.[36]

2. There are many substitutes for children (and sex?) as a source of pleasure, with travel, music, films, television, and consumer goods generally, all serving as alternatives to the joys of parenthood. There is a closer correlation between low literacy and a high birth rate than there is between low per capita GNP and the birth rate.

3. Children lose their role as a built-in system of social security when, with economic progress, the state takes over this function. A benefit of children is thus reduced, meaning a rise in their net cost. In Japan in 1950, 55 percent of those polled answered yes to the question "Do you expect to depend on your children in old age?" but by 1961 the yes answers had declined to only 27 percent.[37]

Even if parents continue to see security in old age, as an important benefit from children, higher survival rates among children mean that fewer need be born in order to ensure that this function is fulfilled. (Preventing 10 deaths among infants yields 1 to 5 fewer births, depending on local circumstances.)[38] Higher life expectancy also correlates more closely with reduced birthrates than does higher GNP.

4. The net money costs of raising children increase with development. Higher education becomes the norm as parents emphasize quality rather than quantity. Families do not live on subsistence farms, so the opportunity costs for food, shelter, and clothing are higher; and there is no income from child labor to offset the increase in expense.

5. The changing status of women has a large impact. With development opportunities widen for them to become part of the paid labor force and to receive an education. They are much less likely than formerly to think of themselves primarily as mothers. Education of the mother (much more than the father) is especially important in reducing the desire to bear children, bringing better knowledge of birth control methods, delay of marriage, and greater opportunity costs of childbearing because the potential mother is more employable. Employability brings in turn less need for support from the children in old age. Educated mothers also tend to desire more education for their children, which raises the costs of procreation. Education of the mother also is correlated with reduced infant mortality, and hence the motive to bear more children to ensure the survival of some is reduced. In Latin America infant mortality is often three to four times greater among the children of mothers with no schooling than among children of those with 6 or more years of education.[39] Demographers thus almost universally recommend that programs to further the education and employability of women be part of official population control policy; such policies are far less successful when the level of female education is low. (The other side of the coin is that the effect of educating females is much reduced where no official program is operating.)[40]

6. Demographers note that greater equality of income distribution also

serves to lessen the desire to produce children among the poorer portion of the population where fertility is high for economic reasons. As discussed above, with more adequate income the economic benefits of offspring decline and the costs rise. Greater productivity in the rural sector and government programs to redistribute income can thus spur a decline in birth rates. Differences in the speed with which these economic factors operate appear important in explaining why fertility adjustments are so variable among countries. In one society the interval between the decline in death rates and the decline in birth rates may be short; in another it may be long. Economics helps to explain why.

In short, the changing balance of costs and benefits leads to a lessened desire to produce children, a sort of reduction in the "demand for fertility."[41]

In the developed countries this higher net opportunity cost for children, including especially mother's time and the costs of education, led to a great decline in the desire to bear children. A similar effect is being felt in the LDCs, in a reflection sometimes pale but, when buttressed by the propaganda, peer pressure, and economic incentives and penalties of official family planning programs, sometimes strong. There is now substantial evidence to support the claim that desires are changing.

First and most important, the declining desire is evident in the demographers' measure called the total fertility rate (TFR). The TFR is an age-specific measure that is obtained by adding the average number of children born to a woman in each age group to arrive at the average number of live births per woman at the end of her childbearing period (age 15 to 44). For the low-income LDCs the TFR was 6.2 in 1975 and 3.9 in 1984.[42] For the middle-income LDCs the figures were 6.1 and 4.4 in the same years. (There remains a large gap between the LDCs and the rich: The developed-country figures went from 2.3 to 1.8.) The TFR figures, incidentally, are not affected by the skewed age distribution of the population; they thus show a much better correlation between rising income and reduced births than does the crude birth rate.

Second, population surveys support the conclusion that the number of women who want no more children has shown a marked increase. The London-based World Fertility Survey reports that 52 percent of Asian women and 53 percent of the Latin American women questioned in a large sample survey wanted no more. In Africa, however, the figure was much, much lower at only 16 percent.

Third, and a mirror image of the last two points, the percentage of the married female population using contraceptives is increasing, sometimes substantially, as seen in Table 8.6.

Where contraceptive use is high, the TFR has typically fallen much more rapidly than the crude birth rate. The larger number of women of childbearing age serves to prop up the latter figure long after the desire to bear children starts to decline.

In numerous countries, however, the declining desire is far less evident. Average contraceptive use among married women in sub-Saharan Africa is only 10 percent and in some (poor) countries the figures are lower yet, as shown in Table 8.7.

A fourth and final manifestation of a lessened desire is that the average age

Table 8.6 PERCENT OF MARRIED WOMEN USING CONTRACEPTIVES

	Latest Year (usually 1983)	1970
Egypt	30	10
Guatemala	25	—
India	35	12
Kenya	17	6
Colombia	55	34
Hong Kong	80	42
Malaysia	42	7
Panama	61	44 (1977)
Peru	41	1 (1977)
Singapore	71	60
South Korea	58	25
Sri Lanka	55	6
Taiwan	61 (1977)	36

For comparison, the 1983 figures were the United States 76 percent, Belgium 85 percent, France 79 percent, Netherlands 75 percent, Japan 56 percent. *Source: WDR 1986*, pp. 230–231. Some earlier issues were also used.

Table 8.7 PERCENTAGE OF MARRIED WOMEN USING CONTRACEPTIVES

	Latest Year (usually 1983)
Algeria	7
Burkina Faso	1
Ethiopia	2
Guinea	1
Ivory Coast	3
Malawi	1
Mali	1
Mozambique	1
Nigeria	5
North Yemen	1
Senegal	4
Sudan	5
Tanzania	1
Zambia	1

Source: WDR 1986, p. 230. Some earlier issues were also used.

at first marriage is increasing. In many LDCs where it was once normal for 14- or 15-year-old females to be married, the average female age at first marriage is now 18 to 20 (Ghana, Indonesia, Jamaica, Kenya, and Pakistan). The average age is still far younger than in the rich countries, where the age at first marriage is now well into the 20s almost everywhere, but age 25 has been attained in Sri Lanka and the Philippines and 24 in Tunisia.

POPULATION MOMENTUM

The higher costs of children and the changing desire to bear them were certainly effective in bringing down birth rates to 10 to 15 per thousand in most of the Western world. Some of these countries (Austria, Belgium, East Germany, Great Britain, Luxemburg, Sweden, West Germany) have virtually reached zero population growth (ZPG) or even a decline. The problem from the perspective of the LDCs is that it took at least half a century for this process to complete itself, and a population explosion did not occur only because death rates declined slowly also.

The LDCs do not have the luxury of time to cope with the problem. At *current* rates of declining growth, the world's total population will not stabilize at ZPG until about the year 2110, at which time the present 5 billion people will have multiplied to 10.5 billion. The very thought that countries even now considered overpopulated will be burdened with more than double their present numbers is staggering. The predicted date of stabilization in 2110 is, incidentally, 50 to 75 years *after* the point at which a country's fertility is just sufficient (one mother bearing one daughter) to replace the present population. That is because, even at a replacement level of fertility, the large number of young people in the population will keep crude birth rates above crude death rates for many years. This population momentum will usually double the ultimate number of people before absolute growth stops.

Table 8.8 gives population projections for a selected group of LDCs: the population size in 1984; the year in which, if present rates of change are projected forward, the replacement level will be reached; the population momentum, or number by which the population will be multiplied between the time one mother bears one daughter and the time when the population stabilizes; and the hypothetical size of the population when this state of zero population growth is reached.

GOVERNMENT FAMILY PLANNING PROGRAMS[43]

Figures such as these explain why government-sponsored family planning programs involving widespread distribution of contraceptives are now so commonplace. It is, of course, impossible both politically and morally to let death rates rise or even to lessen the effort to bring them down, in spite of some academic discussion to the contrary. ("Cuterage" is the term for deliberately allowing mortality to rise.) Only birth control pushed strenuously by government appears to offer much hope of reducing birth rates *before* long-term economic develop-

Table 8.8 POPULATION PROJECTIONS

	Present population (millions)	Year in which one mother will bear one daughter	Population momentum 1985	Projected population when ZPG attained (millions)
Bangladesh	98	2030	1.9	310
China	1,029	2000	1.6	1,600
Ethiopia	42	2040	1.9	204
India	749	2010	1.7	1,700
Indonesia	159	2010	1.8	361
Iraq	15	2025	1.9	71
Kenya	20	2030	2.1	111
Malawi	7	2040	1.9	38
Mexico	77	2010	1.9	196
Nigeria	96	2035	2.0	528
Pakistan	92	2035	1.8	353
Tanzania	21	2035	2.0	123

It should be stressed that any unexpected delay in reducing fertility, which would be reflected in the year replacement level of population growth is reached, could make a large difference in the projected population size. *Source: WDR 1986,* pp. 228–229.

ment brings this about as it did in the rich countries, if, indeed, in some countries income per capita *could* be pushed up substantially without some rein on increasing population.

There is strong evidence from almost all studies that official family planning programs, together with improved social and economic conditions that lower the benefits and raise the costs of children, do reinforce the decline in birth rates. Recent attempts to analyze the interplay of official programs and social and material progress show that all these together have a far greater impact than each acting separately. One study suggests that socioeconomic change alone or a family planning program alone on average has only 1/8 or 1/9 as much effect as the two acting jointly.[44] A recent 63-country survey reported by the World Bank notes that birth rates fell most in countries with official family planning programs and announced objectives, less where there was family planning but no specific objectives, and least where there was no family planning program at all.[45] Since the adoption of objectives and family planning are themselves correlated to the level of social and economic development, including health, education, and basic needs as well as industrialization and income growth, this is not surprising. The lesson is confirmed that family planning, announced objectives, *and* development must be pursued at the same time if a policy to limit population is to be effective.

It might fairly be asked why government is needed at all, since family planning could conceivably be wholly provided by the private market. But private distribution channels are poorly developed in some rural areas. In a private clinic prices may be high, waits long, and travel times tedious. Little private profit (whatever the social gain) may lie in disseminating information. Demand may initially be small or even unknown. Information about the availability of family planning may be very limited; recent survey data from Mexico and Kenya showed over half the married women interviewed did not know where to obtain modern methods of contraception. Reflecting this, surveys in over 40 countries show the number of women of childbearing age who want no more children is greater than the number using some form of contraception. In many countries the percentage of women with this "unmet need" is over 20 percent.[46] All in all, the need for government action seems obvious enough.

Government programs of family planning (in 1985 there were 85 of them) generally involve five different avenues of approach, employable in any combination or all together: (1) advocating a goal by skillful propaganda, (2) raising the legal minimum age of marriage, (3) legalizing abortion, (4) promoting contraception, and (5) providing financial incentives for small families and penalties for large ones.

Goals and Propaganda　It is now widely agreed that a national goal advertised by a skillful program of "marketing" (propaganda) can harness strong emotions in favor of economic development and can change attitudes toward family size. The first step is usually to set a target and advertise it widely. Cases in point are Pakistan's goal of reducing the birth rate from 50 to 36 by 1988 and India's from 40 to 21 by 1996. (Both still have a long way to go.) Singapore's more dramatic target was a birth rate of 18 by 1975 (achieved nearly on time and now below that). Some countries set goals in percentage terms. South Korea aimed at a reduction in growth from 2.9 percent a year to 1.2 percent by 1980 (achieved), while Ghana is aiming at 2.0 percent in 2000. Others aim at ZPG by a target year, such as 2000 as the goal for Bangladesh and Jamaica. Yet others set a target size, such as China's "1.2 billion in 2000."

After the publication of the target come the "media events." In China posters, broadcasts, and word of mouth are used to circulate slogans such as "One child best" in a propaganda program that reaches down to the smallest factory, village, and commune. India's "No-baby year" used the slogans "Two or three children—and that's all! Listen to your doctor, he knows!" and "When you have two, that will do." The advice was repeated on the radio, on movie screens, on billboards, even on matchbook covers. Numerous Central American radio stations have run soap operas highlighting the trauma of excessive family size. In Bangladesh singing teams perform in bazaars; in Pakistan songs in simple language boost family planning; in wealthier Singapore contraceptive propaganda comes with the utility bills.[47] The campaigns focus on making people aware of the costs to the country of population growth; the costs of large numbers of children to the family and to the children themselves; the benefits of smaller families; and the means for limiting size. It is difficult to find a self-respecting program these days that does not boast some similar large-scale propaganda effort.

Minimum Age of Marriage　There have been campaigns to raise the legal age of marriage, often very low by today's Western standards, but not by the standards of yesteryear when Roman Catholic canon law set 12 as the minimum age of marriage for girls. India's campaign to eliminate the child bride is the most well known of these. That country recently moved the minimum age for females from 16 to 18 and for males from 18 to 21. To be sure, even the old Indian law was frequently disregarded, but proponents of the legal change nevertheless expect a noticeable effect on birth rates. In China the legal minimum was moved up to 20 and 22 in 1980. (But this was less than the 23 and 25 being unofficially enforced already, so marriages and births both "blipped" upward, showing at least that such regulations do have some effect.)

Legal Abortion   Abortion can certainly play a role in population control, as shown by the experience of Japan. Abortion in Japan has been credited with two-thirds of the effect in the halving of its birth rate in a 10-year period after World War II.[48]

The poor opinion of the practice held in many countries and cultures will, however, mean that abortion is unlikely to be the main tool of population control in much of the world. It is not often legal in poor countries, with the notable exceptions of China (since 1957) and India. Even South Korea, with its firm stand on population, banned it for a long while, and it is not only illegal but subject to harsh penalties in many Catholic countries. Hindus are also strongly opposed on religious grounds. True, there are many illegal abortions anyway—perhaps as many as 30 or even 50 million annually.

At the United Nations International Conference on Population held at Mexico City in August 1984, there was a bombshell of sorts. The U.S. delegation issued a series of stern pronouncements that it would cease to aid any international organization that provided funds for abortion and backed this up with stringent regulations implemented in 1985. The financing did not involve *U.S.* funds for abortion, as this has not been permitted since the 1970s; nor did it imply direct activity of international agencies in abortion, which the agencies deny vehemently. It involved *any* indirect connection, for example, funding family planning publicity in a country permitting abortion.

The new U.S. regulations are comprehensive. Say a private U.S. committee receiving some official dollars aids a family planning group in India, which in turn funds a local clinic. If that clinic uses all-local Indian funds to perform an abortion, then all U.S. aid to the U.S. committee must be ended. Under the regulations action was taken in 1985 to eliminate the official contributions to the International Planned Parenthood Federation (largest of the private groups) and the U.S. grant to the United Nations Fund for Population Activities (UNFPA), which is currently a quarter of that agency's budget. China was the chief target of the U.S. stance, with the powerful U.S. "right-to-life" coalition charging that Chinese women are forced into abortions and sterilizations against their will. China reacted bitterly in 1985, denying that coercion had been used and claiming (with UNFPA) that the international funds are not related to abortion activities. Apparently to no avail: in August, 1986, the United States announced a complete cutoff of its contribution to UNFPA.

In a world where funds are short—rough estimates of current total spending on family planning in LDCs is about $2 billion, with another $1 billion thought necessary to cover unmet needs—this was a serious development.[49] About a quarter of present spending is covered by aid, with the U.S. government and U.S. private donors funding some 40 percent of that, so the impact could be large. Demographers generally seemed critical of the very conservative U.S. stance, citing an imposition of U.S. values on other, different cultures and pointing out that effective family planning promoted by these agencies actually *reduces* abortion by lowering the number of unwanted pregnancies. But the right-to-life groups who oppose family planning are obviously making an impact; it remains to be seen how great the impact will be on population programs in the LDCs.

Contraception[50]   The promotion of contraception has usually taken the form of birth control clinics and the wide distribution, at low cost or free of charge, of contraceptive materials. Clinics have their problems, and they have often been underutilized or even ignored, especially in rural areas. Sometimes only limited propaganda is undertaken in their support for fear of giving offense. Sometimes they are located in urban areas or centrally in rural areas, with little outreach and no field-workers. Sometimes there is no follow-up, now known to be a fundamental mistake; checking is of great value when motivation is marginal. Sometimes they put together a cultured, educated, often male doctor, with a poor, shy, uneducated woman. The cultural gap is real; it takes equally real effort to bridge it. Many countries have successfully done so by utilizing paramedical staff, mid-wives, and local women already in the program as staff at the clinic.

Even a well-managed clinic will have little impact when the demand for family planning is low. It may take some ingenuity to make a visit more popular, perhaps a literacy or child health program in the same center or even a rural credit scheme.

Another problem is cost. Countries that ask payment for contraceptive materials, even at subsidized rates, may miss the lowest-income group. This is true even of rich countries such as the United States, where economic position and use of birth control are closely correlated. (Ninety percent of women in higher-income groups use one method or another, but of the lowest fifth in terms of income, 40 percent did not want their last child and knew very little about family planning.) Free or very low cost distribution of contraceptives to those with the lowest income is clearly necessary for an effective birth control campaign.

The available data indicate that, of all birth control use worldwide, sterilization accounts for about 33 percent, the pill 20 percent, the IUD 15 percent, and the condom 13 percent.[51] (Diaphragms, injections, spermicides, douches, rhythm, abstinence, withdrawal, and deliberate prolonged breastfeeding are the other methods.) Each of the methods most favored in the developed countries has some special disadvantage in the LDCs, which must be kept in mind by the population planner.

For example, since the pill, as it is now used, must be taken at regular dates in the menstrual cycle, it involves central requirements of literacy and familiarity with the calendar that simply cannot be met by a part, and sometimes a sizable part, of the population in an LDC. Even if this problem were overcome, perhaps by a "morning after" pill, there is still "the test," meaning that the desire to limit births is tested regularly by the need to take the pill on schedule. Side effects such as the possibility of embolism (blood clotting), cramps, and upset to the menstrual cycle can be anticipated and treated in Western society with its ready access to medical care, but are more serious and more frightening for the user when such care is not readily available. This is the main reason why India for a time banned the pill from its government program. (Some advanced LDCs, including Malaysia, Thailand, South Korea, and several countries of Latin America, either use paramedics to screen patients and monitor pill use or provide above-average access to medical care facilities, so lessening the difficulties.)

Similar problems surround the controversial Depo-Provera injection, now the most popular form of contraception in some countries, especially those where a trip to the clinic is time consuming and costly. A single injection of the contraceptive chemical is effective for three months. Made by the U.S. firm Upjohn in a Belgian factory which supplies 80 countries, Depo-Provera remains banned in the United States, Canada, and France due to some negative findings in animal testing. There are also reports where the drug has been administered of side effects including irregular menstruation and a slow return to fertility, which are worse when women are malnourished. A further unsolved problem with the injections is that the drug cannot be removed in case of complications. Work proceeds on ways to implant it under the skin in degradable rods or pellets, which if necessary could be taken out surgically.

Sweden and Britain are the most recent countries with careful drug-approval procedures to allow its sale, joining Belgium, the Netherlands, West Germany, New Zealand, and the Republic of South Africa. The injections are now a major factor in the programs of Jamaica, Mexico, and Trinidad, joining Thailand where they have achieved the broadest popularity. But the United States cannot contribute (due to the laws on drug approval discussed in Chapter 5), and supplies are indeed sometimes tight.

The real need in population planning is for more research. Menses-inducing drugs using hormonal compounds may eventually be effective (China is testing a new pill of this type). A long-lasting vaccine producing antibodies interfering with pregnancy may be available in a decade or so. Drugs for men have been neglected, with nine times more spent on female methods in the late 1970s. At present male contraceptive drugs have exhibited too many adverse side effects for general use, though possibly the recent Chinese work with gossypol, an extract of cottonseed oil, will help. The main problem is that little is spent on developing new contraceptives ($167 million in 1983), and what little there is has fallen some 20 percent in real terms since the late 1970s.

Medical problems are also associated with the IUD, even though the programs of Taiwan, South Korea, and India at one time relied heavily on it. The advantages of the IUD are that it is cheap and simple and requires only one decision every year or two (for insertion and check-up). Where rejection occurs, however, and where there are side effects such as backache, bleeding, and, more seriously, pelvic infection (worse when malnutrition is present), immediate medical care is necessary. The high risk of such side effects, the unavailability of medical care, and the serious consequences of insertions without any examination gave the IUD the poor reputation that has followed it for years.

The condom for males is cheap and has no side effects. It has thus been distributed on an enormous scale. The first Indian government distribution program involved 100 million, sold at only 15 percent of cost. A huge advertising campaign was mounted to support the distribution, and many famous companies, including Lipton Tea, Union Carbide, and Lever Brothers, assisted in making condoms available. (The sale by private firms and organizations of subsidized products as part of a government program is called "social marketing.") They were passed out even by the mailman making his daily rounds. The Indian innovation has caught on, and social marketing is now carried out in at least 30 countries. For example, condoms are nowadays distributed by the trade unions of Antigua and sold cheaply along with tickets by Thai bus drivers. Some 6,000 commercial outlets sell them in Sri Lanka. But the advantages of cheapness and easy distribution are eroded substantially by the need for constant recommitment to the goal of birth control. In fact, *every* act of intercourse requires a decision. This is the great weakness of the condom.

The problem is avoided with sterilization.[52] The vasectomy, or tying of the male's vas ducts, is a simple operation that requires only a local anesthetic and takes less than 10 minutes. A medic can do the job. It does not have to be done in a clinic; a room in a railway station or bus depot will do. The procedure is cheap. There are no ill effects, though there are problems with reversing the operation, and embarrassment can be caused since a vasectomy may not take full effect for some weeks. Given its certainty, and the need for only one (permanent) decision, vasectomy became the central tool of some official programs where overpopulation was an especially serious problem; for example, in India, with large-scale programs pioneered by Madras and Mysore states, and in Bangladesh. But deep-seated fears kept the number of volunteers low. The result was a move toward compulsory sterilization in India, with results discussed in the survey of that country's program in the next section of this chapter. Antipathy toward vasectomy is so pronounced that it is actually illegal in a number of nations, including Burma, Somalia, Spain, and Turkey. Anti–family planning groups in the United States do not seem to approve either; when the Sri Lanka government began in 1981 to pay volunteers for vasectomy, these groups persuaded the Reagan administration to withhold U.S. aid funds from the program. But Sri Lanka continued the practice, recently even quintupling the reward to 500 rupees, and the U.S. funds were eventually restored.

The traditional tubectomies on females are more expensive, more complicated, and harder to reverse and so were much less common. Important technical changes have, however, led to a surge in female sterilization. Laparoscopy involves a small incision, electrocautery, and the use of clips or rings on the tubes. Minilaporotomy, or minilap, draws the tubes outside the abdomen for cutting. Both operations can now be accomplished in outpatient facilities, and minilap (but not laparoscopy) can be done by a nonspecialist surgeon. Much training for minilap is now taking place worldwide. Though not as safe as vasectomy, risks are slight. Reversibility is still problematic, with only about one in five eligible for a reversing operation, in which the success rate is about 60 percent. These new techniques have meant a large shift to female sterilizations. In South Korea vasectomies led before 1977, but by 1979 there were eight tubal ligations on women for every operation on a male. Operations on females now lead in China, Malaysia, the Philippines, and Thailand. They are the only form of sterilization commonly available in almost any part of Latin America.

Financial Incentives.   Taxes and subsidies to promote family planning were once rare, but have become more common following Singapore's pioneering efforts and China's large-scale use of such devices. Both programs are discussed in detail in the following section.

SIX NATIONAL PROGRAMS FOR POPULATION PLANNING

A look at six national programs currently in operation will illustrate how progress is achieved, where innovation is taking place, and why population optimism is on the increase; but it also shows where failure lurks. The programs chosen are all in Asia, where they have received more attention than elsewhere.

Indonesia   The Indonesian program has focused on densely populated Java and Bali.[53] Its success is shown by comparing annual population growth in 1970 on those islands (2.5 percent) with 1978 (1.4 percent). The proportion of women aged 15 to 44 using contraceptives was almost nothing in 1970, but by 1977 had reached almost 40 percent in Java and almost 60 percent in Bali. About 65 percent of those who use contraceptives take the pill, down from earlier years when the pill was used almost exclusively; 20 percent use the IUD. Sterilization is not offered in the Indonesian program.

Success did not come easily. The employment of clinics as the first approach to the problem had little impact for the reasons discussed earlier. Attention then turned to establishing a climate of opinion firmly in favor of birth control. This took a variety of interesting forms. Schools were set up for shadow-play puppeteers, whose traditional art form was then used to broadcast a new message. The army, police, and civil service were asked to use their influence to further the acceptability of family planning. Persuasion of Muslim religious leaders [mallams] was embarked upon, and many became enthusiastic supporters of the program. Gamelan orchestras, that all-male Indonesian form of music-making so familiar to tourists, were coopted into the cause, and nowadays some of these orchestras are made up of women. Classical dancers further advertised the goal. The government turned the effort into a sort of serious game, awarding prizes to communities with the best performance in meeting targets.

The result was a rapid and significant change in the status of family planning. It became popular. There are now 27,000 village pill and condom depots in Java and Bali, many of them in private homes. Local mothers' clubs encourage their use, and "cells" (groups organized to discuss and encourage family planning) are ubiquitous among Javanese women. The negative constraint is an outstanding feature. In Bali each village pavilion displays a map. On the map the houses of the pill-users are colored red, the houses of the IUD-users are colored green, and those of the condom-users are black. Houses of non-users are not colored, and the social stigma attaching to that is clear enough.[54] (Obviously, Indonesian methods would work less well in a less cohesive, close-knit, and centralized environment.)

Thailand   The Thai program is perhaps not so dramatic, but it has succeeded through the efforts of some 7,000 urban and rural health centers in reducing birth rates from 44 in 1960 to 26 in 1984. When the program was adopted in 1970, contraceptive use among Thai women was only 15 percent; the figure was 63 percent in 1983.

Three interesting features are worthy of note. First, Thailand was the first country to receive a population "package deal" from UNFPA. The fund was initially starved for money (only $3.9 million in 1969). Once it obtained some funding (over the $100 million mark in 1973 and currently $150 million) and had some projects underway (over 700 in 80 countries during 1973 and 130 now), it found itself acquiring an unfortunate reputation as the "sterilization agency." The Thai package deal, $72 million over three years funded by the World Bank, IDA, Canada, Australia, Norway, and the United States, was a milestone on the population fund's move toward legitimacy and acceptability in the third world.

A second interesting feature of the Thai program is its pioneering work with birth control inoculation (the Depo-Provera method). Its widespread adoption in the Thai program has brought more favorable notice to this controversial technique.

Finally, the Thais have been innovative in offering incentives through private groups. Rural credit, lower prices for seed and fertilizer, a free pig for a woman to rear, are all tactics used by these private supporters of family planning.

Singapore   The noncommunist country associated above all with family planning is the city-state of Singapore.[55] Singapore starts with two substantial advantages: no organized opposition to family planning on religious, political, or other grounds (there were anti-abortion laws, but these were repealed in 1970) and a booming economy that has destroyed the extended family system and thus all but eliminated a major reason for large numbers of children.

In the Singapore program the IUD proved unpopular, as did the Depo-Provera shot due to reported menstrual disturbance. Reliance is thus on the condom (36 percent of contraceptive use), but much more so on the pill (58 percent), ranking Singapore high on the list of LDCs with the greatest emphasis on that method.

An innovative program focuses on new mothers. "Motivators" interview new mothers in hospitals and attempt to sign them up there and then for family planning. Fifty percent of all those contacted do so. There is then a follow-up home visit by the Post Partum Contact Service (PPCS) to reinforce the decision and give further assistance. The midwives, planning assistants, and social workers who serve as motivators and staff the PPCS are given extensive family planning training. Contraceptives are thereafter made available at a price that includes a large subsidy.

The policies in Singapore that have received the most attention, however, involve its use of law and economics to limit births. Both taxes and national benefits are altered as a weapon of control. The law dictates a mandatory end to maternity work leaves and benefits for women delivering their third child. The cost of childbearing is raised immediately.

Such costs are also directly affected by the policy of scaling maternity fees. Delivery charges rise drastically with additional children. The initial scale, in 1969, started at S$10 (S$ stands for Singapore dollars) for delivery of a first child and rose to S$100 for the fourth and subsequent children. In 1973 the charges were differentiated by income, and the fees have since been raised. The present scale, shown in Table 8.9, covers high, middle, and low incomes and is graduated upward until it reaches the maximum with the fourth and further children for the high-income group or the fifth and further for the middle and low groups. The fee for any given child is remitted if one parent presents evidence of sterilization within six months.

Financial disincentives are also written into the income tax statutes. There is a permissible tax deduction of S$750 for the first and second children, S$500 for the third, and no deduction at all for the fourth or more. Limiting tax deductions and scaling maternity benefits beyond a certain number of children have caught on elsewhere; Ghana, Korea, Malaysia, Pakistan, and the Philippines also use these tools now.

In public housing, where much of Singapore's population lives, priorities for large families have been abolished; those with fewer children receive more space per person. Families with four or more children now get a lower priority in their choice of primary schools, unless the fourth can be proved to be the last because one of the parents has since been sterilized. *Top* priority of choice in schools now goes to the children of sterilized parents. Some studies suggest that these housing and education policies have been the most influential, more so even than the financial disincentives. The potential damaging effects on children in the "4+" bracket—poorer housing, worse schools, lower income because of the taxes—are not much seen because there are nowadays so few families that qualify for the sanctions. In a less successful program, however, these unfortunate side effects could be severe.

Table 8.9   SCALED MATERNITY FEES IN THE SINGAPORE
BIRTH CONTROL PROGRAM (IN SINGAPORE
DOLLARS)

Income group	Charge for first child	Charge for fourth or fifth and subsequent children
High	300	480
Middle	120	360
Low	60	300

The results of Singapore's stringent measures have been astounding. Its birth rate is now down to a level equal to or below the 1960 figure for 14 rich countries; at 17 per 1,000 it is with the single exception of Hong Kong the lowest in the LDCs. Population growth is minimal in spite of one of the lowest death rates ever recorded (Tables 8.3 and 8.5); the 1.1 percent growth rate is as high as it is only because of the great preponderance of young people in the population. Singapore thus stands as an example of what can be done when there is the will and the effort. The most recent wrinkle, in 1984, was a move by the government to *encourage* female university graduates to bear more children, in what appears to be a conversion to the theory that intelligence is inherited.

Neither Singapore nor any other country has used positive economic incentives to the extent that is possible. About 30 countries now use incentive awards of one sort or another, in cash or in kind, but this could be carried much further.[56] A nation could in principle employ "deferred incentives," estimating the eventual budgetary impact of an additional (marginal) child and undertake to make this sum available as a reward for *not* bearing the child. A 1982 estimate of the reduced budgetary costs of permanently preventing a birth in India is $800. (The figure would be higher in richer Singapore.) This could be paid out to women who have no more than two children, perhaps $1,600 for no more than one or $2,400 for none at all. The figures represent a large sum for the average villager. It would be an undoubted incentive and would be an excellent counterweight to the argument that large families serve as social security.

There is, of course, the serious loophole that a woman could take the cash but then go ahead and have a child. To protect against this, there are two possibilities. First, the program could be limited to sterilization, which would be administratively easy. More complicated is the suggestion that the sum be paid over in installments every six months into a blocked savings account (one which cannot be drawn upon), the whole amount forfeited if a child is born. The money would be paid in entirety to a woman at menopause; to keep enthusiasm high, interest on the blocked account could be paid out when it is earned. Critics emphasize that fraud might be altogether too easy if such programs were adopted widely in the LDCs. Monitoring of births would be necessary and would not be easy given the incentive for concealment.

Several small experiments have been instituted along these lines. In south India three tea estates make payments of blocked savings to women at age 45; in Taiwan a local government unit deposits funds for the education of two children, but the funds are forfeited on the birth of a fourth. There is also some local use of the idea in Nepal. The Indian plan started in 1971 and has had a positive impact, but perhaps not as great as anticipated.[57] There are five reasons why. (1) It had less effect in the earlier years because the dollar payments were less. (2) Administration of the plan has not been fully satisfactory. (3) The passbooks showing the values involved were not in the women's possession nor were they seen regularly. (4) No revision was made for inflation. (5) Contraceptives were not easily available so sterilization was used, thus robbing the scheme of some of its rationale.

Bangladesh is currently considering two deferred-incentive schemes, one a nonnegotiable bond for sterilized parents, the other a cash certificate for those who delay a first birth after marriage for three years or a second or third birth for five years. The obvious problem is that if such schemes were extended to the country's entire population, they would be very expensive, some 10 percent of the entire Bangladesh budget for 1982–1983.

China   The successful program of the People's Republic of China has attracted more attention than any other in the last decade.[58] Its birth rate has declined from 39 in 1960 to 19 in 1982; during the period 1970 to 1975 it registered the largest decline ever recorded anywhere during a five-year period. By 1982, 71 percent of Chinese married women were practicing contraception, a figure equal to that of Singapore and above that of the United States at that time. Unfortunately, however, the lessons to be learned from China are not all that clear-cut. The emphasis in its program is on community social pressure; the willingness of people to conform to this pressure is in part a product of thousands of years of social history and in part a result of the revolutionary doctrines of the late Chairman Mao. Duplicating the Chinese feat using Chinese methods would doubtless prove difficult in many another LDC.

China uses late marriage as a main weapon in its battle. Although marrying at 20 for females is legal, the "combined age 50" rule is almost national dogma. (It has recently been somewhat relaxed.) The rule requires that the ages of the couple intending marriage sum to 50 or more. The enforcement is through social pressure.

Family planning is in the hands of small groups of 10 or 20 couples, organized within a neighborhood, factory, or village. They meet once or twice a year to consider the population targets set from above. The targets may be national, regional, or local. Individual births are then allocated within the small group. One couple may receive permission to pursue conception in the forthcoming few months, another may be told it is next in line. Couples successful in conceiving are, after birth, often advised to turn to sterilization now that their family is complete; recall that perhaps 40 percent of the world's sterilized population is Chinese.

Exactly how this pressure mechanism works is not altogether clear, nor is it always easy to understand the conformity to it. There is occasional mention of loss of housing rights, reduced food ration or loss of subsidy on grain purchases, loss of educational priority, and job sanctions for those who defy the groups' instructions. But it seems plain that coercion of this sort was not the norm until quite recently. Also, from 1984 there appeared to be some backing off of the pressure, with somewhat greater willingness to let a couple have a child without permission if they cannot be persuaded otherwise.

Law and economics were invoked toward the end of 1979, at which time the Chinese were expressing some dissatisfaction with the results of voluntarism. Nine Chinese provinces instituted a "baby tax" on couples producing more than two children. (Chinese incentive and disincentive schemes have typically been provincial rather than national.) The tax was in the form of a wage reduction of 5 to 10 percent after the birth of a third child, rising to as high as 20 percent after the birth of a fifth. Conversely, wage bonuses and bigger pensions were awarded to those with only one child.

The Guangdong and Jilin province rules were among the earliest to be known in detail. The Guangdong fines are 10 percent of parents' wages for 4 years when a second child is unplanned, 10 percent for 14 years when a third child is unplanned, and 15 percent for subsequent unplanned children. In addition to the fines, parents are ineligible for promotions or bonuses for the next 3 years. The one-child rewards in Guangdong are cash (5 yuan, or $3.25, per month) or free schooling through high school and free medical care. The rewards must be paid back if a second child is born. Only-children also receive job preferences. In addition, penalties and rewards have been introduced at the group level, where meeting the target brings a 0.2-percent increase in bonus funds for group members, while failure to meet the target brings a bonus reduction of the same amount. In Jilin there is a one-child wage bonus of 50 yuan a year until the child is 15. The private plot a family can farm is doubled in size as a one-child award, and low-cost health care is provided. Income is reduced 15 percent if a second child is born, and another 10 percent for a third and each subsequent child.

During 1981 to 1983 the system of economic rewards and sanctions was extended to much of the rest of China, and 1983 saw the start of a major "one-child" campaign using the slogan "1 + 1 = 1." In all urban areas holders of one-child "glory certificates" (now held by 18 percent of Chinese married women) get monthly payments of 5 to 8 percent of the average monthly wage until the child reaches age 14, along with better housing, free medical care, and priority in schooling. In some urban areas an only child is granted an adult food ration. Breaking the pledge with another child means that all benefits must be returned, including no doubt the glory certificate. Very generally, the state requires reimbursement for the costs of educating a second child. But the Chinese still insist that "patient persuasion by peers" rather than compulsion is the key to their system.[59]

To repeat, few countries can show such extensive deference to group opinion, especially when backed by only mild legal sanctions. The unanimity of purpose needed to run a program of this sort must be rare in the world of the LDCs, and, indeed, in the rich countries as well. But China also has numerous special problems—a huge base of women near or at childbearing age, a poorly developed social security system, a strong preference for boys—all meaning that further progress or even maintaining the present gains may not be easy.

India India had the first official family planning program in the LDCs (1952) and was also the first country to include some physical compulsion in its birth control programs. Partly due to the compulsion, India's experience has had a darker side than that of Indonesia, Thailand, Singapore, and China, and the outcome has not been fully successful.[60]

Here we find the outstanding example of resistance to enforced limitations on population, especially the popular revulsion against the mandatory sterilizations carried out in 1976 and 1977. Vasectomies were central to the Indian program. Before 1976 they had been voluntary, encouraged by the reward of a

10-rupee travel allowance to the place of operation, a free transistor radio, a cash bonus of 75 rupees (about $10),[61] or scholarships for children already born, some cloth, and a large can of ghee (clarified butter used in Indian cooking). At the height of the "voluntary" campaign in 1975 to 1976, 2.67 million vasectomies were performed. There was in addition free hospitalization for females undergoing tubectomy, but this was far less common.

Thereafter, official attitudes hardened. Sterilization was made compulsory for government employees after two children. Laws passed in the states of Maharastra and West Bengal established fines or imprisonment if sterilization was not performed after the birth of a third child.

In many states policemen, teachers, public health workers, and other civil servants were given target figures for the number of people they must "motivate" for the operation. Teachers often had a quota of five; four in Uttar Pradesh. Those who did not meet their motivation targets might have their salaries reduced, be transferred to less pleasant posts, be demoted, even suffer curtailment of their food ration.[62] The *Manchester Guardian* reported (November 1976) that "a 50-year-old schoolteacher, given a quota of four for the year, . . . had been threatened by her superiors with the loss of her house and job unless the numbers were accounted for. A water engineer, given a higher quota, ended up allotting tube wells and irrigated water only to those villagers who would agree to sterilization under his so-called motivation—so that he could claim the numbers." There were also reports of police roundups to fill their own quotas.

In an atmosphere approaching hysteria vasectomies reached 8 million in 1976 to 1977. The birth rate, 48 per 1,000 in 1960, was thought to have dropped to 33 in 1976. Population growth fell below 2 percent for the first time in many years. But Mrs. Ghandi, then near the end of her first term in office, was in political trouble. Thousands rioted in the villages of Muzaffamagar and Kairana, near Delhi, against the compulsory rounding up of married men for vasectomy. The police opened fire; dozens were killed. There were numerous other reports of bloodshed as the opposition mounted.

After Mrs. Ghandi's election defeat, family planning fell into disrepute. Even the name was changed to "family welfare," and vasectomies, voluntary once more, fell to only 800,000 in 1977 to 1978. Other methods did not take up the slack. Most of the 4 million users of the pill and condom lived in cities, where indeed birth rates were and are much lower. The succeeding Desai ("Janata") government put less emphasis on free condom distribution, which dropped nearly by half between April and September of 1977. The IUD also declined in popularity; initial estimates of 5 million insertions per year fell to the 200,000 to 500,000 range. The result was a reversal of the birth rate's downward trend. It rose to 35 per 1,000 in 1977, carrying population growth above the 2 percent mark again. The Janata government turned to emphasizing male virginity until age 25, this with the ring of Chinese policy about it, but in a very different social setting. Legislation boosted the age of marriage from 18 to 21 for males and 16 to 18 for females. (In some states, in the early 1970s, half of all marriages involved girls under 15; some officials were implicated in evading even the weaker laws of the time.) The rural camps set up for vasectomies were abandoned. For some time

Janata officials spoke of compensation to those involuntarily sterilized, but this did not occur.

With the return of Mrs. Ghandi in January 1980, there was some forward movement once again, and the impetus continued after her assassination. Sterilizations climbed to the 2 million mark, but they are now largely (77 percent) female, many in minilap camps. The 660 camps set up in Rajasthan in 1980 were each averaging nearly 100 operations annually. The emphasis on females compares to the 80 percent of sterilizations which were vasectomies under the old Ghandi regime. As so often in family planning programs, women are shouldering the burden. Financial incentives have been improved and play a more important role than formerly. Men get the rupee equivalent of $17 (in Rajasthan) for a vasectomy, which is more than a month's pay for a farm worker. Women get only $13 for a minilap operation, $15 for a tubectomy. (Bangladesh, Sri Lanka, and China have also established rewards for sterilization.) Large Indian industrial firms have recently taken to providing incentives also. The Tata steel works in Jamshedpur is currently paying workers $45 for a vasectomy, for example.

The Indian census of 1981 revealed woeful news. Birth rates reported in the 33 to 35 range during the 1970s appear actually to have been about 37; by 1984 the figure was still a high 33. The results of the Indian program, with its many vicissitudes, have thus been disappointing.

Pakistan   We conclude with an even more pessimistic reference to India's neighbor, Pakistan, which can stand as an example of a failed program. Pakistan has made little progress. Its birth rate was still 42 in 1984, down only slightly from the 49 of 1960 in spite of a $50 million program of education in family planning. Despite a flood of contraceptives, their use was not much increased—only 11 percent of fertile couples use them. Muslim mallams, more conservative than in Indonesia, did not favor the program. The government is now storing large stocks of unwanted and wasted contraceptive materials, a clear reflection of the insufficient desire to use them. The lesson is that this desire must come first, as in Indonesia, unless a country wants to take the risky route of outright compulsion, as did India.

A BRIGHT OUTLOOK?

In spite of failures, there is considerable reason for optimism. The rapid initiation of family planning programs in Catholic Latin America, and the resulting large reductions in birth rates, is a case in point. So is the surge in the popularity of the UN Fund for Population Activities. Indonesia, Thailand, Singapore, and China are outstanding examples of what can be done in a relatively short period. Increased contraceptive use by married women in LDCs and the associated relatively rapid fall in total fertility rates in numerous countries are both causes for satisfaction. The reinforcing effect of programs for family planning, programs for better education, health, and nutrition, and greater equality in income distribution is now recognized; addressing the population issue through a package of all these is now standard. Evidence has not supported the once common belief in "Malthusian traps."

These are the reasons why development economists now view the population problem with much less despair than a decade ago. The battle is by no means won. There is much still to be done, and some countries have hardly started on their march. But there has been progress, substantial in some cases, and there is reason to suppose that a problem once considered uncontrollable will, sooner than expected, be brought under control.

NOTES

1. So does the major part of the World Bank's *World Development Report 1984*, which contains a large amount of useful data and analysis, and on which I have relied in several sections. *WDR 1980* also has a special section. There is an extensive literature, among which I have used Robert H. Cassen, "Population and Development: A Survey," in Paul Streeten and Richard Jolly, eds., *Recent Issues in World Development*, Oxford, 1981; Nancy Birdsall, "Population Growth and Poverty in the Developing World," *Population Bulletin* 35, no. 5 (1980) and her "Analytical Approaches to the Relationship of Population Growth and Development," *Population and Development Review* 3, nos. 1–2 (1977):63–74, 77–92; Geoffrey McNicoll and Moni Nag, "Population Growth: Current Issues and Strategies," *Population and Development Review* 8, no. 1 (1982):121–139; Rodolfo A. Bulatao and Ronald D. Lee, eds., *Determinants of Fertility in Developing Countries*, 2 vols., New York, 1983; Richard A. Easterlin, ed., *Population and Economic Change in Developing Countries*, Chicago, 1980; Timothy King et al., *Population Policies and Economic Development*, Baltimore, 1974; Dorothy Nortman and Joanne Fisher, *Population and Family Planning Programs: A Compendium of Data Through 1981*, 11th ed., New York, 1982; and T. P. Schultz, *Economics of Population*, Reading, Mass., 1981. An overview by Robert McNamara, "Time Bomb or Myth: The Population Problem," is in *Foreign Affairs* 62, no. 5 (1984): 1107–1131.
2. The most well-known work of pro-natalist revisionism is Julian Simon, *The Ultimate Resource*, Princeton, N.J., 1982.
3. Note that domestic scale economies are certainly not crucial to growth. Economies can export to the world and so can thrive without a large national market, as shown vividly by Belgium, Denmark, Luxemburg, and Switzerland in Europe, and by even smaller Hong Kong and Singapore in Asia.
4. *WDR 1980*, p. 39.
5. The following discussion is informed by Michael S. Teitelbaum, "Population and Development: Is a Consensus Possible?" *Foreign Affairs* 52, no. 4 (1974):742–760.
6. These views are generally not held by mainstream Protestant Christians, Buddhists, Taoists, Confucianists, practitioners of Shinto, or liberal Muslims. For Saudi Arabia, see *Population Reports* 6 (March/April 1981):1.
7. Where 85 percent of married women use contraceptives, the highest figure in the non-communist world. (Czechoslovakia reports 95 percent.) See *WDR 1986*, p. 231.
8. Teitelbaum, "Population and Development," p. 745.
9. The works of T. R. Malthus, who argued that unrestrained population growth tends to immiserate the population (see a later section of this chapter), have frequently been a target for Marxist scorn. Note, however, that some communist countries have exceedingly effective programs of birth control.

10. For the numbers, see *WDR 1984,* p. 127. As might be suspected from the references in the text to former French colonies, modern France has a long tradition of boosting the population. French leaders have considered the birth rate low since early in the nineteenth century and encourage births by financial means. Cash loans of over $2,000 are made for eight years to married couples, the debt reduced by 15 percent if a child is born before the end of the period, 25 percent further for each additional child, until the debt is canceled on the birth of a fourth child.

    High cash grants, a birth bonus, additional paid holidays, loans for apartments, long paid maternity leaves, "tenured" jobs for mothers, the discouragement or abolition of abortion, and difficulties in obtaining divorces are the tactics of Hungary, emulated to a lesser extent by Bulgaria, Czechoslovakia, and Romania. See *WDR 1984,* p. 157.

    At an earlier time Nazi Germany followed much the same policy and is the best historical example of emphasis on the military side of the argument. The Nazis used a system of honors and awards for fecund females to boost the birth rate. The *Kreuz Deutsche Mutter,* first class, in gold, was awarded to mothers of six or more children. A silver cross for four or five children, and a bronze cross for three or four feted lesser feats of fecundity.

11. The data in this paragraph are from the *IMF Survey,* March 9, 1981, p. 66, and the *Christian Science Monitor,* September 14, 1982.

12. Taken from Ansley J. Coale, "Man and His Environment," *Science* 179 (October 9, 1970):132–136, and brought to my attention by William J. Baumol and Alan S. Blinder, *Economics: Principles and Policies,* New York, 1979, p. 653.

13. See Gerald M. Meier, *Emerging from Poverty: The Economics That Really Matters,* New York, 1984.

14. See *WDR 1984,* p. 86. The suggested large cost decrease would occur if there were "rapid fertility decline" compared to standard fertility assumptions, as calculated by the World Bank.

15. Work of Joe D. Wray cited by William Loehr and John P. Powelson, *Economics of Development and Distribution,* New York, 1981, p. 227.

16. *WDR 1984,* chap. 7, has a thorough discussion.

17. William Loehr and John P. Powelson, *Economics of Development and Distribution,* p. 229; the data apply to a U.S. city (Cleveland).

18. The study of "territorial imperatives" among animals shows animal behavior can become much more belligerent under crowded conditions. Though there is probably less similarity with human behavior, the examples of Hun, Goth, Vandal, and Viking do indicate that when population is thought to be intolerably high in relation to resources, people can become ill-tempered and acquisitive in their relations with their neighbors.

19. *WDR 1984,* p. 57.

20. See Michael P. Todaro, *Economic Development in the Third World,* 2nd ed., New York, 1981, pp. 165–168, 187.

21. See Don E. Dumond, "The Limitation of Human Population: A Natural History," *Science* 187 (February 28, 1975):713–721.

22. Japan's reduction from earlier high levels was the most rapid ever recorded until quite recently. From 35 in 1920 to 1924, and still high at 30 in 1940 to 1944, the figure fell to 19 in the mid 1960s and 13 in in the 1980s.

23. *WDR 1984,* p. 52.

24. *Ibid.,* pp. 51, 122.

25. *Ibid.,* p. 52.

226

THE POPULATION PROBLEM / 8

26. See Kingsley Davis, "Population Policy: Will Current Programs Succeed?" in Theodore Morgan and George W. Betz, eds., *Economic Development: Readings in Theory and Practice,* Belmont, Calif., 1970, p. 343.

27. In an earlier time period (eighteenth and nineteenth centuries) there was another large improvement in food supplies stemming from a Green Revolution in which North and South American crops spread to Europe, Asia, and Africa, bringing especially potatoes and corn (maize) to many millions of new consumers. The better nutrition that accompanied the new crops meant that a considerably larger population could be supported, a fact dramatized by the famine in Ireland when that country's potatoes were severely damaged by blight in the 1840s. The much larger Irish population made possible by the potato could not be maintained without it, hence the "Great Hunger" and the mass emigration out of the island. A similar, though less obvious, role in African population increase has been played by maize and manioc.

28. See David Morawetz, *Twenty-five Years of Economic Development, 1950 to 1975,* Baltimore, 1977, p. 49.

29. R. H. Gray, "The Decline of Mortality in Ceylon and the Demographic Effects of Malaria Control," *Population Studies* 28, no. 2 (1974):205–229; and T. Paul Schultz, *Economics of Population,* Reading, Mass., 1981, p. 116.

30. The great victories over malaria are discussed by Goran Ohlin, "Population Control and Economic Development," in Morgan and Betz, eds., *Economic Development,* p. 62. The celebration was premature, however. There was a three-fold rise in malaria cases from 1972 to 1976, and by the mid 1980s it was again a serious disease. Sri Lanka for example now reports 2 million cases a year after nearly eliminating it. Partly the recurrence was due to overconfidence as population expanded in mosquito-infested areas. Spraying and drainage were sometimes neglected, and governments failed to maintain the intensity of their programs. DDT-resistant strains of mosquitos were reported from India in the early 1970s, so that more of that ecology-damaging chemical had to be used. The best substitute, malathion, works well, but must be spread more often and costs more; the end result is six times more expensive than DDT. Further and equally discouraging, the malaria parasite was developing resistance to anti-malarial drugs. The search for effective substitutes is a first priority. Attention now focuses on a vaccine that will prevent the disease, said to be only a few years away. Details of the malaria comeback may be found in Everett G. Martin, "Resurgent Use of DDT in World's Malaria War is Worrying Ecologists," *Wall Street Journal,* May 17, 1985.

31. Treatment with saline-glucose solutions, given orally and not dependent on modern hospitals, promises success in the fight against diarrheal disease.

32. *IMF Survey,* March 9, 1981.

33. The only developed countries with a growth rate of as much as 1 percent in 1984 were Ireland and New Zealand; in both the figure was exactly 1.0 percent.

34. See Dumond, "Limitation of Human Population," pp. 714–716.

35. T. Paul Schultz, *Economics of Population,* Reading, Mass., 1981, p. 123.

36. A fourth reason, malnutrition, has now been shown to apply only weakly. Until a short time ago it was believed that malnutrition induces intermittent female sterility, delaying menarche (first menstruation) and hastening menopause. But careful work now indicates only a slightly longer delay in having another child. See Schultz, *Economics of Population,* p. 123, citing sources. It is also now known, contrary to another theory, that malnutrition does not *increase* fertility in a kind of Darwinian defense mechanism.

37. Ronald Freedman, "Norms for Family Size in Underdeveloped Areas," in Charles B. Nam, ed., *Population and Society,* Boston, 1968, p. 222.

38. *WDR 1984,* p. 108.
39. Schultz, *Economics of Population,* p. 119.
40. *WDR 1984,* p. 121.
41. For those with a knowledge of indifference curves, the reduced demand for children can be viewed diagrammatically in Figure 8.1, which shows goods consumed by the parents on the vertical axis and the number of children desired on the horizontal. A set of indifference curves is drawn. *AB* is the original budget line, so that the number of children desired is OX_1. An increase in the opportunity cost of children relative to goods shifts the budget line to *AD* and lowers the number of children desired to OX_2. (If income rises at the same time as the shift in cost, moving the budget line to *C'D'*, then the number of children desired will be OX_3.) The diagram follows Michael P. Todaro, *Economic Development in the Third World,* 2nd ed., New York, 1981, p. 189.
42. But if population-conscious China and India are excluded from the 1984 data, the desire for children in the poorest countries has declined only a little, from 6.2 to 5.9. The figures are obtained by comparing Table 15 in *WDR 1978* to Table 26 in *WDR 1986.*
43. *WDR 1984* was a major source for this section.
44. See the correlations by W. Parker Mauldin and Robert J. Mauldin quoted by Robert Repetto, "Population Policy After Mexico City: Reality vs. Ideology," *Challenge* 28, no. 3 (1985):43.
45. Roberto Cuca, "Family Planning Programs and Fertility Decline," *Finance and Development* 17, no. 4 (1980):37–39.

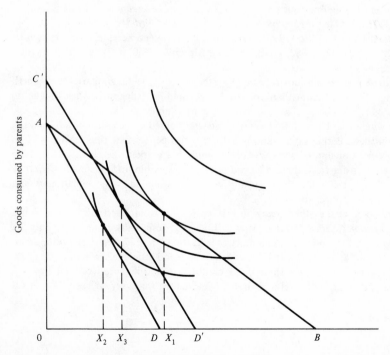

Figure 8.1   Indifference curves relating goods consumed to number of children desired.

46. See *WDR 1984,* Table 3, pp. 196–197.
47. Some of these are from J. Mayonne Stycos, "Prospects for World Population Control," in Morgan and Betz, eds., *Economic Development,* p. 321.
48. This is understandable, given Japan's conservative attitude toward birth control by other means. The pill is not readily available, IUDs were banned until 1974, and an army of medical doctors has a vested interest in continuing abortion as the main line of defense. Thus more than half of all Japanese married women have had at least one abortion and estimates show as many aborted pregnancies as those that come to term.
49. *WDR 1984,* pp. 148, 152.
50. For this and the following sections, I utilized details in many issues of *The Economist,* including May 10, 1980, March 28, 1981, May 30, 1981, January 29, 1983, April 16, 1983, April 30, 1983, December 22, 1984, and January 4, 1986; *WDR 1980* and *WDR 1984;* as well as many articles in the press, including *Wall Street Journal,* February 28, 1983.
51. *WDR 1980,* p. 69.
52. Much of the information in this section is from Jan Stepan et al., "Legal Trends and Issues in Voluntary Sterilization," *Population Reports* 9, no. 2 (1981):E73–E102.
53. See especially *WDR 1980,* p. 68, and *The Economist,* November 25, 1978, p. 74.
54. *WDR 1980,* p. 80.
55. A useful survey article is James T. Fawcett and Siew-Ean Khoo, "Singapore: Rapid Fertility Transition in a Compact Society," *Population and Development Review* 6, no. 4 (1980):549–579. Also see *The Economist,* December 29, 1979, pp. 23–24.
56. See *WDR 1984,* pp. 125–126.
57. See Ronald K. Ridker, "The No-Birth Bonus Scheme: The Use of Savings Accounts for Family Planning in South India," *Population and Development Review* 6, no. 1 (1980):32–46; Todaro, *Economic Development in the Third World,* 2nd ed., p. 194.
58. For details I utilized *WDR 1984,* pp. 124, 178; various articles in *The Economist,* especially January 29, 1983, pp. 31–34, and March 1, 1980, p. 38; and articles elsewhere in the press.
59. The Chinese peer persuasion "rationing" system has some vague similarity to Kenneth Boulding's "Green Stamp Plan" of the 1960s. Boulding suggested, with tongue no doubt slightly in cheek, that children could be rationed by means of transferable stamps, which could be sold for cash to those who wanted more children badly enough to pay for them. Perhaps two stamps could be issued per woman, thus ensuring ZPG. Any unwanted or unused stamps could be sold on a market, thereby accomplishing an income transfer from those who can afford more children to those who feel they cannot. Having children without a stamp would be prohibited by law; violations would presumably be subject to fines.
60. This and some of the other details in this section are from a series by Carol Honsa in the *Christian Science Monitor,* May to June 1981 (especially June 4) and July 30, 1982. Also see Stepan et al., "Voluntary Sterilization," p. E77; *The Economist,* January 7, 1978, p. 58; March 28, 1981, pp. 41, S47–S48; and articles elsewhere in the press.
61. Or 100 rupees if there were three living children, or 150 if there were just two.
62. They did, however, still receive their 10-rupee reward for every successful "motivation."

chapter 9

Human Capital and Productivity

Preventing excess population was the subject of the last chapter. Making the existing population productive and finding employment for it are the subjects of this one. There is general agreement that "human capital" in the form of education, skills, and "maintenance" through health and nutrition are critical components of development, and it is also agreed that making the population more productive through education and health care also makes it more employable.[1] Indeed, the already large disparity in physical capital available to rich and poor countries looks even more formidable if human capital is included as well.[2] But human capital is decidedly not the same as physical capital. It takes a long time to acquire, increasing the risks of obsolescence if conditions change. It does not survive the individual who does the investing. It is not easily transferred to other uses (surgeons may have a huge amount tied up in their training, but it will be useless if they want to switch to designing computers).[3]

EDUCATION AND TRAINING

Private and Social Returns to Education

Education is one of the most important elements of human capital; differences in educational endowments certainly account for some rather large part of the gap in national income per capita between the LDCs and the developed countries.[4] Education involves two difficult questions, one of analysis and one of policy. The first is how the economist is to measure the costs and benefits of education. The second is what type of education best promotes economic development.

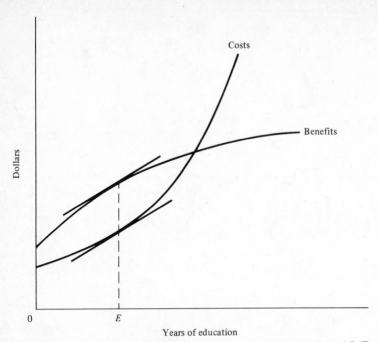

Figure 9.1 Marginal costs and marginal benefits of education. (Michael P. Todaro, *Economic Development in the Third World,* 2nd ed., New York, 1981, p. 307)

As for measurement, the basic principle seems simple: Expand education until the rising marginal costs of providing it are equal to the falling marginal benefits (due to diminishing returns) accruing to society from it. This is shown diagrammatically in Figure 9.1. Since the slopes of the tangent lines are equal at *OE,* marginal costs are equal to marginal benefits at that level of education. Unfortunately, this is not easy to do, and measurement is complicated by several valuation problems.

One such problem is that the private benefits of education may differ substantially from the benefits to society as a whole. Social benefits may rise sharply with primary education because elementary literacy and facility with numbers will make factory workers more productive and because farmers-to-be may gain some knowledge of new technologies in agriculture from their elementary science courses. The direct social benefits from secondary and university education will probably not rise as rapidly (as represented in Figure 9.2). Admittedly, it is difficult to take into account the less direct benefits that some have claimed for education, particularly the higher level of decency and morality in society. Further education arguably brings less crime, more honesty and concern for others, changing attitudes toward tolerance, and civic duty, greater openness to new ideas, greater self-confidence, and higher cultural standards, such as more pleasure from music, art, and reading. Indeed, some studies show that voting, family planning, savings habits, and attitudes toward work are more influenced by schooling than anything else.[5]

Private benefits, however, may be perceived as increasing rapidly at the

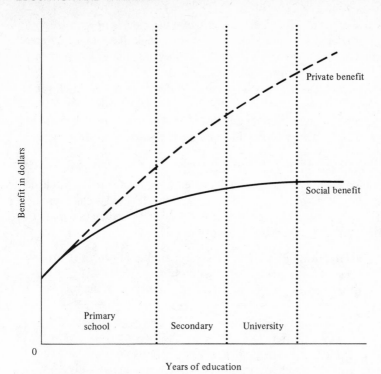

Figure 9.2   Private versus social benefits of education.

secondary or university level whenever high educational attainment is required for job procurement and promotion or whenever wage and salary scales are geared to educational levels, rather than to performance and productivity. George Psacharopoulos has shown that earnings at higher levels of education relative to earnings at lesser levels of education are uniformly higher at every stage in LDCs than in the developed countries. For example, his research revealed private returns to university graduates over 6 times higher than to primary school graduates in Malaysia, Ghana, South Korea, Kenya, Uganda, Nigeria, and India, but only 2.4 times higher in the United States, Canada, and Great Britain.[6] (Note that an argument can be made from these statistics that education has tended to *increase* income inequality in LDCs.)

In such circumstances the demand for secondary and university education will be artificially inflated, and a country may then devote an unjustifiably high amount of money to these activities. The large wage and salary rewards to education may, as we shall see, be due to disequilibrium in the labor market, with resulting heavy unemployment among the more highly educated. (This highlights a problem with rate of return calculations for education. As long-term estimates based on past income data, they will be valid predictions of future rates of return only to the extent that future incomes do not greatly change—and heavy unemployment among graduates would certainly represent one such change.)[7] Typically, the unemployment is highest among those who have completed some high school or college training, but did not graduate.

Another question in valuing the benefits of education is how to treat the "joint product" problem? A graduate engineer will no doubt have a very different level of performance when working with other college graduates as opposed to working with primary school drop-outs.

Still another problem for measurement is differing levels of intelligence, as measured by IQ or by other suitable means. Would these not lead to eventual differences in income even if education levels are the same? And are not those who seek more education sometimes more motivated than those who do not?

In spite of the difficulties of measurement, there have been numerous recent attempts to calculate the costs and benefits.[8] Below is a standard formula for calculating the rate of return for attending university. It divides the increased earnings from university training by the direct cost of the education plus the earnings forgone during the period of education.

$$
\begin{array}{l}
\text{Private} \\
\text{rate of} \\
\text{return}
\end{array}
=
\dfrac{
\begin{array}{l}
\text{average annual} \\
\text{after-tax earnings} \\
\text{of university graduates}
\end{array}
-
\begin{array}{l}
\text{average annual after-} \\
\text{tax earnings of} \\
\text{secondary school graduates}
\end{array}
}{
\left(
4 \text{ years} \times
\begin{array}{l}
\text{average annual} \\
\text{after-tax} \\
\text{earnings of secondary} \\
\text{school graduates}
\end{array}
+
\begin{array}{l}
\text{average annual} \\
\text{private direct} \\
\text{cost of} \\
\text{university study}
\end{array}
\right)
}
$$

(To convert this formula to a social rate of return, before-tax earnings would be used, since from society's point of view taxes are just a transfer. In addition the cost figure must be the full quantity of resources committed, whether included in fees or not.)

The difficulties aside, various studies by the World Bank during the time period 1957 to 1978 reveal social rates of return to education, calculated with similar formulas, as shown in Table 9.1. Note the 27 percent return to primary education in poor LDCs, a figure rarely matched by any capital investment. The returns are a little higher yet for farmer education. Some elementary competence in arithmetic and science, plus basic literacy, was strongly correlated with a rise in agricultural output in 17 recent studies. The output increased by an average of 13.2 percent to 8.1 percent, depending on whether complementary inputs were

Table 9.1 SOCIAL RATES OF RETURN TO EDUCATION, PERCENT

	Primary	Secondary	Higher	Number of Countries
All LDCs	24.2	15.4	12.3	30
Low-income LDCs	27.3	17.2	12.1	11
Middle-income LDCs	22.2	14.3	12.4	19
Developed Countries	[a]	10.0	9.1	14

[a]Not calculated because of small size of control group without primary education (about 20 percent in the United States).
Source: *WDR 1980,* p. 49.

available or not. The latter figure is consonant with a rate of return to primary education of farmers of approximately 30 percent.[9]

Why Education Is Costly in LDCs

One element of education not always appreciated is that, however valuable, its costs are high in the LDCs. Why is this so?

First, the resources needed to provide education are scarce. Teachers must be trained; trained people are much in demand and have other opportunities in business and government; teachers' salaries are therefore high compared to average incomes.[10] In the United States a primary school teacher would receive a wage usually no more than about 150 percent of per capita national income, but because of scarcity, that figure is usually much higher in the LDCs. At the start of the 1970s it was 300 percent in Jamaica, 500 percent in Ghana, and 700 percent in Nigeria. At that time a secondary school teacher in Uganda earned between 2,500 percent and 4,000 percent of national income per head; a college professor 12,500 percent.[11] (Another reason for high salaries is a salary structure inherited from colonial days, especially in Africa.)

Second, high rates of population growth have led to a resulting high burden of dependency, as discussed in the last chapter; this has boosted expenditures.

Third, because of reasons of prestige or because donors of foreign aid want the schools built with that aid to look impressive, school buildings are frequently fancier by comparison to the general architectural standards of an area than is true in the developed countries.

Finally, students can be remarkably coddled, especially at the university level, where extremely generous grants ("bursaries") may be paid to them over and above the free room, board, and tuition that is often made available. The bursaries, a leftover from an elitist past, are often paid to all, even to students from well-to-do families. Of all the reasons for high costs, this one is surely the least defensible. Because of the bursaries, students are attracted for financial rather than educational reasons; funds are diverted away from higher-return primary education; income is transferred in regressive fashion from poor to rich in some countries. Loans or complete abolition, with a shift to higher fees paid by the student, would seem the solution.

As a result, higher education compared to primary education is relatively far more expensive in an LDC than in a developed country. Typically, in the United States and Great Britain there is a difference of about 7 times in the cost per student between primary and secondary schools; for a selected group of LDCs (Ghana, India, Kenya, South Korea, Malaysia, Nigeria, Uganda) the recent figure was 12 times. The figure for primary versus university education was 18 times for the United States and Britain, 88 times for the LDCs.[12] These high costs eat resources; overall in 1980 primary education received only 22 percent of all funding for schooling in LDCs, while university education swallowed nearly 40 percent. There would seem to be a strong argument for shifting funds away from university education and toward primary schooling, which has a higher social rate of return. Needless to say, this move would be difficult since it would tread on the toes of the urban elites who so often hold political power.[13]

The high cost of education has led to swollen budgets for that purpose in the LDCs, which nearly doubled as a percent of GNP between 1960 and 1980 and which are often as large as one-fifth to one-third of all current spending by government. In reaction both to this rapid swelling of educational outlay and to slower economic growth in the 1980s, there has been some recent budget cutting, both as a percent of GNP and as a percent of government revenue, especially in South Asia, the Middle East, North Africa, and Latin America.[14]

THE EDUCATIONAL STRUCTURE IN THE LDCS

The burden of dependency with its masses of young people, combined with the relatively high cost of education, has led to serious difficulties in providing both schools and teachers. But there has also been substantial progress, as can be seen in the following tables that show the numbers enrolled at a given educational level (primary school, secondary school, college and university) as a percent of the relevant age group for that level.

Table 9.2 gives the data for the developed countries. One important result of the high percentages is a corresponding high rate of adult literacy. Of all the developed countries, only two, Ireland and Italy, have literacy rates below 99 percent, and the figure in both is 98 percent.[15]

In the less-developed countries the situation differs substantially. The data for 34 low-income countries (excluding China and India) are shown in Table 9.3.[16] The impression of poor educational opportunities is, however, tempered by the improvement since 1960—the 1960 figures are shown in parentheses. Not everything is revealed by these statistics. They fail to make clear, for example, how far women still have to come before educational equality with men is achieved. The percentage for primary school conceals the fact that the figure is 76 percent for male children, but only 56 percent for female.

This is important not only because it seems "fair" to give women an equal chance, but because education of females carries substantial positive benefits. The

**Table 9.2   PERCENT OF
RELEVANT AGE GROUP
ENROLLED,
DEVELOPED
COUNTRIES, 1983**

Primary school	102*
Secondary school	85
College and university	37**

*Over 100 percent because some outside the age group are enrolled.
**The figure ranges from a high of 56 percent in the United States to a low of 20 percent in Great Britain.
Source: WDR 1986, p. 237.

Table 9.3   PERCENT OF RELEVANT AGE
GROUP ENROLLED, LOW-INCOME
LDCS, 1983 (AND 1960)

Primary school	74	(37)
Secondary school	20	(6)
College and university	2	(1)

Source: WDR 1986, p. 236, for the 1983 data; WDR 1983, p. 196, for the 1960 data.

persuasive evidence of Chapter 8 is that, compared to women with no education or less educated women, more highly educated mothers are able to extract more nutrition from the same level of expenditure on food, there is less mortality among their offspring, they marry later, and their fertility is lower. In all these cases, there is significantly *less* correlation with the educational level of the father. A more highly educated woman is also an earner of higher income, and this, too, aids nutrition because on average more of women's income is used to buy food than is the income of men. Both quality and quantity rise; the effect on nutrition is not nearly so great when the income of men increases. There have, incidentally, been cases of rural development projects that led to greater production of cash crops, but did not safeguard women's income, leading to adverse nutritional consequences and (in what appeared to be an effort to regain lost status) the birth of more children.[17]

The average figures given in the table also do not reflect the wide variance among LDCs. There have been some remarkable primary school successes, including Indonesia 115 percent, Kenya 104 percent, Lesotho 110 percent, Togo 102 percent, Zimbabwe 131 percent and China (not included in the average) 104 percent.[18] But there are also some discouraging cases, such as Burkina Faso 27 percent, Bhutan 25 percent, Mali 24 percent, and Somalia 21 percent.

The averages also do not reflect the very different dropout rates among continents. In the LDCs recently about 40 percent of students dropped out before the fourth year of primary school. In Asia the figure was only some 20 percent (but over 50 percent in populous India and Pakistan), while in Africa it was 54 percent and in Latin America 60 percent. In Brazil's poor, rural northeast, where only 46 percent of the eligible age-group was enrolled anyway (less than half the national average for Brazil), at most only 4 percent of students completed four years of training. Thus wastage appears highest where it can least be afforded.[19] (Dropping out of secondary school is somewhat less common, though still a severe problem—something under 20 percent in Asia and Latin America and approximately double that figure in Africa.)

Finally, the figures do not reflect the strong urban bias in some countries. Funding per pupil in rural schools is often much lower than it is in the cities.

A result of an educational system insufficient in quantity and inadequate in quality is clearly reflected in the statistics for adult literacy. In the low-income LDCs by 1980 still only 40 percent of all adults could read, though this is nearly double the 23 percent of 1960. Not surprisingly, there is often a good correlation between a campaign to increase primary school enrollment and resulting improvements in literacy. Compare the literacy rate for some of the countries mentioned above: Indonesia, Kenya, Lesotho, Zimbabwe, and China, all about 50 percent or above, but Mali 10 percent, and Burkina Faso 5 percent.

The data for the 60 middle-income LDCs give a more favorable impression, and the goal of universal primary education (UPE) is close to attainment in this group (Table 9.4). Literacy shows a corresponding large improvement; 65 percent in 1980, up from 48 percent in 1960. The figures for primary school enrollment in these middle-income countries are most encouraging.

UNEMPLOYMENT AMONG GRADUATES AND CURRICULAR RELEVANCE

A serious problem with education in the LDCs is the disillusionment of those who complete their training and develop expectations as to jobs, income, and prestige based on that training. The expectations may well go unfulfilled. If many wages and salaries are not very flexible in the downward direction, there will be limited capacity to absorb primary and secondary school graduates in jobs outside agriculture.[20] Those educated in rural schools too often tend to think of farming and life in the village as "bush," to use the piquant word much heard in Africa. There is also little inclination to accept a job as an unskilled laborer in the city. Often only a government clerkship or work in the managerial or sales end of a large firm confers adequate status.

At the same time pay scales for those with primary or secondary certificates may be relatively high, originally so set because of the scarcity of such graduates; this was especially true of the colonial governments of Asia and Africa. The educational situation has changed substantially, but sometimes pay scales have not. For example, the pay of government bureaucrats expressed as a percentage of per capita GDP is about 200 percent in the developed countries, but about 300 percent in Latin America and Asia and some 600 percent in Africa. Some bureaucrats are even higher paid: Cameroun 750 percent, Bénin 1,000 percent, Burundi 1,500 percent.[21] The resulting disequilibrium wages have frequently meant a substantial surplus of job applicants and inevitable disappointment.[22]

There are other reasons for the surplus and the disappointment, as we shall see in the next chapter when we examine the enormous rural-urban migrations

Table 9.4 PERCENT OF RELEVANT AGE GROUP ENROLLED, MIDDLE-INCOME LDCS, 1983 (AND 1960)

Primary school	105	(75)
Secondary school	47	(14)
College and university	12	(3)

Source: WDR 1986, p. 236, for the 1983 data; *WDR 1983,* p. 196, for the 1960 data.

of recent years in the LDCs. But whatever the cause, open unemployment rates among young people 15 to 24 years of age are often double the national average. Some recent unemployment rates are Philippine cities 21 percent; Ghanaian cities 22 percent; Bogota, Colombia, 23 percent; and Caracas, Venezuela, 38 percent.[23] Recent Indian government statistics show nearly 2 million unemployed high school and college graduates, while in Sri Lanka recently about 20 percent of all secondary school graduates were unemployed. (It may, of course, be rational for graduates to accept a rather lengthy period of unemployment if the probability of eventually finding a high-paying job is significant. The group of unemployed "turns over" to a degree, some finding jobs as others begin their search. We return to the subject in Chapter 10.

In addition to the problem of finding jobs for graduates and indeed another cause of the employment difficulty, is lack of relevance in the curriculum. Connecting education with economic development is a task yet incomplete. Only a decade ago the situation was much worse, however. There was little concern for rural needs in rural schools. In former British and French colonies there was an overwhelming emphasis on Western history and literature. Students in Ghana and Nigeria, even after independence, would study William the Conqueror and the Magna Carta, but not the remarkable ruler Mansa Musa or the history of the ancient empires of Ghana or Melli or Songhay. They would know of the heritage of higher education in Britain, with its historic universities, but not of the great medieval university at Timbuktu. They would read Dickens and Thackeray, instead of the indigenous literature. (The author's wife, teaching Muslim girls in northern Nigeria long after that country's independence, was required to explain Dickens's *Christmas Carol* to students who knew little of Christmas, had never seen snow or a fir tree, and would have found a pork roast for the holiday completely abhorrent, as to Muslims the pig is an unclean animal. To most of these girls, Scrooge, Bob Cratchitt, and Tiny Tim were mysteries equal to why this book would ever have been included in the syllabus!)

Training in Western history and literature was eventually replaced almost everywhere by a more indigenous curriculum. But the problem still remains, for the traditions of British and French education attached much more prestige to the law and the arts than they did to vocational training in applied science and (especially) agriculture. The same tradition is present in Latin America, which has not been colonized since the early nineteenth century. It is reinforced by religions (Hinduism, Confucianism, Buddhism), that value contemplation or the study of sacred and traditional texts. Whatever the cause, the result can clearly be seen in the statistics. Generally, over 60 percent of university students in the LDCs study arts subjects. Of students in their final year in India's universities, recently 84 percent were in the arts, the law, and the social sciences. Only 7 percent were in science and technology, only 2 percent were in agriculture.[24] Even within fields, this symptom shows: tropical medicine is less prestigious than surgery; architects prefer to design edifices rather than the "standard" sort of building that is usually required; economists gravitate to sophisticated modeling rather than nuts-and-bolts work in the field.[25] All this is a most unfortunate legacy, cultural or colonial, that will not be broken for some time still.

The discouraging realization took hold in the 1970s, that the labor force in the LDCs was growing at unprecedented rates, more than double the European experience of the nineteenth century. Whereas Europe in that century could absorb almost half of its growing labor force into industry, recent statistics show that the low-income LDCs are managing to place less than 20 percent of their additional labor in industrial employment. The figure for the middle-income LDCs is somewhat better, at just under 35 percent.

In response there has been an upsurge in vocational programs to train labor for employment outside of industry or to tailor training specifically for employment in that part of industry where the demand for labor is the largest. Some of these programs have not been overly successful. Kenya's new secondary technical schools and Colombia's comprehensive schools both suffered from their inadequate ties to the labor market. Other schools were too rigid, failing to alter specialist training rapidly as market conditions changed. As with the nonvocational schools, inadequate attention was paid to what the job openings actually were.

An impressive lead in this regard has been given by Singapore, whose Industrial Training Board conducts courses in which class time is combined with on-the-job training in industries where a need is expressed. By focusing on actual needs the program tries to avoid the experience of neighboring Thailand, where in the 1970s government support for the training of technicians was overdone, with 40 percent unemployment among the graduates. Brazil's National Service for Industrial Apprenticeship relies on labor market surveys and detailed analyses of job openings in planning and implementing its training programs. The program is financed by a 1 percent payroll tax that is not charged if a firm agrees to sponsor on-the-job training.[26]

The tying of training to job availability is an idea now spreading widely in both LDCs and developed countries. It has had extensive use in Sweden, West Germany, and Japan and has now been adopted in the United States where it is central to the Jobs Training Partnership Act (JTPA) that dates from 1983.

Other possible policy changes could be made so that human capital formation would accord more closely to a country's development needs. The rate of return data clearly point to the gains from greater emphasis on primary education. In the primary schools curricula could clearly be more attuned to rural needs, including only basic literacy and numerical facility, for illiterate adults as well as for children, with some training in how to improve family life through nutrition, health, child care, and family planning.[27] This is not always easy to accomplish, however, as Mexico discovered long ago. That country in the 1920s and 1930s followed famous educator John Dewey's suggestion that special rural schools be established, but after about a decade faced a reaction in which the rural areas demanded and received the same sort of schools as urban areas; rural people thought their schools were inferior and that they were being discriminated against.[28]

Another change might be to curtail the heavy government subsidization of higher education, shifting the costs to the beneficiary of the education. Job specifications could be redrawn so that high educational attainment is not overemphasized, especially in the government's own civil service. Similarly, the tying of wages and salaries to educational levels could be modified to conform more to market supply and demand.[29] All these steps would reduce the inflated private benefits from higher education and bring them closer to equality with the social benefits.

The undoubted positive externalities from educating more women, already mentioned, could certainly receive more emphasis in the countries that still neglect this resource (some nations continue to count almost no women among their university graduates, for example).

Cutting costs with little loss of quality might be possible. The South Korean Air Correspondent High School is run at a cost only a fifth that of traditional schools, and correspondence schools have also had good success in Brazil, Kenya, and the Dominican Republic, among others. Substituting up-to-date textbooks for more expensive teachers may be possible if at the same time class sizes are allowed to rise somewhat; the better books help to offset the more crowded classrooms. Little loss seems to ensue as classes grow larger until they reach about 50 pupils. Radio and television projects may help and may be cheap. Nonformal education could receive more emphasis.

Some of these proposals would represent a step back from the goal of universal primary education and would thus be both politically charged and highly debatable, but they might also be more cost effective than the enormously expensive UPE, thus allowing the attainment of other objectives as well.[30]

THE "BRAIN DRAIN"

Another area of concern is the "brain drain"—students who go overseas for their higher education and remain and those who are trained at home and then emigrate to the developed countries.[31] Large-scale migration of all types of labor was of course common in the nineteenth century, but was much restricted early in the twentieth century. It came to notice once again in the 1960s, when the Common Market countries began to welcome large numbers of unskilled or semiskilled workers. Yugoslavs and Turks toiled on German assembly lines as "guest workers"; Spanish, Portuguese, Algerians, Moroccans, and other nationalities worked in the factories in various Common Market countries. A similar pattern grew up among the LDCs, especially where a very poor country had richer neighbors. Pakistanis, Jordanians, Egyptians, and Yemenis augment the labor force in the oil states around the Persian Gulf; Burkina Faso supplies labor to the Ivory Coast; workers from Bangladesh go to India; Botswana, Lesotho, Malawi, Swaziland, and others send labor to South Africa. When the labor has not been expensively trained, there may be little loss to the home country and a potential for considerable gain in remittances of hard currency. Remittances from workers abroad yield almost as much hard currency as do exports in Pakistan and Burkina Faso; the migrants are everywhere unusually high savers, building a "nest egg" for their return home.[32]

When the labor is skilled, expensively trained, and perhaps irreplaceable in the short run, the result is far different. Most of the data below are for the United

States, but the brain drain also includes Western Europe, Canada, Australia, and New Zealand. The major impetus for the migration of trained personnel to the United States was the elimination of national quotas in July 1968. The principle of preference based on skills and training is embodied in the present law, the Immigration Act of 1975. In the first year of the new system immigration of professionals to the United States shot to more than double the 1966 figure and for the most part has continued to rise ever since.

The results have been alarming. Over 30 percent of the professional and technical personnel coming to the major countries involved in the brain drain in the last decade and a half has come from the LDCs. This includes engineers, managers, physicians, and nurses. Such immigrants to the United States, formerly very small in total number, during 1969 to 1979 comprised three-quarters of the professionally trained entrants to that country.[33] Preponderantly they came from Asia: The number of professionals coming from the Philippines alone in a recent year (over 9,000) nearly equaled those from all Europe (a little over 10,000).

The drain of doctors from the third world is the most striking case. Of the annual flow of about 3,000 doctors who immigrate into the United States, over 60 percent are from the LDCs. It is said that there are more Haitian physicians practicing in the United States than there are in Haiti. Over 70 percent of Pakistan's newly trained doctors leave the country; the figure is between 50 and 67 percent for the Republic of South Africa; 44 percent of Sudan's engineers, scientists, and doctors have emigrated. Many come to the United States.[34]

In all fields of study recently about two-thirds of the foreign students doing graduate work in the United States stayed as immigrants. The numbers are large. Currently one in eight of all graduate students in the United States is a foreigner; there were 10 times as many foreign students in the United States in 1982 (337,000) as there were in 1954.[35]

All this, of course, brings a large financial transfer. The cost of training is incurred by the LDCs, where funds for education are short, but the benefits are received by the developed world. This "reverse foreign aid" has been estimated for some countries by the World Bank. In 1972 the United States is said to have saved $883 million in education costs, against a loss of $320 million for third world countries spent on educating those who moved. Canada, Britain, and the United States in the period 1961 to 1972 gained in higher income $44 billion more than the income lost by developing countries.[36] On an annual basis some developed countries receive more from this source than they pay in foreign aid (over twice as much for Canada and about 50 percent for the United States and Britain).[37]

But the real losses to poor countries are higher than this. The emigration of a good professor can cause stagnation in a university department, and some courses may not even be given as a result. A key industry (Guyana's bauxite, Turkey's coal and electricity) may be severely handicapped by the drain of its most skilled engineers and managers.[38] The most spirited people, the most enterprising, the better-than-average talents are often the ones to join the drain. Measuring the cost of their education and training may not remotely reflect the true costs.

A contrary circumstance should, however, be noted. If those who leave would otherwise form a frustrated, festering class of educated unemployed, allowing the drain to continue might be a preferred strategy in the short run for a country that lacks the immediate capability to do much about it.[39] There is also a financial contribution from the emigrants abroad in the form of remittances sent home to family still resident there (not included in the calculations of the last paragraph). The $2.6 billion in remittances received by Pakistan, largest of such earners among the LDCs, was in 1982 just over 10 percent of national product. In percentage terms North Yemen is far in the lead with nearly 35 percent of its national product coming as remittances from emigrants working mostly in Saudi Arabia. India and Turkey also earn substantial sums in this way. For most LDCs, however, the totals are small.

Assuming a desire to control the brain drain, what might be done about it? Simply stopping the immigration on the receiving end is one alternative. A number of countries (Britain, Denmark, France, Germany, the Netherlands) have limited the inflow of foreign students and put quotas on individual fields of study. In 1976 Britain greatly increased the fees charged to foreign students.[40] Such measures have obvious negative consequences for the recipient country, however, and risk provoking the charge of prejudice, a charge that touches a sensitive chord in the United States and almost all other developed countries. Instead, a joint approach involving both the developed countries and third world governments seems more promising.

A U.S. contribution has been a system (the J visa) which requires students to leave after the completion of their studies. Britain and other European nations have a similar system of temporary immigration.

The underdeveloped countries have also responded with a range of programs including information, incentives, and service and financial obligations. Kenya, for example, runs a successful recruitment program among its emigrants overseas, based on an original and equally successful British scheme. India sends a weekly list of employment opportunities at home to its students in foreign universities. South Korea and Taiwan have both established (with U.S. help) new science institutes in an attempt to keep the best scientific minds at home. Turkey since 1977 has had a scheme called TOKTEN, assisted by the UN Development Program, which involves the temporary return home on short technical assignment of Turks who have achieved prominence abroad in their field of specialization. The advantages to the emigrant include the fast arrangement of a visit, an easier rapport with colleagues at home than can be managed by a visiting "foreigner," and continuing contact when the Turkish expert returns to his country of residence. Programs similar to TOKTEN have now been adopted by China, Egypt, Greece, Grenada, India, Pakistan, and Sri Lanka. Several nations push this thinking further and *require* a number of years of government service from students educated abroad—three to five years in Tunisia and Colombia; seven years of teaching, research, or administrative work in Egypt for the institution or office that provided the student with a scholarship.

Singapore and Tanzania are more stringent, requiring their students studying abroad to post a bond which is forfeited unless they return. Egypt, too, has a bond and a requirement that scholarship aid must be repaid by those choosing to live abroad. (When the bond has co-signers, relatives perhaps, severe financial hardship can result when a student "jumps ship.") Pakistan attempts to levy a tax on its expatriate nationals. The least popular financial measure is no doubt the high exit tax charged emigrants on their departure from the Soviet Union and a few other countries.

An innovative solution to the problem based on some concrete economic analysis has been recently proposed by Jagdish Bhagwati of Columbia University. He suggests that developed countries place a supplementary income tax on the earnings of emigrants from LDCs living in those rich countries and then channel the funds collected via the UN back to the LDCs for development spending. The rationale for such a tax is compensation for the losses of all those remaining behind in the LDCs, with revenue collected and transferred from the emigrant who has been able to improve his economic position through his employment in a developed country. In support of the tax a moral principle is invoked: The lucky few from LDCs, trained in their homeland and now earning substantially higher incomes in a developed country, should share their gains with those left behind.

Diagrammatically, the case appears as in Figure 9.3. The marginal revenue product curve of skilled labor for a developed country (MRP_{dev}) is shown running from upper left to lower right. The curve for an LDC (MRP_{ldc}) is shown running from a right-hand vertical axis. Before immigration the quantity of skilled labor employed in the developed country is O_1A; in the LDC the quantity is O_2A. The wage, equal to productivity, is RA in the LDC and PA in the

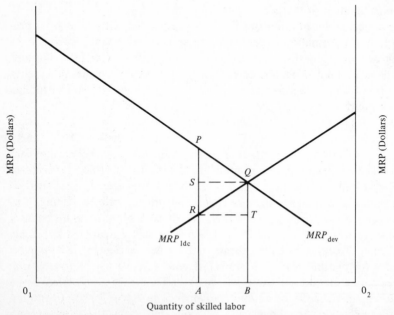

Figure 9.3 Emigration of labor and marginal revenue product. (From Koichi Hamada, "Taxing the Brain Drain: A Global Point of View," in Jagdish Bhagwati, ed., *The New International Economic Order: The North-South Debate,* Cambridge, 1977.)

developed country; earnings are much higher in the latter. When migration opens, AB skilled labor migrates from the LDC to the developed country, the motive for the migration ceasing when labor productivity in the two countries is equalized at QB. National income in the LDC is reduced by the area $ARQB$. A part of this loss is what used to be earned by those who left, $ARTB$. But another part is lost by those who stay behind, RQT. The national income of the developed country will rise by $APQB$; of this the migrants themselves get $ASQB$ (thus gaining $RSQT$ over what they earned in the LDC), while others in the developed country gain SPQ. Here in summary are the main concerns: the loss to the LDC of RQT, the gain to the emigrant of $RSQT$, and the gain to others in the developed country of SPQ. These gains and losses are used to justify the tax, which could be applied to either SPQ or $RSQT$ or both.

In 1978 the LDC Group of 77 endorsed the Bhagwati proposal and recommended changes in national tax laws to bring it into use. There are obvious difficulties. One is the reluctance to bend national tax laws for international purposes. Another is unwillingness to tax refugees from a tyrannical administration. Many educated Iranians, Cubans, Vietnamese, Chileans, and others are working abroad not for the money, but out of necessity or conscience. Under the proposal, how would they be treated? Who would distinguish immigrants who came for gain from those who had to come? But the idea is still an intriguing one. Using 1979 data, it would have yielded some $600 million if applied in the United States, 13 percent of Official Development Assistance in that year.[41]

There is not likely to be a halt or even a slowdown in the brain drain during the next few years. Only stern restrictions, rapid rises in relative income, or the proposed new tax offer much hope. Of these, the first is unpalatable, the second is unlikely to be a solution in the short-run, and the last is rather radical politics in what, for the developed countries, is a rather conservative era. It is one of those clear situations where an attempt at individual betterment is detrimental to a country's development prospects. As such, the issue is likely to be with us for a long time.

FORMING HUMAN CAPITAL : BASIC NEEDS

The emphasis on human capital has helped to increase the appeal of a strategy based on basic needs in health and nutrition.[42] This approach involves an awareness that human capabilities must be maintained before they can be increased; an awareness that if economic growth bypasses a large segment of a country's population, then low standards of public health and nutrition will indeed mean inferior human capital. The approach postulates that the poorest may be unable to obtain income transfers from government because of a lack of political power. It suggests that a dangerous psychological dissatisfaction with the relative affluence of others may arise. It proposes that living standards of the less advantaged part of the population may be improvable more rapidly and at a lower cost in resources if the inadequate standards of health, sanitation, and nutrition are attacked directly, rather than waiting for growth in income to bring them about.[43]

Aside from the argument of sheer speed by comparison with income growth, advocates of basic needs programs argue that this approach will be advantageous in preventing problems that a market system might not recognize or might not cure for some time. (1) Consumers may possibly not, in the absence of a basic needs strategy, optimize their nutrition as income rises. Rice may be substituted for wheat or polished rice for coarse grains for reasons of taste or prestige. Tasty and prestigious crops may bring more profits than the more nutritious but less profitable pulses (legumes) such as chickpeas, lentils, and beans. Nonfood items may be substituted for food. (2) Within households, social strictures may lead to a result where women and children consume less food as a proportion of needs than do men. (3) Health and nutrition may normally be looked after by an extended family of relatives, but an individual without such family ties may be utterly on his or her own unless government fills the breach. (4) With a market system as long as income is unequally distributed, there is no guarantee that malnutrition and poor health will be eliminated; some people because of their poverty will command inadequate supplies of food, impure water, and unsanitary conditions unless government intervenes directly.[44]

That the thrust of these arguments has substantial validity is hard to refute. How else to explain that countries with a strong attachment to basic needs, such as Sri Lanka or China, have attained similar life expectancies to other countries such as Brazil and Mexico on only one-seventh the income per capita?[45] Below we divide the discussion into the two separate areas, health and nutrition.

Health[46]

There is little debate that income growth does eventually lead to improvements in public health. In the developed world, for example, rising income levels led to better water supplies and sanitation; the incidence of cholera and typhoid in Britain declined long before effective treatment was available. Tuberculosis in the United States fell from 200 per 100,000 people to 70 per 100,000 from 1900 to 1930 and then to 30 in the 1950s, *before* chemotherapy was available.[47] The argument that health programs must come first is that, both directly and by improving morale, they will improve labor productivity and the personal sense of well-being (and thus the political climate).

By the 1980s it was plain that developed-country health care was no cheap approach (6 to 12 percent of GNP is spent for such care by the rich, only 1 to 2 percent by the poor). Nor was it the quickest way to improve conditions of health. The emphasis in LDCs turned to universal, basic, *low-cost* treatment. China, with its emphasis on cheap disease prevention especially in rural areas, has been the role model and now boasts health levels about the same as the United States had in the 1930s, remarkable for a country with a per capita income only just over $300.[48] The "barefoot doctors" have been most remarked upon, but local public health personnel of all kinds are numerous in proportion to population and work directly to improve water supplies, sanitation, and nutrition. This primary health care in many LDCs is still more a challenge than a reality, but it remains the focus.

The main reason why LDC death rates stay high is continuing high death rates among children, 132 per 1,000 live births in the poorest LDCs, 220 in Sierra Leone the present record holder, as compared to 9 in the developed countries.[49] Among infants the main cause of death by far (5 to 10 million per year) is the diarrheal condition that *can* come from cholera, but takes many other forms. It is transmitted by human fecal content in soil, food, and water. The new oral rehydration technique for treatment, replacing the older and much more difficult intravenous drip, promises great advances in infant survival from this form of infection and is credited by the World Health Organization (WHO) with already having saved about a half million children every year.[50] Influenza-pneumonia type disease is also a big killer of children (4 to 5 million per year). The two together are responsible for about 40 percent of all deaths from birth to 5 years of age in LDCs; the comparable figure is 2 percent in the developed countries.[51]

Improved water supply would represent a major advance; currently only 31 percent of low-income LDC populations have access to safe drinking water in contrast to over 99 percent in the industrial market economies. But it is costly, $40 per person at 1978 prices plus maintenance.[52]

In many countries the World Health Organization and UNICEF are now sponsoring primary health care programs involving universal, low-cost care. The emphasis in these programs is on community health workers (CHW) with limited training and volunteers who can refer patients to dispensaries and hospitals. The special need for such a new system lies in the scarcity of doctors: 5.8 per 100,000 people in the poorest LDCs; 181 per 100,000 in the developed countries.[53] Adding to the scarcity in many areas is the urban bias; 60 to 70 percent of the doctors in LDCs commonly work in an urban setting. The number is as high as 80 percent in India, and the cities contain only 20 to 30 percent of the population. In Colombia 38 percent of the population is rural, but only 19 percent of the government's subsidies for health go to them. The bias is largely due to the urban location of heavily subsidized, expensive hospitals and the absence of formal health insurance and social security programs in the countryside.[54] One immediate step would seem to be the introduction of, or increases in, the charges for urban hospital patients who can afford it.

There are also serious cost problems, made worse by a preference for modern techniques. India, for example, attains a 95 percent cure rate for tuberculosis with modern chemotherapy, but only 85 percent with cheaper treatment with the drug isoniazid. But by using isoniazid it could reach 100 times more people for the same cost. One country asked the WHO for a computer-assisted whole-body scanner, when the same amount of money could have immunized all children for 10 years, saving perhaps 500,000 lives![55] Partly in reaction to high costs, partly because of reduced economic growth in the last few years, the share of government spending directed toward health fell by some 13 percent between 1973 and 1980.[56]

Nutrition[57]

Better nutrition is another element in the basic needs approach. Ten years ago it was thought that malnutrition was mostly a protein (and some vitamin and mineral) shortage. While protein deficiency is still recognized as a problem, attention has shifted to undernourishment—simply a shortage of food.

Nutritional deficiencies are most common in Africa and Southeast Asia, less so in Latin America and the Middle East. The basic metabolic rate of calorie consumption is about 1,300 calories per day. In 86 poor countries 23 percent of the population or 436 million people are thought to receive less than 1,600 per day.[58] The level of 1,600 has been criticized as not allowing for much physical activity; one study showed that in hard agricultural work consumption can reach 3,500 calories without weight gain (and so, not surprisingly, studies indicate that malnourished farmers work fewer hours per acre cultivated than do the well fed). Depending on the assumptions, the estimates of the number of people chronically undernourished range from 340 million to 730 million, excluding China.[59]

Malnutrition is largely correlated with poverty, so that even relatively rich LDCs, if they have high income inequality, can have serious undernourishment. Malnutrition of children is also correlated (inversely) with the education of the mother, partly due to nutritional information, but no doubt *mostly* due to the enhanced chances of increasing income through work in the market. Inadequacies in nourishment are estimated to contribute to a third or more of infant and child deaths in the LDCs. Girls suffer more than boys (exhibiting the common preference for male children in many parts of the less-developed world), pregnant and nursing mothers more than other women. Nutritional deficiencies are particularly noticeable in very young children, aged 18 to 24 months, just after nursing stops. Weight at this age is often 25 to 40 percent less than average for 15 to 25 percent of the population.[60] Growth may be stunted, and there is the possibility of retardation in mental development when the condition is extreme. The retardation continues on intelligence tests even after the malnutrition is corrected. There are other data, though less confidence can be placed on them, showing that retardation and its continuance can occur even with more mild long-term malnutrition. Immunity processes are also sometimes impaired. One does not often actually *die* from malnutrition, but it is a serious contributing factor to death from many causes.

Malnutrition is much cheaper to prevent than to cure.[61] The hospitals in poor LDCs commonly contain many nutrition cases (in the Caribbean 20 to 45 percent of the pediatric beds are taken up with such cases, 15 percent in India, 80 percent in Guatemala). Even with hospital costs cheap ($7 to $10 per day being a common cost range in the 1970s) prevention of malnutrition in children with a small protein and calorie supplement estimated to cost less than 3¢ per day would surely have been preferable.

What to do about nutrition problems is a major topic for research. In one sense the solution seems simple: It is thought that only about 2 percent of world grain output, if placed in the right hands, would end malnutrition. As we have seen, though, the complication is how to get the food to the poor who need it. Attention has been directed to several sorts of new policy.[62]

1. The level of nutrition among the poor may be improved by raising their income level. Production alone will not suffice; there must be some means to get

the food to the needy, and development targeted toward the lower-income part of the population is one way.

2. Production of the foods eaten by the poor, such as millet, coarse grains, and root crops, might be boosted. These crops have been neglected by agricultural researchers, even though they and other carbohydrate foods provide 75 percent of the calories consumed in the poorest countries (compared to only 30 percent or so in countries above $3,000 in per capita income).[63] Millet and sorghum, for example, do badly in severe drought, and properly directed research might help.

3. Food ration subsidies have proved effective. In Sri Lanka, for example, they get much of the credit for the increase in life expectancies recorded there during the 1970s. In fact, such subsidies are used by all three of the LDCs in which life expectancy is over 60 years. Generally, however, they are *very* expensive, 10 to 20 percent of the government budget in Egypt (where spending on food subsidies in 1983 was over 10 times higher in real terms than it was in 1968), Sri Lanka (where they once reached 24 percent of the budget), and elsewhere. Much of the expense is for food imports. Often the food aid goes to people who do not need it, as in Egypt where wealthy farmers have been known to buy the one-penny bread loaves to feed to their donkeys and other livestock. In Sri Lanka, more than half the benefits from food subsidies went to middle- and higher-income families.[64] The vested interests once established make the aid hard to reduce after it is implemented. If the administration is strong willed, it can use a means test that makes higher-income families ineligible for the aid, as in Sri Lanka during the 1970s. But to introduce a means test is tough politically, as illustrated by the cases of Egypt and Poland.

However tough, many development economists now recommend some variant of the U.S. food stamps as a substitute for across-the-board subsidies. Alternatively, one could subsidize only the foods that the nonpoor do not eat (sorghum in Bangladesh) or allow the subsidy program to run only in the poorest areas (as in projects in Brazil and Colombia).

The supporters of food subsidies should always be on the lookout for repercussions on domestic agricultural output. Imports of foreign food aid to help with the program may depress the local producer price of agricultural commodities. Or prices to consumers may have been kept low because government policy has kept producer prices low, too. We will return to these potentially serious problems later in the book.

4. Another possible strategy is to target any vulnerable groups specifically. Food supplements could be made available to pregnant women and young children only, for example. Such programs tend to be much cheaper, but they run the risk that these same vulnerable groups will find their consumption not really increased because of a family decision to cut the amounts made available to them at home.

5. Finally, rather than providing food, a program might concentrate on food additives and fortification during processing. The difficulty here is that the poor buy little processed food in the first place, and even that from small processors, so that such programs can be uneconomically expensive.

Famines, the extreme of malnourishment, have been the subject of much recent research.[65] They are particularly vicious in that children always make up a disproportionate share of the victims. Many scholars now attribute modern famines not to a fall in the food available to a nation (though this can obviously be a factor), but to local drought leading to a local fall in income, leaving the poor unable to afford adequate food. Since the very poor spend such a high proportion of their income on food (83 percent for the poorest 20 percent of the population in India, still providing fewer than 1,500 calories per day), a fall in cash availability does have a catastrophic potential. Victims may include small and tenant farmers who cannot find work after their crops fail (as in Ethiopia in 1973). Pastoralists who have to trade their cows for food may also find the consequences of drought are severe (as in Africa all across the Sahel in 1973 and again in 1984 to 1985).

The impact is especially hard on the landless, who are mainly casual, unskilled farm laborers. The damage may stem from an employment decline as agricultural output falls. Because of the floods in Bangladesh during 1974, rural landless laborers lost their jobs planting and transplanting rice and thus their income, long before any actual food shortfall showed up. Ethiopia in 1973 to 1974 was suffering from serious drought, but the severe food shortages were localized in areas that were relatively accessible. The major problem was that farmers stopped hiring labor; even though food prices rose only a little, significant numbers of people were less able to buy it. In Bengal during 1943 a rapid rise in the demand for food caused by the wartime boom in urban incomes combined with a poor crop year and poor transport to cause the harm. The food supply was *not* the lowest of the decade, but the upshot was India's last great famine.[66] More important than the availability of food is the *entitlement* to food, to use the word popularized by A. K. Sen of Oxford University.[67] Entitlement can come from personal income, or through membership in an extended family, or through government relief programs. In an unadulterated market system, if entitlements fail among particular classes or occupations, then famines follow.[68]

Even the famine caused by the great drought in sub-Saharan Africa during 1984 to 1985 was not caused by general unavailability of food. The developed countries now mobilize quickly for famine relief in LDCs, and their extraordinary efforts, especially in 1985, for the most part meant that the food was there.[69] Sometimes, however, it was not in the right place, and overloaded transport systems and bureaucratic inefficiencies impeded the relief programs.

The experience emphasized that several seemingly simple steps remain to be taken in coping with emergency famine relief. Data collection to give "early warning" remains poor. LDC governments must respond to initial signals, such as wanderers on the roads following a drought, rather than waiting for signs of actual starvation. Some countries (Sudan, for example) did not ask for food aid until too late; needless hunger ensued. Some countries have foreign trade policies that impeded food imports and government monopolies that mismanaged food distribution. These policies did not help.

The developed countries had to learn that transport to stricken areas is often more crucial than providing the food itself. These countries have never agreed to establish food buffer stocks in famine-prone zones. Further, though many organizations both public and private became involved, their efforts were sometimes little coordinated. There is definite scope for improvement on this score. (The UN World Food Program, dating from 1961, is an extremely valuable agency, serving as a major organizer and clearing house for information, but it and the other multilateral agencies still handle less than 20 percent of all emergency food aid.[70]

Above all, it took a long time to learn that food aid may avert starvation for a time in the particular place where the food is distributed, but it will do nothing to change the conditions that caused the famine. As a result, especially in Ethiopia during 1984 to 1985, the World Food Program pushed the new idea of "food for work" projects, which enabled victims of famine to remain in their villages and on their farms, so that they could maintain their productive assets, even if small, and some measure of independence and self-respect. There they worked on soil and water conservation schemes that resulted in millions of trees planted and hundreds of thousands of miles of new terracing to control erosion.[71] The short-term goal of averting starvation was joined to the laudable long-term goal of altering the conditions that caused the famine in the first place. Another lesson is, where possible, to pay cash wages in relief programs, for then the private marketing system will add to the supply of food. Finally, after the end of the drought the lack of seed and breeding animals must not be overlooked; if it is, there may be a long delay in the recovery.

A Risk of Basic Needs

Few, if any, would disagree with the aims of a basic needs approach discussed in this section. There are, however, two caveats. First, basic needs goals and results are hard to quantify (much harder than income growth, for example) and thus hard to analyze. How does one go about comparing a program that doubles literacy and lowers the incidence of malaria 10 percent with another that halves malaria and increases literacy 10 percent?[72] Since the ramifications are wide and difficult to measure, informed decision making is not easy. (We return to the topic of analyzing costs and benefits in Chapter 11.)

Second, there is always the risk that a basic needs strategy might conflict with some of the means for achieving higher income per head. Any costs of a basic needs program may be far more than offset by increases in labor productivity, but it is certainly conceivable that this might not be so. The funding for a basic needs policy if from domestic taxation might directly reduce saving and investment. The taxes might involve high administrative costs and thus a deadweight loss; they might discourage work effort and entrepreneurship. In Chapter 1 we encountered limited evidence that pointed to the reverse being the case—that higher concentration on basic needs showed significant correlation by country to more rapid income growth. But it would be optimistic indeed to forget the possible negative consequences, and the careful development economist will be alert to their appearance.

Whatever the difficulties in finding reasonable solutions, it is beyond dispute that the basic needs approach did have the effect of focusing far more attention on health and nutrition standards of the poorer part of the population in the LDCs, an effect likely to be a lasting one.

NOTES

1. For a critical review of the subject, see Mark Blaug, "The Empirical Status of Human Capital Theory: A Slightly Jaundiced Survey," *Journal of Economic Literature* 13, no. 3 (1976):827–855. *WDR 1980* focuses on education, nutrition, and health. I have used it frequently.

2. Research by Anne Krueger has led her to conclude that "the difference in human resources between the United States and the less-developed countries accounts for more of the difference in *per capita* income than all other factors combined." See "Factor Endowments and *Per Capita* Income Differences Among Countries," *Economic Journal,* September 1968, p. 658.

3. See Lester C. Thurow, *Dangerous Currents: The State of Economics,* New York, 1983, pp. 178–179.

4. The advanced levels of literacy and numerical facility attained early in their development process appears an especially important cause of the high growth rates attained by some "late developers," such as Japan, South Korea, Taiwan, and Israel.

5. See Pan A. Yotopoulos and Jeffrey B. Nugent, *Economics of Development: Empirical Investigations,* New York, 1976 pp. 186–188; and *WDR 1980,* pp. 47–48.

6. George Psacharopoulos, *Returns to Education: An International Comparison,* Amsterdam, 1973, Table 8.4 (originally brought to my attention by Michael P. Todaro, *Economic Development in the Third World,* 1st ed., New York, 1977, p. 239). See also Psacharopoulos's "Returns to Education: An Updated International Comparison," *Comparative Education,* October 1981; "The Economics of Higher Education in Developing Countries," *Comparative Education Review,* June 1982; and "Education as an Investment," *Finance and Development* 19, no. 3 (1982):39–42.

7. See Yotopoulos and Nugent, *Economics of Development,* p. 195.

8. The formula here is from Psacharopoulos, "Education as an Investment," p. 40, as amended in *Finance and Development* 19, no. 4 (1982):49. A new volume that analyzes the issue is George Psacharopoulos and M. Woodhall, *Education for Development: Analysis of Investment Choices,* Oxford, 1985. T. W. Schultz of the United States won a Nobel Prize in economics in part because of work of this type.

9. *WDR 1980,* p. 48. A book-length study is D. T. Jamison and L. J. Lau, *Farmer Education and Farm Efficiency,* Baltimore, 1981.

10. Most of all in Africa, where teachers' salaries average two or three times higher as a percentage of national income than in Asia or Latin America. See Alain Mingat and George Psacharopoulos, "Financing Education in Sub-Saharan Africa," *Finance and Development* 22, no. 1 (March 1985):35–38.

11. The figures are from Richard Jolly, "Manpower and Education," in Dudley Seers and Leonard Joy, eds., *Development in a Divided World,* Harmondsworth, 1970, pp. 210–211.

12. See Psacharopoulos, *Returns to Education,* Table 8.2 (originally brought to my attention by Todaro, *Economic Development in the Third World,* 1st ed., p. 239).

13. See Emmanuel Jimenez, "The Public Subsidization of Education and Health in Developing Countries: A Review of Equity and Efficiency," *The World Bank Research Observer* 1, no. 1 (1986):118, 125, quoting work by Alain Mingat and J. P. Tan.

14. *WDR 1984,* p. 84.

15. For the literacy rates here and henceforth in this chapter, see *WDR 1983,* pp. 148–149. The standard employed in establishing these percentages is, however, quite low. A

higher standard cuts the percentages substantially, even in the developed countries. Jonathan Kozol in his book *Illiterate America,* New York, 1985, estimates that 60 million U.S. adults are unable to read and understand the Bill of Rights. (There were 171 million Americans over 18 in 1983.)

16. China and India raise the percentages, especially for primary school. The combined figure for these two countries is 96 percent.

17. See especially *WDR 1980,* p. 50; T. Paul Schultz, *Economics of Population,* Reading, Mass., 1981, pp. 117–119; and Constantina Safilios-Rothschild, "The Role of the Family in Development," *Finance and Development* 17, no. 4 (1980):44–47.

18. The data are from *WDR 1986,* p. 236, and are for 1983. Figures over 100 percent are possible because some people older than the relevant age group are in school.

19. *WDR 1980,* p. 47. Some of the figures here are from Todaro, *Economic Development in the Third World,* 2nd ed., pp. 293–294. The last sentence is from Gunnar Myrdal, "Need for Reforms in Underdeveloped Countries," in Sven Grassman and Erik Lundberg, eds., *The World Economic Order: Past and Prospects,* New York, 1981, p. 514.

20. Note that this disillusionment ceases to occur after UPE has been achieved for a number of years. School completion then becomes the norm rather than a special accomplishment. Hence the problem is worse for the poorer countries than it is for the more well-to-do among the LDCs.

21. See *The Economist,* May 25, 1985, p. 110.

22. Some countries, Brazil a notable example along with a number of skill-short oil exporters, have an especially *low* percentage in secondary education and hence a shortage of job applicants with this sort of training.

23. See Todaro, *Economic Development in the Third World,* 2nd ed., p. 41, quoting work by Edgar O. Edwards; and *WDR 1979,* p. 47.

24. From *The Economist,* August 25, 1979, p. 54. It is possible to take a more favorable view of the arts. They are much cheaper to teach than the sciences, so even though the benefits are lower, the *net* result may not be so bad, especially since women have historically been attracted to the arts, and the education of women gives such significant residual benefits. Also, in India's case even a small percentage educated in science and techology in time yields large absolute numbers. India's 2.4 million scientists and engineers (1984) form the largest pool of technical talent outside the United States and the USSR. See Walt W. Rostow, "Economic Growth and the Diffusion of Power," *Challenge* 29, no.4 (1986):30.

25. Compare Todaro, *Economic Development in the Third World,* 2nd ed., pp. 319–321.

26. See *WDR 1979,* p. 53; and *The Economist,* April 28, 1984.

27. Compare Todaro, *Economic Development in the Third World,* 2nd ed., p. 317, citing Philip H. Coombs.

28. From the work of Donald Keesing, quoted by David Morawetz, *Twenty-five Years of Economic Development 1950 to 1975,* Baltimore, 1977, p. 54.

29. See Todaro, *Economic Development in the Third World,* 2nd ed., pp. 308–310.

30. See *WDR 1980,* p. 50.

31. A book-length study is William Glaser, *The Brain Drain,* London, 1978. I also utilized *WDR 1983,* pp. 103–106, and *WDR 1984,* p. 102.

32. *WDR 1984,* p. 101.

33. *WDR 1984,* p. 102.

34. *Ibid.; The Economist,* August 18, 1979, p. 83; and articles in the press.

35. See Vinod B. Agarwal and Donald K. Winkler, "Foreign Demand for United States Higher Education: A Study of Developing Countries in the Eastern Hemisphere," *Economic Development and Cultural Change* 33, no. 3 (1985):623. Most students from abroad go to the United States and Britain. For example, recently 88 percent of Saudi

Arabia's students abroad were studying in the United States; 76 percent for India, and 69 percent for Nigeria.

36. *WDR 1983,* p. 105.

37. *Ibid.*

38. *Ibid.*

39. Compare Bruce Herrick and Charles P. Kindleberger, *Economic Development,* 4th ed., New York, 1983, p. 198, citing Don Patinkin and Harry Johnson in Walter Adams, ed., *The Brain Drain,* New York, 1968.

40. See Alan Smith, Christine Woesler de Panafieu, and Jean-Pierre Jarousse, "Foreign Student Flow and Policies in an International Perspective," and Mark Blaug, "The Economic Costs and Benefits of Overseas Students," both in Peter Williams, ed., *The Overseas Student Question,* London, 1981.

41. The assumptions in the calculation are that 90 percent of those who came stayed, that they earned the U.S. average for their occupation, and that the tax was a flat rate of 10 percent. See *WDR 1984,* p. 102.

42. For the history of this strategy, see Douglas Rimmer, "Basic Needs and the Origins of the Development Ethos," *Journal of Developing Areas* 15 (January 1981):215–238.

43. Compare Paul Streeten, "From Growth to Basic Needs," *Finance and Development* 16, no. 3 (1979):28–31; and the more extended discussion in Paul Streeten et al., *First Things First,* New York, 1981.

44. See David Colman and Frederick Nixson, *Economics of Change in Less Developed Countries,* Deddington, 1978, p. 169; and Streeten et al., *First Things First,* pp. 35–37.

45. Compare Amartya K. Sen, "Development: Which Way Now?" *Economic Journal* 93 (December 1983):753.

46. In this section I drew on *WDR 1980,* pp. 39–40, 53–58.

47. Halfdan Mahler, "People," *Scientific American* 243, no. 3 (September 1980):69.

48. See Morawetz, *Twenty-five Years of Economic Development,* p. 49; and *WDR 1980,* p. 74.

49. The statistics are for 1984, from *WDR 1986,* pp. 232–233. They combine infant mortality (age under 1) with child mortality (age 1–4). Ethiopia's figures total 211 for that year, but because of the famine conditions there they may well be an underestimate. Useful introductions to the problem are UNICEF, *State of the World's Children 1985,* New York, Dec. 1984; and William U. Chandler, "Investing in Children," Worldwatch Paper No. 64, June, 1985.

50. See *WDR 1980,* pp. 54, 56; *The Economist,* November 3, 1984; and Chandler, *Investing in Children,* pp. 21–22.

51. We saw in Chapter 8 that malaria, thought to be under control in the early 1970s, is making a comeback.

52. Sometimes, disappointingly, activities that promote economic growth can also bring an increase in diseases associated with water. Schistosomiasis (carried by snail-borne parasites and causing chronic debilitation) and onchocerciasis (more commonly called river blindness) have been spread by new dams and irrigation canals. The rise of schistosomiasis in Egypt and the Sudan is striking; it causes 1 in 5 deaths currently in Egypt and can rarely be cured in rural conditions. See Mahler, "People," p. 68; and Robert P. Ambroggi, "Water," *Scientific American* 243, no. 3 (September 1980):106.

53. *WDR 1986,* pp. 234–235. The figures are for 1981. China and India, with 48 doctors per 100,000 people, are excluded from the LDC average.

54. See Jimenez, "Public Subsidization of Education and Health," p. 120

55. These examples are taken from Mahler, "People," p. 73.

56. Jimenez, "Public Subsidization of Education and Health," p. 122. The fall was even greater, 20 percent, in Africa.

57. See Nevin S. Scrimshaw and Lance Taylor, "Food," *Scientific American* 243, no. 3 (September 1980):78–88; Thomas T. Poleman, "Quantifying the Nutrition Situation in Developing Countries," *Food Research Institute Studies* 18, no. 1 (1981):1–58; *WDR 1980,* pp. 39–40, 59–64, 89–90; and Morawetz, *Twenty-five Years of Economic Development,* pp. 44–47.

58. This is FAO data reported in Scrimshaw and Taylor, "Food," p. 80.

59. Precise estimates are difficult to make because of data weaknesses. The figures shown are from *WDR 1986,* p. 7.

60. Scrimshaw and Taylor, "Food," p. 81.

61. From the work of Alan Berg, reprinted in Gerald M. Meier, *Leading Issues in Economic Development,* 4th ed., Oxford, 1984, pp. 592, 595.

62. For the following policy analysis, see *WDR 1980,* pp. 45, 62–63; *WDR 1981,* p. 106; *WDR 1982,* pp. 86–87; *WDR 1986,* pp. 90–94; Alan Berg, "Improving Nutrition: the Bank's Experience," *Finance and Development,* 22, no. 2 (1985):32–35; and *Christian Science Monitor,* December 26, 1985.

63. Good work has, however, been done with these foods in several international research centers, including those of India, Colombia, and Nigeria.

64. See *WDR 1986,* p. 93. In that country only 1 calorie in 13 was going to the malnourished.

65. See Shlomo Reutlinger and Jack van Holst Pellekaan, *Ensuring Food Security in the Developing World: Issues and Options,* Washington, D.C., 1986, summarized in Reutlinger, "Food Security and Poverty in LDCs," *Finance and Development,* 22, no. 4 (1985):7–17; Sen, "Development: Which Way Now?" especially pp. 755, 757–760; and Michelle McAlpin, *Subject to Famine,* Princeton, N.J., 1983. There is a summary discussion in *WDR 1986,* pp. 7–9.

66. See *WDR 1982,* p. 89. There have been other famines where war, by causing a food shortage, has been the direct cause of the hunger. Examples include Biafra during the Nigerian civil war in the late 1960s and Kampuchea in the late 1970s.

67. A. K. Sen, *Poverty and Famines: An Essay on Entitlement and Deprivation,* Oxford, 1981.

68. In several works, Sen has called attention to the importance of political pressures in spurring governments to famine relief measures. See "Development: Which Way Now?" pp. 757–759, and the citations there. Such pressures are powerful in India, where no full-scale famines have occurred for many years. But the impulse is less easy to sustain against more mild hunger, which still persists. In China, where grass-roots politics was stifled during the Great Leap Forward, policy mistakes led to what scholars are now calling the greatest famine of modern times during the years 1959 to 1961. Policy problems in Colonel Mengistu's Ethiopia—food distribution not allowed in the rebellious northern provinces, prevention of stockpiling with antihoarding laws that also prohibit private road transport of food, a move toward state farms, a low price policy that discourages private production, and enforced resettlement of hungry refugees in the south—made Ethiopia's experience with famine in 1984 to 1985 worse than it had to be.

69. There is a review of international planning for famine relief by Barbara Huddleston et al., *International Finance for Food Security,* Baltimore, 1984; and see *WDR 1986* pp. 145–148. In the past it took far longer to mobilize large-scale food aid, five years in the case of the African Sahel during the drought of the late 1960s and early 1970s. See *WDR 1986,* p. 147.

70. *WDR 1986,* p. 147.

71. Chandler, *Investing in Children,* p. 41.

72. Compare Gerald M. Meier, *Emerging from Poverty,* New York, 1984 p. 164.

chapter 10

Rural Development

URBAN BIAS, RURAL NEGLECT

The 1970s saw a striking change in attitudes toward the rural areas of the LDCs. Twenty years before, the typical farmer was working by hand on a small plot, facing a hostile climate, with limited inputs of capital and elementary technologies that caused productivity to be very low. Farming was a neglected sector, except by the tax men, whom we last saw in Chapter 4 using their marketing boards and parastatals to tap this accessible source of government revenue. Official policy was usually marked by an urban bias, wherein funds, having been obtained in part through high taxes on farming, were funneled largely to manufacturing and "showcase" projects designed to benefit urban populations. Further reflecting the urban bias, food prices in the cities were held down by subsidies and strict price controls. The budget costs of the cheap food were minimized by enforcing low government procurement prices in rural areas.[1]

Agricultural prices depressed by only one-third through these policies would have been thought relatively generous to the rural sector. In many countries it was not at all uncommon to find farmers receiving prices 50 or even 75 percent below market-clearing levels.[2]

The favored manufacturing sector was frequently sheltered behind high tariff walls, thus raising the prices paid by rural residents for the goods it produced. The protectionist government policies caused a lower level of imports, thus lowering the demand for foreign currencies and causing an overvalued exchange rate. This in turn discouraged agricultural exports and encouraged the import of agricultural commodities. Food still makes up 20 percent or more of all imports in Algeria, Bangladesh, Burkina Faso, Egypt (30 percent!), Haiti, Nigeria, Somalia, Senegal, North Yemen, and several others;[3] government policy decisions are an important reason why. Countries confronted with high food import bills because of their urban bias frequently faced difficulties in finding enough foreign exchange for the industrial development that was taking precedence over agriculture in the first place.

The low-price policies in agriculture might seem highly irrational to a casual observer, but there were reasons much more understandable from the point of view of politicians. They listened to the dubious arguments that rural output is not very responsive to price change; arguments that proved to be incorrect.[4] They considered that high farm prices would chiefly benefit large farmers and hurt the low-income urban poor. They thought that growth required industrialization, which could be financed by taxing agriculture. But they also understood that the support and sympathy of the urban masses are a virtual requirement for staying in office. Concentrated populations when angry are far more troublesome than scattered peasants, and the capital is always urban. Farmers are usually rather inert politically, with poor communications among them and great difficulties in organizing them. They could in many instances be safely discriminated against. Large and influential farmers could be pacified by cheap credit for machines, fertilizer, wells, and the like. The small farmers who benefited little from these government programs thus lost their potential political leadership.

The results for many countries may have been politically acceptable. But the economic consequences were severe, sometimes even horrific. Three examples will make the point. Burma's attempts to keep rice prices low were devastating for production; its once great rice industry sank into a shambles. Ghana's government used a mixture of high taxes on cocoa producers, through its marketing board, and price controls on food to the point where incentives collapsed. So did production. A proportion of what *was* produced disappeared over the border into the Ivory Coast, where prices (3 to 5 times higher, 1980 to 1982) *did* encourage production, or into the thriving black market outside the price control system. These cases were treated in detail in Chapter 4.[5] Similarly, Sri Lanka's production of tea, rubber, and coconuts was dislocated by taxes (averaging more than 50 percent on tea in the late 1970s) that curtailed the export of these commodities. In all cases, an unwanted repercussion was to penalize manufacturing industry, which found its potential domestic markets reduced in size because of stagnation in the countryside. All three countries eventually implemented urgent programs to rectify the perverse incentives, Sri Lanka in the late 1970s, Burma and Ghana in the 1980s. But the shift of government attitudes back toward an emphasis on rural development was initially slow.

In the 1960s came the realization that neglect of agriculture was likely to cause a balance problem, with industrial growth curtailed by slow growth in farming. In the 1970s optimism increased that rural areas, including agriculture but also other rural activities, could provide an economic stimulus toward growth and could even be a "leading sector." Presently, the pendulum has swung very far, with international agencies now giving special attention to rural development;

Table 10.1   AGRICULTURAL GROWTH AND GDP GROWTH IN THE 1970S (BY
             NUMBER OF COUNTRIES)

	GDP growth		
Agricultural growth	Above 5 percent	3–5 percent	Below 3 percent
Above 3 percent	17	5	3
Below 1 percent	2	1	11

Source: WDR 1982, p. 45.

grants for academic research in LDCs now going overwhelmingly for the endeavor; and firm knowledge that few countries have achieved satisfactory overall growth without developing their rural areas.[6] The last statement is supported by World Bank analysis of a 56-country sample, which shows GDP growth closely correlated with agricultural growth during the 1970s. Table 10.1 shows the result.[7]

From the perspective of the 1980s it is not easy to see why there was a spirit of confrontation between agriculture and industry for so long. The idea that a growing manufacturing sector could generate sufficient exports to pay for a large portion of a country's food imports was extremely optimistic to say the least, as often the industries involved had to be protected by tariffs for a long period of time (many still are, as will be seen in Chapters 13 and 14). This implies that the domestic market had to be depended on for growth; if so, then higher incomes in agriculture would serve to enlarge that market.

There also seemed little realization that promoting domestic sources of food might give greater stability of supply, both because bad crop years for overseas exporters might not be bad years at home and because food shipments can be a means for applying political pressure. Some LDCs would not appear to have a comparative advantage in the production of foodstuffs, and as their manufacturing or natural resource output (and population) increase, it would be sensible for them to import more food, paid for by exports. But many other LDCs would seem to have a comparative advantage in producing some foods, and in a fair number of them their governments have employed policies that discourage rural development. For them, the antagonistic policies plus rapid population growth and occasional crop failures force food imports. These imports, running at $21 billion for the LDCs as a whole in 1984, are an expensive burden waiting to be lifted.

It is also difficult to understand the confrontation for reasons of employment. A calculation of the potential for employment in manufacturing takes only a moment and is instructive.[8] Say the labor force is 1,000 workers, and labor-force growth is 3 percent per year, a fairly common figure in the LDCs. Thus the number of workers to be absorbed every year is 30. Given that the manufacturing sector employs about 20 percent of all labor on average (and therefore 200 workers in our example), it would have to absorb 30/200, or 15 percent more labor every year. Labor-force growth in manufacturing at 15 percent per year is an exceptional rate, sometimes attained by some countries, but certainly not by very many. Worse, there is unemployment and underemployment to consider, the two together often a quarter of the whole labor force. To provide jobs for the new entrants *plus* absorbing the un- and underemployed, during say a 10-year period, would mean a rise in industrial employment of almost 30 percent per year, beyond any historical record. It is hardly surprising, therefore, that attention came once again to be directed to agriculture with its demonstrated ability to absorb labor and provide that labor with income. (Do note that this is not the same thing as saying development can proceed easily via agriculture alone. Neither the capacity of the rural sector to absorb labor nor the market for agricultural commodities is usually large enough to allow major long-term development without a significant shift to nonfarm activities.)[9]

RURAL REFORM

We have already discussed the "pull" of urban areas involving the dualism of labor markets. Large wage differences promoted by government legislation and custom have become the main magnet of rural-urban migration. Rural development of agriculture and other activities can be seen as a way to lessen the "push" out of the countryside, thus offsetting the urban "pull."

The numbers involved are huge, and the record of growth disappointing. In the low-income LDCs 71 percent of the 1984 labor force was still in agriculture. The average annual growth rate of population from 1973 to 1984 of 2.6 percent in those years was outstripping the average annual growth rate of agricultural output of 2.4 percent. This rate itself was significantly lower than the 2.7 percent registered from 1960 to 1970. The record is better in the middle-income countries, with 44 percent of their labor in farming, and agricultural output growing faster (at 2.7 percent 1970–84) than population (2.4 percent). Here, too, agricultural production in the previous decade had been increasing faster (3.4 percent per year).[10]

The sheer size of agriculture means that any push out of that sector involves large numbers. Diminishing the push by making agriculture more attractive means raising farm productivity. That in turn is usually thought to mean extensive and thorough reform in the areas of land tenure, farm size, and debt and credit (all discussed in the sections that follow), as well as technological change in agricultural production, which is taken up later in the chapter.[11] Using labor in rural areas but outside of agriculture is another possibility (discussed at the end of the chapter).

Land Tenure

Communal land tenure, where ownership is vested in a village or local ethnic group, is generally thought to inhibit productivity increases. When land is held completely in common, the people who work it often have an attitude of "Take out of it what you can get, put in as little as you can." This was seen historically in the overgrazing of the common in Great Britain. It is seen today in the exploitation of the ocean fisheries. To be sure, much depends on the strength of the community holding that land and the alternative types of private ownership that may succeed the communal tenure. In the Andes countries of Latin America, the large, poorly managed private estates that succeeded the precolonial Indian communal holdings were not obviously more productive.

Similar negative circumstances for productivity occur when farm plots are privately managed, but are shifted about from time to time. (The Russian *mir* system operated this way until the twentieth century.) Since the farmer will not be using the same plot of land the following year, there is an incentive to fertilize inadequately and to skimp on upkeep. Fortunately for farm productivity, economic growth has tended to break down communal land tenure patterns and the practice of shifting cultivation. They still exist, especially in the poorest LDCs, but they are much diminished in number compared to 30 years ago.[12]

Land tenure also involves the question of tenancy arrangements. Some such arrangements can be seriously detrimental to agricultural improvement. A noteworthy case is that of high marginal rents, rising as production rises, with the landlord under no obligation to participate in capital formation or land improvement. Here the tenant's incentive to increase output is diminished to the extent that part of the gain must be paid over to the landlord.

Landlord behavior is not nearly so detrimental when marginal rent is low, there then being an incentive to land improvement. Even high (average) rents appear in a more favorable light when landlords have a high propensity to save and then use these savings for land improvement and capital formation. Historically, this resembles the situation in Japan and England. In India landlords frequently provide production loans to sharecropper tenants, share in the cost of seed and fertilizer, participate in decision making, and take significant interest in productive investment. Similar findings that tenancy is not necessarily less efficient than owner cultivation have been reported by M. Ahmad for Pakistan, Vernon Ruttan and Y. Huang for Malaysia, and S. N. Cheung for prerevolutionary China. In Pakistan, "landlords in general specify contract terms that encourage sharecroppers to adopt new techniques of production."[13] Alas, there are many other cases, especially in Latin America, where landlord behavior was far less beneficial for growth, the land viewed as conferring social status and political power of a semifeudal nature, the landlord a rentier and a usurious one at that, making little effort on improvement.[14] It is not always easy in these cases to distinguish between the effects of tenancy per se and the monopoly element in landlord behavior, as when large estates are the only sellers of land and the only buyers of labor. Some recent efforts at land reform (Ecuador, Sri Lanka) have focused on this issue and have taken the form of fixing rents and establishing security of tenure.

A last, potentially serious problem of tenure is that of inheritance. Where farms are not passed on intact to one heir, as in English primogeniture, they may be split among numerous heirs, resulting in small or dispersed landholdings. The Koran, for example, mandates for Muslims an equal sharing of land among heirs. The resulting small plots may cause special diseconomies, such as having to bicycle from plot to plot, move tools among them, and the like. (In some parts of Sri Lanka this reached the point of time-sharing among heirs, who farm the plots in alternate years.) Agreement among the heirs or merger and consolidation through land purchase can often rectify the damage, but not always, with resulting problems of productivity.

Farm Size

The issue of farm size is another area of land reform. It is clear that in some countries farms are too large for maximum efficiency and that these large estates, if broken up into smaller more productive units, would achieve higher levels of output. On the other hand, there are farms which, if combined to give a larger average size per unit, would lead to higher productivity. It is not unknown to find areas even in the same country, in some of which the economist would prescribe amalgamation of plots and in others the breaking up of the great estates.[15]

Often the issue of size is overshadowed by that of income distribution. Whether or not a large farm is the most efficient economically becomes rather submerged when one realizes that in India 12 percent of rural families control one-half the cultivated land or that in Brazil 10 percent control three-quarters of the farming area. The sociopolitical aspects are most marked in Latin America, where latifundia (large estates) are common. Here, as late as the 1950s, the 1.5 percent of all farms that were over 1,000 hectares in size made up 64.9 percent of the farmed area. The counterpart to this figure is the existence of minifundia —in Peru 88 percent of the farms made up only 7.4 percent of the land, in Guatemala 88.4 percent made up just 14.3 percent of the land, and in Ecuador 89.9 percent made up 16.6 percent.[16] The often-heard litany of a stratified society with no opportunity for peasants to improve themselves, limited capital investment in farming, and the political power of large landowners with a vested interest in things as they are is all too familiar. There has been improvement in a good many countries on this score, but the problems are still considerable. In numerous nations it is still fair to say that the single greatest cause of unequal income distribution is the unequal structure of land ownership.[17]

Large farms are usually not appropriate where labor is plentiful and land is scarce; here it is more economical to maximize the output of the scarce factor, land, by aiming for the greatest possible yield per acre. Small farms certainly do use more labor per unit of land than do large ones. Recent figures from Colombia, for example, show farms of less than 3 hectares using 20 times more labor per hectare than do farms of 50 to 500 hectares.[18] Labor, when lavishly applied to a given unit of land, means more care in land preparation, individual attention to the seedling (including transplanting from seedbeds) and growing plant, and special care in harvesting. Other things equal, output per acre is higher than in mechanized, large-scale farming.

Often the large farm is not a family farm and must utilize hired labor. Without any responsibility and reward of ownership, the work may be both less intense and less careful.[19]

Finally, the larger the farm the more managerial skill is required. If such skills are in short supply in the LDCs, then this represents a disadvantage for farms of great size.[20] It should be added that a land reform that breaks up large holdings, but leaves the new owners without access to credit, technical advice, and reasonable transport, is unlikely to achieve much.

Large farms are more appropriate, however, under different conditions. Where labor is the scarce factor, a more capital-intensive kind of farming is in order. Mechanization of agriculture, irrigation facilities, storage, and so forth may well not be economic on small-size farms. Either amalgamation of small plots or a carefully managed cooperative approach with joint participation will then be necessary.

Mechanization in particular is a problem when farms are small in scale.[21] Machines often cannot be reduced below some minimum size and still perform the required tasks. If irrigation is needed, the tube well must be deep enough to reach the water table and the pump powerful enough to lift the water. Some farm machines cannot be scaled down any further (combine-harvesters, several sorts of picking machinery, tractors powerful enough to break soil with heavy crusts). Used on small-scale farms, they would be both clumsy (turning circle too large) and employed too little of the time to justify the capital outlay. Even a central depot with machines owned by the government or cooperatively is no perfect solution, because by its nature farming demands inputs of machinery during certain fairly short peak periods. Thus the Soviet Union's centralized "machine tractor stations" of Stalin's day were a partial failure. Their machinery was eventually distributed to the collective farms because of the competing demands on the machines at planting and at harvest.

Note that the problem of mechanization is also a reflection of existing technological dualism. Until recently farm machinery has almost always been intended as labor-saving. Only within the past few years have certain countries, Japan and Taiwan especially, pioneered the development of cheap mechanized implements, such as garden tractors and tillers, designed to raise productivity in a labor-intensive setting, increasing output without saving labor. These small machines are making a substantial contribution, though the great oil price increases slowed their continued spread in poor countries.

Another aspect of mechanization is that a good many locations are surprisingly ill-suited to it, even where plenty of land is available. Tropical areas with heavy jungle cover are often highly susceptible to "leaching" when the jungle is cut away and the land is put to farming. Leaching is the process whereby heavy rainfall seeping through the soil removes essential mineral content, leaving a poor and unproductive soil in stark contrast to the previous lush jungle growth. The problem is known right across tropical East and West Africa, northern South America, Central America, and Southeast Asia.

Storage and marketing are further problems when farming units are small.[22] For example, drying equipment is sometimes required, and is uneconomical below some minimum size. Collection and marketing of produce will be an extra burden where farms proliferate and may necessitate cooperative or state marketing or the presence of a competitive system of middlemen. Inputs in small quantities often cost more per unit because transactions costs are high; here again unless there is cooperative bulk buying and heavy competition among middlemen, the cost penalty may be difficult to tolerate. (The middleman often comes in for undeserved criticism in the LDCs. His fees are often thought to represent exploitation when instead they may represent a competitive charge for services made necessary because farm size is small. In spite of fervent beliefs to the contrary, there is little evidence of middleman monopoly in the LDCs.)

Finally, small farmers cannot afford to spend as much on investigating and adopting new techniques; and their smaller resources mean that when shortages of seed, fertilizer, and water strike, they will have less influence on suppliers than large farmers will. In all these cases an efficient market for credit will be needed, as the high fixed costs for small farmers will have to be met with borrowed funds. The rural credit market is, however, often constrained, as discussed in the next section.

Whatever the disadvantages, the weight of the evidence now indicates that the quality of labor advantage on small farms will in many circumstances offset the obstacles.[23]

Rural Credit

Credit is a major issue in poor-country agriculture, in some ways the most important. The problem is simple enough to explain. Income is low, so to cover production expenses and any other cash outlay the demand for loans will be high. Financial capital of all kinds is scarce, with the opportunity cost of funds thus increased. The scarcity of funds may have a marked seasonality, as when farmers must borrow even for next year's seed grain or, as in India, when small holders must rent draft animals and plows. At the same time any extraordinary expense not connected with production (such as marriages and funerals) may also mean more borrowing, and commonly a third or even more of all loans in rural areas are for social rather than productive purposes.[24] Interest rates will reflect a premium for the trouble of administering small loans, and, indeed, a little cash for a few chickens, a new spade, or some seed and fertilizer is often the sort of loan most lacking and most useful to small farmers.[25] There will be a risk premium as well, for several reasons. High default rates of nearly 10 percent are not exceptional: Approximately 25 percent of all loan payments were overdue in a recent 35-country study by U Tun Wai;[26] and collateral is often inadequate. Finally, unless the lenders are local, assessing the degree of risk in lending to farmer X or Y or Z out in the countryside will be difficult.

As a result of these risks, regular commercial banks may avoid rural areas and rural credit. Indeed, in most LDCs noninstitutional sources of rural credit are actually more important than institutional ones. U Tan Wai states that noninstitutional rural credit is 72 percent of the whole in Africa, 72 percent in Asia, 63 percent in the Middle East, and 15 percent in Latin America.[27]

There are exceptions, such as the Philippines and Brazil, where banks predominate in supplying rural credit. Both countries have actually overdone it. In the Philippines rural banks overlent and have generally had to curtail their activity because of their nonperforming loans. In Brazil the large, privately owned

Bank of Brazil was until 1984 empowered by government to create agricultural loans at a fixed interest rate whenever farmers wanted them, which assuredly they did whenever market interest rates generally rose above the Bank's fixed rate![28]

The noninstitutional credit comes mainly from a varied group of professional village moneylenders, traders, pawnbrokers, shopkeepers, landlords, relatives, and friends. In 22 countries surveyed by U Tun Wai, the mean rate of interest on noninstitutional loans was about 40 percent, the median 30 percent.[29] Though these are unadjusted for inflation, they still imply very high real rates. Usually the highest levels are found in Africa, the lowest in the Middle East. Exceptionally steep rates are reported from time to time: 50, 60, or 70 percent, even in countries not suffering from a hyperinflation and occasionally they are higher yet: 200, 300, or even 500 percent per annum have been reported (rarely) in countries with relatively moderate inflation.

There are several repercussions. The large need for credit and its high expense may mean little opportunity for productive investment in farming. Often one hears that farmers are conservative, reactionary, even stupid, unwilling to buy the fertilizer or insecticide or new seed variety that could double their output in a year. How different it all looks when their indebtedness is considered! The reluctance to adopt new methods may be wholly rational if these new methods mean going yet further into debt at very high rates of interest.

The reaction against high interest rates has frequently been a government attack on the moneylenders either by prohibiting their operations or through passage of anti-usury laws establishing maximum permissible interest rates. Such laws have wide popular support. The result often seems to come as a surprise to politicians, but it is highly predictable. The supply of loanable funds available to farmers is reduced, the more drastically the more draconian are the laws. This makes the moneylenders even more unpopular, of course, but what are they to do? Often farmers cannot legally pledge their land or livestock as collateral for a loan, nor can they pledge their crops before harvesting them.[30] (These laws were intended to "protect the farmer.") The result is even less credit available in the agricultural sector, as moneylenders turn to other alternatives for their funds— city property, trucking firms, all the other uses for ready money that are so apparent in the LDCs.

Thus the shortage of credit in agriculture is one of the most persistent problems in development economics.[31] How can it be solved? Commercial banking is an unlikely source of funds because the bankers' knowledge of the risks involved will often be inadequate; they will face some of the serious assessment difficulties referred to earlier.[32] It is possible for government to establish regional rural banks to tap rural saving, especially hoarded currency, and plow it back. India has done so. But such banks are high in cost; each individual's balance is small, there is much traffic in the accounts, and "mobile units" traveling from place to place are expensive. Still, in return for their high expense, they are a way to get some credit to marginal farmers and landless laborers. Another possibility is to establish local credit targets for banks. In Thailand's poor northeast, 60 percent of local deposits must be used for local loans, and 20 percent of deposits for loans in agriculture. This may work to provide more funds if the banks are otherwise profitable enough to stand the costs, but it may, of course, discourage banks from opening at all in disadvantaged rural areas. Even at best, banks will probably charge their other borrowers more to make up for the costs, or pay depositors a lower interest rate, or both.[33] (It is also possible, even probable, that the policy will not be very effective; banks often find ways to circumvent the requirements.) India has followed the path of credit controls on a very large scale in its now-nationalized industry, requiring banks to meet a lending target in the rural sector (16 percent by 1985). Here the credit so provided is the equivalent of a government subsidy. Frequently such subsidies have been tied to particular crops, or to machinery purchases. Neither course is usually very sensible; the first runs the risk of artificially distorting cropping patterns, while the second gives a damaging boost to displacement of rural labor.[34]

One innovation has brought a major improvement. The rural cooperative credit society, with farmers making up the membership, can lower substantially the administrative costs of assessing risks. Where each farmer knows the next, the risks are more clearly evident, and the knowledge so obtained can keep interest rates down. Cooperative credit arrangements are rapidly gaining ground almost everywhere, but particularly in Asia and the Middle East.

Problems remain. The co-op is perhaps a good method of *distributing* funds. It can also obtain discounts in the bulk buying of seed, fertilizer, and pesticides, as well as cutting costs by arranging for local processing and marketing. But it does not automatically generate *new* funds. If credit is to come from outside farming itself, this must involve guarantees to commercial banks loaning to co-ops or funds from the government itself. Noteworthy attempts to fill the gap include Thailand's government credit scheme to reduce interest rates in the farm sector by 40 percent; the combination of land reform with credit availability in Egypt, South Korea, and Taiwan; the provision of combined credit and technical assistance in Brazil's *Operação Tatu;* Kenya's small farmer credit program; and India's Small Farmer Development Agency.[35] In India, between the 1950s and the 1970s, funds flowing through the new co-ops rose from 3 percent to 23 percent of all rural credit, the counterpart of which was a decline in village moneylender credit from about 75 percent to 50 percent of the whole.[36] *After* farm income has started to rise significantly, but not before, co-op banks can lend the savings of members to other members, so reducing the credit problem.[37]

These bright spots are only that, however. The lack of funds in farming remains a notorious obstacle to rural development. Interest rate ceilings staunch the flow of savings to agriculture; requirements for low-cost loans discourage private institutions from participation because they cannot cover their costs. Development banks lend to manufacturing enterprise more than to agriculture, and even the funds that are available are often distributed very unevenly. Applications for small loans (and banks commonly consider even $20,000 to be small) may receive unsympathetic treatment because of alleged high administrative costs.[38] The World Bank reports that subsidized loans rarely reach more than 25 percent of all farmers and that these are usually the larger farmers inclined toward mechanization. (Chile, Colombia, and Mexico are singled out as cases in point.) The smaller the farm, the less chance that credit will be available to the farmer, who thus must do without the high yield seeds, the fertilizer, the pumps, and the pesticides that could transform small-scale agriculture.[39]

An attack on this problem has been mounted by the innovative International Fund for Agricultural Development (IFAD), established in 1977 and jointly financed by the developed countries and OPEC in about a 60-40 split of the costs. IFAD spent some $500 million per year from 1982 to 1984, mostly on loans of modest amounts to peasants with small holdings. The money buys tools or allows loans without collateral to landless laborers for the setting up of a tiny business. IFAD has also found ways to channel loans to rural women, who ordinarily have little access to credit. This small agency (employing only about a hundred professionals) brings credit to villages that have never seen any except from the village moneylender, can boast a spectacular 37 percent average rate of return on its projects, and has a 95 percent rate of full repayment by borrowers. It is an effort long overdue but the agency almost collapsed in 1985–86 when the U.S. challenged the allocation of funding, demanding a 50-50 split with OPEC and a big cut in the U.S. contribution. IFAD was saved after a year and a half of limbo; the 60-40 split was continued and the budget was restored.[40] But it was alarming to realize how close it had come to shutting down. Perhaps a long-term solution to the budget problems of this extremely useful agency would be to allow it to raise funds on world capital markets, as does the World Bank. Needless to say, even IFAD is not likely to be of much help, nor any other rural credit measures, in the countries that still maintain an urban bias of very heavy taxation of the agricultural sector.

AGRICULTURAL RESEARCH: THE GREEN REVOLUTION

Research had a greater impact on agriculture in the 1970s than in any previous decade of this century. The development of new varieties of plants promised such an increase in yields that the term Green Revolution came to be used. The rapid adoption of these crops by third world farmers was a body blow to those who argue that farmers are innately and irrationally conservative and unwilling to change.

For a long period after World War II, however, the results of agricultural research were disappointing. Funds were scarce; Asian and Latin American LDCs were commonly spending on research only 0.1 to 0.8 percent of the value of their agricultural commodities, as opposed to the 2 to 3 percent of Australia, Israel, or the United States.[41] The research that did go on was usually directed to cash crops, often those destined for export, rather than to the crops grown for local consumption. (For example, there was historically little research on the yams, cassava, and other tubers that are staples in Africa, or on the deep-water rice of the Ganges or Mekong delta, or on the beans, lentils, and peas so important for Indian nutrition. Research on improving their yields and making them hardier and more drought resistant would have paid social dividends.)

Often the economics of a crop as opposed to the technical side received too little attention. Much research was focused on West African cotton cultivation even though events showed other crops were economically superior. Shifting cultivation (moving a field every few years, burning off the new plot, leaving the old to a long fallow) was condemned by the experts as technically wasteful, but economists later showed that shifting "slash and burn" techniques may well make sense where labor is scarce and land abundant, as indeed was true in much of Africa where the practice was most used. (Rapid population growth is ending the rationality of long fallow periods over most of its old range.) Too much attention to plants sometimes meant not enough for cheap water catchments, mini-ponds, or terracing in drought-prone regions.

Among the experts there was often a bias toward working with men, instead of with the women who so often have a major role (up to 80 percent in parts of Africa) in the production of food crops. Simple improvements in buckets and the rigging of wells (for women often fetch the water) or in the design of simple wood stoves (for they also fetch the fuel) would free up time, lessen drudgery, and improve the quality of life. Garden projects for vegetables could improve health and provide some income. Tree planting of nitrogen-fixing acacia could in dry climates bring both higher garden yields and some welcome shade. Projects of this type were much neglected until recently. There was a further bias against working with nomadic pastoralists, with the result that population growth among both people and livestock brought overgrazing and consequent unfavorable effects on soils.

The research often concentrated on capital-using techniques, such as mechanized farming, and tended not to emphasize the problems that arose when farming was on a small scale. Sometimes the suggested "improvements" strained managerial ability, as in the many plans for mixed farming with its combination of cropping and animal husbandry. The animals would provide meat and milk, motive power for plowing, and manure for fertilizer. But with education and literacy lacking, inadequate capacity for informed decision making became an obstacle.

Another of the difficulties was how to disseminate information to producers. The original idea of the demonstration plot often proved inadequate to the task.[42] Farmers suspected an economic barrier. The plots seemed to promote high yields rather than high profits, and many an illiterate peasant appreciated the difference (the highest yields will, of course, involve diminishing returns to factor inputs). Needless to say, this economic barrier became even more impenetrable in countries with official low-price policies in agriculture. Farmers also realized they could not operate on the research station's technical plane. They saw excellent land, fine buildings, a first-class irrigation system, special attention to the plots, printed instruction leaflets, and experts whose interests were more with agronomy than economy. Understandably, they ended up ignoring the new techniques as irrelevant to their own circumstances. Meanwhile, the extension workers sent out from the research stations were too often poorly trained and supervised. Sometimes they had numerous other duties to perform, such as collecting production statistics or even census data. Often there was no provision for feedback from farmers to fieldworkers to the agronomists at the stations.[43]

The greatest of all the problems was the combination of risk and low income. The risks in farming are high anyway. Even in the developed world, a change in the weather can have a devastating effect. Add to that the little-studied plant diseases of the LDCs, the pests, and the intensity of weather changes (monsoon failures or floods, African droughts of long duration). Then add the narrowness of markets caused by poor transport and limited storage. Finally, consider an income so low that a mistake might put the farm family below the subsistence level. There emerges an understandable reluctance to adopt new techniques or to specialize completely in crops for the market. Safety first makes sense.[44]

New varieties of trees, shrubs, or plants, although reported to be higher yielding, may in the farmer's mind be untested for risk. One crop failure might not ruin an American or an Australian, but with no cash reserves that risk may be unbearable in Bangladesh or Ghana or Paraguay. If a cocoa tree or coffee bush takes more than a year to bear fruit, replanting with new, more productive strains results in a loss in income for a year or two that may be unsupportable. Finally, risk of crop failure plus a narrow market means farmers have good reason not to specialize in cash cropping. All over the underdeveloped world, farmers continue to grow a large portion of their own food alongside crops for sale on the market (including for export) and often do *not* plant the cash crop at the time that would give it maximum yield. In Nigeria's north, for example, farmers would plant long-maturing seed four weeks late, reducing yields by a third as compared to planting on the "best" date, in order to make time to put in their subsistence crops.[45] As long as high risks and low income exist side-by-side, there is a strong motive against complete specialization. Research *could* focus on cash crops with less than a maximum yield, but a shorter growing season. It *could* search for fertilizers that in small doses give a significant return and aid in minimizing risk. But ordinarily it has not.

Reluctance to innovate and adopt new varieties is sometimes linked to tradition and conservative tastes. New methods may violate some social custom, as with the introduction of higher-yielding, hardier rice in Nepal. The rice would seem to have been an improvement in every way, but because it clung tenaciously to the stalk it required a new threshing process. The old threshing process, however, had both social and religious significance to Nepalese farmers. "Easily overcome," the foreigner might say, but how easy is it to change the Christian's scruples against bigamy or the Muslim's against eating pork?

New methods may also involve subsidiary technology that leads to complications. Such was the case with the steel plow in several widely separated places in Africa and Asia. The plow was much more efficient than the wooden plows and "crooked sticks" that it was intended to replace. But it also required two hands to control it, and farmers from time immemorial had been trained in using one hand to guide the bullock! A new method might also render a major tool obsolete, with no easy way to obtain replacements, as when advisors in Africa recommended planting close together, with the result that the old hoes were too wide for the gaps between the plants. "Perverse conservatism" thus can have an underlying layer of rationality, to which the agricultural researcher should be ever-alert.

Finally, new, cheaper, and more nutritious food varieties have sometimes been rejected by farmers because of their "taste." African farmers cling to their favored but high-cost yam, East Asians to the taste of their old lower-yield rice, and such tastes can be slow to change. Westerners should hardly be surprised, one supposes. The tomato was considered inedible by Europeans for over two centuries after the plant was introduced from the Americas!

The Green Revolution and the HYVs

The early failures of agricultural research should not be forgotten, nor should it be believed that the problems just discussed have been overcome. Research into high-yield variety plants (HYVs) has, however, led to two spectacular break-throughs in recent years, leading to such an increase in yields that the term "Green Revolution" came to be applied. The revolution has not proved to be an agricultural panacea, has certainly caused some unanticipated difficulties, and was for a time in danger of falling victim to the "OPEC Revolution." But the new technical discoveries and their rapid adoption by farmers are a most encouraging aspect of modern development economics, especially since the response of farmers to the new technology belies the claim of "innate, stultifying conservatism" in agriculture.[46]

The story starts with the formation at Los Baños, near Manila in the Philippines, of the International Rice Research Institute. The IRRI, which dates from 1960, was a joint project of the Rockefeller and Ford foundations. For several years its pioneering work on new, higher-yield rice went unsung. It was looking for a hybrid variety with several attributes. Early maturation was desirable, so farmers could obtain two or three crops instead of one or two. More crucial, the new hybrid should be a sturdy plant with a short stalk, to bear a greater weight of rice. The old rice was thin and tall. With large applications of fertilizer and ample irrigation, the rice on the end of the stalk grew so heavy that the plant would dip down into the water with disastrous results.

The solution came after lengthy trials, their length emphasized by the name of the hybrid that resulted. At the IRRI, the eighth cross, in the 288th row, plant number three (and hence IR-8-288-3) was a hybrid, produced by Hank Beachell of Beaumont, Texas, from an Indonesian parent variety called peta and a Taiwanese rice named dee go woo gen.[47] The first HYV, it was released in 1966 with outstanding, even astounding, results. With proper application of water and fertilizer, yields were greater by a factor of three to as much as eight. In Sri Lanka rice yields rose three to four times. In Pakistan the first experiments showed the old rice yielding 1,500 pounds per acre at best, while IR-8 yielded just under 10,000 pounds, a six-fold increase. In India four-fold increases were commonplace. In Japan it has given 16,000 pounds per acre compared to an average of 2,000 pounds for old rice. The effect on production and exports was rapid. Colombia's rice harvest went from 700,000 tons to 1.5 million tons within four to five years after the introduction of IR-8. The Philippines became a major exporter, shipping rice abroad in 1967 for the first time since 1903. Indonesia became self-sufficient in 1984. China shifted from being a major importer to surplus production in the 1980s, HYV rice grown on 80 percent of its cultivated land. By 1976 farmer income from rice in the LDCs had been boosted some $2.6 billion; nowadays the boost is perhaps $5 to $7 billion annually with IR-8 and its improved descendant IR-20. It represents an enormous return on the IRRI's $15 million annual budget, which (in 1984) funded the employment of just 44 senior scientists.

The second of the HYVs was wheat. The Rockefeller-funded International Maize and Wheat Improvement Center (known by an acronym of its Spanish name, CIMMYT[48]) is located at El Batan Mexico. Here Dr. Norman Borlaug of Iowa State University won the Nobel Peace Prize in 1970 for his work with strains of Mexican short-stemmed wheat which, like the rice discussed above, does not bend over after large applications of fertilizer. The research was originally intended to apply to Mexico, but the Norvin 10 dwarfing genes imported from Japan via the United States proved to be hardy on several continents. Under Indian conditions some varieties of the HYV wheat give 2.5 to 3 tons per acre as against the Indian average of 800 pounds per acre for older strains. India imported 18,000 tons of it for seed in 1966, in what has been called a breakthrough in courage as well as in research. The rust disease attacks of the early 1970s were overcome; with more than three-quarters of its wheat acreage now planted in the new varieties, India became self-sufficient in wheat where a short time before it had been the world's second largest importer.

Farmer response was impressive, fueled by the profits to be earned from planting the new seed. In Pakistan and Turkey, for example, wheat output has been growing at 8 percent a year or more, far faster than the rate of population growth. Pakistani farmers found their wheat yields up by 90 percent between 1965 and 1980, following 15 earlier years of declining yields.[49] The total world estimate for the planting of the new wheat varieties was 200 acres in 1965, 31 million acres in 1968, and 50.5 million acres in 1971. By 1980 HYV wheat made up 70 percent of India's acreage, and the figure had reached 82 percent in Pakistan.[50] Old cropping customs were broken rapidly. In India there was some theft of the new seeds, an 11-fold increase in fertilizer use (since 1960), and a highly appropriate comment from the agricultural minister, Dr. Subramaniam, that the allegedly tradition-bound Indian farmer had shown himself responsive to change.[51]

With both rice and wheat, there has been a darker side to the revolution. The new crops require careful and heavy use of fertilizer. Illiteracy is thus a handicap, and cost an even greater one. On the macro level, India was already using 20 percent of its foreign exchange reserves for fertilizer imports even *before* OPEC burst on the scene (the manufacture of artificial fertilizer requires large inputs of petroleum). The problem is exacerbated for India because about half of its natural fertilizer—manure—is dried and used for fuel. Fertilizer is the largest single import item for Turkey (and its HYV wheat) and for many other countries as well, especially in Southeast Asia where fertilizer use grew more than 6 times between 1966 and 1982. OPEC also enters the picture with water, pesticides, and herbicides. The water must often be drawn from tube wells in pumps that run on gasoline or diesel fuel. Some paddy varieties of rice are vulnerable to insects so pesticides are a requirement for high yields. But these in turn are frequently petroleum-based, taking as much as a gallon of gasoline per pound of pesticide. OPEC's rapid and repeated price rises for oil were thus blows to third world agricultural output.

The wheat revolution has actually been more successful than that in rice. The spread of the new rice has been slowed by the special need for water as an input. Only 25 to 30 percent of world rice production is irrigated, meaning that much rice farming has been unable to utilize the new technique. There must not, however, be too much water either. The combination of possible flood and drought explains why only about 40 percent of South and Southeast Asia's rice acreage is presently planted with IR-8 and its descendants. Acreage can now expand with far less rapidity unless massive irrigation projects are completed. The unsuitability of much acreage for the new rice explains why, in Asia, its growth in production has recently slowed to under 3 percent a year. Another problem with IR-8, which was originally thought good for any area of the tropics, is that local miniclimates, insect pests, plant viruses and other diseases, and soil conditions lead to variable yields. Locally specific research proved necessary, and the greatest gains have come when there was enough such research to screen the available varieties, determine where they would do best, and push further breeding efforts to find varieties even better suited to the local conditions. Thus IR-8's most widely-used successor, IR-20, has many variants.

At the IRRI in the Philippines 5,000 to 6,000 crosses each year are presently being made in the search for an acceptable HYV dry rice. Other work pursues a faster maturing rice, such as the IR-50 that is ready for harvest 20 to 25 days earlier than IR-8 and thus gives hope of possibly attaining four crops per year in some areas. In addition, since consumers have not been overly pleased with the chalky taste of the new rice, research is being directed at improving taste. Above all, the research aims to obtain significantly higher yields with lesser applications of expensive fertilizer.

Some other difficulties for all the HYVs are less serious in the long run, but no less galling in the short. Storage, marketing, and transport problems have arisen in handling the new supplies coming to the market at the same time. Surpluses can develop if governments fail to adjust official buying prices downward; India in early 1986 had 24 million tonnes of wheat and rice in storage and was unable to export it, largely due to the subsidized competition of the developed countries.[52] Indonesia and Thailand both had a large rice surplus in 1985. Only with development does a country acquire the capacity to store and ship the much larger quantities involved; only with flexible market policies can supply be equated with demand. To provide adequate storage, transport, and marketing there is a growing trend to replace inefficient government distribution systems with private enterprise, the move explicitly approved by government itself, as especially in India and Bangladesh.[53]

In general it is clear that the HYVs succeed most dramatically when literacy is high, so that instructions can be understood; when landholding is equitable and income evenly distributed, for then risks are less concentrated and credit is more widely available; when the water supply is controlled, especially for rice; when the fertilizer supply and price are both reasonable; and when farm prices are not depressed by government policy (an especial problem in Africa, where the Green Revolution has yet to make a great impact). An agricultural extension service that is available and well-run will be a great help in spreading the new varieties. The extension services of the past, with their too-frequent irrelevance to farmers' needs, have now been much improved on in several countries. India's well-known Training and Visit (T&V) System is a case in point, with regular visits scheduled by extension workers to farmers in their own fields every two weeks, with the workers often drawn from among the most successful of these very farmers. Their advice on spacing, pruning, weeding, and general management has been a productive supplement to the HYVs that they recommend. Contact with farmers has been greatly increased, and a study by Feder and Slade suggests that in India T&V has been responsible for a 7-percent yield increase over 3 years, in addition to the effects of the HYVs themselves. Rapidly, with World Bank support, T&V has spread to more than 40 countries.[54]

Are Small Farmers and the Landless Left Out?

A major problem on the level of the individual farmer, one involving equity, was apparent from the earliest days of the HYVs. The cost of fertilizer, irrigation, and even new seed was a greater burden on the smaller, poorer farmers, whose fixed costs of locating and developing markets and training hired labor were also higher. The deficiency of agricultural credit made the cost barrier even harder to overcome. Thus those farm families (or absentee landlords) with relatively high incomes to start with received greater benefits than poor farmers, and many a landless laborer appeared initially to be passed by entirely. Numerous observers have thus been very critical of the new crops' inability to improve income distribution in agriculture and their capacity to make the distribution even worse. It was said in their defense that they were developed to produce food, not to engineer social change! Even so, critics believed that it would be more difficult than before to alleviate the serious maldistribution of income within the farm sector of most LDCs.[55]

From the late 1970s, however, evidence accumulated that the HYVs during the first decade of their use had exhibited a substantial potential to assist the poor.[56] (1) The HYVs in most countries do produce the main food eaten by the urban and rural poor, so the reduction in the rate of increase in their relative prices was a decided benefit. (2) Typically, the HYVs raised labor requirements per acre substantially, especially for transplanting, weeding, and harvesting.[57] One Indian study on rice quoted by Michael Lipton showed 46 percent more labor income per acre. (This higher labor demand is, of course, seasonal.) Greater labor inputs may be easier for small farmers to organize and apply, bringing advantages to them. More obviously, the higher demand for employed labor would be expected to produce eventual upward pressures on wages. (3) That the initial gains accrued to bigger farms appears to some degree associated with greater risk-aversion on the part of the poorer farmers. Perhaps not surprisingly, the latter looked longer at the results before adopting the technology, and when they did, the adoption was both slower and less complete—the poorer farmers could not afford to make a mistake. One advantage of IR-20 rice is that its yield is less variable than other varieties, with reduced risk that a crop of it will fall much below some modest target. Knowledge of this reduction in the risk of a disaster has helped to spread it. In spite of the remaining risks, however, adoption continued to advance, and at the present time it is clear that the HYVs have spread widely among small farmers as well as large and among tenant farmers as well as landowners. Since the HYVs are scale-neutral for the most part, it is arguable that the *relative* position of many small farmers has even been improved, because the size threshold of small-farm viability has been lowered by the new crops. Government can help. India has made a point of trying to include small holders by distributing Green Revolution kits of HYV seeds, fertilizer, and pesticide. Nearly 5 million were distributed in 1983 and 1984.

Still, there is little doubt that problems of income distribution will persist. Better-off farmers will continue to be the first to adopt the HYVs. Better-off farmers will be able to afford more water control, so important with rice. (A lesson of this is that subsidized credit co-ops and specialized design of irrigation schemes to make it possible for small farmers to participate are especially important.) Even with landless laborers gaining absolutely during the initial decade of the revolution, it is very likely that owners of land and capital profited relatively more, especially since they profit first and thus are in a position to acquire yet more land and capital. The disparity shows in regional terms also. Areas suited to the HYVs gained relative to areas less suited; regional gaps in income increased.

More disquieting is the recent evidence that employment creation from the revolution is now falling.[58] Evidently, farmers, especially the larger ones, have seen advantages in adopting labor-saving technology that cut the demand for new labor. This would give little cause for concern if it were due simply to rising wages as development proceeds, but there appears to be more to it than that. Cheap herbicides have proved to be directly competitive with hand weeding; the use of mechanical threshers, from Japan, Taiwan, or locally produced, is increasing rapidly; mechanized land preparation is advancing steadily; small, inexpensive mechanical reapers and transplanters are in the offing.

Sometimes government policies to subsidize credit or the prices of the new machinery (and overvalued foreign exchange rates with the same effect, as discussed in Chapter 13) are largely responsible, policies in urgent need of reform if relative prices are accurately to measure scarcities. Sometimes large farmers may prefer to tend machines rather than deal with what they see as intractable labor, akin to the industrial bias toward capital met with in Chapter 7. Sometimes, though, the new technology is simply cheaper even with undistorted prices (herbicides), or can avoid losses by faster processing at harvest (machine threshing).[59]

Should these trends persist, they would put an even greater premium on flexibility in LDCs, with a need for greater employment creation in other sectors. At best, the higher incomes to farmers and the lower food prices will lead to a higher demand for goods and services; many of these will be labor-intensive, so providing the jobs that used to be provided in agriculture. But in the short run landless laborers may suffer, which in general they did not during the first phase of the Green Revolution. The extent of the suffering will depend largely on the ability of an economy to adjust rapidly to changed economic circumstances. (This topic is pursued in Chapters 14 and 15.)

A last comment on the HYVs involves the great breakthroughs that might be made in the future.[60] A new maize (corn), with high protein content and good dry-field characteristics, would be a significant advance. Beyond that, cloning via tissue culture would copy the best characteristics of any plant and thus rapidly increase yields. If a gene conferring resistance to weed-killing herbicides could be bred in, the herbicide could be administered much more liberally, promising great increases in yields.[61] Transferring the leguminous (nitrogen-adding) properties of peas, beans, or peanuts to nonleguminous plants of all kinds would represent enormous self-production of fertilizer. (The nitrogen fixation is actually not due to the plant itself but to the bacteria it lives with symbiotically.) Wheat is the current candidate now being focused on. We may barely have seen the beginning, although it would be foolish to count on that in the short run.

Any breakthroughs, however, are unlikely to conserve on land use, and in that statement lies a last troublesome footnote. The combination of progress in agriculture and the population explosion has led to extensive deforestation that promises to bring long-term problems of erosion and loss of soil nutrients. In semi-arid countries, wood consumption will have to drop by as much as half in the next 15 to 20 years.[62] If the drop does not come from new woodstove designs, biodigester technologies, or other technical advances, it will come anyway, willy-nilly.

MODELS OF RURAL-URBAN RELATIONSHIPS

Economists' views of the role of rural areas in development have since about 1950 undergone substantial change. The rural sector was initially seen as a source of inputs for growth via manufacturing, with progress for those remaining in the countryside to come cheaply through so-called community development programs. Now the picture is much different, with hope still high that rural areas have a great contribution to make, but via a quite different route.

Development Models Emphasizing Agriculture as a Source of Saving

The attention given to agriculture in the 1950s revolved around the difficulties associated with increasing domestic saving surveyed in Chapter 4. These difficulties led economists to the construction of several important models that explored the possibility that agriculture might be the source of the saving.

Sir Arthur Lewis (and many others as well) emphasized that the essential breakthrough to growth in the classical era of market capitalism was the emergence of a new social class—the profit-earning entrepreneur—who saves more than the members of other social classes and whose share of national income increases during the development process. When most successful, the saving of these profit-oriented entrepreneurs means extensive reinvestment of their gains and rapid growth in the capitalist sector.

The two best-known models that began from this proposition were those of Lewis himself and of Gustav Ranis and J. C. H. Fei.[63] The Lewis model is known in the literature as "economic development with unlimited supplies of labor," that labor coming from the agricultural sector. The Ranis-Fei model is similar. They directed attention to the possibilities for increasing business saving through rein-vestment, so that development is speeded. An arresting aspect of the models was the concept of "disguised unemployment," a term coined during the Great Depression by Joan Robinson of Cambridge University and applied originally to the taking of jobs at a level of skill below what one was trained for during a time of depressed economic conditions. In the hands of Lewis and other theorists, disguised unemployment came to mean a surplus of labor in agriculture that might be mobilized for employment in a newly developing industrial sector.

The basic assumption of the model is that workers could be transferred to nonagricultural occupations without a country's losing output of food, since at the margin a worker's productivity was so low. Whenever a worker transferred from farm to factory, there would be less consumption of food on the farm equal to what the worker had been consuming before the move, but little or no loss of output. With new income earned in a factory, the former farmer could afford to buy the now-surplus food. The model implied further that there is a perfectly elastic (unlimited) supply of labor available to the modern sector from the traditional sector.

A diagram displaying the marginal product of labor can be used effectively to explain this case. The quantity of labor is shown along the horizontal axis of Figure 10.1, and the marginal revenue product of that labor (the amount of revenue brought to the employer by hiring one more unit of labor) is shown along the vertical axis. The *MRP* of labor *(MRP_L)* is seen to decline as more workers are hired, but the quantity of the other factors of production is held fixed. The diagram shows *OL* as the total quantity of labor available. Of this quantity, *OA* is employed in the modern sector of the economy at a market wage (equal to

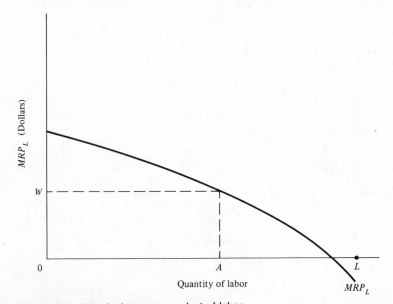

Figure 10.1 Marginal revenue product of labor.

MRP) of *OW*. This leaves, however, an abundance of labor *AL* that must find employment in the traditional sector, largely meaning agriculture. In the diagram this labor is seen to be low in productivity (*MRP* below that of the modern sector) with some workers assumed to have zero *MRP*, or even to have negative *MRP* at and to the right of the point where the MRP_L curve crosses the horizontal axis.

The existence of some labor in agriculture with zero or negative productivity is important. If such a condition exists, it means that some workers can be shifted out of agriculture into industry without sacrificing agricultural output. It remains to be explained, however, how any labor at all would be employed if its marginal productivity is zero or less. The explanation lies in the practice, common in subsistence farming where food is raised for the household's own consumption, of *sharing* the total output among all family members. Everyone has a place at the family cooking pot. Under these circumstances the worker's income is his share of the family output, namely, the average (not the marginal) product of the family. It is certainly conceivable that the average product could be positive when the marginal product of the last worker is zero or below. (If Jim Rice bats 0 for 4 in today's game, that reduces his season's batting average, but not to zero. Mathematically, the logic is the same for marginal versus average product.)

Sir Arthur Lewis, Ranis and Fei, and other proponents of development via the mobilization of disguised unemployment find it important to establish that there is a relatively unlimited (perfectly elastic) supply of labor from farming. If

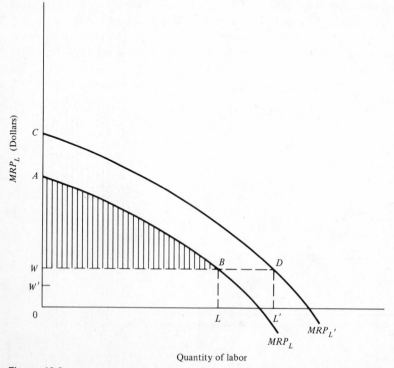

Figure 10.2

labor is perfectly elastic in supply, then saving and investment in LDCs will be subject to some special advantages not found in an already developed country. In the Lewis model any amount of labor is available for transfer out of subsistence agriculture at a constant wage OW, as in Figure 10.2. (Note that this constant wage includes an increment for the expense of moving, the higher cost of living, and the overcoming of inertia equal to $W'W$. In practice the increment may be as much as 30 percent above the average subsistence wage.)

In the diagram, OL labor is originally hired in the modern sector at a wage OW. The total wage bill is thus $OWBL$. But the marginal productivity of labor was higher than OW for all workers except the last employed, with the result that there is a surplus WAB (the shaded area) that need not be paid out and is available for reinvestment. More capital is thus created, with the effect that the productivity of labor is raised. The marginal revenue product of labor shifts from MRP_L to $MRP_{L'}$. More labor is hired in the modern sector (OL'). The surplus available for reinvestment is thereupon raised to WCD. Proponents of the model see the process coming to an end when and if the growth of the modern sector depletes the labor supply in the traditional sector, raising the productivity of labor there and hence raising the wage needed to persuade labor to shift between sectors (in Figure 10.2, this means raising both W' and W). Similarly, technical progress in agriculture could also raise W' and W, as could growing shortages of agricultural commodities that raise the relative price of those commodities vis-à-vis industrial goods. For any one of these reasons, the ability to utilize the model for purposes of development would eventually come to an end.

Note carefully that these models depend on the existence of a perfectly elastic supply of labor available at some constant wage to fuel the labor needs of the modern sector, and with the transfer resulting in no significant loss of agricultural output. Therein lies their most controversial aspect, with a substantial amount of research directed in recent years to detecting a low or zero or negative marginal revenue product of labor in agriculture. There is certainly superficial logic to the claim of disguised unemployment in farming. Some authors point to historical experience for their evidence. Without disguised unemployment, how could a flood of peasant farmers into export production have occurred without some noticeable drop in food supplies? And yet, for Burma's rice, Ghana's cocoa, Uganda's cotton, and Nigeria's palm oil and peanuts in the decades just before and after 1900, export production did increase rapidly without great changes in domestically produced food supplies. How could rapid population growth occur in areas already overpopulated in relation to natural resource endowments and capital stock without contributing to disguised unemployment? How, finally, could the exodus from the farm to the city that has typified many LDCs in recent years take place without reducing farm output, unless there were significant disguised unemployment? Some empirical studies did indeed detect substantial disguised unemployment, including findings of 30 percent unutilized labor-time in Korea and 33 percent in West Bengal.[64]

Criticisms of the Lewis Model   The logic of these arguments proved to be highly debatable, however. Authors attack especially the confusion between zero marginal product at some given time and over the course of an entire year. Say that labor in farming can indeed be found during much of the year with low or zero productivity. May not this be misleading in that it reflects seasonal unemployment, rather than permanently low productivity? During the off-season for farming, farmers may indeed work with low intensity, carrying on temporary low-productivity activities. But during the planting, weeding, and harvesting of the crops, work may be intense, especially under tropical conditions of lush growth. Under such conditions the *yearly* marginal product of labor could be positive; in fact, labor might even be short at the peak times of activity during the farmer's year. If it is added that farmers often carry on various other craft and transport activities during the year and that the need for rest and recuperation is likely to be high in tropical farming, then the conclusion is suggested that output would not stay at the same level if workers were removed from agriculture.[65] A review of the subject by Kao, Anschel, and Eicher concludes that "there is little reliable evidence to support the existence of more than token—five percent—disguised unemployment in underdeveloped countries."[66] A *seasonal* surplus of underemployed, low-productivity labor—perhaps 25 percent of the agricultural labor force during the off-season would not be untypical—seems a much more reasonable proposition.[67]

A number of other objections to the Lewis model have been advanced over the years. One is that the model assumes implicitly that the creation of employment is proportional to the accumulation of capital. But if the new investment embodies labor-saving technology, then MRP_L would not shift symmetrically outward, but might shift instead as shown by the curve $MRP_{L'}$ in Figure 10.3.[68] Then total output grows to $OABL$, greater than $OCBL$, but employment stays the same and so do wages. GNP would rise, but accrue to industrialists. Income distribution problems worsen.

A second difficulty emerged from empirical testing of the model in Egypt and Taiwan. In both countries there was a tendency to choose capital-using investment, with a less-than-predicted tendency to raise employment.[69]

The Prediction Turned Around   The debate over the applicability of the Lewis model was still in progress when it was overtaken by two events, one highly favorable, the other less so. Especially during the 1970s, it became apparent that labor was indeed being transferred from agriculture to the cities, and that farm output (with the major exception of some African countries) was not declining. The absence of a decline was due not to a zero marginal product of labor, but to the technical changes that affected the farm sector of many countries. But, in an ironical twist, it became all too apparent that the movement of labor from rural areas to cities was *greater* than the Lewis model suggested it would be, far surpassing the rates of urban job creation.[70] The modern industrial sector was usually quite unable to absorb anywhere near enough labor to prevent open unemployment and underemployment in low-productivity, low-income jobs.

The concept of *urban* surplus labor now seems more credible than rural surplus labor. New job openings are limited by a capital-intensive bias in manufacturing, fostered by policies such as an overvalued foreign exchange rate that

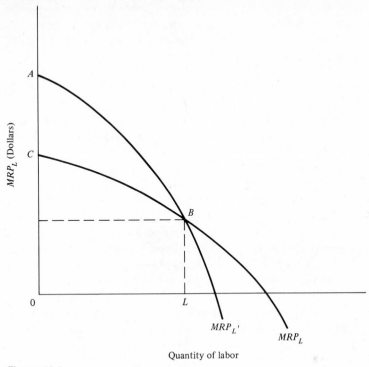

Figure 10.3

promotes imports of capital but discourages exports, exports which in labor-abundant countries would likely be labor-intensive. In many LDCs the growth of manufacturing output has exceeded the growth of *employment* by a ratio of 3 : 1 or 4 : 1.[71]

Wages kept above market-clearing equilibrium in the cities by union pressure, or by strict application of minimum wage laws, or by the payment of relatively high wages by government and foreign corporations are the major cause of urban unemployment. The wage differential with rural areas can be quite spectacular, the size of the gap not foreseen in the Lewis model. Michael Lipton's work has shown that the urban-rural income difference was historically small in today's developed countries, under 2 for Germany, France, Italy, the Netherlands, Britain, and the United States in the nineteenth century and between 2 and 3 for Sweden and Japan. But for most LDCs the current figure is 3 to 4 or even higher (Turkey 6, Mexico 7, Kenya 9, Tanzania 11) or extremely so (Zambia 35, Zaire 41).[72] The increasing flow of labor to the cities has far surpassed the ability to employ it there, at the same time requiring expensive (even though often inadequate) extensions to social services and urban infrastructure that could have been used for productive investment. The numbers are huge. From 1950 to 1975, on best estimate, some 330 million people made the migration, almost a quarter of the entire population of the LDCs in 1950.[73]

Thus the idea that rural disguised unemployment is an advantage for industrialization, a reservoir of labor whose flow to the cities would be in response to job openings there, now looks overly optimistic. But if interpreted as a seasonal very low productivity in agriculture, the Lewis model still offers the hope that new forms of management might be able to utilize the surplus, a topic discussed further along in this chapter.

Rural-Urban Migration

Recently much attention has focused on how individuals decide whether to migrate from a rural area to the city.[74] The most familiar model suggests that an economically rational rural laborer will migrate to a city if the present discounted value of an expected lifetime earnings stream in an urban location exceeds that stream for a rural location by more than the cost of moving.[75] This is a nice application of microeconomic theory to an important human issue and helps us to understand a decision that for those involved is not so easy to make. There will be a risk factor, perhaps as high as 1 in 4, that no job at all will be obtained in the city ("open unemployment") or that employment will be not in a "modern sector" job, but in the informal or "murky" sector of shoeshines, errands, collecting thrown-away containers, handicraft production, and other low-productivity and irregular jobs. This is called "disguised unemployment," "underemployment," or "invisible unemployment." The proportion of the labor force in such low-productivity jobs and with the training and capacity to earn more if better jobs were available is thought to be about 20 percent in Latin America and 40 percent in Africa.[76]

The potential migrant will also have to decide whether "murky sector" employment will cut the eventual chances of getting a modern sector job, and what those chances are. These concerns will be larger the greater the flow of migrants, thus reducing expected earnings and presumably halting the migration altogether when the expected income, weighted for the risk of unemployment, sinks to the level that could have been obtained on the farm. The calculation will presumably take into account some advantages to city life that accrue even to those without a modern sector job. Probably there will be much better access to public services such as water and sewage systems, electricity, clinics, schools, and the mails, even if income earned in the murky sector is very low; and the "bright lights" surroundings will be there anyway. A last consideration is that the new migrants may personally prefer to go back to the country, but considering that they have cut their ties and would lose face if they returned, they find themselves "stuck" with their mistake.

Economic modeling in this area has certainly directed attention to urban unemployment as a function of the urban-rural wage gap. A clear implication of the work is the need for programs to improve productivity in the murky sector of underemployed. Education and training, credit and "extension services," all now familiar in rural development, have been widely ignored in the urban slums of the LDCs. "Rural factories" might find a counterpart in small-scale "slum production," but there has been little progress in this regard either.

Who does in fact migrate from rural areas to the cities?[77] Predominantly the young (age 15 to 29), the more motivated, and consistently the better educated, no doubt because they are aware that many jobs in the city carry educational requirements that do not exist in the country. The closer they are to the city in the first place, and the less productive the farming area in which they live, the more likely they are to pull up their roots. The migration may not be in one big move; the migrants may try life in a small town for a time before moving on.

The effects on the areas they left behind may be striking. Shifts in labor use, involving less labor-intensive cropping patterns and more work for wages, can occur, though seldom an actual drop in farm output. Migrants frequently send remittances to their relatives in the countryside. These aspects of rural-urban migration models have played a part in convincing economists that the large flow of labor into the cities is not so much the problem that it could have been if rural output had declined significantly. To be sure, that still leaves an unemployed or underemployed labor surplus to cope with. But here again the adverse impact can be overemphasized, because the migrants do not appear to be the poorest part of the population, because some will get the modern sector jobs they seek, and because many will be absorbed by the informal murky sector. When the cyclical effect of the early 1980s recession is factored out, there is little evidence that open unemployment in the cities is rising.[78] No palliative will, however, alter the fact that this group can be politically volatile. The disappointed aspirations can represent a real threat to government.

Whatever the dimensions of the threat, it is clear that one solution—using controls to restrict migration or to toss the migrants out of the cities and back to the farm, resorted to from time to time in China, Indonesia, the Philippines, and several African countries—has worked poorly.[79] Better results have accompanied programs to make rural areas more attractive, as we shall see.

COMMUNITY DEVELOPMENT (CD)

The first pillar of conventional wisdom in the economics of rural development was the Lewis model of disguised unemployment available to fuel industrial expansion. The second was community development, or CD, the grand idea that rural areas could improve themselves through their own efforts.[80] The CD movement spread nearly worldwide in the 1950s, and by 1960 over 60 LDCs had CD programs, half of them national in scope. But by 1965 the effort had faltered, and foreign aid support was down dramatically. CD did not disappear. Under other names programs are still encountered most everywhere, but the frequent use of the past tense in the discussion below reflects the disappointment, the retrenchment, and the need for careful assessment of what went wrong.

The main approach was to persuade people to work on CD, or "self-help," projects at low rates of pay or without pay. The well, the road, the clinic, the school, the community center were the common end results of CD. Sometimes food and housing for teachers and other sorts of current expenditure were also provided via self-help organizations, but current costs proved much more difficult to finance in this way than were one-time capital projects.

Several sorts of aims intertwined in community development efforts: the participation of people in improving their own welfare; the use of a seasonal labor surplus in rural areas; the encouragement of local organization, initiative, and mutual self-help with government technical assistance. At the peak period of interest in CD, countries discouraged by the difficulties of capital formation were tempted to view community development schemes as a much easier alternative. In some countries a large scale of self-help effort was achieved. Sri Lanka's Sarvodaya Shramadana movement, beginning in 1958, mounted a full program (it still does in 300 villages, and a partial one in 2,500 more, employing 6,000 full-time worker-advisors). Korea's *Saemaul Undong* dating from 1970 now involves over 30,000 communities.[81] Kenya's Harambee program and the extensive schemes of Indonesia and Tanzania also became well-known. Typically, local people undertook manual work on CD projects during weekends or during periods when agricultural labor is working at reduced intensity, times when the opportunity cost of labor is expected to be low. But experience soon made it clear that salutary warnings were in order if CD projects were to be effective.

It was often forgotten that CD projects were really not free at all and might involve considerable expense to the government. They required administrative personnel for propaganda, organization, and supervision, and such trained staff was a scarce commodity. The programs were often widely scattered, so that the management problems were intractable, involving sluggish coordination, long delays, and a stifling of both enthusiasm and initiative. Government had to pay for the specialized inputs such as cement and reinforcing rods in buildings, for the skilled labor, and for the technical assistance when necessary. The wiring for the school or clinic and the drainage engineering for the road without which it would wash out in the first downpours of the rainy season were not free, and costs of this sort appeared to run from a minimum of around 30 percent to about 50 percent of the money costs of a CD project. (Sri Lanka's Shramadana movement tries to keep budget costs below $1,000 per village, but even that may present a serious fiscal obstacle.) Finally, the fact was sometimes neglected that when a CD project was completed, it required current expenditures financed by the government—doctors, nurses, and medicines in the clinic, teachers and books in the school, and so forth. In remote rural areas any kind of maintenance was difficult to arrange and expensive. Thus, even on the basic ground of low cost, there was over-optimism.

Experience also made it clear that the benefits of the project had to be largely local if enthusiasm was to be generated. Villagers might happily patch or rebuild their road to market, but could not be depended upon in constructing something like the Yugoslav *Autoput,* a superhighway built for long-distance traffic, connecting Italy with Greece, with infrequent interchanges. It was better for purposes such as this to mobilize youth clubs, boy scouts, and international friendship societies than to depend on the villages en route, which saw little advantage in a road to which they could not gain access without a drive of 20 miles. Yet the benefits ought not to be *too* local, as the Peruvian and Indian governments discovered when favoritism toward certain villages, sometimes simply because they were more accessible, was detected in project planning and resented.

Also, where land is privately owned it is possible, even likely, that some landowners would benefit more than others from any given project, such as a road. This, too, dampened enthusiasm and generated jealousies. The same adverse features accrued more widely if self-help worsened a country's income distribution. At times poor areas fell behind when self-help community development schemes, say in education, mobilized less local funding for books and teachers than was the case in more well-to-do regions, particularly urban ones. Northeast Brazil, northern Nigeria, and southern Sudan are cases in point.

CD advisors often found it easiest to align themselves with the traditional village elites. This was comfortable for the advisor and strengthened the elites, but it also explains why little enthusiasm was generated for CD among the poor masses. It is now clear that, within the affected community, the benefits of the project had to be widely felt across all income groups or else general community participation would not be forthcoming. For example, basic needs projects such as a water supply or a health clinic were predictably more popular than a leper hospital; a farm-to-market road was preferred to an airstrip. Projects to raise the local food supply, that could at once have enlisted the poorest, were neglected. In Sri Lanka the Shramadana movement eventually allowed the villagers to choose the projects. But even careful choice often could not cope with the depressed condition of the village poor or the social tensions of unequal income and land ownership. The basic problems were often too much even for a persuasive CD advisor. Even where these problems were overcome, that persuasive advisor may not have been very well trained in any of the technical aspects of agriculture, engineering, road building, well construction, and the like. Having bravely bridged the social gap, the advisor, stretched too thin, found after all he had little to contribute to the village. This was especially a concern in the most broad-based programs.

Thus CD turned out not to be a panacea, or even very successful. But such projects at their best lent an esprit de corps to the development experience, did develop local unity and some identification with the growth process when benefits flowed to all. They served also to give at least a brief period of elementary training in activities beyond the limited horizons of traditional village life. There was at minimum some success in keeping people on farms by bettering their living conditions, rather than further swelling the flow of migrants to the overcrowded cities. Finally (this was a major lesson), abundant and perhaps idle labor was to some extent used to augment the stock of scarce capital with less strain on the financial system than capital investment usually required.

There are thus strong reasons for looking again at CD, fortified with the knowledge of this episode in development history. The new "integrated rural development" (IRD) efforts of the 1970s and 1980s, many of which initially concentrated on relatively expensive basic needs provision and efforts to increase food output, are once more turning to self-help projects, in realization perhaps that the decline of CD was greater than it ought to have been. One hopes that the IRD advisor of today studies closely the informative experience of the CD advisors who came before.

RURAL EMPLOYMENT OPPORTUNITIES

A need rapidly to offset the urban pull and rural push is generally agreed upon. One major outcome of the long debates over the Lewis model and community development was a recognition that slack-season unemployment where labor is abundant is an opportunity for rural manufacturing. New rural-based industry utilizing simple technology, perhaps engaging in processing agricultural commodities, running at different intensities depending on the demand for labor in the fields, offers new hope of a "rural pull." Sometimes this manufacturing already exists, or once did, in the form of village handicrafts such as local weaving, basket making, and so forth. How irrational, in retrospect, when such handicrafts were displaced, further fueling migration, by urban industries using scarce but subsidized capital to produce what surplus labor with low opportunity costs in the farming slack season could do.[82]

Five countries making use of this rural potential are South Korea, Taiwan, Indonesia, India, and China.[83] South Korea and Taiwan have concentrated especially on credit for rural manufacturing and the provision of rural electrical supplies that can be used in the "farm factories." There, farm family members can commute to a rural factory on a schedule that varies with the busy season in farming. The rural factories have had linkages that spur rural small businesses and help to slow migration to the cities (the flow cut by half between the 1960s and 1970s in Korea, where nearly a thousand such factories have been established). With growth, permanent factories have tended to supersede the temporary or seasonal ones.

Indonesia has used its low-cost seasonal surplus of labor for government-managed public works projects. These have included small-scale irrigation, the digging of drainage channels, and the clearing and preparation of land. The joint results are paid employment during the off-season; higher income for farmers because of the increased land area and higher yields brought about by the project; and finally some repayment to the government for its spending because there is now a larger tax base. In India the emphasis is on rural construction during the farming off-season.[84] China has encouraged its rural communes to establish labor-intensive small industries that can absorb the labor freed by the remarkable growth in that country's farm output. It is thought that such rural industry was already producing about 13 percent of China's GDP in 1983, with over 60 million former farm workers employed by rural enterprises and receiving wages considerably above the average return in agriculture.[85]

The lesson provided by these five countries is an important one, unfortunately still to be perceived by some LDCs. Care must be exercised, however. In establishing rural factories, there is the danger that underemployed capital during the farming peak season will replace labor underemployment during the farming off-season. This is an argument for infusing extra labor when necessary, either into farming or into the rural factories. Several countries do this now under government auspices, Cuba with harvest brigades, China with temporary "rustifications," or Tanzania by bussing urban workers.[86] If a market system were operating efficiently, accurately reflecting the true opportunity costs of capital and labor, then market incentives could achieve the same end.

One further realization of the 1970s was that government policy to speed manufacturing at the expense of agriculture seemed to dampen, not aid, economic development. The countries making the most progress and undergoing the greatest structural change were the ones paying close attention to rural-urban balance, that is, to the need to develop agriculture in step with manufacturing.

There is by now a wealth of illustrative experience.[87] The Ivory Coast, Malaysia, South Korea, Taiwan, and Thailand are five good examples of careful attention to rural areas with resulting highly favorable overall effects. Integrated rural development is emphasized in all five. Substantial amounts of public money have gone into rural health and education, land improvement, and irrigation. Agricultural research institutes are well staffed. They all have successful programs of bringing credit to the countryside, the credit backed by a competent extension service. Improvements in village education, health services, water supplies, farm-to-market roads, some electrification, and availability of advice on nutrition and home economics have made the rural landscape more hospitable. All are incidentally easier to provide to a village than to scattered farmsteads. Often national funding is made available to be used at the discretion of local development committees for local projects. All these countries have decentralized decision making to some degree, with good results in improved efficiency. (When decision making is decentralized, it often follows that large, capital-intensive projects fall out of favor to some extent.)

All of the successful countries have been especially diligent in continuing the support of their agricultural initiatives, unlike the many LDCs that are littered with the remains of good projects that failed because the initial effort was not followed up with the less glamorous, but critical day-to-day support work.[88] But the very centerpiece of all the programs is an adequate reward for the rural sector through producer prices that are remunerative and provide an incentive for production. These are not the countries with the onerous taxes on agriculture.[89]

Nor have they used their government funds to subsidize credit, fertilizer, and machinery in unwise ways. In many countries, the first attempts to offset years of rural neglect involved the institution of input subsidies to counter the stringent tax policies.[90] Sometimes these subsidies have been comprehensive, covering seed, fuel, machinery, water, pesticides, and fertilizer. They have been applied especially to fertilizer, usually in the range of 30 to 90 percent of delivered cost; 50 to 70 percent subsidies are common. Often there has been little public opposition. In addition to countering the disincentive effects of heavy taxation, such subsidies are justified as an attempt to overcome rural credit constraints, to encourage rapid technical change in agriculture, to raise the income of the poor, and in general as a way to raise output.

There is little doubt, however, that they have not worked out as their proponents expected.[91] Machinery subsidies seem particularly unjustified, since they usually end up in the hands of the largest farmers with landholdings large

enough to accommodate the equipment, and who then use the financing to
displace labor with capital. Fertilizer subsidies do not have that problem, but they
too often benefit richer farmers more than poor ones. The reason is clear enough.
Because the price is kept low, demand is usually higher than supply so that some
form of rationing must be adopted. With their greater visibility and political
power, better-off farmers are able to shove to the head of the queue. There are
other problems as well. Fertilizer subsidies do not encourage the use of manure,
and chemical fertilizers alone are usually insufficient to maintain soil fertility.
Being distributed by state monopolies in many countries, they may not arrive at
the proper time for application, and may not be tailored to local conditions. The
private competition that could overcome these inefficiencies does not develop,
because government does not permit it to.

On occasion, where a country can afford the expense, one finds these
subsidies carried to irrational extremes. Saudi Arabia pays its farmers a subsidized
price of $14 per bushel of wheat, almost five times the world price. Saudi wheat
growers responded by making the desert bloom with wheat watered from deep
wells, evidence that large enough quantities of cash can boost exports of virtually
anything, no matter how hopelessly uneconomic the unsubsidized activity is.

There is now a growing tendency in many countries to cut back on these
subsidies.[92] But the LDCs with the most successful rural development programs
generally avoided the difficulties in the first place. When subsidies have been paid
in these countries, they have generally been moderate in amount, applied to the
achievement of reasonable goals, and have ended up in hands able to accomplish
the designed tasks. The lesson is a valuable one.

A reflection of the success of the rural effort can be seen in the proportion
of food imported to the LDCs. For the poorest LDCs as a group, food made up
24 percent of all imports in 1960, but only 16 percent in 1982. Some particular
achievements are shown in Table 10.2.

Even where food imports were rising and a country's self-sufficiency was
falling, often the imports reflected not a declining rural sector but instead gains
from trade. Rising incomes and more foreign exchange mean consumers could

Table 10.2 FOOD AS A PERCENTAGE OF ALL MERCHANDISE IMPORTS

	1960	1983
India	21	7
Pakistan	22	14
Kenya	12	9
Cameroon	20	9
Malaysia	29	9
Thailand	10	4

Source: WDR 1986, pp. 200–201, and WDR 1984, pp. 238–239.

now afford wheat products instead of rice and coarse grains. The large grain imports to Mexico, Indonesia, Nigeria, Thailand, and other better-off LDCs, which helped to raise the LDC share of world wheat consumption to 49 percent in 1979 to 1981, thus reflect a taste change spurred by higher incomes.[93]

Prosperous farming has further important ramifications. The higher output means more reasonable farm prices for consumers and more revenues for farmers. The farmers' new income means a market for additional inputs in farming, raising revenues yet again of those providing the inputs. The higher incomes of farmers and suppliers and the income consumers do not have to spend on high-price imported foods mean a larger market for consumer goods generally. The wood, the rubber, the palm products, the oilseeds, and food for processing, all may become direct inputs to domestic manufacturing. Agricultural exports make a contribution to a country's earnings of foreign exchange, which, tapped through judicious taxation, is available for industrial development. Higher saving and higher investment are the result.

The degree to which China has followed this logic in recent years has rightly attracted intense interest.[94] China for many years had a rigid system of state procurement and pricing, but that country has now turned to much higher and more flexible rewards to farmers who successfully increase production. China's guaranteed prices were raised 20 to 30 percent between 1977 and 1979. From 1979 farmers were encouraged to produce crops for private sale at market prices, on both rural and urban farmers' markets, and land can now be "rented" from the rural communes (the Chinese equivalent of collective farms) for this purpose. The communes now have much more leeway than before in setting their own output targets and have some authority to switch production to crops with higher returns. The response in output because of the policy changes and high-yield varieties (and some good weather too) has provoked admiration, even astonishment. There was a production increase of about 30 percent from 1979 to 1984, in the course of which wheat output more than doubled, making China the world's largest wheat grower. The government-guaranteed prices for grains even had to be cut back in 1985 to avoid problems with surplus production. It should be emphasized that this growth occurred without much increase in inputs to agricultural production. There was probably even a fall in the rural labor force, due to the proliferation of jobs in rural enterprises, and in land under cultivation.[95] The impressive results were due instead to more efficient organization and higher motivation.

The reasons for involving rural areas in the development process were too long neglected, but as seen here a salutary reaction has set in with such favorable results that it seems unlikely to be reversed. The reaction could be even more pronounced, incidentally, if developed-country protection against imports of agricultural commodities that they themselves produce were not so intense. Such protection is generally greater than for manufactured goods, as we shall see in Chapter 15. There is thus a limit on present ability to expand exports of these commodities; a reduction in that protection could help to stimulate further output in the LDCs.

The end result is that city and countryside, manufacturing and agriculture, are now seen more as a partnership than as competing sectors. This realization took a long time to come about, and the message has still not reached some segments of official opinion, with policy problems perhaps most pronounced in parts of Africa.[96] But most observers now rate the partnership as a central proposition of development economics.

INCREASING EMPLOYMENT

The struggle for rural development is thus part of a general struggle to increase employment in the LDCs, involving the message of each of the last four chapters.[97] Because labor appears to be in surplus, especially in urban areas, because the surplus is of long standing, and because economic growth has not made a sufficient dent in it, economists have come to advocate more direct assaults on the structural causes of the employment problem.

From Chapter 7: Artificial barriers exist, leading to less labor-intensive technology than would result from a free market. The task is to implement these labor-intensive technologies, so providing more employment, without decreasing output.

From Chapter 8: High population growth can lead to a burden of dependency and hinder capital deepening, thus impeding the growth of productivity and reducing employment opportunities.

From Chapter 9: A poorly educated, illiterate, poorly nourished, and unhealthy labor force is a low-productivity labor force. With wages sticky in the downward direction, there will be difficulties in absorbing the labor.

From this chapter: Agricultural price and tax policies in many countries are disincentives that limit the absorption of labor. Government public services often are targeted to cities rather than rural areas, reflecting an urban bias. Combined with an urban high-wage structure, the result is a flow of migrants that fuels the labor surplus. This flow is so large that no likely rate of economic growth in the modern sector will be able to absorb it.

Hence the general agreement that if the employment battle is to be won, it will require reforms in agricultural policies.

NOTES

1. *WDR 1986* is devoted to policy problems in agriculture. A wide-ranging review is Theodore W. Schultz, ed., *Distortions of Agricultural Incentives,* Bloomington, 1978.
2. *WDR 1986,* pp. 62–65, which documents the case with relative protection ratios and a table that compares internal prices for important agricultural commodities in various LDCs with world market prices, adjusted for transport costs, for the same commodities in the late 1970s and early 1980s. By this time reform had already set in. Tanzania, for example, before its reforms of 1984 and 1985 was paying its farmers about one-quarter to one-half the world market price for their rice, maize, and tobacco. *Ibid.,* pp. 74–75.
3. *WDR 1986,* pp. 200–201, and *WDR 1985,* p. 194. The figures are mostly for 1983.
4. *WDR 1986,* p. 68, notes that supply responses in LDC agriculture are higher than

usually believed, even in Africa where elasticities are supposed to be lowest. The elasticity estimates given in the *WDR* are from studies by Hossein Askari and J. T. Cummings and Pasquale L. Scandizzo and Colin Bruce.

5. See *WDR 1986,* p. 76, for additional details.

6. Again there is an extensive literature. *WDR 1986* treats the topic. A useful and recent survey volume is Carl K. Eicher and John M. Staatz, eds., *Agricultural Development in the Third World,* Baltimore, 1984; George S. Tolley et al., *Agricultural Price Policies and the Developing Countries,* Baltimore, 1982, is also good. Policy problems are analyzed and new approaches suggested in Bruce F. Johnston and William C. Clark, *Redesigning Rural Development: A Strategic Perspective,* Baltimore, 1982; and C. Peter Timmer, Walter P. Falcon, and Scott R. Pearson, *Food Policy Analysis,* Baltimore, 1983. A dependable classic is Bruce F. Johnston and Peter Kilby, *Agriculture and Structural Transformation: Economic Strategies in Late-Developing Countries,* New York, 1975. See also Gerald M. Meier, *Leading Issues in Economic Development,* 4th ed., New York, 1984, part VII.

7. The correlation is shown graphically in *WDR 1986,* p. 80, which covers the period 1973 to 1984.

8. Based on Jonathan Power's example, quoted by Meier, *Leading Issues,* 4th ed., p. 213.

9. Compare Meier, *Leading Issues,* 4th ed., pp. 439–440, citing Michael Lipton, *Why Poor People Stay Poor: A Study of Urban Bias in World Development,* London, 1977. A book-length study of the place of agriculture in providing employment for a rapidly growing labor force is Anne Booth and R. M. Sundrum, *Labour Absorption in Agriculture,* Oxford, 1985.

10. The figures are from *WDR 1986,* pp. 182–183, 228–229, and 238–239; and *WDR 1983,* pp. 150–151.

11. A recent survey with many references is Vernon W. Ruttan, "Assistance to Expanding Agricultural Production," *World Development* 14, no. 1 (1986):39–63.

12. Soviet-style collective farms reflect this difficulty to some extent. Observers have long noted the higher productivity per person and per acre in the cultivation of the "private plot" as compared to the fields of the collective itself.

13. Much of this research is cited by Hiromitsu Kaneda, "Structural Change and Policy Response in Japanese Agriculture After the Land Reform," *Economic Development and Cultural Change* 28, no. 3 (1982):485–486. See also I. M. D. Little, *Economic Development: Theory, Policy, and International Relations,* New York, 1982, p. 174. For the comment on India, see Pranab Bardhan and Ashok Rudra, "Terms and Conditions of Sharecropping Contracts: An Analysis of Village Survey Data in India," *Journal of Development Studies* 16, no. 3 (1980):287–302, and the work of C. H. H. Rao and C. C. Malone. The quote concerning Pakistan is from Ijaz Nabi, "Contracts, Resource Use and Productivity in Sharecropping," *Journal of Development Studies* 22, no. 2 (1986):429–442.

14. The situation is sometimes made less tolerable by racist overtones, as when the land-lords are white and the tenants mestizo, black, or Indian. Caste in India similarly enters landlord-tenant relations.

15. Land reform has historically taken very different forms: collectivization of privately owned farmland into large units, often much larger than before (Soviet Union, China); farmer cooperatives with relocation of former peasant cultivators (Tanzanian ujamaa villages, Mexican ejido cooperatives); transfer of ownership from landlords, usually absentee, to tenants who were already there (Japan, Taiwan, Ethiopia, Mexico); and opening of large estates for new settlement by small cultivators (Kenya). See Michael P. Todaro, *Economic Development in the Third World,* 2nd ed., New York, 1981, p.

278; and the discussion in P. J. D. Wiles, *Economic Institutions Compared,* Oxford, 1977. Two informative sources on farm size and productivity are R. A. Berry and W. R. Cline, *Agrarian Structure and Productivity in Developing Countries,* Baltimore, 1979; and G. A. Cornia, "Farm Size, Land Yields and the Agricultural Production Function: An Analysis for Fifteen Developing Countries," *World Development* 13, no. 4 (1985):513–534.

16. See Celso Furtado, *Economic Development in Latin America,* Cambridge, 1970, pp. 54–55. There is a good section in E. Wayne Nafziger, *The Economics of Developing Countries,* Belmont, Calif., 1984, pp. 125–127.

17. From Todaro, *Economic Development in the Third World,* 2nd ed., p. 278.

18. *WDR 1979,* p. 50.

19. This element is clearly apparent in modern U.S. farming, where even on heavily mechanized farms the relatively smaller ones utilizing family labor tend to be more productive than larger ones employing hired labor.

20. Management problems in large-scale farming are often discussed in connection with Soviet-style collectives and state farms and with some ranches in the western United States.

21. See Gershon Feder, Richard Just, and David Silverman, "Adoption of Agricultural Innovations in Developing Countries: A Survey," *Economic Development and Cultural Change* 33, no. 2 (1985):271.

22. See *WDR 1982,* pp. 81–82, and *WDR 1986,* pp. 85–86.

23. Pan A. Yotopoulos and Jeffrey B. Nugent, *Economics of Development: Empirical Investigations,* New York, 1976, p. 103; *WDR 1980,* p. 42.

24. U Tun Wai, "A Revisit to Interest Rates Outside the Organized Money Markets of Underdeveloped Countries," *Banca Nazionale del Lavoro Quarterly Review* 122 (September 1977):311.

25. *The Economist,* March 28, 1981.

26. U Tun Wai, "Interest Rates Outside the Organized Money Markets," p. 309.

27. *Ibid.,* p. 294.

28. *The Economist,* September 22, 1984, p. 561.

29. U Tun Wai, "Interest Rates Outside the Organized Money Markets," p. 302.

30. There are exceptions. Botswana, for example, has legalized the use of both crops and livestock as collateral.

31. For a study that gives many bibliographical references, see Michael Lipton, "Agricultural Finance and Rural Credit in Poor Countries," in Paul Streeten and Richard Jolly, eds., *Recent Issues in World Development,* Oxford, 1981. The work of Joseph E. Stiglitz has emphasized the importance of imperfect information and the costs of overcoming it. Stiglitz notes in particular how imperfect information has repercussions beyond credit alone, including the link between credit and land tenure arrangements such as sharecropping. His article, "The New Development Economics," *World Development* 14, no. 2 (1986):257–265, refers to several other important articles written by him, some with D. M. G. Newbery, and a wide selection of other works as well. In their extensive and valuable research, Dale Adams and Richard Meyers of Ohio State have discussed subsidized rural credit programs. "How not to do it" is emphasized in Dale W. Adams, Douglas H. Graham, and John D. von Pischke, eds., *Undermining Rural Development with Cheap Credit,* Boulder, Colo., 1984; and in John D. von Pischke et al., eds., *Rural Financial Markets in Developing Countries: Their Use and Abuse,* Baltimore, 1983. Both of these volumes represent important new views on the credit problem.

32. In a few countries (Malaysia, Indonesia) banks have begun to employ local agents,

mainly traders but including even moneylenders, in an effort to reduce the risks of inadequate knowledge. See V. V. Bhatt, "Improving the Financial Structure in Developing Countries," *Finance and Development* 23, no. 2 (1986):21.

33. See Anand G. Chandavarkar, "The Financial Pull of Urban Areas in LDCs," *Finance and Development* 22, no. 2 (1985):26; *WDR 1986,* p. 101.

34. *WDR 1986,* p. 100.

35. From *WDR 1979,* p. 50.

36. See *The Economist,* March 28, 1981.

37. This was an important source of funds for Japanese rural development. *WDR 1986,* p. 101.

38. Compare Todaro, *Economic Development in the Third World,* 2nd ed., p. 471.

39. For a summary of the problems, see Dale W. Adams and Robert C. Vogel, "Rural Financial Markets in Low-Income Countries: Recent Controversies and Lessons," *World Development* 14, No. 4 (1986):477–487. For full treatment, see Adams, Graham, and von Pischke, *Undermining Rural Development with Cheap Credit,* and von Pischke et al., *Rural Financial Markets.*

40. For a time the budget was cut back to less than half the previous figure. See *The Economist,* March 28, 1981; October 17, 1981; January 8, 1983; January 26, February 16, and March 9, 1985. I also drew on articles in the *Christian Science Monitor* and *Wall Street Journal.*

41. For the current figures on agricultural research, see Robert Picciotto, "National Agricultural Research," *Finance and Development* 22, no. 2 (1985):45–47. Picciotto notes that rates of return on agricultural research are now commonly over 20 percent.

42. See *WDR 1982,* p. 73.

43. From Gershon Feder and Roger Slade, "The Impact of Agricultural Extension: The Training and Visit System in India," *The World Bank Research Observer* 1, no. 2 (1986):139–161, especially p. 140.

44. *WDR 1982* and *WDR 1983* have material on farmer behavior, from which some of the cases noted in the text are drawn. A review of the literature is Robert E. Evenson and Yoav Kislev, "Investment in Agricultural Research and Extension: A Survey of International Data," *Economic Development and Cultural Change* 23, no. 3 (1974):-507–521. *WDR 1986,* p. 87, discusses risk aversion in farming.

45. John Russell, "Adapting Extension Work to Poorer Agricultural Areas," *Finance and Development* 18, no. 2 (1981):32.

46. Some of this material is from *WDR 1982,* pp. 69–71 and *WDR 1986,* p. 78. *The Economist* has published frequently on the subject. See the issues of May 13, 1978; March 28, April 18, and July 18, 1981; November 19, 1983; August 18 and August 25, 1984. I also utilized articles in the *Christian Science Monitor,* especially September 18, 1980.

47. Some of the details in this paragraph are from the *Christian Science Monitor,* September 18, 1980, and April 28, 1981.

48. Centro International de Majoramiento de Maiz y Trigo.

49. See "Trends in Grain Consumption in the Developing World, 1960–80," *Finance and Development* 22, no. 4 (1985):12.

50. *Ibid.*

51. As usual, there is room for some skepticism. Most studies, including this section, tend to exaggerate the yield increases delivered by the HYVs to the degree that they cite experimental data from demonstration plots rather than actual field data. And they perhaps overemphasize the role of the international programs such as IRRI and CIMMYT relative to the less-known but valuable research and extension programs

of the LDCs themselves. See Douglas Horton, "Assessing the Impact of International Agricultural Research and Development Programs," *World Development* 14, no. 4 (1986):453–468, especially 465.

52. *The Economist,* June 14, 1986, p. 66.

53. The tendency for public sector marketing to be high in cost and the Bangladesh reform are discussed in *WDR 1986,* pp. 89, 106–107.

54. The T&V technique was originally tested in Turkey during the late 1960s, but since 1977 it has achieved its widest use in India. See *The Economist,* July 5, 1986, pp. 76–77, and the survey article by Gershon Feder and Roger Slade, "The Impact of Agricultural Extension: The Training and Visit System in India," *The World Bank Research Observer* 1, no. 2 (1986):139–161. Also see the same authors' "A Comparative Analysis of Some Aspects of the Training and Visit System of Agricultural Extension in India," *Journal of Development Studies* 22, no. 2 (1986):407–428; and the detailed account by Gershon Feder, Lawrence J. Lau, and Roger H. Slade, *The Impact of Agricultural Extension: A Case Study of the Training and Visit System in Haryana, India,* World Bank Staff Working Paper No. 756, Washington, D.C., 1985.

55. The factors that can delay adoption of the new methods are discussed by Feder, Just, and Silverman, "Adoption of Agricultural Innovations," pp. 255–298.

56. The following three paragraphs of text draw on the survey article by M. Prahladachar, "Income Distribution Effects of the Green Revolution in India: A Review of the Empirical Evidence," *World Development* 11, no. 11 (1983):927–944; and a number of informative articles in *Economic Development and Cultural Change:* Murray J. Leaf, "The Green Revolution and Cultural Change in a Punjab Village," 31, no. 2 (1983):227–270; George Blyn, "The Green Revolution Revisited," 31, no. 4 (1983): 705–725; and Grace E. Goodell, "Bugs, Bunds, Banks, and Bottlenecks: Organizational Contradictions in the New Rice Technology," 33, no. 1 (1984):23–41. Also utilized were Vernon Ruttan, "The Green Revolution: Seven Generalizations," *International Development Review,* December 1977, pp. 16–22; and B. H. Farmer, "The 'Green Revolution' in South Asian Ricefields: Environment and Production," *Journal of Development Studies* 15, no. 3 (1979):304–319; B. H. Farmer, ed., *Green Revolution?* London, 1977; and the review of this volume by Michael Lipton in the *Journal of Development Studies* 15, no. 3 (1979):342–349. There is also a recent volume of papers edited by John W. Mellor and Gunvant M. Desai, *Agricultural Change and Rural Poverty,* Baltimore, 1985.

57. The empirical evidence on growing labor use is cited in S. K. Jayasuriya and R. T. Shand, "Technical Change and Labor Absorption in Asian Agriculture: Some Emerging Trends," *World Development* 14, no. 3 (1986):415–428, especially 417–420. There were some exceptions to the trend toward increased labor use.

58. *Ibid.,* pp. 420–425. The details in this and the next two paragraphs are from this article.

59. For evidence that crucial farming operations are not in general becoming more "timely" because of mechanization, see S. K. Jayasuriya, A. Te, and R. W. Herdt, "Mechanisation and Cropping Intensification: Economics of Machinery Use in Low-Wage Economies," *Journal of Development Studies* 22, no. 2 (1986):327–335.

60. See *WDR 1982,* p. 64; and *The Economist,* November 3, 1984; November 2, 1985.

61. Genetic engineering could also be used as a weapon against the devastating insect pests such as locusts and grasshoppers. New strains of insect disease and methods to spread old ones are being worked on.

62. *WDR 1982,* p. 60.

63. The Lewis model first appeared in a famous article, "Economic Development with

Unlimited Supplies of Labor," *Manchester School,* 22 (1954):139–191. Gustav Ranis and J. C. H. Fei presented their model in *Development of the Labor Surplus Economy: Theory and Policy,* Homewood, Ill., 1964. In this and the next section I benefited from Yotopoulos and Nugent, *Economics of Development,* chap. 12; and from A. Berry and R. H. Sabot, "Labour Market Performance in Developing Countries: A Survey," in Paul Streeten and Richard Jolly, eds., *Recent Issues in World Development,* Oxford, 1981, pp. 149–192.

64. See Warren C. Robinson, "Types of Disguised Rural Unemployment and Some Policy Implications," *Oxford Economic Papers* 21, no. 3 (1969):373. See also Harvey Leibenstein, *General X-Efficiency Theory and Economic Development,* New York, 1978, chap. 4.

65. The question of how the great expansion of cash crop exports from LDCs could have taken place without cutting food output still remains. One explanation is that the most intense periods of labor use in the production of these crops did not correspond exactly to the peak labor demands in food production. For this section, I referred to and utilized Meier, *Leading Issues,* 4th ed., pts. III.A, III.B; and 3rd ed., New York, 1976, pt. III.C, which contain work of R. Nurkse, J. Viner, A. K. Sen, H. Myint, G. Haberler, and Meier himself.

66. Cited by Warren C. Robinson, "Types of Disguised Rural Unemployment," p. 373.

67. Following Yotopoulos and Nugent, *Economics of Development,* pp. 198–205.

68. This diagram follows Michael P. Todaro, *Economic Development in the Third World,* 2nd ed., New York, 1981, p. 236. Also see Bruce Herrick and Charles P. Kindleberger, *Economic Development,* 4th ed., New York, 1983, p. 65.

69. Work of Robert Mabro cited by Subrata Ghatak, *Development Economics,* London, 1978, p. 44.

70. In some countries, migrants from rural areas make up 60 or even 70 percent of urban population increase. See *WDR 1979,* p. 55. In this section, I made use of Gerald Meier's comments in *Leading Issues,* 4th ed., pp. 191–195.

71. From Todaro, *Economic Development in the Third World,* 2nd ed., p. 209.

72. Michael Lipton, *Why Poor People Stay Poor,* pp. 435–437; see also Nafziger, *Economics of Developing Countries,* p. 119.

73. See Dennis J. Mahar, "Population Distribution Within LDCs," *Finance and Development* 21, no. 3 (1984):15–17.

74. Peter Kilby of Wesleyan University made available as yet unpublished material that has been drawn on in this section. The Todaro text, 2nd ed., chap. 9, and William Loehr and John P. Powelson, *The Economics of Development and Distribution,* New York, 1981, pp. 269–274, are informative, and I have used them.

75. The seminal articles on decision making by migrants were Michael P. Todaro, "A Model of Labor Migration and Urban Unemployment in Less Developed Countries," *American Economic Review* 59, no. 1 (1969):138–148; and John Harris and Michael Todaro, "Migration, Unemployment and Development: A Two-Sector Analysis," *American Economic Review* 60, no. 1 (1970):126–142. A recent critique is William E. Cole and Richard D. Saunders, "Internal Migration and Urban Employment in the Third World," *American Economic Review* 75, no. 3 (1985):481–494; and see Todaro's reply "Internal Migration and Urban Employment: Comment," *American Economic Review* 76, no. 3 (1986):566–569. A helpful "Symposium on Advances in Migration Theory" was published as a special issue of the *Journal of Development Economics* 17, nos. 1–2 (January-February 1985), and there is a volume by Richard H. Sabot, *Migration and the Labor Market in Developing Countries,* Boulder, Colo., 1982. An application of sophisticated economic modeling to rural-urban migration in the LDCs is Allen

   C. Kelley and Jeffrey G. Williamson, *What Drives Third World City Growth? A Dynamic Equilibrium Approach,* Princeton, N.J., 1984.

76. *WDR 1984,* p. 88. For recent skepticism on how high the wage differentials actually are, and for evidence that the murky sector has provided more jobs than formerly believed, see Friedrich Kahnert, "Re-examining Urban Poverty and Employment," *Finance and Development* 23, no. 1 (1986):44–47.

77. See the discussion, with numerous sources, in Yotopoulos and Nugent, *Economics of Development,* p. 227. Also see Mahar, "Population Distribution Within LDCs" pp. 16–17; and Todaro, *Economic Development in the Third World,* 2nd ed., pp. 237–238.

78. Kahnert, "Re-examining Urban Poverty and Employment," pp. 44–47.

79. Compare *WDR 1984,* p. 98; and Mahar, "Population Distribution Within LDCs," p. 17.

80. This section utilizes especially Lane E. Holdcroft, "The Rise and Fall of Community Development 1950–65: A Critical Assessment," in Eicher and Staatz, *Agricultural Development in the Third World,* pp. 46–58, and builds on what W. Arthur Lewis had to say in *The Theory of Economic Growth,* London, 1955, especially pp. 59–60.

81. *WDR 1980,* p. 75; *Newsweek,* June 23, 1986.

82. Paralleling the comments by Meier, *Leading Issues,* 4th ed., pp. 210–214.

83. See *WDR 1979,* chap. 8, for the details on the first four countries, and also *WDR 1982,* p. 85. There is a useful analysis in Samuel S. P. Ho, "Economic Development and Rural Industry in South Korea and Taiwan," *World Development* 10, no. 11 (1982): 973–990. For China see the sources cited in note 94.

84. The Maharastra Employment Guarantee Scheme pays the minimum agricultural wage on rural public works located not more than 5 kilometers from a participating village. See I. Singh, *Small Farmers and the Landless in South Asia,* World Bank Staff Working Paper No. 320, 1979.

85. *WDR 1986,* p. 106.

86. See Yotopoulos and Nugent, *Economics of Development,* p. 203.

87. Several volumes that discuss this experience include George S. Tolley, Vinod Thomas, and Chung Ming Wong, *Agricultural Price Policies and the Developing Countries,* Baltimore, 1982; I. Arnon, *Modernization of Agriculture in Developing Countries,* Chichester, 1981; James A. Lynch, Jr., and Edward B. Tasch, *Food Production and Public Policy in Developing Countries,* New York, 1983; and D. Gale Johnson and G. Edward Schuh, *The Role of Markets in the World Food Economy,* Boulder, Colo., 1983. More recently, the comprehensive reforms undertaken by Turkey and Bangladesh have attracted favorable attention. See *WDR 1986,* pp. 106–108.

88. From Reginald H. Green, in Meier, *Leading Issues,* 3rd ed., p. 837.

89. *WDR 1979,* pp. 106–107, and *WDR 1986,* chapters 4 and 5.

90. *WDR 1986,* pp. 95–97.

91. *Ibid.*

92. *Ibid.,* p. 109.

93. *Ibid.,* p. 10. Interference with this process can leave a country worse off than before. In Kenya, for example, government policies to increase self-sufficiency upset a thriving specialized peasant sector, and there is evidence that food marketing actually fell, with an attendant rise in imports. See Michael Cowen, "Change in State Power, International Conditions and Peasant Producers: The Case of Kenya," *Journal of Development Studies* 22, no. 2 (1986):355–384.

94. Three recent analyses of the reform of Chinese agriculture are Keith Griffin, ed., *Institutional Reform and Economic Development in the Chinese Countryside,* Armonk, N.Y., 1985; Dwight Perkins and Shahid Yusuf, *Rural Development in China,* Balti-

more, 1984; and Nicolas Lardy, *Agriculture in China's Modern Economic Development,* Cambridge, 1983. See also *WDR 1986,* pp. 105–106, and *The Economist,* October 13 and 27, 1984; February 2, 1985; and January 18, 1986; *Wall Street Journal,* January 13, 1986; and *WDR 1982,* p. 47.

95. *WDR 1986,* p. 105.

96. During the period 1975 to 1982 the combination of poor policies, high population growth, and (in some years) bad weather caused food output per capita to fall in 23 of 33 African countries for which acceptable data were available. See Shahid Javed Burki and Robert L. Ayres, "A Fresh Look at Development Aid," *Finance and Development* 23, no. 1 (1986):7.

97. Students could continue their study of employment problems with Lyn Squire, *Employment Policy in Developing Countries: A Survey of Issues and Evidence,* New York, 1981.

chapter 11

Planning and the Market

One of the great debates in development economics has involved the role that government planning should play in the allocation of an economy's resources. The essential question is the extent to which an economy should be directed by a government's priorities rather than by the unplanned operation of a decentralized system of market prices. There have been great swings in this debate over the past 30 years, with considerable support for detailed planning among the economists of the 1950s and 1960s, but a substantial reaction against it in the 1970s and 1980s. The debate is by no means settled—perhaps it never will be. To some degree the stand taken in this debate serves as a litmus test as to one's position as a development economist. The proponents of detailed planning are viewed as left of center and perhaps radical by the free marketeer; the free marketeer is labeled conservative or reactionary by the pro-planner. Neither side accepts the other's stereotypes, but they are applied nonetheless.

Planning involves the deliberate, coordinated attempt to alter the outcome that would have emerged with an unimpeded market mechanism. Proponents of planning object to the results of a market mechanism for two reasons: First, the market may not work perfectly, and second, the market, when it works, may produce undesirable results.[1]

MARKET FAILURES

The first objection to a free market system, that is, to decision making based on the search for profit within a system of market prices, is that such a system does not work optimally. The objection is based on several considerations.

1. There may be ignorance and lack of information. This will be especially important for investment decisions where the lifetime of capital goods is long and where the indivisibility of capital makes for "lumpy" investment.

2. Externalities may exist. The investor, employer, and landlord consider the private marginal product, not the social marginal product, of their activities. External economies do not lead to more of a given activity because the externality is reaped by others; external diseconomies are ignored since these costs are not felt by their perpetrator. Akin to this argument, some goods will carry a large element of consumers' surplus to the purchasers; others will not. The mechanism of commercial profitability does not measure the degree of the surplus and thus does not signal increases in the production of goods with large amounts of such surpluses.

3. Monopoly distortions may be widespread in the economy.[2] Though estimates of the degree of monopoly power in the LDCs are rare, there are reasons to believe that such power may be more pervasive than in the developed countries. Antitrust laws are frequently nonexistent, the countervailing power of labor unions is often weak, small markets inhibit competition, and highly concentrated land ownership may mean some monopoly power in the agricultural sector as well as in industry. Profit maximization in a free market does not allocate resources correctly if perfect competition is absent, for then market prices will not be the same as social opportunity costs.

4. Government interference with foreign trade, exchange rates, and interest rates may likewise alter the competitive price structure. Especially when foreign trade is restricted via impenetrable quota barriers, the monopoly power referred to above may be enhanced even further. Again, prices might well be an inadequate reflection of social opportunity costs.

5. A system of market prices may, because of the economic structure of LDCs, require large and destabilizing price changes to achieve useful results. Obstacles and bottlenecks of all kinds may exist. Resources may be immobile. Perhaps there is even a perverse ("backward-bending") response to price changes by labor, farmers, and small businesses. All these constraints may make supply so inelastic that large price changes are needed to call forth small adjustments. (Note the similarity of these points to the structural argument concerning inflation discussed in Chapter 4.[3])

All of these arguments are used to justify planning, and it does indeed take a very dogmatic free marketeer to ignore the market failures entirely. Undeniably, some of the problems discussed above do exist, and wise government action can bring improvements. The debates over planning usually focus not on the existence of various market failures, but on the wisdom of the particular government policy actions to rectify them. Certainly, sufficient serious problems have beset the stronger forms of these actions in recent years to warrant a cautious approach even by planning's committed supporters.

Probably the most controversial criticism of the market is the last, concerning slow or perverse response to market signals. There is a wealth of evidence from agriculture that poor peasant farmers are quick to appreciate new opportunities for profit when these spring up, as in the Green Revolution, or shift to lower-taxed crops (or sell on the black market or smuggle) when taxation hits their staple. It is self-evident that migrants to the cities or overseas are responding in a dramatic way to economic incentives. This is certainly not to claim that all markets in LDCs work efficiently, but it is still a bit of a puzzle how the idea that market responses are generally weak or perverse in LDCs would gain such credence.[4] One is left with at least a suspicion that this claim is a carry-over from the racial attitudes of the old colonial past.

UNDESIRABLE MARKET RESULTS

Even with strong responses, however, a market mechanism might still yield an outcome that politicians (and economists in their policy-making role) may find undesirable; planning may be called for to counter these results. This position is normative, involving a value judgment.

    1. A government may judge that there is a socially undesirable maldistribution of income. If the present distribution is not approved of and cannot be modified through taxes and subsidies, then the market outcome will be considered flawed. The Pareto optimum rule of the textbooks states that economic efficiency is attained when no one's situation can be improved without worsening that of another. The rule will perhaps be thought quite unsatisfactory if it leads to decisions not to improve the lot of a large mass of poor because that would cause some harm to a small group of very rich.

    2. Political leaders may make a value judgment that they should weigh more

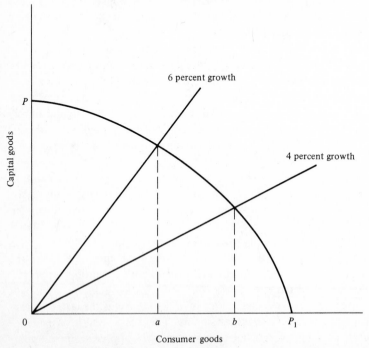

Figure 11.1 Maximizing consumption now or in the future.

heavily than the market does the interests of future generations. If the rate of time discount is high, it means that people tend on the whole to much prefer income now to income later. This, it is said, will cut investment and the ultimate rate of growth. The Galenson-Leibenstein criterion for investment, named for the econo-mists who developed it, illustrates how a planner might choose to extract higher investment now to promote a more rapid rate of growth later. Galenson and Leibenstein suggest that projects be selected to maximize the level of saving and reinvestment, thus maximizing the "rate of creation of investable surplus."[5] Fig-ure 11.1 shows the difference between maximizing consumption now and con-sumption in the future. PP_1 is a production possibility curve, with capital goods on the vertical axis and consumption goods on the horizontal. Choosing a higher percentage of capital goods output yields a faster real growth rate (say, 6 percent), but at a cost of a cut in consumption represented by the distance *ab*.

Figure 11.2 shows the change in consumer goods output over time if a capital-intensive method (K) is selected and if a labor-intensive method (L) is selected.[6] To time T_1 capital-intensive method K sacrifices output of consumption goods. By time T_2 it compensates for the initial loss of output because at T_2 the decrease in consumer goods output, represented by the area ABC is equal to the subsequent increase in output CDE. After T_2, say, 30 years, society is better off. The rate of time discount is thus crucial. If it is very low, K will be preferred; if high, L. A country's leadership might decide to value future consumption higher than does the general public; using the Galenson-Leibenstein argument, it might decide to incorporate projects in its development plan that would result

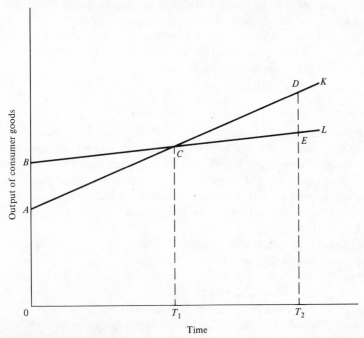

Figure 11.2 Change in consumer goods output over time with capital intensity and labor intensity.

in higher levels of investment than the market would signal. Indeed, many people *themselves* might be willing individually to make sacrifices for future generations, but are discouraged from doing so because of their belief that many others would not voluntarily do likewise.[7] A role for public policy (government planning) is thus called for to ensure that potential "free riders" play their part.

Thus there are both good economic and understandable political reasons why some planning is inevitable, especially where market failures are most pronounced and the distribution of income most skewed. There are clear historical reasons as well. Most LDCs at the end of the colonial period acquired new governments with new leaders committed to growth. To a significant degree, their credibility both at home and abroad depended on delivery of this much-desired "product." The leaders opted for an active and aggressive government role in overcoming shortages, especially shortages of funds for investment. They thought government planning could redress the market failures, direct resources into areas most important for growth and welfare, perhaps even cut down on the volatility of investment that characterizes the business cycle in unplanned economies.

The instincts of these leaders were not necessarily wrong even in countries where the record of planning has been unfavorable. Again let us emphasize that the crucial debate is not so much on the need for some government participation in the development process, but on how pervasive that participation should be, whether the implementation is overzealous, and whether poor planning technique in particular cases confers more costs than benefits. The weighing of trade-offs is central to economics, and this is certainly true of planning.

There is one last point to be made. Care must be exercised in judging this debate. Some observers are much too inclined to compare the unplanned success of some countries with the planning failures of others, and vice versa. Beware: The proper question is what would have occurred in a *given* country under a different policy mix. This is not at all easy to determine.

TYPES OF PLANS

Popular on every continent since India's first five-year plan in 1952, planning has spread almost everywhere in the LDCs. Hardly a country has no development plan at all, and some 300 separate national plans have appeared since the exercise was pioneered.[8] The mathematical technique of planning is sophisticated, as much as or more so than in any other branch of economics, but we shall see that in spite of the brilliance of the technique, the last decade has been kind neither to planners nor to planning itself.

What are the core characteristics of plans? Basically, they are of three main types: comprehensive, indicative, and formal. A comprehensive, or "dirigiste" plan, following the Soviet command model, is aggregate macro planning covering a large part of the economy. An indicative plan involves fully or largely planned government expenditure while private spending is influenced, but not commanded, by tax and subsidy policies within an aggregate planning framework. Finally, a formal plan is more a sketch for strategy than a blueprint actually to be implemented. Indicative and formal planning often emphasize sectoral models that focus on the relations between two or three industries. Such sectoral models are favored by advocates of planning who feel that the aggregate approach has gone too far.[9]

Comprehensive Planning   Comprehensive, Soviet-style planning typically employs direct government command to determine output, with inputs also specified in the plan under the system called "materials balancing." This may be done for a large part of the economy, as in the USSR itself, Eastern Europe, and China, or it may be applied mostly to heavy industry, as at one time or another in Bangladesh, Ethiopia, India, Sri Lanka, Turkey, Algeria, Libya, and several others. Much higher levels of national product can certainly be achieved in this way, as shown conclusively by the performance of the Soviet Union or East Germany. But the general record of comprehensive planning in recent years has not been very satisfactory, and there have been significant defections. Yugoslavia moved away from it in the 1950s, Hungary in the 1960s, China starting in the late 1970s, Turkey and Bangladesh in the early 1980s. All retain vestiges of the idea, but all have much modified its comprehensive character.

In LDCs the major obstacles to comprehensive planning have been weaknesses in information, inadequate staff, and poor coordination of industrial investment. The one econometric tool that could make such planning much more efficient, input-output (IO) analysis, is difficult to operate where the underlying data are weak or missing. IO analysis was invented by Wassily Leontief of Harvard.[10] The planner with an accurate matrix showing where all inputs come from and where all outputs go can ensure that the plan adequately provides for industrial demand as well as consumer demand.

A three-product economy producing electricity, coal, and steel will exemplify what the planners need to know. If consumer demand for electricity rises, and new generators are included in the plan, that will change the necessary output of steel (for the generators) and for coal (both for the steel and for powering the generators). It even alters the demand for electricity, which is used in the mills and in the mines. Planning even this simple economy would thus be a difficult exercise in matching supplies and demands.

If, however, IO analysis can be used to trace these effects, the problem becomes more manageable. A matrix of interindustry flows can be used for the tracing, as in Table 11.1. The vertical columns show inputs, while the horizontal rows show outputs, all measured in dollars. Using this technique, the planner can

Table 11.1.   MATRIX OF INTERINDUSTRY FLOWS (IN DOLLARS)

Outputs ⟶	Electricity	Steel	Coal	Consumer demand	Total
Inputs Electricity	200	200	200	400	1,000
Steel	400	100	200	300	1,000
Coal	200	600	0	200	1,000
Value added	200	100	600	100	
Total	1,000	1,000	1,000		

project what happens throughout the system from an initial change in any box of the matrix and can thereby plan both outputs and inputs with some confidence in the plan's consistency.

Input-output analysis has come to be recognized as elegant in its mathematics and useful to economists everywhere. But there is also a major obstacle to its employment in support of comprehensive planning outside the developed world: IO studies are data-intensive, requiring accurate information far beyond that available in most LDCs. A secondary problem has been the assumption in IO analysis of fixed coefficients, for example, a fixed proportion of coal in the output of steel. This assumption can lead an observer to miss the potential for substituting one input for another and can thus lead to pessimism concerning the ease with which an economy can respond to internal or external disturbances.

Even the countries with excellent planning organizations and where good data are widely available, India, for example, have found comprehensive planning difficult to carry through. By and large, their comprehensive plans have been unable to surmount the shock that a changing economic environment can deliver. Unforeseen events of the 1970s and 1980s, such as the oil crises, the food shock, and the debt crisis, brought formidable and complex problems of reworking the planning structure. Events showed that governments with centralized decision making were no better able to anticipate these crises than governments with less comprehensive planning or none at all.

Indicative and Formal Planning Indicative planning was first invented in France after World War II and spread from there to francophone Africa and Southeast Asia. Some successful economies have used the method, including South Korea, Kenya, Malaysia, and the Ivory Coast. Typically, government expenditure is carefully planned, especially official investment. Government predicts what it expects to happen in the private economy, and if the private sector has confidence in the predictions, it will invest accordingly. Taxes, subsidies, licenses, permits for foreign exchange, "jawboning," and the like can be used to influence private firms in the direction of the plan targets.

The third type of planning, formal, came late. It was largely employed by countries that wanted to develop a national consensus or vision about economic policy and to demonstrate their rational strategies to aid givers. Often the only substantive difference from indicative planning is that actual plan implementation receives little emphasis. The formal variety is found particularly in Latin America, the last large group of LDCs to adopt planning. Formal plans are also found in parts of sub-Saharan Africa, for example, Ghana and Nigeria, and on some Caribbean islands such as Jamaica.

In contrast to comprehensive plans, both the indicative and the formal variety rely primarily on prices and markets. Depending on the degree of government intervention, the price structure will be more or less influenced by price controls in the private sector and the price policies of state corporations in the public sector; plus the usual range of measures affecting credit, labor markets, foreign trade, and the exchange rate. Typically, both indicative and formal planning are more flexible instruments than the comprehensive central plans, with forecasting emphasized instead of targeting, and appraisal of individual projects instead of sectoral materials balancing. R. Agarwala calls this a "learning approach" as opposed to a blueprint strategy, with concentration on "strategic policies" rather than attempting to be comprehensive.

CONSTRUCTING AN AGGREGATE PLAN

Whether the plan is a target actually aimed at with government directing private decisions or a forecast with government only influencing the private sector by means of taxes, subsidies, price controls, and similar means, the aggregate, or macro, planning models will usually be very similar. Often the key difference is not the mathematical appearance of the model itself, but the steps the government is willing to take to enforce implementation. The plans will contain an equation for consumption, saving, and income; a production function relating GNP to inputs of capital and labor; an import function relating imports to national income; equations defining GNP and national income; and a series of constraints. Examples of constraints might be that labor use cannot exceed its supply, that investment cannot exceed domestic saving plus net capital inflows, that imports cannot be larger than foreign exchange earnings from exports plus foreign grants and loans, and that the aggregated plan is the sum of all its sectoral components.

Frequently, a capital-output ratio is employed (see Appendix 1 at the end of the chapter for a full discussion), allowing planners to predict the change in output resulting from a planned level of investment. In many countries utilizing planning, a large share of investment is undertaken by government and is hence directly controllable. The most popular of all the planning tools, the capital-output ratio was important in the work of the late Sir Roy Harrod of Oxford and Evsey Domar of MIT; the Harrod-Domar model is named for them.

The Harrod-Domar model in the hands of development economists relates the level of investment, that is, the growth in the capital stock, to the rate of growth in the national income. Development specialists working with the model discovered that for many countries, an investment of $100 will on average give rise to an increase in national income of between $25 and $33 per year. Or, stated another way, raising national income by 3 percent per year is associated with yearly net investment of 9 to 12 percent of national income. These calculations embody the numerical relation between the amount of investment and the increase in output associated with that investment. Here the relation is between 3 and 4, because $9/3 = 3$ and $12/3 = 4$. Investment (change in capital) is in the numerator, output is in the denominator, hence the name capital-output ratio.

How utterly seductive was the appeal of models embodying such a ratio! The planning commissions in LDCs could see some signs of certainty in them. A given capital-output ratio could simply be plugged arithmetically into a formula. If the planners wanted to shoot for 4 percent growth in income and the capital-output ratio was 4, then the percent of this year's income that ought to be invested would be 16 percent, and this would also be the target for saving. Or, if it was thought that the maximum amount of investment that could possibly be squeezed out of the economy was 10 percent, then the rate of growth in income to be expected would be 2.5 percent per year.

Such simplicity attracted a large following, and even today models embodying capital-output ratios are a fixture of development economics. But the euphoria has long since dissipated. Growth and development are much too complex to permit this simplified sort of analysis, nor is there any guarantee that a ratio holding at one moment will continue to hold in the future. A decade of criticism is distilled here into Appendix 1 to this chapter. Though many of the problems with models utilizing a capital-output ratio are technical in nature, the most serious of the objections is also perhaps the easiest to understand. Concentrating on capital alone leads inexorably to neglect of the noncapital elements in growth. These important elements may be, at worst, completely ignored, or they may be, at best, assumed to increase in just the right proportion as the capital stock increases.

To be sure, additions to capital increase output, and hence the capital-output ratio does have some justification. Think, however, of how much *greater* the increase in output would be if technological change accompanied the capital increase, or if management improved, or if the weather were better this year than last, or if attitudes toward work altered, or if health, nutrition, and education, improved, or if bribery and corruption in government and business were reduced, or if onerous taxation and tariffs were lowered, or if the family system that previously discouraged saving and investment now encouraged it. All these changes are obscured by dependence on models that use a simple capital-output ratio. Any explanation of Japan's economy that uses such a ratio without discussing that country's pronounced emphasis on education and team achievement must be grossly inadequate. Any view of a Green Revolution that limits itself to capital as conventionally defined, without close attention to new seed, fertilizer, water, and extension services is even more deficient.[11]

But all this is convincing logic that there will continue to be a major use for capital-output ratios in which economists can still repose confidence. They do indicate well an improving or worsening "climate" for new investment. In the Philippines, when investment in the period 1978 to 1982 was drawn to industries protected by high barriers to imports, and into low-productivity uses because interest rates were kept artificially low, the capital-output ratio more than doubled. Similar policies in Argentina, along with hyperinflation, raised the ratio from 4.4 in 1963 to 1972 to about 11 in 1973 to 1981. In Morocco, where public sector investment was notably inefficient, the numerous "white elephants" caused the figure to rise from 2.6 in 1965 to 1972 to 6.7 in 1979 to 1982. All these examples show how the capital-output ratio, though much criticized as a planning device, does useful service in measuring trends in the efficiency of investment.[12]

Planning Versus Prices

There is wide agreement that the use of planning *can* be justified because of imperfections in markets. The real debate is what type of planning will do the most good and whether the type of implementation chosen gives better results than the market would. There is, after all, unfortunately no guarantee that even where markets operate inefficiently, government planning will necessarily be an improvement.[13]

A simple correlation between the existence of planning and growth is not especially revealing. There are countries with both little and much planning in all three growth categories, high, moderate, and low. Presumably this is because government can be efficient or inefficient, employing effective or ineffective policies toward saving, investing, and productivity, whether or not the economy is planned.[14] On another plane, however, the record of planning in the LDCs during the 1970s and 1980s is not encouraging. As Albert Waterston points out, plan targets worldwide have been missed far more often than they have been hit, and the misses were more frequent in the 1970s than in the 1960s, and more frequent in the 1960s than in the 1950s.[15] The two main reasons for the misses are outside influences over which the planning country has no control and inside (domestic) problems with the plan.

The outside influences are clear enough. Few plans were sufficiently resilient to survive the two oil shocks, the food shock, the interest rate shock, and the deepest recession since the 1930s, all occurring in the last dozen years. Wholesale scrapping of plan targets was a general result, with the problems most acute where the planning was most comprehensive. Singapore even took the step of bringing its detailed planning effort to a complete halt explicitly because its annual plans were not keeping pace with rapid changes in the outside economic environment or even keeping up with the *internal* growth of the economy.[16] A strong impression from the past decade is that uncertainties in economics have grown, that predictions on the whole have been less accurate than they were earlier, that economic policy, when not flexible, can slip far behind events. Of course, exogenous shocks hit and disrupt unplanned economies as well. Markets, however, transmit the signals that a "shock" is in progress and provide the incentive for rapid reaction and adjustment, whereas planners often have a much slower reaction time.

An excellent example of the inflexibility that characterizes much planning can be found in the network of state-owned and state-run corporations (the parastatals or state-owned enterprises, SOEs) of many economies. The importance of these firms is attested by the fact that they account for approximately 10 percent of national product in the LDCs as a whole and at least a quarter of all capital formation. Sometimes the figure is much higher, over 60 percent, for example, in Algeria, Burma, and Zambia. In Argentina 118 state-controlled firms employ a quarter of the labor force. The government sector in Mexico consists of about 550 companies, with energy, petroleum, newspapers, airlines, railways, banks, and many other industries all nationalized. Brazil has a huge parastatal sector of just under 500 firms (it ran up about 65 percent of Brazil's total foreign debt during the debt crisis). India, Pakistan, Peru, Sri Lanka, Tanzania, and Zaire, among others, also have a very large number of SOEs.[17]

Flexibility of response is likely to be low among the managers of the parastatals.[18] They may be enmeshed in the net of price controls that stifle the signals of any shock, whether external or internal. Often they are not subject to the profit motive, with the government historically subsidizing them to cover any losses. Thus they do not respond rapidly to changing economic conditions; in any case they know that the government will not allow them to fail, because that would cause disruption in an important sector. This, too, limits their responsiveness. Finally, given the public "civil service" nature of their jobs, parastatal managers are often risk-avoiders rather than risk-takers; no penalty attaches to very conservative management, no profit rewards innovation, better decision making, or cost cutting. If an innovation proves unsuccessful, however, the loss would be noticed, the manager would be blamed, and promotion would be jeopardized—all good reasons for avoiding new ways of doing things.

Much of this is less important in industries where demand and supply conditions are relatively stable over long periods, as in the management of a sewer system, say, or public education. But when demand or supply are volatile, lack of flexibility may cause considerable damage. Cases in point include energy-intensive industries such as electric power hard hit by the oil shock, or agriculture which may be subject to severe supply fluctuations, or consumer goods such as shoes where tastes change rapidly. These considerations do not necessarily mean that a free market would be preferable; capital indivisibilities, monopoly possibilities, a weak free market structure, and all the other considerations noted earlier in the chapter might well in any given case justify the development of state enterprise. (Other common justifications advanced either explicitly or implicitly include ideology, generation of employment, regional development, national defense, and self-sufficiency.) Whatever the justifications, however, parastatal performance has frequently been disappointing, the firms overstaffed, poorly managed, inflexible, inert, and dependent on the government budget to make up their losses. Arguably, these firms are the exemplars of Harvey Leibenstein's X-inefficiency, the concept, met with earlier, that given the quantity of resources used, output is less than otherwise could be obtained.[19]

Where parastatals are thought to be essential, in many cases there seems a need for rather thorough reform. Fortunately, there is no iron law that they must always be inefficient, and policy reformation can improve performance. Managers of state enterprises, given clear objectives, with an incentive to succeed (a bonus system perhaps), and with their performance carefully monitored, may respond well. Long-term contracts between government and its parastatals are another possible path to reform. Where the private sector can do the job, the parastatals can be sold off (Mexico has about 250 for sale; Brazil may well sell about 100).[20] Governments always prefer to sell the losers and retain the profitable ones, however, which limits the market. Whatever the steps taken, it seems plain that many such firms in many LDCs still lack flexibility in their operations, and that this is an important cause of inefficient responses to planning challenges.

The recognition by economists that systematic distortions from free-market prices might have systematic unfavorable effects on economic growth grew stronger in the 1970s and represented an important new departure in development economics. Only in 1983, however, was this point driven home statistically in a World Bank analysis that showed significant correlation between the degree of distortion and low growth. The analysis, reproduced here as Figure 11.3, examined the degree of interference in foreign exchange pricing, factor pricing,

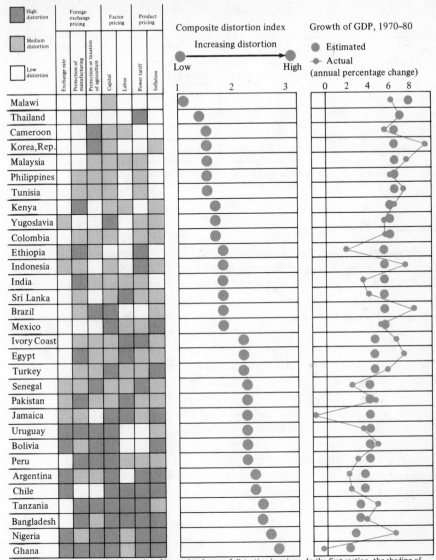

Figure 11.3 Price distortions and growth in the 1970s. (*WDR 1983*, p. 62.)

and product pricing, from which an index of distortion was compiled. High distortion was correlated with low growth (about 2 percentage points lower than average), while low distortion was correlated with high growth (about 2 percentage points higher than average). The regression equations employed suggest that about a third of the variation in growth is explained by the differences in distortion.[21]

The same ranking by degree of distortion is also strongly correlated with the ability to save and with the growth rate of exports, as shown by Table 11.2.

Table 11.2 PRICE DISTORTIONS, DOMESTIC SAVING, AND GROWTH OF EXPORTS, 1970s.

Country grouping	Distortion index (average)	Domestic saving (percent of income, average)	Growth rate in exports (percent per year, average)
Low distortion[a]	1.56	21.4	6.7
Moderate distortion[b]	1.95	17.8	3.9
High distortion[c]	2.44	13.8	0.7

[a]The low distortion countries are the first 10 listed in Figure 11.3, Malawi to Colombia inclusive.
[b]The moderate distortion countries are the 9 countries Ethiopia to Turkey in Figure 11.3.
[c]The high distortion countries are the last 12 listed in Figure 11.3, Senegal to Ghana.
Source: WDR 1983, pp. 60–61.

Planning Difficulties

Within a country planning has tended to suffer from two distinct sets of problems: lack of government support for the targets and difficulties in implementation.[22] Especially when the plan is highly mathematical but the planners are inadequate communicators, political support may be weak because the plan is not understood. Lack of government support can also occur when a plan requires some economic restriction such as a tax, a tariff, or a control designed to lower consumption. Government may pay lip service, but may not have the will to act. Too often the separation of plan formulation from plan implementation contributes to this, because the people who prepare a plan may have little or no authority to establish the policies (taxes, credit, money supply changes) needed to reach the targets. Waterston notes that operating plans can easily degenerate into mere forecasts, projections, and "hortatory instruments" which do not test governmental willingness to carry them out.

Even given the will and the policies, aggregate planning may still face severe difficulties. Weaknesses in underlying information of all kinds may mean the plan is an elegant mathematical facade. As industrial output is easiest to measure, the lack of data in other areas may bias the plan toward large industrial projects as against small projects and endeavors in agriculture. A plan covering the space of several years is subject to interruption because of bottlenecks and poor "time-phasing." Thus delays in construction and equipping or inability to run a project at full capacity because of some shortfall in the planned supply of inputs may be reasons for failure in meeting targets. Unanticipated problems of coordination in a plan are sure to lead to costly bottlenecks. As an example, a plan that involves the simultaneous construction of a road, dam, hydroelectric power station, power grid, and electricity-using industry, if far out of sequence due to materials shortages, transport difficulties, or lack of skilled labor or management, could result in severe waste of resources. Even if the sequencing is adequate, completion under heavy pressure may mean shoddy construction and inefficient operation.

The main bottleneck in planning has usually been, and may well continue to be in the foreseeable future, the acute shortage of qualified personnel. Gerald Meier notes that planning has sometimes been put into effect with spectacular understaffing. Malawi did so at a time when the total number of economists plus accountants in the entire country was six, with no statisticians at all; the Ministry of Planning consisted of four officers, none of whom was an expert.[23] Inadequacies in training, incompetency, systems that shift personnel between departments before a task is fully learned, jealousies among ministries, and the brain drain of the most qualified to developed countries or the World Bank, all reduce the effectiveness of planning performance. Rapid changes of government cut into continuity, and there are even cases (Uganda) where nations utterly unable to maintain law and order nonetheless undertake to plan.[24] Foreign advisors may be thrown into the breach. But the advisor who stays a few weeks, makes the initial decisions (including mistakes), and then leaves the local officials to take the responsibility when these mistakes become apparent does not yield an optimal type of planning. These difficulties appear inherent in underdevelopment and thus would seem little easier to solve than poverty itself.

An objection to the results of aggregate planning that is shared widely by observers concerns its bias toward the quantifiable aspects of growth, as opposed to the nonquantifiable aspects. Recall from Chapter 4 the general agreement that investment in capital, although important, leaves a large part of the growth process unexplained. Technical advance, education and training, and managerial improvement are far harder to quantify, and this explains in part planning's focus on saving and investment. The same is true of population policy. Social and political reform are obviously important, but hard to incorporate in a planning model. Changes in attitudes, motivations, and institutions are often either ignored or are assumed to alter in just the degree needed.

Many economists today advocate a retrenchment to "lighter," less detailed, sectoral planning applying more narrowly to the infrastructure of transport, communications, power, schools, health facilities, irrigation, agricultural support facilities, and the like, all with more emphasis on policies and more dependence on market forces.[25] In spite of this advice, aggregate planning is unlikely to retreat too far because political leaders in the third world will still see some value in it, even if its actual performance in meeting targets leaves much to be desired. There is little in economics that can command national attention as does a country's plan. Its propaganda value may be completely distinct from its value in practice. Creating an image of something major on a national scale, as long as people do not become completely disillusioned, will make for good public relations. The discussions and debates surrounding its birth can serve to focus attention on sensible national growth goals, directions, and choices. Social and political disagreements and disputes that ordinarily lie hidden will be brought into the open, sometimes no doubt for the worse, but sometimes in a manner that may allow them to be addressed rather than ignored.

Furthermore, there are few easier ways to demonstrate inadequacies in data than through a dose of aggregate planning. Statistical departments and services may emerge with more support, and a country may make advances in how its economic data can best be used. True, this may add up to saying that the process of aggregate planning contributes more to economic performance than the execution of the plan; in other words, planning may be most useful when it is not taken too seriously. There are many people in nations with extensive controls that have led to black markets, shortages, corruption, and other serious distortions from allocative optimality, who would undoubtedly agree in full.

In development economics today the tide is running strongly in favor of greater use of the market mechanism and government efforts to strengthen and correct distortions in that mechanism, distortions rather often introduced in the past by planning itself. Building new institutions, such as a banking and credit system, a capital market, agricultural credit organizations, cooperatives, extension services, research and training facilities, and improving the transport, communications, and power systems have tended to take priority over the planning of production.[26] Some governments have come to agree that maintenance of social and political order and the establishment of sound monetary, fiscal, credit, and foreign trade systems ought to take precedence over planning. Coordinating and rationalizing all of these would seem crucial; it is hard to imagine planning faring very well without them. These broad, market-based structural reforms, if successfully established, add up to an economic environment where individual enterprise and initiative are able to operate.

Finally, and perhaps above all, has come the realization that governments must be able to "roll with the punches." Frequent policy revisions to cope with change, large reserves for emergencies, diversified goals, and willingness to move into areas of opportunity are all called for if economies expect to become increasingly flexible.

Flexibility has never been the hallmark of planning, and thus its enthusiasts have been in retreat in recent years, their position staying strongest in countries such as India and China which have potentially very large domestic markets. Even there, however, proponents of prices are on the march, with India's 1981 to 1985 plan putting much more emphasis on the market mechanism and China's move away from rigid central planning attracting worldwide attention.

The Chinese case is fascinating in showing how a rather extreme version of planning can be tempered by market incentives.[27] The movement toward reform started in agriculture in 1978. The traditional communes have been much modified by the "production responsibility system," involving contracts between the commune and a group of farmers. The contracts identify the land to be cultivated and specify the quantity and type of produce to be delivered to the state. They cover access to land for 15 years and can be sold or inherited. Compensation for land improvement is provided for. Most importantly, the group can sell on the newly resurrected free market any excess output above that specified in the contract. This reform plus a large increase in official procurement prices gets much of the credit for the astounding performance of Chinese agriculture in the 1980s.

Industrial reform has proceeded more slowly. The system was initially strict Soviet-style comprehensive planning. Reforms begun in 1984 will much narrow the scope of the plan, allowing competition between the state and a new private sector. Increasingly, prices are being freed. Rather than remitting all profits to the state, firms can now retain sums for bonuses and investment. The industrial reforms are going more slowly than the agricultural reforms, but they still represent a remarkable shift away from comprehensive planning.

SECTORAL PLANNING AND PROJECT APPRAISAL

Sectoral planning and project appraisal, both considerably less ambitious than aggregate planning, have much to offer and are widely practiced. Even the development economists most disillusioned by aggregate planning include many who see a bright future for these tactics.

A focus on certain key sectors can be pursued as part of all types of planning or even when there is no overall plan of any kind. Such a focus recognizes that there are some key sectors where public initiative is essential, even in an economy where private decision making through a price mechanism is generally relied upon. The "social infrastructure" of basic needs—education, health, nutrition, family planning—is one such area where private enterprise may have difficulties. The infrastructure of public utilities, transport, and communication is another. Such investment is very "lumpy," and because of scale economies the industry involved would otherwise be a private monopoly. The combination of planned government expenditures in basic needs areas with a coordinated program of infrastructure development has been an outstanding feature of the most successful plans, such as in South Korea, Taiwan, Malaysia, the Ivory Coast, and Kenya.

A sectoral approach also implies that there are linkages among industries that private investors may not be able to utilize, but a government could. The main reasons for this are lack of knowledge, risk, and limited competition that restricts alternatives. Consider the potential problems of coordination between a small electricity-generating plant and a planned aluminum refinery. In a riskless world of perfect knowledge and competition there would be no obstacle to coordination. The private generating plant would know that an aluminum refinery with a large demand for current was planned and would expand accordingly in anticipation of higher profit. The aluminum promoters would go ahead with their plans, knowing that sufficient electricity will be forthcoming. Coordination takes place smoothly within the private market, and if either party reneges, potential competitors who see the profit opportunity will move to fill the gap.

Consider what may happen, however, in a world of imperfect knowledge, risk, and limited competition. Again, the private generating plant (call it A) is considering expansion, and the private backers of a proposed aluminum refinery (call it B) are considering construction. But A may take into account only the present level of electricity consumption, not knowing that B might be built. B on the other hand calculates its costs on the (expensive) price A is presently charging for its current. Neither goes ahead with its plans. The problem introduced by imperfect knowledge is the lack of any motive for either A or B to increase its scale of operations in the first place if neither knew of the other's plans.

Even if they did know, there is the risk that the plans would not actually be carried out. Neither party wants to move first because of this risk. If the power station expands, but the aluminum refinery is not built, the extra electricity may have to be sold at marginal cost. If the refinery goes into operation, but the generating facility does not expand, then the required amount of current may be high in price. Neither company will move first in a classic case of imperfect knowledge as to what will eventually happen and risk aversion.

The central lesson is that because of imperfect knowledge of the present and future, because of risk, and because there are no acceptable alternative sources of supply or demand, neither A nor B may expand, and this path toward economic growth is blocked. To counter the blockage, some arrangement for coordination and pooling of risks may be advantageous, or even essential.

There have been many attempts in the LDCs to overcome these problems of coordination. In practice, most attempts assume that government participation in capital investment will be necessary to overcome the imperfect knowledge, risk, and limited competition. This idea is central to much sectoral planning, sometimes called "vertical balanced growth." (Other forms of balanced growth, now less fashionable than they were in the past, are surveyed in this chapter's Appendix 2.) The argument is that government participation can provide the coordination by ensuring that A and B will expand at the same time.

This sectoral form of planning, based on the concept of coordinated investment, has proven extremely popular in the LDCs. A major advantage is its adaptability. It can be used to link small projects or large ones. It can apply to two firms or ten. It need not require direct government ownership and operation. Government may function as broker, bringing private firms A and B together around the conference table. Alternatively, government might assume some of the risk of nonperformance. If A and B suffer from inferior entrepreneurship or a shortage of skills, a government advisory team may help. If imperfect capital markets mean limited access to capital, then government loan guarantees will perhaps suffice. At the far end of the spectrum, A and B may be government owned and operated so that the coordination is implemented directly. (Note that private merger of the two firms would have the same effect.) One warning, however. All too frequently unprofitable government enterprise has been established and kept alive with costly subsidies on some fuzzy concept of coordination and vertical balance. The theory can be abused.[28]

Linkages

Sectoral planning via vertical balancing envisages the establishment of industries (or even firms at the lowest level) where a link-up would be most advantageous. Finding where such advantage might lie has been an important part of the work of Albert O. Hirschman, who developed the concept of "linkage."[29] The term refers to the economic connection between a firm's operations and other sectors of the economy. The connection might be a product linkage, which in turn might be forward or backward. It is called forward when a firm's output is much used as an input by other firms and encourages investment by these subsequent users. In our previous example, the forward linkage was from electricity to aluminum production; other cases would be coal to steel, steel to light metal-working, and so on.

It is a backward linkage when a firm's output requires inputs from earlier stages of production and thus encourages investment in these earlier stages. To illustrate backward linkage, reverse the examples above (aluminum to electricity, steel to coal). It was once thought that there was little backward and forward linkage from agricultural and raw materials production, but that was before numerous LDCs did indeed begin to produce fertilizers, simple farm machinery, milling and refining apparatus, and the like. Even Hirschman's reasonable assertion that the linkages may be to industries with technological requirements beyond the capacity of a typical LDC may not stop the effect from operating, since the linkages might attract multinationals from abroad.

In addition to product linkages, which are direct, there are indirect consumption and fiscal linkages, larger or smaller depending on what is produced. When spent, the income generated by a new industry will raise demand across a wide spectrum of consumer goods producers. Even if the new spending goes for imports, a linkage is established to firms able to produce substitutes for those imports. Fiscal links emerge when government taxes the income generated by a new industry and channels the revenue into further productive investment. Such fiscal links may be especially important where a foreign-owned plantation or mining sector has little other impact on the domestic economy.

The options for a sectoral plan may thus come down to a measurement of the linkages, also sometimes called spread effects. Projects with the greatest total linkage are the ones which, once developed, will have the greatest overall effect in promoting further economic activity. Such projects will, it is hoped, become "growth centers" (*pôles de croissance,* as the original French phrase had it), their effects spreading more widely through the economy than would have been the case had there been no consideration of the linkages.

Economies of Scale

Sectoral planning and coordinated investment are related to the existence of scale economies. Coordination is necessary in the presence of imperfect knowledge and risk, so it is argued, because the high cost output of small-scale plants will present obstacles to firms utilizing that output as an input.

This scale argument at base involves economies or diseconomies external to the firm receiving them. The externality is felt, for example, when a firm is producing some output for a small market at suboptimal scale, which then becomes an expensive input to some other firm. The high costs of this input, due to forces outside the latter firm's control, is called a pecuniary external diseconomy to that firm.[30]

Where might we find a pecuniary externality in practice? Take our earlier example of a plant generating electricity on a small scale. The high costs of the current in a given area will presumably slow the development of any industry that is an important user of electricity.

In a riskless world of perfect knowledge, expansion in capacity would occur easily in response to new profit opportunities, bringing larger, more specialized machinery, further division of labor, and thus lower average costs. These economies of scale, note, are *internal* to the firm. In a competitive environment the lower cost means a lower price. To any potential user of electricity, this appears as a pecuniary external economy that may well encourage many other firms to expand their operations. The generating plant might expand further; users of the electricity realize yet more pecuniary external economies. This process goes forward as long as further expansion is profitable. But if the combination of limited knowledge and risk halt the expansion, then scale may remain small with resulting long-term diseconomies.[31]

The argument that small-scale production is high-cost production can be extended and generalized. If a large plant is the only kind that can achieve low long-run average costs *(LRAC),* as in Figure 11.4, then small LDCs with inadequate market size might have to pay a substantial penalty that is detrimental to development. Note carefully, however, that a different view of costs would make necessary a substantial change in the predicted outcome. What if costs fall only a little with large-scale production, as along the solid line of Figure 11.5? Or what if they fall rapidly, but reach a minimum at a fairly moderate level of output, as along the dashed line of the same figure?

Unfortunately, the economic literature on this matter is neither abundant nor entirely conclusive, and the subject seems to be somewhat out of favor. Early work based on U.S. data was done in the 1950s by Joe S. Bain; it suggested that scale economies were an overrated concept. According to Bain, *most* major countries had domestic markets large enough to support several plants of optimal scale in *most* industries. His figures led to the conclusion that numerous industries, both light and heavy, pay only a small penalty or no penalty at all when

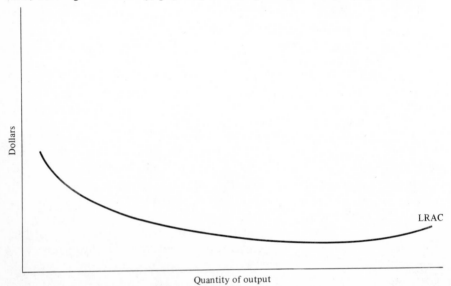

Figure 11.4 Economies of scale with large output.

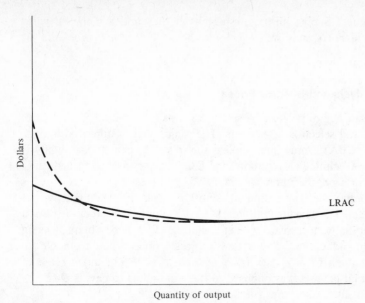

Figure 11.5 Alternative long-run average cost curves.

engaging in relatively small-scale production. Further research in the 1970s by
F. M. Scherer and others working with him confirmed the broad thrust of Bain's
pioneering efforts.[32] To the extent that Bain, Scherer, and the others are correct
(and, of course, to that extent casting into doubt the traditional "received opinion" on the subject), the position of the LDCs is an easier one, with fewer
pecuniary external diseconomies to suffer.

   Work by other scholars over a broad range of countries typically reveals
more mixed results, with scale economies important in some industries, but not
in others where they might logically be anticipated. In 1976 Pan A. Yotopoulos
and Jeffrey B. Nugent surveyed seven studies containing a large number of
estimates. These showed the greatest economies of scale in industrial gasses
(oxygen, chlorine, ethylene, methanol) and in some food processing (beer, fruit
and vegetable canning, sugar refining). But economies were, perhaps surprisingly,
far less important in some other areas (autos, computers, diesel engines, generators, machine tools, petroleum refining, rubber goods, shoes, and fish canning).[33]
There seems no alternative to further careful studies of this type, but it is striking
how few of them have actually been done in the LDCs.

   Where does this leave the small LDC, with a small domestic market and
no prospect of ever achieving scale economies at home? The very asking of the
question reveals the answer, which lies in exporting. A small country's foreign
trade is its avenue of access to a large market—and always has been, as the
developed-country examples of Belgium, the Netherlands, Luxembourg, Austria,
Switzerland, Scandinavia, and New Zealand show conclusively. Small LDCs may
even possess some economic advantages to offset the lack of a large domestic
market. They are frequently freer from the divisive communal tensions of larger
economies, and when they are, economic and political organization are likely to

be less troublesome.[34] Such countries, especially if they find a niche in world markets for their exports, may well overcome the scale economy problem.

Cost-Benefit Analysis and Shadow Prices

A focus on the planning of projects by sector leads us to a next step: techniques for the appraisal and selection of projects. The major tool of appraisal is cost-benefit analysis (CBA), sometimes called the reverse, benefit-cost analysis (BCA).[35] Use of the technique is recent in the LDCs; the very first published study employing CBA in a poor country was in 1972.[36]

Cost-benefit analysis is a method to identify projects that yield positive net social benefits, defined as benefits (willingness to pay) minus costs (compensation required). Conceptually, a measure of net social benefit can be obtained using Figure 11.6's demand curve.[37] Say a new project reduces price from OP to OP_1. Total willingness to pay rises from $ODEQ$ to ODE_1Q_1, an increase of QEE_1Q_1. The actual payment, as opposed to the willingness to pay, is QAE_1Q_1. The net social benefit of the project is here equal to AEE_1.

If all net benefits were realized immediately, the search would be at an end and the highest benefit would identify the most desirable project. There is a complication, however. Some projects come to completion sooner, some later. One must employ discounting to find the net present value *(NPV)* of the net social benefit. The formula is the familiar one which sums the benefits at each time

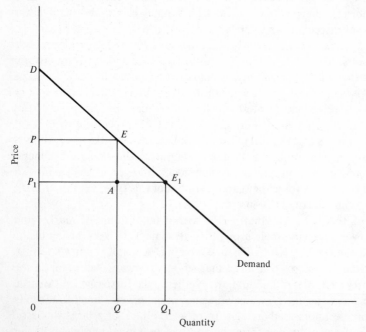

Figure 11.6 Calculating net social benefit. (Subrata Ghatak, *Development Economics,* London, 1978, pp. 138–139.)

period B_{t1}, B_{t2}, B_{t3}, etc., divided by $1 + r$, $(1 + r)^2$, $(1 + r)^3$, etc., where r is the rate of interest. (Often, when detailed information is lacking, a real rate of interest of 10 percent is used in these calculations.) Planners wishing to make a choice among projects would select the ones with the highest *NPV*s. This is a result that most politicians are likely to find convincing, even the ones who have little or no comprehension of the mechanics involved.

A further complication intrudes. What if government controls (direct regulation of prices, an overvalued currency, laws requiring above-market wages in the modern sector, below-market interest rates, tariffs and quotas) plus the existence of external economies or diseconomies mean that project costs do not reflect accurately the costs to society of resources used in a project? Under such conditions, a country appraising projects with the tool of net present value may choose ones that do not really fit the country's actual factor availabilities. Too much of a scarce but price-controlled input may be used; too much capital and too little labor may be involved; export projects may look unprofitable because of the overvalued exchange rate; use of cheap inputs from abroad may be retarded by tariffs and quotas. The list of potentially distorted decisions is as long as the list of distorted prices.

One possibility is an attempt to determine accurately what the market price for any of these *would* have been in the absence of any distortion or externality. This hypothetical price, called a shadow price, could be used in calculating NPV instead of the actual price, which is affected by the controls and does not reflect the externalities.[38] For goods traded internationally, the world price will be an obvious choice, though this would have to be translated at a "shadow exchange rate" if the local currency is significantly overvalued. When there is a risk that the shadow price might change, then sensitivity analysis using alternative values for variables, with probabilities attached, can be used. If a project is assessed with shadow prices weighted for risk, then a positive NPV even under the most pessimistic assumptions would certainly seem to make that project a prime candidate for adoption. Even the effects of projects on the distribution of income could be included by weighting the NPVs, with higher weights assigned to income going to the poor. Project choice with weights for distribution may be an excellent method for achieving greater equality of income whenever political constraints make a direct approach (via taxes, for example) difficult to implement.

The arguments over how to determine accurate shadow prices and whether to employ welfare weights are of long standing.[39] It is hard to deny, however, that even crude shadow pricing, if employed systematically in project appraisal, would lead to less misallocation of investment than actually occurs in countries with a highly distorted price system. At the very least, the use of shadow prices tends to make previous misallocations more obvious. It only remains to warn the beginner in project appraisal that there may be some mystery involved: The government that introduced the distortions in the first place, including its members, allies, and supporters sharing the gains so generated, is often the same government toiling with shadow prices to correct for the distortions. Will there be a willingness to act on shadow prices if there is unwillingness to dismantle the controls and other distortions directly?[40]

And one even more direct warning. A planner can justify just about any project with cost-benefit analysis by manipulating selected assumptions about shadow prices and externalities. The power of government to pick and choose as it wishes is virtually unlimited if its analysts are pliable—and there is plenty of circumstantial evidence that in some countries, from motives of personal gain, fear, or both, they are pliable indeed.

Even with all its problems, however, cost-benefit analysis rightly has a firm place in current development economics. As Andrew Kamarck has said, "Even rough estimates are better than arbitrary, politically determined or purely intuitive decisions."[41] The tool virtually forces economists to widen their view to include more than just the private outlays and revenues of projects. The broader horizons obtained in the exercise result in more and better knowledge, and the knowledge reduces the chances that ill-conceived projects will be undertaken.

NOTES

1. This and the following two sections draw on Harry Johnson and Paul Rosenstein-Rodan as reprinted in Gerald M. Meier, *Leading Issues in Economic Development,* 4th ed., Oxford, 1984, pp. 785–792. (Meier's whole section on planning in this and the 3rd ed., New York, 1976, was valuable to me, as were his comments in *Emerging from Poverty,* New York, 1984, pp. 49, 222–223, and elsewhere; these works were heavily utilized here.) I also drew on Pan A. Yotopoulos and Jeffrey B. Nugent, *Economics of Development: Empirical Investigations,* New York, 1976, p. 398. I. M. D. Little, *Economic Development: Theory, Policy, and International Relations,* New York, 1982, pp. 125–136, is a critical review.
2. See Yotopoulos and Nugent, *Economics of Development,* p. 110.
3. See H. W. Arndt, "The Origins of Structuralism," *World Development,* 13, no. 2 (1985):151–159.
4. Compare Little, *Economic Development,* p. 119.
5. Following Subrata Ghatak, *Development Economics,* London, 1978, pp. 61–69.
6. It is borrowed from A. K. Sen, *Choice of Techniques,* London, 1968, and was brought to my attention by David Colman and Frederick Nixson, *Economics of Change in Less Developed Countries,* Deddington, 1978, p. 253. I drew on their chapter 10 for this section, and also on Ghatak, *Development Economics,* pp. 61–69.
7. UNIDO, *Guidelines for Project Evaluation,* 1972, in Meier, *Leading Issues,* 4th ed., p. 651.
8. See Ramgopal Agarwala, *Planning in Developing Countries: Lessons of Experience,* World Bank Staff Working Paper No. 576, 1985. A recent practical survey of the subject is Warren C. Baum and Stokes M. Tolbert, *Investing in Development: Lessons of World Bank Experience,* New York, 1985. My background on this subject has been informed by W. Arthur Lewis, *Development Planning: The Essentials of Economic Policy,* New York, 1966; Michael P. Todaro, *Development Planning: Models and Methods,* Nairobi, 1971 (and also the chapters on planning in Todaro's *Economic Development in the Third World,* 1st ed., 1977; 2nd ed., 1981); and Albert Waterston, *Development Planning: Lessons of Experience,* Baltimore, 1974. A classic article is Tony Killick, "The Possibilities of Development Planning," *Oxford Economic Papers* 41, no. 4 (1976):161–184. There is much of value in an earlier article by Andrew M. Watson and Joel B. Dirlan, "The Impact of Underdevelopment on Economic Plan-

ning," originally in the *Quarterly Journal of Economics* and reprinted by Theodore Morgan and George W. Betz, eds., *Economic Development: Readings in Theory and Practice,* Belmont, Calif., 1970, pp. 416–423.

9. The classification of plans employed here is suggested in Agarwala, "Planning in Developing Countries." The description in the next few paragraphs draws heavily on this publication.

10. For a short review of the technique by the founding father, more readable than most on the subject, see Wassily W. Leontief, "The World Economy in the Year 2000," *Scientific American* 243, no. 3 (September 1980):207–231. A fuller description is Leontief's *Input-Output Economics,* New York, 1966. A critical discussion of methods is Nural Islam, "Relevance of Development Models to Planning," in Meier, *Leading Issues,* 4th ed., pp. 795–804.

11. See Andrew M. Kamarck, *Economics and the Real World,* Philadelphia, 1983, p. 74.

12. See *WDR 1985,* p. 52. Typically, the economies with the slowest growth are the ones with the highest ratios. The World Bank states that these economies "used twice as much capital to produce each extra unit of GDP than did the high-growth ones." The effect can actually be more significant than the low level of investment itself. See *WDR 1986,* pp. 26–27 which presents the data.

13. Compare Arndt, "Origins of Structuralism," p. 157.

14. See Helen Hughes, *Policy Lessons of the Development Experience,* Group of 30 Occasional Paper No. 16, New York, 1985, p. 16.

15. See the lengthy discussion in Waterston, *Development Planning.*

16. See Hughes, *Policy Lessons of the Development Experience,* p. 16.

17. The data above is taken from *WDR 1983,* chap. 8, and an informative article on parastatals in *The Economist,* February 16, 1985.

18. I drew on Hughes, *Policy Lessons of the Development Experience,* especially p. 20, for this and the next paragraph.

19. Leibenstein presents this important concept and connects it to development studies in his *General X-Efficiency Theory and Economic Development,* New York, 1978.

20. There is a special section on privatization of state-owned enterprises in *The Economist,* December 21, 1985, pp. 71–86. See also Samuel Paul, "Privatization and the Public Sector," *Finance and Development* 22, no. 4 (1985):42–45, for a discussion of what sort of enterprises might be shifted to private ownership and under what conditions.

21. *WDR 1983,* p. 63. The methodology has inspired controversy. For a critique see David Evans and Parvin Alizadeh, "Trade, Industrialisation, and the Visible Hand," *Journal of Development Studies* 21, no. 1 (1984):43–46.

22. This section relies on Waterston, *Development Planning;* Max Millikan in Meier, *Leading Issues,* 3rd ed., pp. 843–846; and Meier himself in *Leading Issues,* 3rd ed., pp. 850–855, and 4th ed., pp. 753–757.

23. Meier, *Emerging from Poverty,* pp. 51–52. Robert Christiansen, an expert on the Malawi economy, has told me that this plan was written by expatriates and generally ignored by the government.

24. P. T. Bauer, *Reality and Rhetoric,* Cambridge, Mass., 1984, p. 28.

25. See Meier's comment in *Leading Issues,* 4th ed., p. 756. I followed Meier's logic in this and the next paragraph.

26. *Ibid.*

27. See William Bird and Gene Tidrick, *Recent Chinese Economic Reforms: Studies of Two Industrial Enterprises,* World Bank Staff Working Paper No. 652, 1985; Luc De Wulf, "Economic Reform in China," *Finance and Development* 22, no. 1 (1985):8–11; *The Economist,* April 26, 1986, pp. 42–43.

28. Compare Wolfgang P. Stolper in Meier, *Leading Issues,* 3rd ed., p. 822.
29. The concept was put forward in Hirschman's well-known book, *The Strategy of Economic Development,* New Haven, 1958. Some of Hirschman's later thinking on the subject may be found in his article, "A Generalized Linkage Approach to Development, with Special Reference to Staples," *Economic Development and Cultural Change* 25, supplement (1977):67–98.
30. The discussion henceforth presumes a knowledge of external economies, so the subject is surveyed in this footnote. External economies may be technological or pecuniary. The *technological* type is familiar from principles of economics textbooks, where output of a good A_1 depends not only on the factors of production L_1 (labor), K_1 (capital), etc., used by the firm, but also on the output A_2 and the factor use (L_2, K_2, etc.), of some other firm or firms. Thus:

$$A_1 = f(L_1, K_1, \ldots ; A_2, L_2, K_2, \ldots)$$

The firm producing A_1 can gain or suffer or not be affected at all, depending on the activities of other firms. Note that this process does not work through the price system. It works instead because one output affects another. The first example in the literature was the "bees and orchard" case, where the apple output (A_1) of Farmer Robinson's orchard is affected not only by Robinson's labor and capital (L_1, K_1), but also by the existence of Farmer Jones's honey-producing bees (A_2), the output of which has a nonmarket effect on the apple crop. The more bees, the better the pollination of the apple trees. Another example might be the draining of land, where a neighbor's work may cut down on the wetness of a farmer's own fields.

   Pecuniary external economies are wider in scope and more important to the case for sectoral planning. These *are* transmitted via the price mechanism, in that they affect the costs and hence the profits of the affected firm. Algebraically, the *profits* P_1 of a firm are dependent on the firm's own output (A_1) and its factor inputs (L_1, K_1), but also on the output of other firms (A_2); this output A_2 is an input to firm number one's operations. Thus:

$$P_1 = f(A_1, L_1, K_1, \ldots ; A_2, \ldots)$$

   For a discussion see Tibor Scitovsky, "Two Concepts of External Economies," in A. N. Agarwala and S. P. Singh, eds., *The Economics of Underdevelopment,* Oxford, 1958.
31. Another sort of pecuniary diseconomy is in the labor market. Say a firm has to start by training unskilled labor up to some suitable standard. In a competitive labor market workers will be hired to the point where their wage equals the marginal revenue product of their labor. Any new firms, however, will have to pay only the going wage rate $W_L = MRP_L$ and not the training costs for any labor that shifts its employment away from the original firm. The knowledge that some of its training costs are sure to be lost is thus a deterrent to the original firm. This problem may justify training subsidies or tax reductions to cover the losses. Note that internalizing the externalities via merger or government operation is an alternative solution.
32. The pioneering work was Joe S. Bain, *Barriers to New Competition,* Cambridge, Mass., 1956. The later research of F. M. Scherer et al. is in *The Economics of Multi-Plant Operation: An International Comparisons Study,* Cambridge, Mass., 1975; it is surveyed together with the work of Leonard W. Weiss and C. F. Pratten in Scherer's *Industrial Market Structure and Economic Performance,* Chicago, 2nd ed., 1980, pp. 91–98.
33. The studies are summarized in Yotopoulos and Nugent, *Economics of Development,*

pp. 152–153. Their methodologies vary substantially and include cost functions, profit rates, value added, and engineering estimates. The results for petroleum refining were mixed. For a recent investigation of the issue, see Martin Williams and Prem S. Laumas, "Economies of Scale for Various Types of Manufacturing Production Technologies in an Underdeveloped Economy," *Economic Development and Cultural Change* 32, no. 2 (1984):401–412.

34. Compare Hughes, *Policy Lessons of the Development Experience,* p. 14. For a recent survey of small-country advantages and disadvantages, see T. N. Srinivasan, "The Costs and Benefits of Being a Small, Remote, Island, Landlocked, or Ministate Economy," *The World Bank Research Observer* 1, no. 2 (1986):205–218.

35. Standard works on the technique are I.M.D. Little and J. A. Mirrlees, *Manual of Industrial Project Analysis in Developing Countries,* vol. 2, *Social Cost-Benefit Analysis,* Paris, 1968; the same authors' *Project Appraisal and Planning for Developing Countries,* London, 1974; P. S. Dasgupta, S. A. Marglin, and A. K. Sen, *Guidelines for Project Evaluation,* New York (UNIDO), 1972; Lyn Squire and Herman G. van der Tak, *Economic Analysis of Projects,* Baltimore, 1975; and E. J. Mishan, *Cost-Benefit Analysis: An Introduction,* New York, 1971. Application of the method in agriculture has its own specialized literature; see J. Price Gittinger, *Economic Analysis of Agricultural Projects,* Baltimore, 1982.

36. See Meier, *Leading Issues,* 4th ed., p. 642, citing I.M.D. Little and D. G. Tipping.

37. The discussion follows the analysis in Ghatak, *Development Economics,* pp. 138–139, along with that of William Loehr and John P. Powelson, *The Economics of Development and Distribution,* New York, 1981, pp. 343–344; and Michael Roemer and Joseph J. Stern, *Cases in Economic Development: Projects, Policies, and Strategies,* London, 1981, pt. III.

38. For recent evaluations of the general theory of shadow pricing, see C. Blitzer, P. Dasgupta, and J. Stiglitz, "Project Appraisal and Foreign Exchange Constraints," *Economic Journal* 91, no. 361 (1981):58–74; and Edward Tower and Gary Pursell, *On Shadow Pricing,* World Bank Staff Working Paper No. 792, 1986. A good critique is Alec Cairncross, "The Limitations of Shadow Rates," in Sir Alec Cairncross and Mohinder Puri, eds., *Employment, Income Distribution, and Development Strategy: Problems of Developing Countries,* London, 1976.

39. Numerous countries have yet to make much use of the technique. Among those that at one time or another have compiled full sets of shadow prices are India, Bangladesh, Sri Lanka, South Korea, Morocco, Kenya, and Jamaica. See Little, *Economic Development,* p. 397.

40. Compare W. M. Corden, "Normative Theory of International Trade," in Ronald W. Jones and Peter B. Kenen, eds., *Handbook of International Economics,* vol. 1, Amsterdam, 1984, p. 105.

41. Kamarck, *Economics and the Real World,* p. 105.

APPENDIX 1: The Capital-Output Ratio

The use of a capital-output ratio as a tool of development promised much, but as its grave weaknesses came to be better understood, it has fallen from favor. Its place in the literature, its importance in development planning, and the enthusiasm felt for it in some quarters to this day, are the reasons for the appendix.[1]

THE INCREMENTAL CAPITAL-OUTPUT RATIO (ICOR)

When we speak of investment leading to growth in income, we are speaking of marginal or incremental changes: Investment is a change in the stock of capital, while growth in income constitutes a change also. In technical terms the relation between them is the incremental capital-output ratio, or *ICOR*. (Sometimes this is also called the marginal capital-output ratio.) The *ICOR* must be carefully distinguished from another, less useful ratio, the average capital-output ratio that relates the size of the capital stock to the size of the nation's income. The *ICOR* is investment divided by change in national income, or $I/\Delta Y$. The average capital-output ratio, on the other hand, is K/Y when K is defined as the stock of capital. It is the *ICOR* which is discussed in the remainder of this appendix.

In the late 1940s two economists, Sir Roy Harrod of Oxford and Evsey Domar of MIT, arrived independently at the same idea. Their work was in connection with developed-country economies, and not with the LDCs. Soon, however, development economists recognized further possible uses of Harrod-Domar theory.

Harrod and Domar suggested that growth in national income Y over time (ΔY), if multiplied by the observed capital-output ratio *(ICOR)*, would reveal the amount of investment I associated with the income growth ΔY. The Harrod-Domar relationship was thus $I = (ICOR)\ (\Delta Y)$. For example, if investment of \$100 this year results in an annual flow of \$25 in new income, the *ICOR* is 4.

Harrod and Domar then introduced saving, which is easy to do since at equilibrium saving must equal investment. We can rearrange the formula to arrive at $\Delta Y = I/ICOR$. At equilibrium, saving equals investment, so if we wish, the I in the formula can be replaced by S. Usually the formula is put into percentage terms so that the *percentage* rate of growth of national income is equal to the *percent* of national income saved and invested divided by the *ICOR*.

In the 1950s and 1960s the observation was made that the *ICOR* for developing countries might be reasonably stable at the level of around 3 to 4 that appeared common in developed countries. Were this to be so, these numbers could then be plugged into the Harrod-Domar formula to obtain the level of saving and investment needed to reach any stated target level of income growth. For example, as noted in the body of the chapter, if the target is a 4 percent growth rate, and the *ICOR* is 4, then the percent of this year's income that ought to be invested is 16 percent of the national income, and this is also the desired target for saving. Or, if it is thought that the maximum amount of investment that can be obtained from an economy is 10 percent, then the rate of growth of national income that will result is 2.5 percent per year.

Very commonly, economists factor in the degree of population growth so as to give a per capita measure:[2]

$$\text{Growth rate in } Y \text{ per capita (percentage)} = \frac{\text{Percent of } Y \text{ saved (invested)}}{ICOR} - \text{Growth rate in population (percentage)}$$

This formulation was used to show that a country must grow at a faster rate if population is increasing if it is to obtain any growth in per capita income. For example, a 4 percent rate of growth in income is needed to get a 2 percent growth in per capita income if population is growing at 2 percent, if the percent saved and invested is 12, and if the ICOR is 3. In the formula above, the numbers would be $2 = 12/3 - 2$.

A CRITIQUE OF THE THEORY

Its indications of certainty gave the theory wide popularity, especially in the development planning commissions of some LDCs. But there are numerous reasons why it must be used with great care, and even why, as a planning tool, the theory is considered to be largely discredited by many development economists in spite of the fact that it remains much used. Several of these reasons are explored below.

1. Using a fixed *ICOR* in planning calculations overlooks several arguments that imply that development itself may change the *ICOR* substantially. Consider the possibility that the *ICOR* may be higher in a typical LDC than in a developed country and that development will cause it to fall.

This will be so if inefficiency, waste, and shortages are present. If an LDC is inefficient in the manufacture of capital goods by comparison to developed countries, which appears so for a wide range of machinery and equipment, then the money value of investment *(I)* needed to obtain a given change in national income (ΔY) may be higher in the LDC, and, of course, a higher ratio $I/\Delta Y$ is a higher *ICOR*. (The importance of this can, however, be somewhat reduced by importing machinery.)

The *ICOR* may also be higher in an LDC because of waste of capital. Extraordinary wastage can certainly be identified in some LDCs, though not in all of them. Tools and machinery are not always handled with care, drivers push their trucks past the breaking point, and inadequate maintenance causes equipment to depreciate more rapidly, especially true in cases of the more complicated forms of machinery. From the pothole that will swallow a car to the airliner that must sit in the open waiting for a repairman to reach it from the United States or the Soviet Union, conditions are conducive to a waste of capital. The waste may be due to poor investment decisions, often caused by inadequate information. LDCs are generally less well mapped and possess less knowledge about minerals, oils, and weather. It is not surprising, says Sir Arthur Lewis, that "great blunders are made." The result may well be that capital tends to stay on the beaten path. If investment, whether domestic or foreign, took a certain track in the past, then it goes there today (as with copper in Zambia, or tin in Bolivia, or bananas in Guatemala) and keeps on going there, with overinvestment in these fields and underinvestment elsewhere, and, of course, a high *ICOR*.

Higher *ICOR*s may also result from shortages of complementary capital. New investment in a developed country can depend on the presence of a good many existing facilities—the electric power grid, the piped water supply, the railway network, the roads, the docks, and so forth. To the extent that these are missing in an LDC, any potential investor may have to provide not only the normal investment to start the enterprise, for example, a mine, but also these complementary capital facilities. The mine is useless without a road or port or electric power. Even when an investor is willing to provide all this, the scale of use may be small. The port may have little traffic, but it still needs (expensive) full-dimension berths for ships and full-size loading derricks. If the generator serves only the mine, its small size implies high-cost electricity. All this means a large amount of investment for each additional dollar of output, another way of saying a high capital-output ratio.

A different argument for a falling capital-output ratio as development progresses is the Colin Clark thesis already mentioned in Chapter 3. We expect development to mean a shift from primary (agricultural) and secondary (industrial) to tertiary (service) activities. Agriculture and industry use more capital than do services. Thus, as the shift to tertiary services is made, the *ICOR* may well fall.

Finally, where population growth is rapid, as it is in many LDCs, a large proportion of investment may have to be devoted to housing, which is a large user of capital. That, too, will mean a relatively high *ICOR* in the LDCs.

It is possible to argue a contrary case: that the *ICOR* in a typical LDC might actually be *lower* than in the developed countries. For example, capital may be particularly productive in terms of income when it is used to develop and exploit new discoveries of natural resources. To the degree that LDCs are locating untapped natural deposits of oil, uranium, iron ore, and other natural resources, at a faster rate than such discoveries are being made in the developed world, each dollar's worth of capital may be more productive in the LDCs. This is identical to saying lower capital-output ratio. (Note that this contention is in almost direct conflict with the complementary capital argument of the last page.) Additionally, because of the scarcity of capital in LDCs, it may be more efficient economically to use less of the expensive capital and more cheap labor. In countries where this is done, we might discover a low *ICOR,* with a little capital investment combined with a large quantity of other factors highly productive in generating income.

The foregoing arguments, taken together, are convincing. It is hard to believe that the *ICOR* for any given poor country will be stable for long periods of time. You expect the *ICOR* to change with development. Using the same *ICOR* in calculations from one year to the next invites mistaken predictions.

2. A second problem with using the *ICOR* in calculating growth is whether to take investment and output gross or net. Since you do not want to talk about investment that simply keeps your capital intact, but instead about the growth of capital, the net figure is the preferred one. However, gross investment is often used along with gross output because the data are more readily available. Related to this, what do you do about working capital as opposed to fixed capital formation? The stocks and inventories of an industry make a difference. A steel industry may greatly increase the need for working capital; the erosion of cottage industry may reduce that need. In any case, working capital is likely to be important, but it is usually ignored in *ICOR* calculations.

3. At first glance, the *ICOR* implies that so much investment in time t will lead to so much income in time t. Clearly, this is oversimplified. The new increase in national income in 1987 will certainly be due in part to investment made before 1987 as well as investment made during that year. There is a gestation period that must be considered. Similarly, output may be below some eventual norm for several years while a particular investment, say, a factory, works up to full production.

Thus the correct relation considered in the *ICOR* should be that between net investment and output after some period of gestation. Different types of capital will have quite different gestation periods. To allow for this, one can use the discounting formula taught in most first-year economics courses. The current interest rate is applied to a flow of output to obtain the present discounted value of the output stream. That formula is:

$$V = \frac{Y_1}{1 + r} + \frac{Y_2}{(1 + r)^2} + \ldots + \frac{Y_n}{(1 + r)^n}$$

with V the present discounted value of an income stream Y_1 in year 1, Y_2 in year 2, up to Y_n in the last year to be measured; and with r equal to the current interest rate. The formula will allow us to calculate the present value of future changes in income caused by investment undertaken this year, but having no effect on income until some later time.

W. B. Reddaway has shown how this problem of a gestation period for investment

Table 11A.1   DIFFERENCE BETWEEN OBSERVED AND REAL ICOR

(1) Year	(2) Capital project starts	(3) Completions	(4) Under construction	(5) Change in income (ΔY_t)	(6) I_t	(7) Observed ICOR $(I_t/\Delta Y_t)$	(8) Real ICOR Lagged Two Years
0	1	0	1	0	$1/4$		$1/2$
1	2	0	3	0	$1\,1/4$		$1\,1/4$
2	4	1	6	$1/2$	$2\,1/2$	5	$1\,1/4$
3	8	2	12	1	5	5	$1\,1/4$
4	16	4	24	2	10	5	$1\,1/4$

can seriously affect measurement of the *ICOR*.[3] In the example in Table 11A.1, the difference between the observed *ICOR* when no account is taken of time lags and the real ICOR when the lags are considered is significant. Column 1 shows a five-year period. Column 2 shows that the number of capital projects doubles every year. Column 3 shows the number of projects completed each year, with a two-year time lag from start to completion. In column 4 we see the number of projects remaining under construction. The resulting changes in national income are shown in column 5. Column 6 calculates the amount of investment in the year shown, equal to one-quarter the number of project starts in the same year plus three-quarters the number of starts in the previous year. The observed *ICOR* is shown in column 7 as $I_t/\Delta Y_t$. It takes no account of the time lag and is noticeably a high figure. Column 8 is the real *ICOR* adjusted for the time lag. It divides I_t by national income two years in the future. With ΔY lagged two years, the *ICOR* is a much lower figure.

Table 11A.1 shows a regular pattern; the information becomes harder to calculate as the pattern becomes less regular. Planning commissions often may ignore the whole problem. Only a few, for example, India's sophisticated planners, pay any serious attention to gestation calculations.

4. Finally, the *ICOR* ignores the question of capacity utilization. It would be possible, obviously, to increase national income with no investment whatsoever if there were capital stock that could be more fully utilized. Even without any change in capacity utilization, there might be a more productive use of existing capital if better methods and techniques of production were applied.

The technical objections posed in this appendix add to the case made in the body of Chapter 11 that capital-output ratios are fraught with difficulties. Those who continue to use them uncritically do so at the peril of making poor predictions and implementing poor policies.

NOTES

1. My main sources for this appendix have been Paul Streeten, "A Critique of the 'Capital/Output Ratio' and Its Application to Development Planning," in Streeten, *The Frontiers of Development Studies,* New York, 1972, pp. 71–116; Bruce Herrick and Charles P. Kindleberger, *Economic Development,* 4th ed., New York, 1983, chap. 8; 3rd ed., chap. 5; and the material on the capital-output ratio in the earlier Kin-

dleberger versions of this text; and Gerald M. Meier, *Leading Issues in Economic Development,* 4th ed., Oxford, 1984, pp. 222–225.

2. The calculation is not exact. For arithmetical accuracy a more complicated formula must be employed, but the one shown works well when the time period involved is relatively short. See Herrick and Kindleberger, *Economic Development,* 4th ed., p. 30.

3. *The Development of the Indian Economy,* Homewood, Ill., 1962, p. 196, to which I was led by Streeten, "Critique of the 'Capital-Output Ratio,' " p. 94.

APPENDIX 2: Models of Balanced and Unbalanced Growth

Models of balanced growth, which predict economic paralysis unless some sort of balance is maintained in the growth process, are now out of fashion. The growth record has been too good in too many countries that did not follow the precepts of balancing. Such models still have their legacy, however. They do point to serious issues of concern, and even their failures, when understood, leave us intellectually richer. This appendix surveys the subject.

Concern with balance in economic growth is extremely common in the development literature.[1] "Balanced growth" refers to the structure of the domestic economy and not to all growth, because a country that exports extensively can still register important progress even if it imports most of its food, other consumer goods, and capital goods in a process that is not "balanced." Indeed, many proponents of balance as a strategy believe international trade is an unsatisfactory avenue to development (a topic of vital importance, considered in Chapters 12 to 15). Their discussions are often carried out with little reference to foreign trade or with the assumption of a closed economy.

Given the closed-economy assumption, it is often said that the small size of the domestic market is a major inhibiting factor for economic development. The detrimental impact of a small market has a long historical tradition in economics: Adam Smith discussed it carefully when he explored the division of labor, and it was a staple topic for the nineteenth century classical economists and for Karl Marx as well.

The reasons for small markets in LDCs can be divided into those of demand and those of supply. Demand is low (for any good or service) because income is low. Even the low level of income is not fully reflective of low demand, however, because a fair proportion of the income in LDCs may come in real and not money terms as subsistence output produced and consumed by the family. Figures already quoted have shown that the subsistence sector often generates as much as a quarter to a third of national income, and perhaps involves as much as 50 to 60 percent of the male work force in parts of Africa. Where the subsistence sector is large, the market must be limited—by the size of a person's stomach, so to speak—as income in the form of subsistence goods by definition cannot be spent on any market. Lack of knowledge and limited horizons, by reducing wants, may also limit market size.

Markets are also limited on the side of supply. Poor transport facilities mean high costs; there may be inadequate communications with areas that might provide alternative sources of supply; facilities for storage may be lacking. For any given product, the local supply is therefore likely to be price inelastic. Grain will serve as an example. Any local shortage might have to lead to a substantial rise in price before supply increases, because the response from local stocks is small, and suppliers elsewhere have little knowledge of the situation and might not be able to afford the transport cost even if they did know. Thus intelligent villagers had better play it safe by growing some of the family's own grain supply in addition to their other work. In short, Adam Smith's dictum of 1776 rings true: "The division of labor is limited by the small size of the domestic market." There are other supply-side considerations whenever institutional arrangements and economic conditions, such as communal land tenure systems, high marginal taxes on output, and problems of nutrition and motivation, hinder a response on the part of producers to greater market opportunities.

The *effect* of small market size has been expressed graphically by Ragnar Nurkse. It creates a so-called vicious circle of economic inhibition, as illustrated in Figure 11A.1. The circle runs thus: (1) The limited market means that any plant producing any product must be small in size, too small to exploit economies of scale. (2) The incentive to invest is thus weak; who will build plants to provide high-cost goods to a small market? (3) The level of investment is therefore low, which means (4) the productivity of labor is low. (5) Low productivity is the root cause of low incomes earned by labor. (6) This low income means in turn a small market for products, which leads us full circle to (1).

Balanced growth as a development theory thus grew out of two separate strands of thought. First, the domestic market is crucial for development and foreign trade is not an acceptable way out; second, the diseconomies of small-scale production are a serious detriment to economic progress. For the time being let us accept both propositions without question.

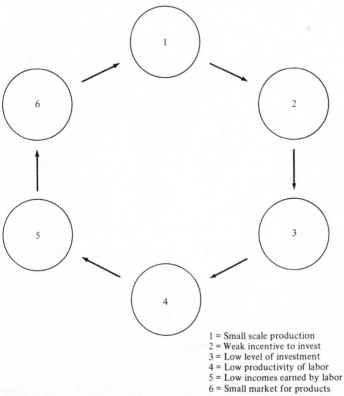

1 = Small scale production
2 = Weak incentive to invest
3 = Low level of investment
4 = Low productivity of labor
5 = Low incomes earned by labor
6 = Small market for products

Figure 11A.1 The vicious circle of economic inhibition. (Adapted from Ragnar Nurkse.)

HORIZONTAL BALANCE

Historically, the first application of these propositions stems from a pioneering insight of MIT's Paul Rosenstein-Rodan, who during World War II considered the following dilemma for development of the soon-to-be-liberated postwar Balkans.[2] What if a country set up a factory producing a product (shoes, said Rosenstein-Rodan) in numbers large enough to realize economies of scale? If the market size is too small, much of the output could not be sold, and the project would fail. What if, however, instead of setting up just a shoe factory, the project were expanded 50-fold? Then there would be not one industry, but "a whole series of industries which produce the bulk of the goods on which the workers would spend their wages." What the one shoe factory could not accomplish "would become true in the case of a whole system of industries: it would create its own additional market."

Nurkse took up this theme.[3] Only a "big push," or "critical minimum effort," as it was sometimes called, could provide adequate demand to offset the uneconomic small-scale production that would otherwise be the outcome. This form of balanced growth soon received the name "balance in consumer demand," or alternatively "horizontal balance."

The theory led to this reasonable conclusion. When an economy reached some adequate size, the inhibiting effects of small markets would tend to disappear. On this score growth was easier as income grew; was more practical for the rich than for the poor. As a policy prescription, though, the theory was woefully lacking. Where would the skills and management for a big push originate, even if plenty of unskilled labor were available? Nurkse apparently assumed that the saving and investment for the push would come from abroad, but with foreign aid and direct investment limited, this appears a counsel of despair. As Hans Singer of the United Nations said so trenchantly, a country with the large supply of resources necessary for balanced growth would not be a poor country.

So the theory languished for a number of years, until it surfaced recently in a different guise. For a time it did appear that populous oil exporters among the LDCs (Mexico, Nigeria, and Venezuela among others) did command sufficient resources to make a big push. The oil exports would provide the capital; the numerous but poor population would provide the potentially large market; a rapid expansion of domestic consumer and capital goods output could provide the higher incomes to make the market real. Skills, organization, and management remained serious constraints, but enthusiasm for the big push was to be found again. The recession of the 1980s and the declining price of oil put such ideas into hibernation. In a few favored countries plans for horizontal balance may once again emerge. In most LDCs, however, the theory is unlikely to have practical application except in the very long run.

UNBALANCED GROWTH

Albert Hirschman carried the concept of balance somewhat further by suggesting that the creation of deliberate *imbalances* might be a superior way to achieve growth. In his well-known book, *The Strategy of Economic Development*, Hirschman contended that plans for horizontal balance overlook the most critical shortage: entrepreneurial skills.[4] The shortage is equally as apparent when management is in private hands as when it is undertaken by government.

From this base is built the theory of "unbalanced growth." In this theory, Hirschman uses the concept of external economies to overcome the basic shortage of entrepreneurial skills. His system involves the creation of a deliberate disequilibrium between two broad sectors of the economy: directly productive activity (DPA), which is industry producing output of goods; and social overhead capital (SOC), which includes public utilities, transport, medical care, systems of communication, and so forth.

The real problem, according to Hirschman, is how to identify the optimal (most efficient) path along which the economy might expand, a path representing "balanced growth" between directly productive activity and social overhead capital. With management skills and entrepreneurial ability in short supply, with data lacking and forecasting weak, how does one know what the most efficient combinations actually are?

This could be done, says Hirschman, by selecting a sequence for expansion that deliberately leads to an imbalance, involving the creation of either external economies or diseconomies, making decisions easier and the choice of direction more obvious. There will thus be a reduction in the need for skilled managers and entrepreneurs, which was, we recall, the original aim.

The imbalance can be created by expanding either DPA or SOC independently of the other. Let us begin by increasing SOC, there being no change yet in DPA. The immediate result of expanded SOC would have to be pecuniary external economies that will stimulate industries engaged in DPA. The next step for the latter is to expand DPA until a balance is once again achieved. A further deliberate increase of SOC could then be made, financed perhaps from the higher national income. The imbalance recurs; the decision for expansion is easy; the economy grows in a fashion that Hirschman calls "development via excess capacity."

The other possibility is initially to expand DPA. The result of this is now very different. Rather than a surplus of SOC, as in the previous example, there is here a *shortage* of it. The signal is again obvious. To correct the shortage, and the resulting pecuniary external diseconomies, SOC will have to be expanded; repetition of this process becomes "development via shortage."

Which form of unbalanced growth should be used in practice? Gunnar Myrdal has been critical of the development via shortage aspect. He argues that not enough attention is paid to the creation of vested interests committed to keeping the monopoly gains generated by this form of development. There is also the problem as to whether unbalanced growth as a strategy is compatible with private profit-making firms. The worry stems from the simple fact that a private firm will be most unwilling to carry an excess capacity of SOC, involving as it does loss of profit; nor will it wish to expand DPA in the absence of supporting SOC, knowing of the cost penalty thus incurred. If used as a strategy, the model would thus presumably require government ownership and operation or government guarantees of one sort or another to the firms making the expansion.

It cannot be said that the Hirschman model has commanded wide enthusiasm in the LDCs. There is the suspicion that if entrepreneurial decision making is really the scarce factor, then government itself might be unable to plan for unbalanced growth with any success. There is much doubt as to whether decision making is really the major constraint in any case, by contrast to capital availability, education, skills, and the like. In many countries plenty of drive and business initiative seem to appear when the channels are open.[5] Finally, there is concern over the costs of the idea if used as a strategy; attempts to test the hypothesis suggest that the greater the imbalances in an economy, the lower is the growth rate.[6]

Whatever its value as a strategy, however, development economists must be thoroughly conversant with the model because so much of third world development experience can be seen in it. Attempts at "balance" fail because of lack of knowledge, bottlenecks in supply, some critical skill absent at the wrong time. Many a development project over the past 20 years can be viewed as an attempt to alleviate an imbalance between SOC and DPA—an imbalance not deliberately created, but existing anyway because earlier investment was not exactly on the path of balance or because a bottleneck developed. This "challenge and response" type of growth is familiar everywhere, in the developed countries (where the textile, coal, and iron "revolutions" in late eighteenth century Britain were notably unbalanced)[7] and in the LDCs, historically and in the here and now. But often the imbalances are much more apparent in the LDCs because the economy is less flexible and alternatives are not so easy to find. The jerky motions implied by the model are thus surprisingly true-to-life, even though the jerks were not intended by policy makers or anyone else. And the picture extends beyond DPA and SOC. With some renaming to include skills, education, and technical improvement, the idea of balancing an existing imbalance can be put into a broader focus using the same analytical tools that Hirschman employed. Unbalanced growth in this sense is the way the world works.

NOTES

1. Everett E. Hagen, *The Economics of Development,* rev. ed., Homewood, Ill., 1975, chap. 7, is a thorough treatment.
2. P. N. Rosenstein-Rodan, "Problems of Industrialization of Eastern and South-Eastern Europe," in A. N. Agarwala and S. P. Singh, *The Economics of Underdevelopment,* London, 1958, pp. 245–255. This well-known article was originally published in the *Economic Journal.*
3. Ragnar Nurkse, *Problems of Capital Formation in Underdeveloped Countries,* Oxford, 1953.
4. Albert Hirschman, *The Strategy of Economic Development,* New Haven, 1958.
5. And if not, then a preferred solution might be to concentrate resources on training new managers and entrepreneurs. See V. V. Bhatt, "Entrepreneurship Development: India's Experience," *Finance and Development* 23, no. 1 (1986):48–49.
6. Reported in Pan A. Yotopoulos and Jeffrey B. Nugent, *Economics of Development: Empirical Investigations,* New York, 1976, pp. 296–297.
7. *Ibid.,* p. 294, citing Paul Streeten.

chapter *12*

Trade and Economic Development

Does international trade lead to economic development?[1] The more or less standard opinion in the nineteenth and much of the twentieth centuries has been "yes." The famous British economist Alfred Marshall thought that trade was a major cause of progress, and his successor at Cambridge University, Dennis Robertson, called trade "the engine of growth."[2] Such opinions are based on the theory of comparative advantage, which argues that if countries produce what they can do best and leave to other nations what they can produce with less efficiency, then real output, income, and consumption will be higher than it could be in the absence of trade. The higher consumption means a bigger domestic market; the higher income lays the basis for expanded investment for domestic production. In turn the wider markets and larger investment lead to even higher income, with further rounds of economic stimulation. Trade also includes imports of capital goods and technical assistance, which speed the progress. Trade is indeed seen as an "engine of growth."

Today such views are much challenged. In a reaction against the previous orthodoxy, many politicians and some economists argue that international trade itself is to blame for underdevelopment. "Dependency theory" and the "theory of unequal exchange" are now popular points of view, arising largely in Latin America following World War II and still propounded most vocally in that region. Among the leading voices of the trade counterrevolution are Samir Amin, G. Arrighi, Arghiri Emmanuel, André Gunder Frank, and Immanuel Wallerstein.[3] Trade is not an engine of growth according to this school of thought. Rather it locks LDCs into an inferior and worsening position in a world trade system dominated by and for the benefit of the rich. A revolutionary change in trading relations is required.

In this chapter we shall explore the arguments that international trade leads to economic development and the case that trade is a poor prospect in the long run. The next chapter considers policies that lessen the beneficial impact from trade and recommended alternatives to those policies. Finally, two concluding chapters survey the dangerous rise of protectionism against manufactured goods and the difficulties facing primary product exporters. These four chapters attempt to give a balanced presentation of the opposing pro-trade and anti-trade viewpoints.

TRADE AS A STIMULUS TO GROWTH

Higher Incomes Through Comparative Advantage

The idea that trade is a stimulus to growth is based on the theory of comparative advantage, which dates back to David Ricardo's famous chapter 7, "On Foreign Trade," in his 1817 book *The Principles of Political Economy and Taxation.* According to this theory, in the absence of barriers to trade, countries will specialize in the production of the goods they produce *relatively* cheaply (that is, goods in which they have a comparative advantage) and will import the goods in which other countries have a comparative advantage. Consumption and real income can thus be higher than in the absence of trade. The Ricardian model is surprisingly apt for modern development studies, since Ricardo chose poor Portugal and rich England to illustrate his case.[4]

The modern form of the theory uses production possibility curves to illustrate Ricardo's point. (Readers familiar with the model may want to skip to the next section.) Figure 12.1 shows the simplest such model, with two countries, Poveria and Penuristan, producing only two commodities, food and clothing. In Figure 12.1a we see that if all Poveria's factors of production were used for food farming, the result would be 80 units of food and no clothing, while if all factors were turned to clothing, 100 units of clothing and no food would be produced. Penuristan's output would be 120 food if it specializes on that commodity or 100 clothing if no food is produced, as in Figure 12.1b. Penuristan is clearly relatively more efficient at producing food than clothing; it is able to turn out more food than its trading partner, but the same amount of clothing. Reversing the logic, Poveria is relatively better at producing clothing, in which it is Poveria's equal; it is no match in food production.

In Poveria 1 unit of food costs 10/8 of a unit of clothing; 1 unit of clothing costs 8/10 of a unit of food. In Penuristan 1 unit of food costs 10/12 of a unit of clothing; 1 unit of clothing costs 12/10 of a unit of food. Under competitive conditions these will also be the price ratios in the two countries, as otherwise there would be an abnormal profit on one of the commodities and a loss on the other, leading resources to shift into the profitable item and away from the loss-maker, and so leading the ratio of prices toward the ratio of costs. Explicitly, the opportunity cost of clothing is lower in Poveria; the opportunity cost of food is lower in Penuristan.

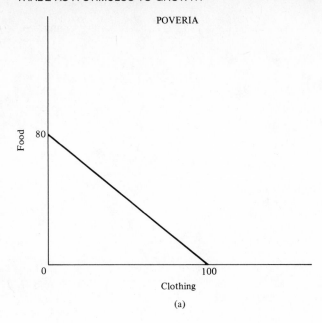

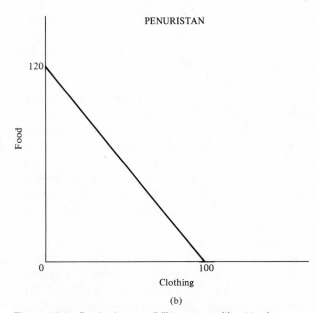

Figure 12.1   Production possibility curves without trade.

Without international trade each country can consume only what it produces. There is no way either can reach a point of consumption outside its curve. This is only common sense, for how could a country's consumption ever exceed production? Yet, in comparative advantage theory this is just what can occur if international trade is allowed to take place. Put the two curves on the same diagram, as in Figure 12.2. What if Poveria specializes on clothing (produced

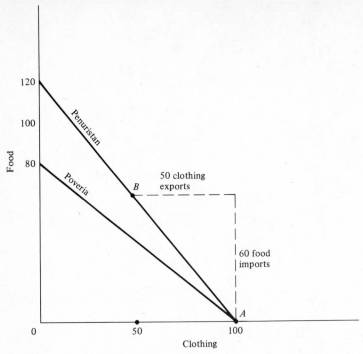

Figure 12.2 Poveria's gain from trade in the model of comparative advantage.

there with relatively greater efficiency, recall) as at point *A* and sells some of it in Penuristan at the latter's prices? (Assume for the moment no transport costs or trade barriers.) Of the 100 cloth output, it could now export say 50 units and buy 60 units of food, since if prices are in the ratio 12/10 in Penuristan then 50 clothing would indeed buy 60 food. *Poveria thus consumes at a point such as* B *outside its production possibility curve.*

Penuristan, too, can gain from trade. In Figure 12.3, Penuristan could specialize on food (at point *C*), which it produces most efficiently, and trade it at the Poverian price ratio of 8 food = 10 cloth. (To show this on the diagram, a dashed line is drawn from 120 food at a ratio of 8/10. That is equal to 12/15, so the line runs down to 150 clothing.) Penuristan can now export perhaps 48 units of food in return for 60 of clothing (because 48/60 is in the same ratio as prices, 8/10 = 12/15). Penuristan can thus also consume outside its production possibility curve, as at point *D*. Plainly enough, exports and imports mean that prices will change. Food, now more abundant in Penuristan, will become cheaper there, but more expensive in Poveria where it becomes scarce. Clothing falls in price in Poveria, rises in Penuristan. Thus the actual price ratio after trade will be somewhere in between the initial 8/10 in Poveria and the initial 12/10 in Penuristan. Whatever the resulting price, trade will allow both countries to consume outside their production possibility curves at the same time. Such is the powerful lesson of comparative advantage, which emphasizes the key point that gains from trade for one country are *not* losses for another. In the model of

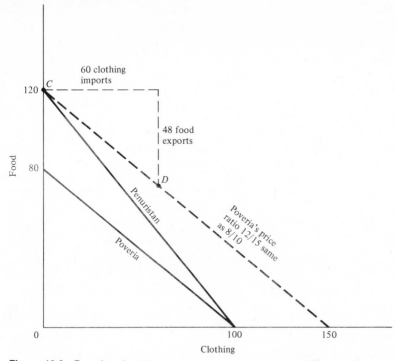

Figure 12.3 Penuristan's gain from trade in the model of comparative advantage.

comparative advantage, trade is a positive-sum game in which *both* participants gain.[5]

Why are comparative costs—and hence comparative advantages—what they are? The modern explanation was developed by the Swedish economists Eli Heckscher and Bertil Ohlin, who called attention to factor proportions as the most important element. Production possibility curves have differing shapes because factor proportions differ: a resource (land, labor, capital) relatively scarce in one country is relatively abundant in another. Basically, the Heckscher-Ohlin idea is the simple one that nations export goods that use intensively their abundant factor and import those goods that embody the greatest amount of their scarce factor. A prediction of Heckscher-Ohlin theory is that labor-abundant LDCs will thus export goods produced with generous inputs of labor, or, as in the case of many agricultural commodities, requiring inputs of such tropical conditions as hot weather and heavy rainfall; that developed countries will import these items and export those that are capital-intensive or contain sophisticated technology. The key point again is that both types of country will be gainers.

The Heckscher-Ohlin model further predicts that trade will increase the income of the most abundant factor, since the exported item employs that factor intensively. (The income of the scarce factor will be reduced, as that factor predominates in the goods that are imported). There is thus a striking conclusion. Whenever these conditions hold, there should be a tendency for a labor-abundant LDC to find its income distribution shifting toward labor, probably leading to more equality. Of course, there may be barriers—monopoly, monopsony, government controls, and any other impediment in the market mechanism can impede the expected result. But the tendency is strong enough so that numerous economists argue that unhindered trade is a workable way to correct for inequalities in income.

The Vent-for-Surplus

Ricardo (and Heckscher-Ohlin) show that international trade allows already employed factors to be reallocated so as to enhance well-being. "Vent" models show how previously unemployed factors can be put to work. Trade may hold even more advantages than implied by Ricardo's model when an underdeveloped country, formerly isolated by high transport costs, is brought into contact with the world trading economy. The initial high transport costs, caused by poor or nonexistent roads, no railways, and the like, may mean that a country has unutilized supplies of productive factors, especially land and labor. Therefore, extensive unemployment or underemployment will be characteristic. Improvements in international transport and communications will provide a market where none existed before, especially for agricultural commodities and minerals. Imported consumer goods become available and are the incentive for increased effort. Trade thus becomes a "vent-for-surplus," in the words first used by John Stuart Mill, building on a concept discussed originally by Adam Smith, and lately made familiar by Hla Myint of the London School of Economics.[6] Examples suggested by Myint include the spurt in the export of rice in Burma, cocoa in Ghana, peanuts in Nigeria and Senegal, and cotton in Uganda.

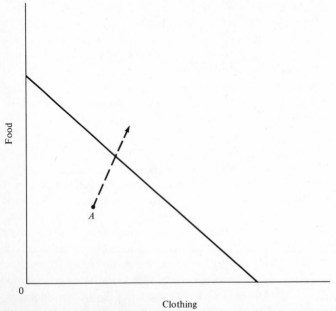

Figure 12.4   The Myint model implies movement to a point outside a given production possibility curve.

The Myint model is portrayed diagrammatically in Figure 12.4. An LDC with the food-clothing production possibility curve shown here finds trade a way to move outside the curve, as in Ricardo's model. But there is more to it, because the starting position at point A was one of heavy un- or underemployment. The opportunity to export means that the unemployed factors can profitably be put to work. The gains from trade are proportionally greater even than in the Ricardo model. (The vent does, however, cease to have its beneficial effect once the underutilized factors are absorbed into production; it is a once-for-all, non-cumulative phenomenon. And since there will be no effect at all in the absence of surplus resources, the model will certainly not apply to all countries.[7])

Dynamic Gains from Trade

Both the standard Ricardian model and the vent model share the problem that trade might leave comparative advantage unchanged over long periods of time. A country specializing in primary product exports produced by large quantities of unskilled labor, with little capital formation and low levels of technical change, may find itself "locked in," for without skills, new capital, education, and technical change, new and potentially more profitable exports will not develop. Proponents of trade see logic in this argument, and that is why many economists believe that the main advantage of trade in development economics is not its static gains as in the Ricardo and Myint models, but in the dynamic advantages of changing factor proportions and hence changing comparative advantage. Dynamic benefits are not pictured with a fixed production possibility curve. Such benefits lead to an outward shift in the curve itself, as in Figure 12.5. There is no guarantee that

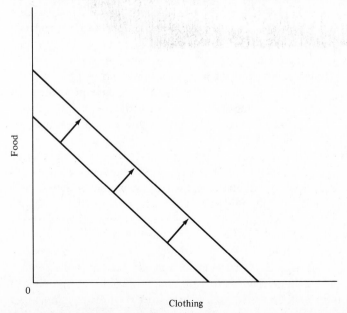

Figure 12.5 Dynamic gains bring an outward shift in the production possibility curve.

dynamic gains must accompany trade. Indeed, we shall see a number of cases where they were largely absent. But there are abundant examples where such gains were powerful, and a strong logical case can be made that, with proper economic management, they can be expected.

Outward shifts in production possibilities can come from imports of consumer goods, of capital goods, and of ideas.[8] New consumer goods have the potential to change tastes, expand wants, and thus encourage the increased application of productive energy. New capital goods may be accumulated, at a price lower than the capital could have been produced at home, when the static gains from trade are invested. The higher level of investment, perhaps financed from the tax revenue generated by the fiscal linkage to exports, can promote both an improved infrastructure of transport, power, health, and education and a greater amount of capital per worker, all raising productivity. These gains are, of course, maximized only if the new investment is wisely made. "Where to invest?" as we have seen in previous chapters, is always a major focus of development strategy.

The import of ideas as embodied in technical and managerial know-how may well be the most important of all the dynamic gains. John Stuart Mill noted the value of contact with different peoples and new ways of thinking. New skills may feed back into other activities; new entrepreneurship can make an impression and can be copied outside its immediate province; the road or rail line built to supply a foreign market with an exported good may be utilized for other economic purposes as well; simplification, standardization, specialization in subprocesses, and assembly line methods may be noted and copied.

At the very least, the mere existence of a popular import demonstrates that a market exists for the product, so reducing the risks for local entrepreneurs who decide to compete. Such dynamic benefits of trade have the potential to contribute a sense of momentum, moving the curve of production possibilities outward. This, together with a dose of learning-by-doing that further reduces costs, may lead to a new comparative advantage that allows some former imports to be produced at home and also allows new exports beyond the initial range of primary product exports to develop. Learning by doing is now thought to be an especially important addition to the standard model of the gains from international trade. If the learning is specific to an industry, it may suggest a development strategy of deliberate early specialization in some selected line of activity. This would presumably be particularly attractive to countries where educational attainment is above average among the LDCs.

We have now seen the three main arguments advanced for trade as an engine of growth: (1) higher incomes through comparative advantage, (2) a vent for surplus, and (3) dynamic productivity gains. It is possible to debate how important the engine is or was for the giant continental-size economies of the United States and the Soviet Union, which do not export more than about 10 percent of their GNP and can depend on a large internal market as a stimulus to growth. For smaller countries, however, international trade is crucial. Among the world's richest countries today are the eight listed on the left in Table 12.1. Without foreign trade it is inconceivable that the standards of living and rates of growth of these nations could have been anywhere near world leadership. And, indeed, economic historians have shown that before these countries became im-

Table 12.1 PERCENTAGE OF GROSS DOMESTIC PRODUCT EXPORTED, 1984

Belgium	77	Bangladesh	8
Denmark	37	Brazil	14
Finland	31	China	10
Netherlands	63	Colombia	12
Norway	48	Ghana	11
Sweden	37	India	6
Switzerland	38	Mexico	18
West Germany	31	Nigeria	16
		Pakistan	11
		Peru	20
		Sudan	10
		Tanzania	11 (1983)
		Turkey	12
		Uganda	11

Source: Calculated from *WDR 1986,* pp. 188–189.

portant trading nations, each of them was relatively underdeveloped compared to neighbors with larger markets and higher levels of foreign trade. The data on the right side of Table 12.1 suggest an important conclusion: For many an LDC trade may currently be too limited to act as an efficient engine.[9]

TRADE AS A HINDRANCE TO GROWTH

The debate on the merits of international trade for developing nations includes several issues. The objections to trade fall into three general categories. First, there is a school of thought that believes the doctrine of comparative advantage is itself fundamentally flawed and that trade is likely to result in "unequal exchange." This is the argument advanced by Arghiri Emmanuel.[10]

Second, it is said that exports from the LDCs fail to stimulate development because of a low multiplier effect from that trade and because there is little "dynamic radiation" from trade. These are called the "enclave" or "backwash" arguments. The complaint is usually made with reference to primary products. Proponents of the backwash arguments often agree that trade along the lines of static comparative advantage may indeed be of benefit to all, but that some countries will benefit far more than others. An initial comparative advantage in high-technology manufacturing tends to be self-perpetuating, it is said, thus locking LDCs into permanent and less profitable production of agricultural goods and minerals with limited impact on the domestic economy.

Third, it is said that the prospects for exports from developing countries (especially primary products) are poor and that the prices of these exports have declined vis-à-vis the prices of goods exported by the industrial world. There is, further, little world capacity to absorb an increasing volume of exports from the LDCs. This is commonly known as the "terms of trade" argument.

All these North-South arguments concerning trade, when taken together, are called "dependency theory" by critics of trade, the words implying the locking of LDCs (the "periphery") into an inferior and worsening trading relationship with the industrial countries (the "center").[11] Various authors have used the word dependency in different ways. Many appear to mean merely that growth is much affected by actions in the metropole or capitalist world. This is, of course, true. In a strong version of this theory, however, the developed countries are blamed for creating underdevelopment. By destroying already existing industries, such as local textile manufacture and handicraft production, and by shifting farming from foods to cash crops for export, the gains from trade were nullified. Even when gains occur, arguably they are dissipated by wasteful consumption patterns introduced from the developed countries, by capital flight to foreign bank accounts for which the urban elite is responsible, and by spending on "security" to maintain that elite in power. In a somewhat weaker version of the theory, the conditions surrounding foreign trade may not have created poverty, but they have prevented development in the LDCs from taking place.[12]

Either way, ending dependence is a synonym for throwing off poverty and grasping control over one's own destiny by lessening the degree of external relationships, including trade, by "delinking" the LDCs from the developed countries. The suggested strategy thus aims toward inward-looking self-reliance. Others consider ending dependence to mean pursuing an independent strategy in one's trade relations rather than lessening the degree of external relationships. In general, the dependency arguments have had less influence among economists than they have had in some other disciplines, such as sociology and political science. The debate has served, however, to identify more carefully the circumstances when trade may not be beneficial.

Arguments that trade is not an engine of growth because of developed-country protectionism and flawed trade policies in the LDCs are less an attack on trade itself than on the particular strategies employed. These arguments are considered in Chapters 13, 14, and 15.

On entering the thickets of this extensive debate, let us do so armed with our usual skepticism. Though trade is very important, it is also easy to overrate that importance. The trade-to-income ratio for the world in 1980 (world exports divided by world income) was only 18 percent. In large countries with a low trade-to-income ratio (India 6 percent, Bangladesh 8 percent, and China 10 percent) a *fourfold* improvement in export prices, with import prices unchanged, would raise national income only in the range of 24 to 40 percent. For India, it would require a rise in export prices of over 16 times to double national income. Obviously, for some important LDCs trade cannot be the only villain. It is important to note that such countries are poor basically because of their low productivity, not because of the conditions facing them in foreign trade.[13]

The Unequal Exchange Argument

"The theory of comparative advantage is one of the few bits of statical logic that economists of all schools understand and agree with" writes Paul Samuelson of MIT.[14] A major exception is Arghiri Emmanuel, who argues that the poverty of the LDCs is *caused* by trade itself.[15] Much of Emmanuel's work considers the terms of trade, low multiplier effects, and the other points of a dynamic nature included in our second and third categories of objections to trade (and examined in detail below). But the remarkable innovation in the Emmanuel argument is that even in a *static* situation, there can be an unequal exchange resulting in losses, not gains, for an LDC engaging in trade. Should this contention ever be proved, it would be revolutionary.

Emmanuel uses capital movements to make his case. International capital movements will, he argues, increase the supply of the scarce factor in capital-short countries (LDCs) and thus lower profit rates there, while at the same time raising them in the capital-abundant countries (the rich). The lower profit component in poor-country prices will mean the prices themselves fall, while in rich countries the higher profit component will boost prices. The capital flows will mean a poor country has to exchange more of its now-cheaper goods for less of the rich country's output. The LDC in this position is worse off than it would have been without trade. This case has attracted wide attention in the underdeveloped world and has been used to justify a strategy of self-sufficiency.

Paul Samuelson has mounted a powerful attack on the Emmanuel position. In his paper "The Illogic of Neo-Marxian Doctrine of Unequal Exchange," he states that the analysis assumes no change along the production possibility curve after the opening of trade.[16] A move toward specialization alters Emmanuel's arithmetic, says Samuelson. "It is a cruel hoax on the laborers in poor countries to pretend that there is some way of increasing their real incomes . . . by choking off trade. . . ." states Samuelson.[17] And, indeed, the arithmetical counterexamples presented by him appear to cast grave doubt on the soundness of Emmanuel's position. We can safely conclude that in its static sense, the Ricardian theory of comparative advantage emerges still useful from this hot controversy, with Emmanuel's alleged flaw in comparative advantage theory unlikely to be proven. That leaves the dynamic objections, that trade *in the long run* brings declining benefits, still to be considered.

Enclave Arguments[18]

A major criticism of trade as an engine of growth, often associated with the Swedish economist Gunnar Myrdal, concerns the linkages and multiplier effects between the trading activity and the domestic economy. The ideal trading activity is easy enough to define. The optimum is a fast-growing export sector with a strong stimulus for investment, local employment, and local income. There would be considerable externalities such as raising skills of the employed labor and heavy purchases of local, rather than imported, raw materials by the export industry (backward linkage in the language of Chapter 11). The labor force would use its new higher incomes to purchase domestically produced consumer goods instead of imports; there will also at optimum be significant forward linkage from exports, as in the case of rice where the brown husks left over after milling can be used for livestock feed.

Imagine the establishment of a canning factory to see the case at its best and worst. This exporter of canned fruits and vegetables provides fertilizer, seed, and technical advice to farmers and gives them long-term contracts. They and the labor employed in the cannery all receive higher incomes leading to a demand for more consumer goods and better food, thus stimulating both local industry and local farming. (These are the backward linkages.) Farmers apply their new knowledge of techniques to other crops, the growing prosperity encourages banks to provide more credit to local farming and manufacturing; cooperatives, brokers, and middlemen, all owing their existence initially to the cannery, have an impact on domestic pursuits as well. The engine rumbles along.

Now consider a more bleak alternative. The cannery fails to gain local supplies, because farmers fear to switch from subsistence production. Raw materials must be imported. Labor is hired at subsistence wages, and the multiplier effect on income is thus very low because there is little to be multiplied. Even those who do earn higher income use almost all of it to buy imported goods.

There are in fact stark examples of enclave economies where exports provided little domestic stimulus. Sri Lanka, then Ceylon, and its tea industry is one such case. The capital equipment for the industry was purchased in Britain, the equipment and the tea were carried on British ships, and the managers were British, importing many of their consumption goods. The profits were largely repatriated to London. Even the labor was imported from India, where it was cheaper. Sri Lanka was left with little in terms of new knowledge, multiplied incomes, and domestic industrialization. The same case has been made for the West Indies by the "New World Group" or "Plantation Economy School." The perpetuation of absentee ownership and the foreign control of refining, marketing, shipping, and all associated finance arguably have political and psychological consequences far beyond the economic impact. All contribute to the inertia that characterizes an enclave economy.[19]

Some writers have concluded that the enclave problem is more serious in the production of primary product exports. Hans Singer of the UN emphasized the lesser degree of capital formation and the smaller "dynamic radiation" through the training of a skilled or semiskilled labor force. He believed industry was more suitable on both counts than agriculture and mining. That there is some validity to his argument is perhaps demonstrated by the examples of Germany in the nineteenth century and Japan in the twentieth.

Many economists are far less certain of the conclusion, however. Dynamic radiation through training is much more likely to be important where agriculture is capital-intensive and based on mechanical skill—and it is not obvious why this path is less desirable than the establishment of manufacturing industry. Nor is there reason to assume that an *unskilled* industrial labor force will yield any external economies whatever in comparison with agriculture. Examples of countries developing through agriculture without sacrifice of external economies are not rare; they include the United States, Canada, Australia, New Zealand, and Denmark. The farmers of Iowa or the Australian outback know considerably more about machinery, marketing, and production than do many city dwellers!

Furthermore, it now is clear that manufacturing industry can lead to enclaves as easily as primary production. The foreign firm that imports a capital-intensive technology may indeed pay relatively high wages and salaries, but does not hire many workers. And the lucky ones who do find employment may adopt a life style that stimulates luxury imports rather than domestic production. Alternatively, domestic industry may be rather capital-intensive, substituting for imports but at the same time relying heavily on imported inputs. Manufacturing in this sense provides not dynamic radiation, but just another enclave.

Most economists agree that "outpost investment" of the enclave sort is common in the LDCs. There is far less agreement, however, that international trade is the reason for the existence of enclaves. Enclaves and low multiplier effects can more realistically be blamed on other causes, impediments that are part of underdevelopment itself and that are not explained by reliance on trade or the nature of exports and imports. For example, a large subsistence sector in agriculture must result in a reduced domestic multiplier effect in rural areas when exports occur. A country such as the Ivory Coast with much cash marketing of food has a decidedly larger multiplier impact from its cocoa and coffee exports than does a country such as Uganda, whose cotton and coffee are grown together with food for the farmers' own family. As a general rule, the poorer a country, the larger its subsistence sector, and therefore the smaller its domestic market and the less the opportunity to spend new income—whether from exports or any other internal activity unconnected with international trade—on locally produced goods. Similarly, the poorer a country is, the more it will be necessary to use imported capital, imported technology, and imported management with high repatriation of profits and salaries.

In addition to a large subsistence sector, another explanation of the existence of enclaves is the mass of unskilled labor available for employment at low wages. There may be overpopulation, unemployment, and a large sector of low-productivity farming. All this means low opportunity costs; with alternatives for employment poor or nonexistent, only a low wage is needed to attract labor into the export sector, as in the Lewis model discussed in Chapter 10. The result is that exporting can become established and can begin to grow appreciably, without as much stimulus to the economy as would be expected in a more developed country, where wages would rise significantly when the new demand for labor affects labor markets. For the same reason, *any* domestic activity in addition to exports (manufacturing for the local market, for instance) would radiate less stimulus to the rest of the economy.[20]

Financial and political institutions may also contribute to enclaves. When a country is very poor, banking and brokerage institutions often do not develop enough to provide further linkages to the rest of the economy from exports. Banks remain highly specialized, lending only for the traditional export crop or mineral. Foreign buyers and indigenous brokers also stay specialized, as when the local coffee buyer will not touch tobacco or cocoa. Frequently, the major reason for this conservatism is risk; with capital scarce and expensive and knowledge limited, neither bank nor broker feels the urge to leave the beaten track.

Another institutional element is the political process, which can work against linkages to and from agriculture. The tax system may, as we saw in Chapter 4, be biased against agriculture. The growing power of the urban work force may result in price controls on food and subsidized food imports, both of which work to raise the urban real wage, but which also inhibit domestic agriculture. Again the enclave is seen to be associated with symptoms of underdevelopment in general, rather than with exporting in particular.

The conclusion must be that even a large initial stimulus from exporting (whether of primary products or manufactures) will not be passed on through a strong multiplier process if the domestic impediments are serious, and that these barriers will also be sizeable for indigenous development based on production for the domestic market.

Some economists argue that the disadvantages of export enclaves have been overemphasized. No doubt, as Alec Cairncross suggests, there is little about an oil refinery that would bring transformation to the agriculture of an oil-producing state.[21] But what about the fiscal linkage of the tax mechanism? Even enclaves with no other conceivable connection to the domestic economy can, after all, be linked to it through the tax mechanism. Primary product enclaves were certainly important in the development of countries such as Japan (silk), the United States and Canada (grain), and Great Britain (first wool, then textiles, which once comprised over 70 percent of British exports). The enclave producing such primary product staples is likely to find a strong linkage to the processing of those staples into semifinished and finished form. Any hindrance to the operation of this linkage will presumably be due more to politics in the developed world, especially high tariffs against such processed items, than to any inherent weakness in trade itself. Even in the "worst case" of the Ceylonese tea discussed above, there were *some* linkages.[22] Railways and ports built or improved to handle the export item were useful for other economic activities. The higher tax revenues financed the first large investment in education and public health; this investment stemming from fiscal linkage became the hallmark of modern Sri Lanka. (Admittedly, in colonial days the tax revenues also paid for the army, the police, and the high salaries of the colonial administrators.) In sum, it would seem far more reasonable to attack the enclave effects of international trade with a combination of taxes and development programs than to attack the concept of international trade itself.

One element in the enclave debate is a rather bracing one.[23] Sometimes those who attack international trade as responsible for enclave development seem to assume that, without such trade and its enclaves, the alternatives would be very bright. Would there, however, have been domestic investment to replace the foreign investment? Would local entrepreneurship be abundant? Above all, would the domestic market be sufficiently large to stimulate a wide range of new economic activity? There might be in all this a logical fallacy of contrasting what did occur (an export enclave) with some idyllic picture of what might have occurred at best. Unfortunately, the result without trade may be far less favorable—a stagnant idleness of the factors of production due to the very limited local market. Export crops or mining or production of some manufactures for export, even when their linkages are low and their future sales prospects not especially inviting, may for dozens of countries be the only plausible way to start the development process. One thinks of the even worse poverty that would be found in Senegal without its peanuts, Uganda without coffee, the Sudan without cotton, Bangladesh without jute, Zambia, Peru, and Bolivia without copper or tin, and, more obviously, Nigeria, Libya, and the Arab states without oil.

The Terms of Trade Argument

The terms of trade argument is a shorthand way of expressing a general pessimism on the prospects for exports from the LDCs, especially when these exports are primary products. Its chief advocates over a period of many years were Raul Prebisch of Argentina, former chairman of the UN Economic Commission for Latin America, and Hans Singer of the UN.[24]

Several different elements are involved in the controversial assertion, all combining to mean that a typical LDC must export more and more to obtain the same quantity of imported goods as before. The argument is often expressed in the following manner. There is a secular (that is, long-run, lasting at least several decades) tendency for the terms of trade to turn against the exports, especially the primary product exports, of the LDCs. It is generally agreed that yearly or cyclical price changes, even when severe and disruptive, are not evidence of a long-run decline, can be due to very different causes, and are subject to other remedies considered in the next chapter.

"Terms of trade" is a measure economists use in attempting to express the relative prices of a country's exports and its imports. There are several ways to calculate the measure, but the most common version, called the commodity or net barter terms of trade, is an index of export prices divided by an index of import prices, P_x/P_m. This calculation is itself turned into an index by setting it equal to 100 for some base year. Then, if in later years, export prices should rise faster than import prices (that is, P_x grows larger than P_m), then the index number would be higher than 100, a so-called favorable movement in the terms of trade. Falling export prices relative to imports would result in an index number below 100, an unfavorable movement in the terms of trade. This most common form is published frequently for almost all countries.

One must be wary of the unqualified proposition that an improvement in the commodity terms of trade is necessarily "good" for a country or a fall in the index necessarily "bad." In most cases this will be true, but a rising index is not always advantageous and a falling index is sometimes favorable. Note that the terms of trade alone says nothing about the resulting total revenues earned. For LDCs as a whole, or for large countries with some ability to influence market conditions, high and rising prices for exports might be reducing rather than increasing earnings, with the volume exported falling proportionately more than the price rise. This will, of course, depend on the elasticities involved. Conversely, lower export prices may stimulate sales and improve earnings. The "best" position is not simply some highest possible commodity terms of trade, but rather some optimum terms of trade that maximizes earnings.[25] More significantly, a fall in export prices and hence an unfavorable movement in the terms of trade might be caused by an increase in productivity in the exporting industries. The greater productivity, leading to an enlarged quantity of exports, may bring higher incomes from those exports even though the price falls. The productivity change causes the price decline, but it would not be correct to conclude that the country's economic situation is now worse.

Economists for a number of years have attempted to calculate a version of the terms of trade that takes productivity changes into account. The major attempt is called the "single factoral terms of trade," a ratio between an index of income accruing to the factors of production engaged in producing for export and an index of import prices. The formula, for some base year and for the year to be measured, is an index of income to a fixed amount of factors used to produce a given quantity of exports divided by an index of import prices. Such a formulation would readily reveal the cases where export prices are falling, but where factor incomes are stable or rising due to improvements in productivity.[26] Unfortunately, it is not easy to calculate the factoral terms of trade because of the difficulties in constructing an adequate index of productivity. Work is advancing, but progress is difficult because acceptable data are so rare. Even when the numbers are not available, however, the policy maker must be careful to make rough estimates, though these will admittedly be imperfect.

Good examples of factoral considerations in practice are the United States and Canada, whose cheap grain captured many European markets in the late nineteenth and early twentieth centuries, and Japan where there was a drastic decline in the commodity terms of trade between 1910 and 1920, again after 1930, and once again from 1960 to 1980.[27] The decline gave a vigorous push to exports, brought new markets, and accompanied rapid increases in per capita income. (Japan had the world's fifth-worst terms of trade performance between 1960 and 1980, the fall being from 150 to 77 with 1975 = 100. For that country, price competition was a key to economic success, not failure.)

It is therefore not enough to say that the commodity terms of trade are deteriorating for the LDCs, who are thus worse off. With this caveat in mind, we now turn to the reasons advanced by those who feel the commodity terms of trade are destined in the long run to decline against the LDCs. Each of these reasons has generated controversy of its own, and the points both pro and con are presented in the section below.

THE TERMS OF TRADE ARGUMENTS AGAINST LDC EXPORTING

The Main Cause for Declining Terms of Trade: Weak Demand for Primary Products

The main theoretical argument focuses on a supposed weakness in the long-run demand for primary products. The argument is commonly associated with Raul Prebisch, Ragnar Nurkse, and Edward M. Bernstein. In this scenario a decline in the commodity terms of trade of the LDCs originates in their dependence on primary product exports, the demand for which rises more slowly than the demand for manufactures, turning prices against the former and in favor of the latter. Several different conditions are alleged to be the cause of this.

First, the demand for food rises more slowly than income rises. This well-known phenomenon is known as Engel's law after Ernst Engel,[28] a nineteenth century Prussian mathematician. Engel's law is certainly correct for the developed countries. For example, the income elasticity of demand for food (the percentage increase in demand accompanying a 1 percent rise in income)[29] in the United States, Canada, and Western Europe is in the range of only 0.2 to 0.3, and American per capita consumption of wheat was about the same in the 1980s as it was in 1900. The elasticities facing LDC food exporters are only a little more encouraging, with their food exports estimated to rise at about 0.6 percent for a 1 percent increase in developed-country incomes. The tropical specialties—sugar, tea, coffee, cocoa, pineapple, bananas—all have income elasticities less than 1.0, and most are lower even than the average 0.6 noted above, ranging from 0.3 to 0.5.[30] (Note that the low elasticities do not apply to exports of *manufactured* goods from LDCs, which on average rose about 2 percent for every 1 percent growth in industrial-country GNP, 1967 to 1981.)

Export pessimists are surely correct in believing that markets for food in developed countries will grow slowly. The pessimism does not extend to the LDCs themselves, however. In these countries, Engel's Law has yet to take full effect, and the income elasticity of demand for food is much higher, nearly 1.0 in India and Latin America, perhaps 0.8 for LDCs as a whole. Sales of food *to* LDCs can surge as income grows, and indeed the vast bulk of recent increases in sugar sales has been to the LDCs themselves. Here the tropical specialties are all expected to be income elastic as consumers in LDCs find they can afford a few more "luxuries."

There is the further consideration that population growth will necessitate far larger quantities of food. The *Global 2000 Report*[31] to the President published in 1980 speaks of a rise in food consumption of perhaps $2\frac{1}{2}$ times in the LDCs between 1970 and 2000, due mostly to larger population size, but also including a per capita rise estimated to be about 10 percent. Real price increases are predicted to lie between 30 and 100 percent during this period, depending on whether population growth is toward the lower or higher end of a suggested range. It will not be possible to bring huge new amounts of arable land into production, according to the Report. There were about 1.48 billion hectares of arable land in 1971 to 1975, and the figure is expected to be only some 1.54 billion hectares by 2000.[32] Thus even with the full effects of the Green Revolution, large amounts of expensive fertilizer and water will be needed to achieve the necessary growth in food production, adding to the eventual price-boosting effect. Price rises in the long term will be even greater if more affluence leads LDCs to shift away, in accordance with "Bennett's law," from the calorie-efficient production of cereal grains and starches and toward the more costly and less efficient production of meat and poultry.[33]

If these predictions are correct, there is at least a possibility that they could outweigh the undoubtedly strong negative effect of Engel's Law. Food exporting might then be a leading sector for at least a few LDCs, those able to produce a large agricultural surplus after feeding their own population. Among the countries where food exporting might give a dynamic stimulus to economic development are, in this view, Argentina, Brazil, Colombia, Indonesia, and Thailand.

Numerous others are potential exporters if the problems of scarce credit, limited capital, and inefficiency discussed in Chapter 10 could be overcome. The long-term prospects for food exporters are thus perhaps not quite as bleak as is sometimes asserted.

A second condition assumed to lead to declining terms of trade for LDCs is a weak demand for primary product raw materials. As income grows in developed countries, demand shifts to service industries with a low ratio of raw materials inputs to final output, as opposed to manufacturing where the reverse is true. Technological change brings economies in the use of raw materials, including larger availability and better processing of scrap metal, electrolytic tin plating that conserves on the quantities of tin, and the like. There is also a substitution of synthetics for natural raw materials, as in the cases of nitrates, cotton and silk (with synthetic fabrics), rubber (with the manmade substitute), copper (with plastics), and so forth.[34]

There is substantial evidence to support this contention. The General Agreement on Tariffs and Trade (GATT) has reported that there was a fall in the industrial-country ratio of raw materials and fuel inputs to total manufacturing output from 25.8 percent in 1938 to 20.8 percent in 1954. The same study shows the ratio of *imported* natural raw materials to total natural raw materials used as inputs declined from 38.9 percent to 29.4 percent (with countries therefore turning when possible to their own sources of supply). During the same time period inputs of synthetics as a percentage of final output nearly quadrupled.

Figures for the United States alone are available over a far longer period of time; they show demand for primary products declining even more sharply.[35] According to the government's Paley Report of 1952, a dollar's worth of output in the year 1900 embodied $0.239 worth of raw materials, but by 1950 the dollar's worth of output contained only $0.128 of raw materials. The Paley Commission went on to estimate what it thought consumption of raw materials would be in the 1970s. Its projections overestimated actual consumption by an average of 46 percent. Richard Cooper of Yale University in his 1975 study of the Paley Report states that the Commission gave too little regard to technical and managerial change as forces for increasing the efficiency of production and the development of substitute materials.[36] Theodore Schultz has demonstrated that real per capita income increased about 80 percent more than real per capita consumption of raw materials between 1904 and 1950. D. D. Humphrey has shown that growing use of synthetics more than offset the 75 percent decline in U.S. tariffs on imported natural raw materials in the 20 years before 1955. On the import side U.S. raw materials imports rose only 23 percent between 1929 and 1955 as against 44 percent for imports as a whole (much less, incidentally, than the growth rate in GNP).[37] Between 1973 and 1984 there was a 20 percent fall in the amount of copper used per unit of GNP, a 30 percent fall for nickel, and 40 percent for tin. One major reason for this is that plastics can substitute for many metals, and though plastics are derived from petroleum, they require less energy than is used in the refining of most metals.[38] It certainly does then appear that LDCs face a serious problem of loosening ties between the rise of income in developed countries and their demand for raw material inputs, and hence declining demand for their primary product exports.

Despite the impressive nature of the arguments, there are serious reservations that do not support the case of the pessimists. Technical change does not always work against the demand for primary products; the reverse may be true. Consider the great increases in demand during the last 30 years for bauxite (the raw material for aluminum), vanadium, uranium, and tungsten. All have demonstrated a high income elasticity. The *Global 2000 Report* projects future demand increases running ahead of world GNP increases for a range of mineral and raw materials including aluminum, industrial diamonds, fluorspar, phosphate rock; about keeping pace with GNP growth for a large group; and falling significantly behind only for a short list including refined copper, iron ore, mercury, nickel, silver, and tin.[39] Even demand falling behind GNP growth is no sign of an unfavorable turn in the terms of trade, because price is also a matter of supply. Diminishing returns in the production of primary products, both mineral and agricultural, can mean rising prices and higher incomes whether or not demand is income inelastic.

This was a traditional position in economics dating back to the work of Ricardo and Malthus on land scarcity. John Maynard Keynes warned of diminishing returns and supply constraints in a well-known *Economic Journal* article of 1923, and this contradictory view was resurrected with the Club of Rome's much publicized *Limits to Growth* report of 1972.[40] Today's developed countries are often heavily dependent on mineral imports (the United States less so than Western Europe or Japan), as is shown in Table 12.2.

The LDCs have most of the world's known reserves of some of these minerals (bauxite 73 percent, chromium 98 percent, copper 57 percent, nickel 64 percent, tin 87 percent). They also hold important quantities (31 percent) of iron ore.

Added to that, the mineral deposits being worked in the LDCs frequently are more richly concentrated than they are in the developed countries. This is true because given the serious transport problems common in LDCs, it makes economic sense to develop only the richer deposits. (Examples include the copper of Chile, Zambia, and Zaire, the iron ore of Liberia and Mauritania, the bauxite of Suriname and Guyana, the tin of Bolivia and Malaysia, and the phosphates of Morocco.) During the OPEC oil crisis the high concentration proved to be a

Table 12.2   MINERAL IMPORTS AS A PERCENT OF CONSUMPTION, 1976

	United States	EC	Japan
Bauxite	88	50	100
Chromium	90	95	95
Copper	16	99	93
Iron ore	35	85	99
Manganese	100	99	90
Nickel	61	90	95
Tin	75	90	90

Source: Global 2000 Report, New York, 1980, p. 205.

major advantage to the LDCs, because mining and processing less rich deposits is energy-intensive. Higher energy prices are thus likely to shift demand to the LDCs, where less energy must be expended per ton of raw material recovered.

Finally, there are many alternative uses for resources in the developed countries. With opportunity costs thus high, when mineral prices weaken, we would expect these countries to shift out of minerals production long before an LDC does so. The United States or Canada would surely cut their copper output in the face of falling demand years before Chile or Zaire would take that decision. The more elastic supply would stand to benefit any LDC remaining in the field.

Thus, as with food, the long-run prospects of mineral raw materials exporters perhaps do not warrant the extreme pessimism with which they are often viewed. Economies in their use and the substitution of synthetics may be considered not as the cause of a problem, but as a response that has the effect of supplementing a low elasticity of supply. The Brandt Commission took this view when it called for new coordinated programs of investment in the LDCs to offset a decade of inattention to minerals as a leading sector and to ward off the diminishing returns the Commission believes will set in from the late 1980s.

A final consideration is the possibility that LDC exports of food and raw materials might displace exports and production in developed countries. Developed nations are also large-scale producers of primary products, and at the start of the 1980s these countries exported almost as many primary products by value as did the LDCs. There is significant direct competition between the two groups in numerous metals, fibers, sugar, fats and oils, and, indirectly, beverages and rubber. Competition tends to imply high price elasticities for individual commodities or countries. Alec Cairncross has pointed out that this high price elasticity, caused by the ready availability of competing primary products in developed countries, might well be responsible for what appears to be sluggish demand for these LDC exports.[41] If this is so, the practical significance would be that price stability, or a measure of price reduction in the LDCs (that is, a worsening of the commodity terms of trade), might actually be advantageous, leading to the eventual capture and retention of large markets at the expense of developed-country producers. More efficient methods in agriculture, more investment in mining, and lower taxes on exports would here be seen as playing on high price elasticities to offset the alleged income inelasticities of demand. (If an exporter is small, then its situation is automatically better; the price elasticity of demand facing it will be high and the market will be able to absorb large percentage increases in that country's output.) Needless to say, if the developed countries maintain or increase their already heavy protection of primary products facing competition from the LDCs, then the optimism of this paragraph would have to be much tempered. (Protection against primary products is treated in Chapter 15.)

The observer attempting to be a fair-minded judge will perhaps conclude from this debate that general predictions of the overall demand for primary products are of far less value to a given country than specific predictions for its individual exports. There will certainly be *some* primary product exports saddled with income inelasticity, subject to substitution through technical change, and unable to capture additional markets with calculated price cutting. Countries in this camp are well-advised to look for alternative exports—perhaps other primary products, perhaps manufactures. But this prescription is not the same as sentencing primary product exports in general to the certainty of declining terms of trade.

The Productivity Argument

The second of the arguments pointing to a decline in the terms of trade is the productivity theory advanced by Hans Singer three decades ago, but still very much a part of the current debate. Singer postulates that economic growth in the developed countries typically leads to higher income in the form of wages because labor supply is relatively inelastic. In Figure 12.6 economic growth increases the demand for labor and pushes up wages. Figure 12.7 shows the contrary position for a labor-abundant LDC, where growth pushes up labor demand, but along a highly elastic supply curve for labor. Adding to the problem, the growth in demand is faster in the rich countries because technical advances are concentrated there. Wage incomes in LDCs thus do not rise or rise less than in the developed world. Goods prices then show a different secular tendency: rising due to increasing costs in the developed world with a less elastic supply of labor; rising more slowly in the LDCs because of the high elasticity of labor supply.

The argument has recently received strong theoretical articulation in an article by Ronald Findlay of Columbia University.[42] Many economists see merit in the argument and agree that it does introduce a tendency for the terms of trade to decline against LDCs. Fortunately for those countries, however, this logic may not apply permanently. As development occurs, labor supplies may become less

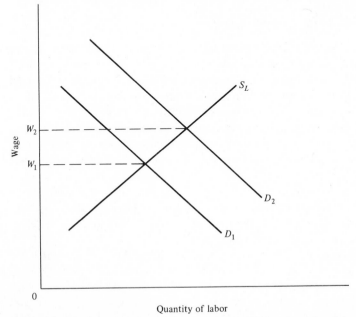

Figure 12.6 Effect of growth on demand for labor and wages when labor supply is relatively inelastic.

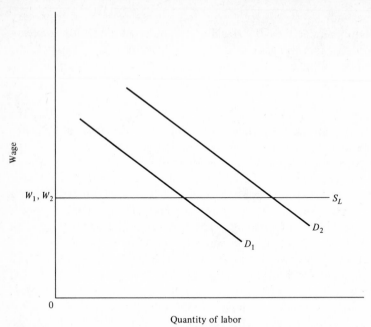

Figure 12.7   Effect of growth on demand for labor and wages when labor supply is highly elastic.

elastic, and the real wage will start to rise as it does in advanced countries. Here is another aspect to the need for limiting population growth.[43]

The Monopoly and Ratchet Effect Argument

The third reason suggesting a decline in the commodity terms of trade concerns rigidities in the market structure of the developed world. The monopoly argument is most closely associated with Raul Prebisch; it involves the familiar "ratchet effect" of economic theory. In the developed countries oligopolistic market structure characterizes industrial markets, with a resulting rent element in prices. In these same countries, but more rarely in the LDCs, strong trade unions bargain with large firms. Under these circumstances a ratchet effect may typify price patterns. Prices normally rise during a boom, with oligopolistic firms passing cost increases on to customers and unions perhaps pushing up wages beyond rises in productivity in a wage-push type of inflation. When a slump follows, both firms and unions work to avoid cuts in prices and wages. Prices rise more easily than they fall in the developed world; there are fewer barriers to the fall of prices elsewhere; the terms of trade turn against the LDCs.

There is debate on this proposition. Charles P. Kindleberger has pointed out that trade union power alone is not enough to explain any such tendency. Firms must also have sufficient market power to pass cost increases through to consumers; otherwise competition in the product market results simply in reduced sales for any country with a cost-push inflation. Nor is it enough to say that there is strong market power within a national market. Only if the power to raise prices is international in scope will this argument work generally for the goods exported by the developed countries. The idea of an international product monopoly in many products does not seem tenable. The impression is actually one of quite intense global competition for most industrial products in world trade, for example, automobiles and trucks, shipbuilding, steel, aircraft, and computers. There is even the possibility that if developed-country monopoly leads to more technical change and hence lowers production costs over time, on this score the terms of trade might even turn in favor of the LDCs. Recent statistical work gives little support to the thesis that an international ratchet results in a long-term decline against poor countries.[44]

Ronald Findlay has stated that as an explanation for terms of trade shifts, the monopoly argument is unconvincing.[45] There is perhaps a growing consensus on this point. The theory retains a kernel of importance, however, that is significant whenever there is monopoly power in a national market sheltering behind tariff or nontariff barriers to trade. Here the effect of the ratchet is to exacerbate domestic inflation. If price rises are caused by higher costs of raw materials inputs, domestically the higher prices tend to remain even if the raw materials costs drop back later in the business cycle. Within a protected national market, then, the ratchet may have substantial importance as a conveyer of inflation.

There is an additional argument that some markets for primary products are rigged on the side of the *buyers*. Such monopsony power may indeed exist in at least a few markets, as we discuss in Chapter 15. To shift the terms of trade further against the LDCs, the monopsony power would presumably have to intensify.

Lack of Flexibility

The fourth and last argument suggesting that the terms of trade will decline against LDC exports is the "inflexibility" theory advanced by Charles Kindleberger. A decline will occur because LDC economies are less capable of rapid shifts in production than are those of the developed world. Labor, land, capital, and entrepreneurial ability do not move as rapidly from one occupation to another because transportation is poor, communications and hence knowledge are limited, literacy is low, and skills in management and government are retarded. Even when decline for an export commodity is predictable, the shift away from that export toward other alternatives is sluggish. This low elasticity of supply for relative price decreases means a country can be locked for a lengthy period into a disadvantageous export, unable to pursue its changing comparative advantage.

Economists generally concede that the overall thrust of this argument is quite true. Inflexibility is common enough in LDC exporting, with the familiar examples of nitrates, jute, cotton, and natural rubber where demand has dropped and of bananas, cocoa, and coffee where new and more competitive sources of supply have emerged. Any country with an export commodity suffering from declining terms of trade due to a fall in demand or greater supply elsewhere will certainly want to consider shifting to alternatives, and where inflexibility hinders this, the situation is a difficult one.

The major weakness in the argument is the implication that primary product exporting is somehow to blame for the inflexibility. The reverse conclusion is more sensible: that inflexibility is the cause of unsuccessful exporting. Note that the argument applies with equal force to any manufactured export from an LDC, and perhaps even more so since tastes change rapidly for many consumer goods. It applies also to producers of import substitutes, who are more likely (if inflexible) to be driven out of business by cheaper imports. Finally, it applies widely even to any domestic economic activity unrelated to international trade, where extra costs are incurred whenever response to changing internal demand and supply conditions is especially slow. It is not the nature of the commodity produced nor of international trade that is at fault here—it is underdevelopment itself. Even so, the Kindleberger position does make a sensible case that the terms of trade might for long periods turn against the slow-reacting LDCs.

To summarize, there is a plausible argument that long-run adverse shifts in the terms of trade might be experienced by LDCs. The risk is greatest for (1) exporters of foodstuffs and (2) exporters of primary product raw materials most subject to economies in use and replacement by synthetics; with the potential for decline more severe if (3) productivity gains result in price decreases in LDCs and (4) poor countries prove less flexible in moving away from exports with declining prospects.

TERMS OF TRADE: THE EVIDENCE

The beginner in development economics might think that all the argument on a supposed secular decline in the terms of trade could easily be settled by an appeal to the facts. Why not just survey the data for the nineteenth and twentieth centuries? Would this not be a conclusive outcome? Alas, it is not so easy to appeal to the evidence. One would want to show the terms of trade for LDCs versus developed countries, but most LDCs achieved independence only recently. Their colonial statistics are spotty and often difficult to assess.

Table 12.3 **TERMS OF TRADE FOR PRIMARY PRODUCTS (HENCE FOR LDCs), INVERSE OF BRITISH TERMS OF TRADE (1938 = 100)**

1876–1880	163
1896–1900	142
1913	137
1928	123
1938	100

Source: From United Nations, *Relative Prices of Exports and Imports of Underdeveloped Countries,* 1949, pp. 21–24.

The Older Evidence for Declining Terms of Trade

The most famous long-term figures are a UN series, based on old League of Nations data, covering the 60 or so years between 1876 and 1938.[46] They were obtained in an unorthodox way. With the figures for LDCs so imperfect, the UN adopted the device of using data for Great Britain, which are excellent and cover a long period of time. Since historically Britain was an exporter of manufactures and an importer of primary products, the UN believed that the *inverse* of Britain's terms of trade would indicate the situation for primary products and hence for the LDCs. These figures, shown in Table 12.3, were first popularized by Raul Prebisch and have been widely used by various UN agencies to show a very long-term decline in the terms of trade. (With much more data available after World War II, it was possible to construct an expanded series showing the terms of trade for the LDCs as a group vis-à-vis the developed countries. These data are considered later in this chapter.)

The data of Table 12.3 certainly seem to support the argument that there has been a significant long-term decline against the LDCs. Grave statistical doubts concerning the British data have arisen, however, generating one of the more durable controversies of development economics. Critics claim that the statistics in the table give the appearance of precise meaning when the question is really very much in doubt. Four main objections have been made to the use of the British data.[47]

1. The British statistics are not a good proxy for the experience of the other industrial countries, and they are thus a misleading indication of primary product behavior. Evidence that this is true can be found in the work of Charles Kindleberger, who found no significant trend in the terms of trade of European industrialized countries *except* Britain down to World War II, and Richard Lipsey's analysis for the United States that also showed trendless terms of trade for American imported primary products against exported manufactures.[48] Theodore Morgan's long time series for seven specific industrial and less developed countries showed disparate results, thus casting doubt on the British data.[49] For example, from 1861 Morgan shows a long rise-fall-rise for India, violent instability for New Zealand with a clear upward trend, a fall-rise-fall for South Africa, a mild rise for Japan to 1900 and a major fall thereafter, and a rise-fall-rise-fall-rise with sharp fluctuations and no clear downward trend for Brazil. Evidence such as this led Gottfried Haberler to conclude that the supply of and demand for primary products are affected by such divergent conditions that movements in a broad, weighted index covering all LDCs or all primary products leave us with little useful information; it led Alec Cairncross to say that averaging the experience of the LDCs is to "presume common elements that may have no real existence."[50]

An UNCTAD study published in 1972 appears to confirm that the magnitude of the decline shown by the British data is misleading. The study, piecing together what information is available for the LDCs, also showed a decline, from 80 in 1900 to 68 in 1938. This decline is less than half that shown by the British (Prebisch) data, 15 percent as opposed to 33 percent for the same time period.

John Spraos has concluded that *some* decline up to World War II did occur, that this took place because Britain's importance in the statistics was large enough to outweigh the rather trendless experience of the rest of Europe and the United States, but that the magnitude of the decline has been exaggerated.[51]

2. A second objection to the British data is that a bias is introduced because primary product exporting is carried on *both* by developed and less-developed countries. Thus it is possible that developed countries as well as LDCs would be disadvantaged by deteriorating commodity terms of trade for primary products. That this *could* be so is illustrated in Table 12.4, showing percentages of world trade in 1979. Note that the rich world actually exported almost as many primary products as did the LDCs.

John Spraos investigated the possibility by looking at U.S. figures for agricultural imports (the larger share of which were tropical products) and agricultural exports (largely temperate zone commodities). He found a slight negative price trend for the imports and a slight positive one for the exports between 1879 and 1938. Data for Europe taken from the work of Kindleberger (for 1872 to 1938) and Maizels (for 1899 to 1937) are largely neutral, there being no noticeable trend either for or against temperate zone or tropical agricultural products. The conclusion is that if full price data covering the LDCs had been available, rather than proxies such as primary product exports and imports, they would not have altered the finding that some smallish deterioration in LDC terms of trade took place in the 60-odd years up to the Second World War.

3. The British data are affected by the problem of FOB versus CIF. The British valued their exports FOB (free on board), not including ocean freight charges. Their imports were valued CIF (cost, insurance, and freight), including the transport costs. Many countries still do the same. The result is that any major shift in transport costs affects only the average price of imports, not exports. Several economists, P. T. Ellsworth most prominently, have estimated that the greater part of the decline in British import prices from 1876 to the outbreak of World War I was due to the introduction of large steam-powered cargo ships built of iron and steel and the international expansion of railway construction. Freight rates in 1913 were in real terms only about 30 percent of what they had been in

**Table 12.4   PRIMARY PRODUCT
EXPORTS AS A
PERCENT OF
WORLD EXPORTS,
BY VALUE
(EXCLUDING
PETROLEUM)**

Exports from	
Industrial Countries	19.0
LDCs	22.9

Source: World Bank, *Commodity Trade and Price Trends,* Baltimore, 1981, pp. 2–3

1870. Thus, says E. M. Wright, it was possible for wool prices to rise 12 percent in Buenos Aires and simultaneously to fall 8 percent in London due to better trans-Atlantic shipping and the completion of the Argentine rail network.[52]

There is, however, new evidence that this bias applied only to about the start of World War I, and that in following years it was canceled out by rising transport costs. The conclusion: There is a transport bias, probably not large, that overstates the long-run decline in the terms of trade against primary products.

4. A fourth objection is made on the grounds that terms of trade data do not reflect quality changes. Many have asserted that quality changes in manufacturing have been far greater than in primary products. Coal today is the same as coal in 1870, but the electric light and motor car did not even exist then and have improved considerably since their invention. Shifts in the terms of trade against primary products are here seen as a justified reflection of the improved relative quality of manufactures.

In rebuttal, the point is made that quality change does after all affect primary products, as with the movement toward higher quality coffee beans, a switch to cotton of longer staple length more suitable for the textile industry, much lower free fatty acid content in peanuts because of innovations in shelling, and much higher iron content per ton of iron ore because of technical advance in mining.[53] Added to this, quality deterioration of manufactured goods can and certainly has occurred with some products.

The research on how to take account of quality change in the terms of trade has been largely experimental in nature. Thus far it gives little support for the charge that the price index for manufactures is inflated because quality change is not included. It is probably reasonable to conclude that there is *some* quality bias for manufactures working to offset the nominal fall in the terms of trade for primary products, but the bias is not as great as the protagonists in the argument have suggested.

Recent Trends in the Terms of Trade

What about the more recent evidence concerning any continuing decline in the commodity terms of trade? The UNCTAD series, which covered 1900 to 1938, has been extended to 1970. In the extended series the deterioration disappears, there being a slight improvement from 1900 to 1970 with temporary peaks in 1912 to 1913 (100) and in 1951 during the Korean War boom (118). Another series, produced from World Bank data in 1978 and judged to be better than that provided by the UN as it covers primary products and manufactures weighted according to their share in LDC exports, shows an extremely slight deterioration between 1900 and 1970, with some improvement between 1938 and 1970. The record from the middle 1950s to 1973 is reasonably clear, with the terms of trade for LDCs and for their primary product exports showing no perceptible decline in this period. After that, the debate becomes muddied because of the oil shocks of 1973–1974 and 1979–1980. Table 12.5 shows that the terms of trade fell sharply for non-oil LDCs, while rising even more sharply for oil exporters.

The decline for the oil-importing LDCs was mostly due to the change in

Table 12.5   TERMS OF TRADE (1975 = 100)

	1960	1980
Low-income LDCs	113	90
Middle-income LDCs		
Oil importers	109	83
Oil exporters	69	135
Developed countries	100	94
Iraq, Kuwait, Libya, Saudi Arabia	26	168

Source: UN data.

oil prices, so that there was a remarkable transfer of welfare not just from rich countries to OPEC, but from many unlucky poor countries to some lucky ones. The episode underscores how misleading it was ever to believe that there is some uniformity of economic behavior that applies to primary products generally. (It is worth noting that since the two oil crises, the terms of trade have rarely been calculated for LDCs as a whole. That figure would have shown large gains, at least until the oil price broke in early 1986. The convention has been to make a separate calculation for oil importers and oil exporters. Needless to say, one way to make movements in the terms of trade appear unfavorable is to exclude the items or countries that performed best during the period considered. The trained observer will keep that point well in mind.)

Other than the fall due to the effects of the OPEC oil shocks, changes in the terms of trade of non-oil LDCs were slight to 1980. After that, they deteriorated sharply for the countries that exported primary products, and in 1985 they were about 20 percent less than their average from 1960 to 1980.[54] The fall was far less serious for the NICs that export mainly manufactured goods. This relative price decline for primary products was presumably a reversible short-term movement caused by the global recession, recovery from which began in 1983. It would thus not be evidence of a secular decline, and has no part in this chapter's debate. (It does, however, point to the problem of price and income instability considered in Chapter 15.)

There is no doubt, however, that the renewed decline in 1985 was unexpectedly sharp, caught economists by surprise, and was cause for concern. The orthodox explanation that temporary slow growth in world trade was the culprit certainly applied in part. Developed-country industrial output that had been growing at 8 percent in 1984 tailed off to only 3 percent in 1985; a major effect of that was a fall in the growth of world trade from 9 percent in 1984 to 3 percent in 1985. For all that, the continuing weakness in primary product terms of trade was extraordinary, and other causal factors were apparently at work. Western Europe's economies were particularly sluggish. That area imports half the world's primary products, and the poor long-term prospects for European growth were thus disquieting for LDC exporters. In food and beverages the high prices of four to six years earlier were apparently having the delayed effect of raising supply in 1985. (After planting, bush and tree crops take several years to mature and reach maximum output.) The Green Revolution was exerting supply effects as well. Finally, perhaps the structural shift away from heavy industry in developed countries and the substitution of synthetics for primary products were having a greater effect than before.[55]

Your author's suspicion is that time will show the 1985 dip was mostly related to temporary demand conditions. If true, renewed world growth would bring quick improvement in the terms of trade. But this diagnosis is not certain, and the situation will have to be carefully watched.

Conclusions on the Terms of Trade

Having completed this survey of the terms of trade and economic development, what conclusions can be drawn from the analysis? Concerning the statistical case, it seems fair to say that the famous original series chosen by Prebisch and his proponents (the British data) exaggerates the decline against primary product exports between 1876 and 1938, but some smallish fall did probably take place, even when the various objections are considered. Between 1938 and 1980 there was considerable improvement with oil included and still some improvement with oil excluded. Taking a longer view from the start of this century to 1980, even with oil excluded there has been no very important decline. I.M.D. Little summarized the debate somewhat sharply: "Any reasonably objective observer would have been saying for many years now that the evidence cannot possibly be held to give grounds for maintaining that there is a trend in the terms of trade against developing countries. Theories have been invented to explain this non-existent trend: they are treated with respect even though they explain what does not exist."[56]

Perhaps the major lesson conveyed by the statistics is that a *general* index conceals as much as it reveals. Some commodities are rising in price, while others fall; some LDCs prosper in their exporting, while others stagnate. Any overall average does not give sufficient information on which to base a country's decisions on whether to export and what to export. Only careful analysis of short- and long-run demand and supply for individual products can do that—and that is often much more difficult than compiling averages. The uncritical use of such averages certainly contributed to the bias against trade encountered for so long in so many LDCs, with costs discussed in more detail in the next chapter.

But it is also true that some primary products and even manufactured exports may be bad bets and that some LDCs will need to worry about declining terms of trade in the long run. Consider that Bangladesh with its jute exports suffered a terms of trade decline between 1960 and 1980 from 201 to 84; Sri Lanka's fell from 203 to 93 as its tea exports stagnated; and Liberia and its rubber (worst performing of all major products) did even more poorly, crashing from 255 to 71. These were the world's worst cases in those years, and their experience was bad indeed.

A country with no good substitutes and slow to adjust (inelastic supply), facing an inelastic and slow-growing demand for its major export, may well find that even strong growth in the export industry results only in a falling price, so exporting away most of the gains from trade. If the country in this fix earns much of its income from exporting; if population growth makes relatively cheaper labor available to the export sector; if cost-reducing technological changes take place in that sector and these are passed on in lower prices; then prospects will be even worse. It is actually conceivable that the growth in the export sector will so reduce export prices as to result in *lower* national income. This has been called "immiserizing growth" by Jagdish Bhagwati; a country in this position would be frustrated indeed.[57]

Fortunately, many LDCs in recent years have shown unexpected flexibility, the elasticities are often high enough so that no problem ensues, and trade among the LDCs themselves gives a prospect of large new markets. Studies often show that earnings from exporting grow even when the commodity terms of trade fall. One recent 19-country study showed that 16 of them raised their earnings from exporting and only 3 earned less, even though P_x/P_m fell for the entire group.[58] In some of the countries, the growth in earnings was large.

But as we have said before, there are no guarantees. The country that spies the onset of immiserizing growth had best be ready; government policy may be essential. The offending export may have to be restricted. (Only under perfect competition would export expansion be pushed when incomes decline as a result; under monopoly or state intervention this would not happen.[59]) Diversification into other exports may have to be pushed. Programs to encourage a more flexible entrepreneurial response may have to be emphasized, including carefully planned infrastructure development, education, freer markets, and the like. Unfortunately, one would expect the least flexible economies, most in need of these safety valves from immiserizing growth, to be also the poorest ones encountering the greatest difficulties in implementing the remedies.

The message of this chapter is that trade has been an engine of long-run growth in the LDCs, and probably remains a good bet for the future, but that governments had better stay constantly alert for signs of difficulty that will require policy actions to correct. We should also note that there is no magic through which even successful trade will automatically solve the many problems considered in earlier chapters, such as inappropriate technologies or population pressure or agricultural backwardness or market imperfections. Here, too, policy makers must simultaneously pursue other strategies if progress is to be made.

To this point we have considered international trade in the long run. The next three chapters will examine the numerous short-run problems that can impede trade as an engine. Booms and slumps in the developed world, oil shocks and food shocks, cause LDC export prices and revenues to swing alarmingly. Protectionist barriers to trade can turn down the steam. All are more painful to the LDCs whose exports are heavily concentrated. The LDCs themselves may adopt trade policies that, however appealing politically, turn out to be economically ill advised. All of these, even though they may be short run in nature, have the capability to derail the locomotive, as we shall see.

NOTES

1. Some parts of this introduction are taken from Jan S. Hogendorn and Wilson B. Brown, *The New International Economics,* Reading, Mass., 1979, chap. 18.
2. See D. H. Robertson, *Essays in Monetary Theory,* London, 1940, brought to my

attention by Ragnar Nurkse in Gerald M. Meier, *Leading Issues in Economic Development,* 4th ed., Oxford, 1984, p. 493.

3. See the major recent survey of the subject, thorough and well written, by Keith Griffin and John Gurley, "Radical Analyses of Imperialism, the Third World, and the Transition to Socialism: A Survey Article," *Journal of Economic Literature* 23, no. 3 (1985): 1089–1143. André Gunder Frank's *Latin America: Underdevelopment or Revolution,* New York, 1970, has been influential; see also his *Lumpenbourgeoisie and Lumpendevelopment,* New York, 1973. A vivid title in this genre is Walter Rodney, *How Europe Underdeveloped Africa,* London, 1972. Dependency theory is reviewed by Theotonío dos Santos, "The Structure of Dependence," *American Economic Review* 60, no. 2 (1970):231–236; and by Gabriel Palma, "Dependency: A Formal Theory of Underdevelopment or a Methodology for the Analysis of Concrete Situations of Underdevelopment," in Paul Streeten and Richard Jolly, eds., *Recent Issues in World Development,* Oxford, 1981, pp. 383–426. The term unequal exchange was made popular by Arghiri Emmanuel, *L'échange inégal,* Paris, 1969, translated into English as *Unequal Exchange,* New York, 1972. The concept also figures in the research of Samir Amin; see especially his *Neo-Colonialism in West Africa,* Harmondsworth, 1973. Also see Edmar L. Bacha, "An Interpretation of Unequal Exchange from Prebisch-Singer to Emmanuel," *Journal of Development Economics* 5, no. 4 (1978): 319–330; Giovanni Arrighi and John S. Saul, *Essays on the Political Economy of Africa,* New York, 1973; and Immanuel Wallerstein, *The Modern World System,* New York, 1974.

4. Compare Gerald M. Meier, *Emerging from Poverty,* New York, 1984, p. 129.

5. International trade textbooks use indifference curves to introduce demand, thus allowing a determination of exactly how much will be imported and exported by the two countries. They also show that diminishing returns, meaning a production possibility curve bowed outward (concave to the origin), do not alter the essence of the model. Comparative advantage theory can easily be put in commonsense terms that have a remarkable validity. The town's best lawyer also is a careful, efficient, and fast-working mower of lawns, but he hires the neighbor kid to mow his lawn, even though the kid works more slowly at the job, for the obvious reason that the high earnings from an extra hour of legal work far outweigh the costs of paying the (less efficient) kid. Or take the dramatic example unearthed by Charles P. Kindleberger of MIT. Billy Rose was a noted impresario of stage and screen in the 1940s and made a fortune in his various promotions. Simultaneously and remarkably, he happened to be a world class speed typist, having won numerous awards and actually holding a world championship in the skill at one time. He would thus have encountered enormous difficulty in hiring a secretary who could type nearly as well as he could. Still he hired secretaries, because even in this extreme case of being the world's best at the job, he could still earn much more in an hour spent manipulating his entertainment empire than he could in an hour of typing. Q. E. D.

6. See Myint's well-known article, "The Classical Theory of International Trade and the Underdeveloped Countries," *Economic Journal* 68, no. 270 (1958):317–337; and his *Exports and Economic Development of Less-Developed Countries,* Fifth World Congress of the International Economic Association, Tokyo, 1977.

7. Critics have contended that development via the vent leads inevitably to dependence on agricultural and mineral exports, both bad bets in the long run. They also argue that the imports of manufactures made possible by the opening of trade can ruin local manufacturing and craft activities, stifling development along these lines. Both points will be returned to later.

8. This and the next paragraph draw on W. M. Corden, *Trade Policy and Economic Welfare,* Oxford, 1974, pp. 327–329; and on Gottfried Haberler's Cairo Lecture reprinted in Gerald M. Meier, *Leading Issues in Economic Development,* 3rd ed., Oxford, 1976, pp. 702–707.

9. In the table, exports are defined as goods and nonfactor services. There are LDCs with higher ratios of exports to GNP. These fall into three groups: the newly industrialized countries, which have found exports a powerful engine in their development; very small economies whose smallness means that exports and imports must bulk large; and big mineral exporters with oil, copper, and the like. Some are shown in Table 12N.1.

10. Emmanuel, *Unequal Exchange.*

11. The survey by Griffin and Gurley, utilized in this section, has an extensive bibliography of the works of the major dependency theorists, including Paul Baran, Celso Furtado, F. Cardoso, O. Sunkel, P. O'Brien, and others, as well as the authors already mentioned in the text and in note 3. A useful book by Anthony Brewer attempts (I think successfully) to capture the essential features of these models in simplified form. See his *Marxist Theories of Imperialism: A Critical Survey,* London, 1980, especially pts. III, IV. How to incorporate into their models the export success of NICs such as the East Asian Gang of Four is a difficult problem for dependency theorists. The subject is examined by John Browett, "The Newly Industrializing Countries and Radical Theories of Development," *World Development* 13, no. 7 (1985):pp. 789–803.

12. From Griffin and Gurley, "Radical Analyses of Imperialism," pp. 1105–1116.

13. Following the logic of W. Arthur Lewis in *Growth and Fluctuations 1870–1913,* London, 1978, p. 244; and see Meier, *Leading Issues,* 4th ed., p. 503.

14. Paul A. Samuelson, "Illogic of Neo-Marxian Doctrine of Unequal Exchange," in

Table 12N.1   PERCENT OF GROSS DOMESTIC PRODUCT EXPORTED, 1984

NICs	
Malaysia	56
Singapore	38 (1983)
South Korea	37
Small countries	
Costa Rica	34
Honduras	27
Jamaica	55
Liberia	40
Panama	36
Papua New Guinea	42
Togo	31
Mineral exporters	
Libya	43
Saudi Arabia	44
Zaire	33 (1983)
Zambia	37

Source: Calculated from *WDR 1986,* pp. 188–189, and *WDR 1985* where 1983 figures are used.

David A. Belsley, Edward J. Kane, Paul A. Samuelson, and Robert M. Solow, eds., *Inflation, Trade, and Taxes,* Columbus, 1976, p. 96.

15. Emmanuel, *Unequal Exchange.*
16. Samuelson, "Illogic of Neo-Marxian Doctrine of Unequal Exchange."
17. *Ibid.,* p. 107. Brewer's *Marxist Theories of Imperialism,* pp. 226–230, advances and discusses other criticisms.
18. The author has made a similar statement on enclave economies in Hogendorn and Brown, *New International Economics,* chap. 18.
19. For an example of the work of the New World Group, see Lloyd Best, "The Mechanism of Plantation Type Economies: Outline of a Model of Pure Plantation Economy," *Social and Economic Studies* 17 (1968):283–326.
20. Even land may have a low opportunity cost where it is underutilized. Lack of population pressure and shifting cultivation with long fallow periods are a signal of this situation.
21. See A. K. Cairncross, *Factors in Economic Development,* London, 1962, excerpted in Meier, *Leading Issues,* 3rd ed., pp. 712–717.
22. From Lloyd G. Reynolds, "Inter-Country Diffusion of Economic Growth, 1870–1914," in Mark Gersowitz et al., *The Theory and Experience of Economic Development,* London, 1982, p. 327, citing the work of J. E. Craig and D. Snodgrass.
23. Suggested by Hla Myint in Meier, *Leading Issues,* 4th ed., p. 504; and Gottfried Haberler's Cairo Lecture, in Meier, *Leading Issues,* 3rd ed., p. 703.
24. Other well-known economists who have supported the view are Charles P. Kindleberger and Benjamin Higgins in the United States and Nicholas Kaldor in Great Britain. In this section I utilized Bo Södersten, *International Economics,* 2nd ed., chap. 12; and Meier, *Leading Issues,* 4th ed., pts. VIII.A, VIII.C, including work of Nurkse, Myrdal, and Meier himself.
25. International trade texts define an income terms of trade, $P_x Q_x / P_m$, that allows such trends to be measured. There is a similar situation on the side of imports. A decline in import prices (P_m) may reduce income in some foreign country, with a resulting fall in the volume and value of exports.
26. There is also a double factoral terms of trade, an index of income to factors producing a given quantity of exports divided by an index of income to factors producing a given quantity of imports. This is of less concern to those interested in calculating a country's command over imports rather than its command over the quantity of foreign factors. It does figure, however, in the thinking of dependency theorists who believe that trade causes LDCs to fall behind rich countries.
27. For the earlier dates, see Benjamin Higgins, *Economic Development,* rev. ed., New York, 1968, p. 624.
28. *Not* Friedrich Engels, as is sometimes assumed.
29. Formally, the income elasticity of demand is: percentage change in quantity demanded divided by percentage change in income.
30. See Michael P. Todaro, *Economic Development in the Third World,* 2nd ed., New York, 1981, pp. 339, 371, citing Alfred Maizels; and Meier, *Leading Issues,* 4th ed., p. 428, citing Bruce Johnston and John Mellor.
31. New York, 1980.
32. This would represent a decline in arable land per capita from 0.39 hectares to only 0.25.
33. The law was observed by a pioneer food economist M. K. Bennett in the 1930s. See Thomas T. Poleman, "Quantifying the Nutrition Situation in Developing Countries," *Food Research Institute Studies* 18, no. 1 (1981):29.
34. Cotton declined from 41 percent of total fiber consumption in 1950 to only 29 percent

in the 1970s. In the same period natural rubber declined from 62 percent to 28 percent of total rubber consumption. See Todaro, *Economic Development in the Third World,* 2nd ed., p. 352.

35. Some of the figures in this and the last paragraph are reported in Hogendorn and Brown, *New International Economics,* p. 409.

36. See Richard N. Cooper, "Resource Needs Revisited," *Brookings Papers on Economic Activity,* Washington, D.C., 1975, pp. 238–245. Cooper notes that the technical and managerial changes were often a response to higher prices and to threats of scarcity. Recovery of scrap metals was not as important a factor as the Paley Commission thought it would be in the two decades after 1952, and Cooper argues that because of this there are great unexploited opportunities for an augmentation of metal supply in the future.

37. The Schultz and Humphrey data and the U.S. import figures are from Ragnar Nurkse in Meier, *Leading Issues,* 4th ed., pp. 493–497; and from lectures by A. D. Knox at the London School of Economics.

38. *The Economist,* August 11, 1984, p. 61; *South,* no. 68 (June 1986):103.

39. Professor Wilfred Malenbaum of the University of Pennsylvania is a leading authority on these "intensity of use" calculations, as they are called.

40. D. L. Meadows et al., *The Limits to Growth,* New York, 1972. That report, however, was criticized for failing to take into account future economies and substitutions in resource use due to scarcity-induced higher prices.

41. Cairncross, *Factors in Economic Development,* reprinted in Meier, *Leading Issues,* 3rd ed., pp. 712–717.

42. Ronald Findlay, "The Terms of Trade and Equilibrium Growth in the World Economy," *American Economic Review* 70, no. 3 (1980):291–299. Note that under normal assumptions the relatively low price of labor will lead to more total employment than if the supply of labor were less elastic.

43. The productivity theory has sometimes been used to justify concentration on industrial production rather than on primary products, but note that its implications affect both sorts of activity so long as labor supplies are relatively elastic.

44. See A. P. Thirlwall and J. Bergevin. "Trends, Cycles and Asymmetries in the Terms of Trade of Primary Commodities from Developed and Less Developed Countries," *World Development* 13, no. 7 (1985):805–817.

45. Findlay, "Terms of Trade and Equilibrium Growth."

46. United Nations, *Relative Prices of Exports and Imports of Underdeveloped Countries,* 1949, pp. 21–24. Note that the 60 years before World War II is not in this context just ancient economic history. It was the high water mark of imperialism. Oligopolistic forms of business organization and stronger trade unions became much more common in the developed countries. Synthetic raw materials were developed. Any long-term tendency for the terms of trade to decline against primary products (hence LDCs) should be clear in this time period.

47. The controversy has recently received a judicious review by John Spraos of University College, London, in a book-length study entitled *Inequalising Trade?* Oxford, 1983. This book grew out of a well-known article by Spraos, "Have the Terms of Trade Declined?" *Economic Journal* 90, no. 357 (March 1980):107–128. Spraos' work is much relied on here.

48. Charles P. Kindleberger, *The Terms of Trade: A European Case Study,* New York, 1956, pp. 239, 263–264.

49. Theodore Morgan, "The Long-Run Terms of Trade Between Agriculture and Manufacturing," *Economic Development and Cultural Change* 8, no. 1 (1959):1–23.

50. Gottfried Haberler, "Terms of Trade and Economic Development," in H. S. Ellis, ed., *Economic Development for Latin America,* New York, 1961, pp. 275–297; and see Meier, *Leading Issues,* 4th ed., pp. 504–505; Cairncross, *Factors in Economic Development,* extracted in Meier, *ibid.,* 3rd ed., p. 714.

51. Spraos notes that had any of the prosperous years between 1925 and 1929 been chosen as a terminal date for the index rather than the depression year 1938, there would have been a large improvement in the terms of trade for LDCs from 1900. He also notes that much of the fall to 68 took place in the last year of the period; in 1937 the figure had been 82, higher than in 1900. It is important to note that the lesson conveyed by any time series may be substantially altered by the choice of beginning and terminal dates.

52. See Morgan, "Long-Run Terms of Trade," for citations and a detailed analysis.

53. One-third of the iron ore in world trade had an iron content of more than 60 percent in 1950; by 1964 the figure was over half. See Spraos, "Have the Terms of Trade Declined?" pp. 117–118.

54. IMF, *World Economic Outlook, 1986,* p. 141.

55. *Ibid.,* pp. 61–63, 139–144. Further studies will undoubtedly show that the shift to synthetics was encouraged by the fall in oil prices during early 1986, assuming the fall is a long-term one.

56. I.M.D. Little, "Economic Relations with the Third World—Old Myths and New Prospects," *Scottish Journal of Political Economy* 22, no. 3 (1975):227, called to my

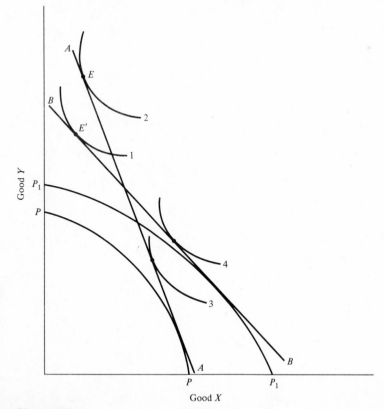

Figure 12N.1

attention in Jagdish Bhagwati's introduction to his *The New International Economic Order: The North-South Debate,* Cambridge, 1977, p. 21.

57. Students with a knowledge of international trade theory will be able to visualize the Bhagwati method by means of Figure 12N.1. *PP* is the initial production possibility curve, with X the exported good and Y other production. Growth (to P_1P_1) favors exports and causes the price of the export to decline relative to that of other goods. This fall in the terms of trade from price ratio *AA* to *BB* gives a new equilibrium *E′* on indifference curve 1, lower than curve 2 with its old equilibrium *E.* Growth has been immiserizing. The result depends on a quite inelastic foreign demand for the export and a high preference by the country for imports. (Had the indifference curves been in a different place, such as curves 3 and 4, growth would not have been immiserizing.) The model in this form is from Subrata Ghatak, *Development Economics,* London, 1978, pp. 168–169.

58. Paul D. Reynolds, *Commodity Agreements and the Common Fund,* New York, 1978, quoting a study by Roy Hensley and Eli Schwartz.

59. See Ronald W. Findlay, "Growth and Development in Trade Models," in Ronald W. Jones and Peter B. Kenen, eds., *Handbook of International Economics,* vol. 1, Amsterdam, 1984, p. 198. Findlay points out that "this example has the virtue of being possibly the simplest illustration of the proposition that it does not *always* pay to rely solely on *laissez-faire* or the 'magic of the market'."

chapter *13*

Trade Policy and Economic Development

In many developing countries, and for a long time, trade pessimism based on the arguments of the last chapter was both persistent and pervasive. To the degree that exports would have effects only of the enclave or backwash variety, with the terms of trade declining in the long run, the outlook was grim. The response by political leaders was widespread adoption of an import substitution strategy involving high tariffs, strict quotas, licenses, and domestic content requirements on production, all designed to encourage the replacement of imports (especially of manufactured goods) by a country's own output. The fewer the imports, the less necessary would be exporting to pay for them, and the less the thralldom to the rich countries. Many people, especially noneconomists, applauded the general idea of self-sufficiency, or "autarky" as it is sometimes called, but experience showed so many penalties had to be paid with such a policy that the good sense of the idea came to be much in doubt.

The purpose of this chapter is to survey the subject of import substitution and contrast it to the opposite and presently much-recommended strategy of removing policy biases and promoting exports. The following two chapters will then consider whether barriers to trade will, now or in the future, make even the pursuit of export promotion unwise.

RATIONAL APPLICATIONS OF IMPORT SUBSTITUTION POLICY

Clearly, some forms of import substitution are eminently sensible.[1] A very poor country with no local manufacturing will find that some lines of production are "naturally protected" by high transport costs. These goods are "market-oriented" and expensive to import; there is a clear advantage in producing them close to the market. Soft drinks and beer contain a great deal of water, and thus the transport costs are high; bottling close to the market is obviously superior to paying for imported water. The water can easily be added by the bottler to the solid ingredients. Furniture can be imported assembled, but much space (between the table legs, for example) is wasted in transport. The volume to be shipped can be reduced if the furniture travels in knocked-down form and is assembled at a local factory near the market. A similar argument applies to cars and trucks. Perishable goods of all kinds are also expensive to ship, and there will be a cost advantage in producing them close to the market. We would not be surprised to find imports of these types of goods rapidly giving way to domestic output, even if merely the assembly of imported components, because of a comparative advantage based on transport.

Import substitution is also economically sensible when there is a comparative advantage based on production costs. Perhaps, as happened widely, colonial governments discouraged early attempts to industrialize. Some industries, such as textile manufacturing, may therefore not have developed, even though they would have been profitable. Imports of these are obvious candidates for substitution. An equally good case for the replacement of imports holds when comparative advantage is changing, perhaps because the capital stock is rising, or human capital in the form of education, skills, health, and nutrition are improving, or learning by doing has enhanced performance. In these cases domestic production may well become a reasonable proposition even though earlier it was not. Similarly, demand may expand so as to allow sufficient economies of scale for production to begin. Many products on the market for years as imports become reasonable candidates for domestic production as income grows, perhaps giving vent to new "middle class" tastes. With adequate demand, it may then pay to provide supportive retail personnel and equipment (the freezers for local ice cream, for example) without which local output will be limited. In all these cases market forces would lead entrepreneurs to compete "naturally" with imports, without the need for a particular government policy to compel its occurrence.

Any firm trying to start up may, however, encounter some special problems. It might take months or even a few years to get the "bugs" out of production, for the workers and managers to learn their tasks, for the purchase of inputs and marketing to go smoothly. Before this is accomplished, even firms that would eventually have a comparative advantage may find they cannot fight the flow of imports from abroad, and so succumb. Borrowing might tide a firm over this difficult infancy, but capital markets may be imperfect so that new entrepreneurs find loans difficult to acquire from private sources. If government budgets are tight, then no assistance may be forthcoming from that source either. In any case, the new firm may have to bear the cost of training workers, who may then be bid away by competitors incurring no costs for training. There may also be strong externalities well worth having for the country as a whole but with little or no effect on the balance sheets of the originating firms, such as technical know-how that then becomes freely available. Lending will not cover these cases even if capital markets are efficient.

For these reasons, early in a country's development some limited protection on "infant industry" grounds may be warranted. Justifications for infant industry tariffs in LDCs are actually more persuasive than they are in developed countries, where capital markets are sophisticated and presumably well able to judge whether an industry has a chance to make good. Protection of "good bets" for a period of, say, four to eight years, with infant industry tariffs kept in the range of 15 to 25 percent, would lead to a form of import substitution that, if not favored by economists who generally advocate improving capital markets or subsidies, would at least be tolerated. The result would be a number of industries whose production would take the place of imports; if the choices were made correctly, these industries would eventually be able to compete without the protection and perhaps even begin to export. In effect, the nation's production possibility curve would move outward.

The model is not just wishful thinking. The United States, Germany, France, and Japan all used it to advantage in their development experience, while the heavy industry of South Korea and Brazil (including steel and autos in both these countries), plus a wide range of manufacturing in these and other NICs, have benefited from a sensible application of the infant industry argument.[2]

GENERALIZED IMPORT SUBSTITUTION POLICY

In contrast to these rational applications of import substitution policy, a fair number of countries have generalized the strategy, using it across a wide range of imports even when there was no present comparative advantage in many of these and no likelihood that changes in factors or in learning would lead toward one. This generalized import substitution strategy was in its heyday during the 1950s and 1960s. While many governments have moved away from it, in some quarters the theory still has a major influence on the public and politicians. The idea seems to be based on a perception that if a substantial amount of some good is imported, then it should be produced locally. Often the justifications center on trade pessimism—either that exporting is an uncertain path to development for external reasons or that above-market wages will hinder exports (see the discussion of dualism in Chapters 7 and 10). Mixed with these reasons is the presumption that important external economies and learning by doing will accompany local manufacturing of an industrial product. Sometimes, as in Latin America during World Wars I and II, the strategy took root because many previously imported goods had become unavailable. Frequently the belief seems to be that the whole manufacturing sector is an infant, inefficient now, but lacking only a dose of protection in order to grow up. On occasion, the preference for domestic industry does not appear to be based on economics at all, but instead on considerations of morale and prestige. The production in some countries of steel or aircraft or cars at a considerable loss are cases in point.

A "typical" policy of generalized import substitution begins by protecting local producers of consumer goods. The umbrella of protection (via tariffs, quotas, licensing of foreign exchange, and other methods to be discussed) is usually not so much directed at capital goods and raw materials. Imports of these goods are thought to be more essential and are generally more difficult to produce or are completely unavailable domestically. Often government decides in the first place which industries it wants to develop; these are the ones to receive the protection.

The High Costs of Generalized Import Substitution

An overall, pervasive policy of import substitution is likely to be a high-cost strategy. More than anything else, it is the recognition of these costs that has turned the great majority of economists against it and explains why the 1980s have seen many LDCs abandoning their commitment to it. This section considers why the costs are high.

Typically, the tariffs, quotas, and licensing of production will be costly for consumers because local prices are raised. (For an analysis of why this occurs, see the box on page 371.) The higher prices percolating through the economy, together with the distortions introduced by the policy controls discussed below, can be an inflationary mixture. It is endlessly fascinating to consider how often general protection means gains for a small group of well-to-do industrialists at the expense of the great mass of the population, who through the higher prices lose some of their access to the imported "inducement goods" that are so effective in stimulating effort. It is estimated that during the late 1960s the profits associated with import protection in some LDCs were running as high as 15 percent of GNP.[3] Not surprisingly, "infant industry" protection is hard to dismantle when the results pay the beneficiaries as well as this. The more quotas are used, the worse this problem will be; they limit imports to a fixed quantity, whereas, if a tariff is in place, import quantities can vary with supply and demand changes. As we saw in Chapter 2, these price-boosting effects of protection lead to an artificially inflated importance of manufacturing in the GNP. Import substitution would look somewhat less appealing if GNP growth were not thereby overstated. I.M.D. Little suggests that growth rates for heavy import-substituting countries are exaggerated by up to about 0.5 percent per year because of the higher prices caused by the policy.[4]

Costs may be much higher yet, though difficult to quantify, because the system of controls will involve unexpected changes in the regulations, extensive red tape, and corruption. (Recently, applications for licenses to import in Tanzania had to be submitted three months in advance; in Indonesia 25 to 100 pages of documentation were required for each piece of equipment imported.[5]) With the quotas and licenses likely to be lucrative for the holder, the incentive for corruption increases. Import substitution can serve to enrich not only favored entrepreneurs, but also government officials, as well as the smugglers and black marketeers who make their living by avoiding the controls. Not without reason is it sometimes said that a market price, rather than a controlled one, is often a better policeman than the real thing!

Industries "growing up" under these hothouse conditions may be profitable enough for their owners, but they can be especially inefficient in a number of ways. Since in so many countries the domestic market is relatively small, there will be no economies of scale such as might have been attained in a larger market (that is, through exporting), and the industry's growth will be limited to the level and growth of local demand. Bangladesh, for example, has an industrial economy only 3 percent the size of Sweden's and 2 percent that of Canada's, and both of these two rich countries are generally thought to need international trade to obtain the benefits of scale economies. India, though its population is huge, has an industrial market estimated to be less than 25 percent that of Germany's.[6] With scale small, any gains from learning by doing will be reduced, as will any other dynamic advances in productivity that might be expected from high-volume output. Inexperienced firms facing little competition (monopoly and oligopoly do tend to proliferate behind the barriers) may turn out products substantially inferior to what could be imported. This will be noticed not only by consumers, but by producers who use the protected goods as inputs, for they will have no place to turn for better quality substitutes.

The character of the industries so established may not be satisfactory. The low barriers against imports of capital inputs mean the financial incentive to produce consumer goods of a "less essential" type is higher even than it would otherwise have been. (The increased attraction involves the principle of "tariff escalation," which will be considered in Chapter 14.) The higher output of less essential products is out of keeping with a goal of self-reliance, so often the initial motive of the policy.

The highest protection of all may apply to luxury goods, since tariffs against them will be thought "fair"; the incentives are then to produce these luxuries at home, for consumption by middle- or high-income consumers. The resulting industrial structure can thus show signs of urban bias, even if unintended. (Discriminatory sales taxes can be used to offset the pull toward luxuries, but these taxes are difficult to collect in the poorest countries, as explained in Chapter 4.) Further, the industries established behind the protective barriers may largely be "assembling" activities, with little value added in production and few prospects for future expansion. From the easy beginnings, every further step may be more difficult because the imports substituted for must be ever more capital-intensive and ever more subject to diseconomies due to small scale. Naturally, the products least difficult to produce and least sensitive to scale were undertaken first. At worst, the process ends with the economy more dependent on imports than before, with self-reliance actually decreased. Any disruption of imports that would formerly have affected only the flow of consumer goods now interrupts the supply of machinery, spare parts, and vital raw materials, causing production stoppages and layoffs.

A striking result is that the foreign exchange costs of the imported raw materials and capital may be higher than the foreign exchange costs of the imported product itself. Such has been the case with a number of products including steel in Bangladesh and Egypt, tin cans in Kenya, autos in Thailand, Nigeria, and Turkey, and jet aircraft in Argentina, Egypt, and India.[7] In short, the confidence that import substitution increases independence is seriously exaggerated, an irony since the search for self-reliance was the justification for the policy in the first place.

An additional effect is that the forced-draft expansion of industry will attract scarce factors of production, including capital and talented entrepreneurs, into the areas where protection has raised profits (see the box on p. 371). The relative cheapness of the imported capital, often exaggerated by interest rate subsidies, will lead to too much capital intensity and excess capacity. Because of the relative capital intensity, often the industries established do not provide as much employment of labor per unit of output as does exporting. (The strong evidence for this assertion is presented in this chapter's section on export promotion.) The artificial cheapness of capital is also very likely a major cause of the surprisingly low level of capacity utilization reported in the industries of many LDCs, and the infrequency of shift work that would utilize capital more efficiently by applying to it larger quantities of abundant labor.

The diversion of resources into the import substitution industries will inevitably penalize exports.[8] Exporting firms will also suffer because they use the expensive protected products as inputs, thus boosting their costs (as explained in the box on page 371). To the extent that the exporters are selling in a competitive world market, they cannot pass on the higher costs to foreign consumers. With exports penalized, there are likely to be chronic shortages of foreign exchange to purchase imports, requiring exchange controls and rationing. These controls themselves may be administered in such a way as to inflict even further damage (as explained in the next section on overvalued exchange rates). Of course, *potential* exporters will be hurt also. Products that could have been exported under "neutral" free-market conditions are poor bets because of the bias. Capital, including foreign investment by MNEs, has no incentive to flow toward export operations.[9] As a case of "what might have been" this harm will be almost invisible to voters, politicians, or dictators. True, there will still be MNEs, but they will be there to take advantage of the high profits available behind the protectionist barriers, competing with local firms for the quota licenses and the foreign exchange permits.

The country engaging in widespread import substitution is likely to discover that the panoply of price controls, foreign exchange rationing, and protection required by the strategy makes its economy less flexible in the face of disturbances from inside or outside. A harvest failure requiring food imports or an OPEC oil shock that boosts fuel and fertilizer bills can raise additional havoc. The extensive controls mean the economy is likely to respond less elastically; low reserves of foreign exchange and little attractiveness to foreign bankers mean that imports may have to be restricted all at once, with consequent contraction of output of any industry using imported inputs.

The results of generalized import substitution seem so doleful that one wonders how such policies have survived. As so often, it is not really hard to understand why. Every tariff, every quota, every import license or foreign exchange permit establishes a profitable vested interest in the maintenance of the system. While society as a whole might lose from it, the favored individual firms —their owners, their managers, their workers—and the government officials who administer the system would all regret its passing and fight hard for its retention. Indeed, when a policy of import substitution is reformed, it is not only economically wise but politically sensible to do it with some gentleness, rather than

SOME COSTS OF IMPORT RESTRICTION

Import restriction attracts resources to a protected industry, raises prices for buyers of the product, shifts welfare from consumers to producers, and involves a deadweight loss.

Figure 13.1 shows the domestic supply and demand for a product that can be imported at the world price OP_w. With free trade domestic firms will produce quantity OQ_1; consumption will be OQ_4; the gap Q_1Q_4 is filled by imports. A tariff P_wP_t will boost prices to OP_t and cut imports to Q_2Q_3. Alternatively, a quota limiting imports to Q_2Q_3 will have the same price-boosting effect; the price rises because of the supply limitation. In either case domestic consumers cut back their consumption of the now higher-priced product from OQ_4 to OQ_3. A further result of either a tariff or a quota is new production by domestic firms Q_1Q_2, as these firms react to the higher price by raising their employment of resources.

Those with a knowledge of consumers' and producers' surplus can also trace the shifts in welfare caused by a tariff or quota and identify a deadweight loss from protection. Consumers' surplus is the area above the price paid and below the demand curve. Before protection, it is P_wP*Z, while after the tariff or quota is applied, it shrinks to P_tP*Y, a reduction of $A + B + C + D$. Producers' surplus is the area above the supply curve, but below the price received. It rises from P_zP_wW to P_zP_tX, a rise of A. Under a tariff government gets tariff revenue equal to the quantity of imports Q_2Q_3 times the tariff per unit P_wP_t, which amounts to area C.

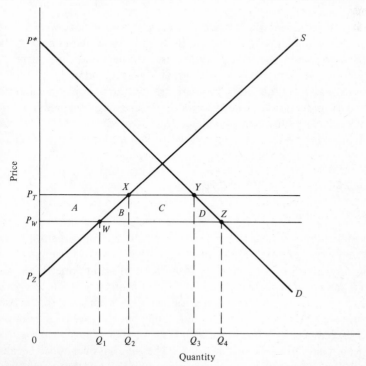

Figure 13.1 Effects of import restrictions.

371

(Under a quota, usually given gratis to importers, C represents a transfer from consumers to those who receive the quota tickets.) Note that the gains to producers and/or the government $A + C$ are not as great as the loss to consumers $A + B + C + D$. The remainder, $B + D$, is a deadweight loss in welfare, a penalty paid by society for choosing a protectionist policy.

Studies in developed countries show quite small deadweight losses from protection, usually 1 percent or less of national product. (Long-run losses are undoubtedly much higher; and the large *transfers* from consumers to producers are not included in the estimates of deadweight loss.) But studies of LDCs suggest much greater damage to those countries, sometimes as much as 9 to 10 percent of GNP or even more. See Bela Balassa et al., *The Structure of Protection in Developing Countries,* Baltimore, 1971; Peter H. Lindert and Charles P. Kindleberger, *International Economics,* Homewood, Ill., 7th ed., 1982, pp. 123–125; and Pan A. Yotopoulos and Jeffrey B. Nugent, *Economics of Development: Empirical Investigations,* New York, 1976, chap. 7. Recent work by Richard Harris emphasizes the dynamic gains from increased competition and from economies of scale. Harris suggests that realizing these through a dismantling of protection would yield a respectable rise in GNP in the range of 2.5 to 8.5 percent. (See his "Applied General Equilibrium Analysis of Small Open Economies and Imperfect Competition," *American Economic Review* 74, no. 5 (1984): 1016–1032.

guillotine-style. Withdrawing the protection totally and all at once would mean not only the collapse of many industries and perhaps a serious recession, but also adamant opposition from the affected interests. At the same time there are potential benefits for setting up a new system that shakes up old ways of thinking and old political bases and alliances. Thus reforming the policy at a moderate pace, with steady reductions of the barriers and increasing freedom from the controls, will make the adjustment economically less painful and politically more acceptable than a once-for-all approach, but will still prepare the way for change.

OVERVALUED FOREIGN EXCHANGE RATES

Causes of Overvaluation

An overvalued foreign exchange rate is the usual result of an import substitution policy. The overvaluation is often put in place by government to support that policy (as has been done most commonly in Africa and Latin America, less so in Asia), but it can result anyway from a high level of protection against imports.

We use overvaluation to mean a price for a country's currency that is fixed above the price we guess would obtain in an unregulated market, for example, 1 U.S. dollar exchanging at a fixed rate of 100 Penuristan penuris when a free-market rate would have been 150 penuris for $1. The penuri is overvalued because it takes only 100 of them to buy a dollar, rather than the 150 that would have been needed if the rate had been market-determined. To keep the exchange rate at a level different from what the market would dictate requires a system of foreign exchange controls enforced by administrative action.

Since everyone will want dollars or other hard currencies at the favorable rate in order to import cheaply (quantity demanded of dollars will exceed supply of dollars when the Penuri price of dollars is below equilibrium, as in Figure 13.2), it will be necessary to do one of three things. (1) Monetary and fiscal policy can be made restrictive, contracting the economy and thus lowering the demand for imports and the foreign exchange to buy it. This will be unpopular, not only with citizens but with economists, who will wonder why one would want to have an overvalued rate at the cost of chronic recession. (2) Borrowing abroad can be pursued to provide an extra supply of foreign exchange, thus financing the deficit. Though obviously not a long-run solution, there has been some use of this, especially by relatively prosperous borrowers such as Argentina, Chile, and Uruguay. In this way overvalued exchange rates contributed to the debt crisis explored in Chapter 6. Given the reduction in private international lending, this tactic is now not practical. (3) Finally, and much more generally, a country can establish trade controls to reduce the spending on imports and a system of rationing for foreign exchange, whereby the limited amount of hard currency available (*OA* in Figure 13.2) is doled out to only a few of the many customers who will want much of it *(OB)* at that price.

Overvaluation based on controls would not occur in a country with a freely floating exchange rate determined by movements in supply and demand. But only

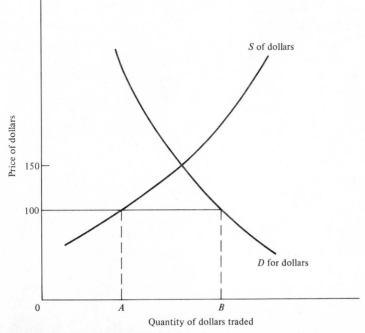

Figure 13.2 An overvalued exchange rate.

a minority of the LDCs allow their rates to float freely. In February 1985 about 40 percent of them had a fixed rate pegged to a major currency. (About two-thirds of these chose the U.S. dollar for their peg.) Another 30 percent pegged their rate to a market basket of foreign currencies. While the remaining 30 percent had floating exchange rates, most often the floats were managed by government controls and interventions, and many of these currencies were overvalued too. In 1983 only three LDCs had freely floating rates: Lebanon, South Africa, and Uruguay. In 1984 and 1985 six more were added to the list as part of required IMF stabilization programs: Dominican Republic, Jamaica, Philippines, Uganda, Zaire, and Zambia.[10]

There are several reasons why overvaluation may be present. As noted above, a country may have chosen an overvalued foreign exchange rate to complement its import substitution policy. The government can give permits for foreign exchange to favored producers. These producers will find it cheaper to acquire imported capital and raw materials than would otherwise have been true, because overvaluation acts as a subsidy to the firms so selected. Protection keeps consumer goods from flowing in freely, and the currency controls keep the demand for foreign exchange limited to the available supply. Even without a government policy of deliberate overvaluation, all other things being equal, the import substitution measures can cause it anyway through the effects of the widespread protection. The tariffs, quotas, and the like will ordinarily cut the demand for foreign goods by pushing up their price. As compared to the situation without the protection, the demand for foreign exchange will thus fall as in Figure 13.3, leading to a lower (overvalued) penuri price for the dollar.

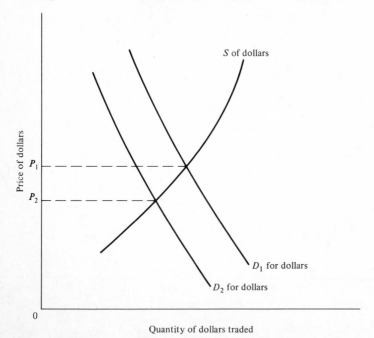

Figure 13.3 Protection and overvalued exchange rates.

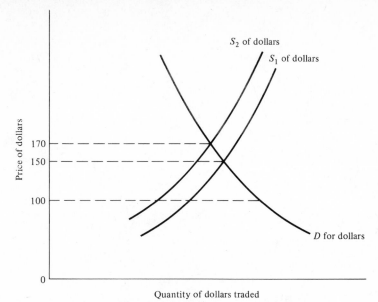

Figure 13.4 Even greater overvaluation as exports decline.

Meanwhile, the overvalued rate makes exporting more difficult, since earners of a dollar from exporting can convert it to only 100 penuris rather than the 150 that a free market would bring. By discouraging their efforts, the country earns fewer dollars, shifting the supply curve of dollars up and to the left as in Figure 13.4. The overvaluation becomes even greater, and at the official fixed rate the system of exchange control will be under yet more strain.

If the rate of inflation is high, that, too, will contribute to growing overvaluation. With domestic prices rising, at the fixed exchange rate foreign goods will appear cheaper at home, and Penuristan's exports will look more expensive to foreigners. Penuristanis will thus want more foreign exchange to buy imports; foreigners will supply fewer dollars to buy that country's exports, with the result that both the supply and demand curves shift as in Figure 13.5, further widening the gap between the fixed official rate and the market equilibrium. The most common reason why exchange rates become overvalued is that rates of inflation are higher in LDCs than in developed countries.

One more reason for the growing overvaluation was (temporarily) true in the period 1980 to 1985. LDC currencies pegged to the dollar were pulled up as the dollar rose in value against other currencies; countries that kept their pegged rates intact gradually found their currencies climbing against the pound, franc, mark, yen, and other currencies.[11]

Further Effects of Overvaluation

A country that keeps its rate overvalued on a long-term basis is likely to find some further unfavorable consequences.[12] The damage to exports will lead to a demand for export subsidies from producers with enough political influence to get them.

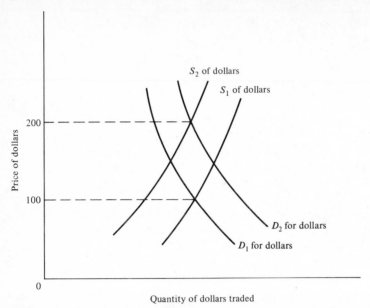

Figure 13.5   Inflation and overvaluation.

This will widen the country's budget deficit alarmingly if enough firms are successful in obtaining them. Since the farm sector in LDCs seldom has this clout, agricultural exports may be especially hard hit. Nor are the subsidies likely to go to the potential exporters, particularly the small ones, that might have found production for foreign markets profitable at a free-market exchange rate.

The armor of protective devices will have to be extended and strengthened at the same time, because any importable good produced at home but not yet protected will be penalized by the overvalued rate (imports will appear cheaper, remember). A perception on the part of the public that the protection will soon be extended, or the exchange controls made tougher, or the overvalued rate abandoned will cause a further rush to buy imports. Crises of this sort do indeed tend to lead toward tighter restrictions all around. In turn the further restrictions on imports, by cutting spending on them, reduces the demand for foreign exchange and thereby perpetuates and adds to the overvaluation that contributed to the problem in the first place.

Just as the existence of quota licenses and other import controls brings rents to the lucky recipients, so, too, do foreign exchange controls. It will be lucrative to acquire the scarce foreign currency; goods imported at the cheap rate can be sold at higher domestic prices, or perhaps sold on the black market. Effort will therefore be thrown into the search for the permits, with attendant politicization of international trade and the high possibility of further corruption. With something to gain, there is also something to offer. Wider and wider spreads the net of bribery and kickbacks, from the circle of favored traders and the administrators of the controls to the auditors, police, politicians, and army officers who might put a stop to the favoritism. Both the bribers and the takers of bribes may well benefit greatly from the status quo, along with the legions of black market exchange dealers who make their living by illegal avoidance of the fixed rate. The police and armed forces may acquiesce for another reason as well; these politically vital arms of government can often count on getting the scarce permits when necessary for their own equipment and thus can buy imports cheaply. (As the London *Economist* has noted only half jestingly, the president's cousins often want to run the department in charge of licensing the foreign exchange—fully understandable from their point of view.[13])

All contributes to the substantial corruption observed in many LDCs that run an overvalued exchange system. Honest behavior may not be the human way, but a free-market rate certainly cuts the potential profitability of corrupt practices in the foreign trade sector. The firms that can make the most efficient use of foreign exchange are then the ones willing to pay the bill for it, rather than ones with the best lobbyists and the attention of the most important politicians.[14]

Eventually, if the official exchange regimen is on the way to breakdown and finance is failing, one expects to see the rise of *countertrade*. This is the encompassing term for practices that avoid the use of foreign exchange. Included are counterpurchase and offsets (you buy from me, I will buy from you), buy-backs (you build a plant for me, I will repay you with output from the new plant), and traditional barter. The size of such practices is unknown, though certainly growing; one study by the General Agreement on Tariffs and Trade (GATT) estimates 9 percent of world trade, while another by the Group of 30 estimates 8 to 10 percent. Agricultural commodities and oil figure most importantly.[15]

Countertrade is not cheap, since it often involves the expensive services of lawyers, consultants, and bankers to work out the deals. (Most big banks have had countertrade departments for several years now.) These costs mean payments in countertrade transactions are usually higher, sometimes up to 30 percent or more, than in cash transactions. There are also many companies that refuse to do business this way, and some developed countries are much opposed to the idea. There have been cases of reduced trade concessions and foreign aid to LDCs pushing countertrade. All of this limits its benefits.[16]

Econometric evidence that the adverse consequences of exchange rate overvaluation are serious was published by the World Bank in 1986.[17] A study covering 24 LDCs during the period 1960 to 1983 examined the relationship between exchange rate misalignment (mostly overvaluation) and growth of both real GDP and exports. The study showed a significant negative correlation, with a 10-percent increase in misalignment associated with an average reduction in GDP growth of 0.8 percent and a reduction in export growth of 1.8 percent.

DEVALUATION OF THE EXCHANGE RATE

Official Devaluation as a Remedy for Overvaluation

With all the demonstrated problems that predictably accompany an overvalued exchange rate, official devaluation of the rate would seem an obvious measure for adjustment.[18] There may even appear to be little choice, given the tendency for imports to increase and exports to stagnate, and with credit drying up as banks refuse any further bail-out. (The IMF typically recommends devaluation as a remedy for overvalued currencies: it played a part in 25 of 35 IMF adjustment programs in 1983, for example.)

But this tool of exchange rate management is intensely unpopular and will often be shunned by the government and the public alike. Why is this so, beyond the obvious point that those who have gained from the overvaluation will lose from the correction? A strong belief that national pride and national strength can be measured by the value of the currency is extremely common and seems almost visceral. The rate becomes symbolic: bringing it down will to many be proof of dependency and even of foreign neocolonialist machination; the country itself should decide, not the IMF or outsiders. Students riot over the issue; politicians wrapped in the flag declare they will never devalue.[19] Devaluing the exchange rate certainly does have its costs, as we shall see, but the intransigent opposition to it often seems to go far beyond any rational weighing of economic costs and benefits.

There is, incidentally, no reason to be surprised at this reaction. It is not a disease that affects the LDCs alone. Winston Churchill, when he was in charge of British finance in the 1920s, insisted on maintaining a strong pound as a monument to British greatness; it was ruinous policy that stifled exports and economic growth. In the 1980s President Reagan argued for many months that the high dollar was a symbol of U.S. economic vitality, even as the export sector rapidly sickened.

What positive results will a devaluation deliver? Though unpopular, it will undoubtedly have a shock effect that can be a valuable part of the political process, a sign of "turning over a new leaf," so to speak. The main hope is that the devaluation will lower the country's price level relative to that of other countries. Much depends on what happens to these prices. Let us trace the possibilities.

If on world markets a country's exports are quoted in a foreign currency such as the dollar, then devaluation will not affect these prices. (Mexico's oil at $25 per barrel will still be $25 even if the peso's value is lowered.[20]) This is common in the trade of the LDCs. But every dollar earned from exporting now means more local currency for the exporter: if the penuri, formerly at 100 to the dollar, is devalued to 150, then each dollar earned from sales abroad raises the revenues of exporters by 50 penuris. If local production costs do not change, profits rise accordingly.

Whether more *dollars* are earned from the exporting will depend crucially on the elasticity of supply of exports. If that is high, greater quantities will be exported and earnings in foreign exchange will rise. Indeed, only a zero elasticity of supply will prevent that from happening. Time helps: the longer the period considered, the more the enhanced profitability of exporting will attract resources into that activity; in the short run there may be little impact.

It also helps if adequate financing is available to expand capacity, if creating new capacity is easy, if a proper infrastructure of transport, communications, and public utilities is in place, and if resources are flexible and so can respond smoothly to market incentives. The transition is even easier if the previously overvalued exchange rate has caused substantial excess capacity in the exporting industry, and if the country has significant unemployment problems (common in LDCs). Then the idle resources can simply be put back to work. Generally, experience shows that the rise in exports will be largest if the protection against imports is liberalized at the same time the currency is devalued. This suggests that unavailability of imported inputs had all along been constraining the growth of exports.

The export-raising consequences of devaluation are joined by a depressing effect on imports. It now takes more penuris to buy a dollar; consumers will thus be less eager to purchase imported goods at their higher price in local currency and will turn to goods produced at home. Exporters, where possible, also switch away from imported inputs and purchase more local production. Both these results take effect at once and increase over time as new substitutes appear and knowledge about them grows. Analytically, any elasticity of demand for imports greater than zero will mean a reduction in dollar spending as prices rise and therefore will cause the demand for dollars to fall. The higher the elasticity, the greater the decline in imports and in the demand for dollars, and thus the more successful the policy.

The reduction in imports may be limited, however, if the country liberalizes its protection at the same time. The fall in the barriers will work in some degree to offset the rise in prices. Also, spending on imports will not be reduced as much if more of them flow in as inputs to the newly expanding export industries, and if the more efficient policies are causing a rise in real national income that fuels the inflow of goods from abroad. These are major reasons why studies often find the overall change in the trade balance is smaller than predicted.[21] Conceivably, the short-run results may even be in the wrong direction, though this will be reversed as exports pick up.

Unfavorable Consequences of Devaluation

The path to an equilibrium exchange rate may not be an easy one, and several warnings are in order. A country that is a major producer of a commodity (Brazil and coffee or Ghana and cocoa), would have to worry about a decline in the world price as production of the export increases. This adverse turn in the terms of trade could be sharp if world demand is inelastic; if the country is heavily dependent on this export, it may find its foreign exchange earnings are falling. Meanwhile, imports are unlikely to be concentrated; buying less of them will probably not depress the world price. The problem will be of no concern to an LDC that has little effect on world commodity prices, and various studies confirm that devaluation almost always raises the local currency returns to the production of exports, so that both the quantity exported and earnings rise.[22] But where a tendency toward an unfavorable shift in the terms of trade exists, it is a strong argument for long-run export diversification.

Perhaps the response of exports will be poor. A country specializing in tree crops that take a long time to bear or mineral products where new mines take years to develop, with its economy inflexible, its infrastructure inadequate, and financing for new projects scarce, may find the results of devaluation disappointing. In recent years some of the world's lowest supply elasticities have been reported for agricultural commodities in troubled Uganda; under such conditions it would be difficult to raise foreign exchange earnings. Where elasticities are so low, supply-side improvements in infrastructure, capital markets, basic needs, and so forth are obviously called for along with devaluation, but, unfortunately, these take a long time to bring about and can be expensive and unappealing to a country in crisis. Even at worst, however, the devaluation will make it potentially more profitable to export *any* suitable commodity, agricultural or industrial, and this incentive takes effect immediately. There is thus at least the hope of long-run improvement.

Another obstacle presents itself if numerous countries that are exporters or potential exporters of the same products all devalue at the same time. When one country devalues, it can compete more strongly against other producers. When many do so, the ability to make inroads into the markets of others is diluted. The more countries that attempt the strategy at the same time, the less well it will work.[23]

The devaluation must be real, meaning that it must not be offset by higher inflation, for then there would be no "expenditure switching" away from imports and toward exports and import substitutes and thus no change for the better. The intended impact is to lower domestic prices relative to other countries (remember that in dollar terms, export and import prices did not change, but all other local prices look lower, at least at the start, to holders of dollars).[24] If the lower domestic prices quickly rise again because of inflation, the benefits of the devaluation are lost.

There is no immediate reason to expect general inflationary consequences. Imported goods do rise at once in local currency prices, but if the demand for imports is elastic, there will be little feedback to the rest of the economy as consumption shifts to domestic substitutes when possible. If the demand for imports is on the contrary inelastic, perhaps because there are no substitutes, then the country's local currency spending on imports will rise. This will be *deflationary* for the economy as a whole, at least until the eventual expansion of export capacity increases revenues from exporting enough to offset it. (Alternatively, there might not be much of a price rise for imports if such goods were largely being purchased before the devaluation at illegal black market prices. The black market would already reflect the "devalued" price of foreign exchange. Prices may even fall because the risk element is reduced.[25])

There may be other deflationary consequences as well.[26] Wages may rise more slowly than the rise of export and import prices (the so-called money illusion), so that income is shifted toward profits. If in turn the owners of capital have a lower propensity to consume *(MPC)* than workers, the macroeconomic effect will be deflationary. If government taxes on exports and imports are by value, then government tax revenue in local currency will rise, and that, too, could be deflationary. Finally, the local currency costs of servicing any foreign debts will rise immediately, and this further leakage of purchasing power is another reason to expect any inflationary consequences to be muted. The domestic deflation that may result from these sources may be severe enough to make a piecemeal and gradual devaluation much more sensible than an all-at-once one.

Even so, there are reasons to fear that the low local prices may not remain so, with the possibility of eventual inflationary consequences after all. The higher output of exports and domestic substitutes for imports may put pressures on factor markets, so that wages and other costs in these sectors start to rise even though the economy generally is suffering from deflation. The resulting "stagflation" is likely to be a serious political problem for the government. That government may also be under intense pressure from unions because workers recognize that the prices of imports and import substitutes have risen and thus that the devaluation has cut their real wage. Perhaps the country has a comprehensive system of indexing incomes to reflect price rises. That, too, will transmit inflationary effects.

Sensible demand management can be of great help in these circumstances, but the government may respond instead with money creation to offset the original deflation and the decline in workers' real wages. If it does so, inflation can speed up to the point where exporting loses the advantages given it by the devaluation, and imports again look attractive. In short, inflation causes the currency once again to be overvalued. There are a significant number of cases where governments have responded in this fashion, canceling the real effects of the devaluation. Domestic monetary policy always has the capacity to ruin the reform; the threat has been particularly severe in Latin America.

At base, the argument that a strategy of devaluation will not work often boils down to an opinion that government will create money to avoid the adverse political effects of the real wage cuts. Entrepreneurs see this as fast or faster than anyone else.[27] If they believe that, following a devaluation, exporting will not be profitable for long because of continuing money-fueled inflation, then they are unlikely to raise the supply of exports in the first place. Fortunately, the evidence supports the view that inflation does not cancel the whole effect of the devaluation. But a good deal of the impact is lost (often about half) when the general price level is allowed to rise, and it is theoretically correct to say that inflation *could* entirely remove any real effect of the policy. All these consequences are dangerous, especially in a country with extensive indexing, politically minded labor unions, and oligopolistic industries.

In these conditions a "crawling" or "creeping" devaluation of the exchange rate, perhaps introduced for some sectors before others via a temporary multiple exchange rate system, may be more sensible than devaluing all at once.[28] It may also be possible temporarily to maintain or enlarge some of the transfer and subsidy programs that could alleviate the decline in labor incomes and counter the political backlash in that sector. The financing could come perhaps from further taxation of high incomes, tighter credit policies to replace cheap credit schemes, and lower defense spending. Of course, each of these steps immediately brings a new political problem of its own; in these circumstances foreign aid and IMF program assistance might help to prepare the path.

It is frequently argued that a devaluation will make the country's distribution of income less equal. This could happen in the short run if exporters' revenues rise while the mass of urban wage earners suffer a fall in their real earnings. In

A "WORST CASE"

All these unfavorable circumstances do not usually come to pass at the same time. They could, however, and it is instructive to examine a case of mismanaged devaluation to see what must be guarded against.

Chile moved away from an import substitution policy in the late 1970s, but neglected to devalue the highly overvalued exchange rate. Other policies, such as 100 percent government bail-outs of failing banks, spurred capital inflows by foreign lenders and caused further overvaluation of the exchange rate. The result was constricted exports, booming imports, and a balance of payments crisis.

When devaluation eventually came, it caused a severe recession. In 1982 Chile's GDP fell 14 percent, far more than could have been expected from the effect of the world slowdown of production occurring (unhelpfully) at the same time. High unemployment was persistent. Meanwhile, Chile's system of almost complete indexation of wages picked up the rising cost of imports and transmitted an inflationary impulse in the midst of recession. Government created money to ease the recession and to make it possible to pay the higher wage bills caused by the indexing.

All in all, the devaluation did not work well, and there are still unanswered questions as to why it did not do so. The episode is an object lesson that there are no unbreakable promises of success in economic policy making.[29]

the long run, however, the factors drawn into exporting will share in the gains, and this will be particularly true in rural areas (which often still contain the greater part of the population) as exports of agricultural cash crops grow. In any case, the rural areas will be less affected by the higher prices of imported goods.

Are There Alternatives to Devaluation?

When a country's foreign exchange rate is badly overvalued, are there any alternatives to devaluation? Yes, several, but all with disadvantages of their own. We have already noted that one could simply deflate the economy with monetary and fiscal policy to cure the excess of imports over exports. But deflating as a strategy is slow and painful, brings high unemployment, and does nothing to promote the exporting that has been suppressed by the overvaluation.

Another alternative is to use foreign exchange controls as a substitute for devaluation. These take effect at once, and since they do not work through the price mechanism, there is no resulting fall in national income as there is with devaluation. On first hearing, these are impressive advantages. But we have already examined these sorts of controls enough to anticipate the problems: the complex regulations are a fertile setting for corruption, as vested interests (import substitution industries, government officials in charge of the policies) rally to their support. The controls are usually stiffest against "nonessential" imports, thus promoting local production of these very goods. Most importantly, controls do nothing to cure the underlying suppression of exports and thus cannot cure the inefficient allocation of resources. That penalty is still paid. The discrimination against exporting *could* be offset by export subsidies, but these also usually discriminate, paid on some goods but not others such as traditional agricultural exports and the products of small firms lacking political influence.

How Much Should a Country Devalue?

Assuming that devaluation is selected as proper policy in spite of the difficulties, what should be the extent of the currency adjustment? This is not an easy question. There is no obvious benchmark. Freeing the exchange rate to float always has the disadvantage that trade in a given LDC's currency may be thin, contributing to high volatility. One would not want Sierra Leone's leone, Burma's kyat, Honduras' lempira, or a hundred others to fall sharply because a new electric generator has been purchased or to rise in a rush because a shipload of export produce has just been paid for. The arbitrageurs who normally iron out these fluctuations may well avoid these currencies because of the unpredictability of government policy and because information about their day-to-day trade is not as good as it is for a developed country. This potential for high volatility explains the reluctance of most LDCs to adopt floating rates.

Elasticity studies that would allow for analysis and prediction are scarce or perhaps have not been done at all. Black markets can give clues, but expectations of future devaluation in these markets may mean the rate there is actually more devalued than a free-market rate would be. Further, trading in a black market is usually limited by the fear of discovery, thus making rates highly unstable due to shifts in even thinner supply and demand than that noted above. Finally, the investigator has to balance the foreign exchange overvaluation against the existing structure of protection, preferential tax and credit schemes, export subsidies, and other government intervention in the market. These have to be taken into account if any are reformed at the time of the devaluation.[30]

EXPORT PROMOTION STRATEGY

The detrimental consequences of generalized import substitution, buttressed by protection and overvalued exchange rates, are all too clear. This package of policies is likely to retard growth in the LDCs, when, as everyone will agree, the goal is to do just the opposite.

It might be thought that the cure would be a policy of export promotion, and indeed that term is widely used.[31] But export promotion does not mean exactly what it says. The term is misleading, in that a literal interpretation would indicate an indiscriminate push for all exports and no attention at all to the replacement of imports. Such a policy would have distortions of its own, in a direction opposite to those of import substitution. We shall avoid this misunderstanding by defining export promotion as the *removal of the bias* toward import substitution. Thus an economically rational replacement of imports, based on comparative advantage, would still be recommended, along with exports of goods, also based on comparative advantage.

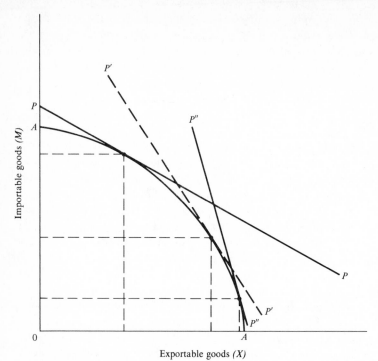

Figure 13.6 Distortions in trade.

Figure 13.6 demonstrates the argument. *AA* is a production possibility curve, with exportable goods (X) on the horizontal axis and importables (M) on the vertical. The ratio *PP* shows a distorted price relationship, with protection, subsidies, discriminatory credit policies, and an overvalued exchange rate all combining to make imports and import substitutes relatively dear and exports relatively cheap. (See how *PP,* if extended to each axis, would show a smaller amount of expensive M goods exchanging for a larger quantity of cheaper X goods.) Entrepreneurs respond with higher quantities of M and lower amounts of X. Were the distortions removed, so that the stimulus for M goods is eliminated, and X goods are now on an equal footing with them (price line *P′P′*), the production of exportables would rise and that of importables would fall. If distortions were introduced to favor exports, for example, subsidies, cheap credit, and an undervalued exchange rate, then the price line would swing to *P″P″*. The case examined in detail here is the middle one, where there is no attempt to maintain a bias of any sort in foreign trade.[32]

Advantages of a Growing Export Sector

Several outstanding advantages should be expected from removing the bias toward import substitution and against exports. Undistorted prices will better reflect the actual scarcities of the factors of production; studies generally show that export-promoting countries have fewer distortions in their price system than do countries with an import substitution strategy.[33]

An immediate and important consequence is job creation. Export promotion will generally create more employment. Labor is usually abundant in LDCs, and comparative advantage should lie in goods that contain a large relative input of the abundant factor of production. A. H. M. M. Rahman noted over a decade ago that 80 percent of the manufactured goods exported by LDCs were more labor-intensive than the factor proportions in world exports as a whole. Studies in a number of countries confirm the heavy use of labor in exporting, for example, in Chile 28 percent more employment per dollar of value added in exports than in import-competing production; double or more in Brazil, Indonesia, and Thailand; and nearly that in Uruguay. In Korea production of manufactures for export was 33 percent more labor-intensive than was production of manufactures for the domestic market and 50 percent more so than in industries that specifically competed against imports.[34] This demonstrated capacity to create employment for unskilled labor in LDCs is a major attraction of an export promotion policy. (If the available labor is relatively skilled, and the country's overall trade strategy is well designed, the employment creation is likely to be greater yet.)

A further consequence of the employment creation is the strong possibility that the distribution of income will become more equal. The growing number of new jobs for thousands and eventually millions of originally unskilled laborers has played a major role in bringing relatively high equality of incomes to Korea, Taiwan, and other export promoters. The effect is certainly not true of *all* exports. Oil revenues have often not contributed much to income equality, and mining also has limitations in this regard. But for agricultural commodities, especially when produced by small holders, and for a wide range of manufactures, the statement seems justified.

The environment in exporting is usually quite different from that found behind protectionist barriers. Large-scale economies are a possibility, since the boundaries of the market are worldwide rather than the nation's own borders. There is a constant incentive to compete more effectively by reducing any internal inefficiencies, whether in choosing how to combine the factors of production, what goods to produce, or how to squeeze the most output out of a given stock of resources (achieving X-efficiency). With no built-in bias toward cheap imported capital, as occurs with import substitution, there is no reason to expect overexpansion of capacity; all other things equal, the likelihood is that capacity utilization in industry will rise. The receipts will be paid in foreign exchange, thus loosening that constraint on development and allowing further imports of capital and intermediate goods.

In short, the resource cost of earning a unit of foreign exchange via exporting is quite likely to be less than the resource cost of saving a unit of foreign exchange via import substitution.[35]

Dynamic Gains from Export Promotion

As always in foreign trade, the static gains may be overshadowed by the less easily measured dynamic gains. As time passes, exporters obtain new insights into technology, design, quality control, organization, and management, especially from buyers in developed countries willing to pass on the latest information.

Large exporting firms spread this knowledge to smaller firms by contracting for inputs. Government agencies can assist in locating suitable subcontractors and helping with quality control. Exports of entirely new products may spring up at once if the developed countries lead in subcontracting to the LDCs. In these circumstances foreign MNEs may provide the specifications, technology, even the capital and joint management. Inflows of direct investment from developed countries are in fact often associated with exporting, and that tendency appears to be increasing.

With the incentives now favoring export expansion, the limited number of old traditional export commodities expands also. This gives more flexibility if supply shocks occur or if problems develop in overseas markets. Banks become more interested in lending because the increasing revenues from exporting make debt servicing easier. In some ways the opportunity may be greatest for the poorest countries. These have the lowest wages, so that their labor-intensive exports will be strongly competitive in world markets. The ease with which technology can be transferred or copied gives broad opportunities for rapid productivity increases in manufacturing, and developed-country protection applies more lightly to the poorest. But the obstacles of imperfect and limited capital markets, low levels of human capital, an underdeveloped infrastructure, and all the other concomitants of severe poverty are obvious limitations. The strong correlation between exporting and economic growth discussed in the next section is, unfortunately, weakest for the poorest.

There is another, largely unsung outcome, that for some countries may well be the most important of all. A market structure of undistorted pricing, with protection and subsidies reduced and with overvaluation of the exchange rate eliminated, leaves far fewer opportunities for corruption. Less is to be gained by lobbying, bribes or concealment; the incidence and costs of lobbying and corruption may drop dramatically.

The potential for dynamic gains is thus impressive. But there is little doubt that a strategy emphasizing growth in foreign trade also increases risks of various types. A country that specializes in a limited range of exported manufactures or primary products might find itself facing unexpected trade barriers erected by the developed countries, with the risk of protectionist action greatest for the most successful exporters. If sharp swings in prices occur, especially of agricultural commodities and minerals, then export revenues may not be very stable. By their nature small countries will be the most vulnerable of all, since because of their size they will usually be specialized in just a few exports. (All of these subjects are returned to in detail in the book's next two chapters, 14 and 15.)

These adverse dynamic effects are not necessarily immutable. Developed countries might be persuaded that their own interests militate against protection. Sensible economic policies in individual countries may make it possible to reduce the impact of price fluctuations, and even international action in pursuit of price stabilization might be taken. Policies to encourage resource flexibility and development itself, which often has the same effect, can reduce the trauma of a declining market for a major export.

Even so, there is no gainsaying that certain sorts of risks do increase in international trade. Then again, there are obvious risks in being poor, too—the risks of hunger, illness, and blighted human potential. If trade based on comparative advantage offers a good possibility of escaping poverty, then even if success is not guaranteed, the idea will command attention. And, indeed, the empirical evidence on growth via trade does command attention, as we see below.

Empirical Studies of Export Promotion

There is abundant evidence of a high correlation between the rate of growth of exports and the rate of growth of GNP. A wide range of studies utilizing both cross-country and time series data are virtually uniform in their conclusion that the relationship between export performance and growth performance is very significant.[36] Anne Krueger, for example, finds that "an increase in the rate of growth of export earnings of one percentage point annually was associated with an increase in the rate of growth of GDP of about 0.1 percentage point."[37]

Correlation does not prove anything about what is cause and what is effect. The usual hypothesis is that the export growth causes the output growth, but the causation *could* be the other way, from GNP growth to exports. Consider that national product may be rising because of human and physical capital accumulation, learning by doing, or new technology inflows to some industries, which thereupon produce more than can be absorbed in domestic consumption. Such industries would export, and here it would be fair to say that the growth caused the exports. An alternative hypothesis would be that exporting and GNP expansion are both correlated to some other causal determinant. Further, one could hypothesize that economic growth will raise the local demand for exported goods and thus eventually reduce those exports. Jung and Marshall, using statistical tests for causality in their 1985 study, found numerous cases where each of these different explanations appeared to be significant.[38]

The important conclusion from this debate is that policies to reduce distortions and increase exports do certainly appear to stimulate growth (see Table 13.1), whatever the immediate cause of the larger exports. Whether the superior performance of export-promoting policies is due primarily to the reduction of distortions in the economic structure or to the dynamic gains from foreign trade is not entirely clear. Export promotion policies appeared to help especially in making adjustments to the oil and food shocks of the 1970s.[39] During this period of disturbances the correlation between an outward-looking policy stance and GNP growth was particularly marked for countries that were pursuing export promotion when they were first struck by the shocks.

Adopting an Export Promotion Policy

For countries discouraged by the results of a generalized import substitution strategy, an important question is how to move toward export promotion with the greatest efficiency and least cost. Without doubt, one of the major topics of modern development economics is how to manage this transition. The start-up is likely to be difficult because of the wide range of politically important groups

Table 13.1 EXPORT GROWTH AND GNP GROWTH, 1960–1973 AND 1973–1981

	Period	Exports	GNP		Period	Exports	GNP
			Real Annual Growth (Percent)				
World	1960–1973	8.1	5.0	World	1973–1981	3.8	2.5
			Countries with "balanced" trade incentives				
Brazil	1968–1973	13.6	11.2	Chile	1975–1980	12.0	7.5
Hong Kong	1962–1973	13.6	10.1	Hong Kong	1973–1981	8.5	9.1
Ivory Coast	1960–1973	11.2	7.6	Ivory Coast	1973–1981	4.5	5.7
Korea	1960–1973	14.0	8.9	Korea	1973–1981	15.7	8.8
Malaysia	1965–1973	8.8	7.1	Malaysia	1973–1981	4.2	7.3
Singapore	1965–1973	12.6	12.7	Singapore	1973–1981	12.1	8.0
Group average		12.3	9.6	Group average		9.5	7.6
			Countries with "inward-looking" trade policies				
Argentina	1960–1973	4.0	4.1	Argentina	1974–1981	5.3	0.4
Chile	1960–1968	3.7	4.4	Ghana	1973–1981	—	−2.4
Ghana	1961–1973	1.5	2.7	India	1973–1978	7.7	5.1
India	1960–1973	3.0	3.5	Pakistan	1974–1981	6.4	5.4
Pakistan	1960–1973	2.9	6.2	Sudan	1974–1981	2.6	3.8
Turkey	1960–1973	7.3	5.9	Turkey	1973–1980	0.3	4.0
Group average		3.9	4.5	Group average		3.7	3.7

Source: Anne O. Krueger and Constantine Michalopoulos, "Developing-Country Trade Policies and the International Economic System," in Ernest Preeg, ed., *Hard Bargaining Ahead: U.S. Trade Policy and Developing Countries,* New Brunswick, N.J., 1985. Also see Shailendra J. Anjaria, Naheed Kirmani, and Arne B. Petersen, *Trade Policy Issues and Developments,* IMF Occasional Paper No. 38, 1985, Table 66.

benefiting from the previous policy of protection, overvalued exchange rates, and so forth. Probably the move is easiest in crisis conditions. A huge balance of payments deficit, hyperinflation, and a drought in foreign lending will concentrate minds wonderfully; even the beneficiaries of import substitution policy will see the need for wholesale reform.

The initial step is to reduce the battery of distortions that gave the bias toward import substitution. Especially important is an immediate reduction of protection; the IMF has required lower trade barriers in the majority of its recent stabilization programs. Import quotas and licenses can be streamlined and relaxed, quantitative restrictions replaced by tariffs, and tariffs rationalized by reducing their dispersion. There may be a devaluation of the exchange rate. Following our earlier advice that the process had better be cautious and gradual to avoid short-run dislocations, the level of tariffs might or might not immediately be lowered; at first the shift away from quotas will be liberalization enough. Further dismantling of protection can follow, accompanied by reductions in the bias against agriculture and the lifting of many price controls. Export taxation should be eased whenever the foreign price elasticity of demand is high, but it can be judiciously maintained for items with low elasticity.

The transition can be facilitated by speeding or eliminating the procedures for the licensing of imports and foreign exchange. Healthy exporting will require the purchase of imported inputs; these must be available, and the price paid must be at world levels, and not higher, if the potential exporter is to compete on even terms. In recent years Korea has computerized its licensing; Brazil and the Philippines have sharply cut the time necessary to obtain the permits; Indonesia and Turkey have put all licensing in the hands of a single department ("one-stop shopping"); India since 1985 has brought more certainty to those who must import components by changing import regulations every three years rather than every six months; Singapore has assigned officials explicitly to cut red tape.[40]

The reduction of protection will encourage entrepreneurs and resources to enter exporting, rather than huddling behind the trade barriers. The new export ventures are most likely to be light manufactured goods of a labor-intensive nature, with low capital-output ratios. The traditional agricultural exports get a boost also. The import substitution that continues will generally be limited to labor-intensive, nondurable consumer goods; many of the less viable industries established under the previous trade regime will not survive as the heat is turned down in the hothouse. Their labor, capital, and management are freed for more efficient uses.

If there is already a domestic market for a product, then a dose of infant industry protection may play a useful role. If not, an infant industry export subsidy might be used. In both cases credit subsidies may be better yet, as they do not raise so many international objections from trading partners. (This should not be overdone, as it is easy to reintroduce a bias against agriculture by such methods.) There are excellent examples of industrial infants making good with the help of government start-up assistance: Brazilian, Mexican, and Korean cars were once infants and so was their steel. The protection and subsidies ought not to be long lasting; the infant should either be grown or allowed to expire peacefully within about five to eight years (following the suggestion of Bela Balassa). Of course, a longer period may be needed to "master" a difficult new technology, but because of compounding, the consumer cost of the protection and the budget cost of the subsidies are then much more likely to outweigh the benefits. Nor should the rate of protection be very high; anything over 10 to 20 percent would raise the costs markedly.[41]

Various promotional tactics can be employed.[42] Exporters may receive tax relief, including holidays on income tax and rebates of sales tax. Subsidies may be granted on credit; government may make available land and buildings at zero or subsidized rent, fund market research, or provide insurance. Government can guarantee credit lines to the overseas customers for the exports. Raw materials, semifinished inputs, and spare parts can be exempted from tariffs and given special import licenses to outflank whatever protection survives. Free trade zones (FTZs) can be established, where no tariffs and quotas apply at all; there are now more than 225 of these in operation worldwide.[43] Manufacture can be undertaken within the zone and the output exported under free trade conditions; any restrictions the country has apply only when the goods cross the boundary of the FTZ. These zones, always carefully policed and often behind real walls, have played a growing part in export promotion strategy during recent years. FTZs are now important in countries as ideologically different as Panama (the Colon FTZ is famous in Central America), Sri Lanka (the FTZ near Colombo originates most of the country's new textile production), and China (14 coastal cities and all of the large island of Hainan are now designated as FTZs).

Mexico has made a major effort with such zones, from small beginnings in 1965.[44] Originally a strip 12 miles deep was designated all along the border from Mexicali in Baja California to Matamoros opposite Brownsville, Texas. Later it was possible to get the same status in the interior. In the zone Mexico's strict rules on foreign investment apply only in part. There is duty-free access to imported raw materials and semifinished goods. Until 1983 the product had to be exported; now 20 percent of output can be sold in the Mexican market. The tariff charged by the United States is only on the value added in Mexico. Since wages are much lower than on the other side of the border, averaging only $4.80 per day in 1984, business has boomed in the assembly plants, which in 1985 produced 29 percent of Mexican exports to the U.S. *Maquiladoras* they are called, from the toll that millers collected in Spanish colonial days for processing someone else's grain. Some 720 *maquiladoras* were operating on the Mexican side in early 1985, up from virtually none in 1979. They employ about 235,000 people, mostly women before 1982 in garments and electronics, now increasingly men in autos and parts, woodworking, and plastics. The most important centers are Ciudad Juarez, Tijuana, and Nogales. If protection cannot be dismantled for political reasons, they are a second-best method to get exports going anyway.

Should entrepreneurship, marketing, or technology prove to be bottlenecks, the country might decide to loosen further the restrictions against investment by MNEs. At an outer extreme monopoly status can be guaranteed to an exporter. In return for the favors government often imposes performance requirements on the recipients of the assistance, mandating export targets and local content requirements.[45]

A government seriously inclined toward export promotion might attempt to emulate the Japanese technique of consultation and liaison between business, public officials, and academics, with frequent and regular discussions of appropriate trade policies. Common in the East Asian NICs, such consultations can be a centerpiece of policy, as in Korea, where the president of the republic chairs the monthly meetings.[46]

By this or other means, encouraging industrial flexibility is extremely important. Among consumers tastes change rapidly, and protection can arise unexpectedly in a key market. Sure knowledge of what exports will be successful five years from now, or even next year, is unobtainable. Helping to instill flexibility is thus an important aim of government policy, far more so than bureaucratic "picking of winners," which is largely mythical—understandably so, since why should a bureaucrat do better at this than an entrepreneur who stands to profit from a correct choice and risks his capital on mistakes? A government can probably accomplish more by not permanently propping up losers than it can by attempting to pick winners; this is an essential element in encouraging flexibility.

The consultation and liaison might advantageously extend to government contacts with MNEs abroad. The surge of investment in the fabrication, subassembly, and processing of imported components in the LDCs, mostly destined for eventual re-export, often involves government negotiations over foreign trade zones and a package of inducements such as low tax and full repatriation of profits. This remarkable development has been spurred by low labor costs and the willingness of rich countries to apply their tariffs only to the value added abroad rather than the complete product.

Trade of this kind, with the developed country as exporter of components and importer of final product, depends on transport costs being low enough for a given item to stand both the outward and the inward shipment. It includes some unlikely examples. The cores of baseballs are exported from the United States to several West Indian islands, their covers are sewn on, and then they are flown back. Similarly, semifinished clothes, gloves, and leather luggage are sewn in Southeast Asia, Mexico, and the West Indies and then re-exported. Data tapes are flown from the United States for keypunching in Barbados and Southeast Asia, India, and even China; sometimes the data are transmitted via satellite. Loose ammunition is exported to Mexico to be put into magazines by cheap labor and then re-exported. Auto components are worked on in Taiwan, Korea, Mexico, Thailand, and India. The semiconductors, valves, and tuners for a variety of electronic equipment are manufactured in Hong Kong, Singapore, Taiwan, Mexico, and elsewhere.[47] Imports of this type to the United States rose by about 30 percent per year from 1966 to 1979, with the largest share from the countries mentioned plus Malaysia.[48]

Export Subsidies

Perhaps more controversial than any other measure for export promotion is government subsidization of the exports.[49] Such subsidies have the plain effect of increasing exports over what they would otherwise have been, as seen in Figure 13.7. Assume that the world price is OW and that since Penuristan is a small country, any quantity of the item can be exported without affecting that price. Penuristan would thus export only AB widgets. By paying a subsidy equal to WS per unit exported, government will cause exports to rise to CD. Local consumption of the product falls, since the price rises; producers would always want to sell at OS including the subsidy rather than accept a penny less for domestic sales. Protection against imports will have to be employed to keep a backflow from entering the country to profit from the above-market price.

If the export subsidies are provided to all exports, then there is a uniform degree of bias and the subsidies are equivalent to a partial devaluation of the currency. If they are doled out selectively, however, they have distortionary impacts similar to a nonuniform structure of tariffs. That in turn could easily cause a country to specialize in the "wrong" exports, that is, those produced less efficiently than some unsubsidized ones.

The General Agreement on Tariffs and Trade in Geneva, the forum for

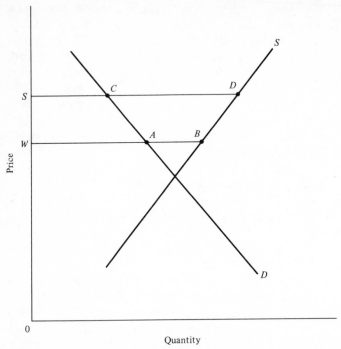

Figure 13.7   Government subsidization of exports.

carrying on negotiations in international trade, has rules on export subsidies. Under the subsidies code dating from the Tokyo Round of 1979, and earlier GATT rules, developed countries cannot legally subsidize exports of industrial products and minerals. Agricultural commodities cannot be subsidized either if that results in the substantial displacement of the exports of other countries. Under the subsidies code, however, LDCs are permitted to use export subsidies for manufactured goods as long as they do not cause serious prejudice to the trade and production of another signatory. The LDC is expected, however, to reduce or eliminate the subsidies as its national product grows; this clause has led to controversy, with the United States insisting on rigorous adherence to it.[50]

The main uses for export subsidies are to encourage infant industries and to offset past policies that have harmed exporting, such as import protection and overvalued foreign exchange rates. Most economists would probably argue that they are unobjectionable or desirable for LDCs, as long as they are phased out when an industry either fails to grow up or becomes competitive. They are less acceptable for the prosperous NICs because capital markets are more able to loan to industries that are developing a comparative advantage, thus tiding them over the period of infancy. It would seem reasonable to allow importing countries to impose countervailing duties against the subsidies only if the subsidized exports have passed some relatively large threshold level and if there is proof of substantial harm so caused. Whether the behavior of the developed countries has been tolerant in this regard is examined in the next chapter.

Disadvantages of Export Promotion

All the measures discussed in the past few pages can clearly be pursued too far, turning export promotion based on comparative advantage into costly export bias. A bias toward export, with firms lacking comparative advantage permanently kept alive by subsidies, is no more defensible than generalized import substitution policy, and no better economics either. Overdoing it is not perhaps as likely, however, since the costs are generally in the government budget and thus highly visible. Another reason why overzealous export promotion is relatively rare is that in many LDCs the initial bias toward import substitution was very strong. Extensive measures for export promotion could be taken and still do no more than correct the underlying imbalance. Furthermore, a major part of export promotion strategy is intended to work through market prices rather than controls. Even if subsidies are granted, the freeing of the price mechanism reduces the damage.[51]

Sometimes governments may use criteria other than comparative advantage in selecting the export industries they want to promote. Malaysia's much-criticized 1985 program seems to fit this description. The tires, furniture, palm oil products, and other goods chosen for emphasis were apparently selected because the raw materials were produced domestically and not because the export promised to be profitable.[52]

Finally, the type of industry established may have limited effects on the economy as a whole. The processing of materials in a foreign trade zone may fit well the description of enclave exporting discussed in the last chapter. Mexicans have often criticized their *maquiladoras* for providing low wages, little training, and little demand for Mexican inputs. (Recently, however, studies have shown both higher wages and skill levels in these plants, and the still stiff Mexican protection means that imported inputs from the United States are usually cheaper.) On top of their enclave character, an MNE's assembly operations may be quite "footloose," quick to move on at any perceived slight. The LDC may have little bargaining strength, there being no control either over the imported input or the output decided on by the MNE and then exported. What does one do with an Apex stereo tuner besides install it in an Apex receiver?[53] This conundrum may give MNEs engaged in the assembly activities more than usual influence in domestic politics. It may also mean that further progress in exporting will be in the hands of foreign firms. Clearly, the decision to welcome this sort of investment carries costs as well as benefits.

Whatever the costs, we have seen that the advantages of a policy mix that promotes exports are large. What remains to be seen is whether the environment will be as receptive to an export promotion strategy in the future as it has been over the past two decades. The major fears are twofold: that world growth will slow, thus providing inadequate demand for new exports by the LDCs, and that the developed countries will increasingly turn to trade restrictions to protect their beleaguered industries. These two topics are currently among the most important in our discipline, and they are the subjects of the next chapter.

TRADE POLICY AND ECONOMIC DEVELOPMENT / 13

NOTES

1. Good general introductions, from which I have drawn, are Bo Södersten, *International Economics,* New York, 1980, chap. 16; Gerald M. Meier, *Leading Issues in Development Economics,* 4th ed., New York, 1984, pp. 388–394, 516–538; Anne O. Krueger, "Comparative Advantage and Development Policy Twenty Years Later," in M. Syrquin, L. Taylor, and L. Westphal, eds., *Economic Structure and Performance: Essays in Honor of Hollis B. Chenery,* New York, 1984, summarized in Krueger, "Import Substitution Versus Export Promotion," *Finance and Development* 22, no. 2 (1985): 20–23; Hubert Schmitz, "Industrialisation Strategies in Less Developed Countries: Some Lessons of Historical Experience," *Journal of Development Studies* 21, no. 1 (1984):1–21; Hubert Schmitz, *Technology and Employment Practices in Developing Countries,* London, 1985; David Colman and Frederick Nixson, *Economics of Change in Less Developed Countries,* Deddington, 1978, pp. 187–202. A classic article that I used is Henry J. Bruton, "The Import-Substitution Strategy of Economic Development: A Survey," *Pakistan Development Review* 10, no. 2 (1970):123–146.
2. Brazil's case is the most recent and is impressive. See the analysis by Simon Teitel and Francisco E. Thoumi, "From Import Substitution to Exports: The Manufacturing Exports Experience of Argentina and Brazil," *Economic Development and Cultural Change* 34, no. 3 (1986):455–490.
3. *WDR 1983,* p. 52. The statement applies to Turkey in the year 1968; an estimate for India is 7 percent in 1964. Since protection in the LDCs is widespread and has overall been rather steady, there is reason to expect that the figure will be high in many countries.
4. I. M. D. Little, *Economic Development: Theory, Policy, and International Relations,* New York, 1982, p. 280.
5. *WDR 1983,* p. 55.
6. See Krueger, "Import Substitution Versus Export Promotion," p. 22.
7. In part from *WDR 1983,* p. 58.
8. For the penalties paid by exporters, see Anne O. Krueger, *Trade and Employment in Developing Countries,* vol. 3, *Synthesis and Conclusions,* Chicago, 1983; and her *Foreign Trade Regimes and Economic Development: Liberalization Attempts and Consequences,* Cambridge, Mass., 1978. See also Jagdish N. Bhagwati, *Foreign Trade Regimes and Economic Development: Anatomy and Consequences of Exchange Control Regimes,* Cambridge, Mass., 1978.
9. For example, the appearance of new exports when Peru liberalized its protectionist policies in the 1950s was both sudden and unexpected. "A notable feature in the diversification of Peruvian exports has been the addition of new products." See Wilson B. Brown, *Government Measures Affecting Exports in Peru, 1945–1962,* unpublished doctoral dissertation, Fletcher School (Tufts University), 1966, p. 66.
10. IMF, *Annual Report on Exchange Arrangements and Exchange Restrictions,* Washington, D.C., 1985, summarized in *IMF Survey,* September 23, 1985; *The Economist,* May 18, 1985, p. 73.
11. *The Economist,* May 18, 1985, p. 73.
12. For the adverse effects, see Guy Pfeffermann, "Overvalued Exchange Rates and Development," *Finance and Development* 22, no. 1 (1985):17–19.
13. January 19, 1985, p. 72.
14. Some countries which once had highly overvalued rates have recently taken to auctioning the available foreign exchange to the highest bidder. Jamaica and Uganda are cases in point, both doing so as part of an IMF stabilization program.

15. There are new studies from the Group of 30, *Countertrade in the World Economy,* New York, 1986; and Bart S. Fisher and Kathleen M. Harte, *Barter in the World Economy,* New York, 1985. *The Economist,* October 5, 1985. p. S21, notes the importance of various products. Other recent articles on the subject include Frieder Roessler, "Countertrade and the GATT Legal System," *Journal of World Trade Law* 19, no. 6 (1985):604–614; and Gary Banks, "The Economics and Politics of Countertrade," *The World Economy* 6, no. 2 (1983):159–182.

16. See Thomas B. McVey, "Why Countries Find Countertrade a Double-Edged Sword," in Group of 30, *Countertrade in the World Economy.*

17. The study, Domingo F. Cavallo, Joaquin Cottani, and M. Shahbaz Khan, "Real Exchange Rate Behavior and Economic Performance in LDCs," was a background paper for the 1986 *World Development Report.* It is summarized on pp. 31–32 of that report.

18. The analysis in this section draws heavily on an article by Graham Bird, "Should Developing Countries Use Currency Depreciation as a Tool of Balance of Payments Adjustment? A Review of the Theory and Evidence, and a Guide for the Policy Maker," *Journal of Development Studies* 19, no. 4 (1983):461–484. See also Karim Nashashibi, "Devaluation in Developing Countries: The Difficult Choices," *Finance and Development* 20, no. 1 (1983):14–17.

19. For a survey of the difficulties, see David B. H. Denoon, *Devaluation Under Pressure: India, Indonesia, and Ghana,* Cambridge, Mass., 1986.

20. If the oil had been priced in Mexican pesos, at 6,000 to the barrel, and the peso were devalued from 240 to 300 pesos per dollar, the dollar equivalent of one barrel sold at 6,000 pesos would fall immediately from $25 to $20. Foreign currency earnings would drop temporarily, until the export quantities rise sufficiently to offset the fall. This so-called J curve effect, named for the reversing pattern of foreign exchange earnings, is fortunately not a problem most LDCs have to worry about, since their exports are so frequently priced in an important foreign currency such as the dollar.

21. See, for example, the lack of a consistent pattern in the 22 episodes of devaluation studied by Anne Krueger in her *Foreign Trade Regimes and Economic Development.*

22. See Bird, "Should Developing Countries Use Currency Depreciation?" p. 465, quoting studies by Cooper, Connolly, Taylor, and Krueger. Norman S. Fieleke, "Price Behavior During Balance of Payments Adjustment," *New England Economic Review,* November–December 1984, p. 42, comes to the same conclusion. There is strikingly little empirical evidence that devaluation causes the terms of trade to deteriorate.

23. See Morris Goldstein, *Global Effects of Fund-Supported Programs,* IMF Occasional Paper No. 42, 1985.

24. How prices change following a devaluation is nicely surveyed by Fieleke, "Price Behavior."

25. See Michael Nowak, "Quantitative Controls and Unofficial Markets in Foreign Exchange: A Theoretical Framework," *IMF Staff Papers* 31, no. 2 (1984):404–431.

26. The effect of devaluation on output can be more complex than described in the text. Several variations are discussed by Liaquat Ahamed, "Stabilization Policies in Developing Countries," *The World Bank Research Observer* 1, no. 1 (1986):97–98, citing numerous sources. This is an area of theoretical debate.

27. Compare Little, *Economic Development,* p. 82.

28. Choosing the speed for a crawl or creep can be a delicate and complex task. See the discussion in Ahamed, "Stabilization Policies," pp. 84–85.

29. Five interesting articles contributed to this paragraph: Arnold C. Harberger, "Observations on the Chilean Economy, 1973–1983," *Economic Development and Cultural*

Change 33, no. 3 (1985):451–462; Sebastian Edwards, "Stabilization with Liberalization: An Evaluation of Ten Years of Chile's Experiment with Free-Market Policies, 1973–1983," *Economic Development and Cultural Change* 33, no. 2 (1985):223–254; Edwards' "Monetarism in Chile, 1973–1983: Some Economic Puzzles," *Economic Development and Cultural Change* 34, no. 3 (1986):535–559; Ricardo Ffrench-Davis, "The Monetarist Experiment in Chile: A Critical Survey," *World Development* 11, no. 11 (1983):905–926; and *The Economist,* August 10, 1985, pp. 60–62. Also see Rodrigo Briones, "The Chilean Malaise," *Challenge* 27, no. 1 (1984):57–60.

30. The subject is surveyed by G. G. Johnson, *The Formulation of Exchange Rate Policies in Adjustment Programs,* IMF Occasional Paper No. 36, 1985. Bela Balassa has led in investigating ways to measure the effects of preferential tax and credit arrangements. See Balassa et al., *Development Strategies in Semi-Industrial Countries,* Baltimore, 1982. I also utilized Michael Nowak, "Black Markets in Foreign Exchange," *Finance and Development* 22, no. 1 (1985):20–23.

31. In addition to the specific references in the following sections on export promotion, I utilized *WDR 1983,* pp. 54–56; *WDR 1984,* pp. 13, 103; *WDR 1985,* p. 70; Meier, *Leading Issues,* 4th ed., pp. 394–405, pt. VIII; Krueger, "Import Substitution Versus Export Promotion," pp. 20–23; Anne O. Krueger, "Trade Strategies and Employment in Developing Countries," *Finance and Development* 21, no. 2 (1984):23–26; and IMF, *World Economic Outlook, 1985,* pp. 182–183.

32. Removing the bias can also be described as establishing an "effective exchange rate" that is the same for both imports and exports. If the official fixed foreign exchange rate is 100:$1, then an importer will, of course, pay 100 penuris in local currency to buy a dollar's worth of imports from abroad. With the structure of tariffs and quotas, however, that dollar's worth of imports sells domestically for perhaps 200 penuris, or the equivalent of $2. In practice, the importer was able to buy $2 for 100 penuris, for an effective exchange rate of 50:$1. Meanwhile, an exporter would receive 100 penuris for each dollar earned, giving an effective exchange rate of 100:$1. This is an import bias. An opposite export bias would occur if subsidies (or cheap credit) were given for each unit exported. If the official foreign exchange rate is 100:$1, an exporter would earn 100 penuris for each dollar's worth of goods exported plus the subsidy from the government of, say, another 100 penuris. That makes 200 in all per dollar, so that the effective exchange rate when exports are subsidized is 200:$1. In the meantime importers must pay 100 penuris to buy $1 for importing; their effective rate is 100 : $1. This is an export bias. If there had been no protection, cheap credit, or subsidies, then both importers and exporters would have faced the same effective exchange rate, perhaps 100:$1. There would be no foreign trade bias. See Meier, *Leading Issues,* 4th ed., pp. 539–540; and Gerald M. Meier, *Emerging from Poverty,* New York, 1984, pp. 178–179, for a discussion.

33. Anne O. Krueger's research on this topic is conveniently summarized in her "Trade Strategies and Employment in Developing Countries," especially p. 25.

34. The evidence is from *WDR 1984,* p. 103; Anne O. Krueger et al., eds., *Trade and Employment in Developing Countries,* vol. 1, *Individual Studies,* Chicago, 1981, and vol. 3, *Synthesis and Conclusion,* Chicago, 1983; A. H. M. M. Rahman, *Exports of Manufactures from Developing Countries,* Rotterdam, 1973, brought to my attention by Colman and Nixson, *Economics of Change,* p. 203; Larry E. Westphal, "The Republic of Korea's Experience with Export-Led Industrial Development," *World Development* 6, no. 3 (1978):347–382; Meier, *Leading Issues,* 4th ed., p. 533.

35. Following the statement in Meier, *Emerging from Poverty,* p. 176.

36. Among the studies are those of R. Emery, 50 countries, 1967; A. Maizels, 9 countries,

1968; C. Voivodas, 22 countries, 1973; M. Michaely, 41 countries, 1977; B. Balassa, 10 countries, 1978; R. Williamson, 22 countries, 1978; O. Fajana, 20 countries, 1979; W. Tyler, 55 countries, 1981; C. Schenzler, 30 countries, 1982; and G. Feder, 31 countries, 1983. See the citations in Woo S. Jung and Peyton J. Marshall, "Exports, Growth and Causality in Developing Countries," *Journal of Development Economics* 18, no. 1 (1985):1–12.

37. See her study *Foreign Trade Regimes and Economic Development* for the statistical detail. The sample size involved was 10 countries. The quotation is from her "The Effects of Trade Strategies on Growth," *Finance and Development* 20, no. 2 (1983):7.

38. Jung and Marshall, "Exports, Growth and Causality," p. 9.

39. Bela Balassa, "Exports, Policy Choices, and Economic Growth in Developing Countries After the 1973 Oil Shock," *Journal of Development Economics* 18, no. 1 (1985): 23–35. Balassa's figures suggest that the improved performance was true even for the poorest LDCs, where the correlation between export growth and GNP growth had heretofore been weaker. See also Balassa's "Policy Responses to Exogenous Shocks in Developing Countries," *American Economic Review* 76, no. 2 (1986):75–78; and his book *Change and Challenge in the World Economy,* London, 1985.

40. All these are noted in *WDR 1983,* pp. 55–56, and in *The Economist.* A variety of IMF stabilization programs involving liberalization of trade policy is described in Shailendra J. Anjaria, Naheed Kirmani, and Arne B. Petersen, *Trade Policy Issues and Developments,* IMF Occasional Paper No. 38, 1985, pp. 84–85.

41. See David Evans and Parvin Alizadeh, "Trade, Industrialization, and the Visible Hand," *Journal of Development Studies* 21, no. 1 (1984):23, for a discussion.

42. IMF, *World Economic Outlook, 1985,* p. 182.

43. For a survey of the zones, see Walter H. Diamond and Dorothy B. Diamond, *Tax-Free Trade Zones of the World,* New York, 1977. Also see D. L. U. Jayawardena, "Free Trade Zones," *Journal of World Trade Law* 17, no. 5 (1983):427–444. For China see *The Economist,* September 14, 1985, pp. 79–80. In many LDCs the array of tax breaks and incentives to attract foreign investment has led to the use of the name "investment promotion zones." In the United States they are more commonly known as "foreign trade zones."

44. See Joseph Grunwald, "Restructuring Industry Offshore: The U.S.-Mexico Connection, *Brookings Review* 1, no. 3 (1983):24–27; U.S. ITC, *Operation of the Trade Agreements Program, 35th Report,* Washington, D.C., 1984, pp. 304–305; *37th Report,* 1986, pp. 179–180; and articles in the *Wall Street Journal.*

45. See IMF, *World Economic Outlook, 1985,* p. 182; and U.S. ITC, *Operation of the Trade Agreements Program, 36th Report,* Washington, D.C., 1985, for examples of such measures.

46. *WDR 1983,* p. 55.

47. Most of these examples are noted by Colman and Nixson, *Economics of Change,* p. 205. A recent volume on overseas assembly activities is Joseph Grunwald and Kenneth Flamm, *The Global Factory: Foreign Assembly in International Trade,* Washington, D.C., 1985.

48. See Schmitz, "Industrialisation Strategies," pp. 10–11.

49. See Belayneh Seyoum, "Export Subsidies Under the MTN: An Analysis with Particular Emphasis on Developing Countries," *Journal of World Trade Law* 18, no. 6 (1984):512–541.

50. U.S. ITC, *Operation of the Trade Agreements Program, 37th Report,* 1986, p. 70. Domestic subsidies to firms, not just on exports but to help cover costs of operation generally, are also legal. The code provides for consultations if harm is caused to

industry in another country. These subsidies used to be less controversial, though recently some developed countries, including the United States, have directed substantially more countervailing duty actions against them.

51. There is a persuasive comment to this effect in Meier, *Leading Issues,* 4th ed., pp. 521–522. Also see his *Emerging from Poverty,* p. 179.

52. *The Economist,* September 7, 1985, pp. 17–18; February 15, 1986, p. 70.

53. Repeating a question asked by Meier, *Leading Issues,* 4th ed., p. 396, and also reflecting the work of G. K. Helleiner quoted there.

chapter *14*

Trade in Manufactured Goods as an Engine of Growth

The general question is the limits to the expansion of any kind of trade. This chapter considers manufacturing, and the next addresses primary products.

Whether manufactured exports can continue to act as a powerful engine of growth largely depends on three main considerations. First, will developed-country GNP rise enough to increase the demand for imports and thus provide a growing market for the LDCs? Second, will developed-country trade barriers arise in response to the export success of the LDCs? Third, will the LDCs lower their high trade barriers against one another? Failure on any of these three counts, but especially the first two, would significantly reduce the likelihood of development led by manufactured exports. Another problem, inconvenient but probably less serious in the long run, is that technological change may cause comparative advantage to alter more rapidly than in the past, leading to a need for greater flexibility and willingness to adapt.

SLOWER DEVELOPED-COUNTRY GROWTH AS A HINDRANCE TO LDC EXPORTS

The 1970s and 1980s brought unmistakable signs of a slowdown in developed-country growth. The slowdown has serious implications for developing countries first because LDC exports still go largely (57 percent not including fuel) to those countries and second because industrial-country GNP and LDC export revenue are closely connected, with a 1 percent decrease in the former associated with about a 1.5 percent decrease in the latter, according to the IMF.[1] The IMF suggests that with oil excluded, the relationship is even more pronounced: for every 1 percent reduction in industrial-country real GDP, about a 2.5 to 4 percent fall in non-oil LDC export earnings can be expected. This in turn is associated with a 0.2 to 0.3 percent decline in the exporters' real GDP, with the figure as high as 0.7 percent for some countries. The terms of trade of primary products reflect a similar close relationship. A recent study by Data Resources, Inc., suggests that when developed-country growth averages less than 2.6 percent annually, commodity prices will fall.[2]

The reasons for the slowdown in developed-country economic growth are complex and not entirely clear.[3] Certainly, "catching up" technologically to the United States was an important spur to German and Japanese growth until the late 1960s, but that has been done. The shift from low-productivity agriculture to higher-productivity manufacturing also fueled growth and is also virtually at an end. The rise of the service economy generally meant a tendency to lower GNP growth, because the productivity of services is harder to increase. Stagflation stemming from the oil shocks played a role. So did labor market rigidities, especially in Europe, with unemployment high in part because wage cuts were politically unacceptable. The great U.S. federal budget deficit together with tight monetary policy led to higher interest rates and crowding out, especially of exporters due to the resulting strong dollar (see Chapter 6 for details). Whatever the reasons, and there is little enough agreement among economists, the end result is irrefutably a slowdown. World GNP grew 6 percent a year in the period 1963 to 1973, and world trade grew 8.5 percent. In the following 10 years of oil shocks and stagflation, 1973 to 1983, those figures slumped to 2 percent and 3 percent, respectively.

It is just as well that LDC exports had swung sharply toward manufactured goods in the 1970s, because these fell far less than did primary products. Agricultural commodities had been 50 percent of LDC export value in 1960; by 1980 the figure had fallen to under 25 percent. Exports of manufactures, on the other hand, rose in that period from about 20 percent to over 30 percent of the total.[4] (The figures vary considerably by region.) In 1965 only 1 LDC exported $1 billion dollars or more of manufactures (Hong Kong), while in 1982 the number was 18. In 1965 19 countries exported $50 million or more; in 1982 there were 45.[5] About four-fifths of this impressive growth was in office and telecommunications equipment, household appliances, textiles, clothing, glassware, furniture, and foot-

Table 14.1   GROWTH IN LDC EXPORTS (PERCENT PER YEAR)

	1965–1973	1973–1980	1980–1982
Total merchandise	7.9	3.4	−0.5
Fuels	8.0	−1.8	−5.1
Other primary products	4.6	5.9	0.6
Manufactures	15.6	12.4	4.1
Services	11.3	9.4	2.6
Total	8.2	4.2	0.0

Source: The Economist, November 26, 1983, p. 73.

wear.[6] As Table 14.1 shows, LDC manufactured goods exports held up far better than their other exports during the oil shocks of the 1970s and the recession of the early 1980s. This was especially true of shipments to the United States, which grew over 80 percent in the four years to 1984, in spite of the recession.

The superior performance of manufactured exports even during the recession is striking. Still, it is even more striking to see so clearly how the development prospects of the LDCs depend in large measure on the employment of sensible economic policies in the developed countries themselves.

DEVELOPED-COUNTRY PROTECTIONISM AS AN OBSTACLE TO LDC GROWTH

The threat of greater protection is the other major obstacle to LDC export growth.[7] It is clear that in any short period of time there is no chance that all LDCs could emulate the export success of the leading NICs. If all LDCs exported as much as a percent of GNP as do Hong Kong, Singapore, South Korea, and Taiwan, then LDC manufactured exports would grow over 700 percent, raising their share of developed-country manufactured imports from about 17 percent to over 60 percent. This would undoubtedly trigger widespread protection against them.[8]

The actual prospects sound considerably better, however. Obviously, different LDCs would begin to export a given manufactured good at different times, so reducing the pressure. A gradual increase in manufactured exports of, say, 10 to 15 percent a year would be much easier to absorb than a huge once-for-all expansion.[9] Some LDCs would export mainly agricultural commodities and natural resources and not manufactured goods. Many of these imports do not compete with developed-country production. Even when they do, given the state of demand, these exports would not be expected to grow nearly as much as 15 percent a year, so relatively little protectionist pressure would be generated from this quarter.

In addition, over time one would expect an increasing proportion of all types of LDC exports to be sent to the LDCs themselves. The percentage increase in such trade from 1973 to 1983 was about a quarter more than the increase of LDC trade with developed countries.[10] It is true that oil made up about half of this, but there is still plenty of scope for expanded South-South trade in manufactures (fastest growing because they have the highest income elasticities of demand), food, beverages, and raw materials. Protection is often stiff in these countries too, however, and that could delay the development of trade among the LDCs. The last section of this chapter considers the problem.

With growing poor-country prosperity, markets there would enlarge, benefiting not just themselves, but also the developed countries that would find new markets for *their* exports. Note that as the exports of major Asian NICs (Indonesia, Malaysia, Philippines, South Korea, Thailand) rose from $64 to $68 billion from 1981 to 1983, their imports rose by even more, $61 to $74 billion. If intra-industry trade burgeons to the extent it has among the rich countries, then products might be both imported in quantity and produced domestically as well.

**Table 14.2 PERCENTAGE SHARE OF
LDC EXPORTS IN THE
DEVELOPED-COUNTRY
CONSUMPTION OF
MANUFACTURES,
1970–1980**

	1970	1980
Australia	2.1	5.5
Canada	1.3	2.1
EC	2.5	4.6
Japan	1.3	2.4
Sweden	2.8	3.8
United States	1.3	2.9
Total	1.7	3.4

Source: The Economist, November 26, 1983, p. 73.

The new markets for developed-country products would lend greater strength to the free-trade lobby, as exporters see where their bread is buttered.[11] The thought that the LDCs (including the oil states) purchased 38 percent of U.S. manufactured goods exports in 1983, more than Japan and Western Europe combined, and an even higher 43 percent of U.S. agricultural exports, seems motive enough to keep the trade channels open. (The figures for the non-oil LDCs are about a quarter less than those for all LDCs.)

"Penetration" by LDC Exports

Much presumably depends on the degree of LDC "penetration" into developed-country markets. If the LDC share of developed-country markets is relatively low, then calls for protection by producers will ring hollow, even if the LDCs are raising their exports rapidly. Currently, that share *is* low (only 3.4 percent for manufactures in 1980), though it is growing as seen in Table 14.2

Even if the import penetration ratios of Table 14.2 were to increase much more rapidly than they have, this would not necessarily be a cause for alarm. Though voters and legislators would deplore higher figures and would argue that competitiveness is eroding, the ratio need not show that at all. Exports to LDCs could be growing as fast or even faster than imports from them. The higher import penetration might signal even greater developed-country competitiveness than before![12]

In fact, the job losses in industries facing competition from these exports *are* far offset by the job gains generated by the increase in industrial-country exports to the LDCs (about three times more, according to the research of J. M. Finger).[13] Amid the rise of protectionist sentiment in the rich countries, it is often not appreciated that these countries sell far more manufactured goods to the LDCs than they buy from them, and that nearly two-thirds of all LDC imports are this sort of good. A recent Morgan Guaranty study shows that a 3 percent cutback in LDC output, easy enough to engineer by increasing protection, would decrease U.S. output by 0.5 percent because of the lost exports. The losses are even greater for Europe (0.8 percent) and Japan (1.1 percent). On this reading, applying protection to the products of the LDCs is "shoot yourself in the foot economics," causing considerably more harm than good at home, not to mention what it does to the LDCs.

The Present State of Protection in the Developed Countries

Protection certainly has the capacity to ruin the engine of growth. What is the present situation? In the developed countries we find a rather surprising mixture of reduced protection in some areas, heavy barriers in others, and an increasing volatility of policy.

For the LDCs the best news comes from the area of tariffs. Here the situation is by and large an encouraging one for trade in manufactured goods. From a trade-weighted average level of over 50 percent in the 1930s, tariffs for manufactures were already down to 7 percent by 1979 when the Tokyo Round of Multilateral Trade Negotiations (MTN) was signed. The MTN will bring these levels down to 4.7 percent for all industrial products in the nine major industrial markets when all cuts are finally in effect on January 1, 1987. (Most major countries have phased these in at a rate faster than originally agreed.) The cuts made in that seven-year period are deep, 34 percent or 39 percent depending on whether the averages are weighted or not.[14]

The Generalized System of Preferences (GSP)

In addition, the LDCs have benefited from special tariff preferences granted to them by the developed countries. An outcome of much publicized negotiations in the 1970s, the Generalized System of Preferences (GSP) was a primary aim of LDC policy makers. It is also constantly held up as a major concession by the rich nations. Some of these reduced their duties rather than eliminating them; some have quotas for duty-free treatment, beyond which normal tariffs apply. The nations of the European Community (EC or Common Market) first offered GSP in July 1971 for 10 years, and in 1981 they renewed the program for another decade. The United States eliminated tariffs on 2,724 categories of imports from the LDCs on January 1, 1976, also for 10 years. This law was renewed in January 1985 for 8½ more years; it will expire on July 4, 1993. By 1985 something over 3,000 products from 114 countries and 26 territories were covered. Manufactures and semimanufactures make up the largest share. By increasing the return on exports from LDCs, the GSP certainly increased trade and thereby has probably contributed to faster economic growth.[15]

In spite of the growth in trade that did occur, there is no escaping the fact that GSP has been a disappointment. One major problem with it is that developed countries unilaterally reserve the right to remove the preferences, both by commodity and by country. From the start the EC excluded all primary products (a serious blow) and base metals to the ingot stage, plus a long list of manufactures and semimanufactures that made up over three-fifths of the dutiable imports from LDCs to the EC. The United States has always excluded textiles, clothing, shoes, some electronic goods, some steels, watches, and glassware. The first four of these are especially important to many LDCs. Goods could also be removed from the preferential list; the United States did so with tungsten, molybdenum, chromium, and vanadium steel products, nuts and bolts, television picture tubes, leather wearing apparel, and sew-on fasteners, among others. In the United States, automatic exclusion was built in under the "competitive need" formula, applied when 50 percent of the total imports of a product came from one country or when imports of a product reached a certain dollar figure ($63.8 million annually in 1985, the figure adjusted every year). In the 1985 law the competitive need exclusions were much tightened and will henceforth be applied when imports hit 25 percent instead of 50 percent, and $25 million instead of $63.8 million. By 1981 there had already been 226 applications of the competitive need formulas, and enforcement, once winked at, has been strict. By 1985, because of the limits, more trade was not given GSP treatment than actually received the reduction in duty.[16] Rule of origin limits also apply, with the requirement that 35 percent of the value of a product be added in the country making the final export. This, too, reduces the application of GSP. By and large, rules of this sort are even tougher in the EC.

Whole countries were excluded by the United States, though not by most other schemes. For political reasons, most communist countries were denied the benefits and so are members of OPEC, even though some of them (Indonesia, Nigeria) are very poor. Recently, Nicaragua, Laos, Iran, Ethiopia, and Afghanistan have also been removed from the list. For economic reasons, the president was permitted to "graduate" a country by limiting the application of the rules (Hong Kong, South Korea, Brazil, Mexico, Israel, and especially Taiwan have been so treated). The EC has also slashed preferences for a similar group of countries.

Under the new U.S. law of 1985 the president has greater authority than before to determine eligibility by country. There is now an automatic phase-out over a two-year period when an LDC's per capita income hits $8,500, indexed to one-half the rise in nominal U.S. GNP. The president can also cancel the preferences if a beneficiary fails to provide reasonable access to its markets. (This rule will not be enforced against the poorest LDCs.) Finally, there is a clause in the new extension requiring recipients to assure "internationally recognized worker rights," including trade unions and "acceptable" conditions of work. This clause could be used to improve sweatshop conditions, but could also conceivably be employed as a protectionist measure against cheap labor in any LDC receiving GSP benefits.[17] Note well that none of this maze of exceptions and limitations would have been possible had tariffs simply been reduced across the board. In that case, the ancient rule of "most favored nation" would have applied, meaning that no country can be specially discriminated against and all must receive the same benefits as the most favored trading partner.

The result is that a fairly modest amount of LDC exports comes in duty-free under GSP, $13.3 billion for the United States in 1985, only 12.4 percent of all imports from eligible LDCs. The figure is a little higher for the EC. (Much tropical produce comes in duty-free anyway.) Even the limited benefits under GSP are heavily concentrated on a few NICs: Taiwan, South Korea, Brazil, Mexico, Hong Kong, Israel, and Singapore, in that order of importance, had 75 percent of the trade qualifying for U.S. GSP treatment; all low-income LDCs had a minuscule 0.5 percent of this trade in 1985.[18]

One last problem with the GSP is that some of the increased trade from the LDCs has been a diversion of developed-country imports from a cheaper source to a more expensive source. If the amount involved had been large, this could have been a fundamental objection. Fortunately, studies by Baldwin and Murray in 1977 and Birnberg in 1979 found a modest sum of about 14 percent of total expansion in GSP trade to the United States, the EC, and Japan was a diversion of this sort. The implication is that developed-country imports from LDCs are not close substitutes for their imports from each other, so little diversion took place.[19]

There seems little doubt that further tariff cuts, as in the Tokyo Round, make more economic sense than does the GSP. Such cuts cannot be trade diverting since they are granted on a most favored nation basis, and for the same reason they cannot be used to discriminate against certain countries. Further, they are permanent unless national and international laws are changed, whereas all GSP programs include time limits. Probably the vast attention given to GSP in the past decade and a half was misplaced. It made the developed countries feel better, and it convinced the LDCs they had won a battle for a concession. Ironically, the broad decline in tariffs negotiated in the Tokyo Round not only brought greater gains to LDCs than GSP ever had, but it also reduced the importance of GSP. If a recommendation may be made, it would be to phase out the preferences and their associated restrictions and discrimination and to replace them with another general round of tariff cuts.[20]

Tariff Issues

It is almost fair to say that tariffs are now a trivial trade barrier, but not quite. There remain a few issues of interest and importance.

Goods of Special Concern to LDCs   Generally, the goods excluded from the GSP were the very goods on which tariff cuts were less generous in the Tokyo Round. For example, the U.S. duties on leather imports were reduced only 4 percent and clothing only 15 percent, compared to an average reduction on all goods of well over 30 percent. The average U.S. tariff on clothing after all Tokyo Round cuts will be 23 percent. There were no cuts at all on footwear and color television sets. The EC acted in similar fashion. Agricultural tariffs were little affected (protection in this area is discussed in Chapter 15). Thus for some goods of special concern to the LDCs, tariffs remain an important obstacle.

Effective Protection   The problem of "effective protection," often called "tariff escalation," is not solved. The direct implication of effective protection is that the nominal or apparent tariff rate, "5 percent on widgets," for example, may differ substantially from the effective or actual rate. Why this is so is not at all self-evident; the now familiar concept did not become standard analysis to economists until well into the 1970s.[21]

Let us explain it with a tale of the tariff on pearls. The nominal rate on strung pearls imported into the United States used to be about 50 percent, for example, $50 for a necklace that could be purchased abroad in Greece for $100. There was no tariff at all on raw pearls. Boring the pearls and stringing them added only about $1 to their value. No sane Greek exporter would ever be willing or able to pay a $50 tariff on the strung pearls, because that would have been a tax of $50 on just $1 of value added for the stringing.[22] The tariff on the strung pearls was "effectively" 5,000 percent, enormously higher than the 50 percent nominal rate. The processing of a raw material or semifinished commodity would not occur in the exporting country under these conditions; all processing would take place in the importer. The conclusion is that whenever the rate of duty is higher on finished commodities than it is on raw materials or semifinished goods, the exporting country will be less likely to undertake the processing, even if otherwise that country would have a strong comparative advantage in doing so.

Table 14.3   EVIDENCE OF HIGH EFFECTIVE PROTECTION

Product	Depth of Tokyo Round Cut (Percent)	Post-Tokyo Round Weighted Average (Percent)
Wood, wood pulp, paper, furniture		
Raw material	54	0.2
Semifinished	38	1.9
Finished	41	4.2
Textiles, clothing		
Raw material	25	0.8
Semifinished	22	11.5
Finished	19	16.7
Leather and rubber footwear		
Raw material	80	0
Semifinished	35	4.4
Finished	11	10.2
Basic metals		
Raw material	82	0
Semifinished	26	3.2
Finished	37	5.9

Source: S. J. Anjaria, Z. Iqbal, N. Kirmani, and L. L. Perez, *Developments in International Trade Policy,* IMF Occasional Paper No. 16, 1982, p. 113.

A formula to calculate the degree of effective protection is:

$$\text{Effective rate of protection} = \frac{(y - b) - (x - a)}{x - a}$$

where x is the international price of the finished commodity, y is the domestic price of the finished commodity, a is the international price of the imported component, and b is the domestic price, including the tariff, of the imported component.[23]

For ease of calculation, say the tariff on strung pearls is only $1; the stringing of $100 worth of pearls also costs $1, and there is no duty on raw pearls. In this case the nominal tariff is 1 percent, but the effective tariff through escalation is:

$$\frac{(102 - 100) - (101 - 100)}{101 - 100} = \frac{1}{1} = 100 \text{ percent}$$

How easy it would be to dismiss a 1 percent tariff, but 100 percent is a different story. The examples in Table 14.3 show that on average, tariff reductions in the Tokyo Round were usually largest for raw materials and smallest for finished products, meaning high effective protection for the latter. A selection of nominal tariff rates for finished products and their raw material (Table 14.4) further demonstrates the extent of the problem.

When all Tokyo Round cuts are in place in 1987, the overall average tariff rate for the industrial countries will be 0.3 percent on raw materials, 4 percent on semifinished manufactures, and 6.5 percent on finished manufactures.[24] Thus even with average nominal tariffs now quite low, tariff escalation still exists, and the LDCs have a legitimate complaint. Almost wholly unnoticed by the general public, their chances for processing what they might be able to do efficiently are

Table 14.4 SELECTED NOMINAL TARIFF RATES

Product	Post-Tokyo Round Tariffs in		
	EC	Japan	United States
Green roasted coffee	5.0	0.0	0.0
Coffee extracts	18.0	17.5	0.0
Cocoa beans	3.0	0.0	0.0
Chocolate	27.0	27.4	6.5
Raw cotton	0.0	0.0	1.9
Cotton clothing	13.7	13.2	8.8
Bauxite	0.0	0.0	0.0
Wrought aluminum	9.7	11.7	2.9
Natural rubber	0.0	0.0	0.0
Rubber products	5.3	4.8	5.3
Hides and skins	0.0	0.0	0.0
Leather goods	11.7	11.0	14.4

reduced. (There is no reason to believe that any conspiritorial malevolence against the LDCs has caused this, incidentally. It is obvious why developed-country manufacturers would lobby for low tariffs on inputs and high tariffs on output.) Whatever the underlying reasons, it is clear that more local processing of primary products could generate substantial earnings for the LDCs. An UNCTAD study using data from the 1970s puts the potential increase for 10 important commodities at 1½ times the value of the unprocessed commodities themselves, not far below the current value of all foreign aid.[25]

"Safeguards" and Unfair Trade Practices   With the decline in tariff rates resulting from the Tokyo Round, a group of protective measures that allow tariffs to be imposed in special circumstances assumed new significance. The group includes temporary safeguard measures, such as escape clause action, and measures to combat "unfair trade practices," such as dumping duties and countervailing duties against subsidies. Fortunately, the Tokyo round codes on dumping and subsidies brought useful progress in these areas, and safeguard action is of little importance. But charges of dumping and subsidization are now an effective way to harass potential LDC exporters and a major route to protection for industries in developed countries.

1. Temporary "safeguard" measures are permitted under GATT's article XIX on behalf of an industry hurt by a surge of imports. In the United States, following a recommendation by the International Trade Commission that an industry has been injured, the president can impose escape clause tariffs or quotas, negotiate voluntary export restraints, or attempt to adjust the industry with assistance for retraining and the like. If protection is imposed, it is temporary, lasting 5 years with a possibility of a 3-year extension.

The ITC recommended escape clause action 14 times in 1976, but in the 10 years since then its use has practically disappeared, recently averaging about 2 cases a year. Safeguard action also finds only slight use in the EC.

The lack of importance is easy to explain. The standards of proof that an industry has been injured are high, the president has wide discretion, protection does not necessarily result, and when it does, its temporary nature is unattractive to industry. Above all, discrimination is not permitted—escape clause duties apply to all trading partners, including those with the power to retaliate. That for the most part has kept governments from supporting safeguard action. In the United States from 1982 to 1983 there were only 5 safeguard investigations, but 262 cases alleging unfair trade practices; in the EC during 1983 there were 2 safeguard cases but 80 "fairness" cases.[26]

2. The first of the unfair trade practices is dumping, defined as selling abroad at a price below that in the home market.[27] The United States extended the definition in 1974 to encompass sales below cost of production; most other countries do not use this extended definition. Under the U.S. antidumping statutes, when dumping is proved, the Department of Commerce applies an anti-dumping duty as an offset and adds on a penalty. The president has no discretion to interfere.

There was an improvement for the LDCs in the Tokyo Round antidumping code, which recognized that special conditions, such as foreign exchange rate overvaluation and high marketing costs, may mean that the home price in LDC markets may not be commercially realistic for calculating dumping. Under the code prices in third-country export markets and cost of production plus a "reasonable amount for marketing costs and profit" will now form the test.

There is also unfavorable news. In a recession economic theory predicts that any firm that cannot cover its average costs of production will continue to produce as long as it can cover its variable costs. This is common practice for U.S. firms, but by law if a foreign firm does it with its exports, this is dumping! Not surprisingly, as the possibilities for protection via this route were understood, there was a large increase in the number of antidumping cases. In the United States in 1984 61 investigations were undertaken, as opposed to just 25 in 1983. Twenty-two new duties were imposed, whereas 5 to 7 a year used to be standard; over half were directed against LDCs.[28] At the start of 1985 109 antidumping duties were in effect, about a quarter against LDCs. Elsewhere, in the EC 20 to 30 cases annually are usual; Australia and Canada use this tool with special frequency.

One unfortunate provision in the U.S. law, fully exploited by protectionist interests, is that nondumping firms from any given country get hit with antidumping investigations right along with the guilty parties, meaning that time and expense must be wasted on a defense.

Most economists would find it reasonable to retaliate against dumping when that tactic is used to run domestic firms out of business and then boost prices to claim the monopoly rewards. This is rare, however, since there would have to be international, not just national, monopoly power, and because the high prices would stimulate domestic competition once again.[29] There is no doubt that even when not predatory, the idea of charging a lower price abroad than at home does seem to violate the producers' sense of fair play. But why is nonpredatory dumping thought to be so bad if a foreign firm charges more at home because it has some monopoly power there? Is it sensible to claim that we, too, should pay monopoly prices for the product? And why is it argued that sales below average cost are "unfair" when domestic firms often do exactly that, on a massive scale, during a recession?[30] Add the thought that dumping, however nasty the word sounds, does benefit consumers by bringing lower prices, and this author reaches a conclusion: The concept of the antidumping laws in the United States and other developed countries is fundamentally unsound; the protection should probably be cut back to counter predatory dumping only.

3. Countervailing duties against subsidies are another remedy for an unfair trade practice.[31] Recently, U.S. firms have been bringing many cases under laws dating back to 1897. These laws require a countervailing duty to be imposed when proof is forthcoming that a foreign government is subsidizing exports to the United States or, under the amendment of 1922, is granting domestic subsidies to a selected industry or group of industries.[32] As with antidumping duties, the president has no discretion to interfere. Other major countries have similar laws.

Until the Tokyo Round code on subsidies, these countervailing duties could be imposed even if no harm or injury had resulted; in a major gain under that code a "material injury" criterion was agreed to. Countervailing duties may still be imposed, but now only when material injury in home markets is shown; injury in third markets is not sufficient. (The fact that there were only 26 signers of the code at the start of 1986 limits the benefits of this clause.) More important for the LDCs, the code recognized that such subsidies are a legitimate tool of development and did not outlaw their use by these countries. The developing countries that signed the code agreed to phase out the subsidies when they are no longer needed for development or for competitive purposes. Disagreements have arisen, with the United States insisting on rapid elimination and the LDCs arguing that the subsidies are needed.

Most economists would probably agree that there is an element of unfairness when exports caused by long-term subsidies harm domestic firms. They would note, however, that there is a world of difference between a subsidy designed to allow the controlled running down of a declining industry or to compensate for some government regulation such as above-market minimum wage laws and a subsidy designed to increase market share at the expense of other producers. All are treated alike under the law. In any case, the United States has clearly shown that it will continue to employ countervailing duties against poor countries when injury is proven. Of the 56 duties in effect at the end of 1984, fully 37 were directed against LDCs, affecting a wide range of commodities including bricks, cement, tile, steel, chemicals, clothing, and lime. Of the 16 new duties imposed in 1985, some three-quarters were applied against LDCs.[33]

One sticky issue was resolved only after several years of acrimony. Mexico is not a signatory of the GATT subsidies code; in fact, it did not even *join* GATT until 1986. The United States continued to apply the old law before the code, imposing countervailing duties against Mexican subsidies even when U.S. firms were not harmed by them; fully 27 cases were brought against that country between 1980 and 1985. This policy was very hard to defend. In April 1985 the United States agreed to an injury test in return for a Mexican undertaking to phase out some of its subsidies.[34]

The new GATT code on this subject failed completely to touch the problem of subsidies and export subsidies for agricultural products. (This failure is considered in Chapter 15.) The code also continued to allow long-term subsidies for export *credit,* which is tantamount to an export subsidy and clearly works thus. The LDCs could not afford to compete this way, but the developed countries could and did, promoting their *own* exports by this means. That led to a brief, but intense export credit war among the major developed countries, in which they competed in cutting interest rates on loans advanced to their export customers. In 1983 an agreement ended the era of subsidized low interest rates, and export credits now track market rates closely. For a time, though, obscure agencies that granted the credits—the U.S. and Japanese Export-Import Banks, West Germany's Hermes, Britain's Export Credit Guarantee Department, and France's Banque Française du Commerce Exterieur—were in the limelight. The abolition of subsidized rates will mean less benefits to LDCs from cheaper imports, but it also puts LDC producers of competing products at less disadvantage.[35]

In the United States, prosecution of two other examples of unfair trade practices have recently been emphasized, especially since President Reagan's speech of September 23, 1985.[36] Under Section 337 of the U.S. trade act, goods can be excluded if they violate patents, infringe copyrights and trademarks, or involve false labeling. Of the 41 outstanding Section 337 exclusions at the start of 1986, 29 were against LDCs, with Taiwan and Hong Kong most heavily represented. The United States has also become more aggressive in responding to foreign government actions limiting access to markets or involving unfair competition under provisions concerning violation of trade agreements (Section 301). Among the small number of present cases are major ones against the tough Brazilian protection of its market for computers and shoes.

These unfair practices are probably less controversial than either the anti-dumping rules or the countervailing duties against subsidies. For one thing, the infringement cases have represented a real and growing problem; for another, the Section 301 cases have generally been limited to especially serious examples of foreign policies that seem to go beyond normal infant-industry protection, and few enough of these. They do, however, represent yet another route by which developed-country trade barriers could intensify.

Nontariff Barriers (NTBs)

The gravest area of developed-country protection against the LDCs is nontariff barriers or NTBs. NTBs hit certain key industries hard, but ignore others altogether. The most important of these barriers are quota-type arrangements, either in the form of a normal quota imposed by the importing country or a voluntary export restraint (VER). Sometimes these are also called orderly marketing arrangements, or OMAs. VERs are analytically quite similar to a normal quota, except that the import licenses awarded under a quota become export licenses usually allocated to foreign producers by the foreign government that agreed to the VER.

Economic theory indicates clearly that quotas and VERs, inflexible and bringing no tariff revenue to the country where imports are limited, carry greater welfare losses for consumers than do tariffs. They are also more profitable for producers receiving the protection whenever demand rises or supply falls, and they have the ability to convert potential monopoly power into actual monopoly power.

NTBs are widespread; the UN Commission on Trade and Development estimates that such barriers exist somewhere in the world against 98 percent of all product types.[37] Unfortunately for the LDCs, these barriers bear more heavily on poor-country exports than they do on the exports of the developed countries, as shown in Table 14.5.[38]

Making matters more serious, this form of protection is intensifying. The percent of imports to developed countries subject to NTBs more than doubled in the United States from 1980 to 1983 and rose by 38 percent in the EC. Several of the most stringent NTBs are directed explicitly at manufactured goods such as textiles, clothing, and shoes in which the LDCs appear to have a comparative advantage. It is clear enough that the main reason this is so is that the LDCs have

Table 14.5   PERCENTAGE SHARE OF IMPORTS SUBJECT TO NTBs, 1984

	Percent of Imports from	
	Developed Countries	LDCs
EC	10.7	21.7
Japan	12.4	14.5
United States	9.2	16.1
All developed countries	11.3	20.6

Source: WDR 1986, p. 23.

less bargaining capacity and ability to defend themselves in trade battles than does an important developed country.

NTBs: Outright Quotas   The incidence of outright, unilateral quotas is fairly low in manufacturing, but much higher in agriculture, as we shall see in Chapter 15. Even in manufacturing, however, quotas are unfortunately more used against the exports of the LDCs than against those of the developed countries. The United States employs them especially against leather goods, textiles and clothing, and until quite recently footwear and some electronic goods. The EC has a longer list that includes all these items plus wood products, paper, glass products, electrical equipment, and transport equipment. (Japan uses unilateral quotas in manufacturing far less than the United States or EC, contrary to a current misconception.)

Arguably, LDC producers suffer more harm from quotas than would other producers for two reasons.[39] First, they are vulnerable because their exports are often concentrated both by product line and by trading partner. Especially susceptible to damage are firms that are independent, not branches of multinational companies, and that sell to small importing firms in rich countries; they have no strong allies to lobby against the protection. Add to that a lack of flexibility and adjustment capacity in some LDCs, and the resulting harm may be difficult to diminish.

Second, the quotas are focused on labor-intensive product groups of interest to poor countries. As always, old industries in developed countries now too labor-intensive to compete on world markets will see great benefits in obtaining protection. The advantages of free trade are, however, much more diffuse; the lower prices of imported goods will affect millions of people and perhaps save consumers billions of dollars, but each consumer gains only a little and so does not camp on the steps of the capitol. The campers are instead the lobbyists for industries seeking the protection. Potential exporters, who would gain as LDCs buy abroad with their new earnings from foreign trade, may not even suspect that they, too, are losers from protection. They may not notice that protection appreciates the exchange rate (see Chapter 13 for details), thus depressing demand for their product. Only later do they see how foreign retaliation has raised barriers against them abroad.

NTBs: The Multi-Fiber Arrangement in Textiles and Clothing   The harm to the LDCs is undoubtedly greatest in the area of textiles and clothing; the most interesting and important trade restrictions concern these products.[40] The products make up 9 percent of world trade, about 27 percent of the total manufactured exports of non-oil LDCs and nearly 30 percent of their exports to developed countries. In numerous LDCs textiles and clothing together are the largest non-agricultural export and provider of employment.

The LDCs have a clear comparative advantage in the many lines of production where low labor costs are crucial, but these are also areas of very long-lasting protection against them. Total trade in these items has grown rapidly, 19 percent in value during 1980 alone, for example. But because of the protection specifically directed against the LDCs, *their* share has grown much more slowly, just 3 percent in value during 1980. In terms of intensity, it would appear that the EC has the least penetrable barriers, while the U.S. barriers are also high. Japan's are lowest among the major countries.

Protection against textile and clothing imports from the LDCs is well organized to say the least. A Multi-Fiber Arrangement (MFA) was put together in 1974, the name indicating that it applies to cotton, wool, and synthetic fibers. There had been a history of many years of protection against textiles and clothing before the arrangement was negotiated. The start of the MFA, a three-year voluntary agreement covering the years 1974 to 1977, sounds rather reasonable. Its stated intention was to codify and simplify the many confusing national protectionist measures of the time and to guarantee steady and orderly growth in textile and clothing exports. Simultaneously, it was to give developed countries time to restructure one of their most labor-intensive industries. A renewal, MFA II, was in effect until MFA III was agreed upon in December 1981. (There were 42 participants in mid 1984.) The agreement lasted until July 31, 1986, and a further extension (MFA IV) has been negotiated.

Central to the original MFA was a promise of 6 percent annual expansion in imports taken from the signatory LDCs. Generally this was a sensible aim, but the developed countries did not live up to the pledge. (Recall the 3 percent figure for 1980 noted above.) Under the clauses permitting protection against market disruption and the risk of market disruption came hundreds of bilateral and unilateral VERs and quotas. MFA III was actually more restrictive than the earlier agreements, and MFA IV is more restrictive yet, both allowing growth rates of well below 6 percent for some countries. The U.S. agreements in 1986 with three big suppliers, Hong Kong, South Korea, and Taiwan, cut their growth rate in the U.S. market to 1.0, 0.8, and 0.5 percent per year respectively, while the EC earlier had achieved 6 to 8 percent *cuts* for these countries in "sensitive" categories. (Between 1981 and 1984 the LDC share of clothing imports to the EC fell from 40 percent to 25 percent.) MFA III was also more comprehensive than the earlier versions, and under it further action was often taken to restrict imports even within an agreed-upon quota.

Let us be entirely clear that these limits on trade in textiles and clothing are discriminatory, applying only to the LDCs and *not* to the developed countries. The MFA does not now and never has controlled the exports of rich countries. Some of these have been doing very well indeed in product lines where labor-saving automation restored comparative advantage. About 70 percent of world textile exports and about 50 percent of clothing exports are done by developed countries. In recent years the top three exporters were not LDCs, but West Germany, Japan, and Italy, in that order. In some years these countries have expanded their textile and clothing exports far more than permitted to LDCs under the MFA.

The MFA has now grown to a Byzantine complexity of 69 clauses and some 20,000 annexes. There are currently about 3,000 bilateral quotas on different countries and products within the arrangement. When changes occur, they usually result in tightened rules. An example in the United States was 1983's less flexible criteria for market disruption. One clause states that a ratio of imports to production of 20 percent or more will now so serve. Another applies if a foreign producer supplies 1 percent or more of total U.S. production of that product or category. "Once any category is restricted," states the agreement, action shall be taken "to ensure that it shall under ordinary circumstances, remain under control for the life of the bilateral agreement that governs our textile relations with the called country." As a result of the policy changes, some 120 "calls" (negotiations that usually led to the imposition of tighter limits) were made in 1984 and a similar number in 1985. These calls often come long after an importer has purchased the goods, substantially increasing the risks of doing business. New rules of origin were also introduced in 1984 to stop one country that had already filled its quota from shipping semifinished goods to another with part of its quota still remaining for completion and export. A bilateral agreement has even been imposed on Guam, which is U.S. territory!

If anything, the rules of the EC are even more complex. Its "sensitive product ranking" limits growth among so-called group 1 items to as low as 0.5 percent per year for one product in the category and an average 2.0 percent for the group as a whole. The so-called "basket extractor mechanism" leads to hundreds of new limits, usually on *non*sensitive products whose exports rose following the strict import limits on the sensitive group. Various measures involve large-scale reduction or elimination of "swing" (excess in one category compensated for by shortfall in another), "carry over" (using the unused portion of a previous year's quota), and "carry forward" (borrowing against the next year's quota).

Surely the last two paragraphs will convince any skeptic that the MFA is almost impenetrable in its maze of detail. Even when imports would otherwise be permitted, the uncertainty facing exporters can surely be appreciated. Nor is there respite in the smaller developed countries. Australia, Canada, and Scandinavia all have relatively stringent protection as well, all involving bilateral agreements. Even the most liberal governments have joined in.

What a fine collection of issues for an economist! One recent estimate is that LDC textile and clothing exports would have been twice as large in 1982 and 1983 if there had been no MFA. (To be sure, the MFA looks better if one assumes that national protection would have been even worse without it.) The bilateral agreements tend to freeze market shares, and unused quotas are not transferred between countries. The most efficient producers, those that have signified their belief in trade, not aid, are the most penalized. The enormous complexity creates uncertainties that undoubtedly have their worst effect on small suppliers with limited expertise and potential exporters who are discouraged.[41] The bilateral agreements create vested interests not just in the protected importing country, but also in exporting countries, where profits accrue to those who have a guaranteed share in a high-price market. This consideration makes small, poor countries more acquiescent than they would be if they took a longer-run view.

Unfavorable effects spread far beyond the LDCs. In the developed countries the protection attracts new resources into what would otherwise have been a declining industry. In 1982 one-third of all textile and clothing establishments in the United States had not been in business six years earlier. In France fully one-fifth of the new manufacturing firms formed in recent years have been in these industries. The inflow of resources adds to political clout and, of course, makes it even harder to remove the protection. The effect on consumers is higher prices for clothing (doubled in the United States), curtains, bedding, towels, rugs, and so forth. The total bill currently is perhaps $12 billion per year in the United States alone, and the impact is regressive because these products take a higher proportion of the income of the poor. Estimates of the cost of each job saved in textiles are in the $40,000 to $80,000 range; for clothing a World Bank study suggests $169,000 in the United States and $124,700 in the EC. There seems little sense in perpetuating such arithmetic.[42]

Finally, note the irony that the industry in the developed countries has already gone through extensive adjustment, with spinning and weaving in the advanced, capital-intensive sector having severely damaged the old labor-intensive part of the industry. Computer-assisted design and manufacture (CAD/CAM) has been important; CAD/CAM explains why countries like Italy and West Germany are now leading textile exporters. Adding further irony, exit from the obsolete part of the industry is easy, there being a good market for used textile machinery. It is even debatable how immobile the labor is in the obsolete plants. We know of "pockets" of immobility—women in areas where female employment is low, girls between secondary school and marriage, elderly workers, and (in the United States) blacks and illegal immigrants—groups who would find it hard to move. On the other hand, labor turnover is high anyway; the work force could be reduced by attrition; and alternatives come more easily when wages are low, since little human capital would be lost in the moving.

In almost all developed countries, however, the combined urge for survival in the obsolete sector and recognition that protection enhances profits in the capital-intensive and prosperous sector have fueled the protectionist push. Few governments can afford to ignore an industry of this size. Its large number of voters and its regional concentration make it a force to reckon with. But the MFA, as Martin Wolf warns us, "like the wreck of a ship on concealed rocks, ... warns the unwary" of the damage that can be caused to LDCs by developed-country protection.[43]

In October 1985 Singapore's Prime Minister Lee Kuan Yew addressed a joint session of the U.S. Congress. Referring mainly to textile protection, he spoke eloquently of the

> economic uplift Japan, South Korea, Taiwan, Hongkong, [and other Southeast Asian LDCs] have had from the free market economies of the West by plugging into their trading and investments power grid. . . . Putting up barriers to America's markets would halt the economic advancement of the free market oriented developing countries. . . . Does America wish to abandon the contest between democracy and the free market on the one hand versus communism and the controlled economy on the other, when she has nearly won this contest for the hearts and minds of the Third World?[44]

The day after the speech, the House passed the Textile and Apparel Trading Act (the Jenkins bill). The bill would have replaced the bilateral agreements with major exporters in effect under the MFA, restricting imports by quotas based on imports in 1980.[45] It would *not* apply to the rich EC or Canada, just to the poor! The effect would have been large, a 35 to 40 percent fall in U.S. imports. Under its terms, Hong Kong's exports would have fallen 13 percent, Korea's 35 percent, Taiwan's 45 percent. Korea estimated that the bill would ruin 500 firms. For countries that did not become major exporters until after 1980, the result would have been to wipe out most shipments to the United States: Thailand − 70 percent, Indonesia − 90 percent, China − 90 percent. *The Economist* summarized it well: "In the great struggle for 2 billion hearts and minds, the rich capitalist world could yet snatch defeat from the jaws of victory."[46] Not to mention the effect on U.S. consumers, who would have paid an additional bill of perhaps $28 billion as textile and clothing prices would have soared higher yet. Fortunately, both for them and the LDCs, President Reagan vetoed the bill in the closing days of 1985. But the bill's supporters in an unusual move arranged to bring up a veto override in August 1986, timed for the start of the 1986 congressional campaign. No doubt anticipating trouble, the administration lent its support to a tougher MFA and tightened some of the bilateral quotas still further. It also proposed the MFA be expanded to cover natural fibers such as linen and silk, and this provision was included in the new MFA IV. But perhaps Lee Kuan Yew's eloquence had had an effect; the veto override, which had been expected to pass handily in the House, failed. The margin, though, was a mere 8 votes.

NTBs: Steel   Steel is a declining industry in the United States and the EC, and comparative advantage has swung toward a small group of advanced developing countries.[47] Seven of them (Brazil, Chile, India, Mexico, South Korea, Taiwan, and Venezuela) had 4 percent of world steel production in 1974, but 10 percent in 1983. U.S. average wages in the industry were $22 per hour in 1984, with wage increases about a third greater from 1950 to 1980 than for all manufacturing, even though productivity increases were slowing rapidly. Labor resisted changes in work rules and crew size; there was high absenteeism and confrontational labor-management relations. Management invested little in the industry, with only two big plants built in the United States since the 1950s. The pattern of high pay and declining relative productivity was broadly similar in the EC. Meanwhile, average wages in Korea's modern steel industry were just $4 per hour. Neither the United States nor the EC could compete with the NICs on the basis of price (except the small U.S. "mini-mills" that use scrap as the raw material). Firms in both areas turned loose their lobbyists to seek protection.

A blizzard of antidumping suits, countervailing duty cases, and escape clause actions hit the U.S. government. Many of these had to be decided during the month of September 1984, in the middle of the presidential campaign. The government caved in, negotiating a large VER on most forms of steel. Though the VER was agreed on with all major producers, the heaviest restraint fell on the poorest countries. The assigned share of the U.S. market for finished steel and steel products for the newly efficient LDCs was 1.9 percent for South Korea, 0.8 percent for Brazil, and 0.36 percent for Mexico. Current estimates are that U.S. steel prices are raised 7 to 10 percent. The EC early in the 1980s adopted a similar structure of bilateral agreements with most steel exporters to limit their shipments.

Protection Against Other Products   Systematic protection against other manufactured exports of the LDCs is generally not as comprehensive as in textiles and steel or when it is, the harm is not generally as widespread.[48] Automobiles can be imported rather freely to most countries as long as they are not Japanese. There is heavy protection against foreign-built ships, but this affects mainly Korea which by 1983 captured 19 percent of all new orders in that year. Shoes were protected in the United States by a VER with Korea and Taiwan from 1977 to 1981, but the VER has expired; the EC does not limit shoe imports from LDCs, though separately Britain, France, and Ireland do have protectionist arrangements; Canada and Australia have tight shoe quotas. Color television sets from Taiwan and Korea (and Japan as well) were hit with a U.S. VER that expired in 1982; some countries in the EC maintain unilateral quotas on a variety of electronic products.

There is no doubt that developed-country protection is an important concern for any nation considering an export promotion strategy. It is clearly directed against the most successful NICs. LDCs forced to move into third markets must compete for a share of a smaller cake. It is unpredictable—an exporter never knows when it will rear its head, and that increases risks. This is true even of trade where access to major markets is currently free or little controlled. Any confidence in recommending footwear or electronics to cheap-labor LDCs has to be shaken somewhat by the dangers of protectionist pressures arising in those product areas too. In some respects the uncertainty and its effect on investment plans may well be worse than the protection itself.

Thus the U.S. Congress, with bills in the hopper during 1985 and 1986 for "reciprocity" (you must buy from us a value equal to what we buy from you) and for a surcharge on imports from countries who have a trade surplus with the United States is a volatile element. The protection can come even in unexpected form. Who would think in an era of high energy prices that an efficient and cheap gasoline substitute would be hit? Yet that is what happened to Brazil's gasohol industry. Brazil's sugarcane can be made into fuel, with output about three times greater than from the equivalent amount of American corn. But, to protect farmers, the U.S. Congress voted a tariff of 63¢ per gallon. (This redoubles the pressure on the Brazilian sugar industry, which, as we shall see in Chapter 15, suffers severe protection against its raw sugar also.)

TRADE ADJUSTMENT ASSISTANCE IN DEVELOPED COUNTRIES TO REDUCE PROTECTIONIST PRESSURE

Both protection itself and its haphazard nature are of great concern to development economists. If the situation were to worsen, the prospects for export-led growth might diminish greatly. Is there anything the developed countries could do to ward off this possibility?[49]

We examined the strong dollar problem in Chapter 6 and noted the damage that it causes exporters and producers of import substitutes. A further significant reason why protectionist pressures have intensified in the United States during recent years is the decline and fall of trade adjustment assistance. At present this is the missing link in trade strategy. Any time imports flow into a country from new sources, there are likely to be dislocation costs associated with the impact. Unemployment may develop in the affected industry along with excess capacity in plant and equipment; these are the short-run opportunity costs imposed by trade flows. The market will in time bring adjustments, but these may be slow and costly if information is imperfect, if transactions costs are high, and if downward rigidities of prices and wages lead to employment problems.

In more detail, the costs to labor from the impact of trade include the sudden obsolescence of specific skills, loss of seniority, pension problems, and the need for geographical relocation with possible high moving costs, capital loss on one's house, and the breaking of family and social ties. (Workers affected by trade flows may have to make greater shifts in occupation and location than is usual when unemployment occurs, since a whole industry may be affected rather than just a firm.) The older the worker, the worse the loss, since age brings more local ties, a greater stake in the pension plan, and higher seniority in a present job, but reduced opportunities in alternative occupations. This is due in part to age discrimination and in part to the specific nature of the skills possessed by experienced workers.

The greatest adverse impact for labor will be in beleaguered industries where wages for historical reasons are far above the national average. Perhaps the high wages are due to an earlier but now eroded productivity advantage or perhaps to protection, with strong labor unions able to extract a share of the gains from the firms in the industry. In such a case it is likely that alternative employment will be at a lower, and perhaps much lower, wage. In communities dependent on a single firm or industry, the damage will perhaps spread more widely, to merchants and anyone else selling goods and services to the now-distressed workers and to all owners of property, who must make up for the decreased property tax collections from the damaged firm or industry. For workers and communities, there is no easy way to insure against all this or to recover quickly. A stockholder can rapidly adjust shareholdings to avoid or reduce losses, but the problems are likely to be more intractable for a worker or for a town.

All these costs explain why a reduction in protection and a shift to freer trade ought to be gradual. Letting attrition do the work is surely less painful than adjusting all at once. These costs also explain why multilateral tariff reductions are better than unilateral ones. When trading partners also cut their barriers, there will be a sharper stimulus for export industries to expand, thus reducing the dislocation costs. Finally, and needless to say, the costs will be cut if the reduction in protection comes during a period of economic growth and not in the middle of a recession when jobs are scarcer everywhere. Recessions are protection's best friend!

The existence of these costs explain the growing enthusiasm for protection in the developed countries. Unlike the "normal" unemployed, those who lose their jobs because of the impact of imports are free to seek tariffs and quotas from congresses and parliaments. Those who stand to lose from the protection—consumers, LDCs, potential exporters to those countries from whom we buy—are less well organized and have less influence. The public is also to a lamentable extent ignorant of the costs, the hidden tax that cannot be escaped. Polls in most developed countries show that the public usually supports additional demands for protection. This emphasizes the importance of public programs for adjustment assistance, which can compensate those with power to do harm, in effect buying them off and simultaneously acting as a "caution" signal that this industry is a declining one. Lack of such programs spurs protection, as politicians note the employment losses in their home district; in turn the protection attracts new resources into the industry.

Adjustment assistance was introduced in the United States in the Trade Expansion Act of 1962. The rules were liberalized in the Trade Reform Act of 1974. The key provision in the 1974 act was payment of 70 percent of the weekly wage for one year to workers displaced by imports from abroad. Workers were also eligible for federally funded retraining. The program of Trade Adjustment Assistance (TAA) attained great size, funded at about $1.5 billion in both fiscal years 1980 and 1981. But with deep budget cuts after the election of President Reagan, Congress just managed to keep TAA alive at $84 million in both fiscal 1983 and 1984, only 5 percent of its former funding. It expired in December 1985. In March 1986 it was renewed for six years with a little more money than before, $25 million for job training, job search, and relocation and $105 million for cash allowances. But it still is the developed world's "least-developed" program, with funding equal only to 8 percent of the old plan's and less than that in real terms.[50]

The loss of trade adjustment assistance is deeply regrettable for those who oppose protection, but not because the old act was particularly well designed. Most of the money was spent for glorified unemployment compensation gleaned by very high paid workers—auto and steel workers took 55 percent of the benefits, for example, much of this paid in the run-up to the 1980 elections. The benefits were paid in such a way, weekly and concurrent with regular unemployment compensation, that they had disincentive effects on finding another job. The counseling and training were laughable; according to Labor Department data, of the 1.3 million workers assisted by the program from 1977 to 1984, only 70,000 (5 percent) enrolled in retraining programs, only 28,000 (2 percent) completed the training, and only 4,500 (0.3 percent) found jobs that utilized their new training. At the height of the program, 35 percent of the workers aided did not even know training was available![51]

Few would defend this. Reform was overdue. But the effects of the virtual scrapping of trade adjustment assistance have contributed to the rekindling of protectionist fires. In the absence of an effective, wide-ranging program, the industries adversely affected by foreign trade will normally and naturally seek the protection of tariffs, quotas, and VERs, as preferable to the not-so-tender treatment of the marketplace. If the benefits of free trade are to be preserved and defended, arguably there must be a move toward more training for workers harmed by trade, who must be attracted and held even by generous cash allowances.

Many claim this is unrealistic in an era when the federal budget deficit must be cut rather than increased. In ordinary circumstances, this is correct. But it must be remembered that protection already costs the American consumer well above $50 billion per year, over 30 times what trade adjustment assistance cost at its highest. According to a study undertaken by the Institute for International Economics, the annual cost to consumers per job retained through protection is often amazingly high: $750,000 yearly in carbon steel, $1 million for specialty steel, $55,000 in footwear under the now expired VER that the industry wants back, $105,000 in autos, and so on.[52]

The clear implication is that workers could be paid large sums to be idle, for example, their entire annual wage, and if the protection were ended at the same time, there would still be great gains. How much more would the gains be if the adjustment assistance were used to train them and transfer them to productive employment. Those who argue the market will do all this without government help overlook the arithmetic of protection, an arithmetic appealing to the protected industry, but which makes no sense for the public as a whole. An effective program of trade adjustment assistance is a potent means to ensure that the gains from trade are shared and that new protectionist barriers are not erected against the LDCs.

Concern for the federal budget should not be allowed to stand in the way because the public already pays far more in the costs of protection than even a greatly expanded program would cost. Indeed, there are effective ways to cut the costs of TAA if so desired. Eligibility could be restricted to workers with longer service (four or five years, say) and certified by their employer as unlikely to be rehired in the near future. Resources could thus be concentrated. Even an expensive program could be funded with ease if all NTBs were converted to temporary tariffs, and if the tariff revenue were used for that purpose.[53] Alternatively, a "protection profits tax" might be levied on protected industries to fund TAA.

The question broadens into one of comparative economics. Is there something to be learned from the experience of others? A good case can be made that some aspects of the Japanese model deserve emulation. The flexibility within that country's economy is especially marked by a willingness to shift resources rapidly from declining industries to areas of increasing advantage.

The Ministry of Trade and Industry (MITI) coordinates this policy. MITI is most well known in the United States for its (largely mythical) attempts to target export winners. It deserves to be far better known for its coordination of programs to buy up and scrap excess capacity in declining industries.[54] Of Japan's shipbuilding capacity, 56 percent was mothballed in 1983 and 1984; 36 percent of ethylene capacity has been scrapped; 58 percent of aluminum capacity was closed down by 1984 with another 28 percent to go by 1986. Further slimming is underway in the pulp and paper industry. (High energy costs were the major cause of the problems.) Japan does well at not staying too long in a losing industry. Workers there seem more willing than those of the United States to shift among plants and among jobs, in part due to the willingness of Japanese companies to cooperate, in part because unions are industry-wide and do not defend particular crafts.

Lester Thurow at MIT argues that the United States has lost some of its willingness and ability to disinvest by closing low-productivity plant. It is as essential to disinvest as it is to invest, he notes, adding that we are simply not very good at accomplishing it. The implication is that capitalism is not being allowed to work; the problem in this view is not so much industrial structure as it is human psychology. This theme has been taken up by some Democrats, who suggest a government industrial policy such as a national industrial development bank or national measures to increase research and development expenditures in "targeted" industries.[55] (Republicans generally oppose these ideas.) Most suggestions for industrial policy in the United States generally are thought to mean keeping industries afloat rather than helping to run them down, and the Trade Adjustment Assistance program has never included funds for closing down operations. As yet this problem has not been grappled with successfully. Many economists (but few politicians) would agree that the economy not afraid to run down its losers, to "de-target" in effect, is the strong economy in the end. As we have seen in this chapter, it is also the economy that does its share in promoting export-led growth in the LDCs.

MONOPSONY BUYING IN THE DEVELOPED COUNTRIES, MONOPOLY IN OCEAN TRANSPORT

Protectionism is not the only impediment to an LDC's exports. If international markets are noncompetitive on the side of the buyer, this, too, will restrict the gains from trade. Certainly, many in the LDCs believe this to be true. Gerald Helleiner has noted that some markets do indeed have a limited number of buyers, especially for a group of agricultural commodities and numerous minerals.[56] Three firms, for example, are responsible for 68 percent of world banana imports. The largest buyer involved in the purchase of cocoa beans has a share of the world market usually between 20 and 40 percent, and it publishes the most important market information on future demand and supply. The top three firms in the industry purchase 50 to 80 percent of the world cocoa crop. One firm buys 25 percent of the world's tea. Twelve buy 80 percent of the world's natural rubber.

Much trade is "closed" in the sense that it is between branches of a multinational enterprise. There are said to be only about 12 independent copper smelters in the entire world who will buy from unintegrated mines. Perhaps only 20 percent of the Western world's aluminum production is marketed outside vertically integrated channels.

There is therefore the possibility that where supply is inelastic, monopsony barriers can restrict the quantity purchased and so reduce the price paid. (The higher the elasticity of supply, the less exploitative a monopsony can be, as supply will simply dry up as prices are pushed down; producers have alternatives and turn to them.) But elasticity is sometimes low, with monopsony pricing thus possible if buying is concentrated. Unifruit's banana empire in Central America (see Chapter 4), copper buying in Chile until the 1970s, and the oil market as rigged by the Seven Sisters in pre-OPEC days (see Chapter 15) are all possible examples.

How serious this problem is at present is open to question. In manufacturing monopsony power seems limited because any exporting LDC can turn to alternative buyers in other countries as long as trade is open. The rapid growth of world commerce in the 1960s and 1970s has presumably limited the problem by intensifying competition. In agricultural and mineral production much capacity is now owned or supervised by government, and the output is sold by government marketing boards or is subject to an export tax or supply restriction. This would resemble the bilateral monopoly model of the textbooks, with "countervailing power" used to offset the monopsony exploitation. The balance might even tilt far in the other direction, as with OPEC's oil surveyed in the next chapter. In one market, grain, where the number of buyers is relatively small, studies have suggested that the large size of the firms is a reasonable reaction to market conditions, and that the monopsonistic consequences are slight.[57] One need only add that countervailing action (by LDC governments negotiating jointly or by developed countries applying their antitrust laws or both) would seem called for whenever monopsony power is uncovered among the firms of the rich countries. For then, more than would be likely at home, there is an indefensible exploitation of the poor by the rich.

Very similar to monopsony in its effect is the rigged market for shipping that faces LDCs in some parts of the world.[58] "Liner conferences," liner meaning regularly scheduled service and conference meaning cartel, set rates in some areas that appear not always to reflect costs closely. There are signs that transport costs are higher for processed goods exported from LDCs than they are for primary products, sometimes two or three times as much as a percent of FOB value, more than justified by the difference in handling costs. It also appears that these costs tend to escalate with the degree of processing. The problem is worse in the least-developed countries, especially in Africa and the Caribbean, than it is elsewhere because the lower level of cargo volume attracts less competition from nonscheduled shipping. Such costs rose sharply as a result of the two OPEC oil crises of the 1970s.

All this is disturbing because analytically transport cost is as much a barrier as is a tariff, reducing the level of trade and its attendant benefits. With transport costs as a percent of goods value about the same as tariff collections before the Tokyo Round, monopoly pricing of transport services is sure to be a serious problem.[59] Efforts to dismantle the monopoly power and encourage competition would seem eminently justified. For those who so believe, it is disappointing to see that the UN Liner Code, negotiated in UNCTAD and now open for signature, permits and even encourages continuation of restrictive practices in ocean shipping. Of the 59 countries that have so far signed, many are LDCs.[60] This paradox is presumably due to the clauses in the code that would guarantee a proportion of cargoes for a signer's own shipping. It seems a clear case of special interest economics and national prestige (boosted by ships flying one's own flag) winning out over economic efficiency.

RAPID CHANGES IN COMPARATIVE ADVANTAGE REQUIRE MORE LDC FLEXIBILITY

An export promotion strategy might encounter one last important obstacle. LDCs can now generally be assured that comparative advantage lies in labor-intensive products, and that this will continue as long as wage levels are relatively low vis-à-vis the developed countries. But what if the advantage of low labor costs is eroded by technical developments that make cheap labor less important? There would still be a comparative advantage, of course, because any country will continue to produce some goods with greater relative efficiency and some goods with less. But the changes in advantage might become harder to predict, faster, and more haphazard, thus increasing the need for adjustment and flexibility. Poorer LDCs may not be good at this.

There is reason to think that some technical developments are leading exactly in this direction. Computer-assisted design and manufacture is based on microelectronics. CAD/CAM, with automatic insertion devices, very large-scale integration, and automated, programmable assembly, does have a capacity to undermine the importance of low labor costs. In effect, the improved machines are better substitutes for labor than the older machines. The ease with which the programmable machines can be shifted among products sharply cuts "down time" and thus lessens the importance of in-plant scale economies. Computers can also be used to cut inventory size and costs by better control over flows, but the positive effect of computer use for this purpose will be far more pronounced when the suppliers of important inputs are located nearby rather than overseas, as the transport can be better monitored and adjusted. Here, too, LDC assembly operations are potentially at a disadvantage.[61]

Already by 1983 in automated semiconductor assembly, Hong Kong's cost advantage had shrunk to only 8 percent lower than U.S. costs, compared to 66 percent lower with the older, labor-intensive, manual technique. "Trade reversal" may occur, since the digital revolution will take place first in the developed countries. Thus some Japanese television set producers have recently been pulling their operations out of South Korea and back to Nippon; GE has closed some of its

Southeast Asian offshore factories and switched its foreign buying to Japanese producers; and other pull-backs have affected the garment and auto industries.

Such developments will make it ever more necessary for LDCs to develop a flexible response. If labor is educated and easy to shift, if a proper infrastructure can support new lines of activity, if management is resilient, and if local banks can provide loans, the difficulties will be minimal. But where an economy suffers from sclerosis, its price system unresponsive because of controls, its producers failing to react rapidly to changed circumstances, alterations in comparative advantage could be a painful experience.

TRADE AMONG THE LDCS

LDC Barriers to Trade

The effects of developed-country protection against manufactures could be partly circumvented by a rapid rise in South-South trade. Unfortunately, the LDCs themselves maintain many barriers to trade, barriers generally even higher than those of industrial countries.[62]

Tariff rates in LDCs typically exceed those of developed countries. An unweighted average is about 32 percent, and maxima in the range of 100 to 150 percent are not uncommon.[63] Actual collections are substantially lower because free importation is often granted to inputs, government purchases, and other products. But countering this are a variety of service charges, stamp taxes, sales taxes collected on imports, and foreign exchange taxes, all of which act like tariffs and leave tariff-type barriers far higher than in the developed countries. Such protection against textiles and clothing is often extraordinary.

Some poor LDCs, especially in Africa, depend on tariffs as a major source of government revenue. (Forty-three countries generated 20 percent or more of government revenue from this source in 1981; 2 earned over 40 percent. The figure is under 1 percent for the United States.) Nontariff barriers are relied on even more heavily, applying to 71 percent (!) of all product groups in a recent survey of 27 LDCs, compared to a little over 20 percent in the developed countries. Quotas have historically been very important, especially in India, Pakistan, Latin America, and Africa.[64]

Local content requirements are common. Mexico, for example, requires auto manufacturers to utilize locally produced parts and materials equal to at least 50 percent of the vehicle's value. Indonesia's law requires an exporting firm selling $750,000 or more to the state sector to buy local goods of equal value to the sale. On occasion an LDC has even refused to join GATT because it wishes to have complete freedom to determine its own trade policy, without being required to abide by the international agreements regulating trade. Mexico has been the most important of these countries, joining in August, 1986, only after a debate of nearly 40 years; another is Iran.

When the protection hits a developed country's exports to an LDC at the same time that the LDC is rapidly increasing its penetration of the former's markets, political friction often arises. This has been especially true of services in recent years, with LDCs becoming ever more avid in protecting them as they have become easier to transport.[65] There is no doubt that politicians often consider some services to be quite "intrusive," from a cultural and political point of view, and few people anywhere would want them in foreign hands. Radio, television, domestic airlines, and the telephone system are cases in point, with foreign operation seldom permitted. Others, however, are kept off limits to foreigners even though they are important for development, and even though free trade would appear to give cheaper access to information processing, professional services, finance, and technology. For example, foreign insurance, banking, data processing, and computer hardware and software are sometimes excluded, even when the developed countries have an obvious, large comparative advantage in them. Brazil especially protects the information and technology sector; perhaps that country's major ongoing controversy in 1986 involved its protectionist measures against telephone switching, computers, and software from the United States and elsewhere. (The new GATT round of trade talks, the "Uruguay Round," is expected to consider protection against services. This is opposed by Brazil and India, but favored by Korea and Southeast Asia, who apparently believe concessions in this area could be exchanged for freer trade in manufactured goods.[66])

Often LDCs apply protection even on goods that are fully competitive internationally and are being exported successfully without a subsidy: textiles, clothing, and shoes for example. For an egregious case, consider that Taiwan is the world's largest producer of umbrellas yet maintains a tariff of 50 percent on umbrella imports; and is a leading exporter of shoes but puts a tariff of 60 percent on many types of footwear imports.[67] This redundant protection appears to be almost inexplicable from an economic point of view, sometimes even silly, since it gives an opening to protectionist interests in developed countries to retaliate. It would seem sensible as a matter of urgent priority to scrap all redundant protection of this sort at the first opportunity.

Earlier in the chapter, we reviewed the concept of effective protection, or tariff escalation. This problem is pronounced in many LDCs because imported inputs to manufacturing are often allowed in duty-free. The high percentages shown in Table 14.6 (all over 25 percent and the most recent figures averaging about 50 percent) show that the barriers to imports of finished manufactures are significantly higher even than indicated by the nominal tariff rates. High dispersion, as exemplified in the table when the maximum rate is far above the average rate, means a greater distortion of incentives than otherwise among sectors of the economy and thus even more problems.

Could South-South Trade Be Encouraged?

In the 1970s South-South trade was growing three times as fast as North-South trade. Though petroleum made up 50 percent of the total, it is also true that 47 percent of LDC manufactures went to other LDCs in 1977. (Asian exports of these goods to LDCs are about twice as large as exports of them from elsewhere.[68]) Services, too, have figured in the expansion, as with the Brazilian construction

Table 14.6   AVERAGE EFFECTIVE RATES OF PROTECTION IN LDC MANUFACTURING (PERCENT)

Country	Year	Average rate	Maximum rate
Argentina	1977	38	
Brazil	1980–1981	44	252 (1967)
Chile	1967	217	1,140 (1967)
Colombia	1979	55	140 (1969)
Dominican Republic	1971	124	
Egypt	1966–1967	42	
Ghana	1968–1970	143	
India	1968–1969	125	
Indonesia	1971	101	5,400 (1971)
Israel	1968	71	
Ivory Coast	1970–1972	72	278 (1973)
Jamaica	1978	50	
Kenya	1967	92	
Malaysia	1974	39	
Mexico	1980	37	
Nigeria	1979–1980	232	
Pakistan	1970–1971	181	595 (1970–1971)
Philippines	1974	59	
Sri Lanka	1979	38	
Sudan	1971	179	
Uruguay	1968	384	1,014 (1968)

Note that these effective rates are not a complete measure of the "pull" of resources into protected industries, because to a greater degree than in the developed countries, price distortions due to controls and overvalued exchange rates also exert an influence.

Source: Taken from Hubert Schmitz, "Industrialisation Strategies in Less Developed Countries: Some Lessons of Historical Experience," *Journal of Development Studies,* 21, no. 1 (1984): 5, Table 1; and Anjaria, Kirmani, and Petersen, "Trade Policy Issues," table 64, p. 149. The country averages are from the work of O. Havrylyshyn, I. Alikhani, I. M. D. Little, T. Scitovsky, and M. Scott. The maxima are from the work of Anne O. Krueger, "Trade Policies in Developing Countries," in Ronald W. Jones and Peter B. Kenen, *Handbook of International Economics,* vol. 1, Amsterdam, 1984 p. 542.

firms whose business has recently boomed because they are experienced in organizing labor-intensive construction. Can steps be taken to increase this flow, thus perhaps circumventing developed-country protection?

It should be understood and stressed that in the abstract there is no reason to encourage South-South trade for its own sake. Comparative advantage will work to identify who will be the largest trading partners. In general one would expect North-South trade to be of greater importance for years to come because factor proportions differ more than in South-South trade, the North offers the larger markets, and LDC protection is higher.[69] However, there is little question that some goods developed for an LDC market will have an appeal for similar market segments in like countries elsewhere and will become profitable exports. In addition, many protectionist LDCs may find it much easier to grant trade preferences to other LDCs than to lower barriers to the developed countries. If this is the only politically acceptable way to reduce protection in a country, then the opportunity may well be worth taking because of the scale and learning effects. If groups of LDCs lower barriers against one another, the result can be larger markets, greater economies of scale, more learning by doing, and more diversification of exports. Especially important is that any backwash effect from specializing in primary products might be avoided by diversifying into manufactures for consumption within the union. The great fear is that such mutual lowering of barriers might be trade diverting, with countries buying from LDCs at higher prices what they used to buy from developed countries at lower prices.

Customs Unions Among the LDCs

The major form of granting trade preferences has been through formation of a customs union. Such unions aim to reduce and eventually eliminate tariffs among the members, while maintaining a "common external tariff" against outsiders. Under certain circumstances a customs union is capable of generating a great increase in trade among its members (called "trade creation" in the literature). Remember that unilaterally reducing barriers against the whole world will achieve the same thing, and without the possibility of trade diversion, but this may not be politically feasible.

A customs union joining a number of countries which previously had high tariffs will be most successful when the following six conditions are met.[70]

1. If the elasticity of demand in the member countries is high, a cut in the barriers against fellow members of the customs union will lower price and cause a large increase in consumption. Much additional trade is generated. The higher the duties in the first place, the more positive the result.

2. If the elasticity of supply in the member countries is high, production within the union will rise rapidly, to take the place of the former imports from nonmembers when a demand increase occurs because of the fall in tariffs.

3. If low-cost producers, for any given good, also belong to the customs union, there will be only a small sacrifice in shifting trade from nonmembers to members. It follows that the larger the customs union the better, for there is more chance that there will be low-cost producers among the membership, so lessening the trade diversion.

4. If the member countries are large, with only a small percentage of their consumption imported, then diversion of trade to a higher-cost source within the union will make little difference.

5. If in negotiating the union the external tariff against outsiders is more or less an average of the previous rates existing in the member countries, then the dispersion of tariffs is likely to be reduced. This is an advantage. When very high and very low tariffs exist together, incentives become skewed toward and away from the various industries concerned. A smaller variation in tariffs means comparative advantage has a greater chance to work.

6. If the union is large enough that its external tariff can affect the world market for an imported item, it may be able to manipulate the tariff to alter the terms of trade in its favor. (It may be able to do the same thing with exports if export taxes are standardized.)

These six conditions are uniformly worrisome for the success of the idea. Consider them one by one. LDC imports often contain a high proportion of essential inputs (capital goods, oil), and demand may be quite inelastic. A poor economy is an inflexible one; LDCs have more government controls over economic activity, an inadequate infrastructure, low levels of literacy, education, etc.; supply may be inelastic as a result. Customs unions often have a rather limited membership, do not contain low-cost producers of manufactured goods, and consist of relatively small countries. The conclusion is that policy makers must be especially alert to possible trade diversion when preference arrangements are made. Even with all these disadvantages, a union still might be worthwhile if the dynamic effects—economies of scale in intraunion sales, higher investment, improved marketing, a greater spur to productive efficiency, better management, and technical change—are large enough to more than offset the trade diversion. But there is no guarantee that this will be so, and the record of such unions so far is not particularly encouraging.

The Experience of LDC Unions

A fair number of attempts at economic integration have been made.[71] One of the earliest and most ambitious was the Latin American Free Trade Area (LAFTA) —Argentina, Brazil, Bolivia, Chile, Colombia, Ecuador, Mexico, Paraguay, Peru, Uruguay, and Venezuela. LAFTA was founded in 1961. It hoped to eliminate all duties in 10 years, but it ran into serious problems of industrial allocation. New industries would obviously be attracted into existence behind the common external barriers, and LAFTA thought they should be allocated by government agreement. This union expired in August 1980, to be replaced by a less-ambitious successor, the Latin American Integration Association (LAIA). Internal duties are not yet eliminated. In something of a protest against the influence of Brazil the giant, an Andean Pact was formed in 1968 as a union within a union. It consists of Ecuador, Colombia, Peru, Bolivia and Venezuela (Chile left it in 1976). As yet it has no common external tariff. In July, 1986, Brazil and Argentina signed an agreement to remove tariffs against each other and to adopt a common customs barrier.[72] Uruguay will join, and others may follow.

The other Latin American preference area was the Central American Common Market (CACM), dating from the Treaty of Managua in 1960. The CACM was a progressive idea for a customs union and an integration of industries plan. It got off to a rousing start, with an eightfold rise in intraunion trade between 1960 and 1969. But strains in the industrial policy developed, and the Soccer War of 1969 saw two erstwhile fraternal members of the Market, El Salvador and Honduras, hurling their armed forces at one another. The CACM quickly collapsed, protectionist barriers were soon again in place, and there has been no improvement since. In early 1984 many frontiers were closed to trade: the Nicaragua-Honduras border because of the near-war there, the Nicaragua-Costa Rica frontier because of unrest in the area, the Guatemala-El Salvador and Guatemala-Honduras frontiers and seaborne commerce between Guatemala and Costa Rica because of various trade disputes.

In the Caribbean area a West Indian Federation fell apart due to internal dissension, and its successor, the Caribbean Community (CARICOM) of 1973, has made little progress. CARICOM's common external tariff has not yet been adopted by a number of countries, with three deadlines for doing so missed in 1985. Trade barriers have been raised, especially by Trinidad and Jamaica. There are allegations of cheating on the rules of origin.[73]

In Asia, the Association of Southeast Asian Nations (ASEAN) was founded in 1967. Its original members were Indonesia, Malaysia, the Philippines, Singapore, and Thailand, with Brunei joining in 1984. It started to move toward a common market in 1976, with heavy tariff cuts in 1977, 1980, and 1984. ASEAN members are successful economies, although a surprisingly low proportion of their trade (17 percent in 1984, little changed since 1970) is among the member countries. Compare the 53 percent of the European Community. Only some 20 percent of *that* limited amount is at preferential rates. There is still no common external tariff; Indonesia has high rates, while Singapore's are virtually zero. The strict rules of origin to qualify for preferences (50 percent of a given product's value added must be local) limit the benefits yet further. ASEAN's attempts to establish joint ventures are proceeding slowly, partly due to the opposition of Singapore, which does not approve of protection.[74]

In Africa the East African Community (Kenya, Tanzania, and Uganda) of 1967 was at its inception perhaps the most widely discussed of all the LDC efforts to form a customs union. But intractable disputes arose, the Community disintegrated, and borders were closed. More successful is the Economic Community of West African States (ECOWAS), founded in 1976. It has been heading toward customs union since 1980 and is scheduled to abolish all tariffs by May 28, 1989. There are foreign exchange problems, however, because the former French colonies in ECOWAS use the strictly managed CFA franc, while other members (Ghana, Nigeria, and Sierra Leone) have had much looser money management and rapid inflation. The influence of Nigeria grates on the poorer members in the same way that Brazil irritates LAIA. Further south, there is a small Central African Customs and Economic Union founded in 1966.

In almost every case progress in these LDC customs unions has come easily at first, as the intraunion duties are lowered initially on goods where there is no local production in any member country. When production already exists in one country, but not the others, progress is not so simple. The country with the lead typically wants to eliminate protection rapidly; the others obstruct in the hope that they can catch up; the advance slows.[75]

The major problem with most of them is that they tend to be weakest when the level of industrialization is low, for then new industries do not spring up easily and are high in cost. There is too much chance for trade diversion and monopoly creation. Often enough, the unions have quite high external barriers against outsiders, which increase the chances of trade diversion. As Anne Krueger has written,

While there is undoubtedly scope for gainful intradeveloping country trade, it seems clear that the type of trade in manufactures that has been encouraged under regional trading arrangements has generally been more the outcome of the import-substitution type of incentives than of the incentives that accompany a genuinely export-oriented trade strategy.[76]

More useful than regional preferences, if they could be arranged, would be *general* trade preferences among all LDCs. Since the wider the customs union, the less the chances of trade diversion, a super union among the LDCs makes good sense. An approach to this—Economic Cooperation Among Developing Countries (ECDC)—was made in the Protocol of 1973, recently including 17 countries and 750 commodities. But the Protocol has not been across the board. The preferences have usually been granted bilaterally on a case-by-case basis, largely on complementary goods and not substitutes. Quotas and other non-tariff barriers remain in place, just as has been true in most of the customs unions discussed above. Effectiveness has thus been limited.[77] Still, the protocol has now developed into a push for a global system of trade preferences (GSTP) that would cover both manufactured goods and commodities and involve reductions in both tariff and nontariff barriers. Negotiations were expected to commence on a GSTP in 1986.[78] The idea seems better than the present one of regional preference arrangements with high barriers against the outside.

Customs Unions with a Rich Patron

A last alternative is for one or more LDCs to join a customs union with a rich country. There is a certain "colonial" pattern to such action, as it usually ties the trade of the LDC partner tightly to the metropolitan economy of the "patron." Counting the aid, technical help, and defense umbrella that may accompany the deal, it may still be worth doing from the LDC's point of view. The oldest of these preferences are those advanced by the EC to the former colonies of its members, the African-Caribbean-Pacific (ACP) states. Lower tariffs and guaranteed access outside quota barriers and VERs are commonly granted to this group.[79]

The United States has two similar unions, one with the Caribbean and the other with Israel. The Caribbean Basin Initiative (CBI), which took effect January 1, 1984, provides for one-way duty-free treatment for 12 years.[80] (The long time frame was thought to be important for planning investments.) CBI was the first U.S. preferential treatment for an entire geographical area. To acquire duty-free status, an article must be imported directly, and 35 percent of its appraised value must be value added in one or more of the beneficiary countries. It is superior to the U.S. GSP scheme because inputs originating in other beneficiaries qualify, as does production in Puerto Rico and the Virgin Islands. U.S. materials also count, up to 15 percent of the total value, in satisfying the 35 percent rule, and that, too, is more liberal than the GSP. There are also fewer listed exceptions to duty-free treatment in the CBI than in the GSP, no "competitive need" restrictions, and no plans to "graduate" countries when they hit a certain income level.

There is a long list of eligibility requirements, many innocuous, so it seems. Guyana, Nicaragua, and Suriname have not qualified for political reasons. The duty-free treatment can be suspended entirely or tariffs lower than MFN tariffs can be imposed under escape clause legislation. All U.S. antidumping and countervailing duty legislation will continue to apply. There is a clause carrying extra safeguards for perishable agricultural commodities.

Finally, there is a list of exceptions. Excluded from duty-free treatment are textiles and clothing subject to export-restraint agreements under the Multi-Fiber Arrangement; certain leather, rubber, and plastic footwear, handbags, luggage, work gloves; certain leather clothing; canned tuna; petroleum and petroleum products; and watches and watch parts if material in them comes from communist countries. Finally and most important, U.S. quota legislation is not affected, so bilateral agreements under the MFA remain in force, as do the prohibitive agricultural quotas on peanuts, cotton, and sugar (all discussed in the next chapter). The sugar exclusion is especially unfortunate since cane sugar production has declined so seriously on the Caribbean islands, to a level only half the 1.5 million tonnes of 15 yeas ago. There is also irony in U.S. moves during 1986 to assist the CBI countries to expand their textile and clothing exports to the United States, while at the same time tightening the MFA's restrictions. The Congress also failed to provide for tax credits to U.S. companies investing in the CBI countries. This had originally been suggested, but was not forthcoming. The result of all the exclusions is that the impact of the CBI has been strictly limited, affecting in 1985 only about $500 million in goods formerly dutiable but now entering duty-free. This is only about 7.3 percent of the region's current total trade with the United States. While not denying that eventual dynamic effects might be large, it is quite clear that the CBI has been gutted by U.S. protectionist interests.

There has, however, been one surprise. Asian business people noted that numerous Caribbean countries were too unimportant in textile and clothing exporting to have been hit with quotas under the Multi-Fiber Arrangement. More than two dozen new firms opened in these fields in 1984 to 1985, and the stage seems set for a CBI boom in these products.[81] One would not want to count on that, however, given the recognized and demonstrated ability of U.S. protectionists to control textile and clothing imports.

The second of the U.S. preference agreements took effect on September 1, 1985, when the United States and Israel agreed to eliminate all tariffs against one another over a 10-year period.[82] The customs union with Israel might appear not very important on the world stage, but it is the first U.S. bilateral arrangement, and it removes virtually all tariff and nontariff barriers. (Escape clause safeguards, antidumping laws, the regulations against subsidies and textile protection still apply.) The new union would appear to pose some threat of trade diversion for Israel, with more expensive U.S. exports substituting to some extent for what Israel could buy at cheaper world market prices. From the Israeli point of view, however, that problem is no doubt completely overshadowed by the further evidence of a strong political and economic alliance with the United States. Any costs of diversion are well offset by benefits in other forms, including aid and military support.

The chief implication of this union, as with the EC's similar and far broader arrangements with the ACP states (and Israel, too), is the tendency for patrons and clients to be cemented into trading blocs, all discriminating against one another, and with the client states becoming wedded to their privileges. Intransigent opposition to the similar imperial preferences of the British and French colonial days was a hallmark of U.S. foreign policy for three-quarters of a century. There is some irony in the United States joining in that game.[83] No single customs union may have the capacity to do much harm, but together, by making trade discrimination commonplace, they could reduce world welfare.

This chapter has considered the problems encountered by LDC exporters of manufactured goods. Our basically optimistic conclusion is tempered by worry about the rise of protectionism. Such a rise would have adverse results far beyond any simple measure of reduced LDC exports. It would also attack directly and reduce the dynamic gains from increased efficiency and scale benefits that trade brings. In the next chapter we consider primary product exports. There we shall find the protectionism even worse against some nontropical commodities, discouraging swings in price and income, and an oil cartel that has had a severe impact on LDCs without oil. For long-term success in primary product exporting, it would appear that some reforms need to be implemented.

NOTES

1. See IMF, *World Economic Outlook, 1986,* Washington, D.C., 1986, p. 11, and *World Economic Outlook, 1985,* Washington, D.C., 1985, p. 179, which gives a slightly higher figure. In 1983 about 40 percent of these exports were manufactures; 23 percent went to North America, 20 percent to the European Communities (Common Market, or EC), and 9 percent to Japan. *Ibid., 1985,* p. 176.
2. The DRI study is cited in Allen Wallis, *Commodity Markets and Commodity Agreements,* U.S. Department of State Current Policy No. 791, 1986.
3. See *WDR 1984,* p. 13.
4. Oil made up most of the balance, rising from about 20 percent in 1960 to over 40 percent in 1980, but, of course, these gains were available only to a lucky few.
5. See *WDR 1985,* pp. 198–199. Though the dollar figures are nominal, even in real terms using 1965 dollars there were still 12 LDCs exporting over $1 billion in manufactures, and all but 1 of the other 6 remaining were close to the billion-dollar figure. In real terms (1965 dollars) 36 countries exported $50 million or more.
6. IMF, *World Economic Outlook, 1985,* p. 176.
7. In the sections on protection in this and the next chapter, in addition to the specific references, I drew frequently on S. J. Anjaria, N. Kirmani, and A. B. Petersen, *Trade Policy Issues and Developments,* IMF Occasional Paper No. 38, 1985 and on that paper's predecessors, S. J. Anjaria, Z. Iqbal, N. Kirmani, and L. L. Perez, *Developments in International Trade Policy,* IMF Occasional Paper No. 16, 1982; and S. J. Anjaria, Z. Iqbal, L. L. Perez, and W. S. Tseng, *Trade Policy Developments in Industrial Countries,* IMF Occasional Paper No. 5, 1981. These works contributed to the way I structured this material.
8. See William R. Cline, "Can the East Asian Model of Development Be Generalized?" *World Development* 10, no. 2 (1982):81–90; and Raphael Kaplinsky, "The International Context for Industrialisation in the Coming Decade," *Journal of Development Studies* 21, no. 1 (1984):76.
9. See the interesting debate between Gustav Ranis and William Cline stimulated by Cline's "Can the East Asian Model of Development Be Generalized"; Ranis, "Can the

East Asian Model Be Generalized? A Comment," *World Development* 13, no. 4 (1985):543–545; and Cline's "Reply" in the same issue, pp. 547–548. Cline, who raised most of the objections noted in the text, agreed with Ranis that a 10 to 15 percent annual rise in exports was probably attainable. An important book that weighs judiciously the prospects of manufactured exports from the LDCs and the consequences of developed-country protection is William R. Cline, *Exports of Manufactures from Developing Countries: Performance and Prospects for Market Access,* Washington, D.C., 1984.

10. See IMF, *World Economic Outlook, 1985,* p. 183. Further data can be found in Anjaria, Kirmani, and Petersen, "Trade Policy Issues," pp. 72–73, Tables 56–60.

11. See E. Lee, ed., *Export-Led Industrialisation and Development,* Geneva, 1981.

12. See Douglas Cleveland, "It's Time to Retire the Import Penetration Ratio," *Challenge* 28, no. 4 (1985):50–53.

13. J. M. Finger, *Industrial Country Policy and Adjustment to Imports from Developing Countries,* World Bank Staff Working Paper No. 470, 1981, pp. 8, 11. Studies dating back to the Leontief paradox of the 1950s confirm that more jobs are created by a million dollars' worth of exports than by replacing a million dollars' worth of imports. Lawrence Krause has reported that the numbers are 111 jobs in exports versus 89 in import replacement. See Krause, "How Much of Current Unemployment Did We Import?" *Brookings Papers in Economic Activity,* no. 1 (1971):421–425, to which I was led by Peter H. Lindert and Charles P. Kindleberger, *International Economics,* 7th ed., Homewood, Ill., 1982, p. 76.

14. See Anjaria, Kirmani, and Petersen, "Trade Policy Issues," pp. 18–19, 22. Using weighted averages introduces a downward bias because a high tariff on an item restricts the amount of trade in that item, thus reducing its weight in the calculation. Unweighted averages avoid this problem, but have the disadvantage of giving equal weight to all items, including those in which there would have been little trade anyway. See Bela Balassa and Carol Balassa, "Industrial Protection in the Developed Countries," *The World Economy* 7, no. 2 (1984):182. The 1987 average rates will be lowest in Japan, 2.9 percent, compared to 4.3 percent in the United States, and highest in the EC members, 5.2 to 6.9 percent. From Alan V. Deardorff and Robert M. Stern, "The Economic Effects of Complete Elimination of Post-Tokyo Round Tariffs," in William R. Cline, ed., *Trade Policy in the 1980s,* Washington, D.C., 1980, p. 676. Strikingly, EC tariffs had been relatively low at the end of the 1970s, but are now relatively high.

15. For estimates of trade expansion under the GSP see Robert E. Baldwin and Tracy E. Murray, "MFN Tariff Reductions and Developing Country Trade Benefits Under the GSP," *Economic Journal* 87, no. 345 (1977):30–46. Also see T. E. Murray, *Trade Preferences for Developing Countries,* London, 1977. The gains in the 1970s were thought to be rather limited, however, only about 4 percent of the trade subject to duty. For a summary of the modeling on the subject and a statement that GSP has increased exports from developing countries, see Robert E. Baldwin, "Trade Policies in Developed Countries," in Ronald W. Jones and Peter B. Kenen, eds., *Handbook of International Economics,* Vol. 1, Amsterdam, 1984, pp. 598–600. Many figures in this section are from U.S. International Trade Commission (ITC), *Operation of the Trade Agreements Program, 36th Report, 1984,* Washington, D.C., 1985, pp. 217–221, and *37th Report, 1985,* Washington, D.C., 1986, pp. 250–252.

16. U.S. ITC, *Operation of the Trade Agreements Program, 37th Report,* p. 251.

17. See Steve Charnowitz, "Fair Labor Standards and International Trade," *Journal of World Trade Law* 20, no. 1 (1986):61–78.

18. For the figures, see Anjaria, Kirmani, and Petersen, "Trade Policy Issues," pp. 152–

154; and the sections on GSP in U.S. International Trade Commission (ITC), *Operation of the Trade Agreements Program, 36th and 37th Reports.* In this section I also utilized U.S. Department of State, "Generalized System of Preferences," *Gist,* February 1985; and Anjaria, Iqbal, Kirmani, and Perez, "Developments in International Trade Policy."

19. See Robert E. Baldwin and Tracy E. Murray, "MFN Tariff Reductions"; and Thomas B. Birnberg, "Trade Reform Options: Economic Effects of Developing and Developed Countries," in William R. Cline, ed., *Policy Alternatives for a New International Economic Order—an Economic Analysis,* New York, 1979. For a summary of the various studies on GSP benefits versus gains from multilateral tariff decreases, see Jaleel Ahmad, "Prospects of Trade Liberalization Between the Developed and the Developing Countries," *World Development* 13, no. 9 (1985):1077–1086.

20. Compare the criticism in the 1985 GATT Wisemen's Report cited by C. Michael Aho and Jonathan David Aronson, *Trade Talks,* New York, 1985, pp. 102, 115.

21. The history and analysis are covered thoroughly by W. M. Corden, *The Theory of Protection,* Oxford, 1971, pp. 35–40, 245–249.

22. The tale is from Don D. Humphrey, *The United States and the Common Market,* New York, 1964, p. 61. In actuality, the pearls were bored and temporarily threaded abroad because these steps did not transform them into "strung pearls" under U.S. law. They were put on a permanent string and provided with a clasp in the United States.

23. Several restrictive assumptions are embodied in the formula, and these are not easy to relax. It assumes producers do not substitute cheaper inputs for more expensive ones as tariffs are imposed, and it does not take into account any effect of quotas. See Peter Kenen, *The International Economy,* Englewood Cliffs, N.J., 1985, pp. 183–184. For another simplified view on how to calculate effective rates of protection, see *WDR 1986* p. 126.

24. See C. Fred Bergsten and William R. Cline, "Trade Policy in the 1980s: An Overview," in Cline, *Trade Policy in the 1980s,* p. 72. There is an analytical study by Stephen S. Golub and J. M. Finger, "The Processing of Primary Commodities: Effects of Developed-Country Tariff Escalation and Developing-Country Export Taxation," *Journal of Political Economy* 87, no. 3 (1979):559–577. With the development of large econometric models in the rich countries, it has become possible to trace more carefully the effects of any change in nominal tariffs, so the subject has gone somewhat out of fashion. But it remains important as an issue for the LDCs. See Kenen, *The International Economy,* p. 184.

25. Quoted in Brandt Commission, *North-South: A Programme for Survival,* London, 1980, pp. 141–142.

26. *WDR 1984,* p. 19. At the start of 1986, there were only 2 safeguard measures in effect in Australia, 4 in Canada, 3 in the EC, and 2 in the United States (heavyweight motorcycles and specialty steel). See U.S. ITC, *Operation of the Trade Agreements Program, 37th Report,* p. 56.

27. See U.S. ITC, *Operation of the Trade Agreements Program, 36th Report,* pp. 196–198; *37th Report,* pp. 230–231, 260–263, 267–270; and Klaus Stegemann, "Anti-Dumping Policy and the Consumer," *Journal of World Trade Law* 19, no. 5 (1985):466–484.

28. Brazil, Korea, Taiwan, and Venezuela are heavily represented. The number of new antidumping duties fell to 11 in 1985.

29. The concept of predatory pricing received a serious rebuff in March 1986, in a 5 to 4 U.S. Supreme Court decision in the case of *Matsushita Electric et al.* v. *Zenith.* In this antitrust case the court held, in a decision that many economists would applaud, that a predatory strategy is highly unlikely in the presence of substantial international competition.

30. A new departure under the dumping laws has been to bring cases against centrally planned economies where average cost is impossible to establish directly because market pricing is not used. In recent cases against China these costs were established by proxy, estimated on what they *would have been* if the product had been produced in Malaysia or the Republic of Guinea (candles) and South Korea (nails). Since labor costs in all these other countries are higher than China's, the method seems flawed.

31. See Gary Clyde Hufbauer and Joanna Shelton Erb, *Subsidies in International Trade,* Washington, D.C., 1984, especially chap. 3; Anjaria, Kirmani, and Petersen, "Trade Policy Issues," pp. 32–33, 103, 110–111; Laurie A. Cameron and Gerald C. Berg, "The U.S. Countervailing Duty Law and the Principle of General Availability," *Journal of World Trade Law* 19, no. 5 (1985):497–507; and U.S. ITC, *Operation of the Trade Agreements Program, 36th Report,* pp. 57–58, and *37th Report,* pp. 5, 70, 184, 230, 271–273.

32. The concept of "upstream subsidies" was included in the U.S. 1984 trade act. Countervailing duties can now be directed against an unsubsidized product if some principal input is subsidized.

33. U.S. ITC, *Operation of the Trade Agreements Program, 37th Report,* pp. 230, 271.

34. *Ibid.,* p. 184.

35. See Hufbauer and Erb, *Subsidies in International Trade,* pp. 68–76; U.S. ITC, *Operation of the Trade Agreements Program, 36th Report,* pp. 77–79 and *37th Report,* p. 88; and Belayneh Seyoum, "Export Subsidies Under the MTN: An Analysis with Particular Emphasis on Developing Countries," *Journal of World Trade Law* 18, no. 6 (1984):512–541. The rates for the poorest LDCs in the first half of 1986 were 8.80 percent compared to 10.95 percent for high-income countries. The "mixed credit" problem, when aid is mixed with subsidized credit, was discussed in Chapter 5 and remains an area of dispute among aid givers.

36. U.S. ITC, *Operation of the Trade Agreements Program, 37th Report,* pp. 5, 235, 237–245, 277–279.

37. Anjaria, Kirmani, and Petersen, "Trade Policy Issues," p. 22.

38. Other studies with different results, some higher than the figures in the table, include Bela Balassa and Carol Balassa, "Industrial Protection in the Developed Countries," pp. 179–196; William R. Cline, *Exports of Manufactures from Developing Countries;* David Greenway, *Trade Policy and the New Protectionism,* New York, 1983; and S. A. B. Page, "The Revival of Protectionism and Its Consequences for Europe," *Journal of Common Market Studies* 20 (September 1981): 17–40. Also see *WDR 1985,* p. 40.

39. This paragraph draws on Anjaria, Iqbal, Kirmani, and Perez, "Developments in International Trade Policy."

40. For this section, I have depended on Anjaria, Kirmani, and Petersen, "Trade Policy Issues," pp. 40–45, 122; David B. Yoffie, *Power and Protectionism: Strategies of the Newly Industrializing Countries,* New York, 1983; Martin Wolf, "Managed Trade in Practice: Implications of the Textile Arrangement," in Cline, *Trade Policy in the 1980s,* pp. 455–482; Bhagirath L. Das, "The GATT Multi-Fibre Arrangement," *Journal of World Trade Law* 17, no. 2 (1983):95–105; U.S. ITC, *Operation of the Trade Agreements Program, 36th Report,* pp. 46–48, 210–211, and *37th Report,* pp. 246–248; and Donald B. Keesing and Martin Wolf, *Textile Quotas Against Developing Countries,* London, 1980. I also consulted articles in *The Economist,* February 5 and August 20, 1983; September 1 and December 22, 1984; May 18, June 29, and July 20, 1985; and January 4, February 15, May 17, and April 5, 1986.

41. For an example of the uncertainties, consider Bangladesh. Your author lectured there in 1982 on behalf of the U.S. government and strongly recommended textiles as a possibility for manufacturing, given that country's energetic and cheap labor (60 to

90¢ per day). Entrepreneurs saw this opportunity too, and clothing exports boomed by 36 times, from 1981 to 1985, to $116 million. Six hundred new firms were established, most in 1985, creating 150,000 new jobs. The United States and Europe thereupon hit Bangladesh with quotas under the MFA. That country allocated them, unwisely, to as many firms as possible, thus making difficult the fulfillment of big overseas orders. Business slumped. After much lobbying, the United States tried to undo some of the damage in 1986 by tripling the quota for at least two years. What were entrepreneurs to think of all this? See *The Economist,* May 24, 1986, p. 67.

42. See "The Consumer Cost of U.S. Trade Restraints," *Federal Reserve Bank of New York Quarterly Review* 10, no. 2 (1985):1–12; *WDR 1984,* p. 40; and *WDR 1986,* pp. 22–23 citing a study by Orsalia Kalantzopoulos.

43. Wolf, "Managed Trade in Practice," p. 482.

44. *The Economist,* December 21, 1985, p. 70.

45. The exact limit was 1980 imports plus 6 percent annually compounded or 1984 imports, whichever was less; 1 percent growth annually would have been permitted thereafter. There were better terms (6 percent growth) for smaller exporters (countries exporting less than 1.25 percent of annual U.S. imports). Mexico and much of the Caribbean also got these better terms.

46. *The Economist,* December 21, 1985, p. 70. Somewhat different estimates of the loss are given in *South,* no. 64 (February 1986):38.

47. For this section, I utilized Ingo Walter, "Structural Adjustment and Trade Policy in the International Steel Industry," in Cline, *Trade Policy in the 1980s,* pp. 483–525; Theresa Wetter, "Trade Policy Developments in the Steel Sector," *Journal of World Trade Law,* 19, no. 5 (1985):485–496; and Anjaria, Kirmani, and Petersen, "Trade Policy Issues," pp. 36–40. There is also a recent Congressional Budget Office study on steel, *The Effects of Import Quotas on the Steel Industry,* Washington, D.C., 1984.

48. Details in this paragraph are mostly from Anjaria, Kirmani, and Petersen, "Trade Policy Issues," pp. 45–52; a longer study is Yoffie, *Power and Protectionism,* which includes other products.

49. In this section, in addition to the specific citations below, I have depended on J. D. Richardson, "Trade Adjustment Assistance Under the United States Trade Act of 1974: An Analytical Examination and Worker Survey," in Jagdish Bhagwati, ed., *Import Competition and Response,* Chicago, 1982; J. D. Richardson, "Worker Adjustment to U.S. International Trade: Programs and Prospects," in Cline, *Trade Policy in the 1980s;* Robert E. Baldwin, *The Political Economy of U.S. Import Policy,* Cambridge, Mass., 1986; and G. Glenday et al., *Worker Adjustment to Liberalized Trade: Costs and Assistance Policies,* World Bank Staff Working Paper No. 426, 1980.

50. Compare Sweden, the best example of a country using a highly active retraining and relocation program. It relies heavily on subsidies to employers to finance the training; this is done only to a very limited extent in the United States. Sweden's current annual spending on these activities (about $3 billion) is greater than the much larger United States has ever undertaken. *WDR 1979,* p. 26, points out that in the (prosperous) 1970s, a remarkable 90 percent of Swedish trainees found new jobs within nine months. In early 1986 that country was able to boast a low unemployment rate of less than 3 percent compared to 10 percent or more in much of Europe and over 7 percent in the United States.

51. In 1985, only 916 workers received job search aid; only 1,692 were granted relocation allowances. See U.S. ITC, *Operation of the Trade Agreements Program, 37th Report,* pp. 228–229.

52. Gary Clyde Hufbauer, Diane T. Berliner, and Kimberly Ann Elliott, *Trade Protection*

in the United States: 31 Case Studies, Washington, D.C., 1986. The major data from this work are summarized in Gary Clyde Hufbauer and Howard F. Rosen, *Trade Policy for Troubled Industries,* Washington, D.C., 1986, especially pp. 20–21.

53. The Roth-Moynihan bill, which did not pass in 1985, would have funded TAA with a 1 percent tariff on all imports. Cash benefits would have been conditional on acceptance of retraining.

54. See *The Economist,* June 30, 1984, p. 57; January 29 and February 19, 1983; and Anjaria, Iqbal, Kirmani, and Perez, "Developments in International Trade Policy," pp. 27–28.

55. See the Congressional Budget Office's report, *The Industrial Policy Debate,* Washington, D.C., 1983.

56. The details are from Gerald K. Helleiner, "World Market Imperfections in the Developing Countries," in William R. Cline, ed., *Policy Alternatives for a New International Economic Order,* New York, 1979; *International Economic Disorder,* chap. 2; "Freedom and Management in Primary Commodity Markets: U.S. Imports from Developing Countries," *World Development* 6, no. 1 (1978):23–30; and other works by Helleiner on the subject.

57. Information provided to me by Wilson B. Brown of the University of Winnipeg.

58. For this section, see Henry McFarland, "Transportation Costs for U.S. Imports from Developed and Developing Countries," *Journal of Development Studies* 21, no. 4 (1985):562–571; Brandt Commission, *North-South: A Programme for Survival,* p. 143; J. M. Finger and A. J. Yeats, "Effective Protection by Transportation Costs and Tariffs: A Comparison of Magnitudes," *Quarterly Journal of Economics,* 90, no. 1 (1976):169–176; and U.S. ITC, *Operation of the Trade Agreements Program, 36th Report,* p. 107.

59. Finger and Yeats, "Effective Protection by Transportation Costs and Tariffs," p. 173.

60. U.S. ITC, *Operation of the Trade Agreements Program, 36th Report,* p. 107.

61. Kaplinsky, "International Context for Industrialisation," has been relied on for this and the next paragraph.

62. This section relies heavily on Anjaria, Kirmani, and Petersen, "Trade Policy Issues," pp. 73–79, 147–150. There is a lengthy catalog of protective measures in LDCs in Office of the United States Trade Representative, *Annual Report on National Trade Estimates,* Washington, D.C., 1985.

63. For a discussion, see M. M. Kostecki and M. J. Tymowski, "Customs Duties Versus Other Import Charges in the Developing Countries," *Journal of World Trade Law* 19, no. 3 (1985):269–286.

64. *Ibid.,* and see W. M. Corden, *The Theory of Protection,* p. 199.

65. See A. F. Ewing, "Why Freer Trade in Services Is in the Interest of Developing Countries," *Journal of World Trade Law* 19, no. 2 (1985):147–169.

66. *The Economist,* October 12, 1985, p. 86; November 30, 1985, p. 67; U.S. ITC, *Operation of the Trade Agreements Program, 37th Report,* p. 114.

67. U.S. ITC, *Operation of the Trade Agreements Program, 37th Report,* p. 197.

68. But trade in manufactured goods among NICs is still quite low, only 6 percent of their total exports of such goods. See Oli Havrylyshyn and Engin Civan, "Intra-Industry Trade Among Developing Countries," *Journal of Development Economics* 18, nos. 2–3 (1985):253–271.

69. Oli Havrylyshyn explores the factor differences and advances criticisms of South-South trade in "The Direction of Developing Country Trade: Empirical Evidence of Differences Between South-South and South-North Trade," *Journal of Development Economics* 19, no. 3 (1986):255–281.

70. There is a thorough examination of customs unions among LDCs, citing many sources, in Constantine V. Vaitsos, "Crisis in Regional Economic Cooperation (Integration) Among Developing Countries: A Survey," in Paul Streeten and Richard Jolly, eds., *Recent Issues in World Development,* Oxford, 1981, pp. 279–329. I benefited from Gerald M. Meier's discussion of when unions among LDCs will be advantageous in *Leading Issues in Economic Development,* 4th ed., Oxford, 1984, pp. 561–566. I also utilized Pan A. Yotopoulos and Jeffrey B. Nugent, *Economics of Development: Empirical Investigations,* New York, 1976 pp. 347–364.

71. See "Market-Integration and Market-Sharing Schemes," in B. P. Menon, *Bridges Across the South,* New York, 1980, pp. 106–111; and *South,* no. 72 (October 1986): 97–98.

72. *The Economist,* November 8, 1980; June 5, 1982; August 2, 1986; *South,* no. 72 (October 1986):96; and Vaitsos, "Crisis in Regional Economic Cooperation (Integration)," in Streeten and Jolly, *Recent Issues in World Development,* pp. 279–329.

73. *The Economist,* September 28, 1985, p. 70.

74. *The Economist,* July 2, 1983; February 15, 1986.

75. See Bruce Herrick and Charles P. Kindleberger, *Economic Development,* 4th ed., New York, 1983 p. 483.

76. Anne O. Krueger, "Trade Strategies and Employment in Developing Countries," *Finance and Development* 21, no. 2 (1984):25.

77. See Rolf J. Langhammer, "Multilateral Trade Liberalization Among Developing Countries," *Journal of World Trade Law* 14, no. 6 (1980):508–515.

78. U.S. ITC, *Operation of the Trade Agreements Program, 37th Report,* p. 95.

79. *WDR 1986,* p. 144, contends that the preferences to the ACP countries have had limited benefits. The margins are slim, trade diversion has predominated, monopsonistic European buyers have captured some of the preferences, and the poorest ACP states have not been flexible enough to take advantage of the arrangement.

80. For this section I have drawn on Richard E. Feinberg and Richard Newfarmer, "The Caribbean Basin Initiative: Bold Plan or Empty Promise," in Richard Newfarmer, ed., *From Gunboats to Diplomacy,* Baltimore, 1984; W. Charles Sawyer and Richard L. Sprinkle, "Caribbean Basin Recovery Act," *Journal of World Trade Law* 18, no. 5 (1984):429–436; U.S. ITC, *Operation of the Trade Agreements Program, 35th Report,* pp. 25–36, *36th Report,* pp. 213–217, 251–253, *37th Report,* pp. 5, 254–256, 287–288; articles in the *Wall Street Journal* and *Christian Science Monitor;* and personal communications from the Caribbean Basin Business Information Center of the U.S. Department of Commerce.

81. *Wall Street Journal,* October 2, 1985.

82. See Sidney Weintraub, "A U.S.-Israel Free-Trade Area," *Challenge* 28, no. 3 (1985): 47–50; and U.S. ITC, *Operation of the Trade Agreements Program, 36th Report,* pp. 26–29, and *37th Report,* pp. 111–112.

83. Richard Pomfret, "The Quiet Shift in U.S. Trade Policy," *Challenge* 27, no. 5 (1984): 61–64.

chapter 15

Primary Product Exporting and Its Problems

Primary product exports face difficulties in addition to the long-run ones associated with the terms of trade issue discussed in Chapter 12. Just as manufactured goods must contend with protectionist barriers, so must agricultural and mineral commodities, though usually only when developed countries also produce the item in question. On top of that, the primary product exporter must also contend with a notorious tendency for the prices of these products to be unstable in the short run. When prices fluctuate violently, so in some degree may the income earned from exporting. This problem has generated interesting and innovative ideas on how to dampen the fluctuations.

DEVELOPED-COUNTRY PROTECTION AGAINST PRIMARY PRODUCTS

The situation is mixed. Clearly, LDCs will never be able to compete in some temperate zone crops for reasons of climate. Just as clearly, many LDC commodity exports face little or no competition from developed-country producers and therefore encounter no protection. A long list of primary products enters free of any duty and is not subject to any other barrier at all. (As we saw in the last chapter, there is still the problem of high effective protection caused by the escalation of tariffs on semifinished and finished goods. The import of *processed* primary products into developed countries is still discriminated against.[1])

In between the commodities which LDCs do not produce and those on which there is no protection is an area of competition where LDCs with a comparative advantage could gain from trade in the absence of barriers. Unfortu-

nately, it is easier to erect barriers against primary products than against manufactured goods because they are so homogeneous—their characteristics cannot
ordinarily be changed to avoid a barrier, as can be true of manufactures.

It is not surprising that little progress has been made in reducing the
barriers to agricultural trade, given the strength of producer interests, especially
in the EC, but also in the United States and Japan. The Tokyo Round tariff
reductions averaged well over 30 percent for industrial goods, but only 7 percent
for agricultural commodities, and only about a third of total agricultural trade
was included in the tariff cuts. Fully 29 percent of LDC exports of these commodities were subject to nontariff barriers in 1983, and the figure is higher than
that in some very rich countries, including Norway, Sweden, Switzerland, and the
whole of the EC.[2] The Tokyo Round failed to liberalize the many national quotas
against agricultural trade. These are legal, there being a GATT rules exemption
covering agricultural quotas, dating from 1955 and instigated by the United
States.

Major protection against imports from the LDCs occurs with sugar, peanuts and peanut oil, beef, cotton, tobacco, and fresh fruits and vegetables. The
situation is worsening: for example the import penetration of sugar from LDCs
into all industrial countries was 7.8 percent in 1970 but only 3.9 percent in 1980;
for beef and veal, the LDC share fell from 2.3 percent to 0.9 percent; for tomatoes
the fall was from 5.3 percent to 4.7 percent. Overall, LDCs produced 63.1 percent
of the world's total agricultural exports in 1961 to 1963; that figure had fallen
sharply to only 48.4 percent in the period 1982 to 1984.[3] The pattern of protection
differs significantly among the developed countries. We examine the salient details below.

U.S. Protection

The U.S. quotas with the most effect on LDCs are the extremely tight ones for
cotton, peanuts, and dairy products (butter, milk, cheese) and the larger but more
damaging one for sugar.[4] All protect a price support program in one form or
another. All involve products that could be important for LDCs; cotton worldwide, peanuts mainly in Africa, dairy products in parts of Latin America, and
sugar in many tropical regions of requisite rainfall.

The cotton quotas currently in force in the United States virtually exclude
imports. Total upland cotton production in the U.S. in 1980 totaled 15,646,000
bales. Total imports were 28,000 bales, or 0.002 percent of the market! The quotas
are by country. Some are not completely laughable, 18,500 bales from Mexico,
for example. But some *are,* such as less than one bale for Iraq, Haiti, and
Colombia. The quota for extra-long staple cotton is almost equally ludicrous,
totaling only 95,000 bales. The higher cost of the protected cotton is one reason
why the textile industry has sought the barriers against LDC exports discussed
in the last chapter.

Peanuts are a similar case. U.S. production is about 1.4 million metric
tonnes a year. The global quota, unchanged since 1953, is 775 tonnes, and even
that 0.00055 percent of the market must pay a high tariff.

The butter and cheese quotas are also extremely restrictive, although this is of concern only to a small number of LDCs. Possible producers face a quota equivalent to 0.06 percent of U.S. butter production, and cheese quotas of 0.3 to 14.0 percent of U.S. production, depending on the type of cheese.

Protectionism in beef is embodied in U.S. law and involves quotas figured on a base adjusted for cyclical domestic production. Although restrictions have not usually been applied in recent years, the strict inspection requirements serve to exclude some beef (and poultry) anyway. On January 1, 1984, imports from 14 countries, including the Dominican Republic, El Salvador, Haiti, Mexico, Nicaragua, Panama, and Honduras, were banned as not meeting U.S. inspection requirements. The ban has only a superficial connection with health and appears principally designed to keep out imports.

The sugar quotas have the worst effect, because sugarcane can be grown efficiently in at least 100 countries, some of them very poor and with no other good export opportunities. Refining may be the start of industrialization; long-run prospects are promising because of the high income elasticity of demand in LDCs. The refusal of Congress to vote sufficient funds for sugar price supports in 1982 led to an imposition of country quotas based on historical performance. (There had been quotas before, dating from the days of the New Deal, but they had disappeared in the 1970s.) U.S. imports of 5 million tons in 1981 were immediately cut back to 2.8 million in 1982, and again to 1.7 million tons (for 10 months) in December, 1985, when the quotas were tightened again. The U.S. share of world raw sugar imports, which averaged over 20 percent between 1960 and 1973, fell to only 10 percent in the early 1980s.[5]

The quotas represent a tremendous lobbying success for the strongly united U.S. sugar producers, of which there are only 11,000 in all. At the start of 1986 sugar was selling on world markets at about 5¢ per pound, up from a little over 3¢ six months before. The U.S. support price, also paid for imports coming in under the quota, was 18¢ per pound. Even 3¢ sugar cannot beat a quota, and thus this appalling price differential is maintained. It is estimated that during the 1982–1983 crop year, U.S. growers gleaned $1.5 billion (well over $100,000 per grower) from this system. The only reason the country was not swamped with domestically produced sugar is that production costs are high. Meanwhile U.S. consumers paid approximately $3 billion more, or about $100 extra for a family of four, for their sugar. Though the quotas were originally announced as a temporary expedient, Congress renewed them for five years in December 1985.

The imposition of the sugar quotas by country has the effect of freezing market shares and making it impossible for potential exporters to follow their comparative advantage. Table 15.1 shows a selection of current quota allocations. Note that some very small countries, Belize for instance, might possibly not be able to compete effectively in a free market with sugar juggernauts such as the Dominican Republic. Logically, then, they will welcome the quotas with their guaranteed access to a high price market. Politically, this can to some degree "buy off" LDC opposition and dilute the force of the argument against them; this principle is obviously fully understood by the sugar lobby.

In 1984 U.S. sugar producers charged that some sugar was slipping into the

Table 15.1   U.S. SUGAR QUOTA ALLOCATIONS, PERCENT

Argentina	4.3
Australia	8.3
Brazil	14.5
Dominican Republic	17.6
Philippines	13.5
South Africa	2.3
Barbados	0.7
Belize	1.1
Guyana	1.2
Haiti	0.3
India	0.8
Mauritius	1.1
Mexico	0.3
Trinidad	0.7

Source: U.S. Tariff Schedule.

country by being included in other products. The government agreed, and in January 1985 it placed additional quotas (sometimes set at the zero level of imports) on sugar-based syrups, sweetened cocoa, pancake and flour mix, sauces, confections, and frozen pizzas(!)—all contain sugar. There was some fraud in 1985; importers permitted to buy cheap foreign sugar, refine it, and re-export it were caught selling in the U.S.—nice confirmation that government measures of this sort are commonly an open invitation to corruption, even in a very rich developed country. A side issue is that expensive high fructose corn sweetener, a sugar substitute, has now become artificially competitive with sugar, so its use is growing. Of course, the corn growers, too, then lobby for the continuation of the sugar quotas against the efficient producers. If a strong statement may be permitted, the whole episode is scandalous economics.

One other recent U.S. program is an outstanding example of how better treatment for farmers at home can compound the difficulties for the LDCs. Rice is a major third world export item, but U.S. rice producers managed to convince Congress in 1985 that they should receive federal subsidies on any exports they make. As a result of these subsidies, in April, 1986, U.S. rice was selling on world markets for about half its 1985 price. The repercussions for the LDCs could be severe.[6]

Japanese Protection

Japan is also highly protectionist, using 22 categories of quotas (it was 500 in the 1960s) plus state trading by the Japan Food Agency, which levies a de facto tariff by reselling to domestic buyers at prices above what the agency paid. Recent studies show costs of the protection amount to more than half the value of total farm output, about 2 percent of GNP, with Japanese consumers devoting 32 percent of their spending to food in 1981, well above the U.S. figure of 20 percent. The Japanese find steaks cost over $20 in their supermarkets, and strict limits on sugar imports raise the domestic selling price in a usual range of 100 to 200 percent over the world price. Farmers receive eight to ten times the world price for rice, though consumers pay "only" five to six times more because of expensive subsidies that have recently been running at about $3.5 billion per year.[7] The very high prices for these products are due to price support programs; these in turn necessitate barriers against imports that would otherwise flood in. The high price supports result in government holdings of surpluses, which then require export subsidies to be rid of them. Farming in Japan is not very efficient, The land laws keep farms small, and two-thirds of the country's rice is produced by people who also hold other jobs. But due to the geographical structure of the voting laws, farmers are politically powerful. The usual reason given by Japanese politicians for these policies, that an island nation is buying food security, does not seem tenable. A war or boycott that cut off imported food would also presumably cut off imported petroleum-based fertilizers, without which Japanese agriculture could not feed the country. Japan could be a major importer of third world rice and beef were reforms to be undertaken. More importantly for its own sake, it could remove one of the reasons U.S. protectionists use when they advocate retaliation against Japanese exports.

Protection in the EC

The most costly protection is in the EC, under the Common Agricultural Policy (CAP).[8] The EC's principal tool is the simple purchase of surpluses at a floor price; there are few provisions for controls on acreage and production. The main protected products of interest to the LDCs are wheat, dairy products, beef, wine, and sugar, especially the latter. All are about 30 to 60 percent higher in price within the EC than their price in world trade. To maintain the supports, imports must of course be restricted. This is accomplished by quotas and by the so-called variable levy, a tariff that rises when world prices fall and vice versa.[9] The quotas on sugar are especially tight, about 70 percent the size of the U.S. quota and available for the most part only to the ACP (African-Caribbean-Pacific) states. The variable levy is considerably more destabilizing for world trade than a constant tariff would be. In a boom year abroad world prices fall, so the tariff is higher; in a poor year abroad prices rise, so the tariff falls automatically.

Thus protected, the EC pursues its purchases to maintain price, with spending on farm surpluses rising 20 percent a year in most years since 1975, to a point where such spending is now over 70 percent of all EC official spending. The resulting "mountains" of surplus commodities in late 1985 were mostly at record highs, as shown in Table 15.2. (On occasion the butter has been fed to cows which then, of course, produce more butter).

Some reforms have been attempted, including quotas on new planting of sugar beets and reductions in some of the support prices. Even so, almost nothing

**Table 15.2   SIZE OF EC SURPLUS
COMMODITY "MOUNTAINS"
AND WINE "LAKE," LATE
1985**

Butter	1.2 million tonnes
Milk powder	0.5 million tonnes
Beef	0.8 million tonnes
Wheat	12.2 million tonnes
Wine	870 million gallons
Sugar	4.8 million tonnes

Source: The Economist, December 21, 1985, p. 36.

can save the CAP from eventually running out of money unless major changes are implemented. Spain and Portugal joined the EC on January 1, 1986. At a stroke that increased the Community's farmed area by 34 percent, its farmers by 38 percent, its farms by 40 percent, but its number of consumers by only 14 percent. Vegetable output will rise by a quarter, fruit by nearly half, olive oil by 59 percent.[10] Unless the CAP prices are changed radically, this will balloon both the surplus and its costs.

The EC members obviously want to get rid of its huge, unwanted surplus. They could dump it or donate it as aid. In 1981, for example, they gave away 928,000 tons of cereals, 150,000 tons of milk powder, and 45,000 tons of butter, much to the LDCs, some to Poland; the mountain has been the source of most EC food aid for African famine relief. They could also sell it cheaply to nontraditional markets, such as the USSR and Iran, as has been done from time to time.

For the most part, though, they have usually subsidized its export to world markets.[11] For the LDCs this amounts to being kicked when you are down. Not only are markets lost because of the protection, but the subsidized EC exports capture other markets outside the Community. In the Tokyo Round of trade negotiations the rest of the world agreed to the subsidies only if the EC did not expand beyond its existing markets, but the expansion has clearly happened. For example, the EC was a net importer of dairy products, sugar, and beef as late as 1974. Now it is the world's largest exporter of dairy products, challenges Argentina as number 2 in beef exports, and is number 3 in wheat. Least forgivable, the Community now produces about 25 percent more sugar (from sugar beets, not cane) than it consumes. That has made it the free world's largest exporter of sugar, all subsidized, of course, at a loss of about $350 on each tonne exported, and now accounting for some 18 percent of world trade in that commodity. The EC's share of all world food exports, only 8.3 percent in 1976, was 18.3 percent by 1981.[12] In the process resources have been retained in agriculture that would otherwise have been pushed out long ago; in 1985 7.7 percent of the EC's labor force was still in agriculture compared to less than half that (3.6 percent) in the generally lower cost United States.

Recently, the Community has been spending on the CAP about $18 to $21 billion annually in direct budgetary costs. One-fourth to one-third of that has been on subsidies for agricultural exports, while the remainder went for price support.[13] These costs do not count the large additional spending by individual EC countries on their farmers, nor the resulting higher food prices for consumers, in Britain perhaps 10 percent over what they would be without the Common Agricultural Policy. The total transfer from European taxpayers and consumers is estimated to range from $60 billion to $70 billion per year; over half the value added in farming comes from these transfers. Even these huge figures ignore completely the costs to LDCs that lose markets in the Community because of the protection and outside it because of the subsidies.

The LDCs pay an even greater penalty because they are now innocent bystanders to an incipient trade war between the United States and the EC on this issue. America is obviously a big loser. Because of the variable levy, the share of the Community in total U.S. agricultural exports fell from 35 percent in 1960 to 25 percent in 1974 and 21.6 percent in 1980; the United States finds third-country markets disappearing because of the subsidized exports. The Department of Agriculture estimates that because of the CAP, nearly $6 billion per year in agricultural exports are lost. The United States brought a complaint to GATT about EC export subsidies for flour, claiming that they violate the prohibition against nonprimary product export subsidies, and retaliated with subsidies on a million tons of flour to recapture the Egyptian market where the EC had made inroads. In 1985 the United States accumulated a $1 billion 3-year war chest to finance subsidized sales mainly to North Africa and the Middle East. A new program, the Bonus Incentive Commodity Export Program (BICEP), distributed free food from surplus government stocks along with regular sales; this particular muscle was first exercised in a sale to Algeria in 1985.

The EC quickly counter-retaliated, boosting its export subsidies on wheat 34 percent in September 1985 and granting extra subsidies on sales to China, a large U.S. customer. Wrangling continued in GATT, with the United States threatening to dump its $3 billion butter surplus in Europe's overseas dairy product markets or put tariffs on beer, wine, cognac, cheese, and wool. Many economists have pointed out that a shift to income support for farmers, and away from farm price supports backed by tariffs and quotas, would bring a major fall in prices for consumers and would not require an export subsidy. But, of course, *efficient* farmers stand to gain much more from support prices plus protection than they do from income supplements. Furthermore, the costs of the supplements would be visible in the budget, whereas higher prices to consumers are far less obviously attributable to government action; thus reform does not occur.

The Results of Protection Against Agricultural Commodities

The clear result of the widespread protection in agriculture is harm for the LDCs in their export markets, and harm to their domestic production as well, since commodity prices are pushed lower by the developed-country export subsidies. For the developed countries, the protection is part of a much wider web of price support and income maintenance for farmers that involves extreme expense.

Quantitative estimates of the impact are large. One recent study by R. Ayers and K. Anderson cited in the *World Development Report* for 1986 uses simulations based on the rates of protection in the period 1980 to 1982, and examines the gains that would accrue if the barriers were removed on the main temperate zone commodities.[14] The resulting cost figures are an underestimate because protection is higher now than it was then, because inclusion of the tropical commodities would raise the benefits even further, and because no account is taken of any dynamic as opposed to static gains. Even with these restrictive conditions, the simulations show that if the developed countries and the LDCs were to liberalize their agricultural trade barriers at the same time, then the former would gain $45.9 billion and the latter would gain about 40 percent of that, or $18.3 billion. (LDCs also protect their domestic markets; in the 15 largest LDC importers, nontariff barriers apply to 31 percent of the commodities traded, compared to only 23.5 percent of their manufactured imports.[15])

The total predicted gains, $64 billion, would be more than double the current amount of foreign aid. This huge amount would seem to hint that reform must be imminent, but not so! The gain of $45.9 billion for the developed countries is actually a net figure, comprising large benefits to consumers and taxpayers but losses to producers, who would lose their price supports. Hence reform does not occur.

Another recent study, by Burniaux and Waelbroeck, considers the most expensive and protective of the developed-country schemes, the EC's Common Agricultural Policy.[16] The study estimates that LDCs as a whole would gain an additional 2.9 percent in real national income by 1995 if the CAP were scrapped.

The largest loss in export revenue to the LDCs is from developed country sugar protection. The costs of this alone ($7.4 billion) are thought to be equal to 30 percent of all foreign aid. The damage is especially severe in Latin America (Dominican Republic, Mexico), the Philippines, and India.[17] Every million tonnes that could be gained back by the LDCs in the world sugar market would yield them about a quarter of a billion dollars when sugar is at 10¢ per pound. But rather than rising, LDC sugar exports to the developed countries have been falling for over a decade in spite of their obvious comparative advantage in this commodity. The situation is deplorable. For beef, the estimated loss of export revenue to LDCs is in the area of $5.1 billion, with the effects concentrated in Argentina, Brazil, and Uruguay.[18] All are presently losing sales to the EC's subsidized beef exports, which cost twice as much to produce. "A triumph of the least efficient over the most efficient," said the Argentine secretary of commerce —and he was right.[19]

It is ironic that, for all the billions of dollars they shower on their agricultural sectors, developed countries do not appear to be buying what they expect to buy from their farming policies.[20] Better-off farmers clearly gain the most whenever farm assistance is tied to production totals; the smaller and poorer farmers gain much less and are still leaving farming, so that the sector as a whole continues to shrink. The assistance gets built in to land values, since land is worth more when the crops grown on it command price supports. Thus those who sell their farms are large gainers while newcomers to farming, having paid high prices or high rents for land, now have a vested interest in opposing reform. Finally, by raising the price of food, the developed-country agricultural policies in effect are an especially regressive form of taxation, a heavy burden on poor consumers. Presumably the public will not stand for this situation forever, but it has certainly lasted for a long time.

The GATT membership has agreed to include agriculture in the forthcoming Uruguay Round of trade talks. But as long as the developed countries support their farmers as they presently do, a solution satisfactory to the LDCs (and economists) will not be easy.

PRICE AND INCOME VOLATILITY IN PRIMARY PRODUCT EXPORTING

There are economic reasons to expect, and evidence to indicate, that price fluctuations for primary products are on average considerably greater than they are for manufactured goods. The pattern of surge and collapse will, it is said, have a serious detrimental effect on the progress of countries exporting these commodities. The price changes may cause the incomes of producers to rise and fall. When they will and when they will not are examined later in this chapter. Income changes, if they occur, will cause a spreading multiplier effect, with the sales of those who supply inputs for commodity producers, and those who produce goods consumed by them, directly affected. The country's tax revenues will swing sympathetically, especially if export taxes are important. The supply and demand for credit is likely to gyrate also and therefore so will interest rates, generating further instability in investment.[21] All the foregoing means development plans will be hit with unpredictable shocks.

The difficulties are greatest when a country is highly specialized in exporting, for then there is little spreading of the risk. Indeed, in recent years some 30 LDCs obtained over 80 percent of their export revenues from no more than three primary products, and there were about 30 more where the figure lay between 60 percent and 80 percent. Oil makes up over 90 percent of the exports of Iran, Nigeria, Venezuela, and the Arab oil states; copper is currently 83 percent of Zambia's total; coffee is 36 percent in Tanzania and 55 percent in Colombia, while alumina is 52 percent in Jamaica. Compare America's largest, corn, which generates about 4 percent of U.S. export revenue.

Specialization obviously increases risk, but this would matter far less if price fluctuations were infrequent. There is plenty of evidence, however, that the swings are both frequent and intense. The average annual fluctuation in 50 primary product prices, expressed as movement away from a trend line, was 13 percent between 1900 and 1958.[22] Since then, the history of wide price swings has continued, as seen in Figure 15.1, which covers the period from 1971 to 1982.

How is it possible that these price fluctuations are so large?[23] The answer lies in the elasticities of the demand and supply curves and in the large shifts that these curves typically undergo. First let us consider the elasticities. Elementary analysis indicates that large price shifts will occur if demand and supply are highly inelastic, as in Figure 15.2. Any small shift either in supply or demand

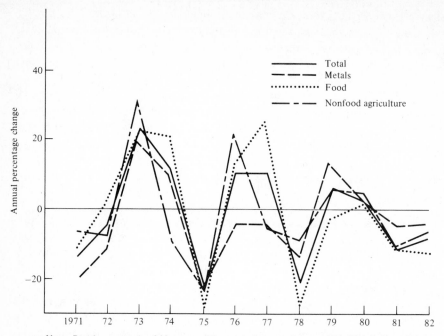

Note: Based on a sample of 33 commodities, excluding petroleum, weighted by current values of developing-country commodity exports, deflated by the manufacturing unit value index.

Figure 15.1   Annual fluctuations in developing-country export prices, 1971 to 1982. (*WDR 1982*, p. 12.)

causes a large change in price. (Figure 15.2a shows a small rise in supply and a large fall in price; Figure 15.2b shows a small increase in demand and a large rise in price.)

Most agricultural commodities do have a very low short-run supply elasticity, often near zero, because it is so difficult to obtain any increase in output

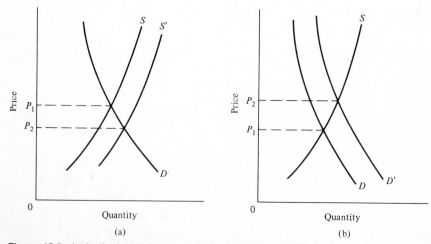

Figure 15.2   Inelastic demand and supply lead to large price fluctuations.

between one harvest and another. The means for increasing yields in the middle of the growing season are very limited. Tree crops (cocoa, coffee, tea, rubber, palm oil) have even greater price inelasticities of supply, as they take several years to bear following a first planting. Mineral production can often be increased only by large-scale investment in mining or drilling, a slow and expensive process. The low short-run supply elasticities are shown in Table 15.3. (The long-run supply elasticities are much higher.)

A low price elasticity of developed-country demand for tropical agricultural commodities is also well documented. Most of the foods and beverages absorb little of the consumer's total food bill, but are also important in most people's lives. By their nature, their use does not expand greatly as prices fall. (Note how well sugar, coffee, cocoa, and tea fit this description.) For the industrial raw materials, such as sisal and jute, the limited uses of the product make demand even less sensitive to price. The demand elasticities are also thus quite low, as seen in Table 15.3. The figures cited are long-run; in the short run they would be lower yet. These low elasticities go a long way toward explaining the long-standing instability of commodity prices.

Variability of short-run supply is the second important factor. For agricultural products, weather is the great unknown. For example, episodes of frost in Brazil ruined the coffee crop once in the 1970s and again in 1986; given the underlying inelasticities, the swings in price were substantial. Epidemic plant diseases are also unpredictable. Adding to the volatility, producers may behave as in the "cobweb theorem," raising and lowering output in response to cyclical price changes in a fashion that reinforces the price instabilities.

Finally, variations in demand can also be large for some products. Though generally not true of the foods and beverages, demand instability certainly affects many minerals because that demand is so closely tied to the business cycle in the developed countries. As income swings in these countries, so demand swings in

Table 15.3   SHORT-RUN SUPPLY AND LONG-RUN DEMAND ELASTICITIES, VARIOUS PRIMARY PRODUCTS

	Price elasticity of supply	Price elasticity of demand
Coffee	0.2	−0.6
Cocoa	0.2	−0.4
Tea	0.1	−0.2
Sugar	0.5	−0.3
Cotton	0.3	−0.4
Rubber	0.2	−0.8
Jute	0.5	approx. 0.0
Sisal	0.5	approx. 0.0
Copper	0.1	−0.2
Tin	0.0	−5.0

Source: From Jere R. Behrman, "International Commodity Agreements: An Evaluation of the UNCTAD Integrated Commodity Programme," in William R. Cline, ed., *Policy Alternatives for a New International Economic Order,* New York, 1979, pp. 118–121.[24]

the LDC producers. Income elasticities of demand as high as 5.0 have been noted (for tin); for many metals and minerals used as inputs, a given percentage rise or fall in output of the final product results in a rise or fall in purchases of the input of approximately the same percent. A "minerals accelerator" has even been reported, with falling demand for a final product resulting in proportionally greater fall in mineral demand as producers draw down their raw material inventories, and vice versa.[25]

How Harmful Is the Price Variability?

Given the obvious ill effects that would seem to stem from highly variable export prices, it may come as rather a surprise to find that degree of harm is quite debatable. Alasdair MacBean's initial study of twenty years ago basically revealed little statistical evidence that instability of export earnings is detrimental to economic growth. Economists were perhaps a bit skeptical at first, but these results have now been replicated a number of times by other scholars.[26] Apparently, the fluctuations in export revenue sometimes even lead to *higher* levels of saving to avoid risks, which in turn leads to a higher level of investment. Anne Krueger writes, "It seems reasonable to conclude that if there are negative feedbacks from instability to growth, they are sufficiently small in magnitude relative to other factors contributing to growth that it is difficult to find robust empirical tests that detect them."[27]

This is ironic, since the most important new departure contained in the debates over a "new international economic order" that occupied much of the 1970s was the ambitious proposal to stabilize primary product prices by means of international commodity agreements. It should be noted, however, that the statistical research on the subject is relatively sensitive to small changes in assumptions and that small countries, where the income swings would presumably be greatest, are typically omitted from the studies. (Small countries are more specialized in their exporting, so the effect on income is intensified. Further, if crop failure occurs, there would be no price rise on world markets to counteract the fall in quantity.) When the swings in income are large and not easily predictable, there would likely be repercussions on entrepreneurial and official behavior. A more cautious approach to investment would then seem justified.

THE ROCKY PATH TO A NEW INTERNATIONAL ECONOMIC ORDER (NIEO)

Every few years the United Nations Commission on Trade and Development holds a large international conference (the last was at Belgrade, Yugoslavia, in 1983) that has come to be a major sounding board for LDC complaints about the world trading order. The first organized calls for a new international economic order (NIEO) were heard in 1974, and by about 1980 the movement was at its peak.[28] NIEO envisaged numerous reforms of varying degrees of defensibility and practicality. In the proposed package at one time or another were extended GSP tariff preferences and enlarged GSTP global trade preferences; removal of high effective protection on processed goods; a brain drain tax, a sea resource tax, a tax on arms and trade; an SDR link; and reforms in the IMF and World Bank. (These topics have already been covered; a look at the index will show where.)

Also in the NIEO proposals, however, were two major schemes for offsetting the variability in primary product prices: the Integrated Program for Commodities (IPC) for stabilizing the prices of numerous important exports and a fund to finance shortfalls in LDC export earnings. These have generated an enormous debate that still continues. We survey that debate in the remainder of this chapter.

NIEO's peak in about 1980 coincided with the election of much more conservative governments in the United States and Great Britain and with the onset of a recession that tended to break down the unity with which the LDCs had pursued the goals of price and income stabilization. By 1986 the enthusiasm felt for NIEO had become much muted, with the developed countries far less supportive, and the LDCs (on the surface, at any rate) more inclined to work through existing institutions rather than pressing for new ones. But an Integrated Program for Commodities did at least get a start, and there are two existing plans for stabilizing export revenues, one run by the IMF and the other by the EC for its associated ACP states.

RAISING COMMODITY PRICES BY MEANS OF INTERNATIONAL AGREEMENTS

International agreements to stabilize the swings in commodity prices or to increase those prices or both have a long intellectual history, and there have been more practical examples than is generally realized.[29] There had been an agreement to restrict sugar output and raise prices as early as 1902, and at the Bretton Woods Conference of 1944 John Maynard Keynes was suggesting an international commodity system. Soon thereafter, the American economist Benjamin Graham advocated that price stabilization for commodities be funded through the use of the resources of the new IMF. Though nothing came of these proposals at the time, they eventually did germinate.

There have always been two distinct alternative arrangements for commodities. One could try to restrict output by means of export quotas or export taxes and so raise prices, or one could maintain an international stockpile ("buffer stock") of a given commodity, adding to it when prices are low and selling from it when they are high, to achieve price stabilization. The two aims are of course very different in their appeal. Producers typically prefer higher prices to stabilization; consumers typically support either stabilization or a free market. Much about the politics of commodity agreements becomes clearer when this is remembered.

Raising Prices by Means of Quotas on Output

Quota arrangements to restrict output have had a much longer history than have buffer stocks. Long ago it was realized that few countries had much chance of influencing world prices through individual action, because a single country generally provided too small a proportion of total supply to affect the world market to any great extent. Only rarely (Chile with nitrates before World War I, Brazil with coffee before World War II, Pakistan with jute and Ghana with cocoa briefly after that war, and Saudi Arabia with oil in the 1970s) has a single country been able to exercise commodity power. The importance of elasticity conditions in determining when it is profitable for a single country to restrict supply was considered at length when we discussed export taxation in Chapter 4.

It was also realized that an individual country's lack of monopoly power might be rectified by cartels of producers. The first attempts on an international level were crude quota arrangements wherein producers agreed to limit output, with the limits usually adjustable according to the state of the market. Generally any fall in prices would be resisted by tightened quotas; less frequently, higher prices would result in liberalized quotas. In a fully formed quota arrangement shares are assigned, usually based on past performance, and the building up of new production capacity in the member countries is prohibited. Within each member a mechanism is put into place for allocating a share of the country's quota to existing producers. In addition to the original sugar agreement of 1902, other early examples include tin (1921), tea (1933), rubber (1934), and coffee (1962). The International Coffee Organization, set up to administer the 1962 agreement, urged its members to limit production by uprooting trees. Brazil, which exported about 40 percent of the world's coffee at the time, tore up a million trees and cut its crop by a quarter.

Economists have traditionally looked askance at quota schemes, not because they cannot work in the interests of the LDCs, but because the circumstances in which they do work are so limited.[30] The price elasticity of demand for the product must be low, meaning consumers cannot easily shift to substitutes if prices are forced up by the quotas. Otherwise, falling sales volume may offset the gain in price. Income elasticity of demand should be high, so that economic growth will cause growth in the demand for the product. There ought to be only a small number of members in the cartel, and they ought to believe that joint action is in their best interests; this will make policing easier and limit the incentives to cheat. Supply should continue to be inelastic even after several years. Thus the entry of new members should be difficult because of technological problems, or absence of a necessary resource such as a mineral deposit, or lack of the right kind of agricultural land. If there are substitute products, the members would prefer the long-run supply elasticities of these substitutes to be low so their production cannot easily expand. Profit maximizing should perhaps not be pushed too far, with prices kept low enough to discourage the entry of competitors who would find high prices attractive. (This is the "limit price" logic of the textbooks.) It helps if the commodity is storable at low cost (metals, oil, rubber, coffee) and does not always have to be dumped on the market as soon as it is produced (bananas, fresh meat). Finally, it will be an advantage if the members of the cartel have similar cost structures and market shares, for then there will be less debate on where to set prices and how to allocate production.

A quota scheme that initially succeeds in raising prices and hence earnings will predictably encourage additional production both in members and in non-members of the cartel and a search for substitutes by consumers. Jere Behrman's study of 51 attempts to raise prices found many did not sufficiently satisfy the conditions noted above; the median length of time before the attempt was abandoned was 2½ years.[31] Behrman concluded that the major cause of failure where quota schemes were employed has been competition among the members, each knowing that if it could increase its market share at the high cartel price, it could greatly increase revenues.

A second important cause of failure has been the development of production in nonmembers. Typically, a cartel attempts to control this by attracting the nonmembers into membership. But this necessitates granting them handsome quotas and so dilutes the advantages of the original members. Another possibility is including consuming countries in the cartel, obtaining their help in policing the agreement. Consumers might be enticed by more generous prices than the cartel would otherwise offer. This has proved difficult, however. Consumers and producers are uncomfortable bedfellows: the cartel may spend most of its time debating the degree of supply restriction and the price to be defended.

Substitute products also pose a serious problem for price-raising cartels. Most important primary products do face potential competition if their prices are raised, as seen in Table 15.4.[32] For some products (rubber, jute) the price of the competing substitutes now governs the market. For others (tin, sugar, copper) it is important. Only a few commodities (coffee, tea) have no direct competitors, and even here the possibility that consumers would switch to other beverages limits any possibilities for price enhancement. Cola drinks, for example, have already made major inroads into the coffee market among the "under 30s" in the United States.

Finally, it should be noted that even if the cartel works perfectly to raise long-run prices and incomes, the results might not be fully desirable from the standpoint of the development economist. LDCs consume these products, too; have-nots lose at the expense of the haves, and the have-nots might be poorer. Nor is there any guarantee that a cartel will do much for the mass of population even in a country clearly receiving benefits. It has not escaped notice that producer interests—plantations, landowners, merchant firms, transport companies,

Table 15.4 COMPETITION FACING IMPORTANT PRIMARY PRODUCTS

Primary product	Competition
Rubber	Synthetic rubber, plastics
Cotton	Other natural and synthetic fibers
Tin	New technology permitting thinner tin plating; plastic can lining; paper, aluminum, and plastic containers
Jute	Polypropylene and polyethylene
Sugar	High fructose corn sweeteners
Copper	Aluminum, glass fiber, plastics
Bauxite	Plastics, aluminum recycling
Cocoa	Artificial chocolate flavoring, vegetable oil extenders

banks—are usually first in line to lobby for cartels of this sort and fierce in their defense.

The Special (and Remarkable) Case of Oil

No one who drove a car in the 1970s needs to be reminded that supply restriction for one product, oil, was and remains a remarkable special case. Understanding why the Organization of Petroleum Exporting Countries (OPEC) succeeded for so long when many commodity cartels had failed is an object lesson that draws together several threads of economic analysis from Chapter 4 and this chapter. On top of that, OPEC is both topical and important.

"In the beginning," before 1973, seven major oil companies (Exxon, Shell, Mobil, BP, Texaco, Socal, and Gulf—the "seven sisters") dominated world markets.[33] In 1972, on the eve of the first great OPEC crisis, the sisters owned over half the noncommunist world's total oil reserves and were responsible for two-thirds of the petroleum produced. (Ten years later, the figures were about a tenth and less than a fifth, respectively.) The sisters in their prime were vertically integrated right from the first exploration to delivery of refined products, and their power was considerable. They squelched Mexico's attempts to sell its oil internationally after that country nationalized its industry in 1936. They were victorious when radical premier Mossadeq of Iran seized oil assets in 1951; no one would buy Iranian oil, and the resulting depression was a major factor in the overthrow of the Mossadeq government.

Typically, Arabian oil was selling in the late 1950s at a "posted price" of $2 per barrel, or somewhat less as discounts from the posted price became frequent. Governments of the producing states took royalties and levied profits taxes based on that price, but these gleanings amounted to only about $1 per barrel. OPEC was formed in response to a cut in the posted price (to $1.80) imposed by the oil companies that had the impact of reducing the tax revenues of the member governments. Initially comprising only five countries, weak, and cautious, it did manage to keep the posted price from falling any further. (Meanwhile, in 1957 the U.S. oil companies succeeded in getting Congress to pass an oil import quota, ostensibly to encourage American companies, but with the result that expensive domestic oil was consumed at a much faster rate than otherwise would have been true.)

The crisis began not with the OPEC membership, but with Libya, then a nonmember. Libya was a special case with a number of smaller companies producing more than half of its petroleum. Radical Colonel Qaddafi had just overthrown conservative King Idris. He pushed through a price increase of 40¢ and gradually nationalized holdings. Since the seven sisters' Libyan operations were relatively unimportant to them, they did little to assist the small firms in resisting the Libyan ruler. These caved in, paid the higher prices and began to buy from the new national oil company. OPEC was stunned. The unsophisticated Libyan colonel and his quite sophisticated advisors had done what no one before had been able to do.

The first results seem small in retrospect. Late in 1970 OPEC demanded and got concessions to match those given to Libya and then achieved further small increases in 1972 and 1973. The oil companies could not seem to present a united front and went along. This stimulus to OPEC's morale came just before the outbreak of the Arab-Israeli "Yom Kippur" war of October 1973. That war brought cohesion to OPEC as never before and served to divide the consuming nations as well. A temporary oil embargo was succeeded by a new sense of determination by OPEC to control production and force prices up. Unilaterally, on October 16, 1973, OPEC raised prices 70 percent from the $3.00 pre-war price to $5.11, then another 128 percent in January 1974 to $11.65, and then again another 6 percent in October 1975, leaving oil in the range of $12 to $13 per barrel, where it stayed for some time.

The second incident was the great Khomeini shock of 1979 to 1980. This time Iran's oil deliveries were sharply cut back, and Iraq's, too, as war broke out between these countries, and the other OPEC members deliberately did not make up the difference. The result was that oil eventually reached $34 per barrel. (The two names Yom Kippur and Khomeini are incidentally convincing testimony that there would have been an oil crisis even if there never had been an OPEC.)

In its heyday OPEC rigged the market by establishing export quotas set in quantity terms. Many of the requisites for a successful quota scheme were present. Both supply and demand elasticity appeared to be low; it would not be easy to develop new sources of supply or substitutes in consumption. There was plenty of political cohesion at first, and the oil could just be left in the ground. One producer, Saudi Arabia, had such vast reserves that its own actions could influence the world price substantially—it could act as policeman.

Analytically, the cartel maintained an "umbrella" price by manipulating supply, as in Figure 15.3. Given the world demand curve *DD*, the cartel needed only to limit total supply to the level *SS* to accomplish its aim of a high price *OP*. The limitation was achieved by agreeing on an overall production figure and

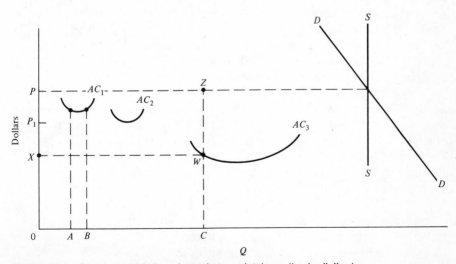

Figure 15.3 Cartel manipulation of supply to maintain an "umbrella" price.

allocating shares of that to each individual member. The policy was effective because at that time (in 1973) OPEC controlled 92 percent of world crude oil exports.

Saudi Arabia (country 3 in Figure 15.3) had much lower costs than some other members, say Ecuador (country 1) and Indonesia (country 2), as shown by the average cost curves AC_1, AC_2, and AC_3. By expanding production Saudi Arabia could easily have driven prices below OP_1 and thereby have eliminated Ecuador and Indonesia from the world market. It did not do so because by tolerating them at the high umbrella price, it vastly increases its profits. (If Arabia's output is OC, its total profit is $WXPZ$.)

The members with high costs either had to agree to stay within their allocated share or somehow be policed. There was always a motive for them to cheat to increase revenues by pushing up their production from some allocated figure such as OA to a higher figure OB. The motive was intense when a country was fighting an expensive war (Iran, Iraq) or spent a great deal on its political activities (Libya) or was very poor (Nigeria, Indonesia). Perhaps they could be accommodated with a Saudi Arabian cut, or perhaps the threat that Saudi Arabia would increase production would suffice to restrain them. There was additional tension between countries with limited, rapidly depleting reserves and those with large reserves. The former would, of course, prefer pumping now at the high cartel price; the latter would prefer a limit price strategy to restrain new exploration and guard against technological change.

The Economic Impact of OPEC   The economic impact of the two oil crises on the LDCs was profound and still continues. Economic growth obviously requires more petroleum in any country that uses trucks and pumps, farm machines, and petroleum-based fertilizer. LDC national incomes were growing rapidly in the 1970s, and these countries found it difficult to economize on petroleum use. Often they were also slow to change fixed low prices for gasoline and oil products, which discouraged conservation, for example, Bolivia's 12¢ per gallon price, raised at last in 1985. Oil consumption in the LDCs grew 64 percent in volume from 1973 to 1984, and even increased per unit of output, from 0.3 million tons of oil equivalent per billion dollars of GNP in 1965 to 0.4 million tons in 1985, as energy-intensive manufacturing increased in importance. Much of the increase was in countries that had the oil (up over 70 percent), but consumption rose nearly 30 percent even in the oil importers. (Simultaneously oil consumption was declining in volume in the rich countries.) Just after the Khomeini shock, the non-oil LDCs were spending as much on oil as they were receiving in foreign aid. Oil imports to South Korea grew to represent 30 percent of the value of all of that country's exports in 1981; for the Philippines the figure was 37 percent, for Turkey 82 percent, for India 83 percent.

The OPEC cartel had indirect effects as well as direct ones. It slowed economic growth in the rich countries and so diminished their demand for LDC exports. It contributed an inflationary impulse felt by rich and poor alike. Even for the oil *exporters,* some citizens of which grew fabulously rich, there were disappointments. These were caused largely by the waste of going too quickly, costly ill-planned projects, and inefficiencies generated by broad new subsidies for consumption. Less obviously, petroleum exports boosted the foreign exchange rate in a "petrodollar" phenomenon, thus depressing other exports, sometimes ruinously. It is startling to learn that the average GNP growth of oil-exporting countries in real terms was lower from 1973 to 1982 than it was from 1960 to 1973.

The Response to OPEC   Slowly, gathering momentum, market forces brought the largely expected response. Because of the special nature of oil, this response was very slow—many economists were already predicting it in 1975 and 1976—but by 1986 clearly it had been powerful. Conservation in the developed countries proved to be possible, as power stations shifted to coal and natural gas, drivers traded in their eight-cylinder gas guzzlers for four-cylinder compact cars, and homeowners turned down the heat and used natural gas and wood. Petroleum input per dollar of GNP fell 17 percent between 1973 and 1983, and imports fell even more, down 40 percent in volume during the same period. Even in the LDCs, where conservation was more difficult, oil as a percent of energy consumption fell from 53.5 percent in 1973 to 45 percent in 1983.[34]

Meanwhile, non-OPEC production soared. Alaska and the North Sea came on line; Britain alone now produces more oil than any OPEC members except Saudi Arabia and Iran. As this occurred, developed-country exports of oil as a percent of the total went from only 3.7 percent in 1973 to 12.5 percent in 1983. Even more impressive was the rise of non-OPEC production in poor countries, Mexico especially but also Egypt, Oman, Angola, Malaysia, China, and others, from 4 percent of total exports in 1973 to 18.7 percent in 1983. In the process Mexico became the world's third largest free-world producer, after the United States and Saudi Arabia. In some LDCs small deposits previously not worth bothering with were brought into production, "topping up" domestic use in countries where major finds are not expected: Cameroon, Ghana, the Ivory Coast, Sudan, Guatemala, the Philippines, and India are cases in point. Elsewhere, efforts were made where possible to develop hydroelectric sites, coal mines, even nuclear power (in Argentina, Brazil, India, Pakistan, and South Korea). Brazil moved quickly into gasohol and ethanol, as we have already noted. By 1985 about 90 percent of that country's new car output was being made to run on ethanol produced from sugarcane; about 20 percent of the present stock of cars runs on this, while gasohol fuels the remainder.[35]

Slowly, but perceptibly, OPEC began to crack. From the $34 per barrel cartel "marker" price just after the Khomeini shock, the marker was down to $29 in 1984 and $28 at the end of 1985. OPEC's share of exports had been 92 percent in 1973, but it was under 70 percent by 1983. The world's oil trade by volume was cut by a third in that period, but OPEC's was cut more than half. Nearly 32 million barrels per day (mbd) had been produced by the cartel in 1979, but by end 1985 the production ceiling was only 16 mbd, and indications were that only 14 mbd were being pumped; idle capacity in percentage terms was not much smaller than that in use. There were constant reports of discounting (cheating) by Iran and Nigeria, and at conference after conference OPEC's spiritual leader,

Sheikh Yamani of Saudi Arabia, could not forge an agreement to close ranks. In January and February of 1986 there were further breaks in the oil market, and Saudi Arabia seemed determined to recapture a large share of that market; the result was the steepest short-term decline in price ever recorded. The economic principles that had stymied all the other primary product cartels this century seemed at last to be catching up with OPEC.

The Future   Given the surprises of the past, it would be foolish to be certain about the duration of any improvements. If OPEC were quickly to regain its ability to control a large share of output, the developed countries would find consumption would not be so easy to cut this time around, since the obvious economies have already been made. But it would also find much more cooperation among those countries, with an International Energy Association pledged to maintain stocks sufficient to replace 90 days' worth of imports, to equalize the drawing down of stocks in case of need, and to share oil in an emergency. The U.S. strategic petroleum reserve of 500 million barrels stored underground, with room for 750 million barrels if desired, is another stabilizing factor.

In addition, governments are now equipped with far more powerful ideas to deal with a cartel than they had in the past. Another python grip by a revived OPEC might face an Adelman scheme, named after a proposal by Morris Adelman of MIT, involving a special sort of oil import quota and secret auctions of the licenses. Adelman suggests that most cartels break because members cheat. He argues that a federal agency as sole purchaser of imported crude oil, with a fixed quota and sale of quota tickets in secret monthly auctions, would encourage cheating because there would be no way to know the price paid unless the cheater revealed it. The cartel countries would bid up the price of the quota tickets if they wanted to increase their sales. Revenues from the auctions could be refunded to consumers or used to subsidize low-income consumers or promote energy research or all three. Any OPEC country not buying a ticket would have to sell more the next month, and so the price cutting would spread.

Market shading could be rewarded automatically with a longer-term contract in the Paul Davidson variant of the Adelman proposal. A discount of 5 percent might result in a commitment for 4 months of purchases, 10 percent for 1 year, 15 percent for 2 years. With that guarantee, there would be even greater incentive for cartel members to cheat. If the cartel breaks because of the strategy, these long-term contracts would have to be subsidized by tax revenue and justified as a response to economic warfare.

If fast, energy-using economic growth or a return of consumer preference for gas guzzlers were to raise demand rapidly, or if politics were to cut off important supplies from one or more areas, then OPEC's relative decline might be arrested.[36] In mid 1986, however, this did not look likely. Conservation was firmly in place, and production from non-OPEC sources remained high. One authoritative estimate in 1986 predicted that if oil stayed in a low $15 to $18 per barrel range, then by 1990 world demand for OPEC oil would be only 24 mbd compared to over 31 mbd in 1979.[37] The result was a brighter outlook on the macro side, with declining oil prices reducing inflation and stimulating real output—perhaps 1.5 percent in each case for a 30 percent cut in oil prices, which at that time did not seem at all out of the question.

That overall outcome would be highly beneficial to most LDCs. For the oil exporters the transition can be cushioned by using the large foreign exchange reserves accumulated during OPEC's heyday. But some oil exporters, notably Mexico and Nigeria, have not accumulated large reserves, and get well over 80 percent of their export revenue from petroleum. Mexico especially would have even more trouble meeting its debt payments, and the already substantial pressure on banks that have lent to that country would intensify. Higher overall world income would, however, allow the financing of a more flexible response, including aid both for the world's Mexicos and the banks if desired. Oil would be again produced where it is most efficient to do so, restoring something of the principle of comparative advantage to an area where for a long time it has been notably absent.

Stabilizing Price by Means of Buffer Stocks

In addition to quota limits on production, the other major method for intervening in world markets for primary products is a buffer stock system that influences prices by buying and selling commodities.[38] Buffer stocks are a poor way to *raise* prices, because obviously the stock must continuously and expensively accumulate the commodity in order to keep prices above the market-clearing level. It could still be done, if financed by the rich countries, but this would be tantamount to foreign aid in another form. If one wants to give aid, direct transfers would be far more efficient because they can be given to the poorest (price support does not necessarily do that) and because much waste would attach to the permanent maintenance of ever larger buffer stocks. In practice quotas have always been the preferred, though risky, tool for accomplishing price increses. Buffer stocks have, however, been favored for *stabilizing* price and have thus been a major element in the proposals for a New International Economic Order.

A suitably managed system of buffer stocks could conceivably dampen the severe short-run price fluctuations that afflict most primary product exporters. The predicted advantages for the LDCs would be a more even collection of tax revenue, a dampened cycle of saving, investment, and command over imported goods, more stability in development planning, and diminishment of any "cobweb" effect of expansion and contraction in response to price instability. A poor LDC might find it no longer necessary to engage in distress sales on the downside of a market when producers are unable to delay sales because of an urgent need for revenue. Consumers tempted to substitute commodities more stable in price for commodities that are more variable might not now do so. Individual producers would find their risks reduced. Since the non-oil LDCs still derive over half their export revenues from commodities, the effects of stabilization would be widely felt. (Recall, however, that in spite of all this convincing logic, there is only very limited evidence showing countries with exports more variable in price do worse at development than those whose export prices are more stable.)

Price stabilization can also promise benefits for consumers. Importers find it difficult to plan for large swings in price. Especially in the inflationary late 1970s, it was thought that these up-and-down swings were contributing to overall inflation via the ratchet effect. In an economy where the oligopolistic form of business organization is common, and trade unions are strong, price rises may occur in a boom, but are resisted in a slump. The high variability of primary product prices might then mean that inflationary impulses are transmitted in developed countries when the prices of their imports from LDCs rise, but deflationary consequences are much muted when price declines follow. Jere Behrman suggested that the gains from avoiding ratchet inflation might eclipse all other reasons for commodity price stabilization; in the late 1970s he estimated $15 billion as the present discounted value of preventing inflation from this cause. Even at the time, however, this argument did not seem to carry much weight with politicians in the developed countries, and with the decline of inflation in the 1980s, its force virtually disappeared.

It remains to ask why official buffer stocks are thought necessary when private trading by commodity speculators buying when prices are low and selling when they are high works toward the same end of stabilizing prices.[39] This is a fair question, and it has not fully been grappled with by proponents of buffer stocks. There are three usual arguments: (1) Private speculation is said to be sometimes destabilizing, with falling prices pushed even lower and rising prices higher. Professional speculation would not work in this fashion, because professionals would want to buy at the low point in order to profit from later sales when prices have risen, and sell at the high point to buy again when prices have fallen. But if there are many amateurs in the market, behaving in a casino or bandwagon fashion, then professionals may find it profitable to speculate on the behavior of these amateurs, rather than on the "normal" trends in the market. (2) An official buffer stock manager might have access to better information, as when government agencies control the marketing of some commodities and keep their statistics and their plans confidential. (3) Finally, a buffer stock might have access to cheaper capital, perhaps from government contributions, than would private speculators.

Though all three of these arguments have some surface plausibility, it is striking how little evidence has been amassed to prove them.[40] All in all, it is a bit of a puzzle how the suggestion for large-scale official buffer stocks could have attracted such support without the presence of definitive evidence of their superiority to private speculation. The arguments in the last paragraph are not necessarily wrong; but they *are* unproven.

The elementary theory of buffer stock operation is simple enough and is analyzed in Figure 15.4. A krypton buffer stock is illustrated. It starts operation with a stockpile of the metal and a war chest of cash; these are its working tools. The market supply and demand for the metal are S and D, respectively. The buffer stock manager must determine a floor and ceiling price at which action will be taken; in the diagram these are OP_c and OP_f. No actions are taken as long as supply and demand equilibrate at prices within the floor-ceiling range. The manager ignores any price changes in this range.

Should either demand or supply (or both) change by enough to give a

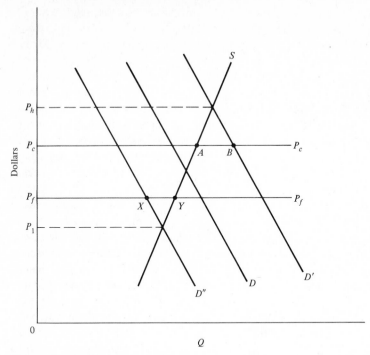

Figure 15.4 Buffer stock operation.

market price above the ceiling or below the floor, however, the buffer stock manager reacts. If, for example, there is an increase in demand for krypton to D', to keep the price from rising to the high level OP_h, sufficient krypton is released onto the market from the buffer stock so that the price does not rise above OP_c. The amount needed is exactly AB. Or, if a decline in demand to D'' would otherwise push prices down to a low OP_l, the buffer stock manager uses some of the cash reserve to buy just enough krypton (XY) to keep the price at OP_f. Supply changes can be analyzed in the same way, with krypton sold from the stock to keep prices from rising or purchased to keep them from falling.

Doubts Concerning Stabilization by Buffer Stocks   Economists have always been skeptical about the efficacy of buffer stocks as a device for stabilization. One concern has been that the stocks, instead of having a stabilizing influence, might actually destabilize commodity markets. The buffer stock must be sufficiently large and adjust with sufficient rapidity to long-term trends in prices, so that it exhausts neither its cash nor its supply of commodity. The buffer stock that runs out of either, because it is too small or because the manager did not pick up an underlying price trend soon enough, could conceivably face a change in price much greater (because of panic and speculative overshooting) than would have occurred with no intervention whatsoever. Certainly, any price change when the stock is "broken" is likely to be very large and very sudden.

In short, it would be a mistake to institute a buffer stock where speculators had a good bet that the stock would run out of money or commodity. That would be an invitation for speculators to buy at the stock's ceiling price, to profit later when the price is pushed through the roof following the stock's collapse. A recent study by Jere Behrman suggests that some $10 billion in funding would be adequate for buffer stocks to stabilize eight important commodities in a +15 percent to −15 percent price range, whereas UNCTAD has been discussing funding of only $4.5 to $6 billion to defend (more expensively) a narrower plus or minus 10 percent range.[41] (As we shall see, only a small fraction even of this inadequate sum has actually been raised.) Note that the size of the stock has to be larger than otherwise because successful buffer stocks would cause *private* stocking by speculators to decrease.

Assuming this problem is overcome, another immediately arises: Stabilizing price does not always stabilize revenue. The layman might assume that doing the first will accomplish the second, but not so. The rather complex economics of this problem depend on the elasticities involved. A reasonable rule of thumb is that stabilizing price stabilizes export revenue when demand shifts are responsible for the price change, but stabilizing price can destabilize export revenue when supply shifts are responsible.

A diagram does much to make this clear.[42] In Figure 15.5 we start with demand and supply curves D and S, a market price OP, and a quantity OQ. In Figure 15.5a a demand decrease to D_1 in a free market causes price to fall to OP_1 and quantity to fall to OQ_1. Total revenue sinks from the original $OPEQ$ to $OP_1E_1Q_1$. Using a buffer stock to stabilize price at OP, however, would cause revenue to producers to be unchanged at $OPEQ$. Similarly, a rise in demand to D_2 causes a higher free-market price OP_2, higher quantity OQ_2, and hence a higher revenue earned $OP_2E_2Q_2$. Stabilizing price at OP would have kept revenue

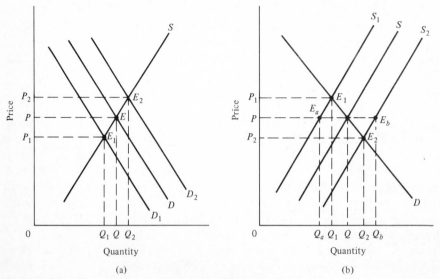

Figure 15.5 Price stabilization and revenue stabilization.

unchanged at *OPEQ.* Rule: Stabilizing price also stabilizes revenue if demand shifts.

Now consider Figure 15.5b in which a supply shift to S_1, due perhaps to a partial crop failure, raises the market price to OP_1 with a lower quantity OQ_1. The fall in volume is compensated for by the rise in price. Stabilizing with a buffer stock would, however, keep the price at *OP,* and by denying the increase would cut revenue substantially to OPE_aQ_a. If instead supply increased to S_2, in a free market revenue would become $OP_2E_2Q_2$, with the revenue lost from the price fall partly offset by the rise in volume. Stabilizing at price *OP* would prevent the price fall, and result in a much higher revenue OPE_bQ_b. Rule: Stabilizing price may destabilize revenue if supply shifts.

All this is worrisome because for most agricultural commodities there are frequent supply changes due to variable weather, the erratic effect of plant diseases and pests, and possible cobweb responses to price changes. The implication of frequent large supply shifts is that to stabilize producer incomes a buffer stock to influence price is not enough; it will be necessary to have a complementary or substitute program of income stabilization. (We return to income stabilization programs at the end of the chapter.)

The two diagrams also show nicely that over the business cycle there are likely to be gains or losses in income to producers if a buffer stock is in operation. Which will be the case again depends on whether there has been a demand shift or a supply shift. In Figure 15.5a a change in demand to D_2 results in revenues of $OP_2E_2Q_2$ if there is no buffer stock, but if a stock is stabilizing price at *OP,* then revenue will be *OPEQ,* meaning an income loss of $PP_2E_2Q_2QE$. If later in the business cycle demand sinks to D_1, then without a stock, revenue would be $OP_1E_1Q_1$, while with a stock revenue would be *OPEQ.* That would mean a revenue gain of $P_1PEQQ_1E_1$. Note that the loss of revenue with a buffer stock and higher demand $(PP_2E_2Q_2QE)$ is greater than the revenue gain with a stock and lower demand $(P_1PEOQ_1E_1)$. Over the business cycle the presence of a price-stabilizing buffer stock would in this case cause a loss of revenue for producers.

Now consider the case of supply shifts in Figure 15.5b. If supply falls to S_1, then revenue without the buffer stock would be $OP_1E_1Q_1$. With a stock stabilizing price at *OP* revenue would be OPE_aQ_a. The resulting revenue loss for producers would be $PP_1E_1Q_1Q_aE_a$. If supply rises to S_2, then revenue without a buffer stock would be $OP_2E_2Q_2$, whereas revenue with a stock would be OPE_bQ_b. There would be a revenue gain for producers equal to $P_2PE_bQ_bQ_2E_2$. Note the reversal from the case of a change in demand: The gain in revenue with a buffer stock and higher supply $(P_2PE_bQ_bQ_2E_2)$ is greater than the loss with a stock and lower supply $(PP_1E_1Q_1Q_aE_a)$. In this case over the cycle the presence of a buffer stock means a gain in revenue for producers.

In his investigations of eight commodities based on logic of this sort, Jere Behrman predicted that a major buffer stock program stabilizing in a plus or minus 15 percent range would bring considerable gains for producers of coffee, cocoa, and rubber, where supply shifts are more important; would bring reduced revenue for producers of copper and tin, where demand shifts are more important; and would be relatively neutral for jute, sisal, and tea.[43] Overall, a rather modest

$600 million net would have been transferred by consumers to the LDCs export-ing commodities. These contrasting results explain why the enthusiasm once felt for buffer stocks even in LDCs has been tempered by the conflicting interests involved.

A final objection, often advanced by rich and poor alike, is that a primary product exporting country is not necessarily a needy country. A large buffer stock program would deliver its major benefits to the largest exporters, and some of these (Brazil, Colombia, Ivory Coast, Malaysia) are rather well off among the LDCs. This, too, introduced a note of discord.

The Integrated Program

Whatever the objections, the NIEO proposals did provide for the establishment of price-stabilizing buffer stocks, under the so-called Integrated Program for Commodities, and a Common Fund to finance them was agreed on in 1980. Originally, 18 commodities, comprising 55 to 60 percent of all LDC non-oil primary product exports, were on the list for eventual action: bananas, bauxite, cocoa*, coffee*, copper*, cotton*, hard fibers* (abaca, coir, sisal), iron ore, jute*, manganese, meat, phosphate, rubber*, sugar*, tea*, tropical timber, tin*, and vegetable oils. Due to reasons of expense or unsuitability for stockpiling, 8 were dropped, and the core commodity list now includes only the 10 marked with an asterisk.

Progress came with a rush. In 1980 the Common Fund negotiations were concluded, with innovative rules that gave 47 percent of the voting power to the LDCs, 42 percent to the developed countries, 8 percent to the East bloc, and 3 percent to China.[44] Serious decisions required either a majority or a two-thirds vote, depending on the issue. The plan for a Common Fund to finance the buffer stock system was based on the supposition that there would be economies in finance. Weather is not the same all over the world, and it was thought some of the buffer stocks would be facing a need to sell, thus obtaining cash, at the same time that others would be using their cash to buy. If pooled financial resources could be used, the cost would be lower than if each buffer stock were funded separately. Research by John Cuddy of UNCTAD indicated that the saving would be large, in the range of 25 to 50 percent depending on different assump-tions about financing the initial stockpiles.[45] (This would not have helped in the recession of the early 1980s, when almost all commodities went down.)

The original financial target was $6 billion, to be contributed by both exporters and importers. Topping up was to be provided by the IMF, particularly its new Buffer Stock Financing Facility (BSFF). Designed to assist IMF members who belong to a buffer stock organization, the BSFF will loan up to 45 percent of the member's IMF quota, additional to any other lending, with repayment over three to five years. Conditionality applies (see Chapter 6 for details). Thus far, the BSFF has been used for financing the commodity agreements in tin, rubber, and sugar. Of the Common Fund's money, three-quarters was intended for buffer stock financing. Most of the rest was to go for programs of research on new uses (so raising demand) and on ways to improve market efficiency. The research programs are generally welcomed by all parties to the debate, as there are no adverse side effects such as accompany quotas and (possibly) buffer stocks.

But progress has been slow, even glacial, since the 1980 agreement. Ratification has proved a tedious process, and the start-up date of March 1982 was badly missed. Ninety countries and two-thirds of the capital are required by the rules; by January 1986, 91 had ratified but these contributed only 58 percent of the capital, well short of the target.[46] The United States, which originally supported the idea, turned against it under the Reagan administration and has not ratified. The $6 billion in financing had to be scaled back to only $750 million, about 60 percent for the buffer stocks, and as just noted even that has not yet been fully raised. By 1986 only three commodity agreements had been set up under the integrated program, rubber in 1979, jute in 1982, and tropical timber in 1983, of which only rubber provides for market intervention. (There were already existing agreements for coffee, sugar, cocoa, and tin, and discussions have been underway on cotton and tea.) Under the Common Fund rules, only rubber, tin, and coffee are now eligible for funds; any other agreements must be funded by the members. Only the coffee, rubber, and cocoa agreements now attempt to stabilize price; the sugar and tin agreements were doing so, but they broke up. The others restrict themselves to promoting research and market development.

At the last UNCTAD meeting in Belgrade, the talk was of eventually devoting $9 billion for 15 commodity buffer stocks, with large IMF contributions from the BSFF and elsewhere to make up any shortfall.[47] But the developed countries viewed the discussions with disquiet, especially when they saw the debate turning toward price raising (to the average of the 1970s) rather than price stabilization along a trend line. There was no agreement. Resistance has become especially pronounced in the United States. Though a member in 1984 of the coffee, sugar, jute, rubber, and tropical timber agreements, it now generally opposes new buffer stocks.

A LOOK AT THE EXISTING COMMODITY AGREEMENTS

A short survey of the existing commodity agreements adds a practical side to the theory and illustrates fully the political turmoil in the area.[48] Some use output quotas, some use buffer stocks, some use both, and some make no attempt to alter market prices.

An *International Tin Agreement* (ITA) was first established in 1956. It is the oldest and for a long time the most successful of the buffer stocks, though when this was written it was enmeshed in the worst difficulties a buffer stock has ever faced. Renewed from time to time, the sixth and latest agreement dates from 1982; in this sixth renewal but not before, consuming countries (excluding the United States) helped to finance the stockpile. The buffer stock was intended to be some 40,000 tonnes; when it is at this size, production quotas are imposed (88,000 tonnes in 1984). Without the quotas the buffer stock's cash reserves would have been dissipated long ago.

The Tin Agreement had a long-standing reputation for success in spite of some disturbing incidents. The price fell briefly through the floor in 1958 and

1982 and broke through the ceiling in 1961, 1964–1965, 1966, 1973–1974, and 1976. Even so, it did work rather smoothly for the most part, and that makes its collapse in late 1985 doubly dramatic. Basically, in recent years the stock was defending a price range that was too high. The quotas kept production down in the members, but that led to substitutions by consumers and new and highly rewarded production in nonmembers, especially Brazil and China. By 1985 about 40 percent of the world's tin was being produced by nonmembers, nearly half of that by Brazil. Twenty years before, nonmembers had been responsible for only 20 percent of world output.

The buffer stock manager struggled resolutely from his headquarters near the London Metals Exchange to buy sufficient tin to keep the price at the floor level. Eventually the stock reached 50,000 to 60,000 tonnes, with another 68,000 tonnes contracted for.[49] On a shocking day in October 1985, the manager announced to the Metals Exchange that he could not fulfill the contracts already made and that the member countries would not come up with the $90 million or so needed to avoid default. The price plunged almost 10 percent in a few minutes and 17 percent in the first week. Amid consternation the London Metals Exchange closed, and so did tin trading around the world. At the time of writing, tin trading was still suspended in London, many lawsuits were in the offing, with over $1.3 billion owed by the members to brokers' banks; a "gray market" trade was being carried on in Europe and America. In April 1986 tin at £3750 per tonne was 55 percent below the price at the time of the suspension. Perhaps a new floor and ceiling price will eventually emerge after some of the excess stock has been sold for what it will bring; it is more likely that we have seen the end of the ITA. If prices stay depressed, hundreds of mines in the LDCs would have to close. Opponents of price-stabilizing buffer stocks have been handed the best evidence they could want that such stocks are actually destabilizing. The mismanagement is likely to have repercussions far beyond the world of tin.

The *International Coffee Agreement* (ICA) dates from 1983, succeeding a 1976 pact, and will expire in 1989. There is a long history of rigging this market with quotas. Brazil tried to do so alone before World War II, several postwar efforts involved quotas, and there was one abortive attempt to form a buffer stock. There still is no such stock, and the present ICA works through quotas (currently 61 million bags per year). These are automatically tightened when the coffee price hits a floor ($1.20 per pound), increased when the price hits a ceiling ($1.40), and suspended at $1.50. Consuming nations belong and help in the enforcement. Allocation of the quotas has been a severe problem, and apparently there are lots of illegal shipments from nonmembers to members in what amounts to a two-tier market. The United States has, atypically, been a participant in the ICA, one reason being political and economic support for Brazil. The great advance in coffee prices in early 1986, caused by Brazilian freezes and drought, brought a rapid relaxing of the quotas.

The *International Cocoa Agreement,* called the ICCA to distinguish it from the coffee pact, dates from 1972. The United States has not been a member. Its third renewal in 1981 was to have involved a buffer stock of 250,000 tonnes, financed by a 2¢ per pound fee on exports. But it soon (1982) exhausted its funds with only 100,000 tonnes in stock. By 1985 it had again built up a cash reserve through its levy on exports, but the planned floor to ceiling price range for the stock ($1.00 to $1.60) was well above the current market price; new competition, especially from Brazil and Malaysia, had driven prices very low. When the current agreement was due for renegotiation in 1985, no replacement could be agreed upon even after months of talks.

The *International Natural Rubber Agreement* (INRA), dates from 1980. It was the first to associate with the Common Fund. The United States is a member and contributor. Rubber has a history of failed attempts to cartelize the market. The Stevenson Plan of 1922 restricted shipments from the then major exporters, Ceylon and Malaya, but other producers responded with increased output so that the erstwhile leaders found their market share down from 70 percent at the start of the plan to 54 percent in 1927, and with no long-run price increase to show for it. A wider arrangement to build stocks in the 1930s raised prices, but because of synthetics there was no further agreement until INRA. INRA uses a buffer stock as its sole method to influence price; at the start of 1985, 270,000 tonnes were in stock. The price was relatively stable, within the floor to ceiling range of 38¢ to 52¢, and the stock was thus inactive during 1983 and 1984. However, prices fell in 1985, and the buffer stock began to purchase. Some 370,000 tonnes had been accumulated by the end of 1985, close to the planned maximum of 400,000 tonnes. The members agreed to raise the money for 150,000 tonnes more. The financial strains of this were severe for Indonesia, Thailand, and Malaysia, all countries already facing a heavy responsibility to rescue the tin agreement at the same time. The INRA buffer stock manager quit his job in 1985, complaining about the political squabbling among the members.

The *International Sugar Agreement* (ISA), dating from 1978 and based in London, fully intended to control price. But sugar prices were so low that production cuts would have had to be huge to bring them up to some "desired" level, and there was no accord on who would cut. The United States was a member. After the agreement expired at the end of 1984, attempts to negotiate a strong replacement failed. A new ISA has been in effect, since January 1, 1985, but it has no economic provisions and is largely a forum for discussion and a fact-gathering organization. The EC, which would not join the predecessor with teeth (recall that its subsidized exports are the single worst problem in sugar today) did join the toothless successor.

The 1978–84 ISA had a buffer stock and export quotas, following a tradition of quotas established earlier in the century. When prices were low, consuming-country members were to limit their imports from nonmembers. When prices were high, "national stocks" held in exporting countries were to be released. But faced with the corrosive and ill-considered sugar policies of the United States and the EC, price stabilization was clearly not going to work, and it did not.

There was an *International Tea Agreement* between 1933 and 1955. In the 1930s export quotas and a virtual outlawing of new plantings did prop the price, while after the war there were few restrictions on output and relatively little impact from the scheme. Discussions on a new tea agreement have thus far failed, largely because of disputes between old and new producers over quota size.

An *International Jute Agreement* (IJA) entered into force in 1984, the second under UNCTAD's Integrated Program. There is no economic intervention, only research and development support, market promotion, and cost control measures. The heavy competition from polypropylene and polyethylene severely limits any chance to raise prices.

A *Tropical Timber Agreement* came into force during 1985, with the United States a member. There is no market intervention, little funding, not yet even a headquarters. It will be restricted to research and development and market promotion only.

Copper has often been mentioned as a candidate for an agreement, and there have been many negotiations. But there is a history of failed cartels that suggest this is a difficult product to cartelize, being too responsive to price on both the demand and supply sides. World markets are large, and an effective buffer stock would be very expensive, costing perhaps $2 billion. In any case, Chile, the biggest supplier and with some of the lowest costs, now seems intent on encouraging sales rather than restricting production.

Hard fibers (abaca, coir, sisal) are on the UNCTAD list, but they receive stiff competition from synthetic substitutes, and there has been little progress toward an agreement. Meat is also on the list, but currently enjoys a strong market, with no agreement likely. Discussions on cotton have mainly focused on the large shift to synthetics that would occur if an attempt were made to raise prices. Bananas are impossible to stock, while vegetable oils are highly competitive with world fats and oils, with too much substitution among them to permit agreed price rises.

To repeat the point made at the start of this section, the practical experience of the international commodity agreements seems to accord rather well with the more pessimistic predictions of how those agreements would, or rather would not, work. It should be remembered, however, that the severe 1980s recession was chiefly responsible for the problem, and buffer stock performance might have been better under more normal economic conditions. In the near future one would expect relatively little forward movement; only time will tell where the idea will go in the long run.

STABILIZING EXPORT REVENUE

A plain implication of our analysis of price-stabilizing buffer stocks is that they would not stabilize income when supply shifts occur. Even highly successful price stabilization will thus not eliminate the fluctuations of export revenue that afflict primary product exporters. For that purpose, some form of income stabilization is needed as a supplement.

It would be fair to ask why, if revenues remain unstable, would one bother with smoothing price at all? Why not focus on revenue stability alone and simplify matters? The answer appears a tactical one. Stabilization of primary product export revenues might be of great value to the LDCs, but it is of little direct value to the buyer of the commodity. Buffer stocks working on price will, on the other hand, promise some benefits to consumers if the fluctuations are dampened.

Consuming nations would, of course, have to come up with large amounts of the funding in either case. This is a major reason why both price and revenue stabilization are often advocated at the same time.

The Compensatory Financing Facility

There are presently two schemes for stabilizing revenue: the Compensatory Financing Facility of the IMF and the Stabex scheme of the European Community that applies to its associated ACP states. The IMF's Compensatory Financing Facility (CFF), dating from 1963, is a revenue-smoothing device that allows lending to countries where a shortfall in export earnings has occurred.[50] Shortfall is measured in a sophisticated manner: A five-year trend in revenue is established statistically, based on the evidence from the previous two years and projections as to what is most likely in the two following years. For the current year, if revenue is below the trend, the member country could originally borrow 25 percent of its IMF quota, now 83 percent of a much larger quota, to cover the deficiency. Repayment is required after three to five years. Under the CFF, between 1977 and 1982 there were 112 loans worth $7.3 billion.

Originally the loans were granted with few conditions, but since 1983 full conditionality applies, meaning that the IMF may require some policy reforms as in its regular lending.[51] Critics of this policy change are quite correct in pointing out that the shortfall may have been caused by a policy action in some developed country, but that no remedial steps are required of them by the IMF. Critics also point out that the loans have to be repaid in a rather short period of time even if earnings continue to fall. It should also be noted that linking the borrowing to quota size is not entirely sensible in that some countries with large quotas export few primary products, while others are very dependent on these exports but have small quotas. A resolution passed at the UNCTAD VI Conference in 1983 called for the establishment of a broader and more liberal compensatory finance scheme within UNCTAD; the developed countries prefer it to remain with the IMF where their votes weigh more heavily.

Stabex

The other revenue stabilizing scheme currently in use is the EC's Stabex, which dates from 1975. The scheme usually covers only exports to the EC, and not to the rest of the world. It is much smaller than the CFF, and less sophisticated in that the shortfall in export performance is based only on the average of earnings in the past four years, with no account taken of the future trend. (The main result is that Stabex always lags behind any inflation or deflation of prices, while the CFF keeps up by making projections of price behavior.)

Stabex is the most distinctive feature, and often the most controversial one, of the Lomé Conventions between the EC and its associated ACP states.[52] (Lomé is the capital of Togo where the three different treaties have been signed.) Under the Lomé III agreement, put into effect in 1985 and due to expire in five years, 48 products of the 66 member countries are covered up to the financial limits of the scheme, now about $648 million. Stabex will pay on a given export even if export earnings are rising on other commodities; this is unlike the IMF's compensatory finance scheme. There are dependency thresholds and fluctuation thresholds, so that the more a country depends on an export, and the more earnings from it fluctuate, the more likely that Stabex payments will be received. (These thresholds are much less restrictive for "least developed, landlocked, and island" countries.)[53] When and if export revenue again increases, repayment is eventually required of all but these last countries, to which the money goes as grants. Contrary to the Compensatory Financing Facility, the loans are interest-free. There is no limit on receipts, also unlike the CFF, which is linked to IMF quotas. In the period 1975 to 1982, Stabex made 205 payments worth about $800 million to 44 countries. Receipts under the scheme were important for some countries; for example, in 1983 10 percent or more of all export revenue in Senegal, Sudan, and Mauritania.

This wide-ranging and liberal idea has, however, faced undeniable problems. The funding is not adequate to meet anywhere near all the legitimate claims. Stabex ran out of money twice in 1980 and 1981, largely because the world recession hit primary products hard following four years of relatively high prices. In both those years only about half the claimed amounts were actually paid. (It should be noted that Lomé III channels much more aid to the LDC members than is involved in Stabex. The treaty also includes development cooperation, rural development, food security programs, and infrastructure promotion as well as income stabilization.)[54] The scheme probably leads to more production of the commodities covered and less of uncovered ones. Certainly non-ACP states with no recourse to Stabex are put at a disadvantage. Finally, potential benefits in agriculture are much diminished since the EC is so restrictive on imports of commodities, especially sugar, that compete with community production.

This last point might not be immediately obvious in the ACP countries, which apparently benefit from handsome treatment under the "Sugar Protocol" of the Lomé Convention. Under this protocol, the EC pays high prices, recently about four times the world price, for the 1.4 million tonnes of sugar delivered under quota to its protected markets. The results are apparently lucrative, with a large share of current production eligible for the preferences. For example, in 1981–82 74 percent of sugar output in Trinidad and Tobago entered the EC under quota to be sold at the high European price. The figure for Barbados was 51 percent, for Guyana 49 percent, for St. Christopher and Nevis 45 percent. Above all ranks Mauritius, which Indian Ocean island usually sells 80 percent or more of its output under the protocol's quotas. (Mauritius holds some 38 percent of the EC's total quota; over 6 percent of that country's national product comes from these sales.[55])

But the handsome treatment is in large part an illusion. The more efficient producers or potential producers of sugar cannot enlarge their markets at the expense of the less efficient; total sales cannot increase within the rather small EC quota, which is less than three-quarters the size of the U.S. limits; resources are drawn into uses where they are less productive as countries with less comparative advantage in sugar production still strive to use their entire share of the quota; non-ACP states are severely penalized. Perhaps above all, the Lomé sugar protocol creates vested interests (the present sugar producers who sell at the profitable EC price) that work to keep their countries tethered in the protectionist camp.

The EC has also had its own objections to the way Stabex has worked. For years it has expressed disappointment that the Stabex payments were going for showcase projects, were simply being added to a country's general revenues with no direct link to development, or were reflecting urban bias. In the 1985 version of the plan the EC insisted on and did receive increased control over the way the payments are used. More funds will flow especially to agriculture and not to general revenue.

The Future for Revenue Stabilization

Whether through the IMF's Compensatory Finance Facility or the EC's Stabex, stabilization of export revenue along some moving trend line as a use of aid funds would appear to lessen the difficulties facing primary product exporters. Yet the enthusiasm has definitely been muted. The developed countries do not say so publicly, but they fear that stabilization will become a compulsory transfer mechanism for aid funds and so oppose further enhancements. Some LDCs, the ones that export few primary products or products unlikely to be covered, are also opposed.

Two reasons for promoting stabilization schemes might still prevail however. Taxpayers in developed countries might possibly persuade themselves, or be persuaded, that aid in the form of funds for stabilization is more acceptable than aid in other forms.[56] Certainly the voters in the United States, Japan, and the EC have been much more ready to channel funds toward their farmers, even rich ones, than toward their own poor as "welfare." Another possibility is that stabilization might be a useful bargaining tool if primary product producers ever develop the cohesion to bargain as a collective monopoly. Admittedly, this is unlikely, but then so was OPEC. Guarding against unwonted developments on the political side by means of an income stabilization program might then appear both useful and cost effective.[57] It is probably fair to say that most economists would favor extensions in this area over enhanced price stabilization, and even more over measures to boost commodity prices. In the present political climate, however, developed-country governments have taken a dim view of all such policies. Again, only time will tell whether the idea of revenue stabilization will resume its advance.

NOTES

1. *WDR 1986,* p. 126.
2. *WDR 1985,* p. 40.
3. See Ron Duncan and Ernst Lutz, "Penetration of Industrial Country Markets by Agricultural Products from Developing Countries, *World Development* 11, no. 9 (1983):771–786; and *WDR 1986,* p. 10.

4. Quota amounts in this section are from the *U.S. Tariff Schedule.* See U.S. International Trade Commission (ITC), *Operation of the Trade Agreements Program, 36th Report,* Washington, D.C., 1985, pp. 53, 212–213, and elsewhere in this and the *37th Report,* 1986, for additional details.

5. For details see U.S. Department of Agriculture, "Sugar and Sweetener," annual reports; Ian Smith, "Prospects for a New International Sugar Agreement," *Journal of World Trade Law* 17, no. 4 (1983):308–324; *WDR 1986,* p. 114; and articles in *The Economist* and the *Wall Street Journal.*

6. For details see *The New Republic,* August 11/18, 1986, pp. 5–6; and *WDR 1986,* p. 125. The *New Republic* article notes that subsidies on U.S. beef sales to Brazil, used in 1986 to be rid of the beef from cows slaughtered to prop dairy prices, result in prices just one-half what Uruguay had been earning in this market.

7. This and some of the other details in this paragraph are from *WDR 1986,* pp. 116, 119.

8. See Brian E. Hill, *Common Agricultural Policy: Past, Present, and Future,* London, 1984; A. E. Buckwell, D. R. Harvey, K. J. Thomson, and K. A. Parton, *The Costs of the Common Agricultural Policy,* London, 1982; Ian R. Bowler, *Agriculture Under the Common Agricultural Policy: a Geography,* Manchester, 1985; *WDR 1986;* U.S. ITC, *Operation of the Trade Agreements Program, 37th Report,* 1986, pp. 143–144, and the constant coverage in *The Economist.*

9. Variable levies are also used by Austria, Sweden, and Switzerland. *WDR 1986,* p. 113.

10. See U.S. ITC, *Operation of the Trade Agreements Program, 37th Report,* pp. 21–26.

11. Agricultural export subsidies are discussed by Gary Clyde Hufbauer and Joanna Shelton Erb, *Subsidies in International Trade,* Washington, D.C., 1984, pp. 68–76 and sources quoted there. Some details in this section are from U.S. Department of State, *Current Policy No. 804,* 1986.

12. The EC thus bears the main responsibility for the rise of the industrial country share of world agricultural exports from 30.5 percent in 1961–63 to 47.9 percent 1982–84, during which time the LDC share fell from 63.1 percent to 48.4 percent. *WDR 1986,* p. 10.

13. The weaker dollar of 1986 means further problems for the CAP. A weaker dollar means U.S. farm commodities will look more attractive abroad. This will require even larger export subsidies than before, and CAP authorities were estimating in 1986 that a new $750 to $800 million supplementary budget will be needed because of the dollar's decline.

14. *WDR 1986,* pp. 129–131. This edition of the *World Development Report* concentrates in part on protection in agriculture.

15. *Ibid.,* p. 144, which points out that South-South trade in agricultural commodities amounted to $21 billion in 1980, 25 percent of the total exports of the LDCs. This trade is growing faster than LDC agricultural exports to the North. Rice, sugar, coffee, and cotton are the most important items. But transport costs are high, the export subsidies of the developed countries are harmful, and information on new markets is poor, problems that will take time to overcome.

16. The simulation by Jean-Marc Burniaux and Jean Waelbroeck is cited in *South,* no. 64, February, 1986, p. 41.

17. The data on sugar are from *WDR 1985,* pp. 40–41. The politics of sugar protection are fascinating. Cuba, the world's largest exporter, ships over half its output to the Soviet Union, receiving in barter a price equivalent to about 50¢ per pound on the 4 million tonnes shipped. (Other customers include Eastern Europe and China.) Meanwhile the United States, which bought 52 percent of the Caribbean's sugar in 1981, was buying only 30 percent in 1983 because of the new quota. The EC pays 21¢ per

pound, four times the current world price, for the 1.4 million tonnes it allows in from its associated ACP states. This can be a windfall for small sugar producers such as Mauritius in the Indian Ocean (83 percent of its output went to the EC in 1984) and Fiji in the Pacific (62 percent), but the small size of the quota, less than three quarters that of the United States, sharply limits the gains. (We return to the EC's sugar scheme later in the chapter). The result is that currently only 20 percent of the world's sugar production is actually traded on free markets; this thinness contributes to greater variability of price than would otherwise be the case.

18. *WDR 1985,* p. 41.
19. *Wall Street Journal,* October 18, 1985. Argentina and Uruguay both once had huge markets in Europe. Even the USSR, Argentina's supporter in the Falklands/Malvinas War, has turned away from Argentina and to the EC for its (cheap) beef purchases.
20. *WDR 1986,* pp. 123–124, 152.
21. W. M. Corden, *Trade Policy and Economic Welfare,* Oxford, 1974, p. 314.
22. See Jan S. Hogendorn and Wilson B. Brown, *The New International Economics,* Reading, Mass., 1979, p. 412.
23. In this and the following sections, I made use of Pan A. Yotopoulos and Jeffrey B. Nugent, *Economics of Development: Empirical Investigations,* New York, 1976, pp. 336–340.
24. I used Behrman's "median of available estimates" where given. As he explains, for a number of reasons these elasticities are probably biased upward to some degree, adding to the strength of the case. The supply figure for tin is Behrman's own, as are the demand estimates for cotton, jute, sisal, and tin. In many cases Behrman's own estimates are lower than the "median of available estimates." The higher long-run supply elasticities are also presented by Behrman. Alternative figures, also high, are in *WDR 1986,* p. 68.
25. See Paul D. Reynolds, *Commodity Agreements and the Common Fund,* New York, 1978, p. 22.
26. See A. I. MacBean, *Export Instability and Economic Development,* Cambridge, 1966. Further studies by Peter Kenen and C. S. Voivodas did not alter the basic conclusion. A nice treatment of the issue is D. Lim, "Export Instability and Economic Growth: A Return to Fundamentals," *Oxford Bulletin of Economics and Statistics* 38, no. 4 (1976):311–322.
27. The statistical evidence supporting the claim that saving and investment rise with instability is in Yotopoulos and Nugent, *Economics of Development,* p. 337. The quotation is from Anne O. Krueger, "Trade Policies in Developing Countries," in Ronald W. Jones and Peter B. Kenen, eds., *Handbook of International Economics,* Vol. 1, Amsterdam, 1984, p. 564.
28. Major survey volumes are William R. Cline, ed., *Policy Alternatives for a New International Economic Order,* New York, 1979; and Jagdish N. Bhagwati, ed., *The New International Economic Order: The North-South Debate,* Cambridge, Mass., 1977. Also see Paul Streeten, "Approaches to a New International Economic Order," *World Development* 10, no. 1 (1982):1–17; and William Loehr and John P. Powelson, *Threat to Development: Pitfalls of the NIEO,* Boulder, Colo., 1983.
29. The subject is surveyed by Fiona Gordon-Ashworth, *International Commodity Control: A Contemporary History and Appraisal,* London, 1984; by Reynolds, *Commodity Agreements and the Common Fund;* and by Christopher P. Brown, *The Political and Social Economy of Commodity Control,* London, 1980. The author has treated the subject with Wilson B. Brown in *The New International Economics,* chap. 19, and the discussion here incorporates some of the same material.
30. This paragraph draws on Allen Wallis, "Commodity Markets and Commodity Agree-

ments," U.S. Department of State *Current Policy No. 791,* 1986; Bruce Herrick and Charles P. Kindleberger, *Economic Development,* 4th ed., New York, 1983, p. 485; and Gerald M. Meier, *Leading Issues in Economic Development,* 4th ed., Oxford, 1984, p. 556.

31. Jere R. Behrman, "Stabilizing Prices Through International Buffer Stock Commodity Agreements," *National Development,* May 1980, pp. 49–54. This article was brought to my attention by Dennis T. Avery, "International Commodity Agreements," *Department of State Special Report No. 83,* June 1981, which was also used for this section.

32. Avery, "International Commodity Agreements."

33. This background is in part from Hogendorn and Brown, *New International Economics,* chap. 17, and sources quoted there. A recent volume analyzing OPEC that I found informative is Abbas Alnasrawi, *OPEC in a Changing World Economy,* Baltimore, 1985. I also utilized IMF, "World Oil Situation," *World Economic Outlook, 1986,* pp. 148–160; *World Economic Outlook, 1985,* pp. 141–155; U.S. Department of State, "International Energy Security: The Continuing Challenge," *Current Policy No. 612,* 1984; and "Energy Trade Problems and Prospects," *Current Policy No. 741,* 1985; "Oil and Energy," *Gist,* September 1985; *WDR 1986,* pp. 50–51; and *The Economist,* January 29, 1983, pp. 57–60; October 15, 1983, pp. 80–86; July 28, 1984, survey section; February 1, 1986, pp. 63–64; and July 12, 1986, p. 97.

34. A United Nations study discussing how the LDCs have coped with the OPEC crisis is *Energy Planning in Developing Countries,* Oxford, 1984. For further analysis see World Bank, *Energy Transition in Developing Countries,* Washington, D.C., 1983. According to *Jane's World Railways* for 1984, London, 1984, the following LDCs still operate coal-burning steam locomotives: Angola, Bangladesh, Burma, Chile, China, Ecuador, Ghana, India, Indonesia, Iraq, Mozambique, Nigeria, Pakistan, Peru, South Africa, Sri Lanka, Sudan, Swaziland, Taiwan, Tanzania, Thailand, Turkey, Uruguay, Yugoslavia, and Zimbabwe.

35. *WDR 1980,* pp. 16–17; Michael Barzelay and Scott R. Pearson, "The Efficiency of Producing Alcohol for Energy in Brazil," *Economic Development and Cultural Change* 31, no. 1 (1982):131–144; *The Economist,* February 22, 1986, pp. 62–63.

36. For an analysis of the potential impact of political problems in the Middle East, see Knut Anton Mork, "What If We Lose the Persian Gulf?" in Paul Wachtel, ed., *Crisis in the Economic and Financial Structure,* Lexington, Mass., 1982.

37. Oxford Institute for Energy Studies, quoted in *The Economist,* March 8, 1986, p. 73; IMF, *World Economic Outlook, 1986,* p. 148. If oil were to return to $27 to $28 per barrel, the Oxford Institute estimates that world demand for OPEC oil would be 17 mbd in 1990.

38. For this section I have utilized Jere R. Behrman, "The Analytics of International Commodity Agreements," in Carl K. Eicher and John M. Spatz, eds., *Agricultural Development in the Third World,* Baltimore, 1984; Behrman, "International Commodity Agreements"; and Christopher P. Brown, *Political and Social Economy of Commodity Control.*

39. The question is asked in *WDR 1986,* chap. 7, which is relied on for this and the following paragraph.

40. Following the statement in *ibid.,* p. 134.

41. Behrman, "International Commodity Agreements."

42. This type of analysis is presented in more detail in Jere R. Behrman, *Development, the International Economic Order, and Commodity Agreements,* Reading, Mass., 1978. I also drew on Ezriel Brook, Enzo Grilli, and Jean Waelbroeck, "Commodity Price Stabilization and the Developing Countries," *Banca Nazionale del Lavoro Quarterly*

Review, no. 124 (March 1978):79–99. Debate on this issue is considered by Walter C. Labys, "Commodity Price Stabilization Models: A Review and Appraisal," *Journal of Policy Modeling,* 2, no. 1 (1980):121–136. This article also considers the welfare implications of stabilization and directs the reader to the earlier studies of B. F. Massell, F. V. Waugh, and Walter Oi.

43. Behrman, "International Commodity Agreements"; and see Ian M. D. Little, *Economic Development; Theory, Policy, and International Relations,* New York, 1982, pp. 337–339.

44. "UNCTAD: Agreement on the Common Fund," *Journal of World Trade Law* 14, no. 6 (1980):541–545; U.S. ITC, *Operation of the Trade Agreements Program, 35th Report,* pp. 127–128, and *36th Report,* p. 84.

45. John Cuddy, "Financial Savings from the Common Fund," *Weltwirtschaftsliches Archiv* 114, no. 3 (1978):499–513.

46. U.S. ITC, *Operation of the Trade Agreements Program, 37th Report,* p. 93.

47. *Wall Street Journal,* January 26, 1983, p. 34.

48. For this section I drew on U.S. ITC, *Operation of the Trade Agreements Program, 37th Report,* pp. 93–105, *36th Report,* pp. 87–98, and *35th Report,* pp. 131–142; Avery, "International Commodity Agreements"; and articles in *The Economist, South, Wall Street Journal,* and *Christian Science Monitor.*

49. Figures differ. I have generally followed "Tin Crisis in London Roils Metals Exchange," *Wall Street Journal,* November 13, 1985. Other details in this section are from *South,* no. 66 (April 1986):15.

50. For details, see Nihad Kaibni, "Evolution of the Compensatory Financing Facility," *Finance and Development* 23, no. 2 (1986):24–27; and *WDR 1986,* pp. 138–139, 141. For a critical review, see Sidney Dell, "The Fifth Credit Tranche," *World Development* 13, no. 2 (1985):245–249; and J. M. Finger and Dean A. Derosa, "The Compensatory Finance Facility and Export Instability," *Journal of World Trade Law* 14, no. 1 (1980):14–22.

51. As noted in Chapter 6, the CFF is now linked to the Cereal Import Facility that loans under similar terms when the price of imported cereals rises. There is an overall limit on borrowing from the two together, currently 105 percent of quota. All is in addition to the limits on normal lending.

52. A few non-ACP poor countries are to be made eligible for Stabex aid in 1986. Details and analysis may be found in Adrian Hewitt, "Stabex: An Evaluation of the Economic Impact over the First Five Years," *World Development* 11, no. 12 (1983):1005–1027; Hamisi S. Kibola, "Stabex and Lomé III," *Journal of World Trade Law* 18, no. 1 (1984):32–51; Gerrit Faber, "The Economics of Stabex," *Journal of World Trade Law* 18, no. 1 (1984):52–62; Michael Blackwell, "Lomé III: The Search for Greater Effectiveness," *Finance and Development* 22, no. 3 (1985):31–34; F. Long, ed., *The Political Economy of EEC Relations with African, Caribbean, and Pacific States,* Oxford, 1980; *WDR 1986,* pp. 139–144; *IMF Survey,* February 4, 1985; *The Economist,* October 13, 1984, p. 58; and January 5, 1985, pp. 39–40; and personal conversations with Pierre-Henri Laurent of Tufts University.

53. The product must account for at least 6 percent of total export revenue in the claim year, and earnings from the product have to fall at least 6 percent compared to the average of the past four years. For the "least developed, landlocked, and island" members, these percentages are a much lower 1.5 and 1.5, respectively.

54. There is also a small (currently $291 million) program for minerals called Sysmin, or sometimes Minex, dating from 1980. Under Lomé III a country is eligible for Sysmin funds if 15 percent of its export earnings come from a covered mineral (copper, cobalt,

phosphate, manganese, bauxite, tin, and iron ore). By special dispensation on a case-by-case basis, the payments will be made on *any* mineral (except oil, natural gas, and precious metals and stones) if they make up at least 20 percent of export revenue. (The figures are 10 percent and 12 percent, respectively, for least developed, landlocked, and island countries.) The payments are used to improve production and infrastructure and to reduce capacity.

55. From *WDR 1986,* pp. 142–143.

56. See M. E. Kreinin and J. M. Finger, "A Critical Survey of the New International Economic Order," *Journal of World Trade Law* 10, no. 5 (1976):504.

57. See John Spraos, *Inequalising Trade?* Oxford, 1983, chap. 8, for a discussion.

chapter *16*

Lessons Learned

Perhaps the best way to put into perspective the lessons learned in this book is to make the attempt to "teach" them to someone else. Of course, mastering one book in development economics doth not a development advisor make; that will require additional years of further training, reading, and often most important of all, field experience. But imagining that we have been asked to serve as consultants to the government of Poveria, to make and explain policy recommendations, can be a useful exercise for a student. Suppose this morning we together find ourselves flying into Poveria's international airport, scheduled this afternoon to discuss development issues in a North-South round table with economists and politicians. Which of the principles of development economics we have studied here would we want to emphasize as most generally useful? Permitting ourselves the freedom to make uninhibited policy recommendations to rich and poor countries alike, what would that advice be?

DEVELOPMENT IS COMPLEX

We begin with what may be the hardest of all lessons for us and for our well-trained colleagues to learn: One must be always open-minded yet skeptical and questioning, always willing to learn from other schools of economics and from other disciplines, and always willing to adjust theory to the reality of empirical evidence. In this field of economics, certainty can come uncomfortably close to intellectual arrogance. The principles we believe to be generally valid all too often will have many exceptions, unavoidable because of the great variety of social, political, and economic conditions in the world of the LDCs. History has had a way of treating poorly some of the most widely supported policy recommendations of the past, the "slaying of beautiful hypotheses by ugly facts" in the words of Thomas Huxley. Even the most used statistics in all our studies, GNP per capita expressed in dollars, is flawed and badly in need of replacement by statistics adjusted for purchasing power.

Then let us admit that our economic modeling does not always capture well the complexity of the barriers to development in the LDCs. We have examined a long list of such barriers, including inadequate knowledge, poor organization, social and religious constraints on women, on ethnic minorities, on entrepreneurship, government policies that distort economic incentives, rule by an economic elite or by the military, corruption, and so forth.

Henry J. Bruton has discussed this complexity in vivid terms as a peculiar production possibility curve.[1] Rather than the smooth curve of an introductory course in economics, the situation may be better represented by a maze with internal constraints that block any number of otherwise promising paths toward the curve, as in the accompanying figure. A country starting at point A will find it cannot move to its frontier in a northwest direction, and that reaching the frontier at any point at all is likely to involve a process of "searching, probing, trials and errors, willingness to abandon trials that are errors."[2] We know that the outer edge cannot be passed until more resources are available, but long before that outer edge is reached, wherever it is, a country may run into internal barriers that are difficult to breach and perhaps were not even anticipated until development caused them to be encountered. An understanding that development is more like negotiating a maze than it is like walking a straight line is humbling no doubt, but it will lessen the sense of surprise when a strategy goes wrong or performs disappointingly and will encourage a flexible approach by economists.

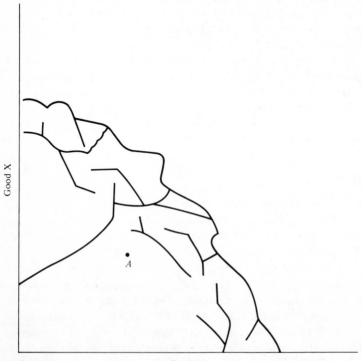

Good Y

POLICY RECOMMENDATIONS FOR THE LDCS

The heart of the development effort is to raise productivity, for this is the key to income growth. In our round-table discussions, we shall ask what the LDCs can do themselves. Promoting domestic saving and investment is a crucial element in productivity increase, but the more difficult the poorer a country is. Government assistance to establish financial institutions can help, and so can the use of market rates of interest, for that will encourage savers and avoid overly great capital intensity. Government budget surpluses financed from tax revenue and made available through lending agencies to private entrepreneurs could play a much more important role than they currently do. But the tax mechanism employed to collect the revenues for these purposes must be carefully managed; it is too easy to discourage saving, penalize agriculture, distort foreign trade, and generate whole-sale tax avoidance with an ill-designed tax system. Possibly the most promising tax for LDCs is the value added tax, with its broad base, its self-policing aspect, and its nonapplication to savings or the interest on savings. To promote both equity and ease of collection, VAT might be charged at a higher rate on luxuries and supplemented with a moderate income tax, might exempt foodstuffs, and might not be collected from petty traders in local markets. The earlier a VAT replaces specific taxes on agriculture and imported goods, the better.

As advisors, we shall insist that it is important to improve the quality of Poveria's population directly. Economic growth could (and with luck probably will) eventually bring this about without government effort, but even if it happens the process is likely to take many years, with the longest delays for those in the lowest income groups. Basic needs programs in education, health, and nutrition can raise productivity now and thereby boost incomes. Primary health care, research on crops consumed by the poor, programs to provide income to the poor including "food for work," and food subsidies based on need are all sensible ideas. By reducing infant mortality and providing some rudimentary welfare measures, such policies can counteract two important reasons for choosing to bear large numbers of children, in turn reducing the burden of dependency and making it easier to increase the stock of capital per head. A well-designed family planning program will work toward the same end, but to the degree that it goes beyond reasonable peer pressure and financial incentives to involve direct compulsion, it will lower the quality of life. By improving conditions in villages and on farms through rural development efforts, including basic needs, higher incomes through research and extension services, rural credit, but also mobilizing the off-season labor surplus for infrastructure improvement and employment in rural factories, policy can reduce the motive for further migration to the cities and improve the lot of the largest part of the population.

Concentrating on the quality of the population also augments the ethical dimension to the economics of development. It reflects a belief that economic growth must be accompanied by humane treatment for the poorest and that growth is not real progress if in spite of it many people, especially children, are still going hungry every day.[3] At the same time policies to rectify extreme uneven-ness in land ownership, including a well-designed land tax, can be a major tool for bringing more equality to the distribution of income.

"Appropriateness" should be a watchword. Appropriate technology means in particular more attention to a country's factor proportions when selecting the type of capital to employ. Appropriate education programs mean more emphasis at the primary level on basic literacy and numeracy, agricultural technique, and health; more emphasis at the secondary level on technical training of the type useful in the development effort and linked to job openings; and less emphasis on expensive university education, especially where the government's spending is focused on the already well-to-do. Emphasis on women's education is important in its own right because it is "fair," because of the neglect of the past, but also because of its positive indirect effects on nutrition and health, and the reinforcement that it brings to efforts to reduce population growth.

Next we turn to the government development policies already in place in Poveria. We have a little list of policies that, if we find them in use, will cause us immediate unease. To be sure, as polite advisors and skeptics of revealed wisdom, even when it is our own, we must give our hosts every opportunity to explain the origins and justifications for these policies, and perhaps we will find their reasoning is convincing. But we are well aware that the policies are on our little list solely because, at many other times and places, they have been counterproductive.

1. *Urban bias.* Is there favoritism toward the cities and a prejudice against the interests of the countryside? Do we find urban wages higher than justified by labor productivity, expensive general food subsidies in the cities, low procurement prices in agriculture, high taxation of farmers via marketing boards and export levies? Are village schools and rural health care far below urban standards? Do rural residents live without electricity, without adequate transport, and without an effective communications system? Do private bank loans and government assistance find their way overwhelmingly to manufacturing enterprise in the cities, and not to agriculture or rural improvement? Then truly we have identified urban bias and rural neglect. In general the greater this bias, the worse the result for a country's past economic growth and its future economic prospects. Even if a country has begun to correct for this bias with subsidies for agricultural inputs and credit, we must examine whether these subsidies go predominately to bigger farmers, whether they encourage misallocations such as a lower demand for agricultural labor, and whether the inputs are distributed inefficiently by government marketing organizations.

2. *Inflationary bias.* Does the government habitually boost its spending by running large fiscal deficits financed by rapid increases in the money supply? Then we shall have to warn our Poverian hosts that, however much they justify the spending as providing capital for development or improving the lot of the poor, the policy will absorb private saving, will repel foreign investment, will risk a hyperinflation that will ravage the growth figures, and will be difficult to stop.

3. *Distortions of foreign trade.* Is the foreign exchange rate sharply overvalued, with heavy protection against a wide range of imports? Is effective protection far more stringent than implied by the nominal rates, and does a high dispersion of tariff rates and quota amounts skew incentives sharply? Behind the trade barriers do we find inefficient "hothouse" industries that could not survive on their own? Does the combination of an overvalued exchange rate and artifi-

cially low real interest rates on government-approved loans mean capital intensity is far higher than we would expect given the relative abundance and cheapness of labor, with labor saving encouraged rather than labor use? Here we have found an import substitution policy that has probably been carried too far. We will strongly consider advising Poveria to eliminate the biases.

By and large, in all these cases we will support the intelligent use of market pricing. The replacement of controls and interventions with market pricing will be a long step forward in erasing the common favoritism toward urban areas and capital-intensive manufacturing, and the production of goods in which the country has no comparative advantage. Facing the market's realities, buyers and sellers in those markets can make more rational economic decisions based more firmly on the information conveyed by those prices, foreign trade can be grounded on comparative advantage, and entrepreneurs are encouraged to deal with people outside their circle of friends, relatives, and political allies. When government undertakes activities, these will preferably be to improve the capabilities of the private sector and to do what that sector cannot do, or does poorly, rather than government operation of activities that could be performed privately, guided by the signals of the market. All too often, when government ownership and operation expands beyond these sensible limits, the activity ends up inefficiently done, at high cost, in politicized surroundings.

But this is decidedly not the same as saying that government activity should be minimized, as some conservatives would have it. There are many areas where well-designed government participation in the development process is essential, and this is likely to be the more true the poorer the country is. An important area is the infrastructure of law and order, finance and banking, the power grid, large irrigation systems, transport, and communications. These activities will require government control or operation because if left to the private sector they might be provided in inadequate amounts or would otherwise be private monopolies. Most of these also possess demonstrable and strong external economies. Public goods such as education, health, family planning, agricultural research, and extension services will also be most successfully organized by government. From the standpoint of efficient production, economic planning in these sectors, with the remainder of the economy following the path indicated by market forces, appears to us much preferable to the more comprehensive forms of output planning. Broad and damaging inequalities of income may remain, however, and if they do government will have to implement programs to raise the productivity and employability of the poor. In examining any government plan, we will cast a critical eye at the degree to which the plan neglects to improve the capacity of the poor to improve their lives.

POLICY RECOMMENDATIONS FOR THE DEVELOPED COUNTRIES

In our round-table discussions we shall also make a number of points about developed-country policies. There is no doubt that our recommendations for important and worthwhile steps for LDCs to take involve costs to these countries that will exceed their available revenues. That is why aid from the developed countries can be crucial, the more so for the poorest LDCs. As advisors, we find ourselves favoring a number of initiatives: raising World Bank capitalization, or gearing, or both; restoring the funds for IDA so valuable to the poorest LDCs; more multilateral aid for the poorest rather than bilateral aid for those who need it less; a new creation of SDRs linked to aid but limited to minimize any inflationary impact; and perhaps a seabed resources tax. But we also agree that aid can be and often has been misused within an environment of damaging economic policies. Structural adjustments in return for the assistance and adequate, preferably international, supervision of its use would seem reasonable requirements.

The aid could be increasingly valuable if a greater amount of it focused on developing more appropriate technologies that utilize labor without sacrificing output and on assisting small farms and small businesses where credit has been especially scarce. Support for funding population programs is essential, including especially the neglected field of research into new contraceptive techniques.

Perhaps above all is the potential for progress in the promotion of trade flows, and the potential for damage if trade barriers are erected against the LDCs. Nothing would be so discouraging for these countries as to find their growth prospects choked off by selfish developed-country protection, nothing more encouraging than stable prospects for following their comparative advantage in trade. In the long term this vital topic transcends the question of aid, which could double or triple in amount and still accomplish little if trade is stifled.

We will admit to grave doubts concerning one major initiative, the international commodity agreements. Attempts to boost price via commodity agreements will succeed only rarely, we suggest, because of the likelihood of consequent supply increase and demand decrease. Even when they do succeed from their members' point of view, the costs they inflict on other LDCs may be severe. Price stabilization is far better, but the example of the tin buffer stock looms ominously as a warning that, rather than bringing benefits, commodity agreements may destabilize expensively. Perhaps the time has come at last to recognize that income smoothing along the lines of the IMF's Compensatory Financing Facility and Stabex are less trouble-prone than price stabilization, can be granted directly in exchange for needed policy reforms, and are a more sensible use of funds.

POLICY RECOMMENDATIONS INVOLVING MUTUAL GAINS

During our discussions in Poveria we will emphasize that progress will be easiest whenever contending parties such as the LDCs and the developed countries can see, or be convinced, that *mutual gains* will result from some possible policy change. Though this was a major thrust of the Brandt Commission report of 1980, the large scope for exploiting such mutual gains is still too little appreciated. All chances should be seized, for positive-sum games will always be easier to play than zero or negative-sum ones.

This recommendation should not be misunderstood. Mutual gain ordinarily does not result in unanimous support, because gain to all countries is not the same as gain to all individuals. It is very difficult to find any policy changes that will leave *every person* better off without any further action by government. Such movements, which harm no one, are easy to bring about, there being no rational opposition to them, but this being so the changes will probably already have been carried out. Another easy case involves policies that bring mutual gain in the sense that the total benefits are sufficiently large so that gainers can and do pay full compensation to losers, leaving society as a whole better off if the policies are adopted. Such "Pareto-optimal" movements will not be resisted on economic grounds either.[4]

But many cases are harder ones. For LDCs, there are two major reasons why losers might not actually be compensated for their losses. First, the tax and transfer mechanisms may not be up to the task, and second, the gainers may think the losers undeserving and therefore will not support the compensation. (This second reason frequently applies in developed countries also.) Those who lose will thus resist, and if they are politically powerful, their resistance may be decisive in preventing the implementation of a policy change that could have been advantageous to all if compensation were paid.

Whether to undertake any given policy change when compensation is not paid then becomes a more difficult question involving some concept of justice and fairness on which there will never be unanimous agreement. There will be some economists who would then state bluntly that no welfare judgment can be made if a policy change makes group A better off and group B worse off.

Such "welfare pessimism" does not appear to be very current among development economists, however. Most appear to take two approaches to the subject when compensation of losers is not possible, and in our round table discussions we will do so too.[5] One is a presumption that adopting sensible policies with the promise of enhanced growth will, in time, be likely to make everyone better off, even those who lose initially. This seems especially apt for an LDC such as Poveria, where even the people who gain from faulty policies are relatively poor, and are likely to gain even more from long-run economic progress than from policy favoritism. The second approach is to take a normative position based on a communal value judgment. Thus, if a proposal would increase aggregate income greatly, and harm a small number of rich slightly, then society might well be comfortable with the decision even if the rich were not compensated for their loss. But if a policy would bring great uncompensated harm to a large middle class, while bringing only a slight net gain to society, then as a value judgment society might be equally comfortable rejecting that policy. In between these easy decisions, the effect of higher income for society as a whole will have to be weighed in a normative judgment against the uncompensated losses to those with higher incomes, and the good chance that through growth losers, too, will eventually gain. There is also the further chance that compensation will eventually be paid after all. Such decisions will no doubt often be difficult, but in many LDCs they will be made easier whenever past policies boosted the incomes of the already wealthy while depressing the incomes of the already poor.

This whole question is extremely important because there is a general perception that gains for the LDCs will be losses for the developed countries, and vice versa. Perhaps more than any other reason, this perception explains why international development conferences have so frequently achieved so little or have even had negative results. What could be constructive negotiations deteriorate all too often into a "vicious circle of suspicion, skepticism, indifference, hostility, and stalemate," with "counterproductive procedures and one-sided agendas."[6] It is self-evident that the LDCs have the most to gain from successful cooperation, since any given improvement in income to a poor person or country will have more significance than the same gain to a rich one. This being so, it would seem crucial that the South take the initiative wherever possible for altering the pattern of negotiations, pressing and prodding for the adoption of positive-sum policies whenever they are identified.

Consider some of the policies involving mutual gains that we have encountered in the course of the book.

1. *Promoting growth.* Policies to promote poor-country economic growth bring obvious benefits. But if the rich countries would themselves adopt policies more oriented toward their own growth (lower budget deficits and interest rates in the United States, deregulation of price-boosting government policies in Europe, encouragement of consumption in Japan, for example), then not only would their own citizens benefit, but the high growth would fuel the export engine of the LDCs. That in turn would generate income there, cause increased exports from the developed countries, and add further to *their* growth in a "virtuous circle." In this regard the significant decline in oil prices, following the apparent breakup of OPEC as an effective price-fixing organization in 1986, is (if it lasts) perhaps the most encouraging news of the decade. This event will indeed work to boost growth in both rich and poor, with enough left over to cushion the blow for the poorest oil exporters such as Nigeria and Mexico.

2. *Restructuring agriculture.* If developed countries would restructure their farm support schemes and reduce their agricultural protection, then consumers there would gain just as LDCs benefit from being able to export far greater quantities of commodities in which they have a comparative advantage. A similar though smaller effect would flow from liberalization of agricultural protection in the LDCs. Recall the World Bank estimate that the overall gains to both groups of countries from dismantling trade barriers in agriculture would in value terms be more than double the amount presently paid out in foreign aid.[7] It should also be noted that there is a surprising amount of complementarity between agricultural production in the LDCs and the developed countries, with growth in one leading to growth in the other. An important recent trend demonstrating this has been the increasing use of imported feedgrains as rising LDC income leads to a greater percentage of meat in the diet.

3. *Reducing protection of industrial products.* In the developed countries oligopolies and trade unions will seek protection to maintain their market power. In the LDCs similar motives plus general import substitution strategies are the cause of the high tariffs and quotas. If both groups of countries were to resist these policies, reducing their protection of industrial products, then each would increase the exports of products in which it has a comparative advantage. An open, multilateral trading system brought huge benefits to the developed countries in the decades since World War II, and trade has been instrumental in the progress

of the most successful LDCs as well. These advantages must not be lost. For political reasons the LDCs may find it easier to promote trade in the context of South-South customs unions. If these are not too trade-diverting, they will be better than the status quo, but an overall reduction of barriers among all countries would be better yet. Estimates that the static gains from reducing protection are rather slight can be disregarded; remember that the dynamic benefits are likely to be far greater than any static gains.

A basic message concerning trade emerged from the previous two chapters. The difficulty in forging new trade policies may not reflect so much a struggle between the developed countries and the LDCs as it does a struggle between abused consumers and taxpayers everywhere, and a much smaller group of farmers, workers, and owners who want to preserve their advantages behind protectionist barriers.

4. *Ending the debt crisis.* The debt crisis of the 1980s, still not ended, has been a serious setback for development, with private bank loans outside of rescheduling agreements having shriveled away. Success in ending the crisis will have manifold favorable effects; it will restore profitability to private lending, bring more financing to the LDCs, promote growth there and thus draw in imports from the developed countries. A sensible prescription: pro-growth policies and lower protection in rich countries so that trade has a chance to work, willingness to undertake structural adjustment in the LDCs, more international assistance to make the adjustment possible and to help in reviving private flows of investment, and more multi-year restructuring of repayment terms on old loans. Not least, the United States must reduce its structural budget deficit, with its attendant upward pressure on interest rates as that country has come to be a giant sponge absorbing the world's largest quantity of financial capital. In general, where relief from debt service is thought necessary, it is better to accomplish it with international loans tied to structural adjustment than with interest caps, debt moratoria, or other methods that penalize the banks. This advice is not based on any particular love for banks, but on the hard-headed ground that private bank loans can be a positive force for development only if the confidence of lenders is restored. The need for international assistance is clearest when, through no fault of its own, a country making bonafide efforts to meet its debt obligations finds that the price of its major export has collapsed in a short period of time. Mexico in 1986 is the most obvious example.

5. *Stimulating capital and technology flows.* Given the importance for development of both capital investment and appropriate technology, keeping open the channels for their flow and stimulating their movement stands to be advantageous both to the LDCs that put them profitably to use and the rich countries that make them available at a profit. A huge potential for mutually beneficial expansion in capital flows exists if the pension funds of the developed world were to purchase equity shares in LDC markets. For then the pension funds could earn the higher average returns often paid in these markets, and the LDCs would receive a welcome infusion of new financing. "Appropriate technology" is an area for research that could yield substantial returns if more international assistance were provided.

All this advice is not meant as a recommendation for "maximum openness" in an economy, with complete free trade and no limits on the operation of multinational companies. In LDCs there are certainly important roles for government policy. These include promotion of infant industry through identifying changes in comparative advantage and overcoming barriers that block the realization of the new advantage, preferably with subsidies but also with tariffs if budget constraints are intense. Behavior of MNEs needs to be monitored and controlled. In all countries, including developed ones, temporary "safeguards" against trade surges are reasonable public policy. For the LDCs, "economic self-reliance" and "reducing dependency" are understandable and laudable goals of government action if they mean policies to encourage diversification into areas of increasing comparative advantage, or prudent promotion of alternative exports to reduce risk in a single-product economy, or judicious controls on MNE behavior, or development of production at home when that promises to be more efficient than importing the product. But if "economic self-reliance" means following policies of blind import substitution, attempting to delink from the world economy, and taking action that repels foreign investment, then we believe the evidence shows a country becomes *less* self-reliant, and *more* dependent, because its economy is weakened. All in all, we advocate a large degree of freedom for trade flows and for investment as the best strategy. Exactly what "large degree" means in practice for any specific country is certainly debatable and cannot be answered by averages or by referring to the experience of rich countries. The answer will vary in different countries at different stages of development and requires careful, specialized research.

FURTHER AFIELD

Since we are economics advisors, we shall avoid political topics during our official sessions, but that will not keep us from making a few salient points as we enjoy a social evening with our hosts. (Though perhaps at some risk of reducing the conviviality!) Too commonly, we shall say, democratic ideals are thought to be irrelevant to economic progress. But the military government of generals, the junta, the dictatorship, with their censorship and rule of bullet not ballot, are likely to mean that the political process is very narrow. Where the political process is narrow, then special interests allied to the oligarchs will glean their reward—appointments to positions of responsibility not based on talent, access to loans at low rates of interest, permits to acquire scarce foreign exchange, licenses to bring in scarce imported goods. Where the political process is not open, where the press is not free, graft and corruption are likely to flourish; little light penetrates to these dark corners. We might hint at our conviction that authoritarian practices may spring up partly because governments find they must become more coercive if they are to continue policies that have such clear losers—the rural sector victimized by high taxes on agriculture, the many would-be business people and farmers unable to borrow because the cheap loan policy makes credit scarce, the exporters ruined by the overvalued foreign exchange rate—and if the winners are to retain their gains. Indeed, authoritarian measures may be needed to *overturn* these policies, because long habituation to their perquisites may make vested interests violent in their defense. Economic growth together with encouragement of democratic institutions may be much the best way out of this dilemma, since growth will reward even those who lose the benefits of discriminatory policies. As economists we are not specialists in these often complicated issues of domestic politics, but we can certainly acknowledge their broad importance.

PESSIMISM OR OPTIMISM?

We have encountered many reasons that could, in our Poverian discussions, justify us in taking a pessimistic view of the development prospects of the LDCs. Slow growth in the developed countries, the debt crisis, the decline of aid, the rise of protection, the politicization of economic policy, the poor performance of Africa are among the many challenges still to be faced in bringing about successful economic development. The task is not easy, and courage is needed whenever the entrenched privileges of some have to give way for the good of many.

Yet there is perhaps a tendency to overemphasize the difficulties. Years ago I first heard the tale of the British colonial official in a lonely African outpost connected by telegraph to the outside world.[8] Over the wire came his message to the capital: *SEND HELP IMMEDIATELY. POST SURROUNDED BY LIONS AND TIGERS.* The capital sent an unexpected answer: *THERE ARE NO TIGERS IN AFRICA.* After some thought there came back the reply: *DELETE TIGERS.*

Like the suddenly educated colonial official of the story, whose willingness to abandon exaggerated pessimism we can applaud, we should avoid overstating the difficulties of poor countries. Their real problems—the lions—are bad enough as they are. Yet there are no tigers and many reasons for hope.

Economic growth, though not uniform, has been more rapid in the LDCs than anticipated by the first generation of development economists. The decline of OPEC, if it endures, will through lower energy costs provide a splendid stimulus to growth in the LDCs and in the rich countries as well. The effects of international trade have been sufficiently favorable that, if its critics are not confounded, they must be at least surprised. Substantial progress has been made in controlling population. Sensible rural development and appropriate technology seem in the ascendant; the more questionable forms of comprehensive planning seem in retreat. Multinationals are now treated with more appreciation for the benefits they bring and more confidence that their costs can be regulated and policed. There appears to be somewhat less acrimony in North-South relations than was true only a short while ago.

Evidence mounts that scarcity of natural resources in any particular LDC, or even the total absence of such resources, is not fatal for development prospects, or even much of a disadvantage, just as was true for now-developed countries such as Denmark, the Netherlands, Switzerland, and more recently and impressively, Japan. Though it is satisfying to have natural resources, these can be imported and processed; the greatest economic successes among the NICs are rather resource-poor (Korea and Taiwan) or have none at all (Hong Kong and Singapore).

A capable and energetic population can overcome this problem, and one begins to suspect that the lack of natural resources may even unleash work effort—a sort of "we try harder" among nations.

Even global resource exhaustion does not command the attention that it did 10 to 15 years ago. During this period the world showed unexpected flexibility in substituting abundant inputs for scarce ones and in searching out new sources of supply. There was also unanticipated willingness among consumers to alter demand patterns as prices rose for goods made from raw materials that were rising in price. Oil was, of course, the major example; few economists predicted how high price elasticities of demand and supply would be after a few years of adjustment. Attention has therefore swung away from resource exhaustion as a primary concern.

IS THERE A TIGER? THE GLOBAL ENVIRONMENT

If there is a lurking tiger after all, it is the increasing concern for the global environment as growth in production continues.[9] There are three major current cases in point. First is the greenhouse effect on world climate, caused largely by the blanket of carbon dioxide produced by the burning of fossil fuels. The world-wide clearing of land, especially deforestation, thickens the blanket because it eliminates the trees and vegetation that work to absorb the carbon dioxide. Second, acid rain from industrial effluents, especially sulphur, harms trees and inland fisheries. Finally, depletion of the atmospheric ozone layer from fluorocarbon release (from aerosol sprays, foams, refrigeration, and air conditioning) threatens to bring hazardous levels of ultraviolet and infrared radiation. Of these three, the first gives the greatest cause for alarm in the LDCs. Acid rain carries sulphur emissions a relatively short maximum distance of some 200 to 600 miles, and corrective technology, though expensive, is available. Ozone depletion remains speculative, and international regulations on fluorocarbons would seem relatively simple if the case against them were shown to be persuasive.[10]

But the greenhouse effect is a more somber story, and if studies confirm that the danger of long-term damage is increasing, then a response will clearly have to be made that involves regulations on types of fuels and on further deforestation.[11] Yet in fairness it would be hard to blame the LDCs for the greenhouse condition or to demand that they move first, because the developed world with its immensely greater production and fuel use is clearly the proximate cause of the problem and will remain so for many years to come. When steps are taken, and presumably as evidence of damage accumulates these steps will come rather sooner than later, the main responsibility to develop the necessary technologies and equipment for control must lie with the rich countries and not the poor. Once these are evolved, they can be made available to the LDCs, who would thus not have to bear the burden of financing their development.

It used to be said that there was only slight concern in the LDCs with environmental pollution. No doubt most people in these countries would assert that square meals are better than clean air, and a choice for higher income against some local degradation in the environment would be an understandable one. As a general rule, decisions to allow or control local pollution can be left to a country's own political process, and indeed the number of LDCs with environmental protection agencies has now grown to well over 100, whereas early in the 1970s the number hardly exceeded 10.

But a serious dilemma threatens to arise. The developed countries are the main cause of the global greenhouse condition, but a warmer climate caused by the greenhouse effect would cause more damage in the tropics, where most LDCs are located, than it would in the temperate zones. Worse from their standpoint, some of the colder parts of the temperate zone may even benefit, much of Canada and the USSR, for example. The very difficult problem would then be that some current emitters would not on grounds of self-interest want to curtail their emissions; and the costs would mostly be borne by tropical LDCs that are not mainly responsible for the global warming. The international agreements that could lead to the substitution of hydro, tidal, wind, nuclear, solar, and geothermal power for fossil fuels might then be especially difficult to negotiate. What agonizing irony it would be for the LDCs if, no agreement in reach, they were forced to watch their landscapes baking in droughts of unprecedented severity, caused by the production successes of developed countries that simultaneously benefit from an improved climate! Could one imagine a more volatile and dangerous recipe for political instability?[12]

Even if this frightening scenario is avoided, however, it contains a pointed lesson. Far larger world populations will make measures to limit environmental damage both more difficult and more expensive. This adds weight to the logic that bringing fertility under control is a vital part of the development effort.

Perhaps the proper frame of mind in which to conclude our discussions in Poveria is to suggest that the greenhouse effect, like all the many other problems of economic development we have encountered in this book, can bring merely a supine response to events or can be viewed as a challenge to be faced with untiring effort and commitment. Much of that challenge lies in overcoming the passivity and inertia of "nothing can be done." We shall take leave of our Poverian hosts with the instructive tale of two salesmen sent to a poor country by a shoe company.[13] The first cabled back, *NO PROSPECTS HERE. NO ONE WEARS SHOES.* The second sent a far different cable: *IMMENSE PROSPECTS HERE. MILLIONS WITHOUT SHOES.* To be sure, there is neither a guarantee that shoes *will* be sold, nor any iron law that sensible economic policies must cause development to take place. But we will not change the world with the gloomy view of the first cable. To do that, we need the spirit of the second salesman.

NOTES

1. Henry J. Bruton, "The Search for a Development Economics," *World Development* 13, nos. 10/11 (1985):1099–1124.
2. *Ibid.,* p. 1116.
3. Echoing Dudley Seers, "The Meaning of Development," in David Lehmann, ed., *Development Theory: Four Critical Studies,* London, 1979, p. 21.
4. "Pareto-optimal" movements are named for the Italian social theorist Vilfredo Pareto

who enunciated the principle at the beginning of this century. An understandable review of Pareto improvements is Edmund S. Phelps, *Political Economy,* New York, 1985, chap. 9.

5. See W. M. Corden, "Normative Theory of International Trade," in Ronald W. Jones and Peter B. Kenen, eds., *Handbook of International Economics,* Vol. 1, Amsterdam, 1984, pp. 66–69, whose analysis I followed here.

6. Thomas G. Weiss, "Alternatives for Multilateral Development Diplomacy: Some Suggestions," *World Development* 13, no. 12 (1985):1187–1209.

7. *WDR 1986,* p. 151.

8. I have seen this in print in *The Economist,* September 26, 1981.

9. The discussion in this section relies on Tom Tietenberg, *Environmental and Natural Resource Economics,* 2nd ed., Glenview, Ill., forthcoming 1987, chapter 16. My thanks to my colleague Professor Tietenberg for allowing me to refer to the typescript of his new edition.

10. The OECD estimates that worldwide fluorocarbon release grew from 164,000 tons in 1950 to 13 million tons in 1983. Though the United States banned its use as an aerosol propellant in 1978, U.S. fluorocarbon release is still one-third of the world total. See Tietenberg, *Environmental and Natural Resource Economics,* typescript chapter 16, pp. 10–11.

11. A 1983 study by the NRC suggests that a warming of surface air between 3° and 8°F. could occur within less than a century. *Ibid.,* p. 16.

12. Well, yes, one could—a "nuclear winter" caused by war. This would perhaps be the greatest irony of them all. Many of the LDCs consider themselves "non-aligned" but this would do them not an iota of good if a nuclear exchange were ever to occur. Then indeed the whole world would be underdeveloped with a vengeance.

13. David Morawetz, "On the Origins of Theories," *World Development* 13, no. 12 (1985):1308.

Name Index

Abramowitz, Moses, 67
Adams, Dale, 288–289
Adams, Walter, 252
Adelman, Morris, 41, 458
Agarwal, Vinod B., 251
Agarwala, A. N., 318, 328
Agarwala, Ramgopal, 301, 316
Agege, Charles O., 145
Ahamed, Liaquat, 110, 395
Ahluwalia, Montek S., 25, 28–30, 40
Ahmad, Jaleel, 434
Ahmad, M., 258
Ahmed, Iftikhar, 17
Ahmed, Ziauddin, 106
Aho, C. Michael, 434
Alikhani, I., 426
Alizadeh, Parvin, 63, 317, 397
Alnasrawi, Abbas, 474
Ambrioggi, Robert P., 252
Amin, Samir, 329, 359
Anderson, K., 446
Anjaria, Shailendra J., 388, 397, 406, 426, 432–437
Ansari, Javed A., 62
Anschel, Kurt R., 276
Arhin, Kwame, 108
Arndt, H. W., 316–317
Arnon, I., 292
Aronson, Jonathan David, 434
Arrighi, Giovanni, 329, 359
Askari, Hossein, 287

Avery, Dennis, 474–475
Ayres, Robert L., 142, 293, 446

Bacha, Edmar Lisboa, 169, 359
Bacon, Robert, 43
Bain, Joe S., 312–313, 318
Baker, James, 115, 158
Balassa, Bela, 371, 389, 396–397, 433, 435
Balassa, Carol, 433, 435
Balasubramanyam, V. N., 143
Baldwin, Robert E., 405, 433–434, 436
Banks, Gary, 395
Baran, Paul, 360
Barber, William J., xiii
Bardhan, Pranab, 287
Barker, B. L., 145
Barro, Robert J., 43, 109–110
Barton, Clifton, 49, 62
Barzelay, Michael, 474
Bauer, P. T., xiii, 62, 90, 143, 317
Baum, Warren C., 141, 316
Baumol, William J., 17, 225
Beachell, Hank, 267
Beckerman, Wilfred, 43
Behrman, Jere R., 449, 453, 460, 462–463, 464–475
Bell, C. L. G., 25, 40
Belsley, David A., 361
Bennett, M. K., 345, 361
Benoit, Emile, 109

Subject Index

499

ISBN 0-06-042853-8

90000

9 780060 428532

Country	GNP per Capita (U.S. Dollars)	Adjusted GDP per Capita (U.S. Dollars)	PQLI	Population (millions)
Mauritius	1090	2040	81	1.0
Mexico	2040	4250	80	76.8
Mongolia	na	na	77	1.9
Morocco	670	1910	49	21.4
Mozambique	220(1980)	1110	40	13.4
Nepal	160	720	30	16.1
Netherlands	9520	8810	98	14.4
New Zealand	7730	7350	96	3.2
Nicaragua	860	2080	71	3.2
Niger	190	910	27	6.2
Nigeria	730	2400	41	96.5
North Korea	na	na	84	19.9
Norway	13940	11480	99	4.1
Oman	6490	na	37	1.1
Pakistan	380	1070	39	92.4
Panama	1980	3390	88	2.1
Papua New Guinea	710	1460	45	3.4
Paraguay	1240	2930	80	3.3
Peru	1000	2860	69	18.2
Philippines	660	1610	75	53.4
Poland	2100	3250	94	36.9
Portugal	1970	4900	86	10.2
Romania	na	2770	92	22.7
Rwanda	280	640	45	5.8
Saudi Arabia	10530	na	45	11.1
Senegal	380	1060	30	6.4
Sierra Leone	310	740	26	3.7
Singapore	7260	5310	89	2.5
Somalia	260	620	17	5.2
South Africa	2340	3710	68	31.6
South Korea	2110	3270	86	40.1
Spain	4440	6380	94	38.7
Sri Lanka	360	1380	85	15.9
Sudan	360	1390	39	21.3
Suriname	3510	3610	78	0.4
Swaziland	790	1960	55	0.7
Sweden	11860	10560	99	8.3
Switzerland	16330	10290	98	6.4
Syria	1620	3790	71	10.1
Taiwan	3000(1984)	4110	92	19.2
Tanzania	210	710	61	21.5